LIPSEY & STEINER/ECONOMICS

RICHARD G. LIPSEY

UNIVERSITY OF ESSEX

& PETER O. STEINER

UNIVERSITY OF WISCONSIN

ECONOMICS

HARPER & ROW   PUBLISHERS   NEW YORK

"... Einstein started from facts—

the Morley-Michelson measurements of light, the movements of the planet Mercury, the unexplained aberrancies of the moon from its predicted place. Einstein went back to facts or told others where they should go, to confirm or to reject his theory—by observation of stellar positions during a total eclipse.

"... It is not necessary, of course, for the verification of a new theory to be done personally by its propounder. Theoretical reasoning from facts is as essential a part of economic science as of other sciences, and in a wise division of labour there is room, in economics, as elsewhere, for the theoretician pure and simple, for one who leaves the technical business of verification to those who have acquired a special technique of observation. No one demanded of Einstein that he should visit the South Seas in person, and look through a telescope; but he told others what he expected them to see, if they looked, and he was prepared to stand or fall by the result. It is the duty of the propounder of every new theory, if he has not himself the equipment for observation, to indicate where verification of his theory is to be sought in facts—what may be expected to happen or to have happened if his theory is true, what will not happen if it is false.

"[Now consider by way of contrast the behaviour of the participants in a current controversy in economics.] . . . None of them takes the point that the truth or falsehood of . . . [a] . . . theory cannot be established except by an appeal to the facts; none of them tests it by facts himself. The distinguishing mark of economic science as illustrated by this debate is that it is a science in which verification of generalisations by reference to facts is neglected as irrelevant. . . . I do not see how . . . [members of the public who survey the controversy] . . . can avoid the conclusion that economics is not a science concerned with phenomena, but a survival of medieval logic, and that economists are persons who earn their livings by taking in one another's definitions for mangling.

"... I know that in speaking thus I make enemies. I challenge a tradition of a hundred years of political economy, in which facts have been treated not as controls of theory, but as illustrations. I shall be told that in the Social Sciences verification can never be clean enough to be decisive. I may be told that, in these sciences, observation has been tried and has failed, has led to shapeless accumulations of facts which themselves lead nowhere. I do not believe for a moment that this charge of barrenness, of past enquiries can be sustained; to make it is to ignore many achievements of the past and to decry much solid work that is being done at this School and elsewhere. But if the charge of barrenness of realistic economics in the past were justified completely, that would not be a reason for giving up observation and verification. It would only be a reason for making our observations more exact and more numerous. If, in the Social Sciences, we cannot yet run or fly, we ought to be content to walk, or to creep on all fours as infants. . . . For economic and political theorising not based on facts and not controlled by facts assuredly does lead nowhere.

"There can be no science of society till the facts about society are available. Till 130 years ago we had no census, no knowledge even of the numbers and growth of the people; till fifteen years ago we had no comprehensive records about unemployment even in this country, and other countries are still where we were a generation or more ago; social statistics of every kind—about trade, wages, consumption—are everywhere in their infancy.

". . . From Copernicus to Newton is 150 years. Today, 150 years from *The Wealth of Nations,* we have not found, and should not expect to find, the Newton of economics. If we have travelled as far as Tycho Brahe we may be content. Tycho was both a theorist and an observer. As a theorist, he believed to his last day in the year 1601 that the planets went round the sun and that the sun and the stars went round the earth as the fixed centre of the universe. As an observer, he made with infinite patience and integrity thousands of records of the stars and planets; upon these records Kepler, in due course, based his laws and brought the truth to light. If we will take Tycho Brahe for our example, we may find encouragement also. It matters little how wrong we are with our existing theories, if we are honest and careful with our observations."

Extracts from Lord William Beveridge's farewell address as Director of the London School of Economics, June 24, 1937. Published in Politica, *September, 1937.*

WHY WE WROTE THIS BOOK: A NOTE TO THE INSTRUCTOR

OUR BASIC REASON FOR WRITING THIS BOOK IS that we wanted to see a text that reflected the enormous changes that have taken place in economics during the last fifteen years. The most important change in this period is that economics has moved very rapidly toward becoming a genuine science. We apply the term *science* neither to praise nor to castigate economics, but to describe its movement toward that characteristic that distinguishes any science: the systematic confrontation of theory with observation. All too often in the past, economic theory has been taught merely as logical analysis and has been, at best, only vaguely related to the world; by the same token, applied economics is too often description unenlightened by any theoretical framework. Economic theory is meant to be about the real world. We seek, by the use of theory, to explain, understand, and predict phenomena in the real world, and our theory must, therefore, be related to, and tested by, empirical observations of the world around us. The student of economics needs to ask at every stage what the relevant magnitudes and quantities are in the real world.

The quotation from Lord William Beveridge that opens this book is our text—in the preacher's sense of that word—and it describes the first of the three main themes that we wish to mention here. Beveridge was

scolding the profession in 1937, but we believe that things have changed, and for the better, and that these changes should be incorporated in the approach used from the elementary course on.

Economics is always changing, but it seems to us that, in the postwar period, there has been a change of such importance that we do ourselves and our students a great disservice if we neglect it. We regard the change as the transition of the brilliant child from his troubled adolescence to the vigor of young adulthood.

Economics is not a stage on which we parade our pet theories and ask to have them admired for their elegance or their conclusions, nor is it a container in which we collect quantities of unrelated institutional and statistical material about the economy. Instead, it is a serious attempt to push back the frontiers of our ignorance about our economic environment in order both to understand it and to control it.

If we are to do this, we must continually be concerned with the relations among theory, institutions, and facts, and every theory must be regarded as subject to refutation. This book is, of course, only an introduction, and we could not in any case have provided a compilation of all that is known by economists. But we have, at every stage, attempted to indicate which data are relevant, and to distinguish between those ideas and theories that have been reasonably well tested and those that have not.

A second major theme of this book is the relation between economic theory and economic policy. The distinction between positive and normative statements is well known to professional economists, but all too often we fail to communicate its significance to our students. Even the best textbooks often manage to convey the idea that economic theory justifies the private-enterprise market economies found in most Western countries, or leave students with such ideas as the ones that the "Law" of Comparative Advantage "proves" that nations ought to specialize in the production of certain goods, or that economics has "proved" that rent and price controls and tariffs are wicked and ought not to be used. The student who can think of good reasons why, under some circumstances, price and rent controls and tariffs might not be undesirable reacts by dismissing economics as medieval scholasticism, or as a fraud perpetrated by whichever political party he happens not to support, and so he should, whenever economics purports to prove such propositions. Economic theory can never show us what we ought to do, but only what will happen if we do do certain things. The uses and the limitations of economic theory in dealing with matters of public policy is a theme that recurs throughout the book.

An appreciation of the relation between economic theory and economic policy is not new to economics. Indeed, many nineteenth-century economists expressed exactly the view we have outlined in the previous paragraph. What is new is, first, the appreciation of how little can be said about policy on the basis of the very general qualitative theories used in the past, and, second, the application of the quantitative revolution of the last fifteen years to matters of policy. Fifteen years of systematic observations have provided us with a much better idea of how things are related to one another quantitatively, and this knowledge has greatly increased the economist's power to say sensible and relevant things about public policy.

The third major feature of the book relates to the way we view our students. Our experience accords with the statistics that show them to be better trained and harder working than the students of a decade or two ago. We have tried in several different ways to be honest with them. No subject worth studying is always easy, and we have not glossed over hard points just because they were hard. We have tried, however, often through many drafts, to make the exposition as clear as we could. We do not approve of slipping particularly hard bits of analysis past the student without letting him see what is happening and what has been assumed, nor do we approve of teaching him things that he will have to unlearn if he goes on in economics (a practice that some teachers justify on the grounds that it is important to get to the big issues quickly).

Every student who continues in economics will soon learn that there are areas where economic analysis is woefully inadequate, but the tradition in elementary economics is to suppress these inadequacies. In this book, we have not hesitated to be critical of economists' conclusions, and we encourage the student to be critical—to ask: Just what *is* the evidence for that conclusion, and what would be required to refute it? Both his education and our subject depend upon careful criticism. We have devoted a good deal of space to examining both sensible and silly criticisms of economic theories. In doing this, we hope to give the student some inkling of how it is possible to criticize effectively, and hence to improve, the existing body of economic theory. Effective criticism of existing ideas is the mainspring of progress in science, and we believe that an introduction to the present state of economics should also be an introduction to the testing, criticism, and evaluation of the existing state of the subject. We do not accept the notion that if you suggest the possibility of criticism to the student he will be led to make hasty and confused criticisms. A student will always make criticisms and evaluations of what he has been taught. His criticisms are much more likely to be informed and relevant ones if he is given both practice and instruction in how to go about challenging what he has been taught.

STUDYING ECONOMICS: A NOTE TO THE STUDENT

THE STUDY OF ECONOMICS CAN BE BOTH IN-teresting and rewarding. To a student not intending to specialize in economics, it can give some understanding of the functioning of the economy and some appreciation of the issues involved in current controversies over economic policy. It may also give him some idea of the methods that have been applied with some modest success in one social science. To the prospective economics special-ist, an introductory book such as this one can be the beginning of a real adventure.

Economics has a cumulative structure; it tends to build on itself from stage to stage. Thus if you understand some concept or the-ory only imperfectly, you will run into in-creasing difficulty when, in subsequent devel-opments, this concept or theory is taken for granted and built upon. Because of its logi-cal structure, quite long chains of reasoning are encountered: if A, then B; if B, then C; if C, then D; and if D, then E. Each step in the argument may seem simple enough, but the cumulative effect of several steps, one on top of another, may be bewildering on first en-counter. When, having followed the argument step by step, you encounter the statement, "Now, obviously, if A, then E," it may not seem obvious at all. This is a problem that almost everyone faces with chains of reason-ing. The only way to deal with it is to follow the argument through several times. Eventu-ally, as you become familiar with the argu-ment, it *will* become obvious that, if A, then E.

Another problem is posed by the fact that economics has a large technical vocabulary. At first, you may feel that all you are being asked to do is to put complicated names to common-sense ideas. To some extent, this is true. At the beginning, economics consists largely of making explicit ideas that appeal strongly to common sense and that you may already hold in a vague sort of way. This is an absolutely necessary step, because loose thinking about vaguely formed ideas is one of the quickest routes to error in economics. Furthermore, the jargon—the single word or phrase given to the common-sense idea—becomes necessary in the interests of brevity as the subject is built up. Try this experiment: Remove all technical terms from the argu-ment of one of the later chapters in this book and replace them with the full verbal descrip-tion of the ideas expressed. You will quickly see how cumbersome the argument becomes. If we are going to put several ideas together to see what follows from them, a single clearly defined word or phrase that refers to these ideas becomes a necessary part of our equipment.

It follows from all of this that a book on economics has to be worked at. It cannot be read like a novel. It is usually a good idea to read a chapter quickly in order to see the general run of the argument and then to reread it carefully, making sure that you understand each step of the argument. You should be prepared to spend a long time on difficult sections. You should not be discouraged if you occasionally find yourself spending an hour on only two or three pages. Paper and a pencil are necessary pieces of equipment in your reading. It is best to follow a difficult argument by building up your own diagram while the argument unfolds, rather than by relying on the finished diagram as it appears in the book. It is often helpful to invent numerical examples to illustrate general propositions. At various stages, the book will ask you to stop and think out the answer to some problem for yourself before you read on. *You should never read on without attempting to do this.*

You will find it useful to make your own glossary of technical terms. The first time a technical term is used, it is printed in italics, so that it may easily be recognized as such.

After you have read the book in this detailed manner, you should reread it quickly from cover to cover. It is often difficult to understand why certain things are done when they are viewed as isolated points, but when you reread the book, much that did not seem relevant or entirely comprehensible initially will fall into place in the analysis.

In short, you must seek to understand economics, not to memorize it. Memorization leads to trouble in economics; theories, principles, and concepts are always turning up in slightly unfamiliar guises. If you have really understood your economics, this poses no problem; if you have merely memorized it, this spells disaster. *This approach is somewhat different from that required by some other subjects, but not necessarily more difficult.*

ACKNOWLEDGMENTS

So many people—teachers, colleagues, students, friends—contributed to this book that it is quite impossible to acknowledge our intellectual debts to all of them. A few people, however, contributed so massively that we must not leave them unmentioned. G. C. Archibald, Kurt Klappholz, and Allen Kelley gave us searching criticisms of major portions of the manuscript. Patrick Geary and Christopher Green gave valuable research assistance. Miss Judith Shapiro contributed materially to the end-of-chapter summaries and questions. Miss Firth Haring's editing improved considerably the readability of the manuscript. Mrs. Sarah Craig, Mrs. Nancy Williamson, and Mrs. Evelyn Dean showed unlimited patience and skill in the almost endless typing and retyping of the manuscript. To all of these people, whether mentioned or not, our gratitude. None of them is to be held responsible in any way for the shortcomings or mistakes that remain.

Any endeavor of this kind takes its heaviest toll on wives and children. To Diana, Mark, Mathew, Joanna, and Claudia, and to Ruth, Alison, and David, our apologies and our thanks.

RICHARD G. LIPSEY
PETER O. STEINER

CONTENTS

PART I. SCOPE AND METHOD

1. The Problems of Economics 3

2. Economics as a Social Science 12

PART V.   MARKET PRICE

35. *Labor Unions, Collective Bargaining, and the Determination of Wages* 379

36. *Interest and the Return on Capital* 397

37. *Criticisms and Tests of the Theory of Distribution* 412

PART VII.   INTERNATIONAL TRADE

PART VIII.   THE MARKET ECONOMY AS A WHOLE

PART IX. THE CIRCULAR FLOW OF INCOME

45. *The Model of the Circular Flow of Income* 525

46. *Equilibrium in the Circular Flow* 545

47. *Household Consumption* 560

PART X.   MONEY, BANKING, AND PRICES

52. *The Nature and History of Money*   627

53. *The Banking System and the Supply of Money*   639

54. *The Demand for Money*   654

55. *The Determination of the Price Level*   660

PART XI.   ECONOMIC GROWTH AND ECONOMIC DEVELOPMENT

56. *Economic Growth*   679

57. *Underdeveloped Economies*   694

PART XII.   CONTEMPORARY PROBLEMS OF MACROECONOMIC POLICY

58. *Macroeconomic Policy*   709

A NOTE ON POSSIBLE COURSE OUTLINES

THIS TEXTBOOK REFLECTS TO SOME EXTENT the way its authors would teach their own course. But not entirely, because we recognize that the needs of students differ: that some want and deserve to have material that goes a bit beyond the average class level, but that some have gaps in their background that need filling. To accommodate the former type, we have included more material than will be assigned to every student. Also, because there are many different kinds of first-year courses in economics taught in colleges and universities, we have included more material than normally would be included in any single course.

Although every teacher can best design his own course, it may be helpful if we indicate certain views of our own as to how this book *might* be adapted to different courses.

First of all, do not be upset by the fact that the book contains fifty-eight chapters and twelve appendixes. Many of the chapters are short, and the over-all length of the book is not excessive. Assigning every page would average out to about twelve pages per lecture in a typical sixty-lecture course. There are a lot of chapters, because we believe it is proper to put separable topics in separate chapters, even if some chapters are only a few pages long. This way, the student can digest a unit as a unit. It is much easier for the instructor who wishes to omit some things and change the order of others to do so on a chapter-by-chapter basis, rather than on a page-by-page basis.

The appendixes are "interruptions" in the flow of the book and can be omitted without destroying its continuity. Some of them, as we note below, are somewhat more advanced and are designed for the honors student; others, such as the ones on the principles of accounting and national-income accounting, include related but tangential material; still others, such as the Appendix to Chapter 4, Graphing Economic Observations, are designed to fill gaps in the backgrounds of some students.

In general, the following appendixes are intended for the more advanced or specially interested students and should not be routinely assigned: the Appendixes to Chapters 10 and 13, Appendix A to Chapter 17, and the Appendixes to Chapters 18, 19, and 21.

None of the material in this book presupposes any background in economics or mathematics, but we do suppose that our readers have had both the motivation to seek a higher education and the ability and training to be admitted to college. Some, but not all, of them are committed to economics, and the choice of material will vary accordingly. Basically, the book we have written is for the full-year course in economics for the student who is seriously interested in what economics has to say and how it goes about saying it, but it may also be adapted to shorter courses.

I. THE ONE-YEAR, OR THREE-QUARTER, COURSE (SIX UNITS OF CREDIT)

A. *Macroeconomics Followed by Microeconomics*

We are aware that at least half of the courses in introductory economics treat macroeconomics before microeconomics. For instructors who prefer this order, the book is readily reversible. The recommended order of chapters is:

CHAPTER 1: The Problems of Economics
CHAPTER 2: Economics as a Social Science
CHAPTER 3: The Tools of Theoretical Analysis
CHAPTER 4: The Tools of Statistical Analysis
CHAPTER 5: Economic Analysis and Economic Policy
CHAPTER 44: The South Col
CHAPTER 45: The Model of the Circular Flow of Income
CHAPTER 46: Equilibrium in the Circular Flow
CHAPTER 47: Household Consumption
CHAPTER 48: Investment and Saving
CHAPTER 49: Fluctuations in the Level of Business Activity
CHAPTER 50: Foreign Trade and National Income
CHAPTER 51: Government and the Circular Flow of Income
CHAPTER 52: The Nature and History of Money
CHAPTER 53: The Banking System and the Supply of Money
CHAPTER 54: The Demand for Money
CHAPTER 55: The Determination of the Price Level
CHAPTER 56: Economic Growth
CHAPTER 57: Underdeveloped Economies
CHAPTER 58: Macroeconomic Policy

CHAPTER 6: What Is the Price System?
CHAPTER 7: The Elementary Theory of Demand
CHAPTER 8: The Elementary Theory of Supply
CHAPTER 9: The Elementary Theory of Market Price
CHAPTER 10: Elasticity of Demand and Supply
CHAPTER 11: Price Controls, Taxes, Agriculture: Some Predictions of the Theory of Price
CHAPTER 12: Elements of Dynamics
CHAPTER 13: The Theory of Household Behavior
CHAPTER 14: The Theory of Demand: Measurements and Tests
CHAPTER 15: Background to the Theory of Supply
CHAPTER 16: The Organization of Production
CHAPTER 17: The Meaning and Measurement of Cost
CHAPTER 18: Choosing a Technique of Production
CHAPTER 19: How Cost Varies With Output
CHAPTER 20: The Very Long Run
CHAPTER 21: Introduction to the Theory of Product Pricing
CHAPTER 22: The Theory of Perfect Competition
CHAPTER 23: The Theory of Monopoly
CHAPTER 24: Price Discrimination
CHAPTER 25: Monopoly and Competition: Implications About Behavior

CHAPTER 26: Monopoly Versus Competition: Implications About Performance

CHAPTER 27: Monopoly and Competition in America

CHAPTER 28: Competition Among the Many: Monopolistic Competition Versus Perfect Competition

CHAPTER 29: Competition Among the Few: Oligopoly Versus Monopoly

CHAPTER 30: Criticisms and Tests of the Theory of the Firm

CHAPTER 31: Distribution: A General View

CHAPTER 32: The Demand for Factors: Marginal Productivity Theory

CHAPTER 33: The Supply of Factors

CHAPTER 34: The Pricing of Factors in Competitive Markets

CHAPTER 35: Labor Unions, Collective Bargaining, and the Determination of Wages

CHAPTER 36: Interest and the Return on Capital

CHAPTER 37: Criticisms and Tests of the Theory of Distribution

CHAPTER 38: Exchange Rates

CHAPTER 39: The Gains From Trade

CHAPTER 40: Tariffs and the Gains From Trade

CHAPTER 41: International Economic Experience

CHAPTER 42: The Notion of General Equilibrium: Interactions Among Markets

CHAPTER 43: Microeconomic Policy

Our own preference would be to assign Chapter 6 ("What Is the Price System?") with Chapters 1-5, as well as later on. Chapters 6 and 44 provide a very quick survey of microeconomics that will benefit the student starting with macroeconomics.

The macro-micro organization is subject to the same omissions as the micro-macro organization described under IB below.

B. Microeconomics Followed by Macroeconomics

With or without the appendixes noted on p. xxviii, the book can be used in its present order for courses of this kind. Some instructors will feel that this course is too "full" for their students, either because they wish to deal with a smaller range of topics in greater detail, or because they wish to increase the amount of nontextbook reading material. These instructors may omit one or more of the following chapters without interrupting the coherence of the book:

1. In Price Theory:

CHAPTER 12: Elements of Dynamics

CHAPTER 13: The Theory of Household Behavior

CHAPTER 18: Choosing a Technique of Production

CHAPTER 24: Price Discrimination

CHAPTER 28: Competition Among the Many

CHAPTER 42: The Notion of General Equilibrium

2. In International Trade:

CHAPTER 38: Exchange Rates

CHAPTER 41: International Economic Experience

or

CHAPTER 39: The Gains From Trade

CHAPTER 40: Tariffs and the Gains From Trade

3. In Distribution:

CHAPTER 32: Marginal Productivity Theory

CHAPTER 33: The Supply of Factors

CHAPTER 34: The Pricing of Factors in Competitive Markets

CHAPTER 36: Interest and the Return on Capital

4. *In Monetary Theory:*

CHAPTER 54: The Demand for Money

CHAPTER 55: The Determination of the Price Level

5. *In the Institutional Material:*

CHAPTER 16: The Organization of Production

APPENDIX B TO CHAPTER 17: Balance Sheets, Income Statements, and Costs of Production: Two Views

CHAPTER 27: Monopoly and Competition in America

CHAPTER 35: Labor Unions, Collective Bargaining, and the Determination of Wages

APPENDIX TO CHAPTER 45: Measuring National Income

In suggesting that some of the above chapters may be omitted, we do not imply that they are in any sense too difficult for the average beginning student, nor that they are unimportant. Each was written for the first-year student, and each, in our view, covers an important part of the subject. These chapters are not, however, essential to an understanding of what follows them. For this reason, they may be omitted without causing the student difficulty with subsequent chapters.

II. THE ONE-SEMESTER, OR TWO-QUARTER, COURSE (FOUR UNITS OF CREDIT)

One-semester courses tend to be of three main types: a one-semester general survey course primarily for nonmajors, a one-semester course with a microeconomics emphasis, and a one-semester course with a macroeconomics emphasis.

A. One-Semester General Survey Course

CHAPTER 1: The Problems of Economics

CHAPTER 2: Economics as a Social Science

CHAPTER 3: The Tools of Theoretical Analysis

CHAPTER 4: The Tools of Statistical Analysis

CHAPTER 5: Economic Analysis and Economic Policy

CHAPTER 6: What Is the Price System?

CHAPTER 7: The Elementary Theory of Demand

CHAPTER 8: The Elementary Theory of Supply

CHAPTER 9: The Elementary Theory of Market Price

CHAPTER 11: Price Controls, Taxes, Agriculture: Some Predictions of the Theory of Price

CHAPTER 15: Background to the Theory of Supply

CHAPTER 16: The Organization of Production

CHAPTER 17: The Meaning and Measurement of Cost

CHAPTER 20: The Very Long Run

CHAPTER 21: Introduction to the Theory of Product Pricing

CHAPTER 22: The Theory of Perfect Competition

CHAPTER 23: The Theory of Monopoly

CHAPTER 25: Monopoly and Competition: Implications About Behavior

CHAPTER 26: Monopoly Versus Competition: Implications About Performance

CHAPTER 27: Monopoly and Competition in America

CHAPTER 30: Criticisms and Tests of the Theory of the Firm

CHAPTER 31: Distribution: A General View

CHAPTER 35: Labor Unions, Collective Bargaining, and the Determination of Wages

CHAPTER 43: Microeconomic Policy

CHAPTER 44: The South Col

CHAPTER 45: The Model of the Circular Flow of Income

CHAPTER 46: Equilibrium in the Circular Flow

CHAPTER 47: Household Consumption

CHAPTER 48: Investment and Saving

CHAPTER 49: Fluctuations in the Level of Business Activity

CHAPTER 50: Foreign Trade and National Income

CHAPTER 51: Government and the Circular Flow of Income

CHAPTER 52: The Nature and History of Money

CHAPTER 53: The Banking System and the Supply of Money

CHAPTER 56: Economic Growth

CHAPTER 57: Underdeveloped Economies

CHAPTER 58: Macroeconomic Policy

This course excludes most of the more technical, and thus time-consuming, chapters. Chapters 3 and 4 could also be omitted.

B. One-Semester Microeconomics Course

Precisely how to organize such a course depends upon how it is designed to fit into the over-all curriculum. Such a course is rarely the only course in economics taken by the students involved, and the choice of material will clearly differ if it is the first course taken or if it follows a "general-education" or related course. Basic material for this course is in Parts I to V (Scope and Method, A General View of the Price System, Demand, Supply, and Market Price), and Part VIII (The Market Economy as a Whole), with some material from Part VI (Distribution), and possibly from Part VII (International Trade). For students without a previous course, the omissions listed in IB1 above would be appropriate; for those with some prior exposure, these chapters might be included and Chapters 6–9 omitted or assigned for review only. But here, even more than above, we must defer to the individual instructor's knowledge of his course.

C. One-Semester Macroeconomics Course

Although the comments immediately above apply to this type of course, there is less variation among one-semester macro courses. The basic course would include:

PART I: Scope and Method

PART IX: The Circular Flow of Income

PART X: Money, Banking, and Prices

PART VII: International Trade

PART XI: Economic Growth and Economic Development

PART XII: Contemporary Problems of Macroeconomic Policy

For students for whom this is to be the only course in economics, the instructor may wish to assign Chapters 6–9, Chapter 11, and Chapter 44 and to omit two of the trade chapters (see IB2 above) and Chapters 54 and 55. Chapter 38 in Part VII cannot be understood without understanding the materials in Chapters 7, 8, and 9.

SCOPE &
METHOD

Chapter **1**   THE PROBLEMS OF ECONOMICS

Why?

WHY IN 1965 WAS THE AVERAGE AMERICAN richer than ever before? Why, at the same time, was poverty in the United States a major problem? What do we mean by riches and poverty? How do they come about? Why do the average living standards of some economies rise rapidly, whereas other economies have a static standard of living over very long periods?

Why in most Western countries do periods of boom and plenty alternate with periods of depression and unemployment? Why, for example, during the entire decade of the 1930s was up to one person in four unemployed? When factories lay idle and raw materials went unused, when everything was available to produce goods that were urgently required, why did nothing happen? Can governments spend their way out of depressions or is the only sound policy one of keeping expenditures equal to tax revenues?

Why do many countries have balance-of-payments crises? What are, or were, the causes of the "dollar problem"? What is the point of international trade, and would we not be better off if we made ourselves self-sufficient?

Why, in the history of the world, have periods of rapidly rising prices alternated with periods of stable and sometimes falling prices? Why do the prices of some commodities fluctuate widely, whereas the prices of others are relatively stable? Why is it that, as with many agricultural products, price fluctuations give rise to large variations in the incomes of those who produce them, whereas, with other products, price fluctuations cause hardly any variation in producers' incomes?

Why has the share of the national income going to labor and to profit-earners shown only minor variations over the last hundred years? What determines the level of wages and what influences do unions have on the share of income going to labor? Why do economists insist that countries with large supplies of money are no richer than countries with small supplies of money?

What influence does the government have on people's welfare? What are the effects of the government's taxation policies? What are the effects of public expenditures? How important to our welfare is the size of our national debt?

These are questions with which economists concern themselves and on which the theories of economics are supposed to shed some light. Such a list may give you a clearer idea of the scope of economics than you could obtain from studying the common textbook definitions.

What Is Economics?

One way of defining the scope of economics is to say that it is the social science that deals with the problems listed above. Most of these problems do, however, have certain features in common.

The problems of economics arise out of the use of resources to satisfy human wants. The resources of a society consist not only of the free gifts of nature, such as land, forests, and minerals, but also of human resources, both mental and physical, and of all sorts of man-made aids to further production, such as tools, machinery, and buildings. Economists call such resources *factors of production* because the resources of a society are used to *produce* those things that people desire in order to satisfy their wants. The things produced are called *commodities*. Commodities may be divided into goods and services: Goods are tangible, like cars or shoes, and services are intangible, like haircuts or education. This distinction, however, should not be exaggerated: Any good is valued because of the services it yields to its owner. In the case of an automobile, for example, the services consist of such things as transportation, mobility, and, possibly, status. (Notice the implication of positive value that is contained in the terms goods and services. Compare bads and disservices.)

In most societies, goods and services are not regarded as desirable in themselves, and no great virtue is attached to piling them up endlessly in warehouses, never to be consumed. What is regarded as desirable is that the individual should have at least some of his wants and needs satisfied. Goods and services are the means by which this end, consumer satisfaction, may be reached. The act of making goods and services is called *production*, and the act of using them to satisfy wants is called *consumption*.

Scarcity

The human wants that can be satisfied by consuming goods and services may be regarded, for all practical purposes in today's world, as limitless. In relation to the known desires of individuals (for better food, clothing, housing, schooling, vacations, entertainments, etc.), the existing supply of resources is woefully inadequate; it is sufficient to produce only a small fraction of the goods and services that people desire. This fact gives rise to one of the basic problems encountered in economics, the problem of *scarcity:* Since there are not enough resources to produce everything we would like, there must exist some mechanism by which we decide what will be done and what left undone; what goods will be produced and what left unproduced; what quantity of each good will be produced; and whose wants will be satisfied and whose left unsatisfied.

Choice

Because resources are scarce, we are forced to choose. By choosing to have more of one thing, we necessarily choose to have less of another. All societies face this problem, and all societies must decide what to produce and how to divide it among the individuals composing the society. Who makes such decisions? Who chooses? In most societies, there are a great many different individuals and organizations that either make or influence these choices. Individual consumers, business organizations, labor unions, farmers, and government officials all exert some influence. One of the differences between the economies of such countries as the United States, the United Kingdom, India, and the Soviet Union is in the amount of influence that different groups have upon the choices. The problem of choice arises over and over again in economics; it will be helpful, therefore, to consider it briefly at the outset. We first consider a trivial example and then one that vitally affects all of us today. It is important to note that the principles involved are the same in both examples.

CHOCOLATES OR GUMDROPS?

Consider the choice that must be made by a small boy who has 10¢ to spend and who is determined to spend it all on candy. For him there are only two kinds of candy in all the world: gumdrops, which are priced at 1¢ each, and chocolates, which sell for 2¢ each. The boy would like to buy 10 gumdrops and 10 chocolates, but he knows (or will soon discover) that this is not possible. (In technical language, it is not a *feasible combination* given his scarce resources.) There is, however, a large number of feasible combinations he might buy: 8 gumdrops and 1 chocolate, 4 gumdrops and 3 chocolates, 2 gumdrops and 1 chocolate, etc. Some of these feasible combinations (such as the last one listed) leave him with money left over, but he is not interested in them. There are only six combinations that are both feasible and that use all of his money. List them. After careful thought, the boy has almost decided to buy 6 gumdrops and 2 chocolates, but, at the last moment, he decides that he simply must have 3 chocolates. What will it cost him to get this extra chocolate? One answer to this question is 2 gumdrops. Economists would say that the *opportunity cost* of the third chocolate is what he must sacrifice in order to get it, which in this case is indeed 2 gumdrops. Another answer is that the cost is 2¢, but given his budget and his intentions, this answer is less revealing than the first one.[1] Where the real choice is between more of this and less of that, the cost of "this" is more fruitfully looked at as what you must sacrifice of "that." The idea of opportunity cost is often more difficult than this simple example suggests, and it will be discussed in more detail in Chapter 17. But it is important to recognize, at the very start of one's study of economics, that every time one is forced by scarcity to make a choice, one is incurring costs.

SWORDS OR PLOWSHARES?

So far in the 1960s about 10 percent of the total resources of the American economy has been devoted to the production of goods for defense. The American people have made a choice between the production of goods for consumption by private individuals and the production of goods for the defense program. This choice is similar in form if not in importance to the one facing the boy deciding what candies to buy with his 10¢. Because the resources of the American society are limited, it is not possible to produce an unlimited supply of both defense goods and consumption goods. If we have full employment of resources and if we wish to produce more defense goods, then we must produce fewer of all other goods, thus reducing the supply of goods available to satisfy the wants of individuals. Indeed, one of the great problems in deciding what to spend on defense is to decide to what extent we are willing to produce fewer goods to satisfy the wants of private individuals.

This choice may be illustrated in a diagram that is extremely helpful at various stages in economics.[2] In Figure 1, we measure

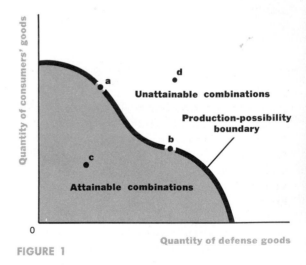

FIGURE 1

1. Of course, given the prices of both goods in terms of money, it is not difficult to compute the opportunity cost in terms of gumdrops.

2. The elements of the problem in which we are interested can be revealed by a choice between two goods. Although the same elements are present in a choice between more than two goods, the statement of the multigood choice problem is complex. The assumption of an economy producing only two goods greatly simplifies the present argument while detracting nothing of importance from it.

the quantity of defense goods produced along the horizontal axis and the quantity of consumers' goods produced along the vertical axis. Any point on the diagram thus indicates some amount of each kind of good produced in the economy. If resources were unlimited, any combination of the two goods could be produced. Because resources are limited, however, some combinations—those that would require for their production more than the total available supply of resources—cannot be obtained. The downward-sloping curve on the graph divides the combinations that can be obtained (such as the ones labeled *a, b,* and *c*) from those that cannot be obtained (such as *d*). Points to the right of this curve, which is often called a boundary or a frontier, cannot be obtained because there are not enough resources; points to the left of the boundary can be obtained without using all of the available resources; and points on the boundary can just be obtained if all of the available

resources are used. The line is called the *production-possibility boundary.* It slopes downward from upper left to lower right because, on this boundary (i.e., when all resources are being used), to get more of one kind of good we must sacrifice some of the other kind, and vice versa.[3]

SUMMARY

Most of the problems of economics arise out of the use of resources to satisfy human wants. Resources are used to produce goods and services that are then consumed. The problem of choice arises because resources are scarce in relation to the virtually unlimited wants that they could be used to satisfy. The concept of opportunity cost emphasizes the problem of choice by measuring the cost of obtaining a quantity of one commodity in terms of the quantity of some other commodity that could have been obtained instead.

Basic Economic Problems

Most of the specific questions posed at the beginning of this chapter (and many other questions as well) may be regarded as aspects of six more general questions that all economies must face, whether they be capitalist, socialist, or communist. Let us consider each briefly.

1. *What goods and services are being produced and in what quantities are they being produced?* This question arises directly out of the scarcity of resources. In terms of Figure 1, we are asking how choices are made between

points such as *a* and *b*. The question of what goods are produced and what are unproduced concerns the *allocation of scarce resources among alternative uses* (a shorter phrase, *resource allocation,* will be used hereafter). The questions "What determines the allocation of resources in various societies?" and "What are the consequences of conscious attempts to change resource allocation?" have occupied economists since the earliest days of economics. Any economy in which resources are scarce in relation to human wants must have

3. The boundary slopes downward, but we do not want to say anything else about its shape at this time. We might have drawn a straight line, which would imply that the opportunity cost of X stayed constant no matter how much we had of it. We might have made the curve convex or concave. The student should regard the shape as drawn in this chapter as wholly arbitrary. Nothing we say in this chapter depends upon the shape of the curve, other than that it be downward sloping.

some mechanism to produce decisions on the problem of resource allocation. In free-market economies, the majority of decisions about the allocation of resources is made through the price system. The branch of economics that encompasses the workings of the price system is called the *theory of price*.[4]

2. *By what methods are these goods produced*? This question arises whenever there is more than one technically possible way in which goods can be made. Generally there are many such ways. Agricultural commodities, for example, can be produced by farming a small quantity of land very intensively, using large quantities of fertilizer, labor, and machinery, or by farming a large quantity of land extensively, using only small quantities of fertilizer, labor, and machinery. Both methods can be used to produce the same quantity of some good; one method is frugal with land but uses large quantities of other resources, whereas the other method uses large quantities of land but economizes on the other resources. Similar possibilities are available with manufactured goods: It is usually possible to produce the same output by several different techniques, ranging from ones using a large quantity of labor and only a few simple machines to those using a large quantity of highly automated machinery and only a very small number of workers. The *theory of production* analyzes why one method of production is used rather than another, and whether or not it matters.

3. *How is the supply of goods allocated among the members who make up the society*? The distribution of the national product among various individuals and groups in the society is clearly of great general interest. Economists have long asked what governs the distribution of the national product among various groups, such as farmers, workers, and owners of companies in a free-market society. To what extent can active government intervention, such as that manifested in the War on Poverty (and in social-security programs, minimum-wage legislation, and the graduated income tax) succeed in altering the distribution of income? What are the consequences of such interventions?

Interest in these problems is as active today as it was a century or two ago when Adam Smith and David Ricardo made their path-breaking attempts to solve them. Such problems are dealt with in studying the *theory of distribution*.

4. *How efficiently are the resources being used*? This question gives rise to two other questions: Is production efficient?, and Is distribution efficient? Production is said to be inefficient if it would be possible merely to reallocate resources and produce more of at least one good without simultaneously producing less of any other good. Any scheme of production that uses all of society's resources but produces inefficiently leads to an output combination that falls inside the production-possibility boundary (at a point such as *c* in Figure 1). It would be possible to get more of either (or both) goods by using more efficient methods of production.

An analogous situation might also arise with distribution. The distribution of the national product is said to be inefficient if it would be possible to redistribute the exist-

---

4. The concept of a free-market economy will be developed at great length throughout this book. It will suffice for present purposes to say that such an economy is one in which most of the choices that are made are achieved by letting individuals buy and sell as they please in uncontrolled markets. The opposite extreme is a centrally controlled economy in which these choices are made mainly by government decree. All actual economies lie somewhere between the two extremes of complete central control and complete absence of it.

ing production among the individuals forming the society and make at least one person better off without simultaneously making anyone worse off.[5]

There is reason to believe that inefficiencies exist in all economies. If they could be removed it would be possible to increase the production of everything simultaneously and to make everyone in the society better off simultaneously. The importance of such inefficiencies, however, depends on their *quantitative* significance. It would not be worthwhile spending time and effort to remove them unless the cost of so doing was more than made up by the gains resulting from their removal. In fact, not enough is known about the quantitative significance of such inefficiencies.

Questions about the efficiency of production and distribution belong to the branch of economic theory called *welfare economics*. A detailed study of this very difficult branch of economics is beyond the scope of this book. Problems of efficiency will, however, be touched upon at many points.

These four questions are related to the allocation of resources and the distribution of goods and are intimately connected, in a market economy, to the way in which the price system works. They are sometimes grouped under the general heading of *microeconomics*. The next two questions have a somewhat different focus, and fall into what is called *macroeconomics*.

5. *Are the country's resources being fully utilized, or are some of them lying idle?* It may seem strange that we should ask this question at all. Surely, you will say, if resources are so scarce that there are not enough of them to produce all of those goods that are urgently required, there can be no question of the resources that are available being left idle. Certainly, no individual or government would *plan* to waste resources that are so scarce. Yet, it is one of the most disturbing characteristics of free-market economies that such waste sometimes occurs. When this happens the resources are said to be involuntarily unemployed (or, more simply, *unemployed*). Unemployed workers would like to have jobs, the factories in which they could work are available, the managers and owners would like to be able to operate their factories, raw materials are available in abundance, and the goods that could be produced by these resources are urgently required by individuals in the community. Yet, for some reason, nothing happens: The workers stay unemployed, the factories lie idle, and the raw materials remain unused. The cost of such periods of unemployment is felt both in terms of the goods and services that could have been produced by the idle resources, and in terms of the terrible effects on human beings who are unable to find work for prolonged periods of time.[6]

We illustrate this kind of problem in Figure 2. The dashed line indicates the production-possibility boundary for the level of employment of resources actually being used.[7] The solid line indicates the position

5. This is possible because in some situations two people will *each* be glad to make a trade with the other.

6. The student with no personal experience of unemployment or depression should attempt to gain some idea of this experience by reading one or two of the many books on the Great Depression of the 1930s. Two such books are George Orwell's *The Road to Wigan Pier* (Harcourt, Brace & World, 1958), and John Steinbeck's *The Grapes of Wrath* (Viking, 1958). Both are also available in paperback.

7. There would be a different production-possibility boundary for every different level of resource use. The boundary in Figure 2 indicated by the dashed line represents about 20 percent of resources unemployed.

of the boundary under conditions of full employment of resources. Unemployment of resources is similar to an inefficient use of them (discussed in Question 4 above) in that they both lead to production inside the production-possibility boundary. They are not the same problem, however, and the remedies are, as we shall see, very different.

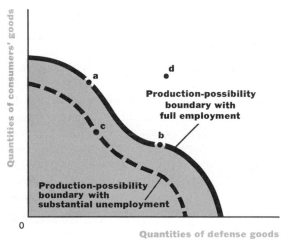

Production-possibility boundary with full employment

Production-possibility boundary with substantial unemployment

Quantities of consumers' goods

Quantities of defense goods

FIGURE 2

It is one of the most important problems of economics to discover why market economies produce such periods of unemployment, *which are unwanted by virtually everyone in the society.* Having discovered why they do, the next problem is to investigate how such unemployment can be prevented from occurring in the future. These problems have long been the concern of economists. Their study was given renewed importance by the Great Depression, when, for nearly ten years, almost all countries experienced heavy unemployment. In the United States and the United Kingdom, for example, labor unemployment during that period was never less than one worker in ten, and it rose to a maximum of approximately one worker in

four. This meant that, during the worst part of the Depression, a quarter of the country's resources was lying involuntarily idle, and this at a time when President Roosevelt said that a third of the nation was ill fed, ill housed, and ill clothed. These problems are studied under the headings of *national-income theory* and *business-cycle theory*.

A great advance was made in the study of these phenomena with the publication in 1936 of *The General Theory of Employment, Interest, and Money,* by John Maynard Keynes. This book, and the whole branch of economic theory that grew out of it, has greatly widened the scope of economics. It has not only added to our knowledge of the problems of unemployed resources, but has provoked prolonged discussion of ways to deal with them. These problems are, however, still with the American economy. The first half of the 1960s has been a period of substantial prosperity, but unemployment in the United States has averaged well over 5 percent of the total labor force during this period. On the other hand, the problem of unemployment has not been serious since World War II in many other economies. In Britain, for example, unemployment has averaged 1.5 percent of the labor force in the first half of the 1960s and it has not risen above 2.5 percent since the war.

6. *Is the economy's capacity to produce goods growing or remaining the same over time?* It is obviously a matter of concern whether an economy's capacity to produce goods and services remains static or grows from year to year. If the capacity to produce does grow steadily, as it has in most Western countries over the last few centuries, then a steady increase in living standards is made possible. Why the capacity to produce grows rapidly in some economies, slowly in others, and not at all in yet others is a critical prob-

lem that has exercised the minds of the best economists from the time of Adam Smith to the present. It is also a major area of interest to today's policy-maker. Although a certain amount is now known in this field, a great deal remains to be discovered. Problems of this type are dealt with in the *theory of economic development and growth.*

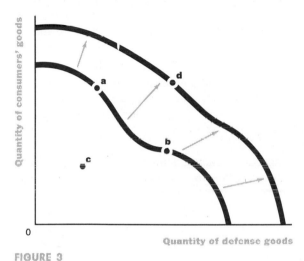

FIGURE 3

Growth in productive capacity can be represented in a production-possibility diagram as a pushing outward of the boundary, as shown in Figure 3. In both of the previous figures, Point *d* was outside of the attainable region. But if the economy is growing in its capacity to produce goods and services, combinations that are unattainable today become attainable tomorrow.

In this chapter we have presented a very general view of the whole subject of economics and have paid particular attention to the interrelation between the various parts of economics that we will deal with in subsequent chapters.

Theory is meant to relate to problems. If the student cannot think of a set of real-world problems to which the theory he is studying might help to provide answers, then either he or the theory has failed. The student is advised to refer back to this chapter when he feels that he has lost sight of the problems to which a particular part of economic theory is directed.

Summary

1. The problems of economics arise out of the use of resources (called factors of production) to produce goods and services that are consumed in order to satisfy human wants.

2. The problem of scarcity arises because wants are limitless while resources are not; thus, all wants cannot fully be satisfied.

3. All societies, faced with the problem of scarcity, must have a means of deciding how much of which wants will be satisfied and how much of which will be left unsatisfied.

4. When there is scarcity, the cost of having something can be viewed in terms of the quantity of something else that you must give up in order to get it. Economists call this concept opportunity cost; it is an important idea and one that will come up repeatedly in this book.

5. Most of the questions met in economics can be regarded as aspects of the following six general questions that arise in all economies: What goods and services are being produced in what quantities? By what methods are they being produced? How is the available supply of goods allocated among the members

of the society? How efficiently are the resources being used? Are the country's resources being fully utilized, or are some of them lying idle? Is the economy's capacity to produce goods growing or remaining the same over time?

QUESTIONS FOR DISCUSSION

1. "The economics of scarcity is obsolete. Surely in America our problems are those of abundance." What do economists mean by **scarcity**? Is it the same thing as poverty? What is meant by scarcity in the above quotation? If the current "War on Poverty" campaign succeeds, would you then agree with the statement?

2. Economists use the term free goods to describe commodities that are so plentiful that everyone can have as much of them as they could conceivably use. How many free goods can you think of?

3. What is the opportunity cost of trying to get a man to the moon by 1970?

4. Take each of the questions on pages 3 and 4 and say which part of economics each comes under and which of the six general questions listed in point 5 of the summary on page 11 each is an aspect of. You may be uncertain about some of the questions, but you should have no trouble classifying most of them.

5. Classify in the same manner as in 4 above each of the following headlines from the *New York Times:*

a. "Unemployment Down Again in May"
b. "New York Post Begins Computer Printing"
c. "Auto Sales Hit New Record"
d. "Coffee Prices Falling"
e. "Canada Expecting Lag in Industrial Expansion"
f. "Rise in Minimum Wage Urged"
g. "Subsidized Ship Lines Charged with Waste"

Chapter **2** ECONOMICS AS A SOCIAL SCIENCE

IN CHAPTER 1 WE BRIEFLY MENTIONED THE kinds of problems with which economics is concerned. We must now consider how to deal with these problems. In other words, having outlined the scope of the subject, we must now consider its method. This discussion of method will occupy us for the next three chapters. Although it may seem a long introduction to someone anxious to learn more about economics, the questions "What can we hope to learn?" and "How can we go about it?" are clearly very important ones. They are also questions about which there is a vast amount of misunderstanding and even superstition.

Economics is generally regarded as a social science, but can economics ever hope to be "scientific" in its study of those aspects of human behavior with which it is concerned? If we are going to talk about science, the first thing we must do is to distinguish between positive and normative statements, for it is

science's ability to make this distinction that has been one of the reasons for its success in the last 300 years.

Positive and Normative Statements

Positive statements concern what *is* and *normative* statements concern what *ought to be*. Positive statements, assertions, or theories may be simple or they may be complex, but they are basically about what *is. Thus, disagreements over positive statements are appropriately settled by an appeal to the facts.* Normative statements, concerned with what ought to be, are inextricably bound up with philosophical, cultural, and religious systems. A normative statement is one that makes a *value judgment*—a judgment about what is good and what is bad. Disagreements may arise over normative statements because different individuals have different ideas of what is good and bad. *Disagreements over normative statements cannot be settled merely by an appeal to facts.*

Let us consider some examples of positive and normative assertions, questions, and hypotheses in order to clarify the distinction.

The statement "It is impossible to break

up atoms" is a positive statement that can quite definitely be (and of course has been) refuted by empirical observations, whereas the statement "Scientists ought not to break up atoms" is a normative statement that involves an ethical judgment. The questions "What government policies will reduce unemployment?" and "What policies will prevent inflation?" are positive questions, whereas the question "Ought we to be more concerned about unemployment than about inflation?" is a normative question. The statement "A government deficit will reduce unemployment and cause an increase in prices" is a very simple hypothesis in positive economics, an hypothesis that could be tested by an appeal to empirical observation, whereas the statement "In setting policy, unemployment ought to matter more than inflation" is a normative hypothesis that cannot be settled by a simple appeal to observation.[1]

The distinction between positive and nor-

1. Having grasped this distinction, the student must beware that he does not turn it into an inquiry-stopping, dogmatic rule. From the fact that positive economics does not include normative questions (because its tools are inappropriate to them) it does *not* follow that the student of positive economics must stop his study of it as soon as someone says the word *ought* Consider the statement "It is my value judgment that we *ought to have* rent control because controls are *good.*" Now it is quite in order for you as a practitioner of positive economics to ask why rent control is good. It may be argued that rent control has certain consequences and it is these consequences that are judged to be good. But the statements about the consequences of rent control will be positive testable statements. Thus the pursuit of what appears to be a normative statement will often turn up positive hypotheses on which our *ought* conclusion depends. There are, for example, probably few people who believe that government control of industry is in itself good or bad. Their advocacy or .opposition will be based on certain beliefs that can be stated as positive rather than normative hypotheses—for example, whether they believe that government control reduces or increases efficiency; changes or does not change the distribution of income; leads or does not lead to an increase of state control in other spheres. A careful study of this very emotive subject will reveal an agenda for positive economic inquiry that could keep a research team of economists occupied for the next ten years.

mative statements follows from the fact that it is logically impossible to deduce normative statements from positive assumptions, and *vice versa*. Thus, if I think something ought to be done, I can deduce other things that, if I wish to be consistent, ought to be done; but I can deduce nothing about what is done (i.e., is true). On the other hand, if I know that two things are true, I can deduce other things that must be true, but I can deduce nothing about what is desirable (i.e., *ought to be*).

To take an example, suppose I believe (1) that it is a moral principle that one ought to be charitable to all human beings. Then, if I am told (2) that the inhabitants of China are not Christians but are human beings, it follows (3) that one ought to be charitable toward the Chinese. We have thus deduced from (1) and (2) a normative principle about how we ought to behave; no positive statement about how we do behave can be deduced from (1) and (2). Now, suppose someone else comes along and says, "Ah, you ought not to be charitable toward the Chinese because moral principles dictate that you should only be charitable toward Christians." If we now get into an argument about whether or not we should be charitable toward the Chinese this argument will turn on our value judgments about how one ought to behave. These are questions on which reasonable people sometimes just have to agree to disagree. If both sides insist on holding to their views on charity, and even if both are perfectly reasonable men, there is no civilized way of forcing one to admit he is wrong.

Now, assume I say (1) that capital punishment is a strong disincentive to murder and (2) that the Chinese abolished capital punishment after the Revolution so that (3) the number of murders must have risen in China since the Revolution. These two fac-

tual statements, (1) and (2), and the deduction that follows from them are all positive statements. We can deduce nothing about the moral desirability of abolishing capital punishment from statements (1) and (2), even if we were certain they were correct. Now let us say someone else comes along and says, "The number of murders has not risen in China since the Revolution; in fact the number has fallen." If he holds this view he must deny one or other of my first two positive statements. He might deny it by saying, for example, that capital punishment is actually an incentive to commit murder, or he might deny it by saying that, although they pretended to abolish capital punishment as a propaganda move, in fact the Chinese retained it after the Revolution. In both cases we are disagreeing over factual statements. If we gathered enough facts and if we are both reasonable, one of us can be forced to admit he is wrong.

Economics, like other sciences, is concerned with questions, statements, and hypotheses that could conceivably be shown to be wrong (i.e., falsified) *by actual observations of the world*. We do not have to show them to be consistent with the facts tomorrow or the next day; we only have to imagine factual evidence that could show them to be wrong. *Thus an appeal to the facts is an appropriate way in which to deal with them.* Other questions, including normative ones, cannot be settled by a mere appeal to empirical observation. This does not, of course, mean that they are unimportant. We must decide such questions as "Should we subsidize higher education?" and "Should we send food to Red China?," but we must decide them by means other than a simple appeal to facts. In practice, we usually tend to settle such questions by voting on them.

So far then, we have said that the separation of the positive from the normative is one of the foundation stones of science and that scientific inquiry, as we normally understand it, is confined to positive questions. We must now consider in more detail just what the scientific approach is and how scientific theories are developed and used.

The Scientific Approach

Very roughly speaking, the scientific approach consists in relating questions to evidence. When presented with a controversial issue, the scientist will ask for the evidence both for and against. He may then take a stand on the issue dictated by his assessment of the evidence. This stand will be taken with more or less conviction depending on the weight of the evidence. If there is little or no evidence, the scientist will say that, at present, it is impossible to take a stand. He will then set about searching for relevant evidence. If he finds that the issue is framed in terms that make it impossible to gather evidence for or against it, he will then usually try to recast the question so that it can be answered by an appeal to the evidence.[2] This approach to a problem is what sets scientific inquiries off from other inquiries.[3] In some fields, the scientist, having reframed the question, is then able to generate observations that will provide evidence for or against the hypothesis. *Experimental sciences,* such as chemistry and some branches of psychology, have an advantage because it is possible for them to call up relevant evidence on command. Other sciences, such as astronomy and economics, cannot do this. They must wait for time to throw up observations that may be used as evidence in testing their theories.

The ease or difficulty with which one can collect or even manufacture evidence does not determine whether a subject is scientific or nonscientific, although many people believe that it does; it is merely one of the factors determining the degree of ease with which the scientific inquiries of various fields can be pursued.[4] The way in which scientific inquiry proceeds differs radically, however, between fields in which laboratory experiment is possible and those in which it is not. In this chapter we consider general problems more or less common to all sciences. In Chapter 4 we shall deal with problems peculiar to

2. One of the really challenging problems to the scientist is to find out how to pose a question in the general spirit of the problem in which people are interested and in a form capable of being answered by reference to evidence. There is no formula for this; it is a real art and one of the most difficult of all problems.

3. Other approaches might be to appeal to authority, for example, to Aristotle or the Scriptures, to appeal by introspection to some inner experience (to start off "all reasonable men will surely agree"), or to proceed by way of definitions to the "true" nature of the problem or concepts under consideration.

4. It is often thought that scientific procedure consists of grinding out answers with reference to blind rules of calculation and that it is only in the arts that the exercise of real imagination is required. This view is misguided, for there are no set rules for the framing of questions. It is a step that often requires great imagination. Also, the collection of relevant evidence often requires ingenuity (e.g., the Michelson-Morley experiment). What the scientific method gives is an impersonal set of criteria for answering some questions; but what questions to ask and exactly how to ask them and exactly how to obtain the evidence are different problems requiring, upon occasion, great feats of imagination.

the nonexperimental sciences, which must accept observations in the forms in which they are thrown up by the actual world of experience.

THE SCIENTIFIC ATTITUDE IN EVERYDAY LIFE

It is often said that we live in a scientific age. Over the last several hundred years the citizens of most Western countries have enjoyed the fruits of innumerable scientific discoveries. But the scientific advances that have so profoundly affected the average citizen have been made by an extremely small minority of the population. These advances have generally been accepted without even the slightest idea either of the technical nature of the discoveries involved, or of the attitude that made them possible. If we take as a measure of the influence of science the degree of dissemination of the fruits of science, then we live in a profoundly scientific age, but if we take as our measure the degree to which the general public understands and practices the scientific approach, then we are definitely in a prescientific era. Indeed, the scientific method of answering questions by appealing to a carefully collected and coordinated body of facts is a method that is seldom adopted by the public.

Consider, for example, the arguments that periodically occur over the national debt. Some people may oppose the national debt because they believe that a good moral code

requires that the government finance its expenditures entirely by taxation. These people, however, are making value judgments; they are taking a normative approach to a positive matter. The great majority of arguments about the national debt are not of this type, but are, rather, predictions about observable behavior and thus belong to the field of science. One line of argument is that if we increase the size of the debt we will have inflation. Another is that if we have a debt we will transfer responsibility for paying for our activities to a later generation. A more extreme view (but still a common one) is that a growing debt is bound to lead to a crisis and to a collapse of confidence in the government. These are factual assertions on which evidence can be brought to bear.

It is truly amazing how people can become committed to such viewpoints without considering the available evidence. A survey of the press whenever the issue arises will show that most of the reasons on which these viewpoints are based are profoundly unscientific. How many participants in the discussion know, for example, what our experience with the national debt has been over the past thirty years? Yet it would seem to be impossible to have an informed discussion on the issue without this fundamental knowledge.

Many hotly debated issues of public policy are positive and not normative issues, but the scientific approach to positive issues is very often ignored when they are debated by the public.

A Science of Human Behavior?

Is it possible to conduct a scientific study in the field of human behavior? For example, would it be possible to conduct a scientific study of such subjects as the national debt

or capital punishment? It is often argued that the natural sciences deal with inanimate matter, which is subject to natural laws, whereas the social sciences deal with man, who has free will and cannot, therefore, be made the subject of inexorable laws. In discussing this problem it is important to distinguish between the behavior of individuals and the behavior of groups.

In many cases, social sciences such as economics do make predictions about the behavior of individuals. In economics we predict, for example, that under a set of carefully specified circumstances a fall in the price of a commodity will be associated with an increase in the consumption of that commodity. If we observe one individual for whom this does not hold then we must say that our prediction has been falsified. In most cases, however, we are concerned not so much with one individual's behavior as we are with the behavior of a group. We do not really care what each consumer does when the price of Oldsmobiles falls as long as we have a pretty good idea of what all consumers will do. This means that as long as we can say what any one individual will *probably* do, we can be fairly safe in saying precisely what a large group of individuals *will* do. Fortunately, there are many cases in both the natural and the social sciences in which we can predict with remarkable accuracy how the group will behave, although we cannot necessarily predict accurately the behavior of every single member of the group. No social scientist can predict, for example, when an individual is going to die, but death rates for large groups of individuals are stable enough to make life insurance a profitable business. It could not be so if group behavior were capricious. Also, no social scientist can predict what particular individuals will be killed in auto accidents on the next holiday weekend, but he can come very close to knowing how many in total will die.

The more objectively measurable data he is given concerning, for example, the weather on that weekend and the number of auto sales that year, the closer will he be able to predict the total number of deaths.

Successful predictions about the behavior of large groups are made possible by the so-called statistical law of large numbers. Very roughly, this law asserts that random movements of a large number of individual items tend to offset one another. This law is based on one of the most beautiful constants of behavior in the whole of science, natural and social, and yet it can be derived from the fact that human beings make errors! This is the *normal curve of error*, which the student will encounter in elementary statistics. Ask any one person to measure the length of a room and it will be almost impossible to predict in advance what sort of error of measurement he will make. Thousands of things will affect the accuracy of his measurement and, furthermore, he may make one error today and quite a different one tomorrow. But ask a thousand people to measure the length of the same room and we can predict within a very small margin of error how this *group* will make its errors! We can assert with confidence that more people will make small errors than will make large errors, that the larger the error the fewer will be the number of people making it, that the same number of people will overestimate as will underestimate the distance, and that the average error of all the individuals will be zero.[5] Here then is a truly remarkable constant pattern of human behavior—a constant on which most of the theory of statistical inference is based.

If a common cause should act on all the members of the group we can predict suc-

---

5. For purposes of measuring the error we define the "true" distance to be that measured by the most precise instruments of scientific measurement (whose range of error will be very small relative to the range of error of our thousand laymen all wielding tape measures).

cessfully what the average behavior of the group will be, even though any one member of the group may act in a surprising fashion. If, for example, we give all of our thousand individuals a tape measure that understates actual distances then we can predict that, on the average, the group will now understate the length of the room. It is, of course, quite possible that one member who had in the past been consistently undermeasuring distance because he was depressed psychologically will now overestimate the distance because the state of his health has changed (but something else may happen to some other individual which will turn him from an overmeasurer to an undermeasurer). Individuals may do peculiar things for reasons which, as far as we can see, are inexplicable, but the group's behavior, when the inaccurate tape is substituted for the accurate one, will none the less be predictable (precisely because the odd things that one individual does will tend to cancel the odd things that some other individual does).

If group human behavior were in fact random and capricious, there would be absolutely no point in trying to predict anything on the basis of sample surveys. The fact that 80 percent of the people sampled said they intended to vote for a certain candidate would give no information about the probable outcome of the election. Today's information might be totally reversed tomorrow. That there are discernible trends in election polls is proof of the fact that in politics people do not act at random.

Of course, it does not follow from anything that has been said so far that people never change their minds, or that future events can be foretold by a casual study of the past. Stu-

dents sometimes think in terms of a simple dichotomy: Either there are historical laws apparent to the casual observer or there is random behavior. They observe a prophet extrapolating a trend[6] make an utterly mistaken prophecy and conclude that, because the prophet cannot prophesy, human behavior is random and thus unamenable to scientific study. The election of Harry Truman in 1948, in spite of the predictions of almost all the polls that he would be defeated, is often cited as a case against the scientific inquiry into voting behavior. What it showed, however, is that a substantial proportion of the electorate can change their minds at quite a late date in the election campaign. But the fact that we can ask the question "Why did they change their minds?" shows that we do not believe that such changes are totally random and capricious. Whatever they may argue in the abstract, almost everyone proceeds as if human behavior were not random. Baseball fans do so when they take bets on who will win the pennant in the American League and Presidential aspirant Nelson Rockefeller did so when he dropped out of the race after the 1964 California primary. Both acts imply that there is some stability in human behavior.

To sum up, human behavior is not capricious; it exhibits more or less stable relationships with other factors that influence it. The significant question is now a *quantitative* one: How much stability is shown by human behavior and how much behavior appears to be random? This is an empirical question. It cannot be settled by *a priori* arguments; it can only be settled by careful and patient observation.[7] Only patient observation can answer this question, just as only patient observation can answer any positive question.

6. To "extrapolate a trend" is to prophesy that some change will take place in the future (e.g., a rise in the birth rate) merely because it has been taking place in the past.

7. *A priori* is a phrase commonly used by economists. It may be defined as that which is prior to actual experience, or as that which is innate or based on innate ideas.

The person who, when presented with evidence the implications of which he does not like, merely asserts that it is irrelevant because human beings are quite likely to do something totally different tomorrow is taking refuge in a medieval position. The weight of the evidence is against him. In trying to establish whether a particular facet of human behavior shows sufficiently stable relations with respect to certain factors influencing it as to be predictable,[8] the social scientist seeks the answer not in prejudice, hunches, and general considerations of human nature, but in an appeal to carefully collected and comprehensive evidence. In some cases he must conclude that, within the limits of present knowledge, a particular facet of behavior is unpredictable; in other cases, and there are many such cases in the social sciences, he finds that he can predict group human behavior within a remarkably narrow margin of error.

THIS IS AN ATTEMPT TO TREAT ECONOMICS AS A NATURAL SCIENCE BY USING EMPIRICAL
METHODS TO PROVE GIVEN ASSUMPTIONS. THIS TREATMENT IGNORES THE UNIQUENESS OF
ALL HISTORICAL EVENTS AND, WHAT'S MORE, REJECTS THE A PRIORI FOUNDATION ON WHICH OUR
UNDERSTANDING OF HUMAN ACTION STANDS.

The Nature of Scientific Theories

We all know that the natural sciences progress through the development of theories. We also know that these theories account for observed phenomena and that they sometimes suggest quite unexpected new phenomena which can then be investigated.[9] We must now ask a number of questions about scientific theories, paying special attention to the use of theories in economics.

WHAT IS THE PURPOSE OF THEORIES?

Theories grow in answer to the question "Why?" Some sequence of events, some regularity between two or more things is observed in the real world and someone asks why this occurs. A theory attempts to explain why. One of the main functions of a theory is to predict as yet unobserved events. Thus, for example, national income theory predicts that a government budget deficit will reduce the volume of unemployment.[10] The simple theory of market behavior predicts that, under certain specified conditions, the introduction of a sales tax will be accompanied by an increase in the price of the commodity concerned and that the price increase will be less than the amount of the tax. It also allows us to predict that, if there is a partial failure of the potato crop, the total income earned by potato farmers will increase. Thus a theory arises in an attempt to explain, or to account for, certain observed phenomena, and a successful theory has the major practical result that it enables us to predict in advance the consequences of various occurrences.

TRUE IN THEORY BUT NOT IN PRACTICE?

All we actually observe in the world is a sequence of events. Any explanation whatsoever of how these events are linked together is a theoretical construct. Theories are what we use to impose order on our observations,

8. The prediction would take the form: If the influencing factors change in such and such a way, the behavior will change in some stated way.

9. There was, for example, the famous implication of the relativity theory that light waves passing close to the sun would be bent perceptibly by the sun's gravitation.

10. A budget deficit arises when the government spends more than it raises by way of taxes. This is not so simple a prediction as might appear at first sight. What it means and how it can be tested is considered in Chapters 51 and 58.

to explain how what we see is linked together. Without theories we would only have a shapeless mass of meaningless observations. If we are to make any sense at all of what we see, the choice is not one between theory and observation but between better or worse theories to explain our observations.

The next time you hear someone say, "That may be true in theory but not in practice" (or, indeed, the next time you say it yourself) you should immediately reply, "All right then, tell me what does happen in practice." It is almost certain that you will not be told facts but will be given an alternative theory—a different explanation of the facts. The speaker should have said, "The theory in question provides a poor explanation of the facts" (i.e., it is contradicted by some factual observations) and that his alternative theory is a better one.

WHAT IS A THEORY AND HOW DOES ONE TEST THEORIES?

A theory consists of (1) a set of *definitions* that states clearly what we mean by various terms, (2) a set of *assumptions* that defines the conditions under which the theory is to apply, and (3) one or more *hypotheses* about the way in which the world behaves. Hypotheses may be simple assertions or they may be logical deductions from the assumptions. In the former case, we sometimes refer to them as assumptions; in the latter case, we refer to them as implications. The implications that are deduced from the assumptions can be tested against actual empirical observations and we can then conclude either that the theory is refuted by the

facts, or that it is consistent with the facts.

Assumptions about behavior made in a theory often cause the student real concern. Consider a theory that starts out: "Assume that there is no government." "Surely," says the reader, "this assumption is totally unrealistic and I cannot take seriously anything that comes out of the theory." But this assumption may merely be the economist's way of saying that, whatever the government does, even whether or not it exists, *is irrelevant for the purposes of his particular theory.* Now, put this way, the statement becomes an empirical assertion, and the only way to test it is to see if the predictions which follow from the theory do or do not fit the facts that the theory is trying to explain. If they do, then the theorist was correct in his assumption that the government could be ignored; the criticism that the theory is unrealistic because we know that there really is a government is completely beside the point. Assumptions, however, are used in economics for other purposes, particularly to outline the set of conditions under which a theory is meant to hold. Consider a theory that assumes that the government has a balanced budget. This may mean that the theorist intends his theory to apply only when there is a balanced budget; it may *not* mean that the size of the government's budget surplus or deficit is irrelevant to the theory. The student may find it confusing that an assumption may mean many different things in economics. When he encounters an assumption in economic theory he should, therefore, do two things: ask what information the assumption is intended to convey,[11] and remember that it is not always appropriate to criticize the simplifying assumptions of

---

11. For example, that the world *actually* behaves, or is, as assumed; that the factor under consideration is irrelevant to the theory; that the theory only holds when the condition specified in the assumption actually holds; and that a convenient fiction is being introduced to formalize some quite complex piece of human behavior.

a theory on the grounds that they are unrealistic. It is important to remember that all theory is an abstraction from reality. If we did not abstract we would merely duplicate the world and would add nothing to our understanding of it. A good theory abstracts in a useful and significant way; a bad theory does not. If the student believes that the theorist has assumed away something that is important for the problem at hand, then he must believe, and try to show, that the *conclusions* of the theory are contradicted by the facts.

A theory enables us to predict as yet unobserved events. What is the nature of a scientific *prediction,* and is it the same thing as being able to prophesy the future? The critical point to notice about a scientific prediction is that it is a conditional statement that takes the form: *If* you do this *then* such and such will follow. *If* you mix hydrogen and oxygen under specified conditions, *then* water will be the result. *If* the government has a large budget deficit, *then* the volume of employment will be increased. It is most important to notice that this prediction is very different from the statement: "I prophesy that in two years' time there will be a large increase in employment because I believe the government will decide to have a large budget deficit." The government's decision to have a budget deficit or surplus in two years' time will be the outcome of many complex factors, emotions, objective circumstances, chance occurrences, etc., none of which can be predicted by the economist. If the economist's prophecy about the level of employment turns out to be wrong because in two years' time the government does not have a large deficit, then all we will have learned is that the economist is not a good guesser about the behavior of the government; we will not have refuted any economic theory. However, *if* the government does have a large deficit (in two years' time or at any other time) and *then* the volume of employment does not rise, we have refuted a (conditional) scientific prediction in the field of economic theory.[12] It is the conditional nature of scientific predictions that causes so much difficulty when we try to test the theories.[13]

In testing a theory we confront its prediction about the world with observations taken from the world. Let us take, for example, the simple economic theory that predicts that *if* a sales tax is levied on the product of a competitive industry, *then* the price of the product will rise, but by less than the amount of the tax. It is not claimed that this prediction holds only for the years 1945-1970, or only in odd-numbered years, or only in the United States and Germany but not in France and Paraguay. The prediction says that this result will hold *whenever a sales tax is levied in a competitive industry.* The theory is unbounded both in time and in space. We can imagine amassing such a weight of contradictory evidence (cases in which sales taxes in competitive industries either caused prices

12. Economic forecasting is not synonymous with economic prediction. Forecasting is a type of conditional prediction that attempts to tell the future by discovering such relations between economic variables as: the value of Y at some future date depends on the value of X today, in which case future Y can be predicted by observing present X. Many conditional predictions are not of this form; those that relate the Y today to the value of X today provide significant and useful relations that allow us to predict that, if you do this to X you will do that to Y, without allowing us to forecast the future.

13. The problem of testing is the subject of Chapter 4, but the essence of the problem is this: Suppose a theory tells us that, under specified conditions, X and Y are supposed to vary together, but we observe that they do not vary together. Have we refuted the theory, or did the specified conditions not hold? In laboratory sciences, we can control for the required conditions, but in nonlaboratory sciences we cannot, and thus we must use more sophisticated techniques to test theories.

from the class of nonscientific statements by the fact that it is possible to imagine the existence of enough unfavorable evidence to force us to regard a scientific statement as false, whereas it is never possible to be forced to regard a nonscientific statement as being falsi-

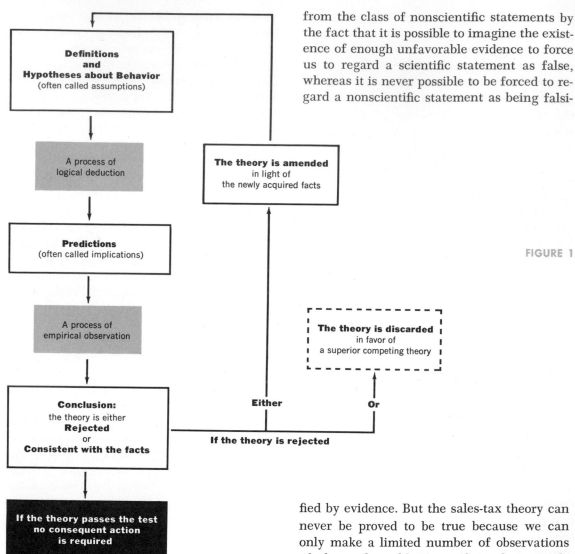

FIGURE 1

to fall, or caused them to rise by more than the amount of the tax) that we would be forced to reject the theory as giving misleading predictions about what would be observed to happen in the world. Indeed, the class of scientific statements is distinguished

fied by evidence. But the sales-tax theory can never be proved to be true because we can only make a limited number of observations of the real world. Even if we have made many observations that agree with the prediction, it is always possible that in the future someone will make a set of observations that refutes the theory. Thus, it is possible to conclude, after testing a theory against real-world observations, either that the theory must be rejected or that it is consistent with the existing observations. It is not possible to conclude that the theory has been proved correct.[14] Thus, if we really want to give a pet theory a run for its money to show that it is a good theory, we should not try to find a lot of facts that agree with it, seeking thereby to confirm it (it would be a pretty measly theory if we could not find some facts that agreed with it), but rather we should ask what tests would expose the theory to a serious chance of being upset by observable facts. The more critical the test, the greater will be our satisfaction if our theory passes the test. Our discussion of theory and tests is summed up in Figure 1.

WHEN IS A THEORY REJECTED?

Up to this point we have spoken as if it is an easy matter to decide when to reject a theory as being inconsistent with factual observations. With almost all economic theories, however, it is no such easy matter. As we explain in Chapter 4, we only expect our theories to hold within some margin of error. Thus it is rarely, if ever, possible that we can decide to reject some theory on the basis of a single crucial observation. Most often what happens is that evidence tends to accumulate which is more or less at variance with the predictions of the theory. Eventually, as the mass of evidence against the theory becomes impressive, someone comes forward with a new theory that is in closer agreement with the evidence than the original theory. The old theory is then abandoned.

In general, theories are abandoned when they are no longer useful, and they cease to be useful when they cannot predict the consequences of actions better than the next best alternative.[15] When this happens they are replaced by the best alternative. We should not be upset by this process. It is one means by which we learn new, surprising facts.

Any developing science will continually be having some of its theories rejected; it will also be cataloguing observations that cannot be fitted into, or explained by, any existing theory. These observations indicate the needs or directions required for the development of new theories or for the extension of existing ones.[16] On the other hand, there will be many implications of existing theories that have not yet been tested, either because no one has yet figured out how to test them, or merely because no one has got around to testing them. These untested hypotheses provide the agenda for new empirical observations.

Economics is no exception to this general rule. There are many observations of the world —for example, the distribution of the national product between wages, profits, and so on— for which there are at the moment no satisfactory theoretical explanations. On the other hand, there are many predictions—for example, that free international trade will make the earnings of labor less unequal between countries—that no one has yet satisfactorily tested. Thus the serious student of economics must not expect to find a set of answers to all possible questions as he progresses in his study. He must expect very often to encounter

14. For more detailed consideration of the rejection of statistical hypotheses, see Chapter 4.

15. In an advanced science, the alternative will be another competing theory. If there is no competing theory, we can compare the theory with predictions based on naïve views, such as "This year will be just like last year"; "Any change observed in the past will go on in the future"; and so on.

16. The development of a new theory to account for existing observations is often the result of real creative genius of an almost inspired nature. This step in the development of science is the exact opposite of the popular conception of the scientist as an automatic rule-follower. One could argue for a long time whether there was more original creative genius embodied in a first-class symphony or a new theory of astronomy. For a fascinating study of the creative process, the student should read Arthur Koestler, *The Sleep Walkers* (Macmillan, 1959), especially the section on Kepler.

nothing more than a set of problems that provides the agenda for further theoretical and empirical research. Even when he does find answers to problems, he should accept these answers as tentative; he should ask, even of the most time-honored theory, what observations he could make that would lead to a rejection of this theory. Economics is still a very young science and many problems in it are almost untouched. There can be little doubt that some of you who are now studying this book will elect to become professional economists and will find yourselves not too many years from now publishing a theory to account for some of the problems mentioned herein, or making a set of observations that will refute some time-honored theory described within these pages.

One final word of warning: Having recommended disrespect for the authority of accepted theory, it is necessary to warn against adopting an approach that is too cavalier. No respect attaches to the person who says: "This theory is for the birds; it is *obviously* wrong." This is too cheap. To criticize a theory effectively on empirical grounds one must demonstrate, by a carefully made set of observations, that some aspect of the theory is contradicted by the facts. This is a task that is not easily or lightly accomplished.

Summary

1. In this chapter we have considered what it means to say that economics is a social science.

2. It is necessary to distinguish between positive questions that concern what *is,* and normative questions that concern what *ought to be*.

3. The scientific approach to positive questions is to relate them to a carefully collected body of systematic evidence.

4. A social science uses the same general approach as a natural science. Fortunately, human beings exhibit sufficiently stable responses to certain stimuli that regularities can be observed, that theories can be erected to link the responses (the effects) to the stimuli (the causes), and that these theories can be used to predict how single individuals and how groups of individuals will react in as yet unobserved situations.

5. Theories that link events together in some causal sequence are tested by seeing if the predicted effect (e.g., a rise in the amount of butter bought) does or does not follow each time the cause is observed (e.g., a fall in the price of butter). If the theory consistently fails to pass this test, it must be amended or discarded.

QUESTIONS FOR DISCUSSION

1. Make five statements of your own about the size of the U.S. national debt. (It does not matter if your statements are actually correct, but you should confine yourselves to ones you think *might* be correct.) Classify each of your statements as positive or normative. If your list contains only one type of statement, see if you can add a sixth that is of the other type. How might you go about checking on the validity of those statements that you have classified as positive?

2. "If human behavior were completely capricious and unpredictable, life insurance could not be a profitable business." What other activities would

also be impossible or at least a waste of time?

3. Would the number of persons traveling on the New York subways at various times throughout the day increase or decrease if the fare were doubled for journeys begun between 5 P.M. and 6 P.M.? Is your answer a positive or a normative statement? How could we settle the matter if two of you give very different answers to this question?

4. In view of the evidence in Fig. A5, on page 56, and in Fig. 1, Chapter 49, what would you say about the validity of an economic theory that predicted that the economy tended to settle down in a stable situation of full employment of all resources that was disturbed only by occasional and short-lived bouts of unemployment?

5. "If the scientist finds that the issue is framed in such terms that it is impossible to gather evidence for or against it, he will then usually try to reword it, so that it can be answered by an appeal to the evidence." How might you begin to do this in the case of the following general assertions? "The American school system is the best in the world." "The American system of government is the best in the world." "The provision of free medical care for the aged will inevitably end in socialized medicine for all, and socialized medicine will destroy our high standards of medical practice by destroying the doctor's incentive to do his job well."

Chapter 3 THE TOOLS OF THEORETICAL ANALYSIS

THERE ARE TWO MAJOR SETS OF TOOLS WHICH the economist uses and with which the student must acquire some familiarity. The first set is composed of all the apparatus of logical deduction used to discover the implications of theories. Logical deduction allows the economist to discover the implications of his assumptions, and thus to deduce from his theories predictions about observable events.

The second set of tools is composed of all the techniques of statistical analysis that the economist requires when he comes to test his theories against empirical observations. At that stage, he seeks to discover how well his theories stand up when confronted by the facts. The present chapter is devoted to the tools of logical, or theoretical, analysis. Chapter 4 considers the tools of statistical analysis.

The Methods of Theoretical Analysis

We have already noted that an economic theory consists of a set of definitions, a set of assumptions, and one or more hypotheses about the way in which the world behaves. The economic theorist has the task of discovering what is implied by these hypotheses. He seeks to make statements such as, *if* costs vary in a certain way with output and *if* businessmen seek to make as much profit as they can, *then* a tax on the businessman's sales will have effects X, Y, and Z both on the level of output and on the price at which the product is sold. The hypotheses of economic theory are hypotheses about the relations between two or more things (e.g., the relation between the price of a commodity and the amount of it that people wish to buy). These relations may be described in words, formulated mathematically, or, if there are no more than three variables involved, graphically illustrated by using coordinate geometry. Once formulated in a precise way, implications of the hypotheses may also be derived by verbal argument, mathematical analysis, or geometry. Geometry is, of course, a branch of mathematics. Since we wish to distinguish geometrical from other mathematical techniques and to avoid the cumbersome expression "mathematical techniques other than geometry," we shall hereafter distinguish between "geometrical" and "mathematical" methods. Euclideans, forgive us.

Which method is best? This is analogous to asking whether a razor is a better tool than an axe. The answer depends upon what the task is, and on the capabilities of the person using the tool.

Verbal reasoning has the advantage of appealing to common sense at every step and, if the theory is simple, of being the easiest way of making deductions. It has the disadvantage of being long-winded; even in slightly complex theories it becomes cumbersome, and, as theories get progressively complex, it breaks down completely. In many cases, it is virtually impossible by verbal methods to say whether or not a given conclusion is implied by the assumptions of a theory.

Geometrical analysis has the advantage of pictorial appeal. Most people find it easier to comprehend a relation between two elements when a picture of it is drawn than when it is stated in an algebraic equation. The major drawback of geometry is that it is necessarily limited to three dimensions and, for most practical purposes, to two dimensions. We cannot show on a simple graph a relationship involving four factors when each one depends on the other three. Since such relations are common in economics, this is a serious drawback. Great ingenuity has been shown by some economic theorists in inventing dodges, such as two-dimensional graphs that show the relationship between more than two factors. But beyond a certain degree of complexity these graphs become extremely cumbersome and difficult to follow. Also there is a definite limit beyond which geometrical techniques cannot go; when that limit is reached, the tools of simple coordinate geometry prove inadequate.

At a certain stage of complexity, more elaborate mathematical analysis becomes an absolute necessity, but often, even before this stage, a mathematical treatment is much simpler than a geometrical or verbal treatment. The advantages of mathematics are generality and power; it is possible to handle very complex theories with relative ease if mathematics is used. The disadvantages are that, for many people, a mathematical treatment lacks the intuitive appeal of a verbal explanation or a simple geometrical treatment. And, for simple problems, the high-powered techniques of mathematics can often be more unwieldy than the lower-powered techniques of geometrical and verbal analysis.

To a great extent these methods are interchangeable; anything that can be done by using words or geometry can also be done by using algebraic notation; most of what can be expressed in words can be expressed geometrically and vice versa. Some problems that are done mathematically, however, cannot be done rigorously in verbal or in geometrical analysis. Where various methods can be used, the choice among them will be dictated by considerations of convenience, economy, and the techniques at the command of the practitioner and of the audience at which he is aiming.

Since a great deal of simple economic theory, both traditional and modern, is based on the assumption of simple relationships between two or three variables, geometrical techniques can be used extensively. However, in intermediate and advanced theory the relationships become more complex. For this reason most introductory textbooks rely almost exclusively on verbal and geometrical analysis, whereas an increasing number of advanced works rely almost exclusively on mathematical analysis, using only a few geometrical illustrations to give readers a feel for the more general analysis. We shall follow the usual practice and rely on verbal and geometrical argument; where this is insufficient, we shall point out how the matter might otherwise be demonstrated. In some ways, this decision is to be regretted since the trend in economics is undoubtedly toward dealing with more complex hypotheses that benefit from (even when they do not absolutely require) mathematical treatment. In the next section of this chapter, we introduce the basic mathematical language that is used to *express* hypotheses in a mathematical way. We urge *every* student to invest one hour (if it takes that long) in learning this language. It will pay him large dividends.

In subsequent chapters, we provide, in special footnotes and appendixes indicated by a dagger (†), mathematical statements, and in some cases proofs, of propositions treated in other ways in the text. These footnotes and appendixes are, of course, optional.

Expressing Hypotheses: The Concept of a Functional Relationship

The idea that one thing depends on another is one of the basic notions behind all of science. The gravitational attraction of two bodies depends on their total mass and on the distance separating them, attraction increasing with size and diminishing with distance; the number of murders in a country is thought to depend on, among other things, the severity of the penalties for murder; the amount of a commodity that people will buy is observed to depend on, among other things, the price of the commodity: The higher the price, the less will people buy. When mathematicians wish to say that one factor depends on another, they say that one factor is a *function* of the other. Thus we say that gravitational attraction is a function of the mass of the two bodies concerned and the distance between them; that murder is a function of the severity of punishment for it; and that the quantity of a product demanded is a function of the price of the product. One of the virtues of mathematics is that it allows us to express very compactly ideas that require a long-drawn-out verbal expression.

There are two steps in giving compact symbolic expression to the relations we have just described. First, we give each concept a symbol, and, second, we designate a symbol to express the idea of one factor's dependence on another. Thus, if we let G equal gravitational attraction, and M equal the mass of two bodies, and d equal the distance between two bodies, we may write

$$G = f(M, d),$$

where f is read "is a function of" and means "depends upon." The whole equation defines an hypothesis and is read "Gravitational attraction is a function of the mass of the two bodies and the distance between them." This is the same as the verbal statement with which we began.

The second hypothesis, that the number of murders depends on the severity of punishment for murder, may be expressed as

$$K = f(S),$$

where K is a measure of the frequency of murders and S is a measure of the severity of punishment for being convicted of murder. The functional relationship is read "The frequency of murders is a function of the severity of the punishment for being convicted of murder." Notice that this is not necessarily a statement of fact, but is, rather, a theory that may or may not prove to be borne out by the facts once we look at them.

Consider the hypothesis

$$D = f(p),$$

where D equals the quantity demanded of some commodity, and p equals the price of the commodity. State in words what this expression says.

The expression

$$Y = f(X)$$

says that Y is a function of X. It means that Y depends upon X. Until we have defined what X is and what Y is, it says nothing at all about the world; but as soon as we define Y and X, we are making a statement about a relationship between them.

The quantities X and Y in this functional relation are called *variables*. Variations in one of these quantities are associated with variations in the other quantity. The notation often looks frightening to the student, especially to someone who did not get on well with his high-school mathematics. However, once one becomes familiar with it, this notation is extremely helpful, and since the functional concept is basic to all science, worth mastering.

The expression $Y = f(X)$ merely states that Y is related to X; it says nothing about the form that this relation takes. Does Y increase as X increases? Does Y decrease as X increases? Or is the relation more complicated? Take a very simple example where Y is the length of a board in feet, and X is the length of the same board in yards. Quite clearly, $Y = f(X)$. Further, in this case we know the exact form of the function, for length in feet (Y) is merely 3 times the length in yards (X), so we may write $Y = 3X$. This *equation* specifies the exact form of the functional relation between Y and X and provides a rule whereby, if we have the value of one, we can calculate the value of the other. If, for example, we should want to know the value of Y when X is 6, we replace X with 6 and the equation tells us to multiply 6 by 3. We obtain 18, which is the value of Y. Clearly, this operation could be repeated for any conceivable value of X and the corresponding value of Y calculated. This example is not typical of all functional relationships because it is in fact true by definition. It is not an hypothesis because it is not capable of refutation. It merely states in functional form the relation between the definition of a foot and a yard. It is nonetheless useful to have a way of writing down relationships that are definitionally true.

Now consider a second example. Let C equal the total spending of a nation on all consumption goods in one year, and Y equal the total income of all persons in the nation in the same year, and let us state the hypothesis

$$C = f(Y), \quad \text{or, more specifically,} \quad (1)$$

$$C = .75Y. \quad (2)$$

Equation (1) says that we hypothesize that national consumption depends upon national income. Equation (2) says, more specifically, that expenditure on consumption will be three-quarters (.75 times) as large as national income. The more specific equation, Equation (2), expresses an hypothesis about the relation between two observable magnitudes. There is no reason why Equation (2) *must* be true; actually, it might not be consistent with the facts.[1] But those are matters for testing. What we do have in the equation is a concise statement of a particular hypothesis.

Thus the general fact that there is a relation between Y and X is denoted by $Y = f(X)$, whereas any precise relation may be expressed by a particular equation such as $Y = 2X$, $Y = 4X^2$, or $Y = X + 2X^2 + .5X^3$.

If Y increases as X increases (e.g., $Y = 10 + 2X$), we say that Y is an *increasing function* of X or that Y and X *vary directly with* each other. If Y decreases as X increases (e.g., $Y = 10 - 2X$), we say that Y is a *decreasing function* of X or that Y and X *vary inversely with* each other.

Economic theory is based on relations between various magnitudes (e.g., the quantity demanded of some commodity is related to the price of that commodity; the amount spent on consumption is related to national income). All such relations can be expressed in the form of mathematical equations, and it is this fact among others that gives mathematical analysis importance in economics.

The Error Term

The examples of functional relations considered above were all *deterministic* ones in the sense that they were expressed as if they held exactly: Given the value of X we knew the value of Y exactly. The relations considered in economic theory are seldom of this deterministic sort.[2] When an economist says

that the world *behaves* so that $Y = f(X)$, he does not expect that knowing X will tell him *exactly* what Y will be, but only that it will tell him what Y will be *with some margin of error*. This error in predicting Y from a knowledge of X arises for two quite distinct reasons. First, there may be other variables that also

---

1. Indeed, we know, and shall subsequently see that there is more to explaining consumption than this. This example is considered further in Chapter 47.

2. Of course, an equation that expresses a definition will hold exactly. If, for example, we break up a person's income (Y) into spending (C) and saving (S), and define savings as all income not spent, then we write $Y = C + S$. This equation, which is called a definitional equation, is true exactly. We have defined our terms so that it must always hold; there is nothing anyone can do to invalidate the equation. On the other hand, if we believe that people always spend three-quarters of their income and save the other quarter, we write $C = \frac{3}{4}Y$, $S = \frac{1}{4}Y$. These two equations are called behavioral equations because they tell us what we are assuming about people's behavior. Such equations need not hold exactly; indeed they need not hold at all. We might, for example, observe someone spending only one-tenth of his income and saving nine-tenths, in which case neither of the latter equations would hold, although of course $Y = C + S$ is still true (by definition).

affect Y. When, for example, we say that the demand for butter is a function of the price of butter, $D_b = f(p_b)$, we know that other factors will also influence this demand. A change in the price of margarine will certainly affect the demand for butter, even though the price of butter does not change. Thus we do not expect to find a perfect relation between D_b and p_b that will allow us to predict D_b exactly, from a knowledge of p_b. Second, we can never measure our variables exactly, so that, even if X is the only cause of Y, our measurements will give various Y's corresponding to the same X. In the case of the demand for butter, our errors of measurement might not be large. In other cases, errors might be substantial as, for example, in the case of a relation between total spending on consumption goods, C, and total income, Y, earned in the nation: $C = f(Y)$. In this case our measurements of C and Y may be subject to quite wide margins of error, and we may observe various values of C associated with the same measured value of Y, not because C is varying independently of Y, but because

our error of measurement is varying from period to period.

If all the factors that affect the measured value of Y other than X are summarized into an *error term*, ϵ, we write $Y = f(X, \epsilon)$. This says that the observed value of Y is related to the observed value of X as well as to a lot of other things, both observational errors and other causal factors, all of which will be lumped together and called ϵ (the Greek letter epsilon). In economic theory, this error term is almost always suppressed, and we proceed as if our functional relations were deterministic. When we come to test our theories, however, some very serious problems arise precisely because we do not expect the functional relations of our theories to hold exactly.

> It is extremely important, both when one comes to interpret a theory in terms of the real world and to test a theory formally against empirical observations, to remember that the deterministic formulation is a simplification, and that the error term is really present in all our assumed and observed functional relations.

Can Economics Really Be Expressed in Mathematical Terms?

One sometimes hears the argument that although it is all right to use mathematical equations to express the behavior of gases, or planets, it is impossible to do so with human beings, because there are too many variables that affect their behavior.[3] Such a criticism cannot mean literally that mathematical formulation cannot handle enough

variables, for indeed it can handle any number.† What it may mean is that mathematical notation will not by itself specify hypotheses about the way in which the large number of possibly relevant variables affect whatever it is we are trying to predict. This is, of course, true: Mathematical notation cannot specify anything that the person who writes down

---

3. This proposition is sometimes argued on the grounds that human behavior is too complex to be made the subject of scientific laws and that mathematics is too rigid to be used to describe anything but deterministic scientific laws. The first point was dealt with in Chapter 2, and the second point is wrong, both because terms expressing random variations are easily accommodated in mathematical analysis and because all scientific predictions also contain error terms.

† Suppose we believe that Y is a function of six variables that we denote $X_1, X_2, X_3, X_4, X_5, X_6$. We may write $Y = f(X_1, X_2, X_3, X_4, X_5, X_6)$.

the notation does not specify. There may, indeed, be many aspects of his problem that he does not understand, or about which he does not have even enough hunches to permit him to formulate hypotheses, but this is his limitation, not the limitation of his technique.

The implication in this kind of criticism is often that verbal statement can somehow overcome ignorance of or vagueness about what the person is considering. Of course it cannot. Verbal statement can often mask fuzziness, but that is hardly an advantage. It is an *advantage,* not a disability, of mathematical formulation that it exposes precisely what is being said as well as what is being left unsaid. If we accept the view that, somehow, verbal analysis (or "judgment") can solve problems, but if we are unable to state the considerations that lead to these solutions, then economics is not a science but a medieval mystery, in which the main problem is to be able to distinguish between the true and the false prophet.

Graphing Functional Relationships[4]

Consider the following simple functional relationship:

$$Y = 150 - 10X,$$

which tells us not only that Y depends upon X, but that it depends upon it in a very specific way. For any specified value of X we can determine the corresponding value of Y. Table 1 presents the value of Y for selected values of X. We can represent these six points on a coordinate grid as in Figure 1(i). These selected values are not the function itself. Suppose we wished to indicate the value of Y for every conceivable value of X between zero and 20 (including such values of X as 11.237, for which $Y - 37.63$). Compute and plot as many points as necessary to satisfy yourself that they all lie on the straight line that we have drawn in Figure 1(ii).

Once we have plotted this line, which *is* the function $Y - 150 - 10X$ in the interval from $X = 0$ to $X = 20$, we have no further need for the coordinate grid, and the figure will be less cluttered if we suppress it, as in Figure 1(iii). For some purposes we do not really care about the specific numerical values of the function; we are content merely to represent it as a downward-sloping straight line. We have so represented it in Figure 1(iv). We have replaced the specific numerical values of the variables Y and X with the letters *a*, *b*, *r*, and *s* to indicate specific points. What does Figure 1(iv) tell us? It says that if we increased the quantity of X from *Oa* to *Ob*, we could expect Y to decrease from *Os* to *Or*.

TABLE 1   **SELECTED VALUES OF THE FUNCTION Y = 150 — 10X**

When X	Then Y
0	150
5	100
10	50
15	0
20	−50

4. Some students will find this section totally unnecessary in view of their previous background. We include it because we intend to rely heavily on graphical presentations, and there must be no doubt about what the graphs mean.

The beginning student may feel we have lost ground at this stage, but it is in this form that most diagrams appear in economic texts. Let us see why.

The great advantage of illustrating functional relations graphically is that we can easily compare different sorts of relations without specifying them in precise equations. Suppose we wish to consider the effect of a change in the wage rate (w) on the quantity of labor used in an industry (D), and are curious as to the importance of the shape of the functional relation $D = f(w)$. We draw a figure like Figure 2. We are then able to compare two different functional relations in quite general terms. If, in one industry, the quantity of labor used does not change very much as the wage rate changes, the graph of the relation $D_{L1} = f(w)$ will be very steep, as is curve D_{L1}; a fall in the wage rate from Os to Or causes demand to increase from Oa to Ob—that is, by the amount ab. If, in a second industry, the quantity of labor demanded varies a great deal as the wage rate varies, then the graph of $D_{L2} = f(w)$ will be flatter, as is curve D_{L2}, so that the fall in the wage rate from Os to Or will cause demand to go up from Oc to Od—that is, by an amount cd. The graph is drawn without numbers or grid merely to prevent it from being cluttered up with irrelevant details. The grid is, of course, always understood to be there, and, when required, we draw in the necessary grid lines. For instance, the coordinates of Point x in Figure 2 are Os and Oc, and the grid lines $x's$ and xc are drawn in because they are needed. If you find this

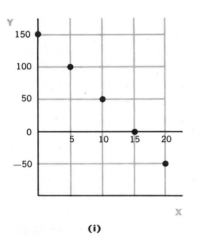

(i)

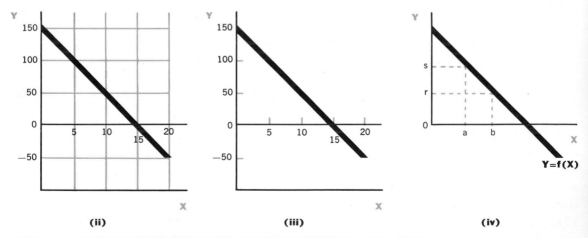

(ii)   (iii)   (iv)

FIGURE 1   **DIFFERENT REPRESENTATIONS OF THE FUNCTION Y = 150 − 10X**

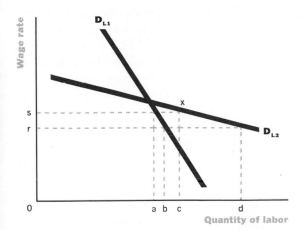

FIGURE 2   **THE RELATION BETWEEN THE QUANTITY OF LABOR DEMANDED AND THE WAGE RATE**

at all difficult you should redraw all graphs on graph paper until you feel at home with graphical analysis.

DERIVING IMPLICATIONS FROM FUNCTIONAL RELATIONSHIPS

So far, we have discussed the various ways in which functional relations can be described, verbally, geometrically, and mathematically. When the economist has laid out the functional relations of his theory, he must then discover what is implied by these relations. He wishes to make statements such as "If relations a and b hold, then relation c must necessarily hold as well." In the process of making logical deductions from his theories, he may again employ verbal, geometrical, or mathematical forms of reasoning. His main concerns will be (1) to ensure that his reasoning processes are correct so that he correctly discovers what is implied by his theory, and (2) that they are efficient so that he discovers everything that is implied by his theory.

Examples of this process in economics cannot be given until we have a rigorously specified theory of some aspect of the economy. You will encounter many examples in Chapter 11, at which time you will be referred back to the present chapter. In the meantime, let us consider the following problem in elementary algebra:

A father's age is two and a quarter times his son's age. The sum of the father's and the son's ages is 52. How old are father and son?

We have two conditions and we have to discover what is implied by them with respect to the ages of father and son. Do not read on until you have provided a verbal, a geometrical, and an algebraic solution to this simple problem in logic.

The Concept of "Marginal" Changes

The idea of the *magnitude* of the changes in one variable in response to changes in another variable is extremely important in economics. We expect, for example, the total cost of producing any good to vary with the total quantities produced, $TC = f(Q)$, and we are interested in *how much* the cost increases for a given increase in quantity produced. One way to examine this question is to ask "How much does cost change if we change the quantity produced by one unit?" Suppose that adding one unit to output increases total cost by $2. We would say that the *incremental* (or *marginal*) *cost* of the additional output was $2 per unit. In general, we can find the incremental change in the equation $Y = f(X)$ by the following ratio:

$$\frac{\text{the change in } X}{\text{the change in } Y}.$$

Where the change in X is very small we speak of it as the *marginal* change in Y due to a change in X. We shall use the concept of marginal changes very often in the chapters that follow.

There is a precise mathematical method of handling problems arising from the question of how one variable changes as another variable on which it depends also changes. The branch of mathematics that deals with these problems is the *differential calculus*. There is not space here for a consideration of the methods of the differential calculus. Since the basic marginal tools of economic analysis are merely applications of derivatives, some study of this concept will bear dividends for the student who intends to continue in economics, but a knowledge of the calculus is not necessary in order to read this book. In fact, one can usually obtain a degree in economics without such knowledge, but those who do have some understanding of the calculus will undoubtedly find it a great help.[5]

Summary

1. An economic theory consists of a set of definitions and a set of hypotheses about how the world behaves. The implications of a theory can be discovered by verbal argument, geometrical analysis, or symbolic reasoning using the tools of algebra and other branches of mathematics.

2. Any hypothesis about how two or more things are related can be expressed in functional notation. $Y = f(X)$ says that Y is a function of X and means that Y varies in a systematic way as X varies.

3. The general functional form does not tell us how one variable changes as the other changes. This precise information is given in an equation such as $Y = 4X^2$, or $Y = 2 + 3X$.

4. An hypothesis about how two things are related can also be shown on a graph. A precise relationship can be shown on a graph using a numbered scale. A less precise relation (say we only know that X rises as Y rises) can be shown on a graph without a numbered scale where only the general shape of the line matters (i.e., whether the line slopes upward or downward and whether it is curved or straight).

5. In economics, we seldom have deterministic relations that tell us exactly what X will be given a knowledge of Y. Our relations usually allow us to determine the value of Y only within some margin of error from a knowledge of X.

6. The error in predicting Y arises from two distinct causes, both of which are usually present: the omission from our theory of other factors that also influence Y, and errors of measurement in either X or Y. Errors of either kind will lead to predictions based upon the theory that do not conform to our observations.

7. In elementary economic theory, we usually ignore this error term, but it is crucially important when we come to test our theories against actual observations.

5. An introduction to the ideas of the differential calculus plus a review of very elementary arithmetic, algebra, and geometry can be found in W. W. Sawyer's excellent little book *Mathematician's Delight* (Penguin, 1955). A somewhat more advanced treatment may be found in Taro Yamane, *Mathematics for Economists* (Prentice-Hall, 1962). The student who wishes to make a serious study of mathematics on his own is best advised to tackle R. G. D. Allen, *Mathematical Analysis for Economists* (Macmillan, 1953).

QUESTIONS FOR DISCUSSION

1. "The quantity of ice cream cones a group of children buy depends upon the heat, expressed in degrees Fahrenheit, the price of an ice cream cone, and their average allowance."

a. How would you write, in the functional notation that you have learned in this chapter, the foregoing statement? Be sure to explain what any symbols you use mean.

b. Will the quantity they buy vary directly or inversely with the heat? Directly or inversely with the price of an ice cream cone? With average allowance?

c. Can you predict what will happen if the temperature falls by 10° and the average allowance rises by 5¢? If not, what further information about the function would you need?

2. State a precise equation that is a specific example of the general hypothesis: "The higher the average tuition fees at private universities, the greater the number of students applying to state universities."

3. Turn to the problem on p. 33.

a. Set up and solve the two equations corresponding to the two conditions.

b. Draw the two equations on the same graph. What does the graph show about the solution? Plot the following solution on your graph and show what is wrong with it: Father's age = 45; son's age = 7. Is the father's age too big or too small? Now do the same for father's age = 34; son's age = 18.

4. Suppose we wanted to test the hypothesis that grades in college vary directly with College Board scores, and we select a certain college for testing.

a. Write this hypothesis as a function and draw it as a graph.

b. If, out of 96 students in a class, 92 have the same rank in average grades as in Board scores, but four do not, would you say the hypothesis is refuted?

c. If you think the hypothesis is refuted, explain why. If you do not think so, explain how the omission of an error term in the specification of the hypothesis could lead you to think it was refuted by the observations in question. What does the error term stand for in *this* instance? (Give concrete examples, if you can.)

d. "I do not think the hypothesis has been refuted, so it must have been proved." What do you think about this attitude?

e. If you believe that the hypothesis predicted well, would you say that high Board scores *cause* high grades? If you don't think this is quite correct, what *would* you say?

APPENDIX TO CHAPTER 3 SOME COMMON TECHNIQUES

CERTAIN GRAPHICAL AND MATHEMATICAL concepts are frequently encountered in economic analysis. In this appendix we deal briefly with the ones most frequently used in this book. Only the barest outlines are possible, and the student who wishes a fuller treatment of the ideas expressed here should fill in his knowledge by reading the appropriate references listed in footnote 5, page 34. We suggest that you merely skim this appendix at this time and make a list of the concepts discussed. When you meet them later in the text, return to this appendix and read the appropriate discussions carefully.

Terminology of Functional Relations

In Chapter 3 we used the expression $Y = f(X)$ to denote a functional relation between X and Y. Sometimes we wish to deal with more than one functional relation and to denote that, although we do not know their exact form, the two relations may be different. It could be, for example, that in one case $Y = 3X$, whereas in the other $Y = 0.5X$. This may be indicated in any one of several ways, for example:

$$Y = f(X)$$

and

$$Y = g(X),$$

where the f and g indicate that we are dealing with two different relations between X and Y.

The choice of letters used to indicate a functional dependence is, of course, arbitrary, but sometimes letters can be selected to indicate the particular dependence in question. Assume, for example, that both X and Z are functions of Y, possibly $X = 10 + 3Y$ and $Z = 5 - 2Y^2$. Although we could write

$$X = f(Y)$$

and

$$Z = g(Y),$$

it is often more convenient to write

$$X = X(Y)$$

and

$$Z = Z(Y).$$

On the other hand we might wish to deal simultaneously with two different relations between X and Y, for example, $X = 3Y$ and $X = 2 - 6Y$. In this case we could write

$$X = X_1(Y)$$

and

$$X = X_2(Y),$$

where the numerical subscripts distinguish the two different relations. This choice of letters to indicate the particular functional relation in question will

be illustrated many times throughout this book.

The fact that various notations are used to indicate functional dependence can be confusing, but the intention of the author will usually be obvious from the context.

Necessary Conditions and Sufficient Conditions

It is common in popular discussion to confuse necessary and sufficient conditions. Many futile arguments have been caused by one person arguing that a condition was sufficient for a result and another arguing that it was not necessary, each thinking he was contradicting the other when, in fact, both were correct. Consider, for example, a club that normally admits only males who are graduates of Harvard, but that is also willing to admit all male U.S. Senators, whatever their background. Being a male senator is thus sufficient to admit you to the club, but it is not necessary to be one. Being a male is a necessary condition for admission (since no females are admitted on any terms), but it is not a sufficient condition. Being a graduate of Harvard is by itself neither necessary (since non-Harvard graduates who are senators can be admitted) nor sufficient (since female graduates of Harvard are not admitted). We may summarize the conditions for admission as follows:

To be male is necessary but not sufficient.
To be a male senator is sufficient but not necessary.
To be both a male and a

Harvard graduate is sufficient but not necessary.
To be a Harvard graduate is neither necessary nor sufficient.
To be a senator is neither necessary nor sufficient.
To be *either* a male graduate of Harvard *or* a male senator is necessary and sufficient.

In general, a necessary condition is something that must be present but by itself may not guarantee the result. A sufficient condition is something that, if present, does guarantee the result but that need not be there for the result to occur. A condition (or set of conditions) that is necessary *and* sufficient must be there and, if there, is enough to guarantee the result.

In this club, the necessary and sufficient condition for entry is a compound either-or condition: to be either a male graduate of Harvard or a U.S. Senator. If, however, another club were set up that was open to all former members of the U.S. Senate and to no one else, then to have been a senator would be a necessary and sufficient condition for entry into the club.

Dependent and Independent Variables

Suppose we say that Y is always three times as large as X. Two other ways of saying the same thing are to say that X is one-third as large as Y and that Y minus three X must be zero. We can write

$$Y = 3X,$$

$$X = \tfrac{1}{3}Y,$$

and

$$Y - 3X = 0.$$

These are three ways of writing the same functional relation. To express the same three forms in general terms, we can write

$$Y = g(X), \qquad (1)$$
$$X = h(Y), \qquad (2)$$

and

$$f(X, Y) = 0. \qquad (3)$$

Equations (1) and (2) are called the explicit forms of the function. In (1) Y is written as an explicit function of X. Equation (3) is called the implicit form of the function. All the terms are gathered onto the left-hand side and the whole expression is thus equal to zero. In which of the three forms we choose to write the function is clearly only a matter of convenience. Any one can be transformed into the others merely by transferring terms from one side of the equation to the other.

The term on the left-hand side of (1) and (2) is called the *dependent variable* and the terms on the right-hand side are called the *independent variables* (or variable, if there is only one). As far as mathematics is concerned the distinction between dependent and independent variables is quite arbitrary: $Y = f(X)$ necessarily implies $X = g(Y)$. The convention may be used, however, to express information we have about the causal relation between the variables. Assume, for example, that crop yield (C) depends solely on the amount of rainfall (R).[1] This allows us to write

$$C = C(R). \qquad (4)$$

But if knowing the amount of rainfall is sufficient to allow us to deduce the amount of crop, then knowing the amount of crop is sufficient to let us deduce the amount of rainfall. Thus we also have

$$R = R(C). \qquad (5)$$

As far as mathematics is concerned, it does not matter which of these two ways we choose. But, of course, the causal relation is clearly defined in this case. The amount of rainfall influences the crop yield; the crop yield does not influence the amount of rainfall.

As a matter of convention, whenever we think we know the direction of the causal link between variables we write the causes as independent variables and the effects as dependent ones. Thus, as a matter of convention, we would use Equation (4) instead of Equation (5). Again, if we wanted to say crop yield (C) depended on fertilizer (F), sunshine (S), and rainfall (R) we would write

$$C = C(F, S, R). \qquad (6)$$

In Equation (6), C is the dependent variable and F, S, and R are the independent variables.

Exogenous and Endogenous Variables

In economic theories it is convenient to distinguish between *exogenous* and *endogenous variables*: Endogenous variables are ones that are explained *within* a theory; exogenous variables are ones that influence the variables but are themselves determined by factors outside of the theory. Assume, for example, that we have a theory of what determines the price of apples from day to day in New York. The price of apples in this case is an endogenous variable—something determined within the framework of the theory. The state of the weather, on the other hand, is an exogenous variable: It will influence apple prices but will be uninfluenced by these prices. The state of the weather will be unexplained by our theory; it is something that happens from without, so to speak, but it nonetheless influences our endogenous variable, apple prices, because it affects the demand for apples. Exogenous variables are sometimes referred to as *autonomous variables*.

Stocks and Flows

Some of the most serious confusions in economics have arisen from a failure to distinguish between *stocks* and *flows*. Imagine a bathtub half full of water with the faucet turned on and the plug removed; you have in mind a model similar to many simple economic theories. The level of water in the bath is a stock—an amount that is just there. We could express it as so many gallons of water. The amount of water entering through the faucet and the amount leaving through the drain are both flows. We could express them as so many gal-

---

1. This is a simplification for purposes of illustration, but crop yield certainly depends partly on the amount of rainfall.

lons, *per minute or per hour*. A flow necessarily has a time dimension—there is so much flow *per period of time*. A stock does not have a time dimension —it is just so many tons or gallons or heads.

The amount of wheat produced is a flow; there is so much flow per year or per month. The amount of wheat sold is also a flow—so much per month or year. The amount of wheat stored (produced but unsold) in the granaries of the world is a stock; it is just so many millions of tons of wheat. The distinction between stocks and flows will arise many times throughout this book.

Identities and Equations

The distinction between *identities* and *equations* is important and subtle. An identity is a relation that is true for all values of the variables; no values can be found that would contradict it. An example of an identity is $(x + y)^2 \equiv x^2 + 2xy + y^2$, which expression is true for any numerical value of x and y. It should be noted that identities are usually written with a three-bar sign and that the expression $y \equiv x$ is read y is identical with x. Identities are statements compatible with any state of the universe.

Equations are relations that are true only for some values of the variables but that can be contradicted by other values. Thus the expression $y = 10 + 2x$ is an equation. It is written with a two-bar or equals sign and is read y is equal to ten plus two x. This expression is true, for ex-

ample, for $x = 2$ and $y = 14$, but not for $x = 2$ and $y = 2$. Equations can be used to state testable hypotheses, since they make statements that are true for some states of the universe but false for other states; identities cannot be used to state testable hypotheses, since they make statements that are true for all states of the universe.

Identities, therefore, tell us nothing about the world. They cannot be the "basis" of any theory (although they can be used very helpfully to convey definitions of terms) and they can usually be reduced to the form $y \equiv y$ which, although true, is hardly very enlightening. Consider, for example, the statement

$$y = c + s, \qquad (7)$$

where y is a man's income, where c is his expenditure on goods and services, and where s is the amount he saves. As it stands we do not yet know if this is an identity or an equation. If y is defined as the amount of money the man earns, c as the amount he actually spends on goods and services, and s as the amount he puts in the bank, then the equation expresses an hypothesis about what people do with their incomes. This is because there are other things the man might do with his income, such as giving it to his nephew. Now, however, let us keep the above definitions of y and c, but define s in terms of y and c: s is defined to be all income not spent on consumption. Thus by definition we have

$$s \equiv y - c. \qquad (8)$$

Equation (7) becomes an identity,

$$y \equiv c + s. \qquad (9)$$

We fool ourselves if we think we have learned anything from (9), for, if we substitute (8) into it, we get

$$y \equiv c + y - c,$$

which, of course, reduces to

$$y \equiv y,$$

which is true for *any* values of y, c, and s.

Confusion between equations and identities has been a ready source of error in economics. One of the most perplexing habits of economists is to warn the student about the nature of identities and then to introduce national-income theory with several pages of identities claimed to be the foundation of the theory.[2]

Some Conventions in Functional Notation

Assume we are talking about some sequence of numbers, say, 1, 2, 3, 4, 5, . . . If we wished to talk about one particular term in this series without indicating which one, we could talk about the ith term, which might be the 5th or the 50th. If we now want to indicate terms adjacent to the ith term, whatever it might be, we can talk about the $i - 1$th and the $i + 1$th terms.

By the same token we can talk about a series of time periods, say, the years 1900, 1901, and 1902. If we wish to refer to three adjacent years in any series without indicating which three years, we can

---

2. For a criticism of this practice, and references to places where it is used, see K. Klappholz and E. J. Mishan, "Identities in Economic Models," *Economica,* May, 1962.

talk about the $t-1$th, the tth, and the $t+1$th years in the series.

Now consider some functional relation, say, one between the quantity produced by a factory and the number of workers employed. In general, we can write $Q = Q(W)$, where Q is the amount of production and W is the number of workers. If we wished to refer to the value of output where 10 workers were employed, we could then write $Q_{10} = Q(W_{10})$, whereas, if we wished to refer to output when some particular, but unspecified, number was employed, we could write $Q_i = Q(W_i)$. Finally, if we wished to refer to output when the number of workers is increased by one above the previous level, we can write $Q_{i+1} = Q(W_{i+1})$. This use of subscripts to refer to the value of the variables where they take on particular numbers is a most useful notation and one that we shall use at various points in this book.

We may also use time subscripts to indicate a lagged relation between variables. A lagged relation between X and Y is one in which the value of Y at any point of time depends on the value of X at some previous point of time. Let us say that the amount produced of a product is a function of its price; so we write $Q = Q(p)$, where Q is the amount produced and p is the price of the product. Production takes time, and what is produced today may not be much influenced by today's prices. If we divide time into months and assume a three-months' lag in output, then we have $Q_t = Q(p_{t-3})$, which says that the amount

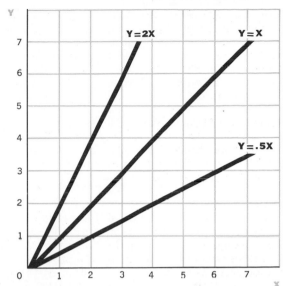

FIGURE A1

produced today depends on what the price was three time periods ago, which in this case is three months ago.

Another convention is used to save space when there are many independent variables in a function. Let us say that Y depends on 6 variables X_1 to X_6. We could write this as

$$Y = Y(X_1, X_2, X_3, X_4, X_5, X_6),$$

but this is rather cumbersome, so, instead, we write

$$Y = Y(X_1, \dots, X_6),$$

where the dots indicate that the intervening numbers are understood to be present.

Now assume that Y is a function of some number of variables but we do not wish to say exactly how many. We can say that Y is a function of n variables X_1 to X_n. Now the omission of intermediate numbers is necessary, for, until we know what number n stands for, we cannot say how many variables there are. In this case we write

$$Y = Y(X_1, \dots, X_n).$$

Straight Lines: Slopes and Tangents

Consider the following functional relations:

$$Y = 0.5X,$$
$$Y = X,$$
$$Y = 2X.$$

These are graphed in Figure A1. You will see that they are all straight lines through the origin. This is also obvious from the fact that if we let $X = 0$ in each of the above relations Y also becomes 0. In the first equation, Y goes up half a unit every time X goes up by one unit; in the second equation, Y goes up one unit every time X goes up one unit; and in the third equation, Y goes up two units every time X goes up one unit.

We now introduce the symbol Δ to indicate a change in a variable. Thus ΔX means the value of the change in X and ΔY means the value of the change in Y. In the first equation if $X = 10$ then Y is 5 and if X goes up to 16, Y goes up to 8. Thus, in this exercise, $\Delta X = 6$ and $\Delta Y = 3$.

Next consider the ratio $\Delta Y/\Delta X$. In the above example it is equal to 0.5. In general, it will be noted that, for any change we make in X in the first equation, $\Delta Y/\Delta X$ is always 0.5. In the second it is unity and in the third the ratio is always 2. In general, if we write $Y = bX$, then the ratio $\Delta Y/\Delta X$ is always equal to b.†

We now define the slope of a straight line to be the ratio of the distance moved along the Y axis to the distance moved up the X axis. We start at the point (X_1, Y_1) and then move to the point (X_2, Y_2). The change in X is $X_2 - X_1$ or ΔX as indicated. The change in Y is $Y_2 - Y_1$ or ΔY. Thus the ratio $\Delta Y/\Delta X$ is the slope of the straight line. This slope tells us the ratio of a change in Y to a change in X.

In trigonometry the tangent of an angle is defined as $\Delta Y/\Delta X$; thus the slope of the line is equal to the tangent of the angle between the line and any line parallel to the X axis. In general, the larger the ratio $\Delta Y/\Delta X$ the steeper the graph

of the relation. In Figure A1 three lines corresponding to $\Delta Y/\Delta X = \frac{1}{2}$, 1, and 2 are shown. Clearly, the steeper the line the larger the change in Y for any given change in X.

Now consider the following equations:

$$Y = 2X$$
$$Y = 10 + 2X$$
$$Y = -5 + 2X.$$

These are graphed in Figure A2. It will be observed that all three lines are parallel, i.e., they have the same slope. In

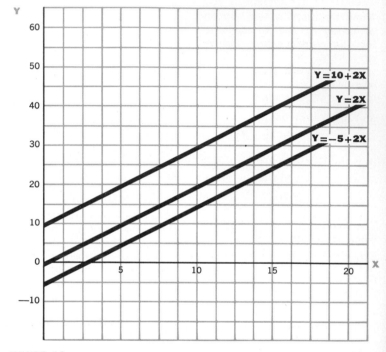

FIGURE A2

† This is easily proved as follows: Select some arbitrary value of X, called X_1, and calculate the corresponding Y_1; now take a second value of X, called X_2, and find the corresponding Y_2. This gives us

$$Y_1 = bX_1$$

and

$$Y_2 = bX_2.$$

If we subtract one equation from the other we obtain

$$Y_2 - Y_1 = bX_2 - bX_1,$$

or

$$Y_2 - Y_1 = b(X_2 - X_1),$$

but we have already used the term ΔY to describe the change in Y and the term ΔX to describe the change in X (i.e., $\Delta Y \equiv Y_2 - Y_1$ and $\Delta X \equiv X_2 - X_1$). Thus we may write

$$\Delta Y = b\Delta X,$$
$$\frac{\Delta Y}{\Delta X} = b.$$

all three $\Delta Y / \Delta X$ is equal to 2. Clearly, the addition of a (positive or negative) constant does not affect the slope of the line. This slope is influenced only by the number attached to X. In general, we may write the equation of a straight line as

$$Y = a + bX.$$

Now, by inserting two values of X, say X_1 and X_2, and finding the corresponding Y's, we get

$$Y_1 = a + bX_1$$

and

$$Y_2 = a + bX_2,$$

and, by subtraction,

$$Y_2 - Y_1 = b(X_2 - X_1)$$

or

$$\Delta Y = b\Delta X$$

$$\frac{\Delta Y}{\Delta X} = b.$$

The constant a disappears when we subtract and so does not influence the slope of the line. What the constant does is to shift the line upward or downward parallel to itself.

Nonlinear Functions

All of the examples used so far in this appendix and most of the examples in the text of Chapter 3 concern linear relations between two variables. A linear relation is described graphically by a straight line, and algebraically by the equation $Y = a + bX$. It is characteristic of a linear relation that the effect on Y of a given change in X is the same whatever the values of X and Y from which we start. The graphical expression of this is that the slope of a straight line is constant.

Many of the relations encountered in economics are nonlinear ones. In this case the relation will be expressed graphically by a curved line and algebraically by some expression more complex than the one for a straight line. Two common examples are as follows:

$$Y = a + bX + cX^2$$

and

$$Y = \frac{a}{X^b}.$$

The first example is a parabola that can take up various positions and shapes depending on the signs and magnitudes of a, b, and c. Two examples of parabolas are given in Figures A3 and A4. The second example becomes a rectangular hyperbola if we let $b = 1$, and then the position is determined by the value of a. Three examples where $a = 0.5$, 2.5, and 5.0 are shown in Figure A5.

There are, of course, many other examples of nonlinear relations between variables. In general, whatever the relation between X and Y, as long as it can be expressed on a graph it can also be expressed by means of an algebraic equation.

Maximum and Minimum Values

Consider the function

$$Y = 10X - 0.1X^2,$$

which is plotted in Figure A3. It will be observed that Y at first increases as X increases, but after a while Y begins to fall as X goes on rising. We say that Y rises to a *maximum*, which is reached in this case when $X = 50$. Until $X = 50$, Y is rising

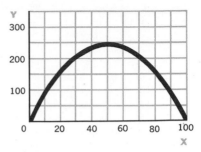

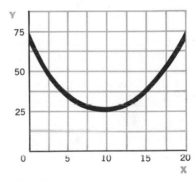

as X rises, but after $X = 50$, Y is falling as X rises. Thus Y reaches a maximum value of 250 when X is 50.

A great deal of economic theory is based on the idea of finding a maximum (or a minimum) value. Since Y is a function of X, we speak of *maximizing the value of the function*, and by this we mean that we wish to find the value of X (50 in this case) for which the value of Y is at a maximum (250 in this case).

Now consider the function

$$Y = 75 - 10X + 0.5X^2,$$

which is graphed in Figure A4. In this case, the value of Y falls at first while X increases, reaches a *minimum*, and then rises as X goes on increasing.

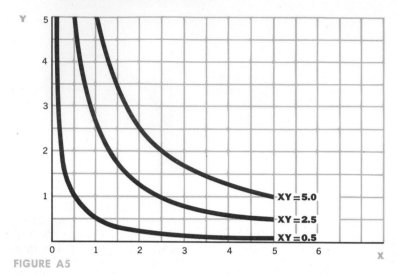

FIGURE A5

In this case, Y reaches a minimum value of 25 when X is 10. Here we speak of *minimizing the value of the function*, by which we mean finding the value of X for which the value of Y is at a minimum.

Functions of More Than Two Variables

In most of the examples used so far we have been considering the relation between only two magnitudes. In most interesting cases we are concerned with the relation between more than two things. The demand for a good might depend, for example, on the price of that good, on the price of a number of competing products, on the price of products used in conjunction with the product with which we are concerned, and on consumers' income. For example, the demand for butter will depend on the price of but-

ter, the price of margarine, the price of bread, and how rich or poor consumers happen to be.

When we wish to denote the dependence of Y on several variables, say, V, W, and X, we write $Y = Y(V, W, X)$, which is read Y is a function of V, W, and X.

In mathematics and in economics we are often concerned about what happens to Y as X varies on the assumption that the other factors that influence X are held constant at some stated level. There are many ways to denote this and we shall use the following notation:[1]

$$Y = f(X) \Big|_{\substack{V = V_o \\ W = W_o.}}$$

The symbols to the right of the bar tell us what is being held constant and at what level. The above example is read Y is a function solely of X with V held constant at the level V_o and W held constant at the level

W_o. In a particular example, we might state the actual levels of V and W. If, for example, W were held constant at 10 and V at 5 we would write

$$Y = f(X) \Big|_{\substack{V = 5 \\ W = 10.}}$$

Partial Derivatives

Students who do not know mathematics are often disturbed by the frequent use in economics of arguments that depend on the qualification "other things being equal" (for which we often use the Latin phrase *ceteris paribus*). Such arguments are not peculiar to economics. They are used successfully in all branches of science and there is an elaborate set of mathematical techniques available to handle them.

When mathematicians wish to know the approximate ratio $\frac{\Delta Y}{\Delta X}$ (i.e., how Y is changing as X changes) when other factors that influence Y are held constant, they calculate what is called the *partial derivative of* Y *with respect to* X. This is written symbolically as $\frac{\partial Y}{\partial X}$. We cannot enter here into a discussion of how this expression is calculated. We only wish to note that finding $\frac{\partial Y}{\partial X}$ is a well-recognized and very common mathematical operation, and the answer tells us approximately how Y is affected by small variations in X when *all other factors are held constant.*

---

1. Here we introduce some notations that henceforth will be used only in footnotes marked by a dagger.

QUESTIONS FOR DISCUSSION

1. A state university admits the following students: All state residents who have a C average; and all out-of-state residents who have a B average. State one necessary and one sufficient condition for admission.

2. $W = 7X - 9Y$. Which is the dependent variable and which the independent ones? Write the equation in the implicit form.

3. What does it mean if I say that I have a theory of the price of land in which population is an exogenous variable?

4. Is the amount of money you have in the bank a stock or a flow? What about the amount of money you spend? What about the national debt?

5. Which of the following could be expressed as identities and which as equations? Write down the expression described in each case.

 a. "A monthly telephone bill expressed in dollars is .04 times the number of message units used plus a one-dollar service charge."

 b. "Take a number; double it; add two; subtract three; multiply by five; add five; divide by ten. I bet the answer is the same as your original number."

 c. "Define all expenditure in the American economy as being either goods for defense or goods for civilian uses. If the percentage devoted to defense goes up, I bet the percentage devoted to civilian uses goes down."

6. In the sequence 2, 4, 8, 16, 32, . . . , can you describe the relationship between the ith number and the $i + 1$th number?

7. Express in functional notation the proposition that next year's wheat crop depends on last year's wheat price.

Chapter 4 THE TOOLS OF STATISTICAL ANALYSIS

THE ROLE OF STATISTICAL ANALYSIS IS twofold. First, we wish to use observations from the real world to test our theories. Second, we wish to use such observations to give us measures of the quantitative relations between economic variables. Testing and measurement are the purposes for which statistical tools are needed. In this chapter we consider them both.

Economic theories are meant to predict the outcome of various changes in which we are interested; they are meant to tell us that if certain things are done then certain things will happen and certain other things will not happen. When we intervene in the economy to bring about a particular result, we are relying on some economic theory that links our act of intervention to the result that we desire (i.e., the theory predicts the consequences of our intervention). But it is always possible that some theory about how events in the economy are related may be wrong; if we act on the basis of an incorrect theory, we will not obtain the desired results—indeed, we may bring about results opposite to the ones that we desire. It is critically important to know whether our economic theories do or do not predict the outcome of various changes in the economy within some acceptable margin of error.

Testing

In order to determine whether or not they do just this, we seek to test our theories against the evidence of what actually happens in the economy. Testing theories against observations is not a task that is lightly accomplished (or briefly described). We cannot accept a single conflicting observation as disproving any theory. There are two major reasons for this. First we can, and often do, make errors of observation. Thus, if we make a single observation that seems to refute our theory, we do not reject the theory until we have ruled out the possibility that we have made a mistake in what we think we saw.[1] Second, we can never be certain that our theory includes all the forces at work. Indeed, in economics we are usually certain that we have left out of our theory some things of potential importance. What we wish to know is whether our theory is able to predict events in the world within some reasonable margin of error. This is something that cannot be settled by making a single observation. It can only be settled by considering the weight of a mass of evidence.

As a first step in seeing how we go about testing theories in economics, we must distinguish between laboratory and nonlaboratory methods.

LABORATORY SCIENCES

In some sciences, it is possible to obtain all observations from controlled experiments made under laboratory conditions. In these experiments, we hold constant all the factors that are thought to affect the outcome of the process being studied. Then we vary these factors one by one while we observe the influence that each variation appears to have on the outcome of the experiment.

Suppose we have a theory that predicts that the rate at which a substance burns is a function of the chemical properties of that substance and the rate at which oxygen is made available during the process of combustion. To test this theory, we can (1) take a number of identical pieces of some substance and burn them, varying the amount of oxygen made available in each case. (This allows us to see how combustion varies with the quantity of oxygen used.) We can then (2) take a number of substances with different chemical compositions and burn them, making available identical amounts of oxygen in each case. (This allows us to see how combustion varies with chemical composition.) Or (3), since chemical composition is complex, we can vary one facet of a com-

---

1. It has been said that there is hardly an accepted theory of physics that is not refuted daily by some schoolboy operating in a high-school laboratory somewhere in the country. Such isolated "refutations" do not worry physicists, although they would be worried if some day almost every schoolboy in the country should begin to make observations that appeared to refute some accepted theory.

plex chemical compound at a time. (This allows us to see how combustion varies with each facet of the composition.)

In such an experiment, we never have to use data that are generated when both chemical composition and the quantity of oxygen are varying simultaneously. Laboratory conditions are used to hold other things constant and to produce data for situations in which factors are varied one at a time.

NONLABORATORY SCIENCES

In some sciences we cannot isolate factors one at a time in laboratory experiments. In these sciences observations are still used to establish relationships and to test theories, but such observations appear in a relatively complex form, because several things are varying at the same time.

Consider, for example, the hypothesis that one's health as an adult depends upon one's diet as a child. Clearly, all sorts of other factors affect the health of adults: heredity; conditions of childhood other than nutrition; and various aspects of adult environment. There is no possible way to examine this hypothesis in the manner of a controlled experiment, for there is no way in which we can find a group of adults whose diet as children varied but for whom all other influences affecting health were the same. Are we to conclude that the hypothesis cannot be tested because other factors cannot be held constant? No, because to do so would be to deny many advances in medicine, biology, and other sciences concerned with humans —and, therefore, with fluctuating, unconstant factors—made during the last hundred years. To conclude that our hypothesis cannot be tested is tantamount to saying that it would be impossible to discover anything about the relation between chemical composition, amount of oxygen, and speed of combustion if these factors could not be controlled separately. Although the problem is more difficult if both chemical composition and amount of oxygen vary from one experiment to another, it should be obvious—and statistical theory provides a formal proof— that the separate relation between combustion and chemical composition and between combustion and amount of oxygen could still be discovered if enough experiments were made. Testing is harder where one cannot use laboratory methods, but, fortunately, it is still possible.

In a situation in which many things are varying at once, we must be careful in our use of data. If we study only two people and find that the one with the better nutritional standards during his youth has the poorer adult health record, this would not disprove the hypothesis that a good diet leads to better health. It might well be that some other factor has exerted an overwhelming influence on these two individuals. The less healthy man may have lived most of his adult life in a disease-ridden area of the tropics, whereas the more healthy may have lived in a relatively pleasant part of temperate North America. Clearly, a single exception does not disprove the hypothesis of a relation between two things as long as we admit that other factors can also influence the outcome.[2]

How can we test an hypothesis where many things vary at once? One method that is sometimes available is to find a large number of people for whom the "other things" are

---

2. Note how often in ordinary conversation a person advances a possible relation (e.g., between education and some facet of a man's character) and how someone else will "refute" this theory by citing a single counterexample (e.g., "my friend went to that school and did not turn out like that").

very nearly equal and examine how (to continue our example) their adult health is related to their diet as children.

If we cannot select data chosen in such a way that other things were held equal, we have to fall back on more formal statistical techniques that have been designed to unscramble the separate effects of several influencing factors, all of which are changing simultaneously. The most common technique used for this task is called *regression analysis*. You will encounter it in elementary statistics. The most important aspect of statistical analysis for present purposes may be stated as follows:

> The techniques of statistical analysis show how, given enough observations, it is generally possible to identify the relationship, if one exists, between two variables, even though other things are also varying.

The Statistical Testing of Economic Theories: An Example

Economics is a nonlaboratory science. It is rarely if ever possible to conduct controlled experiments with the economy. Millions of *uncontrolled experiments* are, however, going on every day: Housewives are deciding what to purchase in the face of changing prices and incomes; firms are deciding what to produce and how to produce it; and governmental bodies are intervening in the economy with taxes, subsidies, and controls. All of these acts can be observed and recorded. Thus a mass of data is produced continually by the economy. One of the basic problems of statistics is how to make sense of data arising from uncontrolled rather than controlled experiments. Most things in which we as economists are interested, such as the volume of unemployment, the level of prices, and the distribution of income, are influenced by a large number of factors, all of which vary simultaneously. If we are to test our theories about relations in the economy, we will have to use those statistical techniques that were designed for situations in which other things could not be held constant.

Let us consider, by way of an example, a simple hypothesis about the factors determining the amount of money spent on food by households in the United States. We shall advance the hypothesis that the larger the household's income the larger will be its expenditure on food, or, to use the language of Chapter 3, that household expenditure on food varies *directly* with household's income.

Let us say we start by observing three households. Our data are recorded in Table 1.

TABLE 1   **FOOD EXPENDITURE AND TOTAL INCOME FOR THREE U.S. HOUSEHOLDS**

Household	Expenditure on food	Total household income per year
1	$2,000	$3,000
2	1,900	6,500
3	1,500	8,750

These data may lead us to wonder if our hypothesis is wrong, but, before we jump to that conclusion, we also note that "by chance" we may have happened to have selected three households that are not typical of all the households in the country. Possibly, we say, the expenditure on food is influenced by factors other than income and possibly these other factors just happen to be the dominant forces in these three cases.

To check on this possibility, we select a

large number of households in order to reduce the chances of consistently picking untypical households. Suppose we do this by selecting 100 households from among our friends and acquaintances. A statistician points out, however, that our new group is a very *biased sample,* for it contains households from only a limited geographical area, probably with only a limited occupational range, and possibly with incomes very similar to one another. (Since we are especially interested in how expenditure on food *varies* as income varies, this last point is likely to be a very serious one.) It is unlikely that this sample of households will be representative of all households in the U.S., which is the group in which we are interested.

The statistician suggests that we take a *random sample* of 1,000 households. A random sample is chosen according to a rigidly defined set of conditions that guarantees, among other things, that every household in which we are interested has an equal chance of being selected. Choosing our sample in a random fashion has two important consequences: First, it makes it very unlikely that our sample will be unrepresentative of all households, and, more important, it allows us to calculate just how likely it is that our sample is unrepresentative in any given aspect by any stated amount. The reason for this is that our sample was chosen by chance, and chance events are predictable.[3] This second result is very important because it allows us to make statements about the probability that all households in the U.S. will differ by any quantitative amount from the households in our sample.

For each member of the sample we collect certain information, including, in this case, the income of the household and the expenditures on food. We represent these data on a *scatter diagram.* In Figure 1, a scatter diagram, we measure income along the horizontal axis and expenditure on food on the vertical axis. Each dot represents one household and its position on the graph tells us the income and food expenditure of that household. (Every student who is not already familiar with this basic kind of graph should now read the appendix to this chapter.)

The scatter diagram in Figure 1 suggests that there is some tendency for expenditure on food to rise as income rises. The relationship is not perfect, however, for there is considerable variation in food purchases that cannot be associated with variations in households' incomes. There are, for example, 11 households in our sample with incomes of $6,000 and the chart reveals that their expenditures on food vary from $500 to $2,500.

Using standard tools of statistical analysis we can now do the following three things: First, we can "fit" to these data a line that represents our best estimate of the actual relation between household expenditure on food and household income. (Draw such a line on Figure 1.) Second, we can obtain a measure of the percentage of the variations in household expenditure on food that can be accounted for by variations in household income. Third, we can apply a "significance test" to discover the chances that the relation we have discovered in our sample does not exist for the whole population and has arisen by chance because we just happen to have selected households that are not representative of all households in the U.S.

It is clear from the scatter diagram that

3. This may sound paradoxical at first. But consider this: If you pick a card from a well-shuffled deck of ordinary playing cards, how likely is it that you will pick a heart? an ace? an ace of hearts? If you know the answers to these questions (and we will bet that most of you do), you must believe that chance events are predictable.

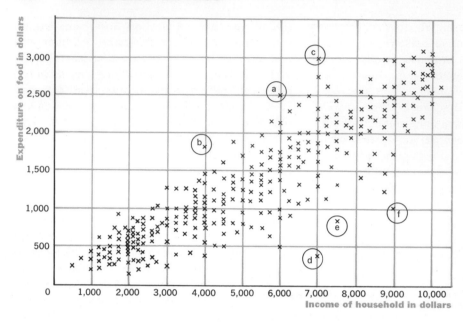

FIGURE 1

HOUSEHOLD INCOME
AND EXPENDITURES
ON FOOD

we cannot account for all of the variations in households' expenditure on food by the variations in household income. If we could, all the dots would be on the line. We may wish to look for some other factor that might also exert a systematic influence on food expenditure. We ask ourselves what could make one household with an income of $6,000 spend twice as much on food as another household with the same income. We look at the data we collected about the households that appear in Figure 1 as extreme points. The observations marked a, b, and c in Figure 1 represent households whose expenditure on food is well above the typical amount associated with the same level of income. Let us say that we discover that most of the households in this class contain a large number of children. The households represented by Points d, e, and f spend less on food than we would expect, given a knowledge of their income, and we discover that most of these households contain only one or two persons. This leads us to put forward the hypothesis that household expendi-

ture on food is higher the larger the number of persons in the household. We project this hypothesis on a scatter diagram. We investigate this hypothesis by classifying households according to the number of members and looking at the expenditure on food by each class of household.

We see immediately that some relation between food expenditure and number of persons in the household does exist: Food expenditure tends to rise as the number of persons in the household rises. The relation is far from perfect, however, for there is considerable variation in expenditure on food that cannot be accounted for by the number of persons in the household.

But this does not surprise us since we already know that expenditure on food is associated with the size of household income. This suggests that we should try to look at one of these two factors, holding the other constant. One way in which we can try to do this is by cross-classifying our data as shown in Table 2.

Each *row* of this table exhibits the effect

of family size on expenditures on food for a given level of income. Each *column* shows the effect of income on expenditures on food for a given size of household.

TABLE 2   **HOUSEHOLD EXPENDITURES ON FOOD CLASSIFIED BY INCOME AND FAMILY SIZE**

Household income in dollars per year	Number of Persons per Household			
	1–2	3–4	5–6	7 or more
Less than $2,000	300	450	510	805
2,000–3,999	790	900	960	1,100
4,000–5,999	950	1,100	1,200	1,250
6,000–7,999	1,200	1,600	1,880	2,010
8,000–9,999	1,800	2,200	2,550	2,800

After seeing these data, we form the hypothesis that variations in household expenditure are the net result of two causes: variations in household income and variations in number of persons per household. We can now apply the statistical techniques of *multiple-regression analysis* to determine, first, the most likely estimate of the separate effects on household food expenditures of variations in household income, number of persons constant, and of variations in number of persons per household, household income constant; second, a measure of the proportion of the total variation in food expenditure that can be explained by associating it with variations both in income and in number of persons per household; and, third, how likely it is that the apparent relations we have found in our sample between food expenditure and income and between food expenditure and number of persons result because (by bad luck) we chose a sample of households that were not representative of all the households in the U.S.

Statistical Hypotheses[4]

Statistical techniques can help us to measure the nature and strength of economic relationships, and can tell us how probable it is that a certain result has occurred merely by chance. What they cannot do is to prove that an hypothesis is either true or false. Nor can they tell us when we should accept or reject the hypothesis.

CAN WE PROVE AN HYPOTHESIS IS TRUE?

Most hypotheses in economics are what may be called universal hypotheses.[5] They say that, whenever certain specified conditions are fulfilled, cause X will always produce effect Y. We have already pointed out that universal hypotheses cannot be proved to be correct, because we can make only a finite number of actual observations, and can never rule out the possibility that we shall make a sufficient number of refuting observations in the future.

CAN WE PROVE AN HYPOTHESIS IS FALSE?

By the same token, we cannot get a categorical disproof of a statistical hypothesis. Consider the hypothesis "Most crows are

4. See Chapter 3, pages 29–30, for the distinction between statistical and deterministic hypotheses.
5. See Chapter 2, page 21.

gray." We observe 50 crows; 49 are black and 1 is gray. Have we disproved the hypothesis? The answer is No, for it is *possible* that this was just bad luck, and that if we could observe all the crows in the world it would indeed prove to be the case that most are gray. Although we have not disproved the hypothesis, we have learned something from our study of 50 crows and, if we have to make a decision about the grayness of all crows, we will be very much better off for having this information. In particular, we are likely to suspect that our hypothesis is not correct. The question of decision-making is considered below. In the meantime, we may ask if there are *any* cases in which observations can categorically disprove an hypothesis. Consider a case in which the proposition admits of no exceptions. Had we said "All crows are gray," our observations would indeed refute this deterministic hypothesis. But what if the hypothesis had been "All crows are black"? If our observations were certainly accurate, this too would have been refuted: One gray crow refutes the hypothesis that all are black. But are we sure that the odd bird was a crow? Are we sure that what looked like a gray crow was not a black crow that had dust on him? Errors in observation may always be present. For this reason, an hypothesis cannot be refuted on the basis of a single observation.

THE DECISION TO REJECT OR ACCEPT IS SUBJECT TO ERROR

We have seen that in general we can neither prove nor refute an hypothesis conclusively, no matter how many observations we make. Nonetheless, we have to make decisions and act as if some hypotheses were

refuted (i.e., we have to reject them) and we have to act as if some hypotheses were proved (i.e., we have to accept them). Just as a jury can make two kinds of errors (finding an innocent man guilty, or letting a guilty man go free) so can the statistical decision-maker make two kinds of errors: He can reject hypotheses that are true, and he can accept hypotheses that are false. Like a jury, he can also make correct decisions.

DECISION RULES

We noted above that the decision to accept or reject an hypothesis is subject to error. In statistics, although we cannot eliminate the possibility of error, we can control it. The method of control is to choose the risk we are willing to take of rejecting an hypothesis if it is in fact correct. Conventionally, we use cut-off points of 5 percent or 1 percent. If we use the 5 percent cut-off point, we say that we will regard an hypothesis as rejected if there exists less than one chance in twenty that we could have made the same set of observations if the hypothesis were correct. Using the 1 percent decision rule we give the hypothesis a greater measure of reasonable doubt: We reject hypotheses only if the results we observe could have happened by chance one time in 100.

When action must be taken, some such rule of thumb is necessary. But it is important that you understand, first, that we can never be *certain* that we are right in rejecting a statistical hypothesis and, second, that there is nothing magical about our arbitrary cut-off points. The cut-off point is a device used because some decision has to be made. You should also note that decisions can always be reversed should new evidence come to light.

Quantitative Measurement of Economic Relations

So far we have considered whether certain observations support certain general hypotheses. Certain data, for instance, support the hypothesis that households' expenditure on food increases as households' income increases. This, however, is not enough. It is important to quantify such qualitative statements. In this case, we should like to say that households' expenditure on food increases by, say, 10¢ for every $1.00 that households' income increases.[6]

Economic theories are seldom of much use until we are able to give quantitative magnitudes to our relations. For estimating such magnitudes, our common sense and intuitions do not get us very far. Common sense might well have suggested that expenditure on food would rise rather than fall as income rose, but only careful observation is going to help us to decide whether it typically rises by 10¢ or by 20¢ for every increase of $1.00 in income.

One of the major uses of statistical analysis is to help us to quantify our relations. In practice, we can use actual observations both to test the hypothesis that two things are related and to estimate the numerical values of the function describing such a relation, if it exists.

Very often the result of a statistical test of a theory is to suggest a new hypothesis that "fits the facts" better than the previous one. Indeed, in some cases just looking at scatter diagrams (or making a regression analysis) uncovers apparent relations that no one anticipated, and leads the economist to formulate a new hypothesis. The student should refer again to Figure 1 on page 22, to see where such hypotheses enter the circuit.[7]

Summary

1. The economy produces a great deal of data that are relevant to our economic theories. These data occur in a noncontrolled fashion because many things are changing at the same time.

2. The techniques of statistical analysis allow us to estimate the separate influences of a large number of causal factors when all factors are varying simultaneously, provided we have a large enough sample of observations.

3. Use of random samples allows us to determine the probability that any relation we discover in our sample was a chance result, occurring because we just happened to pick an unrepresentative sample.

4. We never expect any relation that we discover to be perfect because we shall always

6. The actual quantitative relation is somewhat more complex and this simple one is used solely for purposes of illustration.

7. Hypotheses that originate from data are sometimes called *inductive* hypotheses in contrast to *deductive* ones. But in any science, the sequence of theory and testing and theory and testing is continuous. The question of which came first, theory or test, is quite analogous to the debate over the chicken and the egg.

make some errors of observation and because we shall almost always leave out some causes that may exert some influence on the events we are studying. *For this reason, virtually all economic hypotheses and predictions are statistical ones and not deterministic ones* (i.e., they are expected to hold only with some margin of error).

5. This means that we can never categorically prove or refute economic hypotheses and predictions. We can and do decide to accept or reject them on the basis of established statistical procedures that tell us how large the risk is of rejecting hypotheses that are in fact true.

6. Statistical testing not only tests but it also measures the quantitative magnitudes of any relations that are found. It also may suggest new or amended further hypotheses that are to be treated like any other new hypothesis and as such be subjected to new and further tests.

QUESTIONS FOR DISCUSSION

1. Explain why you agree or disagree with the view that a single contradictory observation refutes an hypothesis.

2. A classic example of biased sampling was the attempt made by *Literary Digest* in 1936 to predict the result of the Presidential election. They forecast a substantial Republican victory, and their subsequent demise is often attributed to this error. They used a survey method, taking their sample from a random selection of names in telephone directories. Can you spot the flaw? Remember that all this happened in 1936. Would the same bias have existed if the exercise had been conducted in 1964?

3. "The simplest way to see that capital punishment is a strong deterrent to murder is to ask yourself whether you might be more inclined to commit murder if you knew in advance that you ran no risk of ending in the electric chair, the gas chamber, or on the gallows." Comment on the methodology of social investigation implied in this statement.

4. "If you want to know the effects of a new tax cut on unemployment in the U.S., there is no sense in studying what happened when taxes were cut in other countries or in the U.S. in the past; the circumstances were bound to be different so that these experiences are of no relevance to what will happen in the U.S. if taxes are cut now." Comment on this view in the light of what you have studied in this chapter.

APPENDIX TO CHAPTER 4 GRAPHING ECONOMIC OBSERVATIONS

THE POPULAR SAYING "THE facts speak for themselves" is almost always wrong if there is a large number of facts. We need theories to explain how facts are linked together and we need summary measures to assist us in sorting out what it is that the facts do show in relation to theories. The simplest means of providing compact summaries of a large number of observations is through the use of tables and **graphs.**

In this appendix we are concerned with the two kinds of graphs that are most often used to represent observations in economics, the *scatter diagram* and the *time series*. Scatter diagrams and time-series graphs are limited to the dimensions of a piece of paper; therefore, they can be used only to depict the variation of two variables.

The Scatter Diagram

Suppose we have taken a sample of 100 men for the purpose of studying the relationship between height and weight.

TABLE A1

Individual	Height	Weight
A	5′ 3″	130
B	5′ 8″	160
C	5′ 9″	155
D	5′11″	180
E	6′ 2″	185

Table A1 shows the information about five of them, but we have data about the other 95 as well.

Figure A1 plots the five points on a graph in which the vertical axis measures weight and the horizontal axis measures height. Each observation in Table A1 is represented by a small circle in the graph whose coordinates show the height and weight of the subject concerned. Thus Point B in the figure refers to the individual called B in the table, whose height is 5′8″ and whose weight is 160 pounds. The student should label the other four points in the graph to be sure he understands exactly what each one stands for. Since we are interested in the relation of height and weight in general (rather than B's height and weight in particular), we usually leave off the labels identifying the points.

Figure A2 shows the scatter diagram for our full set of 100 observations. The five observations of the previous chart appear as dots, the rest as crosses.

The usefulness of the scatter diagram is that, once it is drawn, the relationship (if there is one) often leaps to the eye. In Figure A2 we have drawn a line to suggest this relationship.

Not only can we see immediately from the diagram that there is a relation, but we can gain some idea of its nature: whether it is best described by a straight line or by a curve, and if by a line, then of what slope. We can also gain some idea of the *strength* of this relationship by seeing how close the points come to lying on one particular line or curve; if the points lie exactly on a line or curve, the relationship is deterministic; if they are scattered very widely around the line, the relationship is rather weak. The line in Figure A2 shows the average relation between weight and height, and the scatter of the actual observations around

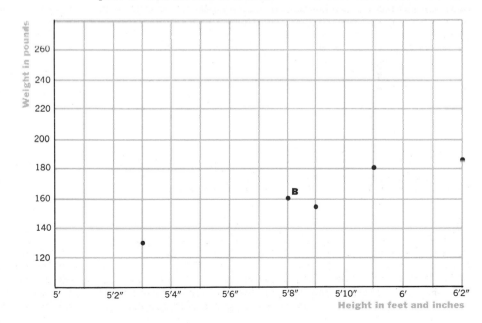

FIGURE A1

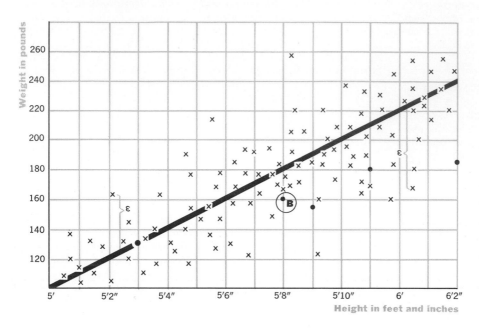

FIGURE A2
**RELATION
BETWEEN HEIGHTS
AND WEIGHTS OF
100 INDIVIDUALS
SELECTED
AT RANDOM**

TABLE A2   **TOTAL PERSONAL CONSUMPTION EXPENDITURE IN THE U.S., 1929–1964**

Year	Consumption in billions of dollars	Year	Consumption in billions of dollars	Year	Consumption in billions of dollars
1929	79.0	1941	81.9	1953	232.6
1930	71.0	1942	89.7	1954	238.0
1931	61.3	1943	100.5	1955	256.9
1932	49.3	1944	109.8	1956	269.9
1933	46.4	1945	121.7	1957	285.2
1934	51.9	1946	147.1	1958	293.2
1935	56.3	1947	165.4	1959	313.5
1936	62.6	1948	178.3	1960	328.2
1937	67.3	1949	181.2	1961	337.3
1938	64.6	1950	195.0	1962	356.8
1939	67.6	1951	209.8	1963	375.0
1940	71.9	1952	219.8	1964	399.3

SOURCE: *Economic Report of the President*, 1965.

the line gives an idea of the strength of the relationship.[1] The fact that the points do not all lie on the line indicates that the relationship is not exact. Data of the kind used in this example are often called *cross-sectional data*. We are (in our example) comparing the heights and weights of different people at the same time rather than studying the height and weight of a single individual as he grows from infancy to adulthood. Cross-sectional studies are very important in economics. We may look *across* households to see the relationship of consumption patterns to incomes. We may look *across* states or industries to see the relationship of unemployment rates to the size of the defense contracts

1. It is inconvenient just to trust our eyes to draw such a line. Elementary statistical theory shows us how to *fit a line* to the data so that the line best describes the average relation.

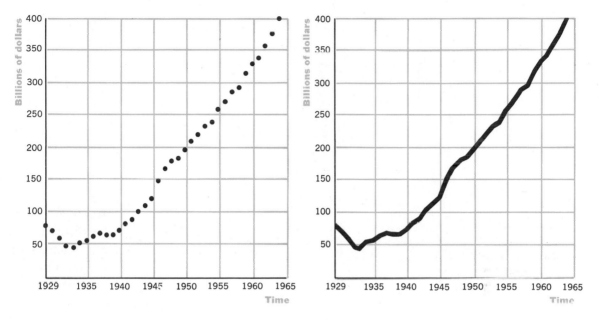

FIGURE A3   FIGURE A4

received. We may look *across* countries to see the effect of the quantities of natural resources on economic well-being. And so on.

The Time-Series Graph

Suppose we have the data on personal-consumption expenditure in the U.S. shown in Table A2.

We now plot this information on a diagram, as shown in Figure A3. Time is one variable, and personal consumption expenditure the other. But time is a very special variable in that the order in which successive events happen is not unimportant. 1933 followed 1932. They were not two independent and unrelated years. (By way of

contrast, individuals A and B were independent and unrelated.) For this reason, it is customary to draw in the line segments connecting the successive points, as we have done in Figure A4. Such a chart is called a *time-series graph* or, more simply, a *time series*.

Another example of a time series is presented in Figure A5, which illustrates an important difference between a scatter diagram and a time series. As a series of dots on a scatter diagram, no significant relationship between unemployment and time would be visible. But the series shows there is a very marked and regular pattern or fluctuation in unemployment over this period. This phenomenon, the business cycle, as we call it, leaps to the eye.

A closer look at the time series suggests further questions: How fast is unemployment changing over time? Is it changing a great deal or only just a bit? If we look, for example, at the years 1908–1909, we see that unemployment was almost constant at 8.5 percent, whereas in 1891–1892, unemployment rose from 3 percent to 6.3 percent—a huge rate of change over a short period of time. We conclude that when unemployment is changing a great deal over time the graph is steep, and when it is changing only a little over time the graph is flat. The geometrical shape of the curve gives a picture of how much the variable on one axis is changing for given changes in the variable on the other axis.

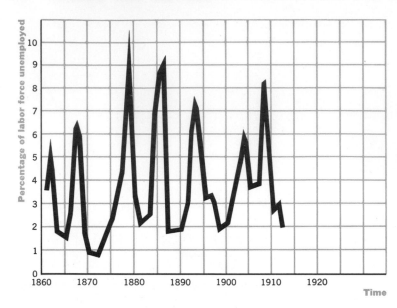

FIGURE A5 **PERCENTAGE OF THE UNIONIZED LABOR FORCE UNEMPLOYED IN BRITAIN, 1861– 1913**

QUESTIONS FOR DISCUSSION

1. It is often said that most economic variables move together and that, since everything in the economy seems to be more or less related to everything else, it is not possible to distinguish between true and false theories about what is causally connected to what in the economy. Test this view for yourself by drawing a scatter diagram relating two economic series chosen haphazardly. Pick any two tables in this book giving postwar data for the American economy and plot one series on the X axis and one on the Y axis. (Such tables can be found scattered throughout the book.) Draw three scatter diagrams, using six series altogether. What do you think now of the hypothesis that all economic series move together?

2. Collect data about monthly temperatures in some U.S. city. Plot two time series, one for maximum and one for minimum temperatures. Plot a scatter diagram showing the relation of maximum and minimum temperatures.

3. What would a time series of variable X look like if X were varying in a completely random fashion over time? Compare your time series for X with Figure A5 on page 56.

Chapter **5** ECONOMIC ANALYSIS AND ECONOMIC POLICY

POSITIVE ECONOMICS HELPS US TO UNDER-stand and to predict economic behavior. Man, by nature curious about his environ-ment, wants to predict this behavior in order that he may control his environment and adapt it to his needs.

The Pervasiveness of Policy Decisions

All governments have economic policies. Governments derive their policy authority from their police power—indeed, the words policy and police come from the identical Greek word, *politeia*.

Some governments may lean toward a policy of *laissez faire*, or noninterference; others aim for a policy of strict control over every facet of the economy. Even the decision not to act, to let nature take its course, is a policy decision. In a democratic country, policies are determined by procedures and are decided under rules that have been adopted with the consent of the majority; in a dictatorship, policies may largely express the will of a small group. In a free-market economy, for example, many "decisions" are left to the market. This type of decision is as much a policy decision as the decision of the government to levy a tax on cigarettes. Not every facet of policy is debated anew every year; indeed, many policy decisions now in force (such as giving unions the right to organize and women the right to vote) were made decades ago. At any one time only a few major policy decisions are being debated that receive a great deal of attention. (In 1964, the tax cut and the War on Poverty were perhaps the most debated economic policies; in 1965, Medicare received major attention.) And, in any one year, thousands of economic policy decisions are made by local, state, and federal governments that never become the subject of serious public debate.

The Relation Between Ends and Means

Any policy action has two aspects: the ends that the decision-makers are attempting to achieve, and the means by which the de-sired ends are to be achieved. The United States Government pursues simultaneously many broad policy goals, such as justice, progress, national security, and economic stability. To achieve its goal of justice, it may decide to improve the economic status of disadvantaged groups—the needy, the aged, Negroes, the mentally defective. To achieve its goal of stability, it may decide that unemployment or inflation must be controlled, or foreign-exchange imbalances corrected. Once such a decision is made, it is translated into a number of more specific goals. The broad concern with justice may eventually be expressed, for instance, in a national minimum-wage law.

Economists asked to evaluate some particular policy—a minimum-wage law, say—must ask themselves two questions: What is the specific objective this law is meant to achieve?, and What is the general objective of the policy-maker? The economist will have no chance of understanding the minimum-wage legislation unless he can relate this policy both to the objective it is designed to serve and to the underlying goal that dictated that objective. To take a different example, a change in the tax laws providing for an investment credit is designed to stimulate investment, which is an objective pursued in order to promote economic growth. The economist asked to evaluate this policy must ask whether it *will* stimulate investment, whether this stimulation will contribute to economic growth, whether there are feasible alternative policies, and what the costs are that are involved. The person who criticizes the policy of the tax credit on the ground that it helps the big corporations but does nothing

for the farmer is not coming to grips with the real issue: If the investment credit increases the amounts businessmen invest, either because it increases their incentives or because it provides them with available funds, it will lead to an increase in production and thus help to realize the goal of economic growth. No one particular policy measure will contribute to the achievement of all our policy goals. It is the economist's business to determine if it contributes to some of our goals and at what cost.

Some people sometimes speak as if economic theory *justified* certain policy objectives. For example, it is not uncommon to hear someone say that the policy of rent control is *economically unsound;* or that the policy of agricultural price supports is *economic nonsense;* or that the only *valid* economic policy is to charge a price that covers costs. Such viewpoints often represent an effort to dismiss a policy without thinking through its consequence. Every time a student encounters the catch phrase "economic nonsense," his every critical faculty should be aroused. "What does this really mean?," he should ask. "Why is it dismissed as nonsense?" In other words, he should try to determine whether the speaker has made a value judgment. As we pointed out in Chapter 2, it is impossible to deduce a statement about what ought to be from statements about what is. Positive economics concerns what *is;* it cannot, therefore, produce statements about what *ought* to be.

The Role of the Economist

Let us take a specific issue of policy to see in more detail what we can and cannot expect from economics. Consider the position

of an economist asked to examine the case for and against rent control (i.e., government-fixing of the rent of private dwellings).

How should the economist go about evaluating rent control? First, he should ask what goals rent control is meant to achieve. He might find that rent control is intended to redistribute income from rich to poor, to ensure a minimum standard of housing for everyone, and to maintain general housing standards. Next, he must ask if rent control does in fact help realize these policy goals. If the answer is No, then that is the end of the story. The case against rent control is clear: It does not achieve the objects for which it is intended. If the answer is Yes, then further study is necessary. Let us consider, as an example, the goal of income redistribution. Rent control, if effective, means that the tenant pays less rent than he otherwise would, and the landlord receives less income than he otherwise would; thus rent control redistributes income from landlord to tenant. But, in the real world, do landlords tend to be richer than their tenants? If a survey shows that most tenants are in fact richer than their landlords, the economist can conclude that there is a case against rent control, not because rent control is unjust or unethical, but because it does not achieve the policy goal for which it was being used. If, however, the survey indicates that most tenants have lower incomes than their landlords, then the economist will conclude that rent control *is* a means of obtaining the desired goal of income redistribution.

The economist must next ask if rent control has effects that conflict with other policy objectives. It may be, for example, that although rent control provides low-cost housing, it simultaneously causes the appearance of more slum areas. When one measure helps to achieve one goal but hinders the attainment of another, it is necessary to decide which of these goals is preferred. The economist considers the alternatives to see if there are other measures that will achieve the goal

at a lower sacrifice both in terms of operating costs and in terms of setbacks to other policy objectives. It may be, for example, that the progressive income tax redistributes income from rich to poor with more certainty and precision and with fewer undesired side effects than does rent control.

The economist must now determine if it is feasible to adopt the alternative means. In other words, when faced with evaluating a policy measure for achieving some goal, he must ask whether other measures that are feasible at this time and place would better achieve the desired goal.

If, having done all this, the economist concludes that rent control *does* achieve the desired policy, that the undesirable effects in other directions are judged (by the policy-makers) to be less important than the desirable effects in achieving the stated policy goal, and that there are no other practicable measures that would better achieve the goals, he will then conclude that there is a strong case in its favor.

There are many pitfalls in attempting to apply this procedure. First, the economist himself will usually have strong views on the particular measure he is attempting to assess. If he does not like the measure, he is likely to be relentless in searching out possible unwanted effects and somewhat less than thorough in discovering effects that help to achieve the desired goals. It is difficult to guard against an unconscious bias of this sort.

Second, it is easy to forget that the statements that emerge from standard theory are *predictions*, the validity of which, in particular instances, can only be established by empirical testing. The economist might, for example, "demonstrate," on the basis of a current economic model, that rent control would cause landlords to spend less on repair-and-maintenance than they would in its absence. He then might conclude that one of the valid arguments against rent control is that it will lead to inadequate repairs to housing when he *should* say that standard theory *predicts* that rent control will have these consequences (generally held to be undesirable) in regard to repairs to housing. The confidence that we place in this prediction must depend on the extent to which the general theory from which the prediction has been extracted has already stood up to severe testing. If the general theory has rarely or never been tested, then we should not have much confidence in this particular prediction until it has been tested itself. If, on the other hand, the theory has been extensively tested in other contexts, we should examine the particular case in hand to see if it differs from other tested cases in circumstances that our theory suggests to be relevant. Thus, if as is so often the case, we are dealing with theories that are substantially untested, at least in a relevant context, we must conclude that the theorist can only predict for us certain consequences of rent control; these

predictions tell us what to look for when we turn to a study of the world. It is a common pitfall in considering policy measures to think that the job is done once the economist has predicted the likely effects; at this stage the job has just begun.

It is the role of the economist not only to analyze the consequences of a proposed policy (or to compare two or more policies), but also to suggest policies. Given a statement of the objectives, economic analysis can be used to invent or publicize proposed policies that have not been previously under consideration. Congress in 1946 established the Council of Economic Advisors to serve the President.[1] There is no doubt that the Council has played an important role in forming U.S. economic policy. Walter Heller, Chairman of the Council from 1961 to 1964, was instrumental in initiating and generating support for the tax cut of 1964. A more recent proposal of Professor Heller's, to return part of federal tax revenue to the states, has not been adopted, but it is a controversial one that is much debated.

Conflicts of Policy

Governments have a multiplicity of policy goals. It is quite impossible for a government to fulfill all of these goals simultaneously. Although one measure will bring us closer to some of our objectives, it may take us further away from others. For this reason, if for no other, policy decisions are subject to disagreement and debate. *Any* policy action limits someone's freedom, but if it is a means to a preferred choice of goals, or a preferred distribution of income, policy-makers may well choose the policy that will reap the

greater benefits. Unemployment compensation, for example, may hinder the quickness with which labor moves from labor-surplus to labor-scarce occupations, thereby increasing the total unemployment in the country, but at the same time it may protect unemployed families from debilitating hardship. Which is more important—to protect some families from hardship or to risk raising the over-all level of unemployment? Economics cannot answer such philosophical questions, but someone must provide the answers, for de-

1. The Council was created by the Employment Act of 1946, the purpose of which was "to promote maximum employment, production, and purchasing power" within the framework of free competitive enterprise.

cisions have to be made. It is not sufficient for governments to decide which objectives are worth pursuing; they must also decide on some *rate of substitution* between them. They must decide how much of one it is worth sacrificing in order to get more of the other.

The significance of this point is frequently overlooked. It is never enough to show that a proposed policy advances one of society's objectives. Virtually any proposed action meets such a test, and usually the exactly opposite action also meets it. (For example,

one might argue that increasing the corporate income tax and spending the increase on needy children would increase the equity of the distribution of income. But cutting corporate taxes and reducing the amount spent on needy children might stimulate corporate expenditure for research and development, and thus contribute to progress and efficiency.) What must be shown of some proposed policy is that it advances certain of our objectives sufficiently to overcome the cost in terms of the amount that it moves us away from other objectives.

Summary

1. Economic theories provide us with explanations of how events are related. We are interested in understanding these relations because we are curious to understand how the world works, and because we wish to intervene to bring about changes that we regard as desirable.

2. We may distinguish between the ends, or goals, of policy and the means by which these goals are to be achieved.

3. Economics does not provide a basis for passing judgments on ends, for whether society ought to pursue a particular end requires value judgments, and this takes us beyond the scope of positive economics.

4. Economics can be used to study the relation between ends and means. We can ask (a) if the means chosen will achieve the desired ends, (b) what side effects on other objectives will be brought about by the policy adopted, and (c) whether there are other feasible policies that would achieve the desired objectives more easily or at lower cost in terms of undesired side effects.

5. Policy objectives often conflict with

each other. Here the economist can try to discover the facts about such conflicts. Is it really true, for example, that full employment and stable prices are incompatible, and, if so, how much more inflation is required to secure a stated reduction in unemployment?

6. Even when economics is successful in providing satisfactory theories of the consequences of various actions, we cannot expect to be able to answer all our questions about what we ought to do on the basis of economic analysis. At best we can hope to answer from within economics such questions as "Given that we have certain objectives, which policies will effectively achieve these objectives and which policies will not?" We can also look to economics to tell us whether two policy objectives are in conflict or whether they can be achieved simultaneously. We must, however, look outside of economics for the answer to such questions as "Given that we cannot simultaneously achieve two policy objectives, which one should be the more important in our scale of values?"

QUESTIONS FOR DISCUSSION

1. Explain why the government cannot avoid making policy decisions on the power of labor unions, the welfare of the small businessman, and federal aid to education. Was there a policy about wages before any minimum-wage laws were passed?

2. Minimum-wage laws are often advocated as a means of ensuring some basic standard of living for all citizens. Discuss the relevancy to this issue of the following assertions. Which are positive statements?

a. "Minimum-wage laws only result in unemployment. It just isn't worth it to firms to hire some unskilled workers at a cent more than they're getting."

b. "I believe it would be better to provide low-paid workers with subsidized housing."

c. "Low-paid workers are lazy, and have only themselves to blame."

d. "The minimum-wage laws do nothing to solve the race problem."

e. "The minimum-wage laws *hurt* the Negro's chances of employment."

f. "Minimum-wage laws interfere with the natural right of businessmen to run their establishments as they please."

g. "Minimum-wage laws are economically unsound."

h. "Inflation can result from workers being paid more than they are now."

i. "People have a right to what they can produce by their own efforts and to nothing else. If they cannot earn a living wage by their own efforts, then they should be allowed to starve to death."

Do not worry too much about the economics of these statements right now; concentrate instead on their relevance, logic, and testability.

3. Discuss the following: "A careful study has shown that students living in apartments earn significantly lower grades than students living in dormitories. The administration has *therefore* decided to ban apartment living." What does this reveal about the administration's policy goals? What does it reveal about the theory that the administration is using to interpret the observed events?

A GENERAL VIEW OF THE PRICE SYSTEM

Chapter 6 WHAT IS THE PRICE SYSTEM?

ALL ECONOMIES ARE FACED WITH THE PROBLEM of scarcity, for, as we pointed out in Chapter 1, there are not enough resources to produce all the goods and services that could be consumed. It is, therefore, necessary to choose between what to produce and what not to produce and to allocate the available resources among their various possible uses. In a market society, this allocation is the outcome of millions of independent decisions made by consumers and producers all acting through the *market mechanism*. Our first task in this book is to familiarize ourselves with the market mechanism. In this chapter, we give a short intuitive view of the workings of the market; in subsequent chapters, we formalize this view into a definite theory of the market and, at the same time, consider the empirical evidence relating to this theory.

A Change in Demand

By a *change in demand* we mean a change in the willingness of consumers to purchase a particular product. How does the market react to such a change? Imagine that consumers develop a greatly increased desire for Brussels sprouts and a diminished desire for carrots. This development might be a matter of fashion, sparked by some quite minor cause,

65

or it might be the result of a successful advertising campaign on the part of an association of Brussels-sprout producers: "Eat Brussels sprouts, grown *above* ground." Whatever the reason, there has been a major shift toward sprouts and away from carrots.

What will be the effects of this shift? Consumers will buy more Brussels sprouts and fewer carrots. Production, however, remains unchanged, and a shortage of Brussels sprouts and a glut of carrots develops. In order to unload their surplus stocks of carrots, merchants reduce carrot prices—in the belief that it is better to sell them at a reduced price than not to sell them at all. On the other hand, merchants find that they are unable to satisfy all their customers' demands for Brussels sprouts. Sprouts have become a scarce commodity and so the merchants charge more for them. As the price rises, fewer people are willing and able to purchase sprouts. Thus, by making them more expensive, the demand for them is limited to the available supply.

Farmers begin to observe a rise in the price of Brussels sprouts and a fall in the price of carrots. Brussels-sprout production has become more profitable than in the past, for the costs of producing them remain unchanged at the same time that their market price has risen. Similarly, carrot production will be less profitable than in the past because costs remain unchanged at the same time that prices have fallen. Attracted by high profits in Brussels sprouts and deterred by low profits or possibly losses in carrots, farmers expand the production of sprouts and curtail the production of carrots. Thus, the change in consumers' tastes, working through the price system, causes a reallocation of resources— e.g., land and labor—out of carrot production and into Brussels-sprout production.

As the production of carrots declines, the glut of carrots on the market diminishes and carrot prices begin to rise. On the other hand, the expansion in Brussels-sprout production reduces the shortage and their price begins to fall. These price movements will continue until it no longer pays farmers to contract carrot production and to expand Brussels-sprout production. When the dust settles, we end up in a position in which the price of sprouts is higher than it was originally, but lower than it was when the shortage sent prices soaring before output could be adjusted, and in which carrot prices are lower than they were originally, but higher than when the initial glut sent prices tumbling before output could be adjusted.

We can now see how the transfer of resources takes place. Carrot producers reduce their production; they will therefore be laying off workers and generally demanding fewer factors of production. On the other hand, Brussels-sprout producers expand production; they will therefore be hiring workers and generally increasing their demand for factors of production.

Labor can probably switch from carrot to sprout production without much difficulty. If, however, there are certain resources, a certain type of land, say, that is better suited for sprout-growing than for carrot-growing, the demand for, and hence the price of, this land will be affected: When farmers increase their sprout production, their demand for those factors especially suited for sprout production increases also and this creates a shortage of such resources and a consequent rise in their price. On the other hand, with carrot production falling, the demand for land especially suited for carrot-growing is reduced. A surplus results and the price is forced down.

Thus, factors particularly suited to sprout production will earn more and will obtain a higher share of total national income than before. Factors particularly suited for carrot production, on the other hand, will earn less and will obtain a smaller share of the total national income than before.

SUMMARY

1. A change in consumers' tastes causes a change in demand, which in turn causes a shortage or a surplus to appear. This in its turn causes market prices to rise, in the case of a shortage, and to fall, in the case of a surplus.

2. The variations in market price affect the profitability of producing goods—profitability varying directly with price. In search of profits, producers will shift their production out of less profitable lines and into more profitable ones.

3. The attempt to change the pattern of production will cause variations in the demand for factors of production. Factors especially suited for the production of commodities the demand for which is increasing will themselves be heavily demanded so that their own prices will rise.

4. Thus the change in consumers' tastes sets off a series of market changes that causes a reallocation of resources in the required direction.

The theory that deals with Point 1 is the theory of determination of market price through demand and supply. Point 2, which concerns the reaction of producers to market changes, is part of the theory of production. Point 3 is dealt with in the theory of distribution.

A Change in Supply

Now consider another change—this time on the side of producers. We assume that, at existing prices, farmers are more willing to produce sprouts than in the past and less willing to produce carrots. There are many things that could cause such a change. It might be brought about by a change in the costs of producing the two goods—a rise in carrot costs and a fall in sprout costs—or it might be brought about by a change in the tastes of farmers: Everything else being equal, including the profits to be earned from carrots and sprouts, farmers might just prefer to grow sprouts rather than carrots.

Now what will happen? For a short time, nothing at all, for the existing supply of sprouts and carrots on the market is the result of decisions made by farmers at some time in the past. But farmers now begin to

plant fewer carrots and more sprouts, and soon the quantities on the market begin to change. The quantity of sprouts available for sale rises and the quantity of carrots falls. A shortage of carrots and a glut of sprouts results. The price of carrots consequently rises and the price of sprouts falls. As carrots become more expensive, fewer people buy them, and as sprouts become cheaper, more of them will be purchased. The rise in carrot prices and the fall in sprout prices now acts as an incentive for farmers to move back into carrot production out of sprout production.

We started from a position in which there was a shortage of carrots, which caused carrot prices to rise. The rise in carrot prices removed the shortage in two ways; first, by reducing the demand for carrots, which became progressively more expensive to purchase, and, second, by increasing the supply of carrots, which became progressively more profitable to produce. We also started from a position in which there was a surplus of Brussels sprouts, which caused their price to fall. The fall in price removed the surplus in two ways; first, by encouraging the consumers to buy more of this commodity, which became progressively cheaper, and, second, by discouraging the production of this commodity, which became progressively less profitable to produce.

These examples illustrate many of the important features of the price system. The allocation of resources is a result of decisions on the part of both producers and consumers. A change in the conditions either of consumers' demand or of producers' supply affects the allocation of resources and thus also the final pattern of production and consumption in the economy. The *mechanism* by which these changes occur is through changes in prices and profits.

It is often remarked that in a free-market society the consumer is king. Such a maxim reveals only half the truth. Prices are determined by both demand and supply. A free-market society gives sovereignty to two groups, producers and consumers, and the decisions of both groups affect the allocation of resources.

Under certain very special conditions, known to the economist as conditions of *perfect competition,* the producer loses his sovereignty and becomes a mere automaton responding to the will of the consumer. These very special conditions are described in Chapter 22. Aside from this special case, however, the producer has at his command, and actually does exercise, considerable power in the allocation of resources in the economy.

This general picture of the working of the price system has left untouched many problems. Before we can handle these problems, we must formulate the ideas given in this chapter into a more precise theory of price. This will be done in the following chapters.

Empirical Evidence

There is a great deal of empirical evidence showing that, for many agricultural commodities and industrial raw materials, the price system works very much as described in this chapter. In any retail or wholesale produce market, prices can be observed to react to the state of demand and supply, prices rising when there is a shortage and falling when there is a surplus. Even the most casual observation of agriculture will

enable one to observe farmers varying their production of different crops as market prices vary. A much more difficult question is whether or not it is valid to generalize this view of the price system into a theory of the prices of all commodities: agricultural goods, manufactured goods, and services. This question must be postponed until after the theory of price has been developed more fully in subsequent chapters.

Summary

1. In this chapter we have surveyed the way in which the price system works in allocating resources among the various uses to which they could be put.

2. A rise in demand or a fall in supply will cause a shortage to appear. A fall in demand or a rise in supply will cause a surplus. The effects of shortages and surpluses can be summarized as follows: A shortage causes prices to rise, a surplus causes them to fall. A rise in the price of a commodity increases the profitability of producing that commodity, while a fall in price diminishes profitability. In search of maximum profits, producers will be induced to increase production of goods whose price has risen and reduce production of goods whose price has fallen. The attempt to change the pattern of production will cause changes in the demands for factors of production. The demand for factors used in making commodities whose production is increasing will rise, and hence their price will rise. The demand for factors used in making commodities whose production is decreasing will fall and their price will fall. The change in the prices of factors will attract resources out of contracting industries and into expanding industries.

In this way, changes in demand and supply set off a series of market changes that cause a reallocation of resources in the required direction.

3. A free-market society gives sovereignty to two groups, producers and consumers. The decisions of both groups affect the allocation of resources.

QUESTIONS FOR DISCUSSION

1. George Bernard Shaw, in explaining the subject matter of this chapter in *Fabian Essays in Socialism*, posed the following hypothetical situation: "The exertion of the Salvation Army might create such a demand for tambourines as to make them worth four times their cost of production." Can you explain what will happen to the allocation of resources between, say, tambourines and trombones, in such an instance? How would this allocation come about?

2. Trace out, in a manner similar to the analysis in this chapter, the effect of a change in consumers' demand away from cigarettes and toward cigars as a result of the publication of an official report linking cigarette smoking (but not cigar smoking) with both heart disease and lung cancer.

3. What will happen, according to the theory sketched in this chapter, if there is a rise in the cost of producing barley relative to the cost of producing oats?

4. What will happen if, on a particularly fine day in April, there is a sudden and temporary increase in the demand for ice cream? What will happen if the exceptionally good weather and the exceptionally high demand continues this way all summer?

5. If goods are expensive because they are scarce, why aren't rotten eggs high-priced?

Chapter 7 **THE ELEMENTARY THEORY OF DEMAND**

IN CHAPTER 6, WE SAW THAT THE MARKET price of a commodity is influenced by the demand of consumers for the commodity, and by the supply of the commodity that producers offer for sale. The first step in developing a

formal theory of market prices is, therefore, to consider the determinants of consumers' demand and producers' supply. Demand is considered in this chapter and supply in Chapter 8.

Consumer Expenditures

The American consumer spent almost $400 billion on goods and services in 1964. What did he spend it on, and why? He spent it on durable and nondurable goods and he spent it on services. (See Table 1.) The question of *why* he spent it as he did is the one that interests the economist. Why did the fraction of consumer income that was spent on food decline from over one-third in 1910 to one-fifth in the 1960s? Why did American consumers spend a negligible percentage of their income on automobiles in 1920, 4 percent in 1929, only 2 percent in 1932, and 6 percent in the early 1960s?[1] Why do they now heat their homes with electricity, oil, and natural gas when twenty years ago they used coal? Why has their gasoline consumption increased so rapidly? Why do Amer-

TABLE 1 **PERSONAL CONSUMPTION EXPENDITURES, 1964, IN BILLIONS OF DOLLARS**

Durable goods		57
Automobiles and parts	24	
Furniture and household equipment	24	
Other	9	
Nondurable goods		177
Food	92	
Clothing	33	
Other	52	
Services		165
Housing	46	
Household operation	22	
Transportation	11	
Other	86	
TOTAL		399

SOURCE: Adapted from the *Survey of Current Business*, April, 1965.

1. In 1943, 1944, 1945, they spent less than 1 percent in each year. Why?

ican consumers spend less on cotton goods and more on synthetic fabrics such as nylon and Dacron than they did ten years ago? Why do people who build houses in Norway rarely use brick, whereas it is commonly used in Great Britain? Why do the majority of middle-class British families have someone who lives in to look after the children, whereas very few middle-class American families do? Why have the maid and the washerwoman become so rare in the American home? Why have the vacuum cleaner and the washer become commonplace?

To answer these questions we need to know, among other things, what determines the demand for commodities.

In this chapter we shall concentrate not on the individual household, but rather on the demand of *all* households for commodities. Of course, what all households do is only the sum of what each household does, but as we indicated on page 17, it is often easier to find explanations of group behavior than of individual behavior.[2]

What Determines Demand?

The amount of a commodity that households wish to purchase is called the *demand* for the commodity. Demand is a flow.[3] We are concerned not with a single isolated purchase, but with a continuous flow of purchases, and we must therefore express demand as so much flow per period of time— 1 million oranges *per day,* say, or 7 million oranges *per week,* or 365 million *per year.* We now introduce six hypotheses about the factors that are important in influencing household demand and about the direction that those influences take.

1. *The demand for a commodity depends upon the tastes or preferences of the members of society.*

If it becomes fashionable to have color television, the flow of expenditures on color television sets (and probably on all television sets) will increase. This does not mean that everybody will buy one, but some people will, and demand will increase. Some changes in tastes are passing fads, like hula hoops and skate boards; other changes in taste are permanent, or at least long lasting, like the American's dedication to having his own car, or his switch to filter cigarettes and ball-point pens.[4]

The economist often regards tastes as given and changes in these tastes as exogenous and therefore as outside his province. Tastes are thought to arise out of the basic wants and needs of human beings and as such are more nearly in the realm of the biologist and the psychologist than of the economist. Changes in taste may, however, be the result of economic activities. The whole purpose of advertising, on which American industry spends in excess of $10 billion per year, is to change

2. By a household we mean all the people who live under one roof and who make, or are subject to others making for them, joint financial decisions. In the appendix to Chapter 13 we consider the theory of the behavior of individual households.

3. See the appendix to Chapter 3, page 37.

4. A Soviet visitor to this country recently remarked that he was appalled by the way in which cars sat idle most of the day. We are, indeed, a country in which cars wait for people, not the other way around.

people's tastes, and there is little doubt that it succeeds. Why else would people buy electric can openers? *Other people* influence taste also. Keeping up with the Joneses creates a *bandwagon* or *demonstration effect:* The quantity and quality of a good one person buys depends upon the quantities and qualities other people buy. A man may develop a taste for fine wine after tasting some, but he may also develop it after discovering that serving it enhances his prestige. In any case, people have tastes and preferences, and these preferences change. When they do, the demand for some commodities increases and for others declines.

2. *The demand for a commodity depends upon the size of the population.*

As population grows, more people need to be fed, clothed, housed, and entertained, and thus demand increases as population does. Economists treat population change as another exogenous determinant of demand.

3. *The demand for a commodity depends upon the level of income of the average household.*

In most cases, the larger is average income, the larger will be the quantity of a particular commodity demanded.[5] Although we have hypothesized that the quantities demanded of virtually all commodities will increase as income increases, they will not increase in the same proportions. Thus changes in income are likely to cause very different percentage changes in the demands for different commodities. When the population is poor, much of its income must go to basic necessities: food, clothing, and shelter.

As it becomes richer, it will buy more (and more expensive) food, clothing, and shelter, but it will also spend more on luxury items.[6] The relative decline of food and other non-durable goods in the over-all consumption pattern and the rise in the importance of durable goods and housing is in large part due to the rise in income.

4. *The demand for a commodity depends upon the distribution of income among households.*

Imagine a society, an oil-rich sheikdom, say, in which the average income, though seemingly high, has been obtained by averaging the very low incomes of the vast number of poor households and the very high incomes of the few enormously wealthy ones. We would expect this society to have a very different pattern of demands from a society in which the same average income is distributed more equitably.

5. *The demand for a commodity depends upon the price of that commodity.*

Our hypothesis is that the higher the price, the lower the quantity of the commodity that will be demanded. Goods and services are desired to satisfy wants and needs. Since there are almost always alternative ways to satisfy these wants, and since incomes are limited, when the price of a certain good or service rises some people will choose to substitute other goods or services. The increase in the wages of domestic servants and the corresponding decrease in their use in the United States dramatically illustrates this hypothesis. The housewife has had to make do without a servant, but she has substituted

---

5. There are some commodities, known as inferior goods, for which this is not the case. See Chapter 14.

6. What is a luxury and what is a necessity is itself a relative matter. Many people consider hot running water, automobiles, appliances, and movies luxuries. Once they get accustomed to them, however, they may regard them as virtual necessities.

washing machines, vacuum cleaners, and frozen foods to lighten her burden. The relevant aspect of a price change is that the price changes *in relation to other commodities*. One way in which a commodity's relative price can fall is for its price to fall while other prices remain constant. Another way is for its price to remain constant while other prices rise. Let us examine the effect of changes in *other prices* more fully.

6. *The demand for a commodity depends upon the prices of many other commodities*.

With a decrease in the price of a *substitute* commodity (one that satisfies the same needs as the original), we can expect a decrease in the demand for the original. Silk and cotton have been less sought after as the price of nylon and Dacron has fallen. Bricks and lumber are substitutes as building materials. In the American West and in Norway, where forests are numerous, timber rather than brick provides the basic material for housing. In most of the American Northeast and in Britain, where lumber is scarce and expensive, brick, relatively cheap, is used instead.

When commodities are *complements* (that is, when they tend to be used together), a fall in the price of one will be expected to lead to an increase in the demand for the other. A fall in the price of automobiles, for example, would lead to a rise in the demand for gasoline. The reason is that an increase in automobile use, which is expected to follow from a decrease in the price of automobiles relative to other goods, will lead to more use of automobiles and (at the moment) automobiles must have gasoline in order to run. Would a rise in the price of gasoline lead to a decrease in the sale of automobiles? Does the complementary relationship work both ways?[7] Of course, in cases where commodities are neither close substitutes nor complements, we expect the demand for one commodity to remain virtually unchanged when the price of a second commodity changes (e.g., bread and washing machines).

The Demand Function

The above hypotheses about what affects the demand for a commodity are not alternative ones but are rather a set of influences all of which are supposed to apply. Demand for a commodity is a function of tastes, population, average income, distribution of income, the price of the commodity, and the prices of other commodities.[†]

Because this is quite a complicated functional relationship, we will not succeed in

---

7. Clue: In Britain, where gasoline costs about 65 cents per American gallon, most cars produced are small and, therefore, economical in their use of gasoline.

† This can be stated formally for commodity 1, which we will assume to be the one whose demand we study in this chapter, as:

$$D_1 = f(T, F, \bar{Y}, Y^*, p_1 \text{ and } p_2, \ldots, p_n),$$

where
D_1 = demand for commodity 1
T = tastes
F = population
$\bar{Y}$ = average income
Y^* = distribution of income
p_i = price of commodity i $(i = 1, 2, \ldots, n)$

developing a *simple* theory of demand or price if we consider what happens to demand when population, prices, incomes, and tastes all change at once. To get around this problem, we use a device that is frequently employed in economic theory: We assume that all except one of the independent variables are held constant; we then allow this one factor (e.g., price) to vary, and consider how demand varies with it, *on the assumption that all other things remain unchanged*, or, as the economist is fond of putting it, *ceteris paribus*.[8] After that, we then allow some other term, income say, to vary, and consider how, *ceteris paribus*, demand varies as income varies.

In principle we could take each variable in turn. In this chapter we shall look in some detail at two of them.

THE DEMAND FOR A COMMODITY AND ITS PRICE

We now assume that everything that can affect demand other than the price of the commodity in question is held constant.† The hypothesis for this relation is that for all commodities, the demand increases as the price of the commodity falls—income, tastes,

and all other prices remaining constant. As its price falls, a commodity becomes cheaper relative to its substitutes, and it is, therefore, easier for the commodity to compete against these substitutes for the purchaser's attention. Conversely, a rise in price leads consumers, in the aggregate, to buy less of that commodity and more of competing commodities. If, for example, Brussels sprouts become very expensive, some (or all) housewives will reduce their purchases of sprouts, possibly replacing them by some other green vegetable. If, on the other hand, Brussels sprouts become very cheap, some housewives will be induced, up to a point, to buy more sprouts and less of other vegetables whose prices are now high relative to the price of sprouts.

The relation that we have been considering between the demand for a commodity and the price of that commodity may be illustrated on a graph by plotting the price of the commodity on the vertical axis and the quantity demanded on the horizontal axis. A curve can then be drawn showing the quantity the consumer will wish to purchase at various alternative market prices.

This curve, which shows the relation between the price of a commodity and the amount of

---

8. The student is often disturbed by his frequent encounters with *ceteris paribus* arguments in elementary economic theory. It is certainly important to know how any two things are related to each other (e.g., how the demand for a commodity is related to its own price), and, in order to deal with these questions, *ceteris paribus* arguments are necessary. When employing such relationships, however, one must never forget the assumption that the relation holds only *if* other things remain unchanged. Many serious errors have resulted from applying a *ceteris paribus* prediction to real-world situations in which the other things did not, and indeed could not, remain unchanged.

The student should now reread the section on Partial Derivatives in the appendix to Chapter 3 (p. 42), in which the problem of *ceteris paribus* reasoning is discussed.

† In the language of the appendix to Chapter 3 (see p. 42), we are about to examine

$$D_1 = f(p_1) \quad \left| \begin{array}{l} T = T_o \\ F = F_o \\ \overline{Y} = \overline{Y}_o \\ Y^* = Y^*_o \\ p_2, \ldots, p_n = p_2^o, \ldots, p_n^o. \end{array} \right.$$

that commodity consumers wish to purchase, is called a *market demand curve,* and it is drawn on the assumption that income, tastes, and all other prices remain constant.

THE MARKET DEMAND CURVE

An example of a demand curve is shown in Figure 1. In this example, households will purchase 30 million pounds of beef per month if the price is 60¢ a pound; they will purchase 100 million pounds per month if the price is 30¢, but only 20 million pounds per month if the price is 70¢.[9] If the price

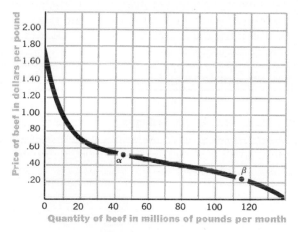

FIGURE 1   **A DEMAND CURVE**

should rise to $1.65, consumers will cease to purchase the commodity altogether; if it should fall to zero (i.e., if the beef becomes free), they will consume 140 million pounds per month. Check other points on the curve to find out what quantity consumers would wish to purchase at various market prices.

A single point on the demand curve indicates a single price-quantity combination. For example, Point α indicates that *if* the price were 54¢ a pound households *would like to buy* 45 million pounds per month; Point β shows that *if* the price were 22¢ households *would like to buy* 115 million pounds per month.

The whole demand curve is a representation of the complete functional relation between quantity demanded and price. Economists often speak of the conditions of demand in a particular market as being given or known. When they do so they are referring not just to the particular quantity that is being demanded at the moment (i.e., not just to a particular point on the demand curve), but, rather, to the whole demand curve, to the complete functional relation whereby desired purchases are related to all possible alternative prices of the commodity.

The market demand curve is the most emphasized of the relations in the demand function. Why? Much confusion exists on this subject. *We do not imply (or believe) that price is the most important determinant of demand.* In the earlier sections of this chapter, we discussed other important factors, and if one had to choose a single most important variable, it would probably be income. (We do not, however, have to choose, as will become clear in a moment.) The reason we focus on this way of representing the demand function is that we are working toward the theory of what determines market price; thus it is convenient to have price as one of our two variables. We now introduce five hypotheses about the influence of other variables on the demand curve.

9. Behind this type of graph lies either a mathematical formula or a table listing selected values of the demand curve. The student who is confused should reread the section "Graphing Functional Relations" in Chapter 3. In most future graphs we will drop the grid and the numbers. The reason for this is that in real-world applications we usually know what the approximate shape of the demand curve will be, but we seldom, if ever, have sufficiently precise knowledge to plot a curve exactly on a numbered graph.

Shifts in the Demand Curve

1. The effect on the demand curve of a change in income.

It has already been stated that, in the case of most commodities, a rise in income, *ceteris paribus*, will cause an increase in demand. Therefore, if the incomes of all households rise, we shall find that, whatever the price we consider, there will be an increase in the

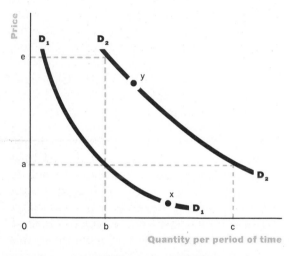

FIGURE 2   **AN INCREASE IN DEMAND**

amount that is demanded at that price. Graphically, the whole demand curve shifts to the right. The curve shifts, for example, from D_1 to D_2 in Figure 2. The curve D_1 shows the relation between the price of the commodity and demand, on the assumption that income is held constant at some level, Y_1; the curve D_2 shows the relation between demand and price, on the assumption that

income is also held constant, but at some other level, Y_2, which is greater than Y_1. The shift of the curve from D_1 to D_2 indicates an increase in desired purchases at every possible price. For example, at the price Oa desired purchases increase by the amount bc from Ob to Oc. Another way of showing that the shift from D_1 to D_2 does represent an increase in demand is to show that, for any given quantity, a higher price will be paid than previously. For example, the quantity Ob can be sold at the price Oa when the demand curve is D_1, but the same quantity can be sold for the much higher price Oe when the demand curve is D_2.[10]

2. The effect on the demand curve of a change in the prices of other goods.

Here the effect depends on whether the good, whose price changes, is a complement or a substitute commodity. Consider, for example, the effect on the demand curve for gasoline of a rise in the price of cars. When the price of cars rises, fewer cars will be bought and hence less gasoline will be bought at each possible price of gasoline. Thus the rise in the price of a complementary good, cars, shifts the whole demand curve for gasoline to the left, indicating that at each price less will be bought than previously. What will be the effect on the demand curve for gasoline of a rise in the price of public transport? People will be more inclined to use their own cars and more gasoline will be purchased at each price than

10. Thus a rightward shift in the demand curve indicates an increase in demand in the sense that more is demanded at the same price and that a higher price would be paid for the same quantity. It is, of course, true that the amount demanded at Point y on D_2 is less than the amount demanded at Point x on D_1. This comparison merely shows that, in spite of the increased desire to purchase the good, a sufficiently large rise in price can reduce the quantity actually demanded to an amount lower than it was originally.

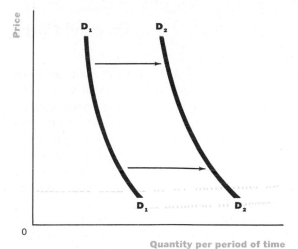

(i) A rise in demand—when more is demanded at each price—can be caused by a rise in income; a rise in the price of a substitute; a fall in the price of a complement; a change in tastes in favor of this commodity; an increase in population; a redistribution of income to groups who favor this commodity.

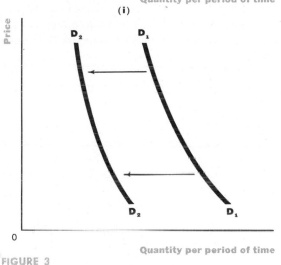

Quantity per period of time

(ii)

FIGURE 3

(ii) A fall in demand—when less is demanded at each price—can be caused by a fall in income; a fall in the price of a substitute; a rise in the price of a complement; a change in tastes against this commodity; a decrease in population; a redistribution of income away from groups who favor this commodity.

previously. Thus a rise in the price of a substitute good shifts the demand curve to the right, indicating that, at each price, a larger amount will be demanded than previously.

3. *The effect on the demand curve of a change in tastes.*

A change in tastes in favor of a commodity will mean that, at each price, more will be demanded than previously, so that the whole

demand curve will shift to the right. On the other hand, a change in tastes away from a commodity will mean that, at each price, less will be demanded than previously, so that the whole demand curve will shift to the left.

4. *The effect on the demand curve of a change in population.*

Population increases will increase the quantity demanded at each price because there will be more buyers, so that the whole demand curve will shift to the right. Population decreases will (for analogous reasons) shift the demand curve to the left.

5. *The effect on the demand curve of a change in the distribution of income.*

We expect that a change in income will change the demand curve. Income redistribution involves some groups gaining income and others losing income. The groups that gain income will usually prefer different goods than will the groups that lose income. Goods preferred by the income gainers will find their demands increasing, and the relevant demand curves will shift to the right. Goods preferred by the groups losing income will find their demand curves shifting to the left.

Figure 3 summarizes this discussion of the effects on a demand curve of changes in other things that are assumed constant when the curve is drawn. We do not neglect such changes if we are prepared to examine shifts in the demand curve as well as movements along it.

THE DEMAND FOR A COMMODITY AND AVERAGE INCOME

Instead of starting with price, we might have started with any other variable. We illustrate this here by examining the relation of demand to average income, assuming all other variables in the demand function to be constant.† Normally, we would expect a rise in income to be associated with a rise in the demand for most goods. There are two possible exceptions: In some cases, a rise in income might leave demand completely unaffected. This would be the case with goods the desire for which is completely satisfied after a certain level of income is obtained. Beyond this level, variations in income would have no effect on demand. This is probably the case with many of the more inexpensive foodstuffs. It is unlikely, for example, that the demand for salt would be affected by either an increase in average income from $6,000 to $7,000 per year, or by a decrease in average income from $6,000 to $5,000 (although the demand for salt might well be influenced by income changes if income were as low as, say, $1,000 per year). In other cases, it is possible for a rise in income beyond a certain level to lead to a fall in the demand for a particular commodity. Such a relation is likely to occur when one commodity is a cheap but inferior substitute for some other commodity. When incomes are low, money might be saved, for example, by using horsemeat or powdered milk. But at higher levels of income many households might feel that they were able to change to beef and whole milk. Thus, as income rose beyond a certain level, the demand for powdered milk and horsemeat would fall and would possibly reach zero as income attained a level at which the consumer ceased to worry about spending a few cents more or less per day on milk or meat. Commodities the demands for

---

† In this section we examine:

$$D_1 = f(\overline{Y})$$

$$\left. \begin{array}{l} T = T^o \\ F = F^{\,o} \\ Y^* = Y^{*o} \\ p_i = p_i^o \ \text{for all } i. \end{array} \right.$$

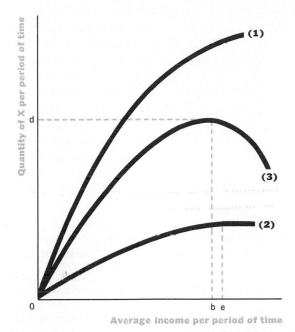

THE RELATION BETWEEN THE DEMAND FOR A COMMODITY AND A HOUSEHOLD'S AVERAGE INCOME

which fall as income rises are called by the economist *inferior goods*.

These relations are illustrated in Figure 4. The three curves indicate different functional relations between income and the demand for a commodity, tastes and all prices being held constant.† Curve 1 illustrates what is possibly the most common case: the one in which a rise in income brings about a rise in purchases at all levels of income. Curve 2 illustrates a case in which purchases rise with income up to a certain point (income Oe) and then remain unchanged as income varies above that amount. Curve 3 illustrates the case of an inferior good where purchases first rise with income up to a certain level (at income Ob where purchases are Od), but then fall as income goes beyond that level.

We leave as an exercise to the student the task of taking one of these curves (say, 1) and tracing out the effects of changes in each of the variables assumed to be held constant.

Summary

1. Demand for a commodity is the amount that households wish to purchase. This quantity is a flow, and so we express it as so much *per unit of time.*

2. We hypothesize that demand is determined by tastes, size of population, household income, the distribution of income among households, the price of that commodity, and the price of other commodities.

3. We hypothesize that for all commodities the quantity demanded increases as the price of the commodity falls, income, tastes, and all other prices remaining constant.

4. This relationship is illustrated graphically by a demand curve that shows how much will be demanded at each market price.

5. The demand curve will be shifted to the right by a rise in income (unless the good is an inferior one), a rise in the price of a substitute, a fall in the price of a complement, a rise in population, and a change in tastes in favor of this commodity. The opposite changes will, of course, shift the demand curve to the left.

---

† *Each* of these curves is described by the function in the previous footnote. We are now specifying something about the *form* of the function.

QUESTIONS FOR DISCUSSION

1. When we draw a market demand curve for a commodity, showing the quantity households wish to purchase at various prices, what things do we assume remain constant?

2.*a.* If there is a rise in the price of butter, what do you expect will happen to the demand for margarine? What term would you apply to the relationship between butter and margarine?

 b. Draw a figure illustrating both the original demand curve and the new demand curve for margarine. Which way does the demand curve shift, to the right or to the left? Explain why a shift of the curve in this direction illustrates this change in demand.

3. What would you predict would happen to the market demand curve for oranges as a result of the following?

a. a rise in average American income;

b. an increase in the birth rate;

c. an intensive advertising campaign that convinces most people of the importance of a daily quota of natural Vitamin C;

d. a fall in the price of tangerines;

e. a government program that raises the income of the poor people in America by taxing richer people but leaving total income the same;

f. a fall in the price of oranges.

5. If the price of beef rises, what do you expect to happen to the amount of beef purchased? What "other things" are you assuming constant that you consider important?

6. Name a few changes that you would expect to increase the demand for gasoline; a few that would decrease it; a few that would not affect it. What about the demand for one particular brand of gasoline?

7. As average income rises what do you expect to happen to the demand for radios, automobiles, used automobiles, books, university education, public transport, newspapers, rice, television sets, magazines, whiskey, fur coats, salt?

8. Trace out what would happen to curve 1 in Figure 4 if there were:

a. a change in tastes toward that commodity;

b. a change in tastes away from it;

c. an increase in population;

d. an increase in the price of that commodity;

e. an increase in the price of a complement to that commodity;

f. an increase in the price of a substitute for that commodity.

Chapter **8** THE ELEMENTARY THEORY OF SUPPLY

NATIONAL PRODUCTION OF GOODS AND SERVICES in 1964 reached $623 billion. Two broad classifications of *what* was produced are given in Tables 1 and 2. The economist is primarily interested in *why and how* the decisions were made that led to the particular selection of goods and services.

Why has total production doubled between 1947 and 1964? Why has this growth occurred unevenly among industries? Why, for example, did the chemical and petroleum industries grow six times as fast as the mining industries and eight times as fast as industries producing primary metals? Why did the aluminum industry grow faster than the steel industry? Why, even within a single industry, did some firms prosper and grow,

TABLE 1   GROSS NATIONAL PRODUCTION, 1964, IN BILLIONS OF DOLLARS

Sales of durable goods	118	
Sales of nondurable goods	188	
Sales of services	244	
Construction	69	
ALL SALES		619
Increases in inventories		4
TOTAL		623

SOURCE: Adapted from the *Survey of Current Business*, April, 1965.

TABLE 2   PERCENTAGE DISTRIBUTION OF PRODUCTION BY MAJOR INDUSTRY GROUPS, 1964

Manufacturing	29
Agriculture, forestry, fisheries	4
Wholesale and retail trade	16
Finance, insurance, real estate	10
Transportation, communication, public utilities	8
Services	12
Government and government enterprises	14
Other	7
TOTAL	100

SOURCE: Adapted from the *Survey of Current Business*, April, 1965, Table 6.

others hold their own, and still others decline and fail? Why, and how, are firms and industries born?

How are goods produced and crops grown? What is automation and how does it occur? Is automation a response to labor unions and wage increases, or does it have a logic of its own? Why do methods of production of the same commodity differ in different countries? All of these questions are aspects of the single question: *What determines the supply of commodities?* This chapter deals with this basic question in a very preliminary way.

A more detailed discussion of supply decisions is in Part V.

Decisions about what to produce, how to produce it, and how much to produce are made in a free-market economy by units called *firms*. (See Chapter 16 for a definition of a firm.) For the present, think of firms as the groups and individuals who make decisions about the production and sale of goods.[1]

What Determines Supply?

The amount of some commodity that firms wish to sell is called the *supply* of the commodity. Supply, like demand, is a flow: It is so much output per day, per week, or per year.

We now introduce four hypotheses about the considerations that are important in influencing firms' willingness to supply a good and the direction these influences take.

1. *The supply of a commodity depends upon the goals of firms.*

If drug companies prefer to engage in the production of medicines rather than rat poison because it makes them feel more important in society, we expect more medicines and less rat poison to be produced than if producers held all commodities in equal regard. If producers of some commodity want to sell as much as possible, even if it costs them some profits to do so, more will be sold of that commodity than if they wanted to make maximum profits. If producers are reluctant to take risks, we would expect smaller production of goods whose production is risky.

Economists usually assume that the goal of firms is to maximize profits. This is an hypothesis, and like all hypotheses, we may wish to reject it in favor of an alternative hypothesis. If we do, our predictions about the quantities that will be supplied will change.

2. *The supply of a commodity depends upon the state of technology.*

The enormous increase in production per worker that has been going on in industrial societies for about 200 years is very largely due to improved methods of production. These in turn have been heavily influenced by the advances of science. But the Industrial Revolution is more than an historical event; it is a present reality. Discoveries in chemistry have led to lower costs of production of well-established products, like paints, and to a large variety of new products made of plastics and synthetic fibers.[2] The new electronics industry rests upon transistors and other tiny devices that are revolutionizing production in television, high-fidelity equipment, computers, and guidance-control systems. Atomic energy is used to send submarines under the polar cap and, unless it is used to exterminate the human race, it will one day be used to build canals and to extract fresh water from the sea. At any time what is produced and how it is produced depend upon what is known. Over time, knowledge changes and so do the supplies of in-

1. We shall assume in this chapter that all goods produced are sold, and thus that there is no need to distinguish between goods produced and goods sold.

2. The most recent use of plastics to come to our attention is plastic grass—ideal for the man who does not like to spend time mowing his lawn and ideal too for golf courses in the desert.

dividual commodities. Since knowledge is rarely lost, most *inventions* and *innovations*[3] tend to increase supplies of commodities.

3. *The supply of a commodity depends upon the price of that commodity and the prices of other commodities.*

We expect that the higher the relative price of a commodity, other things being equal, the greater the quantity of it that firms will wish to supply. Goods and services are produced by firms in order to earn profits. The relative profitability of different commodities affects the profitability of the industries that produce them. New firms or established firms seeking new products to produce will tend, *ceteris paribus*, to undertake production in those industries with higher possibilities of profit.

Some of the clearest examples are found in the field of agriculture. Increases in the price of wheat lead some farmers to shift lands to wheat production and away from corn and soy beans. A similar, but smaller increase in the supply of wheat occurs in the case of a decrease in the price of corn, for although some corn farmers will shift to wheat, others will shift to hogs or soy beans. In general, the effect on the supply of one commodity is greater in response to its own price than to the price of another commodity. The reason is that in the latter case there are usually several alternative goods to which producers of the commodity whose price has declined can turn.

In one sense, every product is in competition with every other one for the attention of a producer whose objective is profits. In fact, much of the production of new products comes from the expansion of existing firms into new but somewhat related lines. In

manufacturing, particularly, the multi-product (and multi-industry) firm is commonplace. General Motors not only makes all manner of cars, trucks, and other vehicles; it makes washing machines and refrigerators as well. General Motors might (but is unlikely to) start producing movies. In 1964, the Columbia Broadcasting System acquired the New York Yankees. Can you see any connection between owning a series of television-broadcasting facilities, a record company, and a baseball team? The decision of a firm to enter a new industry, or to produce a new product is one of the most basic and important decisions it makes. It is also a complex one. Here we can say that relative profitability is an extremely important consideration and that the prices of the commodity relative to other prices is an important determinant of profitability.

4. *The supply of a commodity depends upon the costs of factors of production.*

We expect that the supply will decrease if there are increases in the prices of factors that are very important to the production of the commodity. The effect is through the anticipated influence of factor prices on profits. A rise in the price of one factor will cause a larger increase in the costs of making those goods that use a great deal of that factor than in the costs of producing those commodities that use a relatively small amount of the factor. For example, a rise in the price of land will have a large effect on the costs of producing wheat and only a very small effect on the costs of producing automobiles. Thus a change in the price of one factor of production will cause changes in the *relative* profitability of different lines of production; this will cause producers to shift from one

---

3. *Invention* is defined as the discovery of new techniques and *innovation* as the introduction of them into actual production.

line to another and so cause changes in the supplies of different commodities. Factor prices may affect supply in another way as well. Changes in relative factor prices (labor becoming more expensive relative to ma-

chinery) will tend to cause changes in the techniques of production, and these may lead to the introduction of new technology, which will in turn tend to increase supply. This possibility is discussed in Chapter 18.

The Supply Function

The hypothesis that emerges from the discussion above is that the supply of a commodity is a function of the goals of firms, technology, prices of commodities, and the prices of factors of production.†

Let us examine the relation of supply to one of the variables upon which it depends, holding each of the others constant. The variable we choose most often to examine is the price of the commodity. We note that this is not necessarily because it is the most important determinant of supply, but rather because it is most convenient for our purposes.

THE SUPPLY OF A COMMODITY AND ITS PRICE

We now assume that everything that affects the supply of the commodity other than its price is held constant.†† There is much that needs to be said on the relation between

supply and price. For the moment we shall content ourselves with the intuitively plausible hypothesis that the quantity of a commodity produced and offered for sale will increase as the price of the commodity rises, and decrease as the price falls (i.e., quantity and price will vary directly with each other). This hypothesis has a strong common-sense appeal, for the higher the price of the commodity, the greater the profits that can be earned and thus the greater the incentive to produce the commodity and offer it for sale. The hypothesis is known to be correct in a large number of cases. For the time being we shall assume it to be generally correct.

THE SUPPLY CURVE

This hypothesis can be illustrated in a graph that measures price on the vertical axis and quantity on the horizontal one. Figure 1 is such a graph and the curve shown

---

† The supply function for commodity 1 is:

$$Q_1 = f(G, H, p_1, p_2, \ldots, p_n, w_1, w_2, \ldots, w_m),$$

where
$Q_1 = $ the supply of commodity 1
$G = $ goals of producers
$H = $ the state of technology
$p_i = $ price of the ith good $(i = 1, 2, \ldots, n)$
$w_i = $ prices of the ith factor of production $(i = 1, 2, \ldots, m)$

†† We assume, in our notation, that:

$$Q_1 = g(p_1) \quad \left| \begin{array}{l} G = G_0 \\ H = H_0 \\ p_i = p_i^o \, (i = 2, \ldots, n) \\ w_i = w_i^o \, (i = 1, 2, \ldots, m) \end{array} \right.$$

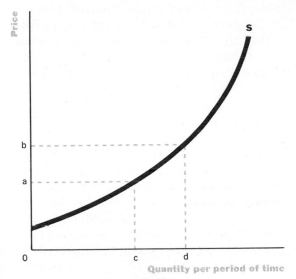

FIGURE 1   A SUPPLY CURVE

on it is called a *supply curve*. It shows the quantity producers will wish to make and to offer for sale at various alternative prices of the product. When the economist speaks of supply he is referring to the whole supply curve, which shows what would be supplied at each price. A *change* in supply thus means a shift in the whole curve so that either more or less is supplied at each price than was supplied previously. A shift in the whole supply curve must be due to a change in some factor other than the price of the commodity. When we wish to refer to a movement from one point on a curve to another point on the *same* curve, we speak of a change in the quantity supplied. Such a movement can only be brought about by a change in price. Just as in the case of demand, it is most important to distinguish between a shift in the whole

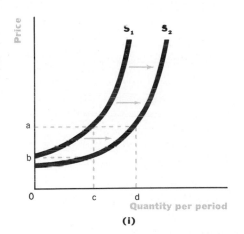

(i)

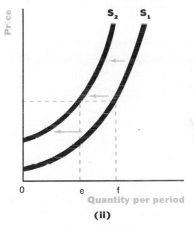

(ii)

(i) An increase in supply—when producers wish to supply more at each price—can be caused by some kinds of changes in producers' goals; improvements in technology; decreases in the prices of other commodities; decreases in prices of factors of production that are important to this commodity.

(ii) A fall in supply—when producers wish to supply less at each price—can be caused by some kinds of changes in producers' goals; loss of technical knowledge (unlikely); increases in the prices of other commodities; increases in prices of factors of production that are important to this commodity.

FIGURE 2   SHIFTS IN SUPPLY

supply curve and a movement from one point to another along a given curve.

In the supply curve shown, if the price is *Oa*, suppliers desire to sell *Oc*. If the price increases to *Ob*, the suppliers desire to increase the quantity supplied to *Od*.

SHIFTS IN THE SUPPLY CURVE

An increase in supply is illustrated in Figure 2(i). A movement from S_1 to S_2 represents an increase in supply in that at any price more is supplied than previously. At the price *Oa*, for example, the amount *Od* will be supplied whereas previously only the amount *Oc* would have been supplied. The rightward

shift of the curve also means that the same quantity will be offered at a lower price than previously. The price of *Oa*, for example, would call forth a supply of *Oc* when the supply curve was S_1, whereas a price of only *Ob* is all that is now necessary to call forth the quantity of *Oc*. Both of these comparisons indicate an increased willingness on the part of producers to make the commodity and offer it for sale. A shift of the supply curve in the opposite direction, as shown in Figure 2(ii), indicates a reduction in supply.

The causes of shifts in supply are changes in any one of the determinants of supply other than the price of the commodity. Some of the possibilities are summarized in Figure 2.

Summary

1. Supply of a commodity is the amount of the commodity that firms wish to sell. (Firms are defined as the units who make decisions about the production and sale of goods.)

2. We hypothesize that the supply of a commodity will depend on the goals of firms (the most common goal assumed is profit-maximization), the state of technology, the price of that commodity, the price of all other commodities, and, finally, the costs of factors of production.

3. We hypothesize that the supply of a commodity increases as its price increases.

4. This relationship is illustrated by an upward-sloping supply curve that shows how much of a commodity will be supplied at each price.

5. The supply curve shifts to the right (an increase in supply) if the prices of other commodities fall, if the costs of producing the commodity fall, or if producers become for any reason more willing to produce the commodity. The opposite changes shift the supply curve to the left (a decrease in supply).

QUESTIONS FOR DISCUSSION

1. *a.* What do you think has been the effect on the supply curve of chickens of the innovation of large-scale, cost-saving methods of broiler production (often referred to as factory farms)?

b. Suppose a successful campaign by the ASPCA convinces chicken farmers of the cruelty of their ways, and many abandon the new methods despite some loss of profits. What will happen then?

c. Suppose there is an increase in the price of land suitable for broiler production. What is the effect on the supply curve of broilers?

2. What will be the effect on the supply curve of hogs of a fall in the price of corn? What will be the effect on the supply curve of corn of a fall in the price of hogs?

3. Draw a curve showing the amount firms will supply at every different cost of producing a unit of the commodity, holding all the other factors, including price, constant. Show what you think will happen with a change in each of the variables held constant.

4. What will happen to the supply of cars if the following occur?

a. an increase in the price of trucks;

b. a fall in the price of steel;

c. introduction of a better assembly-line technique;

d. an increase in the desire of auto manufacturers to be highly esteemed by the nation, rather than to earn as much money as possible;

e. an increase in the price of cars.

Chapter 9 THE ELEMENTARY THEORY OF MARKET PRICE

IN THIS CHAPTER WE SHALL COMBINE OUR theories of demand and supply into a theory of the determination of market prices. We have already described our *dramatis personae*—households and firms. We must now describe their stage—the market. What do we mean by a market?[1] A market is an area over which buyers and sellers negotiate the exchange of a well-defined commodity. The actual geographical area covered by a single market will vary greatly with the commodity.

In the case of wheat, the market is the whole Western world; in the case of strawberries, it may only be a small area including and surrounding one city; in the case of haircuts, it may only be a neighborhood within one city. For the present, we shall confine ourselves to markets in which there is a large enough number of buyers and sellers so that no one of them has any appreciable influence on price. This is a very rough definition of what economists call *competitive markets*.

1. It is easier to understand some of the subtle complications involved in trying to give precise meaning to a market after one already understands the outlines of the theory of price and for this reason a detailed consideration of this question is postponed until Chapter 21.

What Determines Market Price?

What happens in the market for a particular commodity, say, asparagus? Goods are sold by firms and bought by households and we have already developed in the last two chapters an elementary theory of supply and demand. We now bring these two theories together and use them to develop our theory of market price.

In Figure 1, we plot the price of asparagus on the vertical axis, and we draw both a demand and a supply curve on the same diagram. The market demand curve shows the amount of asparagus that households would like to buy at each market price, assuming that population, incomes, tastes, and all other prices remain constant; and its downward slope shows that quantity demanded and price are assumed to vary inversely with each other. The supply curve shows the amount of asparagus that producers will wish to grow and sell at each market price, assuming that their goals, the state of technology, the prices of factors of production, and the prices of all other commodities remain unchanged. The upward slope of the supply curve shows that the quantity supplied and the market price are assumed to vary directly with each other.[2]

Look at the point at which the two curves intersect. This point corresponds to a market price of 70¢ per pound. The amount demanded is 1,000 units and the amount supplied is also 1,000 units. Thus, at the price of 70¢, the amount consumers wish to buy is exactly the same as the amount producers wish to sell. Provided that the demand curve slopes downward and the supply curve slopes upward throughout their entire ranges, there will be only one price, 70¢ in this case, at which the quantity demanded is equal to the quantity supplied.

Now consider any price higher than 70¢, say 90¢. At this price, consumers wish to buy 400 units, whereas producers wish to sell 1,450 units. The quantity supplied exceeds the quantity demanded by 1,050 units. It is easy to see (checking a few examples will ensure that you do) that for any price above 70¢ quantity supplied exceeds quantity demanded. Such situations are characterized as having *excess supply*. The higher the price, the greater the excess supply.

We now introduce the hypothesis that, when there is excess supply, the market price will fall. Producers, unable to sell some of their goods, may begin to ask lower prices for them; purchasers, observing the glut of unsold commodities, may begin to offer lower prices. For either or both of these reasons prices will fall. This hypothesis is illustrated in Figure 1 by the arrow indicating a *downward pressure on price* at all prices above 70¢.

Now consider prices below 70¢, say 20¢. At this price, consumers desire to purchase 1,850 units and producers desire to sell 220 units. There is an *excess demand* causing a shortage of 1,630 units of asparagus. Again it is clear (but, again, check a few examples) that at all prices below 70¢ the quantity demanded exceeds the quantity supplied. The lower the price, the larger the amount of excess demand.

2. We shall assume throughout this chapter that market demand curves do slope downward and that market supply curves slope upward. Limiting cases, such as a vertical supply curve and a horizontal demand curve, are sometimes of interest. They require some modification of the statements made hereafter, but you should have no difficulty in making the appropriate modifications when they are required.

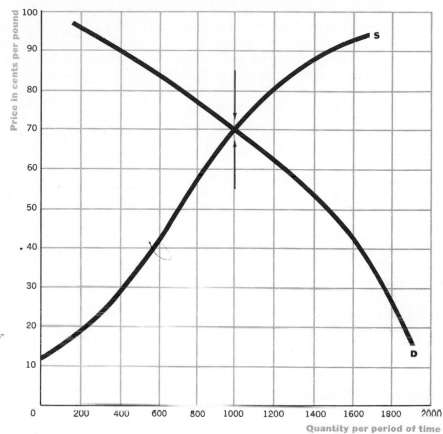

FIGURE 1   DETERMINA-
TION OF EQUILIBRIUM
PRICE AND QUANTITY
IN A COMPETITIVE
MARKET

We now introduce the hypothesis that, when the quantity demanded exceeds the quantity supplied, market price will rise. Individual purchasers, unable to fulfill all their requirements, may begin to offer higher prices in an effort to get more of the available goods, and suppliers, able to dispose of more than their total production, may begin to ask higher prices for the quantities that they have produced. For either or both of these reasons prices will rise when demand exceeds supply. This hypothesis is illustrated in Figure 1 by the arrow indicating an *upward pressure on price* for all prices below 70¢.

For any price above 70¢, according to our theory, prices tend to fall, and for any price below 70¢, prices tend to rise. At a price of 70¢, there is neither an excess of demand creating a shortage nor an excess of supply creating a glut; supply is equal to demand and there is no tendency for the price to change. The price of 70¢, where the two curves intersect, is the price that equates demand and supply; it is the price toward which the market price gravitates; and it is the only price at which there is neither a shortage nor a surplus. This price is called the *equilibrium price*. The term equilibrium means a state of balance; according to our theory, such an equilibrium occurs when demanders desire to buy the same amount that suppliers desire to sell. Since there is neither excess supply nor excess demand there is no cause for price to change.

When demand equals supply we say that the market is in a state of *equilibrium*. When demand does not equal supply we say that the market is in a state of *disequilibrium*.

We may now summarize our simple theory of price as follows:

Hypotheses
1. *Demand curves slope downward continuously.*

2. *Supply curves slope upward continuously.*
3. *An excess of demand over supply causes price to rise; an excess of supply over demand causes price to fall.*

Implications
1. *There is no more than one price at which demand equals supply. In the language of economic theory, equilibrium is unique.*
2. *If either the demand or supply curve shifts, the equilibrium price and quantity will change. (The actual changes are considered below.)*[3]

Shifts in Demand and Supply

What is the effect on the equilibrium price of shifts in the demand and supply curves? In Figure 2 the original demand curve is D_1 and the supply curve is S_1. We now assume that the demand curve shifts to D_2. This increase in demand might, for example, be the result of a rise in incomes. The original equilibrium price is Oe and the quantity Oa. When the demand curve shifts, excess demand develops because, at price Oe, demand is Oc, whereas supply remains at Oa. As a result of the excess demand, ac, price will rise toward the new equilibrium price of Of. At this price demand equals supply. The new equilibrium quantity bought and sold is Ob; the rise in price from Oe to Of reduces the quantity demanded from Oc to Ob, whereas it increases the quantity supplied from Oa to Ob.

We conclude that a rise in the demand for a commodity (i.e., a rightward shift of the demand curve) causes an increase in both the

equilibrium price and the equilibrium quantity bought and sold.

When the demand decreases (i.e., when the demand curve shifts to the left), there will be a decrease both in the equilibrium price and in the equilibrium quantity bought and sold. This can also be seen in Figure 2 if we visualize a shift in the demand curve from D_2 to D_1. Equilibrium price decreases from Of to Oe and equilibrium quantity from Ob to Oa.

The effect of a rise in supply is shown in Figure 3. The shift in the supply curve to the right, from S_1 to S_2, indicates an increase in supply; at each price more is now offered for sale than was previously offered. This time, however, the shift of the curve causes a glut to develop at the old equilibrium price. When the curve shifts, the quantity offered for sale increases from Oa to Od but the quantity demanded remains unchanged at Oa. The excess supply causes prices to fall.

3. For a long time it was thought that the following inference could be drawn from these hypotheses: The market will be *stable* in the sense that, if the price moves away from its equilibrium level, it will move back toward, and will eventually return to, the equilibrium level. This inference cannot be drawn from this theory. The problem of stability is dealt with in Chapter 12.

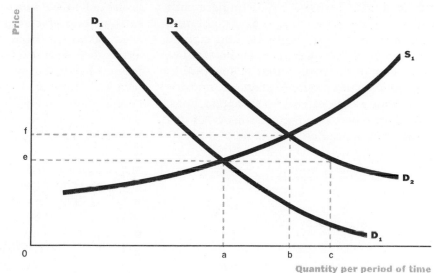

FIGURE 2   THE EFFECTS
OF A SHIFT IN THE
DEMAND CURVE

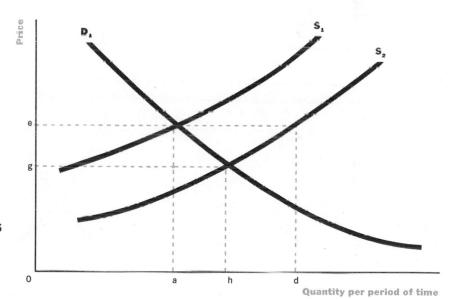

FIGURE 3   THE EFFECTS
OF A SHIFT IN THE
SUPPLY CURVE

As prices come down, the quantity supplied diminishes and the quantity demanded increases. The new equilibrium price is at Og, where the quantity supplied and the quantity demanded are equal at Oh. Thus an increase in supply (i.e., a rightward shift in the supply curve) causes a fall in the equilibrium price and a rise in the equilibrium quantity.

The effect of a decrease in supply (i.e., a leftward shift in the supply curve) will be an increase in the equilibrium price and a decrease in the equilibrium quantity. This can be seen in Figure 3 by assuming a shift in the supply curve from S_2 to S_1. Equilibrium price increases from Og to Oe and equilibrium quantity decreases from Oh to Oa.

We now have a theory that is beautiful in its simplicity and yet, as we shall see, unusual in its wide range of real-world applications. For all its shortcomings, the theory of the determination of price by demand and supply is one of the finest examples of a theory that is both simple and powerful.

THE "LAWS" OF SUPPLY AND DEMAND

It is common to refer to the four propositions that we have just developed as the "laws" of supply and demand. A natural law, something that is necessarily true and that

is proved to be true, is an eighteenth- and early nineteenth-century concept. It has long been discarded from the natural sciences, although traces of it still linger on elsewhere. Even the great "laws" of Newton have been refuted. Scientific theories are now accepted not as laws but as hypotheses that will sooner or later be refuted and replaced by other more embracing hypotheses. In economics, the "laws" of supply and demand are nothing more than predictions that follow from competitive price theory. If we take them as hypotheses about the world (see Chapter 11), they are open to testing but never to absolute proof or absolute refutation (see pp. 49–50). There is considerable evidence that, in many markets, the hypotheses are not widely at variance with the facts; in other markets—especially those for manufactured goods—it is not so clear that the

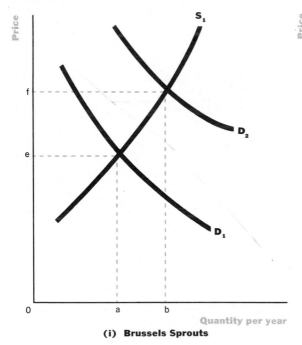

(i) Brussels Sprouts

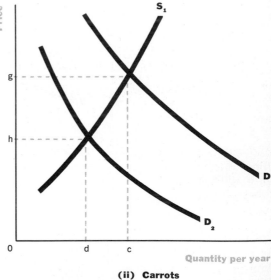

(ii) Carrots

FIGURE 4   THE EFFECTS OF AN INCREASE IN THE DEMAND FOR BRUSSELS SPROUTS AND A DECREASE IN THE DEMAND FOR CARROTS

hypotheses come near to being consistent with the facts. In general, however, we should not speak of "laws"; we should speak rather of hypotheses that appear to be at least somewhere near the mark in a considerable number of cases.

AN EXAMPLE

In Chapter 6 we discussed in a preliminary and intuitive way the effects of a rise in the demand for Brussels sprouts and a fall in the price of carrots. Part, though not all, of that example can now be formalized in terms of our newly developed theory. The market for sprouts is illustrated in Figure 4(i). The original demand and supply curves are D_1 and S_1. The original equilibrium price

is Oe and quantity is Oa. Now the demand curve shifts to D_2. At the original price of Oe there is now an excess of demand over supply. Our theory tells us that if excess demand exists, prices will rise and production will increase until we reach the new equilibrium price, Of, at which demand is again equal to supply at the output Ob. These results —an increase in both price and output of sprouts—were predicted in our earlier discussion. What we cannot yet do is to describe the sequence of events that lead from the first equilibrium to the second. Nothing in our theory tells us this.[4] The effects on carrots are the reverse of the effects on sprouts, and are shown in Figure 4(ii). The decrease in demand leads ultimately to both a lower price and a lower output.

Summary

1. A market is an area over which buyers and sellers negotiate the exchange of a well-defined commodity. A competitive market is one in which there is a large number of buyers and sellers, no one of whom has an appreciable influence on price.

2. The theory of the determination of price and quantity in competitive markets is that these prices are determined by the forces of demand and supply.

3. At any price higher than the one indicated by the intersection of the demand and supply curves, the amount supplied is greater than the amount demanded. We call this a situation of excess supply and we hypothesize that when it exists price will fall.

4. At any price lower than the one indicated by the intersection of the demand and supply curves, the amount demanded exceeds the amount supplied. We call this a situation of excess demand and we hypothesize that when there is excess demand price will rise.

5. At the price indicated by the intersection of the demand and supply curves, there is neither excess demand nor excess supply. This is the price toward which the actual price will gravitate and it is the only one at which there are neither upward nor downward pressures on the price. This price is called the equilibrium price.

6. From our hypotheses we obtain two implications: that there is no more than one

---

4. We do not know, for example, how long it takes carrot producers to shift to the production of sprouts or how long, once they have made the decision, it takes for the sprouts to come on the market. These matters are discussed in Chapter 12.

equilibrium price, and that if either curve shifts the equilibrium price and quantity will change in the manner summarized in the adjacent table.

7. These propositions are often called the "*laws*" of supply and demand, but we must remember that they are really *hypotheses* that appear to predict rather well in a considerable number of cases.

TABLE 1

The Cause	The Effects	
	Equilibrium price will:	Equilibrium quantity will:
A rise in demand	rise	rise
A fall in demand	fall	fall
A rise in supply	fall	rise
A fall in supply	rise	fall

QUESTIONS FOR DISCUSSION

1. What does the word *market* mean in everyday usage? List ten different kinds of markets. How many of them fit our rough definition of a competitive market?

2. Who are the participants in a market? What information about each do we assume?

3. Which two hypotheses lead to the implication that there is at most only one equilibrium price? Draw a diagram in which there is no equilibrium price and explain in words why this comes about.

4. You are told that the price of wheat has risen and that there was either a shift in demand or in supply. What other piece of information would allow you to deduce which shift had occurred? (Experiment by drawing graphs to illustrate the two possible cases; notice any differences between the two.)

5. If there is a rise in the price of margarine, what do you predict will happen to the equilibrium price of butter and to the quantity bought and sold? If there is an increase in the cost of making butter, what would you predict?

6. How do you reconcile the hypothesis that the quantity demanded varies inversely with the price with the statement that a rise in demand will lead to a rise in price?

7. "The effect of price changes often eludes analysis. For example, two of the food groups that have shown absolute decreases in consumption per capita—flour and potatoes—have also shown decreases in price relative to the prices of all foods. Consumption of meat per capita has been rising in the face of an increase in relative prices." This statement about American consumption changes since the 1930s comes from the report of a full-scale investigation into the future patterns of resource allocation. Do the changes elude *your* analysis? (Remember that demand depends on variables other than price. Remember also that shifts in demand induced by changes in variables other than the commodity's own price will cause the price to change.) How would you reword the passage to make clear what you think did happen?

Chapter **10** ELASTICITY OF DEMAND AND SUPPLY

The Responsiveness of Demand: Why It Is Important

Consider the effects of the decrease in the supply of carrots analyzed in the previous chapter. In doing this we shall assume that the equilibrium price is the price that actually rules in the real world.

In Figure 1, we have represented a fall in the supply of carrots by a leftward shift in the supply curve. In each of the two parts of the figure the initial equilibrium is at price Oc and output Oa. But in (i) the effect of the shift in supply to S_2 is a slight rise in price, cd, and a large decrease in quantity, ab. In (ii) the effect of the *identical* shift in the supply curve from S_1 to S_2 is a large increase in price, cd', and a relatively small decrease in quantity, ab'. Clearly, a given shift in supply has very different effects, depending upon the shape of the demand curve.

Since the supply-curve shifts are the same, the difference between the two cases clearly lies in the different ways in which the quantity demanded by consumers responds to changes in price. In the first case, the quantity demanded varies greatly with price, and a

small rise in price restores equilibrium by choking off the excess demand (ea). In the second case, the quantity demanded is very insensitive to price changes and equilibrium is restored only when the price rise has been sufficient to call forth the extra supply necessary to satisfy the almost unchanged demand.

What would happen if the government adopted a number of measures to persuade farmers to produce more of a certain crop? It might, for example, pay a subsidy to farmers for growing this crop; it might give tax relief; or it might engage an educational campaign through the Agricultural Extension Service. If the government is successful, then at every possible price of the product there would be an increase in the quantity that farmers would be willing to produce. Thus the whole supply curve of the product would shift to the right. This may be illustrated in Figure 1 by assuming that the supply curve shifts from S_2 to S_1. Figure 1(i) illustrates a case in which the quantity that consumers demand is very sensitive to price

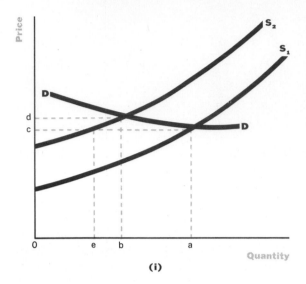

(i)

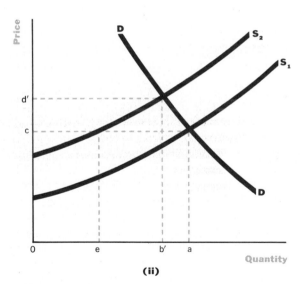

(ii)

FIGURE 1   **THE EFFECTS ON PRICE AND QUANTITY OF A DECREASE IN SUPPLY WHEN COMBINED WITH DEMAND CURVES OF VARIOUS SLOPES**

changes. The extra production brings down price, but because the quantity demanded is very responsive, only a small change in price

is necessary in order to restore equilibrium. The effect of the government's policy, therefore, is to achieve a large increase in the production and sales of this commodity and only a small decrease in price. Figure 1(ii) illustrates a case in which the quantity demanded is quite unresponsive to price changes. As before, the increase in supply at the original price causes a glut that brings price down. But this time the quantity demanded by consumers does not increase very much in response to this fall in price. Thus price continues to fall until, discouraged by lower and lower prices, farmers reduce the quantity supplied very nearly to the level attained before they received the increased incentive to produce. Thus the effect of the government's policy is to bring about a large price fall and only a very small increase in the quantity produced and sold.

In comparing the cases illustrated in Figure 1(i and ii), we see that the government's policy has exactly the same effectiveness as far as farmers are concerned (the supply-curve shifts are identical). But the effects on the equilibrium price and quantity are very different, because there are different degrees to which the quantity demanded by consumers responds to price changes. If the purpose of the government's policy is to increase the quantity of this commodity produced and consumed, then the policy will be a great success when the demand curve is similar to the one shown in Figure 1(i), but it will be a failure when the demand curve is similar to the one shown in Figure 1(ii). If, on the other hand, the main objective of the government's policy is to achieve a large reduction in the price of the commodity, the policy will be a failure when demand is as shown in (i), but a great success when demand is as shown in (ii). Evidently the shape of the demand curve is of some importance.

Elasticity: A Measure of the Responsiveness of Demand to Price Changes

When considering the responsiveness of the quantity demanded to changes in price, we may wish to make statements such as the following: "The demand for carrots was more responsive to price changes ten years ago than it is today," or "The demand for meat responds more to price changes than does the demand for green vegetables." If we wish to make such comparisons, we require a measure of the degree to which quantity demanded responds to changes in price.

In the previous examples we were able to make comparisons between the two demand curves in Figure 1(i) and (ii) on the basis of their geometrical steepness, because the curves were both drawn on the same scale.

Thus, for any given price change, the quantity changed more on the flatter curve than it did on the steeper one. It can, however, be very misleading merely to inspect a *single* curve and to conclude from its general appearance something about the degree of responsiveness of quantity demanded to price changes. Consider the demand curve shown in Figure 2 (i). This curve appears rather flat, but, by a mere change in scale, we can make the demand curve *showing the identical information* appear to be steeper, as in Figure 2 (ii).

Instead of gaining a vague general impression from the shape of demand curves we might note the actual change in quantity

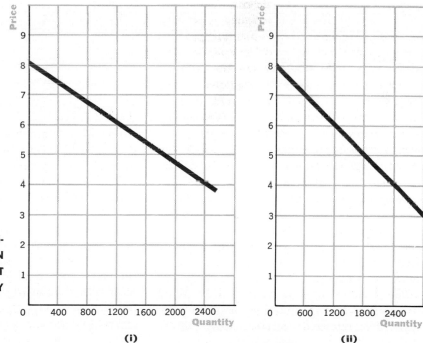

FIGURE 2 **A SINGLE DEMAND CURVE PLOTTED ON GRAPHS USING DIFFERENT SCALES ON THE QUANTITY AXIS**

(i)   (ii)

demanded in response to a certain price change. But this would still leave us unable to compare degrees of responsiveness for different commodities. Assume, for example, that we have the following information:

TABLE 1

Commodity	Reduction in price	Increase in quantity demanded
Beefsteak	$.20 per pound	9,000 tons
Men's shirts	.20 per shirt	5,010 shirts
Radios	.20 per radio	100 radios

Are we to conclude that the demand for radios is not so responsive to price changes as the demand for beefsteak, because a 20-cent cut in price gives quite a large increase in demand for beefsteak, whereas an equal price cut has very little effect on the demand for radios? There are two problems here. First, a reduction in price of 20¢ will be a large price cut for a low-priced commodity and an insignificant price cut for a high-priced commodity. The price reductions listed in Table 1 represent very different fractions of the total prices. Thus it is more revealing to know the percentage change in the price of the various commodities. Second, by an analogous argument, knowing the quantity by which demand changes is not very revealing, unless we also know the level of demand. An increase of 10,000 tons is quite a significant reaction of demand if the quantity formerly bought was, say, 15,000 tons, but it is only a drop in the bucket if the quantity formerly demanded was, say, 10 million tons.

Table 2 shows the original levels of, as well as the changes in, price and quantity. What we really need to know is how large the price decrease is *expressed as a percentage of the original price,* and how large the increase in

TABLE 2

Commodity	Original price	Change in price	Original quantity	Change in quantity
Beefsteak	$ 1.33	$.20	120,000	9,000
Men's shirts	6.67	.20	167,000	5,010
Radios	80.00	.20	10,000	100

quantity is *expressed as a percentage of the quantity originally being sold.* This information is recorded in Table 3.

A large percentage change in the price of beefsteak brought about a much smaller percentage change in quantity purchased. On the other hand, although the increase in the number of radios purchased was only 100, this is quite a large percentage change in the quantity *in comparison to the percentage change in price that brought it about.*

TABLE 3

Commodity	Percentage change in price	Percentage change in quantity	Percentage change in quantity Percentage change in price
Beefsteak	15	7.5	0.5
Men's shirts	3	3	1
Radios	0.25	1	4

ELASTICITY: A FORMAL DEFINITION

As a measure of the responsiveness of demand to changes in price we now define *elasticity of demand* (symbolized by the Greek letter η) as:

$$\eta = -\frac{\text{Percentage change in quantity}}{\text{Percentage change in price}}.$$

The figures in the last column of Table 3 are computed by this formula. There are two small points that arise in applying this definition that often confuse beginning students. Both can be cleared up by examining Table 4, which shows the calculation of the elasticity of demand for a case in which a fall in price from $50 to $49 is accompanied by a rise in quantity demanded from 20 to 22 million tons.

When we deal with a percentage change we must define the change as a percentage of something. Should it be the original amount, or the new amount? In Table 4 did quantity increase by two-twentieths (10 percent) or by two-twenty-seconds (9 percent)? For very small changes it will not matter, and elasticity is properly used only for small changes. But in numerical examples it is often convenient to use larger changes. We will in such cases use the *original* amount in computing percentage changes.

The second point is that every change has a sign attached to it; it is either an increase

TABLE 4

	Original amount	New amount	Change in amount	Percentage change in amount
Quantity	20	22	+2	$\frac{+2}{20} \cdot 100 = 10\%$
Price	50	49	−1	$\frac{-1}{50} \cdot 100 = -2\%$

$$\eta = -\frac{+10}{-2} = +5$$

(+) or a decrease (−). Since demand curves slope downward, the change in quantity will always have the opposite sign from the change in price. The minus sign in the definition of elasticity is simply designed to "neutralize" this negative relation between price and quantity changes and thus to make elasticity of demand a positive number. This is a matter of convenience only, and it has no more profound justification than that.

Numerical Values of Elasticity of Demand

Consider the elasticities of demand shown in the last column of Table 3. The figures show that the percentage change in the quantity of radios demanded was four times as large as the percentage change in price that brought it about; the percentage change in the quantity of men's shirts demanded was equal to the percentage change in their price; and the percentage change in the quantity of beefsteak demanded was only one-half of the percentage change in price that brought it about. We must conclude that, in the sense defined, the demand for radios is more responsive to price changes than is the demand

for men's shirts, which in turn is more responsive to price changes than is the demand for beefsteak.

The numerical value of elasticity can vary from zero to infinity. Elasticity is zero if there is no change at all in quantity demanded when price changes: Demand does not respond to a price change. The larger is elasticity, the larger is the percentage change in quantity for a given percentage change in price. As long as the elasticity of demand has a value of less than one, however, the percentage change in quantity is less than the percentage change in price. When elasticity is equal to one, then the two percentage changes are equal to each other. When the percentage change in quantity exceeds the percentage change in price, the value for the elasticity of demand will be greater than one.

When the percentage change in quantity is less than the percentage change in price (elasticity less than one), the demand is said to be *inelastic*. When the percentage change in quantity is greater than the percentage change in price (elasticity greater than one), the demand is said to be *elastic*. (See Table 5.) This terminology is most important, and the student should become familiar with it.

Notice that a demand curve may not have the same elasticity over every part of the curve. Consider, for example, the straight-line demand curve in Figure 3. Because it is a straight line, a 10-cent reduction in price always leads to the same increase in quantity (1,000 units). But in the upper part of the demand curve, where price is $2.00 and quantity is 1,000 units, a 10-cent reduction in price is only a 5 percent reduction, but the 1,000-unit increase in quantity is a 100 percent increase. Therefore, elasticity is 20. At the other end of the demand curve, where price is 50¢ and demand is 16,000 units, a reduction of 10¢ in price (20 percent) leads to the same 1,000-unit increase in demand, but this amounts to a percentage increase of only 6.25 percent. Elasticity is thus $\frac{6.25}{20} = 0.31$.[1]

The graphical representation of demand curves of various elasticities is presented in Figure 4. Zero elasticity occurs when the quantity demanded does not change as the

TABLE 5   **ELASTICITY: MEASURES, MEANING, AND NOMENCLATURE**

Numerical measure of elasticity	Verbal description	Terminology
Zero	Quantity demanded does not change as price changes	Perfectly (or completely) inelastic
Greater than zero, but less than one	Quantity demanded changes by a smaller percentage than does price	Inelastic
One	Quantity demanded changes by exactly the same percentage as does price	Unit elasticity
Greater than one, but less than infinity	Quantity demanded changes by a larger percentage than does price	Elastic
Infinity	Purchasers are prepared to buy all they can obtain at some price and none at all at an even slightly higher price	Perfectly (or infinitely) elastic

1. A downward-sloping, straight-line demand curve does not have a constant elasticity over its whole range. The only two cases in which a straight line does have constant elasticity is when it is vertical (elasticity zero) or horizontal (elasticity infinite).

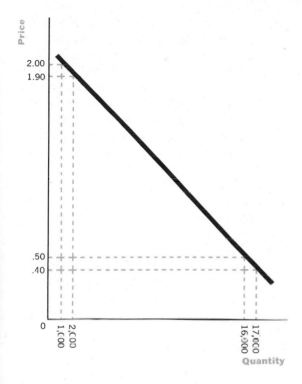

FIGURE 3

price changes. The graph of a demand curve of zero elasticity will thus be a vertical straight line indicating that the same quantity is demanded whatever the price. Unit elasticity occurs when a given percentage change in price brings about an equal percentage change in quantity at all points on the curve. The graph of a curve of unit elasticity over its whole range is shown in Figure 4 (ii).[2] A demand curve of infinite elasticity means that there exists some small price reduction that raises the demand from zero to infinity. This case occurs when, at some price, consumers will buy all that they can obtain of the commodity (an infinite amount if they could get it), while at an even slightly higher price they would buy nothing at all. In Figure 4 (iii), demand is zero for all prices above Oa, but at price Oa demand is infinite. This unlikely case turns out to be a very important one when, in the theory of production, we come to study the demand for the output of a single firm whose output is a very small part of the total market supply.

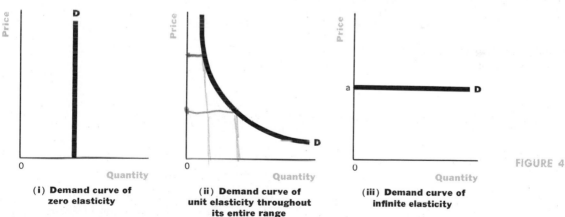

(i) Demand curve of
zero elasticity

(ii) Demand curve of
unit elasticity throughout
its entire range

(iii) Demand curve of
infinite elasticity

FIGURE 4

2. Students are often puzzled why a curve of convex shape is implied by constant elasticity. The reason is that if the ratio $\dfrac{\text{percentage change in quantity}}{\text{percentage change in price}}$ is to be kept constant, the equal absolute price cuts must be met with larger and larger absolute increases in quantity. Thus, geometrically, the curve must get flatter and flatter as price becomes lower and lower. This increasing flatness of the demand curve indicates, of course, an increasing responsiveness of the absolute quantity demanded to equal absolute price changes.

Elasticity of Demand and Changes in Total Revenue

The total amount of money that consumers spend on a commodity determines the amount of revenue received by the people producing and selling the commodity. A fall in consumers' expenditure usually means a fall in the incomes of the producers. Thus the question of the effects of changes in price on the total amount spent by purchasers is a matter of some importance. A cut in price does not necessarily mean a fall in total expenditure. Whether expenditure rises or falls when price falls depends on the reaction of the quantity demanded. If a small cut in price brings about a large increase in quantity demanded, then total expenditure will rise, but if the quantity demanded does not increase greatly, a cut in price will lead to a fall in total expenditure.

Examine the demand curve illustrated in Figure 5. When the price is $2.00 the quantity demanded is 10,000 units *per year*. A 5 percent reduction in price (to $1.90) causes

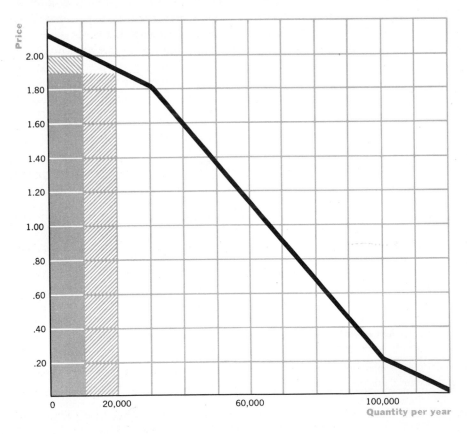

FIGURE 5 **THE CHANGE IN TOTAL REVENUE RESULTING FROM A CHANGE IN PRICE**

demand to double from 10,000 to 20,000 units (elasticity of demand is thus $100/5 = 20$). Total expenditure rises from $20,000 at the price of $2.00 per unit to $38,000 when the price falls to $1.90. In this case, where the demand is highly elastic, a fall in price leads to a rise in the total amount spent on the commodity.[3]

When the price is 20¢, total demand is 100,-000 units. A 50 percent price reduction from 20¢ to 10¢ increases demand by only 10 percent—from 100,000 to 110,000. Thus, elasticity of demand is $10/50 = 0.20$. In this case, the total expenditure falls from $20,000 to $11,000 when the price is cut. Thus, with the highly inelastic demand, a fall in price leads to a fall in total expenditure.

You have seen from the above example that a fall in price when demand is highly elastic causes total expenditure to increase, whereas a fall in price when the demand is highly inelastic causes total expenditure to fall. This suggests that there should be some intermedi-ate elasticity for which price changes leave total expenditure unchanged. This, in fact, occurs when the elasticity of demand is equal to one. In this case a reduction in price is exactly balanced by the increase in quantity sold so that total expenditure remains unchanged. If price falls by 1 percent, quantity purchased rises by 1 percent; if price rises by 1 percent, quantity purchased falls by 1 percent; thus total consumers' expenditure remains constant in the face of price changes.

If elasticity of demand exceeds unity, a fall in price increases total consumer expenditure, and a rise in price reduces it. If elasticity is less than unity, a fall in price reduces total expenditure and a rise in price increases it. If elasticity of demand is unity, a rise or a fall in price leaves total expenditure unaffected.[4]

Total, Average, and Marginal Revenue

In the preceding discussion, all the ideas relating to the three important ways of showing how revenue varies as the quantity sold varies were introduced. We now define these terms formally and show how they are related to elasticity.

1. *Total revenue* is the total amount received by sellers of the commodity; this

---

3. Note that total consumers' expenditure is equal to price times quantity. Geometrically, this is equal to the vertical coordinate multiplied by the horizontal coordinate of the point in question; this is equal to the area of the rectangle defined by the coordinates of the point in question. Two such areas, representing 10,000 units at $2.00 per unit and 20,000 units at $1.90, are shaded in Figure 5.

4. These statements are exactly correct when elasticity is defined in terms of the derivative of quantity demanded with respect to price. They are only approximately correct when elasticity is defined in terms of finite changes in price and quantity. This point is elaborated in the appendix to Chapter 10. The student who knows the calculus should adopt the following definition of elasticity: $\eta = \dfrac{dq}{dp} \cdot \dfrac{p}{q}$. The student who does not know the calculus need not be unduly worried. He can operate satisfactorily with the definition used in the text as long as he realizes that all statements made are only approximately correct.

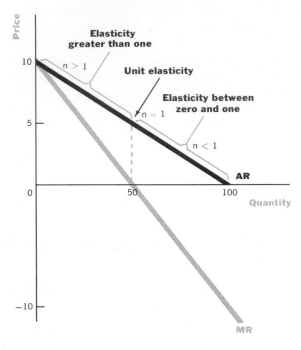

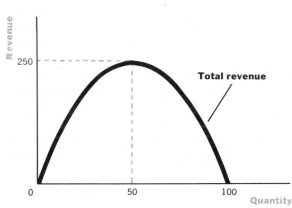

FIGURE 6

amount is equal to the total amount spent on the commodity by purchasers.

$$TR = pq,$$

where TR is total revenue, q is quantity sold, and p is the price at which it is sold.

2. *Average revenue* is the amount of revenue received *per unit* sold. This is, of course, the price of the product.

$$AR = \frac{TR}{q} = p.$$

3. *Marginal revenue* is the change in total revenue resulting from the sale of one more unit of the commodity.[5]

$$MR = TR_{n+1} - TR_n,$$

where MR is marginal revenue, TR_{n+1} is total revenue when sales are at the rate of $n + 1$ units per period, and TR_n is the total revenue when sales are at the rate of n units per period.

Total, average, and marginal revenues are three different ways of showing how revenue varies with quantity. They are not independent of each other because as soon as we have, say, a demand curve showing how average revenue varies with quantity this implies a unique total revenue curve indicating how total revenue varies and a unique marginal revenue curve indicating how total revenue changes as more or less is sold.

Figure 6 shows a straight-line demand curve and the corresponding total and marginal revenue curves.†

At the upper range of the demand curve

5. This is an approximate definition based on finite changes. The precise definition of marginal revenue is the derivative of total revenue with respect to quantity.

† The equation of the demand curve in Figure 6 is $AR = p = 10 - .1q$. The equations for the other curves are derived as follows:

$$TR = pq = 10q - .1q^2$$
$$MR = \frac{dTR}{dq} = 10 - .2q.$$

elasticity exceeds unity. This means that total revenue is rising as quantity increases so that the total revenue curve is upward sloping. Since total revenue is increasing as quantity is increasing, marginal revenue must be positive. At the point at which the elasticity of demand is unity, total revenue no longer increases as quantity sold increases. Total revenue in fact reaches its maximum value when marginal revenue is zero. Once we go past this point we reach the range over which the demand curve is inelastic. This means that total revenue falls as more is sold so that the total revenue curve is now downward sloping. Since increases in sales reduce total revenue, it follows that marginal revenue (the change in total revenue resulting from selling one more unit) must be negative. Once the quantity sold reaches 100 the price has been driven down to zero and total revenue has thus also fallen to zero.

These relations between total, average, and marginal revenue will be useful when we come to develop a theory of price.

What Determines Elasticity of Demand?

A great deal of work has been put into the measurement of demand elasticity. In Chapter 14, page 159, you will find a table giving some demand elasticities that have been measured. There is no special interest in the ones that are given here and they are presented only to give you some idea of economists' range of empirical knowledge on this subject.

One of the most important determinants of elasticity is undoubtedly the degree of availability of close substitutes. Some commodities, like margarine, cabbage, pork, and Fords, have quite close substitutes—butter, other green vegetables, beef, and other similar makes of cars. A change in the price of these commodities, *the prices of the substitutes remaining constant,* can be expected to cause quite substantial substitution—a fall in price leading consumers to buy more of the commodity in question and a rise in price leading consumers to buy more of the substitute. Other commodities, such as salt, housing, and all vegetables taken together, have few, if any, satisfactory substitutes, and a rise in their price can be expected to cause a smaller fall in quantity demanded than would be the case if close substitutes were available.

The following hypothesis about elasticity of demand is commonly advanced:

There are certain commodities, called luxuries, *which can easily be dispensed with and which have highly elastic demands because, when their prices rise, consumers stop purchasing them. There are other commodities, called* necessities, *which are essential to life, and which have almost completely inelastic demands because, when their prices rise, the consumer has no choice but to continue to buy them. Most goods fall into one or other of these classes, entertainment being an example of the former and food an example of the latter.*

There is nothing logically wrong with this hypothesis; it is quite easy to imagine a world that behaved like this. The only problem is that the hypothesis does not describe *our* world; the hypothesis is refuted by the facts. In all of the demand studies that have been made, there is no observable tendency for commodities to fall into two groups, one with very low elasticities and one with very high elasticities. There seem to be goods with all possible sorts of elasticity, a few with very low ones, a few with very high ones, and the remainder with intermediate ones.

To a great extent elasticity depends on how widely or narrowly a commodity is being defined. It is true, of course, that food and shelter are necessities in the sense that life cannot go on without some minimum quantity of them, and it is possibly true that foods as a whole would have an inelastic demand. It does not follow from this, however, that any one food, for example, white bread or corn-flakes, is a necessity in the same sense. Thus there is no reason to believe that the demand for any one food cannot and will not fall greatly as a result of a rise in its price.

Other Demand Elasticities

The general purpose of demand elasticity is to provide a measure of the degree to which demand responds to some change. So far, we have considered the response of the demand for a commodity to changes in the commodity's own price. It is also important to know how demand responds to changes in the prices of other goods and to changes in incomes.

CROSS-ELASTICITY[6]

The responsiveness of demand to changes in the prices of other commodities is called *cross-elasticity of demand*. It is defined as

$$\frac{\text{percentage change in quantity demanded of good } X}{\text{percentage change in price of good } Y}.$$

Cross-elasticity can vary from minus infinity to plus infinity. Complementary goods will have negative cross-elasticities and substitute goods will have positive cross-elasticities. If X and Y are complements, a fall in the price of X will lead to an increase in the consumption of both X and Y. The changes in the price of X and the quantity of Y will have opposite signs. If X and Y are substitutes, a fall in the price of X will increase the quantity of X consumed but will reduce the quantity of Y consumed; therefore, the changes in the price of X and in the quantity of Y will have the same sign.

The closer the relation of substitutability or complementarity, the larger the quantity reaction for any given price change and thus the larger the numerical value of the cross-elasticity. If the two goods bear little relation to each other, then we would expect their cross-elasticities to be close to zero.

INCOME ELASTICITY

The responsiveness of demand to changes in income is termed *income elasticity of demand,* and is defined as

$$\frac{\text{percentage change in quantity demanded}}{\text{percentage change in income}}.$$

For most goods, increases in income lead to increases in demand, and income elasticity will be positive. For inferior goods, where a rise in income leads consumers to demand less of the commodity, income elasticity will be negative.

Look back now to Figure 4 in Chapter 7, which plotted several curves relating demand to income.[7] Whenever a curve is rising, income elasticity is positive. When demand is

6. This section on cross-elasticity may be omitted.

7. Such curves are sometimes called *Engel's curves.*

unaffected by the level of income, as in the right-hand portion of the curve labeled (2), income elasticity is zero. When the curve declines, as in (3), income elasticity is negative.

These curves illustrate a widely accepted hypothesis: Income elasticity of a particular commodity varies as income changes. The reaction of demand to changes in incomes is likely to vary with the level of income. Thus, for example, at very low incomes nothing at all may be spent on fine percale sheets, and over this range the income elasticity of demand for this type of sheet will be zero. As income rises, however, the consumer may become wealthy enough to begin to dispense

with inferior substitutes and to buy percale sheets. As income rises, for a while the consumption of percale sheets will expand rapidly and, over this range, the income elasticity of demand will be high. At higher levels of income, however, the consumer will be able to purchase all the percale sheets he wants, and further increases in his income will leave the demand for them unchanged. Over this range income elasticity of demand will again be zero. Beyond some point the consumer may shift from percale sheets to silk sheets for part of his consumption, and demand may actually decline. The curve relating income and consumption for such an example is shown in Figure 7 below.

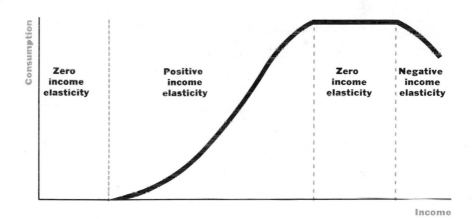

FIGURE 7

Elasticity of Supply

Now that we have considered the responsiveness to price changes of the quantity demanded by consumers, what about the responsiveness to price changes of the quantity supplied by producers? The elasticity of supply is defined as the percentage change in quantity supplied divided by the percentage change in price, and it is a measure of the degree to which the quantity supplied re-

sponds to price changes. Figure 8 illustrates three cases of supply elasticity. The case of zero elasticity is one in which the quantity supplied does not change as price changes. This would be the case, for example, if suppliers persisted in producing a given quantity, Oa in Figure 8 (i), and dumping it on the market for whatever it would bring. Infinite elasticity is illustrated in Figure 8 (ii).

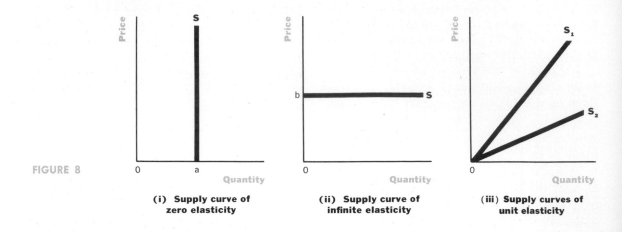

FIGURE 8

(i) Supply curve of
      zero elasticity

(ii) Supply curve of
       infinite elasticity

(iii) Supply curves of
        unit elasticity

The supply elasticity is infinite at the price Ob, because nothing at all is supplied at lower prices, but a small increase in price to Ob causes supply to rise from zero to an indefinitely large amount, indicating that producers would supply any amount demanded at that price. The case of unit elasticity of supply is illustrated in Figure 8 (iii). Any straight-line supply curve drawn through the origin has, in fact, an elasticity of unity. For a proof of this, see the appendix to this chapter, page 111.

Summary

1. The elasticity of demand is defined as the percentage change in quantity *divided by* the percentage change in price. (Since the change in quantity is in the opposite direction from the change in price, we insert a minus sign in the definition so that our measure will be positive.)

2. The possible range of elasticities and the terminology used to describe them is summarized in Table 5, page 100.

3. A straight-line demand curve does not have a constant elasticity unless it is horizontal (infinite elasticity) or vertical (zero elasticity). Otherwise, along one straight-line demand curve, the higher the price, the higher the elasticity.

4. The elasticity of demand for a commodity depends to a great extent on the number and adequacy of available substitutes, and, consequently, on how narrowly or widely the commodity is defined.

5. Total revenue is quantity sold *times* the price. Average revenue is total revenue *divided by* the quantity sold, which is the same thing as the price. Marginal revenue is the change in total revenue resulting from an increase in the rate of sales by one unit.

6. Two other demand elasticities are frequently encountered. Cross-elasticity of demand is defined as the percentage change in the quantity of good X demanded *divided by* the percentage change in the price of good Y. If X and Y are complements cross-elasticity is negative; if they are substitutes cross-elasticity is positive; if they are neither it is zero. Income elasticity of demand is defined as the

percentage change in quantity demanded of good X *divided by* the percentage change in income. For most goods income elasticity is positive; for inferior goods it is negative.

7. Elasticity of supply is measured in the same way as elasticity of demand. It is defined as the percentage change in the quantity of good X supplied *divided by* the percentage change in the price of X. A supply curve of zero elasticity is a vertical straight line; a supply curve of unit elasticity is a straight line through the origin; and a supply curve of infinite elasticity is a horizontal straight line.

QUESTIONS FOR DISCUSSION

1. What types of elasticity of demand have you learned about in this chapter? Describe what each one measures. What do they have in common?

2. Why do we use percentage changes rather than absolute changes in measuring elasticities? What examples can you think of to illustrate the advantages of this definition?

3. During World War II, many families were forced to use margarine for the first time. After the war, many laws that forbade the coloring of margarine were repealed, and manufacturers invested large sums of money to make their product more attractive and to advise consumers of what they had done. In 1957, the Department of Agriculture published estimates for the pre- and postwar elasticities of butter. One was approximately 1.35 and the other was approximately 0.35. Which do you think was which?

What do you think happened to the cross-elasticity of demand between butter and margarine?

4. Consumption of beer in America declined from 25.1 gallons per capita per year in 1947 to 23.2 gallons in 1962, although the relative price of beer did not rise. What might this indicate about the income elasticity of demand for beer? Why do you think this is so?

5. What do you think the elasticity of supply of fresh fish would be on any one day (i.e., if we related a change in the price on that day to any induced change in the quantity supplied on the same day)? How is this elasticity likely to be influenced by the available methods of refrigeration?

6. If the demand for food is inelastic, does it follow that the demand for hamburgers is inelastic?

†APPENDIX TO CHAPTER 10
A FORMAL ANALYSIS OF ELASTICITY

ELASTICITY OF DEMAND MAY BE defined as the ratio of the percentage change in the quantity demanded to the percentage change in price.[1]

This measure is an approximation to the measure involving the *derivative of quantity demanded with respect to price.*

We shall first consider the percentage definition and then consider the definition using a derivative.

Let us first define a number of terms:

$\eta \equiv$ elasticity of demand
$\epsilon_S \equiv$ elasticity of supply
$q \equiv$ the original quantity

$\Delta q \equiv$ change in quantity
$p \equiv$ the original price
$\Delta p \equiv$ the change in price

We have defined elasticity of demand as

$$\eta \equiv \frac{\text{percentage change in quantity}}{\text{percentage change in price}};$$

1. In Chapter 10, as in most elementary treatments, we defined elasticity of demand as the negative of this amount so that it would be a positive number. It is convenient in formal analysis to drop this simplification.

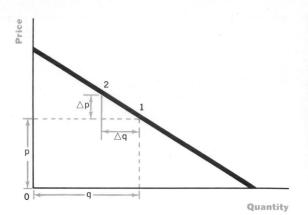

FIGURE A1

on the line. Therefore, its reciprocal, $\Delta q/\Delta p$, must also be constant. We can now infer the changes in η by inspecting the ratio p/q. Where the line cuts the price axis, quantity is zero so the ratio p/q is infinity, thus $\eta = \infty$.[2] As we move down the line, p falls and q rises steadily, thus p/q is falling steadily so that η is also falling. At the q axis the price is zero so the ratio p/q is zero. Thus $\eta = 0$.

2. *Comparing two straight-line demand curves of the same slope, the one farther from the origin is less elastic at every price than the one closer to the origin.* Figure A2 shows two parallel straight-line demand functions. Pick any price, say Op, and compare the elasticities of the two curves at that price. Since the curves are parallel, the ratio $\Delta q/\Delta p$ is the same on both curves. Since we are comparing elasticities at the same price on both curves p is the same and the only factor left to vary is q. On the curve farther from the origin quantity is larger (i.e., $Oq_2 > Oq_1$) and hence p/q is smaller and thus η is smaller.

It follows from Theorem 2 that parallel shifts of a straight-

$$\eta \equiv \frac{\Delta q/q}{\Delta p/p} .$$

By inverting the denominator and multiplying, we get

$$\eta \equiv \frac{\Delta q}{q} \cdot \frac{p}{\Delta p} .$$

Since it does not matter in which order we do our multiplication (i.e., $q \cdot \Delta p \equiv \Delta p \cdot q$), we may reverse the order of the two terms in the denominator and write

$$\eta \equiv \frac{\Delta q}{\Delta p} \cdot \frac{p}{q} . \qquad (1)$$

We have now split elasticity into two parts: $\Delta q/\Delta p$, the ratio of the change in quantity to the change in price, which is related to the *slope* of the demand curve, and p/q, which is related to the *point* on the curve at which we made our measurement.

Figure A1 shows a straight-line demand curve by way of illustration. If we wish to meas-

ure the elasticity at Point 1, we take our p and q at that point and then consider a price change, taking us, say, to Point 2, and we measure our Δp and Δq as indicated. Now, the slope of the straight line joining Points 1 and 2 is $\Delta p/\Delta q$ (if you have forgotten this, refer to the appendix to Chapter 3, p. 40), and the term in equation (1) is $\Delta q/\Delta p$, which is the reciprocal of $\Delta p/\Delta q$. We conclude, therefore, that the first term in our elasticity formula is the reciprocal of the slope of the straight line joining the two price-quantity positions under consideration.

We now develop a number of theorems relating to straight-line demand curves.

1. *The elasticity of a downward-sloping straight-line demand curve varies from infinity* (∞) *at the price axis to zero at the quantity axis.* We first notice that a straight line has a constant slope so that the ratio $\Delta p/\Delta q$ is the same anywhere

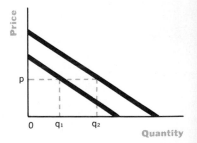

FIGURE A2

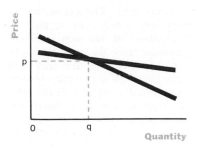

Price

p

0   q

Quantity

FIGURE A3

line demand curve lower elasticity (at each price) when the line shifts outward, and raise elasticity when the line shifts inward.

3. *The elasticities of two intersecting straight-line demand curves can be compared at the point of intersection merely by comparing slopes, the steeper curve being the less elastic.* In Figure A3 we have two intersecting curves. At the point of intersection p and q are common to both curves and hence the ratio p/q is the same. Therefore η varies only with $\Delta q/\Delta p$; on the steeper curve $\Delta p/\Delta q$ is larger than on the flatter curve, thus the ratio $\Delta q/\Delta p$ is smaller on the steeper curve than on the flatter curve, so that elasticity is lower.

4. *Any straight-line supply curve through the origin has an elasticity of one.* Such a supply curve is shown in Figure A4. Consider the two triangles with the sides p, q, and the S curve, and Δp, Δq, and the S curve. Clearly these are similar triangles. Therefore the ratios of their sides are equal, i.e.,

$$\frac{p}{q} = \frac{\Delta p}{\Delta q}. \qquad (2)$$

Elasticity of supply is defined as

$$\epsilon_S = \frac{\Delta q}{\Delta p} \cdot \frac{p}{q}, \qquad (3)$$

which, by substitution from (2), gives

$$\epsilon_S = \frac{q}{p} \cdot \frac{p}{q} \equiv 1. \qquad (4)$$

5. *With a straight-line demand curve, the elasticity measured from any point p, q, according to Equation (1) above, is independent of the direction and magnitude of the change in price and quantity.* This follows immediately from the fact that the slope of a straight line is a constant. If we start from some point p, q, and then change price, the ratio $\Delta q/\Delta p$ will be the same whatever the direction or the size of the change in p.

6. *The result in Theorem 5 does not hold for any demand function other than a straight line.* Figure A5 shows a demand curve that is not a straight line. We desire to measure the elasticity from Point 1. What-

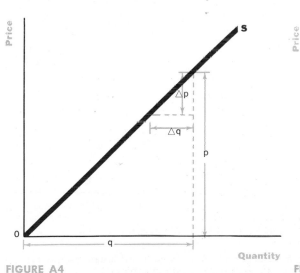

FIGURE A4

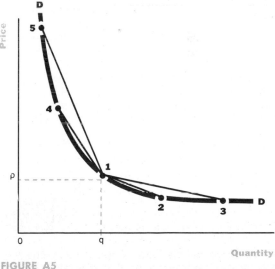

FIGURE A5

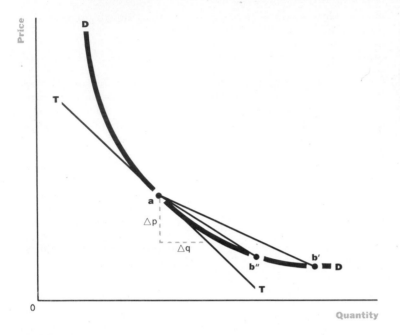

to price change at a point dq/dp and we define this to be the reciprocal of the slope of the straight line (i.e., $\Delta q/\Delta p$) tangent to the demand curve at the point in question. In Figure A6 the elasticity of demand at a is the ratio p/q (as it has been in all previous measures) now multiplied by the ratio of $\Delta q/\Delta p$ measured along the straight-line tangent to the curve at a. This definition may now be written

$$\eta = \frac{dq}{dp} \cdot \frac{p}{q}. \qquad (5)$$

The ratio dq/dp as we have defined it is in fact the differential-calculus concept of the derivative of quantity with respect to price.

This elasticity is the one normally used in economic theory. Equation (1) may be regarded as an approximation to this expression. It is obvious by inspecting Figure A6 that the elasticity measured from (1) will come closer and closer to that measured from (5) the smaller the price change used to calculate the value of (1). In (1), change the price so that we move from a to some Point b; the ratio $\Delta q/\Delta p$ is the reciprocal of the slope of the straight line joining a and b. The smaller the price change that we make, the closer Point b comes to Point a. The closer b comes to a, the closer the slope of the line joining a and b comes to the slope of the line tangential to the curve at a. If the slopes of these two lines get closer together so also do the reciprocals of the slopes and, thus, so do the elasticities measured by (1) and (5). Thus, if we consider (1) as an approximation to (5), the error will

ever changes we make, the ratio p/q is given but the ratio $\Delta q/\Delta p$ will vary according to the size and the direction of the price change. We have already seen that $\Delta q/\Delta p$ is the reciprocal of the slope of the line joining the two points considered. If we lower price by a large amount so that we move from 1 to 3, the ratio $\Delta q/\Delta p$ is the reciprocal of slope of the line joining 1 and 3. If we make the price cut smaller, so that we go from 1 to 2, the slope of the line is larger than that joining 1 and 3, so that its reciprocal will be smaller. Thus our measured η from the point p, q will be smaller if we make a small price cut than if we make a large one. By a repetition of the same argument we can show that, if we raise price, so that we move from 1 to 4, we will get

a smaller elasticity than when we lowered price, whereas, if we move from 1 to 5, the elasticity will be even smaller than it was when we moved from 1 to 4.

Thus our elasticity measured from Point 1 will vary depending on the direction and the magnitude of the price changes which we happen to make. This result is very inconvenient. The reason for it is that, when we take a big Δp, we are averaging the reaction of Δq to Δp over a whole range of the demand curve, and, depending on the range that we take, the *average reaction* will be different.

If we wish to measure the elasticity at a point we need to know the reaction of quantity to a change in price at that point, not over a whole range. We call the reaction of quantity

diminish as the size of Δp diminishes.

7. *The relation between elasticity and total revenue.* Students who understand elementary calculus may wish to see a simple proof of the proposition that when total revenue is at a maximum, elasticity of demand is unity (see Figure 6, p. 104). By definition:

$$\eta = \frac{dq}{dp} \cdot \frac{p}{q} \qquad (6)$$

From the demand curve:

$$q = f(p) \qquad (7)$$

Differentiating (7):

$$\frac{dq}{dp} = f'(p) \qquad (8)$$

Substituting (7) and (8) into (6):

$$\eta = \frac{f'(p)p}{f(p)} \qquad (9)$$

Now consider total revenue:

$$TR = p\,q$$

From (7)

$$TR = p\,f(p)$$

$$MR = p + \frac{dp}{dq}f(p)$$

A necessary condition for TR to be a maximum is: $MR = 0$

$$p + \frac{dp}{dq}f(p) = 0$$

$$\frac{dp}{dq}\frac{f(p)}{p} = -1, \text{ and, recognizing}$$

$$\frac{dp}{dq} = \frac{1}{f'(p)},$$

we have $\dfrac{f(p)}{pf'(p)} = -1$, whence

$$\frac{pf'(p)}{f(p)} = -1 \qquad (10)$$

But by (9) the left-hand side of (10) is the elasticity of demand. Thus it is a necessary condition for total revenue to be at a maximum that elasticity should be unity.

QUESTIONS FOR DISCUSSION

1. Can you write income elasticity of demand in the same way as we have written price elasticity?

2. Assume that two studies of the elasticity of demand for strawberries are made. The first shows elasticity of 1.34 at $p = 25\not c$; the other shows elasticity of 1.26 at $p = 30\not c$. Can the two observations have both come from the same straight-line demand curve? Why or why not? If both studies are competent, what conclusions might explain the findings?

3. Two straight-line demand curves have the equations $Q = 3 - 10p$ and $Q = X - 10p$. At a price of $2, elasticity of demand is greater for the first demand function than for the second. What do you know about the value of X?

4. Show that when marginal revenue is positive, the demand curve is elastic.

Chapter **11** PRICE CONTROLS, TAXES, AGRICULTURE: SOME PREDICTIONS OF THE THEORY OF PRICE

CAN THE THEORY WE CONSIDERED IN CHAPTERS 7–10 provide us with useful predictions about how real prices and quantities will actually behave? Yes, it can, and in this chapter we will see how.

The propositions that we have derived and others that we shall derive in this chapter can be viewed in two different ways. First, they can be considered merely as logical implications of our theory of price. For example, the proposition that an increase in demand raises the equilibrium price and quantity traded is a logical deduction from our theory and, unless generations of economists have all made the same gross error of logic, we must accept it as being incontrovertible that this proposition is implied by our theory. Second, they can be regarded as predictions about what will happen in the world under certain stated conditions. From this second point of view, the correctness of our theory is an empirical matter.[1]

In order to confront the theory with the real world, we advance the hypothesis that actual prices in the real world are relatively close to equilibrium prices most of the time, and that, if the equilibrium price changes, the actual price moves fairly quickly toward the new equilibrium price.

The simple theory of the determination of market prices through demand and supply is extremely powerful and can be applied to a large number of real-world situations. The cases studied in this chapter are examples intended both to illustrate how demand and supply theory can be used, and to give you practice in using it. It is a mistake to try to commit these particular cases to memory; you should seek to understand them, so that when either slightly different or totally new situations turn up (as they always do), you will be able to apply the theory to them and discover what is predicted about each situation that arises.

Price and Wage Controls

MAXIMUM-PRICE LEGISLATION

It is common in wartime, and not unknown in peacetime, for governments to pass laws fixing the prices at which commodities may be sold. In this section we shall confine our- selves to the setting of maximum prices (sometimes called ceiling prices) and in the next section we shall go on to consider the effects of setting minimum prices. What would you expect to be the consequences of a system in which some prices are not left completely free to be determined by de- mand and supply?

Figure 1 shows the demand and supply curves for some commodity. The equilibrium price is *Oa* and the equilibrium quantity is *Ob*. We now wish to know what would hap- pen if the government were able to enforce a maximum price at which this commodity were to be sold. If the maximum price were set above the equilibrium price, the govern- ment intervention would have no effect. The equilibrium price would still be attainable and the market equilibrium would be in no way inconsistent with the maximum-price law. On the other hand, suppose the maximum price

1. You should now reread two earlier passages. First, read the section "True in Theory but Not in Practice?," on pages 19–20. It is of course quite possible that a proposition follows logically from the postulates of a theory but that the proposition is refuted by experience. We then conclude that the whole theory is a bad one and that at least one of its assumptions about behavior must incorrectly describe what actually happens. Read also the section on the "laws" of supply and demand on page 92. Of course, *given the theory,* cer- tain conclusions about equilibrium prices necessarily follow. But this does nothing to establish whether or not these conclusions allow us to predict correctly what will happen in the world. The ability of a theory to predict is a question that can only be answered on empirical grounds—i.e., by actually looking to see if what does happen is what the theory predicts will happen.

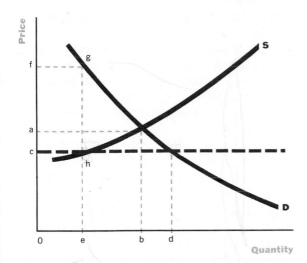

FIGURE 1   **PRICE CONTROL AND BLACK MARKETS**

is set at a level below the equilibrium one, say at Oc. The equilibrium price would no longer be legally obtainable. Prices must be reduced from Oa to Oc, and as a result the quantity demanded will expand by bd, from Ob to Od; the quantity supplied, on the other hand, will fall by be, from Ob to Oe. Thus a shortage of the commodity will develop, the quantity demanded exceeding the quantity supplied. (In Figure 1 the excess demand is equal to ed.)

We now have our first predictions about the effect of price control in a competitive market:

The setting of maximum prices will either have no effect (maximum price set at or above the equilibrium) or it will cause a shortage of the commodity and reduce both the price and the quantity actually bought and sold below their equilibrium values.

In the case of effective price ceilings, production is not sufficient to satisfy everyone who wishes to buy the commodity. Price is not allowed to change so as to allocate the available supply among the would-be purchasers (see Chapter 6 on how the free market does this). It follows that some other method of allocation will have to be adopted. Our theory does not predict what this other method will be, but it is not difficult to enumerate those alternatives that experience has shown to be likely to arise. If stores sell their available supplies to the first customers that arrive, then people are likely to rush to those stores that are rumored to have supplies of any commodity of which there is a severe shortage; long lines will develop and allocations will be made on a first-come–first-served basis. In wartime Britain, the rumor that a shop was selling supplies of some very scarce commodity was sufficient to cause a local stampede. Housewives often spent days tracking down such rumors and then hours standing in line before being able to gain entrance to the shop. Usually, the supplies would be exhausted long before all of them were served. Another system may develop if storekeepers themselves decide who will get the scarce commodities and who will not. Goods may be kept under the counter and sold only to certain customers, for instance, to regular customers. During the war, to move from one town to another meant losing one's status as a "regular" in many shops. Unless one was a regular, it was very difficult indeed to obtain cigarettes and liquor, both of which, though unrationed, were subject to price control. Or the storekeeper might sell only to people of a particular color or religion or to those with other affiliations of which he approved. Allocations made by storekeepers may be called *allocations by sellers' preferences.*

If the *central authorities*[2] dislike the some-

2. We shall use the term *central authorities* as well as the term *the government* to mean those public officials who make policy decisions. In a complex governmental system such as the American one, there are not only many levels of government (federal, state, and municipal) but also many executive, legislative, and judicial authorities at each level. We shall not, in this book, always need to distinguish among them.

what arbitrary system of allocation that grows up, they can ration the goods, giving out ration coupons sufficient to purchase the quantity *Oe* in Figure 1. The authorities can then determine, as a conscious act of policy, how the available supply is to be allocated: The coupons might be distributed equally among the population, or they might be distributed on the basis of age, sex, marital status, number of dependents, or any other criterion they wish to adopt. Thus we are led to predict the following:

Where there is a feeling against allocation on the basis of first-come–first-served or of allocation by sellers' preferences, effective price ceilings will give rise to strong pressure for a centrally administered system of rationing.

Next we observe that, under certain circumstances, price control with or without rationing is likely to give rise to a *black market*. A black market is one in which goods are sold illegally at prices above the legal maximum price. For many products there are only a few large producers but a great many retailers and, although it is easy to police the producers, it is difficult to locate all those who are, or could be, retailing the product, much less to police them. Although the government may be able to control effectively the price that producers get for their product, it may not be able to control effectively the price at which retailers sell to the public, and it certainly cannot control the sale of ration coupons by those who prefer money to the rationed good. What would you expect to happen in this case? First, the amount produced would remain unchanged at *Oe* in Figure 1 because the producer would continue to receive the controlled price for his product. At the retail level, however, a black market would arise, because purchasers would be willing to pay very much more than the controlled price for the limited amounts of the commodity that are available. If the whole quantity were sold on the black market, it would fetch a price of *Of* per unit. The total amount paid by consumers would be *Oegf;* of this, the total amount of the illegal receipts of black marketeers would be *chgf*. The theory predicts that the potential for a profitable black market will always exist whenever effective price ceilings are imposed. The actual growth of such a market depends on there being a few people willing to risk heavy penalties by running a black-market supply organization and a reasonably large number of persons prepared to purchase goods illegally on such a market. It is an interesting comment on human nature that a case has never been documented in which effective price ceilings were not accompanied by the growth of a black market.

It is unlikely that all goods will be sold on the black market, because there are some honest people in every society and because the central authorities always have considerable power to enforce their price laws. Thus we would normally expect not the extreme situation described above but rather a situation in which some of the limited supplies would be sold at the controlled price and some at the black-market price.[3]

An economist can evaluate a black-market situation only when he knows what objectives the central authorities hope to achieve with their price-control policy. If they are mainly concerned with an equitable division of a

3. Demonstrate that the higher the fraction of the available supply sold at the controlled price, the higher the black-market price for the remainder.

scarce product, it is very likely that effective price control on manufacturers plus a largely uncontrolled black market at the retail level produces the worst possible results. If, however, they are mainly interested in restricting the total supply available for consumption in order to release resources for other more urgent needs, such as war production, the policy works effectively, if somewhat unfairly. Where the purpose is to keep prices down, the policy is a failure to the degree that the black market succeeds in raising prices.

There is much evidence confirming these predictions. Practically all belligerent countries in both World War I and World War II introduced schemes setting ceilings on prices well below free-market equilibrium levels. These schemes were always followed by shortages, then by either the introduction of rationing or by the growth of some method of allocation, such as allocation by sellers' preferences, and finally by the rise of a black market. These schemes were more effective in limiting consumption than in controlling prices, although they did restrain price increases. Peacetime price controls have been less frequent and much less successful in their major objectives. Many countries have tried to control rentals of houses and apartments for private use. Such rent control schemes have usually produced shortages, private-allocation systems, and a black market. For example, in order to make up the difference between the controlled rent and the free-market rent, the landlord may charge the new tenant a grossly inflated sum for a few shabby sticks of furniture.

MINIMUM-PRICE LEGISLATION

Governments sometimes pass laws stating that certain goods and services cannot be sold below some stated minimum price. In the United States today, minimum-wage laws specify "floors" for different kinds of labor. (The general minimum wage today is $1.25 per hour, but there are some exceptions.) There are also certain laws called variously resale-price maintenance and fair-trade laws that limit the ability of sellers to sell below prices set by the manufacturers. Before reading on, ask yourself what our theory predicts about the effects of minimum prices.

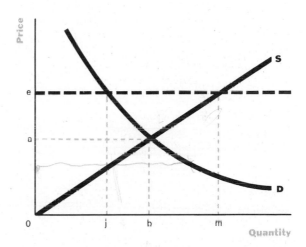

FIGURE 2   **A COMMODITY SUBJECT TO MINIMUM-PRICE LEGISLATION**

The case of a commodity subject to minimum-price legislation is illustrated in Figure 2. The free-market equilibrium price is Oa, and the equilibrium quantity traded is Ob. If the minimum price is set below the equilibrium price then it has no effect on the market. The attainment of the free-market equilibrium and the fulfillment of the minimum-price law are perfectly compatible. On the other hand, if the minimum price is set above the equilibrium, say at Oe, the free-market equilibrium will be legally unobtainable. The actual price will be *Oe*, and at that price there will be an excess of supply over demand. Suppliers would like to sell *Om*, but purchasers are only willing to buy *Oj* at the price *Oe*. The actual amount bought and sold will thus be *Oj*. This leads us to our first prediction about minimum prices:

The setting of minimum prices will either have no effect (minimum price set below the equilibrium) or it will cause a surplus of the commodity to develop with the actual price being above its equilibrium level but the actual quantity bought and sold being below its equilibrium level.

In this case there is, at the prevailing price, no scarcity of the controlled commodity. Therefore we predict that alternative allocative systems will not grow up. There will, however, be a shortage of purchasers, and potential suppliers may compete in various ways for the available customers. Methods of price cutting will be sought, some of which find loopholes in the law and some of which merely flout it. For example, discount houses, in states that enforce fair-trade laws, have become "buying clubs" in which one can purchase a life membership for a dollar. There will be no opportunity for a set of black-market operators to take over the distribution of the product, since there is nothing to be gained by buying at the controlled price and selling at the free-market price. Thus we predict the absence of an organized black market in this case.

Most countries have minimum-wage laws. Applying our theory to the labor market is a bit of a jump in the dark, but a theory developed later does allow us to use a downward-sloping demand curve for each type of labor. If we hypothesize that our theory of competitive markets will apply to a labor market, we can make the following predictions about minimum-wage laws:

---

1. *Where the law is effective it will raise some of the wages of those who remain in employment.*
2. *It will lower the actual amount of employment (by* bj *in Figure 2).*
3. *It will create a surplus of labor that would like to but cannot obtain jobs in the occupation affected (*jm *in Figure 2).*
4. *It will create an incentive for some workers to try to evade the law by offering to work at wages below the legal minimum.*
5. *It will not lead to the rise of an independent group of black marketeers.*

There is ample evidence confirming most of these predictions. The illegal entry into Texas and California of Mexican farm laborers during the harvesting season, for instance, is well known. (These laborers are known as "wetbacks" because they were supposed to have swum or waded across the Rio Grande River in order to evade immigration officials.) The empirical validity of Prediction 2 is a matter of dispute when minimum-wage laws are applied across the whole economy. We cannot go into this controversy here but we shall raise it again in Chapter 35.

It is remarkable how many predictions our simple theory yields about the effects of price control and it is remarkable how many of these predictions have been shown to be accurate. It is interesting, and a little depressing too, to see how often legislators are prepared to pass price-control laws without showing any apparent appreciation of the likely effects of such measures.

A DIGRESSION: METHODS OF ALLOCATING SCARCE COMMODITIES

We raised above the question of alternative methods of allocating scarce commodities among potential consumers. Since it is almost always true that people would like to have more of a commodity than is in fact available, it is necessary to have some way of rationing the available supply. In a dictatorship this may be done by the central authorities. In a free-market society it is done by the price mechanism. When there is excess demand, price rises, and this encourages production and discourages consumption. Price continues to rise until, at its equilibrium level, the rate of consumption is equal to the rate of production. Thus market price does the rationing. If price is held constant at a level below the equilibrium one, the available quantity must be allocated in some other way: by storekeepers on the basis of their preferences, on a first-come–first-served basis, or by government rationing, with coupons distributed on any one of a number of principles.

Because goods are scarce, there must be *some* system of allocating them among potential consumers. It is sometimes argued that the price system provides the best (in an ethical sense) way of doing this. But there is nothing in positive economics that can prove that the price system as it functions in the real world provides an ethically better method of allocating goods than some other system. Positive economics merely attempts to show the consequences of allocating scarce goods by various methods. Any decision about which method ought to be adopted will be a better-informed one if the decision-makers understand the actual effects of different methods.

It is sometimes said that the price that equates demand and supply, *Oa* in Figures 1 and 2, is the *natural* price, whereas other prices are *artificial ones*. This is emotive language that should be avoided, if possible, since it is likely to give the impression that the natural price is in some sense the best price. All that can be said on the basis of positive economics is that the price *Oa* is the one that equates demand to supply *through the mechanism of price*. If other prices are enforced, alternative methods of equating demand to supply will have to be used.

Public Finance: Tax Incidence

What is the effect of taxes placed on the sale and purchase of commodities? What is the effect, for instance, of the excise tax on luggage, or automobiles, or gin? Do such taxes leave prices unchanged or do they cause prices to rise? Does the producer pay the tax or is he able to pass it on to the consumer through higher prices? Many such age-old controversies are to be found in the field of tax theory.

As a first step in discovering what our theory predicts about these issues, we must consider the effect of a tax on the supply of a commodity. Look at Table 1, which shows the supply schedule for an imaginary commodity.

The supply schedule indicated by Columns 1 and 2 is graphed in Figure 3, and is labeled S. The schedule shows the relation between the price that the producer obtains for his commodity, and the amount that he is willing to sell. If no tax is levied, then the seller

TABLE 1   DERIVATION OF A SUPPLY CURVE WHEN AN AD VALOREM AND A SPECIFIC TAX IS LEVIED

1	2	3	4
		If a tax of $1.00 is placed on the sale of this commodity, it must be *sold* for the price listed in Column 3 if the producer is to *receive* the amount listed in Column 1	If a tax equal to 25 percent of the after-tax receipts of the seller is levied on this commodity it must be *sold* for the price listed in Column 4 if the producer is to *receive* the price listed in Column 1
If the supplier receives the price listed below he will offer for sale the quantity listed below			
Dollars per ton	Tons supplied per month	Dollars per ton	Dollars per ton
1	0		
2	500	3	2.50
3	1,000	4	3.75
4	1,500	5	5.00
6	2,500	7	7.50
10	4,500	11	12.50

receives the whole market price for which the commodity is sold. If, however, a tax is levied on the sale of a commodity, then the seller will receive on each unit that he sells the market price of the commodity *minus* the amount of the tax. *In order that he should receive the same amount per unit as he was receiving prior to the tax, the market price must be raised by the full amount of the tax.* This is illustrated in Column 3 of Table 1 with the example of a specific tax of $1.00 per unit. If producers are prepared to sell 500 tons when they obtain $2.00 per unit, then 500 tons will be supplied at a market price of $2.00 when there is no tax, but at a market price of $3.00 when the tax is levied. If producers are prepared to sell 2,500 untaxed tons at $6.00 per unit, then they will sell 2,500 tons at $7.00 when the $1.00 tax is levied. Assuming that the willingness of sellers to

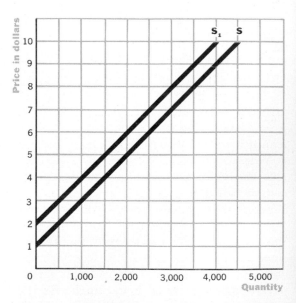

FIGURE 3   THE EFFECT OF A TAX ON THE SUPPLY CURVE OF A COMPETITIVE INDUSTRY

supply the commodity is unchanged, then, after a tax has been levied, every quantity sold will have a market price higher by the full amount of the tax than the one previously required. This shift in the relation between market price and quantity supplied is illustrated in Column 3 of Table 1 and by the supply curve S_1 in Figure 3.

> The effect of a tax on a commodity, therefore, is to shift every point on the supply curve vertically upward by the amount of the tax.

In this example we have used a fixed tax of $1.00 per unit. Precisely the same conclusion follows if we examine a tax that is a fixed percentage of the value: The supply curve will shift upward by the full amount of the tax. Column 4 of Table 1 provides the data and Figure 4 plots the supply curve after taxes. (For the remainder of this section we shall, for brevity, deal only with the specific tax, but you should repeat the argument and draw the graphs for the case of the ad valorem tax as well.)

But price depends on demand as well as supply. Before we can say anything about the price, we must add a demand curve. (See Figure 5.) The original equilibrium price is $5.00, and the quantity traded is 2,000 units. If, following the imposition of the tax, the price rises by the full amount of the tax from $5.00 to $6.00, then the quantity demanded will fall and there will be an excess of supply over demand. This will cause the price to fall until it reaches the equilibrium point where the new supply curve cuts the demand curve. In the example illustrated in Figure 5, the new equilibrium price is $5.66. This is the price that will be paid by consumers. When the tax of $1.00 per unit is deducted, the producers will receive a unit price of $4.66. Thus, in this example, the tax has the effect of raising the price paid by consumers by 66¢ and lowering the price

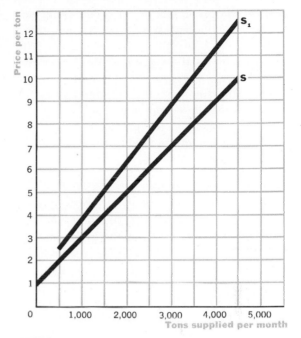

FIGURE 4

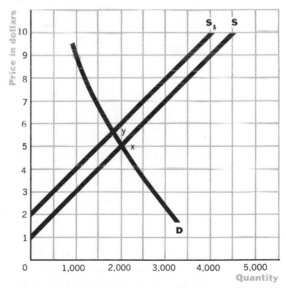

FIGURE 5   THE EFFECT OF A TAX ON THE PRICE OF A COMMODITY

received by producers by 34¢. The *incidence* of the tax falls two-thirds on the consumer and one-third on the producer. The term incidence is used to describe who pays the taxes levied.

The following general prediction can easily be shown to follow from our theory by replacing the numbers of the previous specific example with the letters used in general reasoning.

As long as the demand curve slopes downward and the supply curve upward, the imposition of a tax will raise the price paid by consumers and lower the price received by producers in both cases by an amount less than the amount of the tax.

THE INFLUENCE OF ELASTICITY OF DEMAND AND SUPPLY

Figure 6 repeats the supply curves of Figure 3, but combines them with two different demand curves representing two extreme

cases: a perfectly inelastic demand curve in Figure 6 (i) and a perfectly elastic demand in Figure 6 (ii). In the case of the perfectly inelastic curve, the equilibrium price increases by the full amount of the tax; in the case of the perfectly elastic curve, the equilibrium price is unchanged in spite of the shift in the supply curve. This suggests the following general prediction:

The more inelastic the demand for a commodity, the greater the rise in the price paid by the consumer and the less the fall in the price received by the producer as a result of the imposition of any given tax.

The derivation of this prediction is illustrated in Figure 6 (iii). Look at demand curve D, which intersects the original supply curve, S, at an equilibrium price of $5.00. Note the post-tax equilibrium price given by the intersection of the original demand curve with the new supply curve S_1. Now consider *pivoting* the demand curve through the original

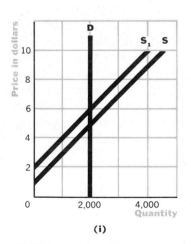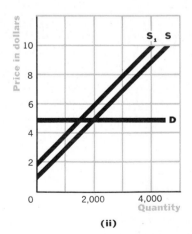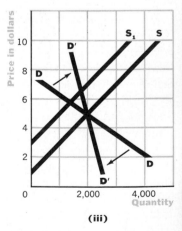

(i)   (ii)   (iii)

FIGURE 6   **THE EFFECT OF A TAX ON PRICE AND QUANTITY, GIVEN DEMAND CURVES OF VARIOUS ELASTICITIES**

equilibrium point, as shown in Figure 6 (iii). Clearly, the steeper, and thus the more inelastic, the demand curve, the greater the rise in price paid by consumers and the smaller the fall in the price received by producers.

We have relied on graphical analysis to derive the above predictions, but the argument can be stated verbally without too much difficulty. The case of the completely inelastic demand curve means that consumers insist on buying the same quantity of the commodity whatever the market price. If the price rises by the full amount of the tax, there will still be no change in the quantity demanded, and, since there will also be no change in the quantity supplied (because the price received by producers will be exactly the same as it was before the tax was levied), then the price that equates demand and supply will be higher than the original one by the full amount of the tax. In this extreme case the incidence of the tax falls entirely on consumers.

The case of the perfectly elastic demand curve means that consumers will purchase as much of the commodity as they can obtain at the going price but will purchase nothing at all at any higher price. Thus, any increase in price will reduce demand to zero. The only possible market price is the original one, and, providing some producers are willing to sell goods at that price, then the original price must also be the new equilibrium one. In this case the tax falls entirely on the producer.

Empirical evidence relating to these pre-dictions is not easy to obtain. If prices were generally constant then all we would have to do would be to observe price changes in competitive markets after the raising or lowering of tax rates. Unfortunately (for the purpose of testing these predictions), prices are constantly changing because of continual shifts in demand and supply due to the growth of real incomes, changes in technology, changes in tastes, inflations, deflations, and a host of other factors. To discover, in such a changing situation, the influence of taxes on prices is a very difficult job of economic measurement and one that cannot be accomplished by casual observation.

It is impossible here to summarize such evidence as does exist. We can only assert the general conclusion, which, we believe, commands general, if not universal, assent: In the case of those raw materials and agricultural products that are sold on a competitive market and in the case of real estate for rental, the burden is probably shared by consumers and producers and the division of the burden is roughly what one would expect on the basis of the elasticities of demand and supply. In the case of manufactured goods that are not sold on competitive markets (see Chapter 29), it is less certain how the burden is shared and it is at least *possible* that taxes are passed on completely to consumers through higher prices, either because producers are not trying to maximize profits or because long-run supply curves are perfectly elastic.

The Problems of Agriculture

The "farm problem," as it is called, is one of the most perplexing for U.S. policy-makers. Four million farmers with their families constitute 7 percent of the population and provide 8 percent of the total labor force, but earn less than 4 percent of national income. This situation alone makes the farmers' problems dramatic. Farmers are a major political force in a large number of states. They wield a political influence (especially in the Senate) disproportionate to their numbers. Over the last three decades, the government has tried a wide variety of farm policies. Parity, production controls, crop insurance, and price supports are terms that are constantly seen in the press. What is the nature of the farm problem? Many aspects of it emerge from our theory of market supply and demand.

AGRICULTURAL PRICE FLUCTUATIONS

The farmer's crop is subject to variations due to many factors completely beyond his control: Pests, floods, and lack of rain are capable of drastically reducing his expected output and exceptionally favorable conditions can cause production to greatly exceed his expectations. What does our theory predict about the effect of these unplanned fluctuations on the prices of agricultural commodities and on the incomes of farmers?

A supply curve is meant to show *desired* output and sales at each market price. If there are unplanned variations in output then actual production and sales will diverge from their planned level. The supply curve in Figure 7 shows the total quantity farmers

desire to produce and offer for sale at various prices. If the price were Oa, then planned production would be Ob, but actual production will vary around this planned amount, owing to causes beyond the farmers' control. Two demand curves are drawn in Figure 7. One

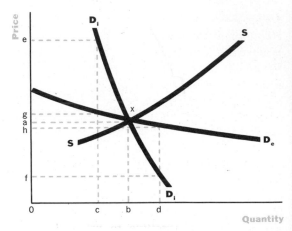

FIGURE 7   **VARIATIONS IN PRICE CAUSED BY UN-PLANNED VARIATIONS IN SUPPLY**

is relatively elastic and the other is relatively inelastic over the price range from Oe to Of. Planned production at the equilibrium price is Ob, but unplanned fluctuations are assumed to cause actual output to vary between Oc and Od. If there were no unplanned fluctuations in production, price would settle at Oa and quantity at Ob. If, for example, the actual production is Oc, then a shortage will develop; prices will rise to Oe in the case of demand curve D_i and to Og in the case of curve D_e. In each case demand will be reduced to a point at which it is equal to the supply available. If, on the other hand, conditions are particularly favorable, actual production will exceed planned production; a surplus will occur and price will fall. If, for example, production is Od, then price will fall to Of in the case of curve D_i and to Oh in the case of curve D_e. In each case the fall in price is sufficient to call forth enough extra demand to absorb the extra unplanned supply, but the fall is large in the case of curve D_i and small in the case of curve D_e.

Unplanned fluctuations in supply will cause price variations in the opposite direction to the supply changes (the bigger the supply, the lower the price) and, for given supply fluctuations, the price changes will be larger, the lower the elasticity of demand for the product.

Although we relied on geometrical analysis to derive the above prediction, verbal reasoning would have led us to the same conclusion. High elasticity means that the quantity demanded is very sensitive to price changes. When there is a crop failure, a small increase in price will be sufficient to choke off the quantity demanded until it is equal to the greatly reduced quantity supplied; when there is a bumper crop, a small fall in price will be sufficient to call forth the additional demand necessary to buy up the larger supply. Low elasticity, on the other hand, means that the quantity demanded is not very responsive to price changes. People will try to purchase roughly the same amount of the commodity

regardless of its price. Thus, when there is a crop failure, a very large increase in price is necessary to reduce the quantity demanded to the level of the available supply, and, when there is a bumper crop, a very large price reduction is necessary to persuade consumers to purchase the whole supply available.

What are the effects on incomes of farmers?[4] Here the relations are a bit more complex, but they all follow immediately from the results established above. If the good in question has an elasticity of demand greater than unity, then unplanned increases in supply will raise farmers' receipts and unplanned decreases will lower farmers' receipts. If the demand for the product is inelastic, consumers' total expenditure on the product, and thus farmers' revenues, will rise when price rises and fall when price falls. Thus, good harvests will bring reductions in total farm revenues and bad harvests will bring increases in farm incomes![5] When demand is inelastic, a given percentage change in the harvest will cause a much greater percentage change in price. To illustrate: A 20 percent fall in production might cause a 50 percent rise in price, in which case total farm revenue would rise by 20 percent. A 20 percent rise in production might cause a 40 percent fall in price, in which case total farm receipts would fall by 28 percent.

If demand happened to be unity, then farmers' revenues would not vary as output and prices varied, because every change in output would be met by an exactly compensating change in price, and total expenditure would remain constant.

---

4. Although we make predictions here about the receipts of farmers—their revenues, or money received from sale of crops—their receipts are closely related to their incomes. We can, without risk of serious error, extend these predictions to incomes.

5. This is only true if demand is inelastic over the relevant range. It does not follow that every individual farmer's income must rise (after all, some farmers may have nothing to harvest); it only follows that the total income of all farmers must rise.

We now have the following predictions:

---

1. *Unplanned fluctuations in output can cause every conceivable type of fluctuation in farmers' gross income.*
2. *Farm revenue and farm output will vary in the same direction whenever demand for the product is elastic.*
3. *Farm revenue and output will vary in opposite directions whenever demand for the product is inelastic.*
4. *The fluctuations in revenue will be larger the more the elasticity of demand for the product diverges from unity in either direction.*

Evidence on these predictions is fairly abundant. Unplanned fluctuations in supply occur frequently in agriculture. Where the prices of such goods are left to be determined by the free market, large price fluctuations occur. The demand for many agricultural goods is, however, quite inelastic. In these cases, very large price fluctuations occur together with the peculiar situation that when nature is unexpectedly kind and produces a bumper crop, farmers see their incomes dwindling and when nature is moderately unkind and supplies fall unexpectedly, their incomes rise. The interests of the farmer and of the consumer appear to be exactly opposed in such cases.

AGRICULTURAL-STABILIZATION PROGRAMS

In free-market economies, agricultural incomes tend to fluctuate around a low *average* level. Agricultural-stabilization programs have two goals: to reduce the fluctuations and to raise the level of farm incomes. Most countries now operate some sort of scheme to reduce agricultural fluctuations. *Parity,* the notion that farmers' incomes should be raised to the level of the rest of the population's, has been the keynote of U.S. farm policies since the New Deal. The two policies, producing stable incomes and producing reasonably high incomes, can, as we shall see, often conflict.

Figure 8 shows the demand and supply curves for some agricultural product. The supply curve shows planned production at each price and, if production could be planned with certainty, price would settle down at the equilibrium level of *Oa*. Although planned production is at *Ob*, actual production fluctuates around that level, say between the quantities *Oc* and *Od*. In a free market prices will thus fluctuate between *Oe* and *Of*.

One method of preventing these fluctuations in prices and incomes is for the individual farmers to form a producers' association that tries to even out the supply actually coming on to the market, in spite of variations in production.[6] There is no point in an individual farmer holding some of his production off the market in an effort to force up the price. Since one farmer's production is a completely insignificant part of total production, the farmer who sold less would only reduce his income without having any noticeable effect on price. But if all farmers get together and agree to vary the supply coming on to the market, then, collectively, they can have a major effect on price.

Under the conditions depicted in Figure 8,

---

6. Such organizations take many forms, ranging from the producers' cooperatives, (often called co-ops) to the newest national association, the National Farmers' Organization (NFO), which is militant in trying to persuade farmers to join in holding supplies off the market. The American Farm Bureau Federation and the American Farmers' Union are more interested in political than in direct market activities.

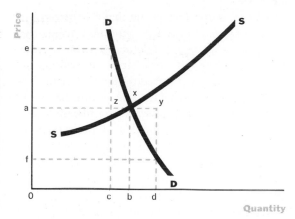

FIGURE 8 **POLICIES DESIGNED TO STABILIZE PRICE IN THE FACE OF UNPLANNED FLUCTUATIONS IN SUPPLY**

a producers' association might be quite successful in keeping the price at *Oa* and incomes at the level indicated by the area of the rectangle *Oaxb*. What would the association's policy have to be? Any excess of production over *Ob* would have to be stored away unsold. If, for example, production for one year were *Od*, then *bd* would have to be added to the association's stocks and *Ob* sold at the price *Oa*. Any deficiency of production below *Ob*, on the other hand, would have to be made good by sales out of the association's stocks. If production were *Oc*, for example, then *cb* would be sold out of stocks, making total sales again equal to *Ob* at a price of *Oa*. In this way the producers' association could keep sales, price, and incomes stabilized in spite of fluctuations in production. Provided that the level of sales to be maintained (*Ob* in Figure 8) were equal to average production, then the policy could be carried on indefinitely. If, on the other hand, an attempt were made to keep the price too high, so that sales were less than the average amount produced, then, over a number of years, additions to stocks would exceed sales from

stocks, and the level of stocks held would tend to increase. The successful policy is the one that keeps sales constant at *Ob* (by adding to, or subtracting from stocks) and, since income accrues to the producers when the goods are actually sold on the market, incomes will be stabilized at *Oaxb*.

What will happen if a producers' association is not formed or is not successful but if the government attempts to stabilize the incomes of farmers by entering the market itself, buying in the open market, adding to its own stocks when there is a surplus, and selling in the open market, thus reducing its stocks, when there is a shortage? If the government wishes to stabilize farmers' incomes, what policy should it adopt? Should it aim, like the producers' association, at keeping prices constant at all times? Before reading on, try to work out the consequences of a government policy designed to keep price fixed at the level *Oa* in Figure 8 by buying goods when production is in excess of *Ob* and by selling goods when production falls short of *Ob*. The government is assumed not to consume any of the commodity but only to hold stocks; thus all its purchases are added to its own stocks and all of its sales are out of these stocks.

If the average level of production around which the year-to-year figure fluctuates is *Ob*, then there is no reason why the government should not successfully stabilize the price at *Oa* indefinitely. This policy would not, however, have the result of stabilizing farmers' incomes. Farmers will now be faced with an infinitely elastic demand at the price *Oa*: Whatever the total quantity produced, they will be able to sell it at the price *Oa*; if the public will not buy all the production, then the government will purchase what is left over. If total production is *Od*, then *Ob* will be bought by the public and *bd* by the government to add to its own stocks. Total farm income in this case will be the amount indicated by the area of the rectangle $Oayd$ (the quantity Od multiplied by the price Oa). If total production in another year is only Oc, then this quantity will be sold by farmers and the government also will sell cb out of its stocks so that price will remain at Oa. Total farm income will then be the amount indicated by the rectangle $Oazc$ (quantity Oc multiplied by the price Oa). It is obvious that if prices are held constant and farmers sell their whole production each year, then farmers' incomes will fluctuate in proportion to fluctuations in production. This government policy, therefore, will not eliminate income fluctuations, but it will reverse their direction. Now bumper crops will be associated with high incomes and small crops with low incomes.

What, then, must the government's policy be if it wishes to stabilize farmers' incomes through its own purchases and sales in the open market? Too much price stability causes incomes to vary directly with production, as in the case just considered, and too little price stability causes incomes to vary inversely with production, as in the free-market case originally considered. It appears that the government should aim at some intermediate degree of price stability. If the government allows prices to vary exactly in proportion to variations in production, then incomes will be stabilized. A 10 percent rise in production should be met by a 10 percent fall in price, and a 10 percent fall in production by a 10 percent rise in price.

The government policy necessary to achieve the requisite price fluctuations is described in Figure 9. The analysis becomes a bit difficult at this stage and you should draw your own graph, building it up step by step as the argument proceeds, using Figure

9 only as a guide. Copy D and S from Figure 9. As before, planned production is Ob, and the price that equates demand with planned production is Oa. Actual production, however, fluctuates between Oc and Od, and these fluctuations, given the very inelastic demand curve D, could cause price to fluctuate between Or and Oi. Now construct through point x (the equilibrium point when actual production is equal to planned production) a curve of unit elasticity throughout its whole range. This constructed curve is the dotted rectangular hyperbola in Figure 9, labeled $\eta = 1$. If Ob is produced and sold at price Oa, total income is that indicated by the rectangle $Oaxb$. The dotted curve now gives us the market price that must rule if production and sales are allowed to vary but income is to be held constant at $Oaxb$.

Consider first what happens if production is Od. Market price must be held at Oj ($= dn$) if income is to be unchanged. But, at market price Oj, the public only wishes to purchase Oq ($= jp$); it is therefore necessary for the government to buy up the remaining production, qd ($= pn$), and add it to its stocks. Farmers' total sales are Od at price Oj, and, since the dotted curve is a rectangular hyperbola, it follows that income $Ojnd$ is equal to income $Oaxb$.

Now consider what must happen if production is equal to Oc. If farm income is to be unchanged, then the price must be allowed to rise to Ot (the area of rectangle $Otkc$ is equal to the area of rectangle $Oaxb$). But at the price Ot, the public will wish to buy Om ($= te$), so that the government must sell cm ($= ke$) out of its stocks.

If this policy is successful, there will be smaller fluctuations in the price of this product than there would be if price were determined on a completely free market. And, also, total income of the producers will be

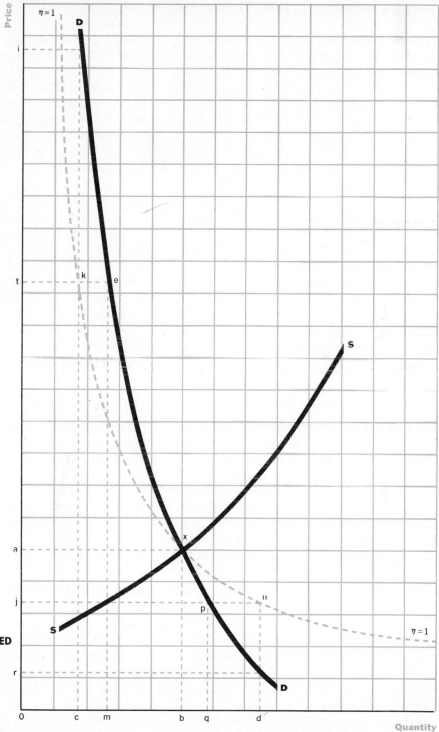

FIGURE 9 GOVERN-
MENT POLICIES DESIGNED
TO STABILIZE INCOME
IN THE FACE OF
UNPLANNED FLUCTUA-
TIONS IN SUPPLY

stabilized in the face of fluctuations in production. Finally, the government scheme should be self-financing. In fact, if we ignore costs of storage, the scheme will show a profit, for the government will be buying at low prices (below Oa)—the lower the price the more it buys—and it will be selling at high prices (above Oa)—the higher the price the more it sells. Whether or not the scheme actually shows a profit will depend on the costs of storing the crops from the periods of glut when they are purchased until the periods of shortage when they are sold. In any case, this scheme has a financial advantage over one in which the government completely stabilizes prices, for, in the latter scheme, there will necessarily be a loss: All purchases and sales will be made at the same price, Oa, leaving no trading profit to set against the costs of storage.

PROBLEMS WITH STABILIZATION POLICIES

The above analysis is meant merely to illustrate the many types of schemes that could be used and to show how, once the details of the schemes are specified, our theory of price can predict the consequences of each scheme. If such schemes have all of the advantages outlined above, why is there so much trouble with most of the government's stabilization schemes? One of the major problems arises from the absence of perfect knowledge, combined with political pressure applied by farmers. Demand and supply curves are never known exactly, so the government does not know what the average production will be over a number of years at various prices. The government does not, therefore, know exactly what level of income it can try to achieve while also keeping sales from stocks approximately equal to purchases for stocks over a large number of years. Farmers can apply strong pressure on any government to fix income at too high a level.[7] If the level of income, and hence price, is fixed too high, then the government will find it necessary to buy unsold crops most of the years and will find only a few years when actual production is low enough for sales to be made out of stocks. In this case, stocks will build up more or less continuously, and the time will come when no more can be stored. When this happens, the stored crops will either have to be destroyed, given away, or dumped on the market for what they will bring, thus forcing the market price down to a very low level. If the crops are thrown on the market and allowed to depress the price, then the original purpose for which the crops were purchased, price stabilization, is defeated. If the crops are destroyed or allowed to decay, then this means that the efforts of a large quantity of the country's scarce factors of production (the land, labor, and capital that went into producing the stored goods) have been completely wasted.[8] Furthermore, the government's plan will now show a deficit, for goods will have been purchased that cannot be sold at all. This deficit will have to be made up by taxation, which means that people in cities will be paying farmers for producing goods that are never consumed.

When schemes get into this sort of difficulty, the next step is often to try to limit the production of each farmer. Quotas may be

---

7. Farmers have (for better or for worse) a degree of political influence out of proportion to their actual numbers, owing to the fact that it takes far fewer rural votes than it does urban ones to elect a member of Congress.

8. The waste is also a vexing moral problem. But if the stored crops are given away or sold to needy countries a political storm often results.

assigned to individual farmers and penalties imposed for exceeding the quotas. Or else, as has been done many times in the past, bonuses may be paid for leaving land idle, for plowing crops under without harvesting them, or for other means of cutting back on production. Such measures attempt to get around the problem that too many resources are allocated to the agricultural sector by preventing these resources from producing all that they are capable of producing. The morality of such measures takes us outside the scope of positive economics, which does not, of course, mean that the student should not pursue the question.[9]

RESOURCES IN AGRICULTURE: THE LONG-PERIOD PROBLEM

Even if the temptation to set too high a price is avoided, there is still a formidable problem waiting to wreck many agricultural-stabilization programs. This problem results from the fact that the productive capacity of almost all economies is growing over time. In the United States, the actual increase in production has averaged about 2 percent per year over the last fifty years. The rise in production has been the result of the increased productivity of the working force, owing to better health, better working conditions, and more and better capital equipment. Workers in most sectors of the economy can produce more per head than they previously did. If the allocation of resources were to remain unchanged, there would be an increase in the production and hence in the supply of each commodity in proportion to the increase in productivity in that industry. If the productivity increases

are spread generally throughout the economy, then the increases in actual production will also be generally spread throughout the economy.

The real incomes of the population will also increase, on the average at a rate equal to the production increase. How will the people wish to consume their extra income? The relevant measure in this case is the income elasticity of demand, which measures the effect of increases in income on the demands for various goods. If, to take the simplest case, all goods have unit-income elasticities of demand, then the proportion in which the various goods are demanded will not change with income, and an x percent rise in income will lead to an x percent rise in the demand for every good. It is known, however, that income elasticities vary considerably among goods, and that most goods tend to have different income elasticities at various levels of income. For example, at the level of income achieved in advanced industrialized countries, many foodstuffs have very low income elasticities, and many manufactured goods have high income elasticities.

Assume that productivity expands more or less uniformly in all industries: The demands for goods with low income elasticities will be expanding slower than the supplies; excess supplies will develop, prices and profits will be depressed, and it will be necessary for resources to move out of these industries. Exactly the reverse will happen for goods with high income elasticities: Demand will expand faster than supply, prices and profits will tend to rise, and resources will move into the industries producing these goods. Table 2 illustrates the point just made. It gives a simple numerical example of an economy

9. There are many excellent introductions to the normative issues in farm policy. The interested student is urged to read one of them. See, for example, D. G. Johnson, *Trade and Agriculture: A Study of Inconsistent Policies* (John Wiley, 1950). He will have little difficulty fitting the institutional material he finds there into the theoretical framework we have suggested.

TABLE 2

	Agriculture	Manufacturing
Production originally was	50	50
Production after productivity change, if there were no reallocation of resources, would be	100	100
Income elasticity of demand is	0.50	1.5
Therefore quantity demanded after rise in income is	75	125
Therefore surplus or shortage is	25 (surplus)	25 (shortage)

divided into an agricultural and a manufacturing sector. Originally, resources are divided equally between the two sectors. Productivity then doubles in both sectors. The incomes of all consumers double and the income elasticity of demand for manufactured goods is higher than the income elasticity of demand for agricultural goods. The rise in productivity causes a surplus equal to one-quarter of the agricultural production, and a shortage equal to one-quarter of the manufactured-goods production. Thus it will be necessary for resources to move out of the agricultural and into the manufacturing industries. Furthermore, if the productivity increases are going on continuously, there will be a *continual tendency* toward excess supply of agricultural goods and excess demand for manufactured goods.

In a free-market economy, this reallocation will take place under the incentives of low prices, wages, and incomes in the declining sector, and high prices, wages, and incomes in the expanding sector. Look at Table 2 again. Because supply exceeds demand in the agricultural sector, prices will fall and incomes of producers will fall. Because too much is being produced there will be a decline in the demand for farm labor and the other factors of production used in agriculture, and the earnings of these factors will decline. At the same time, exactly the opposite tendencies will be observed in manufacturing. Here demand is expanding faster than supply; prices will rise; incomes and profits of producers will be rising; there will be a large demand for the factors of production used in manufacturing industries, so that the price of these factors, and consequently the incomes that they earn, will be bid upward. In short, manufacturing will be a buoyant expanding industry and agriculture will be a depressed and contracting industry.

In a free-market society, the mechanism for a continued reallocation of resources out of low-elasticity industries into high-elasticity ones is a continued depressing tendency on prices and incomes in contracting industries and a continued buoyant tendency on prices and incomes in expanding industries.

Now what is the effect that all this will have on the kind of government stabilization policy considered earlier? Generally, there are two motives behind agricultural-stabilization policies: first, to secure a *stable level* of income, and, second, to provide a *high level* of income. Frequently, in a wealthy community where real incomes are expanding year by year, many feel that the agricultural sector *ought* to share in this prosperity. Stabilization programs often aim at providing the farmer with an income on a parity with incomes earned in the urban sector of the economy.

Positive economics has nothing to say about the ethics of such a policy; it merely tries to discover its consequences. The main problem is that a program that succeeds in giving the rural sector a high level of income may frustrate this reallocation mechanism and, unless some other means of reducing the size of the rural sector is found, the discrepancy between demand and supply will continue to grow until it reaches unmanageable dimensions. If productivity continues to increase in the rural sector while income elasticity of demand for its products is low, then the excess of supply over demand will get larger and larger as time passes. If the government insists on trying to maintain agricultural prices and incomes, it will find that, as time goes by, it is necessary to purchase ever-larger surpluses. If incomes are guaranteed, there will be no monetary incentives for resources to transfer out of the agricultural sector. Unless some other means is found to persuade resources to transfer, then a larger and larger proportion of the resources in the industry will become redundant. If, on the other hand, the government does not intervene at all, leaving the price mechanism to accomplish the resource reallocation, it will be faced with the problem of a more or less permanently depressed sector of the community. The government may not be willing to accept all of the social consequences of leaving this sector to fend for itself.

Do not jump to the conclusion that economics proves that governments ought not to interfere with the price mechanism because the risks are too large. Such a conclusion cannot be *proved;* it is a *judgment,* which depends on a valuation of the gains, losses, and risks of such intervention. Positive economics, by providing some insight into the workings of the price mechanism, can be used to predict some of the consequences of such intervention and thus to point out problems that must be solved in some way or another if the intervention is to be successful. If the problem of reallocating resources out of the rural sector is not solved, then intervention to secure high and stable levels of farm incomes will be unsuccessful over any long period of time. Our notable failure to solve the farm problem is a case in point.

Summary

1. The cases examined in this chapter are intended only as examples of the use of price theory in explaining actual situations.

2. The setting of maximum prices in a competitive market will either have no effect (price set above the equilibrium one) or it will cause a shortage of the commodity and reduce both the price and the quantity bought and sold below their equilibrium values.

3. If the available supply is not rationed by price, it will be rationed by some other method. It may be rationed on a "first-come–first-served" basis or on the basis of "sellers' preferences." Or, the central authorities may intervene by introducing a coupon-rationing scheme with the coupons distributed among potential buyers on the basis of any one of a number of possible criteria.

4. The theory predicts that the potential for a profitable black market exists whenever effective price ceilings are imposed, because it will then pay a group of middlemen to buy at the legal price and sell at the free-market (illegal) price.

5. The setting of minimum prices in competitive markets will either have no effect (the minimum price set below the equilibrium price) or it will cause a surplus of the commodity with the actual price being above the equilibrium level but the actual quantity bought and sold being below it. In this case, producers will have an incentive to sell at a black-market price, but there will be no incentive for a group of middlemen to buy at the legal price and sell at the free-market price.

6. The effect of a tax on a commodity produced under competitive conditions is to shift the supply curve upward by the amount of the tax. The theory predicts that the imposition of a tax will raise the price paid by consumers and lower the price received by producers in each case by less than the amount of the tax. The more inelastic the demand curve and the more elastic the supply curve, the greater the proportion of the tax that is paid by consumers in higher prices.

8. One aspect of the farm problem is the tendency for prices and incomes to fluctuate due to unplanned variations in supply. If the demand is inelastic, supply and farm incomes fluctuate in opposite directions. The lower the elasticity of demand, the larger the fluctuations in prices and incomes for given fluctuations in supply.

9. A second aspect of the farm problem is the attempt to secure for farmers a level of income that is comparable with incomes in other sectors of the economy. But the low income elasticity of demand for most farm products together with the high rates of growth of productivity in farm production is working against the farmer. The continuing downward pressure of relative farm prices and incomes is a mechanism for reallocating resources in a free-market society out of low income elasticity industries into high ones. There is no easy solution to the "farm problem."

QUESTIONS FOR DISCUSSION

1. "The very success of the OPA [Office of Price Administration] in regulating rents has therefore contributed greatly to the demand for housing, and hence to the shortage, for housing is cheap relative to other things." (From Milton Friedman and George Stigler, *Roofs or Ceilings? The Current Housing Problem*, 1946.)

Interpret this statement and draw a diagram to illustrate the situation. In what sense is it correct to say that rent control actually contributes to a housing shortage? In what sense is it misleading? Does it follow logically that because there are abuses of price controls we should never use such devices?

2. Consider the following statement made by a gasoline dealer in World War II: "If we did do away with it [rationing and price control] we would stop the black market; therefore, we should do away with it." Are the man's statements correct? What do you think about his appreciation of the problem, considering that U.S. troops were consuming 25 million gallons of gasoline per day?

3. In wartime Britain, the submarine campaign reduced the imports of eggs to an average of one egg per person per week. What would have been the consequences if the price system had been allowed to allocate the available supply among the potential consumers? Why do you think the government decided to ration eggs (and all other scarce commodities) instead?

4. "Since the demand for these exceeds the supply, applications should be made well in advance." This is from a university catalogue's description of married students' quarters. Comment on the allocative system being used by the university authorities.

5. What effect would the payment of a subsidy of so many dollars per unit produced have on the price and quantity in a competitive market? Under what circumstances would the subsidy be passed on fully to the consumer in terms of lower prices? Under what circumstances would the whole subsidy be appropriated by the producers? Is the subsidy more likely to lower the price paid by the consumer if the demand is elastic or inelastic and if the supply is elastic or inelastic?

6. "The success of American agriculture has benefitted everyone but the farmer." Explain the background of this quotation from the 1965 *Congressional Joint Economic Report* in the light of what you have learned in this chapter.

Chapter **12** ELEMENTS OF DYNAMICS

IT TAKES FIVE YEARS FOR A NEWLY PLANTED rubber tree to reach maturity and to begin to yield latex. It takes five months for a newly hatched chicken to reach maturity and to begin to produce eggs. It takes time before the production of any commodity can be increased, and the time required varies greatly from one commodity to another. Does it matter?

The first thing to notice is that there is a gap in time between the decision to produce more of a commodity and the actual increase in production. The length of this gap will depend on a number of factors, but the two most important are the extent to which there is any productive capacity that is not being used at the moment, and the time that it takes to expand productive capacity. If the owner of a rubber plantation wishes to produce more rubber in response, say, to a rise in the market price of rubber, he will be able to increase actual production fairly rapidly if there exist stocks of mature trees not now being tapped for raw rubber. But once such stocks of unused capacity are utilized (and often they will not exist at all) then it will take at least five years before the desire to change production is translated into an actuality. The gap between a change in the desire to produce goods and a change in actual production is called a *supply lag*.

Every commodity has its own characteristic, and often quite complex, supply lag. For example, farmers can meet an increase in the demand for milk to some extent almost immediately by not throwing away skimmed milk, to a greater extent within twenty-seven months by not slaughtering calves at birth but waiting until they reach maturity and produce milk, and to an ever-increasing extent as the larger number of adult cows gives birth to a larger number of calves. First, therefore, producers stop wasting existing supplies; second, they lower the slaughter rate among newly borne calves; and, finally, they increase the total number of births once there has been an increase in the total number of mature cows.

Statics and Dynamics

Before we inquire further into the importance of the supply lag, we should note that, up to now in our study of economics, we have ignored it. We must now look more critically at the method we employed in previous chapters. The theory of taxes provides an example of this method. (Refer back to Figure 5 in Chapter 11.) A tax on a commodity shifts the supply curve vertically upward by the amount of the tax. The new equilibrium price is above the old one, but not by the full amount of the tax. This theory thus produces the predictions that the effect of a tax is to raise the unit price paid by consumers by less than the full amount of the tax, and to lower the unit price received by producers, again by less than the full amount of the tax.

These conclusions refer to a comparison of the new equilibrium position, y, with the original equilibrium position, x. This is the method of analysis we used in all chapters heretofore. Suppose we wish to form an hypothesis about the effect of some change in the data, the introduction, for example, of a tax or a change in the conditions of demand. We start from a position of equilibrium and then introduce the change to be studied. The new equilibrium position is determined and it is compared with the original one. The differences between the two positions of equilibrium must be due to the changes in the data that were introduced. This analysis, which is based on a comparison of two positions of equilibrium, is called *comparative static equilibrium analysis*. This rather cumbersome expression is usually abbreviated to *comparative statics*.

Theories based upon comparative statics will be of most interest if our concern is with predicting where a market will settle down after all the effects of some change have been worked out. Since, in an ever-changing world, such a final settling down will never be observable, it might appear that comparative statics is useless, but this is not the case. If, in response to some change, the relevant variables move in the direction of their equilibrium values (in what has been called "pursuit of equilibrium"), then statements such as "in response to an increase in demand, price will rise" will be predictions and will be testable. Further, in comparing two different situations, such as two industries with different demand elasticities, it is not necessary that the two industries actually be in equilibrium, but only that they do not depart from it in a systematic manner.[1] Comparative statics thus has a substantial range of relevance. *What it can never do* is to give us any information about how the variables will behave as they move from one position of equilibrium to (or toward) another. We might wish to predict, for example, how price and output of rubber would change from *year to year* in response to a change in demand in a situation in which the final equilibrium could not be reached until ten or fifteen years after the original demand shift occurred. In such cases, as we shall see

1. Our theories, it will be recalled, have "error terms." One reason for this error is a departure from equilibrium. If these errors are not systematic the procedures of statistical analysis permit us to test the validity of the hypothesis that the two situations differ from one another in the manner predicted by the static predictions of the theory.

in a moment, the market may never settle down in a position of equilibrium, and, in these cases, our predictions derived from static-equilibrium theory are very likely to be contradicted by the actual behavior of the market.

In summary we can say that, although theories based on the technique of comparative static analysis are adequate for dealing with many problems, they cannot be used to handle two important classes of problems. First, they cannot be used to predict the path that the market will follow when moving from one equilibrium to another, and, second, they cannot predict whether or not a given equilibrium position will ever be attained. Indeed, when an equilibrium is not attained, predictions based on the assumption that it will be are likely to turn out to be empirically false.

For purposes of studying behavior in situations other than equilibrium, we use *dynamic analysis,* which may be defined as the study of the behavior of systems, single markets or whole economies, in disequilibrium situations.

Market Fluctuations

In Chapter 6 we discussed in an intuitive fashion the effect of an increase in the demand for Brussels sprouts. In Chapter 9 we were able to formalize some of this discussion in terms of the theory of equilibrium price. (Reread the discussion on page 93 before reading on.) We were not able, however, to formalize the discussion of the movement between the initial and the final equilibrium because we did not have a dynamic theory. Let us consider this problem in more detail, with reference to Figure 1.

The rise in the demand for Brussels sprouts raises the equilibrium price from Oe to Ov and the equilibrium quantity bought and sold from Oa to Oc. What happens when supply reacts to price with a time lag? When the original increase in demand occurs it may not be possible to produce any more sprouts until another crop can be raised. In the intervening period, the whole effect of the rise in demand will have to be taken out in a price increase. If supply continues to come on the market at a rate of Oa while the demand rises from D_1 to D_2, then the price will rise to Of.

This is the price that equates the new demand to the unchanged supply. If price reacts quickly it may rise to Of within a week or two after the rise in demand and stay there until more sprouts can be raised. But at the price Of farmers would like to produce and sell Ob sprouts. They may well plan to produce at that rate instead of at the equilibrium rate, Oc—indeed, there is as yet no

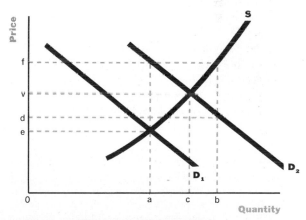

FIGURE 1   **SUPPLY REACTS TO PRICE WITH A TIME LAG**

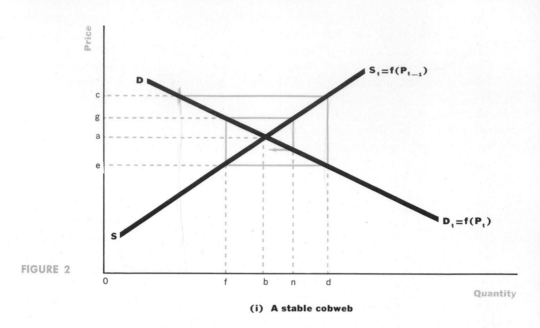

FIGURE 2

(i) A stable cobweb

signal to tell them that Oc is the "correct" rate at which to produce. If, when the newly planted sprouts reach maturity, the rate of production suddenly expands to Ob, then price will fall drastically. Indeed, the price that will clear the market is now Od. But this will lead after a lag to a contraction in supply. At this point we may well begin to wonder whether the market will ever reach equilibrium.

The Cobweb

We shall now introduce an elementary dynamic theory that accounts for some of the aspects of behavior observed above. In this theory, we assume that producers' output plans are fulfilled, but with a time lag, and we show how *planned* changes in supply can give rise to oscillations in market behavior.[2]

All supply decisions take time to implement, so that supply coming onto the market at any one time is always the result of decisions made in the past, whereas decisions made about production in the present always have their effect on the actual supply coming forward to the market only at some time in the future. In cases in which the time lag is short, it can often be successfully ignored, but in many cases in which the lag is longer it is of critical importance. In order to study the ideas of dynamic theory, we introduce only the simplest possible time lag, but even

2. In Chapter 11, we applied comparative-static analysis to a very simple case of agricultural-price fluctuations. In that example we assumed that planned supply did not change and that the price fluctuations were caused by unplanned exogenous changes in supply.

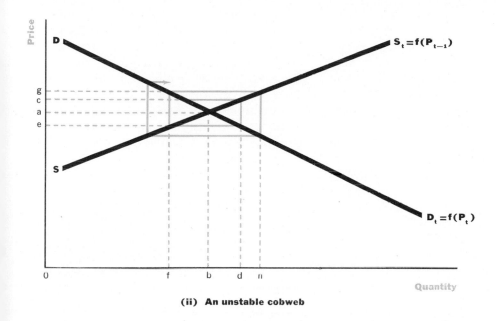

(ii) An unstable cobweb

this will be quite sufficient to cause us a lot of trouble! This simple time lag is one in which this year's price has no effect whatsoever on this year's supply, and in which the full adjustment to this year's price is made all at once next year.[3]

Farmers look to the existing market price when deciding what crops to plant this year, and thus next year's supply depends on this year's price and this year's supply depends on last year's price.†

Such lags are typical of agricultural products, such as wheat, oats, and barley, that give one crop annually.

A market subject to such a simple one-year time lag is illustrated in Figure 2 (i). The demand curve shows the relation between the price ruling in any year and the quantity that will be demanded in the same year; the supply curve shows the relation between the price ruling in any one year and the supply that will come onto the market in the following year. The price that equates demand and supply is Oa. At this price, Ob units will be produced and sold.

What will happen if this equilibrium is disturbed? If in one year, year t, the price is Oc, farmers will plan to produce Od in the following year. In that year (year $t + 1$) Od will come on the market, and, in order that Od

---

3. In this case we say the time lag is a *one-period lag;* if it takes several periods (years in this case) for the full supply reaction to a single price change to occur, we say the time lag is a *distributed* one (i.e., it is spread over time).

† In the terminology of the appendix to Chapter 3 (page 39), $S_t = f(p_{t-1})$, which is read supply at time period t depends on the price of the product ruling in the previous time period, $t - 1$, where time periods are measured in years.

may be sold, the price must fall to *Oe*. The price of *Oe* will induce farmers to produce the quantity *Of*. When this quantity comes on the market in the following year, year *t* + 2, the price will rise to *Og*. This price will call forth a supply of *On* the next year, year *t* + 3, and this will depress the price below *Og*. It is clear from this that, in the market described by Figure 2 (i), the price and quantity will oscillate around their equilibrium values in a series of diminishing fluctuations, so that, if nothing further disturbs the market, price and quantity will eventually approach their equilibrium levels.

In Figure 2 (ii) exactly the same argument applies as the one given in the previous paragraph. Reread that paragraph for a description of the process in this market. Note that the oscillations get larger and larger so that the equilibrium is never restored.

The market in Figure 2 (i) has a *stable* adjustment mechanism, whereas that in Figure 2 (ii) has an *unstable* adjustment mechanism. A stable equilibrium is one that will be restored if it is disturbed; thus the actual price and quantity will tend toward their equilibrium levels. An unstable equilibrium is one that will not be restored if it is disturbed; thus the actual price and quantity will tend away from their equilibrium levels.

What is the difference between these two markets that makes one stable and the other unstable? Try to answer this question before reading further. The difference between the two markets is in the relation between the slopes of the demand and the supply curves. In Figure 2 (i) the demand curve is flatter than the supply curve. The absolute quantity demanded changes more as price changes than does the absolute quantity supplied. Any

excess demand or supply can be eliminated with only a small price change, and the price change in turn causes only a very small change in supply in the following year, and hence the supply change has only a small effect on next year's price. In Figure 2 (ii) the supply curve is flatter than the demand curve: The *quantity* supplied responds more to price changes than does the *quantity* demanded. When there is excess supply, a large price fall is necessary to call forth the required demand. This price fall causes a large reduction in next year's supply (because supply is very responsive to price). Next year there is a large shortage, and a very big price increase is necessary to reduce demand to the level of the available supply. This price rise causes a very large increase in supply in the following year; so we go on in a series of alternating periods of ever-increasing surplus and shortage.[4]

In the case of the unstable equilibrium, the oscillations get bigger and bigger. There is nothing in our theory so far to prevent these oscillations from becoming infinitely large. In practice, however, we should not expect this to happen; we should expect that the oscillations would tend to reach limits. A full theory of such a market would require an analysis of these limits.

What we have established is that, in the unstable case, the operation of the competitive price system does not tend to remove any disequilibrium; it tends rather to accentuate it.

The cobweb model in Figure 2 is a very simple one in which supply plans are always fulfilled (actual supply equals planned supply), planned supply in one year depends

---

4. This argument is, of course, only an intuitive one. Mathematical analysis, however, easily shows that the market is in fact stable if the supply curve is steeper than the demand curve and unstable if the supply curve is flatter than the demand curve.

solely on the price ruling in the previous year, and the market price is always such as to equate current demand and current supply. It is evident that more interesting and complex models would arise if we allowed actual supply to deviate from planned supply due to such uncontrollable factors as weather conditions; if we allowed for a time lag in the adjustment of *price* to the state of excess demand; if we allowed the actual response of supply to a change in price to be more complex—the response thereby occurring gradually over several time periods; or if we allowed for some form of learning process on the part of farmers so that planned supply would not depend solely on past prices but also on what farmers expected to happen in the future. Situations of this sort become quite complex and they cannot be handled without the help of mathematical analysis, and therefore we omit them in this book. The simple cobweb model in Figure 2 introduces dynamic theory, illustrates its importance in providing theoretical explanations of fluctuations in prices and quantities, and emphasizes that there may be problems for which a satisfactory explanation cannot be found in static theory.

Summary

1. In previous chapters, we ignored the possibility of a supply lag—a gap, that is, between a change in the desire to produce goods and a change in actual production. In order to consider such questions, we must use dynamic analysis, which is the study of the behavior of systems in disequilibrium situations.

2. In one of the simplest dynamic theories of market fluctuations, we assume that producer's output plans are fulfilled, but with a time lag, and we show how planned changes in supply can give rise to oscillations in market behavior. We assume a simple time lag such as occurs when farmers look to this year's price in deciding what crops to plant next year. Demand, however, depends on this year's price.

3. If the market is in equilibrium, the supply coming onto the market will be the same from one year to the next, and the market price will be such that people will just be willing to purchase the available supply. What will happen if the equilibrium is disturbed? If the price rises above the equilibrium value in any one year, planned production will rise and next year's supply will be greater than this year's. As a result, price will fall. Because of this price reduction, plantings will be reduced and, the following year, supply will fall and price will rise. This will lead to an increase in supply in the following year, and so on.

4. A market is stable if these fluctuations diminish so that the actual price approaches the equilibrium one. A market is unstable if these fluctuations increase so that there is no tendency for the actual price to approach the equilibrium one. We call this a simple cobweb model; it is just one example of a dynamic model, but it shows that there are some problems that static theory cannot handle.

QUESTIONS FOR DISCUSSION

1. What is the difference between static and dynamic analysis? What are some of the limitations of statics?

2. What do we assume in a simple cobweb model?

3. Draw a graph from the following equations:

$$D_t = 100 - 6p_t$$
$$S_t = 4p_{t-1},$$

where S and D are supply and demand and where the subscripts t refer to time periods. Is the system stable or unstable? Formulate a different demand equation that would change your conclusion.

4. What would happen in a cobweb model if both the demand and supply curves had the same slopes, but were opposite in sign?

DEMAND

Chapter **13** THE THEORY OF HOUSEHOLD BEHAVIOR

IS THE EFFECT ON A HOUSEHOLD'S CONSUMPtion different if its income rises than if the prices it pays for goods fall? Does an increase in the general level of prices hurt everybody? Does it hurt anybody? Can we predict the effect of changes in relative prices on households' behavior? To answer these and other similar questions, we must go behind the market demand curve, whose determinants we studied in Chapter 7, to look at the millions of independent decision units whose aggregate behavior is summarized in that curve.

In this chapter we consider the different effects on a household's consumption of changes in relative prices, absolute prices, and incomes. In the appendix to the chapter we go from a theory of rational household behavior to a theory of the demand curve of a single product and then to a theory of the market demand for a product.

The Household

The basic decision unit in our theory is the household. In Chapter 7 we defined the household as "all the people who live under one roof and who make, or are subject to others making for them, joint financial decisions." What this amounts to is an hypothesis that the household can be treated as a single unit and that it follows a set of consistent rules for decision-making that are independent of who actually makes the decision within the household. We are thus abstracting from many of the problems within a household; as with other theories, the test of the "validity" of these abstractions is whether or not they help us to construct a theory that proves useful empirically.

Our main purpose in this chapter is to distinguish between the effects on households' expenditures of changes in incomes, relative prices, and absolute prices. We shall consider a single household faced with the choice between only two goods, X and Y.[1] In Figure 1 the quantity of good X is measured on the horizontal axis and the quantity of Y is measured on the vertical axis. Any point on this graph represents a combination of the two goods. Point α, for example, represents 40 units of X and 60 units of Y.

THE BUDGET LINE

We now construct a *budget line,* which shows all those combinations of the goods that are just obtainable, given the household's income and the prices of the two commodities. Assume, for example, that the household's income is $120 per month, that the price of Y is $2 per unit, and the price of X is $4. What combinations of X and Y are open to the household? First, it could spend all its money on Y, obtaining each month 60Y and no X (this combination is indicated by Point a on the figure). It could also buy 30X and no Y (Point b on the figure). Other combina-

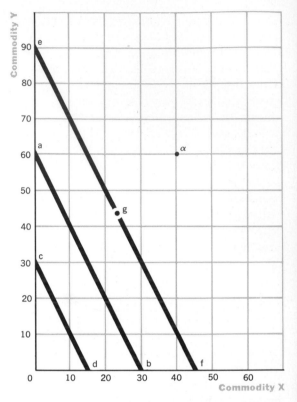

FIGURE 1   CHANGES IN THE CONSUMER'S INCOME CAUSE CHANGES IN HIS BUDGET LINE

tions open to it are 58Y and 1X, 56Y and 2X, 54Y and 3X; in fact, since X costs twice as much per unit as Y, the household must give up 2Y in order to obtain one more X. In the language of Chapter 1, the *opportunity cost of X is 2Y.* All the possible combinations of X and Y open to the household are shown by the straight line *ab* in Figure 1. Pick a few points on this budget line and check that they indicate combinations of X and Y that exactly exhaust the household's income. Check a few

1. The choice between two goods is sufficient to display most of the problems in which we are interested in this chapter. The argument can be generalized to any number of goods, but graphical analysis can then no longer be applied and some quite difficult mathematics is required. A numerical illustration is used in Figure 1 to make the argument easier to follow.

points between *ab* and the origin (e.g., the point 20Y and 10X) to see that they fail to exhaust the household's income. Finally, check that points above the line *ab* (e.g., 50X and 20Y) represent combinations for the two goods that the household cannot buy, given the existing prices and its income.

It is assumed that these goods are the only ones available to the household and that the household will be on its budget line and never inside it, because, unless the wants of its members are totally satiated, the members will always prefer more goods to fewer goods. It is also assumed, for purposes of the present argument, that there is no saving.[2]

CHANGES IN INCOME

What happens to the budget line when income and prices change? If, for example, the household's income is halved from $120 to $60 per month, prices being unchanged, then the amount of goods it can buy will also be halved. If it spends all its income on Y, it will now get 30Y and no X (Point *c*); if it spends all its income on X, it will get 15X and no Y (Point *d*). All possible combinations open to the household appear on budget line *cd*. Note that this line is parallel to budget line *ab*, but closer to the origin. Since prices are unchanged, the household must still give up 2Y for every additional X it wishes to purchase. The slope of the line indicates this opportunity cost, for it shows how much Y must be given up to get another unit of X. The fact that *ab* and *cd* both have the same slope indicates that the opportunity cost of X in terms of Y is the same in both situations.

If the household's income rises to $180, it will be able to buy more of both commodities than it could previously. If it buys only Y

it can now have 90Y (Point *e*); if it buys only X it can have 45X (Point *f*); if it divides its income equally between the two goods it can have 45Y and 22½X (Point *g*). All the combinations of X and Y now available to the household appear on budget line *ef*.

We conclude that variations in the household's income, with prices constant, shift the budget line parallel to itself, inward toward the origin when income falls, and outward away from the origin when income rises. Draw your own figure and sketch on it budget lines for incomes of $100 and $40 per month.

CHANGES IN PRICES

What happens when prices change? Line *ef* in Figure 2, which is the same line *ef* that we discussed in connection with Figure 1, is based on an income of $180, a price of X of $4, and a price of Y of $2. Now assume that the price of Y remains unchanged while the price of X changes. Say, for example, that X falls from $4 to $2. The household can now buy either 90X, if it devotes its whole income to that commodity, or 90Y, if it purchases only Y. The combinations available to the household appear on budget line *eh*. Check a few points on this line to see that the combinations of X and Y indicated exactly exhaust the household's income of $180 when X and Y are both priced at $2.

Now assume that the price of X falls to $1, the price of Y remaining constant at $2. The new budget line indicating all the combinations available to the household is *ei*. A comparison of budget lines *ef*, *eh*, and *ei* shows that changing one money price changes the *slope* of the budget line; the lower the price of X, the flatter the budget line.

2. Saving could be made one of our variables, X or Y, in which case it would appear on one of the axes.

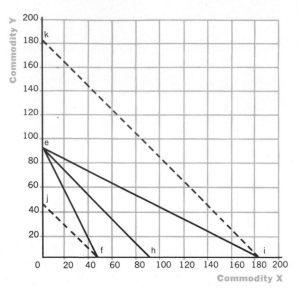

FIGURE 2   **CHANGES IN PRICE CAUSE CHANGES IN THE BUDGET LINE**

Now let us try changing both prices in the same proportion. If we start from budget line *eh* (income $180, X and Y priced at $2) and double both prices then we will halve the amount of both goods that the consumer can purchase. The budget line now becomes *jf*, because the income of $180 will now buy 45Y and no X, 45X and no Y, or any combination of X and Y on the straight line joining these two points.

Now let us go back to line *eh* ($180 income and a $2 price for X and Y) and halve *both prices*. The consumer can now have twice as much of both commodities as previously and the budget line moves outward to *ki*.

We notice that changing both prices in the same proportion shifts the budget line parallel to itself in the same way as an income change shifted it. Before reading further, go back to Figure 1, take budget line *ab* (income = $120, Y = $2, and X = $4), and determine what *price changes* would shift the budget line to *cd* and to *ef*.

RELATIVE PRICES AND OPPORTUNITY COSTS

The reason why changing both prices in the same proportion shifts the budget line parallel to itself is that the slope of the budget line indicates the opportunity cost of one commodity in terms of the other. An equal proportionate change in both prices leaves this opportunity cost unchanged. For example, if Y costs $2 and X costs $4 then 2Y must be given up in order to get 1X; if Y costs $4 and X costs $8 it is still necessary to give up 2Y to get 1X. In fact, as long as the price of X is twice the price of Y, it will be necessary to forego two Y in order to obtain one more X. More generally, the amount of Y that must be given up to obtain another unit of X depends only on *the relation between the price of* Y *and the price of* X. If we take the money price of X and divide it by the money price of Y we have the opportunity cost of X in terms of Y (the quantity of Y that must be given up to get one more X). This may be written:

$$\frac{p_x}{p_y} = \text{opportunity cost of X in terms of Y,}$$

where p_x and p_y are the money prices of X and Y. It is apparent that changing both prices in the same proportion leaves the ratio p_x/p_y unchanged. In economics, this ratio is called a *relative price*, which is the term used when any price is expressed as a ratio of another price. Relative prices are to be distinguished from money prices, which are called *absolute prices*. For example, if we say that the price of X is $2 we are speaking of an absolute price; if we say that the price of X is twice the price of Y, we are speaking of a relative price. This one relative price ($p_x = 2p_y$) is consistent with an infinite number of absolute prices as long as the absolute price of X is twice that of Y: for instance, $p_y = \$1$ and $p_x = \$2$ satisfy the equation as does $p_y = \$10$ and $p_x = \$20$.

Conclusions from the Analysis

We have now reached a number of conclusions that are of extreme importance for demand theory. Reread this chapter if you cannot prove them for yourself.

1. A change in money income with money prices (and thus necessarily relative prices) constant shifts the budget line parallel to itself, inward toward the origin when income falls and outward away from the origin when income rises.

2. An equal percentage change in all absolute prices leaves relative prices unchanged, and, if money income remains unchanged, it will shift the budget line parallel to itself, inward toward the origin when prices rise and outward away from the origin when prices fall.

3. Multiplying all money prices by the same constant, λ, while holding money income constant, has exactly the same effect on the budget line as multiplying money income by $1/\lambda$, while holding money prices constant. For example, doubling all money prices has the same effect on the budget line as halving money income.

4. A change in relative prices causes the budget line to change its slope.

5. An equal percentage change in all absolute prices combined with a percentage change in income of the same magnitude, and in the same direction as the price change, leaves the budget line exactly where it was before the changes occurred.

All of these conclusions except the last one were illustrated in Figures 1 and 2.

As an illustration of conclusion 5, consider the budget line *eh* in Figure 2. This budget line was originally obtained from an income of $180 with prices of $2 for both X and Y. What will happen if the household's income doubles to $360? The budget line will shift to *ki*, since the household can buy twice as many units of both commodities as it could previously. But what if prices double from $2 to $4? This cuts the household's consumption possibilities in half, and it is back with budget line *eh*. (A few numerical calculations will verify that $180 with a $2 price for X and Y can buy exactly the same combinations of goods as can $360 with a $4 price for both commodities.)

Predictions from the Analysis

The five conclusions listed above are matters of logic. The effects of various changes on the budget line are incontrovertible. In order to translate these conclusions into predictions about household behavior, we advance the hypothesis that household's market behavior depends solely on the tastes of the members of the household and on the location of the household's budget line. Another way of wording this hypothesis is to say that the household's behavior depends on *real* rather than on money variables. This behavioral hypothesis along with the five propositions above will allow us to make testable predictions about the behavior of households. Conclusion 3 leads us to the following prediction:

The change in a household's market behavior will be the same if either its income changes by λ or if all money prices change by 1/λ.

And Conclusion 5 leads us to predict that:

The household's market behavior will be unaffected if its money income and all money prices change simultaneously by some multiple λ.

Strictly speaking, these predictions apply only to households that do not have any significant quantity of bonds, cash, or other assets whose value is fixed in money units and whose real value thus changes when money prices change. The extension of demand theory to cases in which households have assets is difficult, and properly belongs in a more advanced text. In the meantime, we note that the above predictions apply to those households for which currently earned income is the main determinant of current expenditure. We should also note that the great majority of all households fall in this class.

Real and Money Income

We can now make the important distinction between *real income* and *money income*. Money income measures a household's income in terms of some monetary unit, so many dollars or so many pounds sterling; real income measures a household's income in terms of the command over commodities that the money income confers. A rise in money income of x percent combined with an x percent rise in all money prices leaves a household's ability to buy commodities, and hence its real income, unchanged. When we speak of the real value of a certain amount of money, we are referring to the goods and services that can be bought with the money; we are referring, that is, to the *purchasing power* of the money.

ALLOCATION OF RESOURCES: THE IMPORTANCE OF RELATIVE PRICES

Our theory of price predicts that the allocation of resources depends on the structure of *relative prices*. If the money value of all prices, incomes, debts, and credits were doubled, there would, according to our theory, be little noticeable effect. The economy would function as before, the same set of relative prices and real incomes would exist, and there would be no incentive for any reallocation of resources; the only difference would be that the money level of all prices and incomes would be doubled.

This prediction is an implication of our theories of the behavior of households and of firms. We have already seen that doubling money prices and money incomes leaves the household's budget line unchanged and so, according to the theory of household behavior, it gives its members no incentive to vary their purchases. As far as the producer is concerned, if all prices—both of final goods and of factors of production—double, then the relative profitability of different lines of production will be unaffected, as indeed will the real level of profits in all lines of production.[3] Thus producers will have no incentive

3. Since all prices and costs will have doubled, money profits will have doubled, but the purchasing power of these profits will be just what it was before the change occurred.

to alter production rates so as to produce more of some things and less of others.

If, on the other hand, relative prices change, then our theory predicts that resources will be reallocated. Households will buy more of the cheaper goods and less of the expensive ones, and producers will expand production of those goods whose prices have risen relatively and contract production of those goods whose relative prices have fallen (since they would be less profitable lines of production).

The theory of prices and of resource allocation that we have developed so far is thus a theory of relative, not of absolute, prices.

INFLATION AND DEFLATION: THE IMPORTANCE OF ABSOLUTE PRICES

The average level of money prices is called the *price level*. If all money prices double, we say that the price level has doubled. An increase in the price level is called an *inflation;* a decrease is called a *deflation*. If a rise in all money prices and incomes has little or no effect on the allocation of resources, it may seem surprising that so much concern is expressed over inflation. Clearly, a person who spends all of his income, and whose money income goes up at the same rate as money prices go up, loses nothing from inflation. His real income is unaffected. One of the problems of inflation, however, is that some incomes, such as annuities and pensions, are fixed in dollar terms, and many contractual obligations, such as bonds, mortgages, and life insurance, are stated in money terms. A patriotic American who bought a Series E Defense Bond from the U.S. Government in 1940 for $75 may have been pleased to receive $100 in 1950 when he cashed it in. But this $100 only bought him goods worth $58.23 in 1940 prices. A widow who raised and educated a family on an annuity of $200 a month during the 1930s has great difficulty living alone on the same annuity in the 1960s.

Let us examine this point more carefully: Assume that A borrows $100 from B. The lender, B, is giving up command over a certain quantity of goods and passing this over to A. If the price level then doubles, A will still have to repay $100 to B, but this $100 will purchase only half as many goods when it is repaid as it would have when it was borrowed. Thus B receives back from A money sufficient to buy only half as many goods as he could have bought with the money he originally lent to A. Inflation thus lowers the real value of all debts—that is, it reduces the quantity of goods and services that can be purchased with the money. The person who has borrowed money gains from inflation because the sacrifice in terms of goods and services in repaying the debt is reduced, whereas the person who has loaned money loses because the real value of the money returned is less than the real value of the money originally given up. By the same token, anyone who saves money, buys ordinary life insurance, or in any other way disposes of his savings so that he gets a certain money return, loses by inflation. An inflation of 3 percent per year will reduce the purchasing power of a sum of money to one-half its original amount in 23.5 years. Thus one of the effects of inflation is to reduce the real value of all debts, savings, and fixed money incomes.

A second consequence of inflation arises from the fact that all adjustments do not take place instantaneously. If the price level were to double, most money incomes would probably double eventually, so that the real value of all incomes would be restored to their original level. In the process, however, some groups will manage to increase their incomes quickly, whereas other groups will increase theirs only slowly. In a state of continuous inflation, those groups whose money incomes rise quickly gain at the expense of those whose money incomes rise only slowly.

The theory of the determination of the absolute price level is discussed in Chapter 55 of Part X.

Summary

A household's consumption behavior is hypothesized to depend upon its money income and the prices of goods it buys. A change in either of these will change its consumption possibilities as represented by its budget line. Lower prices and higher incomes are to some extent equivalent for the household, and they shift the budget line in identical ways as long as relative prices remain constant. If relative prices change, the budget line changes slope, and there is no income change that is equivalent.

The significance of changes in absolute prices is the different ways in which they affect different households. In an inflation, those with fixed incomes, those who are lenders, and those who find their income rising more slowly than the price level will be worse off than those who are borrowers and those who have incomes rising more rapidly than the price level. Reverse results occur in periods of deflation. Inflation and deflation thus lead to a redistribution of income among households in the economy.

QUESTIONS FOR DISCUSSION

1. Draw a budget line for a teenager whose total consumption out of her allowance is for cokes and records. Cokes cost 10¢ each, records cost 75¢, and her allowance is $4.50 a week. Draw a new budget line illustrating what happens when the price of cokes increases to 15¢. Assume that her allowance is cut to $3. Draw her new budget line and determine what price increases would have had the same effect as the cut in her allowance.

2. Explain why an increase in money income shifts the budget line outward and an increase in prices shifts it inward.

3. What is the significance of the slope of the budget line?

4. If money incomes rise, and absolute prices rise as well but more slowly than money incomes are rising, what happens to real income?

5. Bill and Ben each have $100 and each plan to buy a tent and a sleeping bag for a camping trip they intend to take next month. The price of the tent is $60 and the price of the sleeping bag is $20. Bill buys his equipment now and stores it in the basement. Ben keeps his money in the bank, but when he goes to buy his equipment in a month's time he finds that prices have changed. The price of the tent has gone up to $66 and the price of the sleeping bag has gone up to $22. Who is better off, Bill or Ben? Which of the boys would have been better off if the price of the sleeping bag had gone up to

$24, but if the price of the tent had fallen to $52? If the price of the sleeping bag has risen to $30 and the price of the tent has fallen to $50, which of them is better off? Who is better off if the price of the sleeping bag has fallen to $18 and the price of the tent to $48? Would you advise people to hold money or goods if you thought an inflation was imminent? What would you advise them to do if you thought a deflation was imminent?

APPENDIX TO CHAPTER 13 HOUSEHOLD AND MARKET DEMAND CURVES

FROM THE THEORY DEVELOPED in Chapter 13, we can derive implications about the slope of the demand curve for the individual household.

The Income and the Substitution Effect

We have distinguished three causes of changes in the budget line: changes in absolute prices, changes in relative prices, and changes in incomes. We have also seen that the effect of the changes can all be reduced to some combination of a change in the slope of the budget line and a parallel shifting of the budget line. This suggests that we try to split up all changes in the budget line into two pure changes: a real income change that is a parallel shift of the line without any change in slope, and a relative price change that is a change of slope without any shifting of the budget line. We do this in order to measure the effects of each of these changes on household behavior. This then allows us to predict the outcome of changes in incomes, absolute prices, and relative prices.

Assume we have a household whose initial budget line is *ab* in Figure A1. Assume that, initially, this household chooses the combination indicated by Point $a(Ov$ of Y and Os of $X)$. Now assume that the price of X falls, the money price of Y and the household's income remaining constant. The new set of possibilities open to the household is indicated by the budget line *ac*. Assume that it now chooses the combination $\beta(Ot$ of Y and Ou of $X)$ from all of those available to it. More of both X and Y are consumed.

This fall in the price of X has something of the same effect as a change in income, because it makes it possible for the household, if it so wishes, to have more of all commodities. In Figure A1, the price fall makes the total shaded area newly available to the consumer; combinations indicated by points within this area were not available at the original set of prices. Points within Area 1 indicate newly available com-

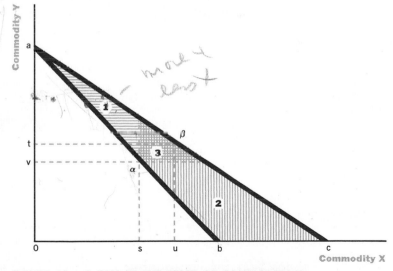

FIGURE A1   A FALL IN THE PRICE OF COMMODITY X

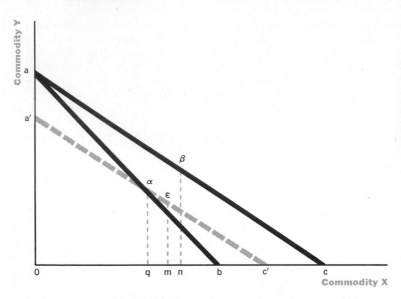

FIGURE A2 **THE INCOME EFFECT AND THE SUBSTITUTION EFFECT**

(the household being able to have more of all goods), which is called the *income effect*. To do this, we can imagine ourselves reducing the household's income until there is no income effect of the change in price—i.e., until the household is no longer able to consume more of all goods than it was consuming originally. To do this, we reduce its income until, *at the new set of prices,* it is just able to buy its original bundle of goods. Graphically, reducing income with relative prices constant at (Oa/Oc) means that the line ac slides inward toward the origin, parallel to itself, until it passes through the point α. This is shown in Figure A2 by the broken line $a'c'$.

1. X becomes cheaper relative to Y, but, simultaneously, income is reduced, so that the household can just buy the same amount of goods that it was buying originally. The household may move from α to some other point on $a'c'$; say it moves to ϵ. The change in the quantity of X purchased (from

binations containing more Y but less X than was consumed at α. Points within Area 2 indicate newly available combinations containing more X but less Y than was consumed at α. Points within Area 3, however, indicate newly available combinations containing both more X and more Y than was consumed at α.

We now break up this movement from α to β into two parts, one movement due to the pure change in relative prices, which is called the *substitution effect,* and the second movement due to the change in real income

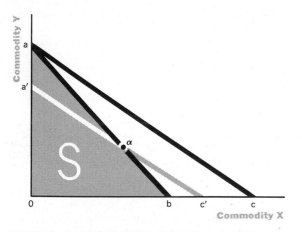

FIGURE A3 **PROOF THAT THE SUBSTITUTION EFFECT IS NONNEGATIVE**

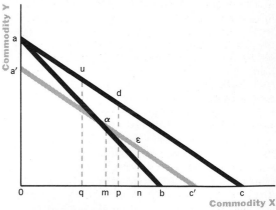

FIGURE A4 **NEGATIVE INCOME EFFECTS**

Oq to Om) is the *substitution effect*—the effect solely of a change in relative prices. Generally, we expect the household to buy more of the relatively cheaper good, X, and less of the relatively more expensive good, Y. That is, we expect ϵ to be to the right of α.

2. Relative prices are now held constant at their new level and the household's income is returned to it. Graphically, the budget line moves outward, parallel to itself, until it is returned to the position ac. The movement from the intermediate position, ϵ, to the final position, β, is the *income effect*. Mn more of X is bought because, with relative prices constant, the household's income rises.

What will happen if a fall in the price of X is accompanied by a sufficient reduction in the household's income so that it can just purchase its original combination of goods indicated by the point α? In Figure A3, the budget line moves from ab to $a'c'$. Now the household can choose any combination of goods on budget line $a'c'$. Look at segment $a'\alpha$ of this new budget line. Points to the left of α were available in the first situation; they are, therefore, part of the set S, which was originally rejected in favor of α. Since α is still available in the new situation, it follows that if the household behaves consistently, α cannot be rejected in favor of a point on the segment $a'\alpha$. On the other hand, points on the segment $\alpha c'$ lie outside of the original set S; they were not available in the original position and there is thus no inconsistency in choosing any point to the right of α in preference to α. Thus the household either

stays at α or it moves to the right along the segment $\alpha c'$, which means that, either it consumes the same amount of X (the good whose price has fallen), or it consumes more of it. We conclude, therefore, that, given our assumption, the substitution effect can never lead the household to buy less of the commodity whose price has fallen; it either buys the same as, or more than, it was buying before the price fell.

THE SLOPE OF AN INDIVIDUAL HOUSEHOLD'S DEMAND CURVE

When the price of X falls, there is an income effect as well as a substitution effect. If X has an income elasticity of demand greater than zero (i.e., if it is not an inferior good), the income effect will lead to an increase in the purchases of X (Point β will lie to the right of point ϵ in Figure A2). Since the substitution effect cannot be negative, an income elasticity of demand larger than zero is sufficient to ensure that more X will be purchased when its price falls (i.e., Point β will lie to the right of Point α in Figure A2). This means that the demand curve, which shows the quantity of X demanded at alternative prices of X, will slope downward to the right.

On the other hand, a negative income elasticity is not sufficient to ensure that the household will buy less of the good when its price falls; this will happen only if the negative income effect is *large enough* to outweigh the substitution effect. Figure A4 illustrates two cases of a negative income effect. The initial budget line is ab and the household's initial

position is at α; purchases of X are at Om. The price of X now falls so that the budget line shifts to ac. To measure the substitution effect we reduce income until the household is just able to buy its original combination of X and Y indicated by Point α; this gives the budget line $a'c'$. Assume that it now buys the bundle of goods indicated at ϵ, purchasing mn more X on account of the substitution effect. Now assume that X is an inferior good so that the income effect will be negative, and examine two possible cases. In the first case, the income effect causes the household to move from ϵ to d on the new budget line ac. It buys np less X on account of the income effect, but this is not sufficient to overcome the substitution effect, *and the household is observed to increase its purchases of X by* mp *as a result of the fall in its price.* In the second case, the income effect is stronger and the household moves from ϵ to u as a result of the rise in its income, thus reducing purchases of X by amount nq. *The household is observed to reduce its purchases of X from* Om *to* Oq *as a result of the fall in the price.*

THE SLOPE OF THE MARKET DEMAND CURVE

Conceptually, the market demand curve is the aggregation of the demand curves of the households in the market. The relation between the demand curves of individual consumers and the market demand curve is illustrated in Figure A5, where, for simplicity, we deal with a market containing only two individuals. We assume

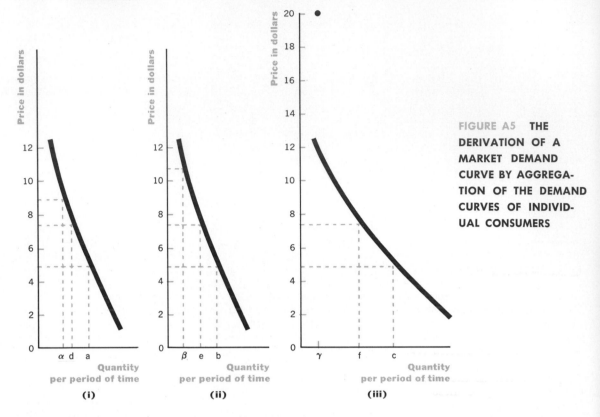

that we know the complete demand curve for each individual and we show these curves in Figure A5 (i) and A5 (ii). From these individual demand curves we have derived the market demand curve in Figure A5 (iii), which merely shows how much will be demanded at each price by both individuals.

Geometrically, we derive the market demand curve in (iii) by horizontally summing the two individual curves in (i) and (ii). At a price of $5, for example, individual (i) demands Oa and individual (ii) demands Ob; the total demand is $Oa + Ob = Oc$, which quantity is plotted in Figure A5 (iii)

against the price of $5. At a price of $7.50, individual (i) demands Od, while individual (ii) demands Oe, and total demand is $Od + Oe = Of$. Thus the market demand curve is to be thought of as the horizontal sum of all the demand curves of the individuals in the market.[1]

In practice we seldom have

1. When summing curves, students sometimes become confused between vertical and horizontal summation—mainly because they try to memorize the process rather than using their common sense. In *vertical summation,* lay off the equal distances $O\alpha$ and $O\beta$ in curves (i) and (ii), which represent the same quantity demanded by each consumer. These quantities correspond to prices $9 in (i) and $11 in (ii). Now, in Figure (iii), lay off $O\gamma$ ($= O\alpha = O\beta$) and plot it against the price $9 + $11 = $20. This point now relates a certain quantity to the sum of the prices that individuals (i) and (ii) are separately prepared to pay for this commodity. (This information is of no interest to us in the present context.) Remember that *every graphical operation can be translated into words.* The advantage of graphs is that they make proofs easier; the disadvantage is that they make it possible to make silly errors. To avoid these, you should always translate into words any graphical operation you have performed. Ask yourself: "Does this make sense and is this what I meant to do?" For example, a market demand curve is meant to tell us total purchases at each price, and hence it is obtained from individual curves by adding up the *quantities* de-

information about individual demand curves although we often do have evidence about the general slope of market demand curves. The derivation of market demand curves by summing individual curves is a theoretical operation. We do this because we wish to understand the relation between individual curves and market curves.

A downward-sloping demand curve for each and every household is a sufficient but not a necessary condition to obtain a downward-sloping market demand curve for a commodity. If a few households always act in an inconsistent fashion, then the market curve will still slope downward as long as the bulk of the households behave consistently. Also, if all households occasionally behave inconsistently, then market curves will still slope downward as long as at any one point in time the bulk of households are behaving in a consistent fashion. Thus the conditions for an upward-sloping market demand curve are, roughly stated, either that the bulk of all households have a large negative income elasticity for some good that accounts for a large part of their total expenditure,[2] or that at any moment in time the bulk of all households should be behaving in an inconsistent fashion. Empirical evidence suggests that rarely, if ever, are either of these conditions fulfilled in practice.

QUESTIONS FOR DISCUSSION

1. Draw a budget line assuming some given income and money prices of two goods X and Y. Show a 10 percent rise in the money price of X. Show a 10 percent fall in the money price of Y. Compare these two cases with respect to the substitution effect, the income effect, and the total effect of the change.

2. What condition is necessary for the substitution effect to be nonnegative? Why do we say that it might be zero?

3. The original good for which it was asserted that the demand curve sloped upward was that of potatoes in Ireland in the last century. Explain why more potatoes might be consumed when their price rose, and less when their price fell. What conditions are necessary for such "Giffen goods" to exist?

4. "Sometimes I buy more strawberries when they are expensive than when they are cheap. I can afford to be inconsistent once in a while." Does such behavior refute the hypothesis of downward-sloping demand curves?

(continued)

manded by each consumer at given prices, not by adding the *prices* that each consumer would pay for some given quantity. But see Chapter 43 for a case where vertical summation is required.

2. In order to get a significantly large negative income effect, two conditions are necessary: The good must have a large negative income elasticity of demand, and the good must form a large part of the consumers' total expenditure.

Chapter **14** THE THEORY OF DEMAND: MEASUREMENTS AND TESTS

IN THIS CHAPTER, WE DISCUSS THE DIFFICULT but crucial problems of testing the demand theory developed in Chapters 7 and 13 and of measuring its specific relations.

In Chapter 7, we introduced the theory of the determinants of market demand. According to the theory of demand, the quantity demanded of a commodity is influenced by consumers' tastes, population, total consumers' income, distribution of income among households, the price of the commodity, and all other prices.[1]

Now we have to answer two questions: Is it possible to test this theory against evidence in a situation in which it has a real chance of being refuted? In other words, do we have a genuinely refutable hypothesis about the determinants of demand? And, is there evidence about the quantitative extent to which the relations hypothesized are capable of explaining actual observed variations in demand?

Is the Theory Testable?

In order to be able to test the theory summarized above, we have to determine if observed changes in demand can in fact be accounted for by changes in the variables population, prices, incomes, and tastes. A refutation would presumably occur if we observed a significant amount of variation in demand that could not be accounted for by changes in these factors. But in order to make such an observation, we would have to know when and how these *explanatory variables*

had changed. It is possible to observe directly changes in population, prices, and consumers' incomes. Unfortunately, it is not possible to observe changes in tastes: What we usually do is to *infer* changes in taste by *observing* changes in demand. Thus, when we come to account statistically for observed changes in demand, we will very likely account for as much as is possible on the grounds of price and income variations and then ascribe the remaining variations to

1. This relation has already been stated fully in the daggered note on page 73.

changes in tastes. As long as we cannot tell when tastes have changed, other than by looking at demand, we can always account for any change in demand by *asserting* that tastes have changed. Thus, if we have no independent way of knowing when tastes have changed and when they have remained constant, we cannot test the theory summarized by the equation in the footnote on page 73: The theory as it stands is consistent with any conceivable set of real-world observations; it is, therefore, irrefutable.

We cannot refute the theory of the determinants of demand because we cannot measure tastes (at least we cannot do so at present). We can, however, measure the other determinants of market demand, and we can ask what proportion of the variations in demand can be accounted for by variations in the factors that we can measure. Even though we could not formally refute the theory of demand, we would not be very interested in it—and indeed for practical purposes we would discard it—if we were unable to account for much of what happened to demand by associating changes in it with observable changes in the other factors that are supposed to influence it. Table 1, which gives data for a number of demand studies, shows that in fact quite a large proportion of observed variations in demand can be accounted for by variations in these other measurable variables. Therefore, our theory of demand is useful, since it does seem to identify measurable variables that do account for a high proportion of observed variations in quantity demanded.

If the equation in the footnote on page 73 does not provide a testable theory, it does provide a useful set of categories into which the factors influencing demand may be divided. Let us look at each of the individual factors and once again ask our two questions: Does the theory specify the relation in such a form that it could be refuted given enough evidence? Can the hypothesized relation account for much of the variations that are observed to occur in quantity demanded?

TABLE 1 PRICES AND INCOME ELASTICITIES FOR SELECTED FOODSTUFFS IN THE U.K.

Commodity	Income elasticity	Price elasticity	Percentage of variation accounted for by changes in income, own price, and prices of related goods
Flour	—	.79	53
Home-produced beef and veal	.34	.41	64
Home-produced mutton and lamb	.70	1.47	70
Bacon and ham	.55	.88	71
Poultry	1.17	.27	33
Cream	1.71	.69	69
Oranges	.92	.97	52
Sugar	.09	.44	74
Meals away from home	2.39	Not estimated	Not estimated

SOURCE: Richard Stone, *The Measurement of Consumers' Expenditure and Behaviour in the United Kingdom, 1920–38* (Cambridge University Press, 1954), Vol. 1.

THE INFLUENCE OF THE PRICES OF OTHER COMMODITIES

In Chapter 7, we made a distinction between goods that are complements to one another and those that are substitutes.[2] Consider the demand for commodity X. The demand for X will *vary inversely* with the price of a complementary commodity (i.e., when the price falls demand for X will rise), and will *vary directly* with the price of a substitute commodity (i.e., when the price falls, demand for X will fall). There may also be a group of commodities variations in the price of which leave demand for X unchanged. These commodities lie on the boundary that divides the goods that are substitutes for X from those that are complements to X.

These three reactions—demand for X rises, falls, or remains unchanged when the price of some other good varies—cover all conceivable possibilities: There is nothing else that could possibly happen. So far we merely have a set of labels to attach to all possibilities. We do not have a testable theory unless we have a way of *deciding in advance* which goods are substitutable for, and which are complementary to, X. A general theory that would allow us to predict in advance for all goods which are complements and which substitutes does not exist, and so we must conclude that there is no testable theory of the relation between demand for one commodity and the prices of other commodities.

In order to justify spending time on these relations, they must provide a useful method of classifying all possible occurrences into significant categories. And in fact they do just that. They provide a series of labeled categories in which our real-world observations, once made, can be accumulated. There are now two possibilities. First, actual empirical

2. See page 73.

observations can sometimes tell us which commodities are complements and which are substitutes; then we could add this knowledge to our theories in order to predict in advance the effects on different markets of changes in such factors as costs, prices, and taxes. Second, technical data can sometimes tell us the same thing, particularly if we consider the demand for inputs in the process of production. Steel plates, electric welders, and welder operators are complementary. Thus we can predict that a fall in the price of any one will lead to an increase in the demand for all three. Cranes and crane operators, steam shovels and trucks, trains and rails, roads and fences, any piece of equipment and its human operator are all examples of pairs of goods that are complements for each other. You can easily expand the list. Construct a similar one for substitute inputs. There are also many consumers' goods for which we can predict complementarity or substitutability in advance. Complementarity would, for example, exist between electric razors and preshave lotion, ordinary razors and razor blades, ordinary razors and shaving cream, golf clubs and golf balls, grass seed and lawn mowers, electric stoves and electricity, and marriage and the services of obstetricians. If we feel that the technical data tell us which goods are substitutes and which are complements, then we can predict in advance the effect of a change in the price of one good on the demand for the other. As the above examples show, we are able to do this in a very large number of cases.

THE INFLUENCE OF CONSUMERS' INCOMES

Just as with a change in relative prices, it is possible for an increase in income to have only three effects: to cause the demand for a commodity to rise, to fall, or to remain unchanged.[3] There are no other conceivable possibilities. There is, therefore, no general refutable theory of the relation between income changes and changes in the demand for commodities.

Income elasticity of demand, which shows the relation between changes in income and changes in demand, is, nevertheless, a useful concept, providing that observations can be used to give it empirical content. If we have discovered, by observing the real world, which goods have low-income elasticities and which goods have high-income elasticities, and if we have reason to expect these elasticities to remain fairly stable over time, then we can predict in advance many of the effects of cyclical fluctuations and of economic growth, both of which phenomena cause systematic changes in incomes. We can also observe that a significant proportion of actual changes in demand can be associated with changes in income. Thus this particular relation is an important one in accounting for what happens to demand.

THE INFLUENCE OF THE PRICE OF THE COMMODITY

In this case the possibility of obtaining a general refutable theory looks a little more hopeful, at first glance. We usually expect demand curves (relating the quantity demanded of some commodity to its own price) to slope downward—that is, we expect price and quantity to vary inversely with each other.[4] This relation has often been referred to as the "law" of demand. It now appears that we have a genuine testable hypothesis that says that price and quantity cannot vary directly with each other (i.e., demand curves

cannot slope upward) and that would be refuted by the observation of such a relation.

Two problems arise: First, we still have no independent indicator of a change in tastes. Say we observe a situation in which there is an increase in both the price and the demand for one commodity, but in which all other prices and incomes remain constant. We can always explain this apparent refutation of the "law" of demand by saying that tastes must have changed in favor of this commodity at the same time as its price rose. This "alibi" can certainly be used with effect to explain away a single conflicting observation. We will be uncomfortable using the same alibi over and over again, however, and we will begin to suspect a fault in the hypothesis that demand and price vary inversely with each other. What we now have is a problem in statistical testing.[5] We are not prepared to throw away a theory after only one conflicting observation. But we are prepared to abandon it as soon as the probability of making a given set of observations if the theory is correct diminishes drastically. Thus, statistically, the theory is testable. If demand curves are observed to slope upward, so that we have to make very special and unlikely assumptions about how tastes just happened to have changed *each time* prices changed, we will prefer to reject our theory that demand curves slope downward. There is a great deal of evidence, however, that demand curves do slope downward. The predictions of the theory have—with one notable exception—always been found to be in agreement with the facts.

The second problem is a more fundamental one. The theory of household behavior that we developed in Chapter 13 admits of the possibility that some demand curves could slope upward. The famous case in which

3. See pages 78–79, and Figure 4, page 79.   4. See pages 74–75.   5. See pages 49–50.

this is reputed to have happened is the "Giffen case." Sir Francis Giffen, a Victorian economist, is reputed to have observed and measured that an increase in the price of potatoes during the 1845 potato famine in Ireland led to an increase in the consumption of potatoes. This was presumably due to the adverse income effect of the price rise and the fact that potatoes are an inferior good.[6]

A totally different kind of case is that in which consumer satisfaction depends not only on the commodity but on the price he has paid for it. The consumer may, for example, buy diamonds not because he particularly likes diamonds per se, but because he wishes to show off his wealth in an ostentatious but socially acceptable way. In the words of Thorstein Veblen, he indulges in *conspicuous consumption*.[7] He values diamonds precisely because they are expensive; thus, a fall in their price might lead him to stop buying them and to switch to a more satisfactory object of ostentatious display. If enough consumers acted similarly, this could lead to an upward- rather than a downward-sloping demand curve for diamonds.[8] Unless we have an independent way of predicting in advance which curves will slope upward and which will slope downward, we always have an alibi for any apparent

refutation of the law of demand: Whenever we observe the demand curve for a single commodity sloping upward we need not say "The law is refuted"; rather we might say "Now we have found the odd case in which the negative-income elasticity is the dominant factor influencing demand."

Thus we must conclude that the theory of the slope of the demand curve does not make a categorical enough prediction to render it potentially refutable with any certainty. Indeed, the strong assertion "all demand curves slope downward" is believed to have been refuted in any case.

We do, however, have very strong evidence that most (indeed, virtually all) market demand curves do slope downward. For practical purposes, we can regard the hypothesis of the downward-sloping demand curve as useful and in conformity with the evidence.

We can go, and have gone, farther than this. We have a reasonable idea of the value of demand elasticity in many cases. Thus, not only do we know that the demand curve slopes downward, we also know, within a reasonable margin of error, how steeply it slopes downward. Reasonably precise knowledge about demand curves is a necessity if we are to make real-world applications of the demand and supply theory developed in

---

6. Economists were initially interested in the Giffen case because it provided an apparent empirical refutation of the "law" of demand. We now realize (and we demonstrated it in the appendix to Chapter 13) that our theory of household behavior does not predict that all demand curves slope downward. If the good in question is an inferior good, there is nothing inconsistent in a household buying more of the good when its price rises. The income effect of the price rise is the same as if income had been reduced and, since the good is an inferior one, the income effect leads to more being consumed. It is quite possible that this income effect could be stronger than the substitution effect that leads the household to consume less of the good whose price has risen.

7. This phrase is drawn from Veblen's interesting and provocative book, *The Theory of the Leisure Class* (1899), which is available in paperback.

8. To the best of our knowledge, no one—with the possible exception of Giffen—has ever observed statistically an upward-sloping *market demand* curve. A moment's thought about the industrial uses of diamonds and the masses of lower-income consumers who could buy diamonds only if they were sufficiently inexpensive would seem to suggest that upward-sloping *demand curves for individual consumers* are much more likely than upward-sloping *market demand curves* for the same commodity.

this book. If we knew nothing at all empirically about them, then the theory of demand is devoid of any real-world application. If we do have this knowledge, then we can predict in advance the effects of changes in

many factors, such as taxes, costs, the amount of competition in a particular market, and so forth. The more accurate is our knowledge of the shape of these curves, the smaller will be the margin of error in such predictions.

Measurement of Demand

This leads us directly to a discussion of the problems of the measurement of demand. Three of the most famous names in this field are Henry Schultz of the University of Chicago, Richard Stone of Cambridge University, and Herman Wold of the University of Uppsala, Sweden.[9] Many difficult problems must be overcome before we can obtain even an approximate measure of the response of demand to price changes from empirical data.

Some of these problems are of a very technical nature and cannot be appreciated without a knowledge of statistical theory.

One of the most important problems can, however, be illustrated simply. We start by assuming that all situations that we observe in the real world are equilibrium ones, in the sense that they are produced by the intersection of demand and supply curves. If, as in Figure 1 (i), the demand curve stays put

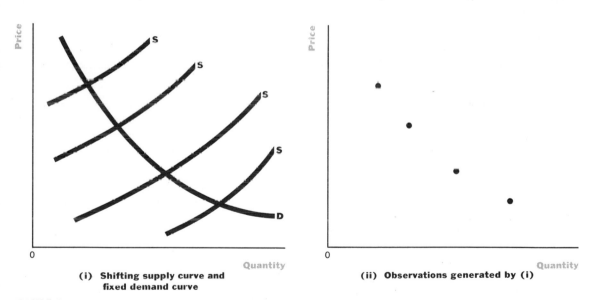

(i) Shifting supply curve and fixed demand curve

(ii) Observations generated by (i)

FIGURE 1

9. H. Schultz, *The Theory and Measurement of Demand* (University of Chicago Press, 1938; reprinted, 1957); R. Stone, *The Measurement of Consumers' Expenditure and Behaviour in the United Kingdom, 1920–38* (Cambridge University Press, 1954); H. Wold and L. Jureen, *Demand Analysis: A Study in Econometrics* (John Wiley, 1953).

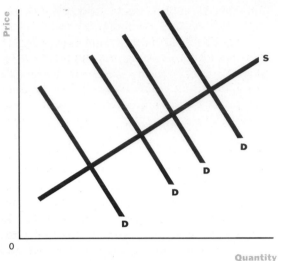

(i) **Shifting demand curve and fixed supply curve**

(ii) **Observations generated by (i)**

FIGURE 2

while the supply curve moves up and down, possibly because of crop variations in some agricultural commodity, then the price-quantity observations illustrated in Figure 1 (ii) will be generated. If we draw a line through these observed points, we will have a good approximation to the demand curve in Figure 1 (i).

Now assume, as in Figure 2 (i), that the supply curve stays put while the demand

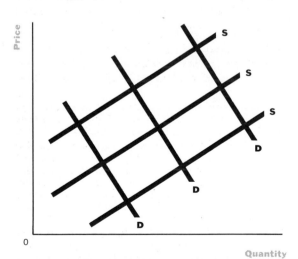

(i) **Shifting demand and supply curves**

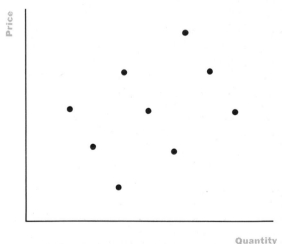

(ii) **Observations generated by (i)**

FIGURE 3

curve moves about, owing perhaps to changes in the number of consumers or in their incomes. Now the price-quantity relations that will be observed are those given in Figure 2 (ii). If we draw a curve through these points, we will obtain a fair approximation to the supply curve in Figure 2 (i).

So far so good. But now what happens if both curves shift, as in Figure 3 (i)? In this case we will obtain a series of points that will be very unlike either the demand or the supply curves that generated them. A few such points are shown in Figure 3 (ii).[10]

This difficult problem is not insurmountable. A proof of the solution to the problem belongs to a textbook in econometrics and we can only assert the solution here without attempting to prove it. The key to *identifying* both the demand and supply curves in Figure 3 (i), given the observations in Figure 3 (ii), is to relate the demand and supply to other variables as well as price—supply to one variable and demand to *some other variable*. For example, we might relate supply of the commodity not only to the price of the commodity but also to its costs of production, and we might relate demand not only to the price of the commodity but also to consumers' incomes. Provided that both of these other factors, cost of production and income, vary sufficiently, it will now be possible to determine the relation between supply and price as well as the relation between demand and price.[11]

Why Is the Measurement of Demand Important?

Much work has been done on the measurement of demand and demand elasticity. This work is of great value because it provides our theory of price with empirical content. If we knew *nothing* about demand elasticities, then all of the exercises we have gone through in previous chapters would have very little application to the real world.

A somewhat different view of the importance of empirical measures of demand is held by some economists. We shall quote from a classic statement of this view by Lionel Robbins:[12]

Our *a priori* deductions do not provide any justification for saying that caviar is an economic good and carrion a disutility. Still less do they

10. A careful statement of these problems in the measurement of demand (without any hint as to how they might be solved) can be found in E. J. Working, "What Do Statistical Demand Curves Show?," *Quarterly Journal of Economics*, 1927; reprinted in *Readings in Price Theory* (American Economic Association, 1953).

11. Most of the work done on the measurement of demand has kept to the assumption that every observed point lies on the intersection of a demand and a supply curve. A potentially fruitful source of demand measurement would seem to follow from dynamic theory, where time lags occur in the adjustment of price to the state of excess demand. In this case, it is possible to observe disequilibrium situations, and the information that is available about the speed at which prices are changing can be used to infer something about the difference between demand and supply at that price. Here is a virtually untapped source of fruitful research for the student interested in both theoretical and empirical economics.

12. L. Robbins, *An Essay on the Nature and Significance of Economic Science* (Macmillan, 1932), pp. 98–101. Every economics specialist should read this provocative work. It contains the classic statements of many views still held by economists. It also states a view on the nature of economic theory and its relation to empirical observations that is directly contradictory to the one presented in this book. For a view much closer to the one presented here, however, see the same author's "The Present Position of Economics," *Rivista Di Economica*, September, 1959.

inform us concerning the intensity of the demand for caviar or the demand to be rid of carrion. . . . But is it not desirable to transcend such limitations? Ought we not to be in a position to give numerical values to the scales of valuation, to establish quantitative laws of demand and supply? . . . No doubt such knowledge would be useful. But a moment's reflection should make it plain that we are here entering into a field of investigation *where there is no reason to suppose that uniformities are to be discovered.*

A simple illustration should make this clear. Suppose we are confronted with an order fixing the price of herrings at a point below the price hitherto ruling in the market. Suppose we are in a position to say, "According to the researches of Blank (1907–1908) the elasticity of demand for common herring (*clupea harengus*) is 1.3; the present price-fixing order therefore may be expected to leave an excess of demand over supply of two million barrels."

But can we hope to obtain such an enviable position? Let us assume that in 1907–1908 Blank had succeeded in ascertaining that, with a given price change in that year, the elasticity of demand was 1.3. What reason is there to suppose that he was unearthing a constant law? [The demand for herrings depends on many things: fashion, theological views, the availability of other foods, the distribution of income, the current state of the art of cooking, etc.] Is it possible reasonably to suppose that coefficients derived from the observation of a particular herring market at a particular time and place have any *permanent* significance—save as Economic History?

The above argument runs somewhat as follows: "I can think of no reasons why the relationship in question (e.g., the relation between demand and price) should be a stable one; I can in fact think of several reasons why it should not be stable; I conclude, therefore, that in the real world the relationship will not be stable, and attempts to *observe* whether or not it is stable can be ruled out on *a priori* grounds as a waste of time." This argument is rather a curious one, and it appears, although it may not have been the author's intention, that it could have been used to stop at an early stage the investigations that produced *observations* of practically every stable relation we know.[13]

The first criticism of the passage quoted is, thus, that *a priori* arguments, although they may strongly suggest the hypothesis that certain relationships will not be stable ones, can never establish this. Only empirical observations can demonstrate such propositions about the real world. Even if the *a priori* arguments turn out to be correct most of the time, there always exists the possibility that in a few cases they will be wrong. Only empirical observation is capable of discovering the case in which the *a priori* argument is wrong.

The second major criticism of the passage

13. For example:

a. Draw up a list of all the factors that influence or could be imagined to influence a falling body. Clearly, since most of these factors are variable, we will find no constant, stable relations in the realm of falling bodies—i.e., the law of gravitation is *a priori* impossible.

b. Observe in detail the complex, varied, and variable behavior of four or five gas molecules. Clearly, there can be no stable laws about the behavior of gas—i.e., Boyle's law is *a priori* impossible.

c. Draw up a list of all the factors that cause a person to make a mistake when we ask him to measure a given distance. Clearly, there can be no stable relations regarding human errors—i.e., the normal curve of error is *a priori* impossible.

d. Consider the number of factors that might affect expenditure on consumption goods. (In order to make the argument seem really conclusive, carry on your list until you run out of paper—you will have no trouble doing this, for the number of factors that *might* affect consumption is infinite.) Clearly, it will be impossible to find any stable relation between consumption expenditure and a few variables such as the level and distribution of income—i.e., such stable statistical relations as have actually been found are *a priori* impossible.

is that it is of critical importance to *economic theory* to know just how variable any given relationship is. If, for example, tastes are so variable that demand curves shift about violently from day to day, then all of the comparative static-equilibrium analysis of the previous chapters would be useless, for only by accident would any market be near its equilibrium and this would only occur momentarily. If, on the other hand, tastes and other factors change extremely slowly, then we might do very well to regard the relation between demand and price as constant for purposes of all predictions of, say, up to twenty or fifty years. Even if we could show, on *a priori* grounds, that every relation between two or more variables used in economic theory was necessarily not a stable one, it would be critical for purposes of theory to know the quantitative amount of the lack of stability. Only empirical observations can show this, and such observations are thus important for economic theory as well as for economic history.

Let us consider an example of this point. The relation between the demand for herrings and their price might have been so variable that the elasticity of demand was 1.37 in 1903, 0.01 in 1905, 8.73 in 1906, 1.00 in 1907, and 41.2 in 1908. If demand for all goods varied in such a capricious way, price theory would be of very little use, for we would be unable to predict the effects of the sort of shift in costs, taxes, etc., that we have been considering. If, on the other hand, all the measures of the elasticity of demand for herrings over a period of twenty years lay between 1.2 and 1.45, then we could predict the effects of various changes in the herring market with a close degree of accuracy and with a high degree of confidence. We would be astounded, and indeed we would suspect

a fraud, if a large number of measures of the elasticity of herring demand, made in several places and over a large number of years, all produced the value of, say, 1.347. What we want to know, however, is *how much* spatial and temporal variation there is in the demand for herrings. Only empirical observations can settle this question.

Finally, even if we find substantial variations in our relations, we want to know if these variations appear capricious or if they display a systematic pattern that might lead us to expect that herring demand is related to other factors. We might, for example, find a strong but sometimes interrupted tendency for the elasticity of demand of herrings to fall over time. We might then find that this systematic variation in price elasticity could be accounted for by income variations (as the population gets richer its demand for herrings is less and less affected by price variations and so the demand becomes more and more inelastic). We might now find that a high proportion of the changes in herring demand could be accounted for by assuming *a stable relation* between demand on the one hand and price *and* income on the other. In general, what looks like a very unstable relation between two variables may turn out to be only part of a highly stable relation between three or more variables.

All of this leads us to the following conclusion: The theory of demand and price can have few applications to the real world without some empirical observations of quantitative magnitudes. Empirical measurements are critical to economic theory. Without some knowledge of the stability or instability of a particular relation (e.g., the relation between price and quantity), we cannot use economic theory to make useful predictions about the real world.

MODERN MEASURES OF DEMAND

A great deal of work has been done in recent years on the theory and measurement of demand.[14] Particular interest has attached to the demand for consumers' durables, such as cars, radios, refrigerators, television sets, and houses. Demands for these types of goods are particularly interesting because they constitute a large fraction of total demand and because such demands can be quite variable from one year to the next. Since the commodity is durable, it can always be made to "make do" for another year, thus purchases can be postponed with greater ease than can purchases of nondurables such as food and services. If enough households decide simultaneously to postpone purchases of durables for even six months, this decision can have a major effect on the economy.

Summary

1. In this chapter, we examine the testability of demand theory.

2. Since we cannot measure tastes directly, the theory is not refutable as it stands. We can, however, examine those variables that we can measure to see if they account for a significant proportion of the variation in demand. If they do not, we would not be very interested in the theory. But, as it happens, there is a large number of demand studies in which a significant proportion of the variations in demand for various commodities has been successfully accounted for by variations in prices and incomes.

3. We examine the relation between demand and each of the variables that are assumed to influence it to see if a testable theory is implied in each.

4. The difficulty with the *relation between demand and other prices* is that all possible relations are admitted by the theory. Unless we have a way of determining from technical data which goods are complementary and which are substitutes, we do not know what to expect from the relation between the demand for good X and the price of some other good. In the absence of such knowledge, the theory tells us nothing about the world, and we cannot rule out in advance any possible situations. In such a situation, the theory becomes both irrefutable and uninteresting. Fortunately, in a large number of cases we do know in advance whether we expect the goods to be substitutes or complements, and so we can use the theory to predict.

5. The same problem arises with the relation between demand and *consumers' incomes;* according to our theory, an increase in incomes can cause the demand for some good, X, to rise, to fall, or to remain unchanged. Fortunately, the income elasticities that we measure do either remain stable over time or change over time in a stable fashion. Thus we *can* use knowledge about the pattern of such elasticities observed in the past to predict the consequences of future changes in incomes.

6. There are two difficulties in testing what is often called the "law" of demand. The first difficulty is the problem of taste changes, which can always be used to explain away any apparent refutation of the "law." Such

14. See, for a survey of recent literature, Robert Ferber, "Research on Household Behavior," *American Economic Review*, March, 1962.

an alibi will do for isolated refutations, but if we had to use it continuously we would prefer to reject the theory. The second difficulty is that we admit an exception to our theory when we admit the existence of "Giffen goods." Almost all demand curves that have been studied, however, have been observed to slope downward, so the hypothesis that virtually (if not quite) all demand curves slope downward can be regarded as in conformity with the large body of existing evidence.

7. When we come to measure demand, we encounter a difficulty known as the "identification problem": When both demand and supply curves are shifting, it is not possible, by observing price and quantity data alone, to determine the shape of either curve. The problem has been solved, and, as long as demand and supply depend on observable things other than the price of the commodity, it is possible to discover the shape of the two curves from observable data.

8. The argument is sometimes advanced that our measurements will be of no use because there is no reason to expect to find stable relations in economics. This argument is unacceptable, both because it does not establish that we *will not* find such relationships and because it is important to know just how unstable any relationship is that we wish to use as a basis for prediction.

QUESTIONS FOR DISCUSSION

1. Why are we interested only in refutable theories? Shouldn't we prefer irrefutable ones? (Hints: What good is a theory that predicts that anything can happen? A theory that says that only some things can happen must say that other things cannot happen.)

2. What do we mean when we say that there is a ready-made alibi to explain away any apparent refutation of some theory? Why do we say that tastes provide such an alibi in demand theory? What would we need to do in order to remove this particular alibi?

3. Assume you have a theory that predicts that every time you put 40¢ in a slot machine a package of cigarettes will drop out. If an earthquake occurred just after you put your 40¢ in the machine, would you regard the theory as refuted if the cigarettes did not come out of the shattered machine? What would you think if, every time you put 40¢ in the machine, an earthquake occurred and you did not get your cigarettes?

4. We hypothesized that demand for a commodity is influenced by the prices of other goods. Even if all other factors influencing demand were known to remain constant, what difficulty would we have in testing this hypothesis?

5. Draw a diagram that illustrates the identification problem in the measurement of demand and supply curves.

6. Criticize both of the following statements:

a. "I have calculated the elasticity of demand for winter lemons and have found it to be precisely .943."

b. "Since there are so many reasons why the elasticity of demand may shift, it is a waste of time making any such measurement."

Which statement do you think is the more dangerous to the progress of economics? Why?

SUPPLY

Chapter **15** BACKGROUND TO THE
THEORY OF SUPPLY

IN CHAPTER 8, WE HYPOTHESIZED THAT THE supply of a commodity depends upon many factors, including the goals of firms, technology, the price of the commodity, prices of other commodities, and prices of factors of production. In the elementary theory of price outlined in Part II, we assumed the existence of a supply curve relating the quantity of goods that firms wished to sell to the price of the commodity. We must now take a more detailed look into the theory of supply to find out how the decisions of individual producers determine the quantities of goods actually supplied to the market. This requires attention to producers' goals, to the choices they have, to the information they get, to the signals to which they respond, and to the institutions in which they operate.

A theory of supply, or, as it is often called, a theory of production, is needed in order to answer a whole host of important questions: If consumers want more of a commodity how can they get it? How quickly? How expensively? How certainly? How will a subsidy, or a tax, or a new law, or an invention affect supply? How does the kind of market in which firms operate affect the price and quantity of goods available to consumers? Will large firms be more efficient than small ones? Will they become monopolies? Why do firms merge? What are the causes and consequences of advertising? Will the existence

173

of labor unions, minimum-wage laws, and antitrust laws make much difference to what is produced and how it is produced?

This is but a sample of the many questions that we cannot answer without a theory of production. In an introductory book, we cannot answer them all, but we can outline the basic theory of production, use it to examine some of these questions, and, what is at least as important, we can see what other informa-tion would be required to permit complete analyses of these questions.

The theory of production, like all useful theories, involves substantial abstraction from the variety of institutions and kinds and forms of behavior that it is designed to ex-plain. The basic definitions and simplifica-tions used in the theory are given below. Some of these are discussed in detail elsewhere in this book.

The Nature of the Firm

In economics, the *firm* is defined as the unit that makes decisions with respect to the production and sale of commodities. Along with other basic economic units, such as households, governments, and labor unions, firms constitute the major actors in the drama of economic activity.

The concept of the firm covers a wide variety of actual business undertakings. At one extreme, there is the owner-operated firm, such as the family-operated grocery store or the small manufacturing company, in which all important decisions are made by a single person. At the other extreme, there is the large corporation, such as the General Motors Corporation or the Ford Motor Company, in which decisions are made by many different persons. Not all decisions of a large organization are made by the same people or in the same way. Nor are they all equally important. To take an example, when the Ford Motor Company decided to intro-duce a new model car, someone made the decision to do so. Someone decided to call it the Edsel. Someone decided how and where to produce it. Someone decided how to pro-mote its sales. In the face of disappointing sales, someone decided it had all been a mis-take and that the Edsel should be abandoned. We can, however, assume that the different decision-makers were united by the fact that they shared common goals—the manufacture of successful automobiles and other products that earn profits for the owners of the Ford Motor Company.

Economic theory assumes that the same principles underlie each decision made within a firm and that the decision is uninfluenced by who makes it. It is thus assumed that the persons making the decisions and the kinds of organization in which they work can be abstracted from, and that the firm can be regarded as a decision-making unit that has objectives and that makes decisions designed to achieve these objectives.

Whether a decision is made by a small independent proprietor, a farmer, a plant manager, or the Board of Directors of the Gen-eral Motors Corporation, that decision-maker is, as far as theory goes, the firm for the purposes of that decision. The great bulk of the productive activity of the nation is car-ried on by large corporations where it is difficult to identify the source of every decision.[1] Criticisms of the theory of the firm because of its neglecting to identify either decision-makers or the institutional structure within which decisions are made are discussed in Chapter 30. Some competing hypotheses about actual business behavior are also discussed at that time. The final test of whether or not such factors can be legitimately ignored is an empirical one: If the theory that we develop by ignoring these factors is successful in predicting the outcome of the kind of events in which we are interested, then we can conclude that we were correct in assuming that these factors could be safely ignored.

The Motivation of the Firm

We assume that the firm makes decisions in such a way that its profits will be as large as possible. In technical language, we assume that the firm *maximizes its profits*.

Profits are defined as the difference between the value of the sales of the firm and the costs to the firm of producing what is sold. This definition leads us to look carefully at sales and at costs. In the elementary theory of the firm we assume that the rate of production is kept exactly equal to the rate of sales. Thus, when considering the sales revenue of the firm, we can treat the value of production and the value of sales interchangeably since they are identical.[2] The definition and measurement of cost is a difficult matter and it is discussed in Chapter 17.

The assumption of profit maximization provides a principle by which decisions of firms can be predicted. The economist predicts the firm's behavior in regard to the various choices open to it by studying the effect that making each of the choices would have on the firm's profits. The economist then predicts that the firm will select from the alternatives open to it the one that produces the largest profits. If actual firms do seek to maximize profits in a reasonably informed fashion, they will make the choices that the economist predicts they will make. In this case, the theory will be successful in predicting the behavior of firms. If actual firms seek to do something very different from maximizing profits, they will not make the choices predicted by the economist. In this case, the theory will be unsuccessful in predicting their behavior and the theory's predictions will be refuted when we test them against the facts.

Why do we make this assumption? First, because it is necessary to make *some* assumption about what motivates decision-makers if the theory is to predict how they will act. Second, a great many of the predictions of theories based upon this assumption have been confirmed by observation. Third, there is no general agreement that an alternative assumption has yet been shown to yield substantially better results.

1. The corporate form is so important that we devote all of Chapter 16 to it.
2. This simplification, which neglects such complications as inventories and goods in process, is appropriate to an introductory book. It can be removed without seriously affecting any of the conclusions reached in the present treatment.

The assumption has, however, been criticized, and alternatives have been suggested. These are examined in Chapter 30.

CHOICES OPEN TO THE FIRM

In the theory of production, as in the real world, the firm must decide what to produce, how to produce it, and in what quantities to produce it.

Initially, we shall assume that the firm produces a well-defined single product. How this product is to be produced is the heart of the theory of production, and in what quantities it is to be produced is an integral part of the theory of price. Both are discussed at length in subsequent chapters of Part IV and in Part V. The remainder of this chapter is designed to prepare for this discussion, as well as to lay the groundwork for the discussion of costs.

Factors of Production

Production is something like a sausage machine: Certain *factors,* such as raw materials and the services of capital and labor, are fed in at one end and some product emerges at the other. The materials and factor services that are fed in at the one end and used in the process of production are often called *inputs* and the products that emerge at the other end are often called *outputs.* One way of looking at the process is to regard the factors as being combined to produce the output. Another way, equally useful, is to regard the materials and factor services as being used up, or sacrificed, in order to gain the output.

Each distinct input into the production process can be regarded as a *factor of production.* There are literally hundreds of factors of production entering into the output of a specific good. Among the factors entering into automobile production are, to name only a few, sheet steel, rubber, spark plugs, electricity, night watchmen, accountants, fork-lift operators, managers, and painters. We can group these inputs into four broad classes: (1) those that are inputs to the automobile manufacturer but outputs to some

other manufacturer, such as spark plugs, electricity, and sheet steel; (2) those that are provided directly by nature, such as land; (3) those that are provided directly by households, such as labor; and (4) those that are provided by the machines used in the manufacture of automobiles.

This last class of inputs—machines—is one of the distinguishing features of modern as opposed to primitive production. Instead of making all consumers' goods directly with the aid only of such simple tools as nature provides, productive effort goes into the manufacture of tools, machines, and other goods that are not desired in themselves but only as an aid to making further goods. Such tools are called *capital goods*, which we define as man-made aids to further production. The use of capital goods renders our production processes *roundabout*. Instead of making what we want directly, we engage in a roundabout process, first making the goods that we need in order to help us make what we finally want.

In many cases, production is very roundabout indeed. For example, a worker may be employed in a factory making machines that are used in mining coal; the coal may be burned by a power plant to make electricity; the electricity may provide power for a factory that makes machine tools; the tools may be used to make a tractor; the tractor may be used by a potato farmer to help in the production of potatoes; and the potatoes may be eaten by a consumer. Such roundabout production is worthwhile *if* the farmer using his tractor can produce more potatoes than could be produced if all the factors of production involved in this roundabout chain were to apply themselves directly to the production of potatoes (using only such tools as were provided by nature).

For many purposes, including ease of exposition, it is convenient to speak of certain broad types of factors the services of which contribute to production. A popular classification is *land, labor,* and *capital*. Land, so used, includes all primary products; labor includes all human services; and capital includes all man-made aids to further production.[3] You should never lose sight of the fact that these broad designations may cover very different things and that, for many problems, attention to a more detailed list of factors is essential.

Technical and Economic Efficiency

In general, there is more than one way to produce a given product. Indeed, if this were not the case there would be no need for firms to face the decision of *how* to produce. It is possible to produce agricultural commodities by farming a small quantity of land very intensively, combining a great deal of labor and capital with each acre of land; it is also possible to produce the same commodities by farming a great deal of land very extensively, using only a small amount of labor and capital per acre of land.

Consider the printing of this book. It would have been possible to set the type for this book in at least four ways: by using a linotype machine, by using a monotype machine, by photocomposition, or by assembling the individual letters and spaces by hand. Which

process is best? If the output is the same, the best process is the one that uses the fewest inputs or, in other words, the one that is technically most efficient. *Technical,* or *technological, efficiency* measures use of inputs in physical terms; *economic efficiency* measures use in terms of costs.

A simplified illustration will make the distinction clear. Suppose we assume that a product uses only two factors of production, which we shall call capital and labor, and the state of technology is such that our engineers tell us there are only four known ways to produce the desired output, which is 100 units per month. Which method shall we use? The methods are summarized in Table 1.

Method B is *technologically inefficient* because it uses more of both resources than

---

3. In the example of the automobile manufacturer we found four classes of inputs: land, labor, capital, and other products that were the automobile industry's inputs but the outputs of other firms. If we trace these "inputs" back to the firm that provided them, we will find that they were produced with the four types of inputs. Eventually, however, if we continue to trace all products back to their sources, we will find that all production in the economy can be accounted for by the services of *three* kinds of inputs: land, labor, and capital. The other products appear only because the stages of production are broken up between different firms so that at any one stage a firm is using as inputs goods produced by other firms.

KNOWN WAYS TO PRODUCE 100 UNITS OF OUTPUT PER MONTH

| | Quantity of Inputs Required | |
	Capital	Labor
Method A	6	200
Method B	10	250
Method C	10	150
Method D	40	50

Method A,[4] and is thus clearly wasteful. Among Methods A, C, and D, Method A is more efficient in its use of capital but most labor-using. Method D conserves labor, but uses much more capital. Method C is intermediate between them.[5] On an over-all basis, all three are *technologically efficient* because no one uses less of all resources than the others.[6]

Economic efficiency involves choosing from among the technologically efficient combinations the one that represents the least sacrifice for the firm. The sacrifice of Method A is whatever it costs to purchase the services of 6 units of capital *plus* the cost of hiring the

services of 200 units of labor, and similarly for Methods C and D. The economically most efficient method is the one that costs the least. Table 2 deals with three assumed sets of factor prices. It shows that economic efficiency will depend on factor prices. Given the quantity of inputs required (see Table 1), Method A is most efficient with Case I prices, Method C is most efficient with Case II prices, and Method D is most efficient with Case III prices.

RESOURCE ALLOCATION: THE PRINCIPLE OF SUBSTITUTION

Economic efficiency as we have defined it makes the choice of a method of production depend upon the relative prices of factors. In the example just used, when capital is very expensive relative to labor (Case I), the efficient firm uses a production method (A) that uses very little capital and a great deal of labor. (See Table 1.) If the price of capital relative to labor decreases, as happens when we move from Case I to Case II, and from Case II to Case III, it "pays" to shift to

ECONOMIC EFFICIENCY DEPENDS ON FACTOR PRICES

| | Factor Prices per Unit | | Total Cost of Factors | | |
	Capital	Labor	Method A	Method C	Method D
Case I	$50	$3	$900	$950	$2150
Case II	20	5	1120	950	1050
Case III	15	5	1090	900	850

4. It might also be so classified because it uses the same amount of capital and more labor than Method C.

5. The student who is tempted to consider Method D technologically most efficient because it uses only 90 units of all resources should think twice.

6. Students with a background in engineering or physics will note that "technical efficiency" is itself a broader concept than engineering efficiency. An engineer may judge the efficiency of a steam engine according to the percentage of the potential energy in the fuel that is actually produced as power by the engine. Technical efficiency concerns the quantities of *all* factors of production used, while engineering efficiency concentrates on just one.

methods of production that use *less* labor and *more* capital.[7]

The principle of substitution says that (for a given set of technical possibilities) efficient production will substitute cheaper factors for more expensive ones.

This principle is a logical proposition. It tells us how the economically most efficient method of production necessarily changes as relative factor prices change. If we now add to this our behavioral assumption that firms are profit maximizers and so will choose the method of producing any given output that involves the least cost, we get the following prediction about substitution in the real world:

The methods of production will tend to change if the relative prices of factors change. Relatively more of the cheaper factor will be used and relatively less of the more expensive one.

As a rough rule, it may be suggested that the scarcer a factor of production in the economy, the higher its price.[8] Because of this, the principle of substitution leads the firm to economize in the use of resources that are scarce and to be more lavish in the use of factors that are plentiful.

Thus, it is neither surprising (nor indicative of inefficiency) to discover that methods of producing the same commodity differ in different countries. In the United States, where labor is highly skilled and very expensive, a steel company may use very elaborate machinery to economize on labor. In India, where labor is abundant and capital very scarce, a much less mechanized method of production may be appropriate. The American engineer who feels that Indians are way behind Americans because they are using methods Americans discarded as inefficient long ago may be missing the truth about economic efficiency in use of resources. The suggestion, often made, that to aid underdeveloped countries we need merely export American "know-how" may be incomplete.

It appears that the price system does lead profit-maximizing firms to take account of the nation's relative factor scarcities when deciding which of the possible methods of production to adopt. One must avoid jumping to the conclusion that whatever productive processes are produced by the market are always the best possible ones and that they should never be interfered with. There is, however, a strong common-sense appeal in the idea that any society interested in getting the most out of its resources take account of the relative scarcity of its resources in deciding what productive processes to adopt. To the extent that the relative prices of factors of production do reflect the approximate relative scarcities of these factors, private firms seeking their own private profit will be led to economize on factors that are generally scarce.[9]

---

7. In Case I, one unit of capital is equivalent in cost to $16\frac{2}{3}$ ($= \frac{50}{3}$) units of labor; in Case II, the ratio is 4 ($= \frac{20}{5}$); and in Case III, 3 ($= \frac{15}{5}$).

8. In a country with a great deal of land and a small population, Australia for example, there will be a large supply of land relative to the demand for it, and its price will be low; because labor is in short supply, however, the wage rate may be high. In a small country with a large population, Holland for example, the demand for land will be high relative to its supply. Thus the rental of land will be very expensive relative to the wage rate. This problem is discussed in Chapter 34.

9. The reason why we have been cautious in the statements of this paragraph is that factor prices do not necessarily perfectly reflect scarcity to society. Private cost is not always social cost. Current scarcity is not always future scarcity, etc. Some of the issues here are discussed later in this volume.

Summary

1. The firm is the unit that makes decisions with respect to the production and sale of commodities. We assume that the same principles underlie each decision made within a firm and that the decision is uninfluenced by who makes it. It is thus assumed that the persons making the decisions and the kinds of organizations in which they work can be abstracted from, and that the firm can be regarded as a decision-making unit that has objectives and that makes decisions designed to achieve those objectives.

2. The firm must decide what products shall be produced, in what way, and in what quantities. We assume that the firm makes these decisions in such a way as to maximize its profits.

3. Materials and factor services fed into the process of production are called inputs; the products that emerge are called outputs. One outstanding feature of modern capitalism is the use of capital goods, which are man-made aids to further production.

4. We often find it convenient to divide factors of production into categories. One common classification is land, labor, and capital. Land includes all primary products, labor all human services, and capital all man-made aids to further production.

5. Efficiency is a measure of the relative amount of input necessary to produce a given output. We distinguish between technical efficiency, which measures units of input in physical terms, and economic efficiency, which measures them in terms of costs.

6. The principle of substitution says that (for a given set of technical possibilities) efficient production will substitute cheaper factors for more expensive ones.

7. If we add to the principle of substitution our behavioral assumption that firms are profit-maximizers, we derive the following prediction: The methods of production will tend to change if the relative price of factors changes; relatively more of the cheaper factor will be used and relatively less of the more expensives ones.

QUESTIONS FOR DISCUSSION

1. What assumption do we make about the goals of firms? How will we ever find out if we are wrong?

2. What choices are open to a firm? In this chapter, how do we assume the neighborhood grocer's decisions would differ if he entered into a partnership?

3. List the important inputs and outputs of the type of firm called a university. Do the inputs seem to fall into any categories?

4. If something is technologically efficient, is it necessarily economically efficient? What about the reverse?

5. Why do you think that different methods of farming are used in America, Holland, and India?

6. "If technocrats could rule the economy unhampered by businessmen, their prices and their profits, a new era of productive efficiency could be initiated." What do you think of this statement?

Chapter **16** THE ORGANIZATION OF PRODUCTION

WE SAW IN CHAPTER 15 THAT STANDARD theory abstracts from the institutional setting in which decisions are made. It is assumed that all firms, whatever their structure, make decisions to maximize their profits. Of all the assumptions of standard theory, the one that the structure of the firm can be ignored is the one that has come under most frequent and most sustained attack. Once we have de-

veloped the standard theory, we shall devote considerable attention to such criticisms. In order to understand what we are abstracting from, and in order to consider the criticisms of our abstractions, you must understand the nature of the modern business organization.[1] In this chapter, we discuss this organization and also consider a few hypotheses that have been advanced about it.

Proprietorships, Partnerships, and Corporations

There are three major forms of business organization, the single proprietorship, the partnership, and the corporation. In the single proprietorship, there is a single owner who is personally responsible for everything done by the business. In the partnership, there are two or more joint owners each of whom is personally responsible for everything done by the business. In the corporation, the firm is regarded in law as having an entity of its own and the owners are not each personally re-

sponsible for everything that is done by the business.

In the United States today, there are about 5 million single proprietorships (not counting agriculture), 1 million partnerships, and over 1 million corporations. These figures may be misleading. Corporations account for more than two-thirds of the nation's privately produced income. In the important sectors of manufacturing, transportation, public utilities, and finance, corporations do virtually all

1. This chapter also introduces you to much of the elementary terminology of business organization and finance. Without a knowledge of the meaning of these terms, you will be unable to strike any contact between what you have learned from this book and what you read in magazines or newspapers about the world of business.

of the business. In trade and in construction, they do about half of the total business. Only in agriculture and in services (e.g., medicine, law, barbering, accounting) is the corporation relatively unimportant.

THE PROPRIETORSHIP AND THE PARTNERSHIP: ADVANTAGES AND DISADVANTAGES

The major advantage of the single proprietorship is that the owner can readily maintain full control over the firm. He is the Boss. The disadvantages are, first, that the size of the firm is limited by the capital the owner can personally raise, and, second, that he is personally responsible in law for all debts of the firm.

The partnership overcomes to some extent the first disadvantage of the proprietorship but not the second. Ten partners may be able to finance a much bigger enterprise than could one owner, but they are still subject to what is called *unlimited liability*. Each partner is fully liable for all of the debts of the firm. This liability is independent of the amount of money a particular proprietor may have invested in the firm. Thus, if a tenth partner makes $1,000 available (or $100, or nothing, for that matter) when he joins a firm that subsequently becomes bankrupt with debts of $100,000, then this individual, together with the other nine partners, is fully liable for the $100,000. If none of the other partners should have salable personal assets, whereas the tenth partner has a house, a car, furniture, and some investments, he may lose all of his possessions so that the debts of the partnership can be cleared. Obviously, a man with substantial personal assets will be unwilling to enter a partnership unless he has com-

plete trust in all the other partners and a full knowledge of all the obligations of the firm. As a direct consequence of unlimited liability, it is difficult to raise money from many persons through a partnership because of the need for all of the partners to have complete confidence and trust in each partner and to have a full knowledge of all the firm's business. An investor may be willing to invest $1,000, but not be willing to jeopardize his entire fortune; if, however, he joins a partnership in order to do the former, he cannot avoid doing the latter.

THE CORPORATION: ADVANTAGES AND DISADVANTAGES

The corporation is regarded in law as an entity separate from the individuals who own it. It can enter into contracts, it can sue and be sued, it can own property, it can contract debts, and it can generally incur obligations that are the legal obligations of the corporation, *but not of its owners*. This means that the corporation can enter into contracts in its own right and that its liability to adhere to such contracts can be enforced only by suing the corporation, not by suing the owners.[2]

The corporation issues shares that are purchased by the general public. The company obtains the money paid for the shares, and the shareholders become the owners of the company. They are entitled to share in the profits of the company, which, when they are paid out, are called *dividends*. They are also entitled to split up the assets of the company should it be liquidated, after all debts are paid off.

This method of finance means that the owners of the firm cannot all be the mana-

---

2. The right to be sued may not seem to be an advantage. It is an advantage because it makes it possible for others to enter into enforceable contracts with the corporation.

gers. The line of control is as follows. The shareholders (and there may be tens of thousands of them) elect a board of directors. The board of directors is supposed to act as a cabinet. It sets broad issues of policy and appoints senior managers. The managers are supposed to act as civil servants and to carry out the wishes of the directors, translating the broad lines of policy laid down by the directors into a series of detailed decisions.

The most important aspect of a joint stock company from the point of view of its owners is that they have *limited liability*. Should the company go bankrupt, the personal liability of any shareholder is limited to the amount of money that he has actually invested in the firm by purchasing its shares. Since the shareholders and the corporation are regarded as separate entities, the shareholder is not liable to lose his personal assets in order to meet the firm's obligations. The great advantage of the joint-stock, limited-liability company is that it can raise capital from a very large number of individuals each of whom gets a share in the firm's profits, but who, beyond risking the loss of the amount he actually invests, has no liabilities. Thus each investor knows his maximum risk exactly, and he may sit back and collect his dividends without knowing anything about the policy or operation of the firm that he, along with many others, actually owns.

The disadvantages (from the point of view of the investor) are, first, that he may have little say in the management of the firm (for example, if the owners of a majority of the shares decide that the corporation should not pay dividends, an individual investor cannot compel them to pay him his share of the earnings); and, second, that the corporation is subject to income taxation, as are the investor's dividends.[3]

The corporate form is employed wherever very large enterprises are found. The reason is that it has decisive advantages over any other form in being able to raise the large sums of capital required for major enterprises. Historically, wherever and whenever large accumulations of capital in a single firm were required, the limited-liability, joint-stock company developed. The corporate form is not usually found in service industries or agriculture because these do not need large quantities of capital to function.

THE RISE OF THE MODERN CORPORATION

Although historians have found roots of the corporation in Roman Law and in the medieval guild system, the direct predecessor of the modern corporation was the chartered company of the sixteenth century. The Muscovy Company, granted a charter in 1555, and the East India Company, chartered in c. 1602, are famous early examples of joint stock ventures with limited liability. These companies were granted charters by the Crown to make possible trade by Englishmen with particular regions. The special needs of having large numbers of investors involved in the financing of a ship that would not return with the cargo for years—if it returned at all—made this *exceptional* form of organization seem desirable. In the next three centuries, the critical attributes of the trading company, large capital requirements and risk, were recognized to exist in other fields as well, and char-

---

3. Debate in the United States over this "double taxation" of income has existed for decades. Whether taxation of corporate income is fair, whether there are offsetting privileges, and the nature of the consequences of double taxation are matters for a course in public finance, and we shall not discuss them in this book. See Harold Groves, *Financing Government* (Holt, Rinehart & Winston, 1964), for an introduction to the issues.

ters were increasingly granted in the fields of insurance, turnpikes and canals, and banking, as well as foreign trade. The Industrial Revolution, which made the large firm efficient, extended these same problems to many more fields, and, during the nineteenth century, the demand for a general rather than a special privilege of incorporation became strong. General laws permitting incorporation with limited liability, as a matter of right rather than special grant of privilege, became common both in England and in the States during the latter half of the nineteenth cen-

tury; today incorporation is relatively routine, although subject to a variety of state laws. Moderate fees are charged for the privilege of incorporation, and competition among the states for the incorporation fees has served greatly to liberalize the conditions for incorporation throughout the country. Delaware is an example of a small state that at one time had a highly disproportionate share of incorporations owing to its permissiveness. In the insurance field, Connecticut took the lead and most insurance companies founded before 1930 have Connecticut charters.

Financing the Modern Corporation

The money that a firm raises to carry on its business is called its *capital*. This money may be borrowed from outsiders or subscribed by the owners of the firm. We therefore speak of the firm's own capital and its borrowed capital.

The plant and equipment (and all the man-made aids to further production) owned by the firm are referred to as its *capital equipment* or *capital goods*. This use of the same word, capital, to refer to both an amount of money and a quantity of goods can be confusing, and the terms *money capital* and *real capital* are sometimes used instead. Most often the single term capital is used interchangeably. It is usually clear from the context whether a sum of money or a stock of equipment is being referred to.[4]

Firms raise capital in several ways. The most important of these are (1) selling *shares, stocks,* or *equities* (as they are variously called) either by private or public sale;

(2) borrowing by the sale of *bonds* or *debentures;* (3) borrowing from banks; and (4) reinvesting the firm's profits.

STOCKHOLDERS

The owners of the firm are its stockholders, persons who have put up money to purchase shares in the firm. They make their money available to the firm and risk losing it in return for a share in the firm's profits. Stocks in a firm often proliferate into a bewildering number of types. Basically, however, there is *common stock* and *preferred stock*. Common stock usually carries voting rights and has a residual claim on profits: After all other claims have been met, including those of holders of preferred shares, the remaining profits, if any, belong to the common-stock holders. The dividends earned by the stockholder may be zero or positive. There is no upper limit to the possible profits

4. The two uses are not totally independent of each other, since much of the money capital raised by a firm will be used to purchase the capital goods that the firm requires for production.

that may be earned by the company and hence to possible dividends that could be paid out to common-stock holders.

Preferred stocks may be voting or non-voting, cumulative or noncumulative. Basically, the difference between preferred stock and common stock is that preferred stocks carry with them a right to a preference over common stocks to any profits that may be available after other obligations have been met, but also a stated maximum to the rate of dividends that will be paid per dollar originally invested.

BONDHOLDERS

The bondholders are creditors, not owners of the firm. They have loaned money to the firm in return for a promise to pay a stated sum of money each year by way of interest on the loan, and also to repay the loan at some stated time in the future (say, five, seven, or ten years hence). This promise to pay is a legal obligation on the firm's part whether or not profits have been made. If these payments cannot be met, then the bondholders can force the firm into bankruptcy. Should this happen, the bondholders have a claim to the firm's assets prior to that of any of the shareholders. Only if the bondholders and all other creditors have been repaid in full can the shareholders attempt to recover anything for themselves.

The disadvantage of raising capital through the sale of bonds is that interest payments must be met whether or not there are any profits. Many a firm that would have survived a temporary crisis had all its capital been share capital has been forced into bankruptcy because it could not meet its contractual obligations to pay interest to its bondholders.

If a member of the public buys a bond from a firm, he cannot get his money back from the firm until the expiration of a stated period of time; if, for example, he buys a ten-year bond, the bond will be redeemed by the company (i.e., the loan will be paid back) ten years after the bond was issued. If the individual wishes to get his money back at an earlier date, the only thing he can do is to persuade someone else to buy the bond from him. Similarly, if an individual buys shares newly issued by a company, then he hands over money to the company and becomes one of its owners. Once this has been done, he cannot get his money back from the firm (except in the unlikely event that the firm is liquidated). If he wishes to withdraw his capital from the company, the only thing he can do is to persuade someone else to take over his piece of the firm by selling his share to that person.

THE STOCK MARKET

A market where existing issues of stocks and bonds are sold by one individual to another is called a stock market. The selling of shares on the stock market indicates that the existing ownership of the company is being transferred; it does not indicate that the company is raising new money from the public, although some new issues *are* sold on the stock market.

The company is, nevertheless, interested in the price of its shares on the stock market, because this price indicates the degree of confidence that investors have in the future earning power of the company. That confidence (or lack of it) will greatly affect the firm's ability to raise funds by selling new issues of stocks or bonds, should it so desire.

REINVESTED PROFITS

For the established firm, as distinct from the new one, an additional very important means of obtaining funds is through the reinvesting, or plowing back, of the firm's own profits. This has become an extremely important source of funds in modern times and over $10 billion per year is obtained for investment in the United States in this fashion. One of the easiest ways for the controllers of the firm to raise money is to retain some of the firm's own profits rather than pay them out as dividends to shareholders. If the shareholder does not wish his profits to be reinvested there is very little that he can do about it.[5] In many cases, firms pay out a standard dividend to their common-stock holders year after year, holding back any profits in excess of this amount, and paying dividends out of reserves when current profits fall short of the amount necessary to make such dividend payments. Common stocks on which a standard payment is made year in and year out in spite of fluctuating profits are a very far cry from the original idea of a common stock, which yielded little or nothing in bad times and very high returns in good times.

The Widespread Ownership of the Modern Corporation

In some giant corporations a small group or family provided most of the original capital, and the firm grew with little or no sale of securities to the public. American examples are the Ford Motor Company, which until 1956 was wholly owned by the Ford family; the Great Atlantic and Pacific Tea Company (Hartford family); E. I. Du Pont de Nemours and Company (Du Pont family); and the Aluminum Company of America (Mellon family). At the other extreme the giant American Telephone and Telegraph Company had in 1964 more than 2 million shareholders of common stock, no one of whom owned as much as 1 percent of the total.

Between these extremes lie the great bulk of corporations. The characteristic pattern of corporate ownership is that tens of thousands or hundreds of thousands of shareholders own minute fractions of the total, while dominant groups (often including other corporations) hold from 3 percent to 20 percent of the voting stock.

THE CONSEQUENCES OF WIDESPREAD OWNERSHIP

The days of the single proprietor who was both the owner and the manager of a company are gone forever in major areas of the business world. Diversification of ownership is a major characteristic of modern business. Does it matter? The following three hypotheses have been advanced about the consequences of the diversification of corporate ownership.

1. *The Hypothesis of Minority Control. Because of the widespread distribution of shares, the owners of a minority of the stock are usually able to control a majority of the voting shares and thus to exercise effective control over the decisions of the corporation.*

---

5. Unless he can persuade a majority of the shareholders to agree with him. Of course, the dissident shareholder can sell his share of the company.

Let us see how these results might occur. Each share of common stock has one vote in a corporation. Any individual or group controlling 51 percent of the stock clearly controls a majority of the votes. But suppose one group owns only 30 percent of the stock and the remaining 70 percent is distributed so widely that few of the dispersed group even bother to vote; in this event 30 percent may be the overwhelming majority of the shares actually voted.[6] How large a percentage is actually required to control the majority depends on the pattern of ownership and on whether there has been a major effort to collect proxies. A colorful, but rare, phenomenon in corporation history is the "proxy fight" in which competing factions of stockholders (or management) attempt to collect the voting rights of the dispersed and generally disinterested stockholders. In general, a very small fraction of shares, sometimes as small as 5 percent, actively voted may exercise dominant influence at meetings of stockholders.

Another aspect of minority control is made possible through the device known as a *holding company*. Suppose, in a certain corporation, call it A, ownership of 20 percent of the stock would give dominant control. Now a new corporation, which we shall call B, is formed. B purchases 20 percent of the stock in A. Corporation B can now control A. But no more than 51 percent of the stock of B is required to control the stock in A. Indeed, if 20 percent ownership of B is sufficient to control B's affairs, an amount of money equal only to 4 percent of the value of A's stock (20 percent of 20 percent) is required for a group to gain control of B and thus of A. Now suppose a new corporation, C, is formed to purchase 20 percent of Corporation B. . . .[7]

2. *The Hypothesis of the Separation of Ownership from Control. Because of diversified ownership and the difficulty of collecting stockholders or proxies, the managers rather than the stockholders exercise effective control over the decisions of the corporation.*

The argument offered in support of this hypothesis is as follows: In order to conduct the complicated business of running a large firm, a full-time professional management group *must* be given broad powers of decision. Although managerial decisions can be reviewed from time to time, they cannot be supervised in detail. If the managerial group behaves badly it may later be removed and replaced, but this is a drastic action and a disruptive one, and is infrequently employed. Within very wide limits then, effective control of the corporation's activities does reside with the managers, who need not even be stockholders in the corporation. Although the managers are legally the employees of the stockholders, they are able to remain largely unaffected by them. Indeed, they characteristically ask for, and typically get, the proxies of a very large number of stockholders and thus perpetuate themselves in office.

3. *The Hypothesis of Intercorporate Control Groups. Whole sectors of the economy are effectively controlled by small groups of people through the mechanism of interlocking directorships.*

If each member of a small group holds directorships in several companies, the group can control the boards of directors of many

6. Shares must be voted at the annual meeting of stockholders. They may be voted in person or by assigning a "proxy" to someone who will be attending.

7. This pyramiding of control via holding companies has no limits in logic, but it is limited in both law and in practicability. It should also be mentioned that holding companies serve many purposes other than the rather suspect one described here.

different companies without being so obvious as to have the identical set of persons on each and every board. By controlling the boards of directors, this group can exert effective and relatively unostentatious control over the companies themselves.

This hypothesis requires not only that interlocking directorships should be common, but also that boards of directors should be able to control the policies of corporations in ways that would not be approved of by managers or by stockholders. This hypothesis is in conflict with the second hypothesis, for one cannot hold simultaneously that managers make the effective decisions, ignoring the interests of shareholders and directors, and that directors make the effective decisions, ignoring the interests of managers and shareholders. One can hold either the second or the third hypothesis, but not both simultaneously.

THE SIGNIFICANCE OF THE HYPOTHESES

These hypotheses have received a vast amount of empirical attention since they were first posed three decades ago.[8] Although it is fairly easy to assess the evidence for and against them, it is more difficult to decide what their economic significance is should they be accepted. The hypothesis of minority control is widely accepted; it is usually observed to be the case that the owners of a minority of the shares in a corporation are able to exercise effective control over the election of a board of directors. The hypothesis of the separation of ownership from con-

trol is widely but not universally held. The hypothesis of intercorporate control groups has some adherents but is not generally accepted, although there is formidable evidence that interlocking directorships exist on a large scale.[9] There does not seem to be any evidence, however, that the common directors exert any significant influence altering the firm's behavior from what it would be if no such interlocking existed. The significance of these hypotheses for economics depends on whether, if true, the behavior of the firm would be significantly different from what it would be if the hypotheses were false.

As far as the behavior of the firm is concerned, the hypothesis of minority control is only important if the stockholders are able to exert a significant influence on its behavior, and if the controlling minority have interests and motives different from the holders of the majority of the firm's stocks. If all stockholders are mainly interested in having the firm maximize its profits, then it does not matter, as far as economics is concerned, which set of stockholders actually influences the firm's policy. There is no accepted evidence to show that controlling groups of stockholders do in fact seek objectives different from those sought by the holders of the majority of the firm's stocks.

For the hypothesis of the separation of ownership and control to be important it is necessary that the managers should be able to exert effective control over business decisions and that they should wish to act differently from the way the stockholders and

8. See especially the pioneering study by Adolf A. Berle, Jr., and G. C. Means, *The Modern Corporation and Private Property* (Macmillan, 1937); and R. A. Gordon, *Business Leadership in the Large Corporation* (University of California Press, 1945; reprinted in paperback, 1961).

9. Some individuals are directors of many corporations. This may be because they represent banks or other investment groups that finance corporations or because they are "big names" who lend authority to the corporation or because they are merely highly valued for their advice. The mere fact that individuals may hold many directorships means that many corporations will have at least one director in common with many other corporations.

directors wish to act. If the managers are motivated by a desire to maximize the firm's profits—either because it is in their own interests to do so or because they voluntarily choose to reflect the stockholders' interests—then it does not matter that they have effective control over decisions. If the managers wish to pursue goals other than profit maximization, then the behavior of the firm will be different according to whether the managers or the owners exercise effective control. In Chapter 30, we shall consider a theory that takes the separation of ownership and control as its starting point and that then proceeds on the assumption that managers are motivated by desires other than to maximize the profits of the firm. This is a genuine competing hypothesis and the only way to choose between it and the hypothesis that the managers seek to maximize the firm's profits is to confront the predictions of each theory with factual observations and see which better predicts the observed phenomena.[10]

Other Questions

The economist is interested in more than the effect of the corporate form on the decision-making process of the firm. Does the corporate form contribute to more efficient production by fostering the establishment of larger firms than could otherwise be organized? Does the corporation, insofar as it encourages reinvestment of earnings, affect (for better, for worse) the allocation of resources between investment and consumption? Does the corporation change the nature of market processes either as a seller of goods or a buyer of factors? Does the corporation centralize economic power? Many of these questions are discussed in detail later in this book.

Summary

1. The three major forms of business organization are the single proprietorship, the partnership, and the corporation. The single proprietorship has a single personally responsible owner. The partnership has two or more personally responsible owners, each with un-

10. Perhaps a word or two more about the interests of managers is in order here. Stockholders elect directors who appoint managers. Directors are supposed to represent stockholders' interests and to determine broad policies that the managers merely carry out. In fact, the links are typically weak enough so that top management often does truly control the destiny of the corporation over long periods of time. As long as directors have confidence in the managerial group, they accept and ratify their proposals, and stockholders characteristically elect and re-elect directors who are proposed to them. Although the members of the top management group need not be stockholders, they usually do hold sizable amounts of the stock in the corporation that they manage, this stock often being acquired as a direct result of bonuses or compensation for their services. Although managers of giant corporations as a group usually own less than 2 percent of the corporation, so also do most other similar sized groups of stockholders. Most top managers of successful corporations are wealthy men much of whose wealth is represented by stock in their own companies. For example, when Charles Wilson left General Motors to become Secretary of Defense in 1952, it was disclosed that he owned $2.5 million of General Motors stock.

limited liability. Its major disadvantage is the difficulty of raising large amounts of money because of the unlimited liability of each partner. The corporation is recognized as a legal entity; its owners, or shareholders, have a liability that is limited to the amount of money they have actually invested in the organization.

2. Corporations can raise money in three main ways: by selling shares (also called stocks, equities, or part-ownerships) in the firm; by selling bonds (also called debentures), which are evidences of debt, since the firm owes the money to the bondholder and has a legal obligation to pay it back; and by reinvesting (or plowing back) its own capital.

3. The characteristic pattern of American corporate ownership today is a group of tens or hundreds of thousands of shareholders, most of whom hold minute fractions of the total stock, but with dominant groups holding from 3 to 20 percent of the voting stock.

4. The hypothesis that widespread ownership of shares confers control on a minority group who have a controlling block of shares is widely accepted. This minority control will only affect the behavior of the firm if the controlling minority have interests that differ from the mass of the shareholders.

5. The hypothesis that because of the widespread ownership of the corporation stockholders cannot exert effective control over the managers so that the latter have the real control of the organization has some serious, but by no means universal, support. This managerial control will affect the behavior of the firm only if the managers have goals that differ from those of the stockholders.

6. The hypothesis that a small group of individuals effectively *controls* a large section of the economy through the mechanism of interlocking directorates is not widely accepted (although the fact of interlocking directorships *is* accepted).

QUESTIONS FOR DISCUSSION

1. List a few businesses best suited to each of the following forms: Single proprietorship, partnership, and corporation.

2. Two owners of a partnership decide to incorporate their business. Because the state law requires at least three owners to every corporation, they each take 49 percent of the stock and give the remaining 2 percent to their secretary. The process of incorporation is a slight nuisance; it is time-consuming and at the moment it confers a certain tax disadvantage on them. Why on earth did they incorporate?

3. Victorian novels, like Thackeray's *Vanity Fair*, were full of wealthy businessmen who went

bankrupt because their businesses failed. Why is this less common today?

4. What is the primary function of the stock market? Do you think that the market for the shares of a very large corporation is similar to the *competitive* markets we discussed earlier? Why or why not?

5. If a lull in business in the economy is expected, which prices do you think will fall further, steel shares or bonds issued by U.S. Steel?

6. What sort of evidence do you think you might need in order to test the three hypotheses about corporate control given in this chapter? What is the importance of these three hypotheses to our theory of supply?

Chapter **17** THE MEANING AND MEASUREMENT OF COST

What Is Cost?

WE HAVE INTRODUCED THE HYPOTHESIS THAT, in making decisions about production, firms seek to maximize their profits. The profit from production consists of the difference between the value of the outputs and the value of the inputs. The *value* of the inputs used in production is the *cost* of the output achieved.

Notice our use in this definition of the word *value*. We are concerned not only with the physical quantities of the factors of production used, but with a monetary measure that permits us to add up such unlike units as man-hours of labor, tons of coal, and board-feet of timber and to compare them in the aggregate with the value of the output produced. A production engineer can tell his plant manager that, in order to achieve 100 units of output, he used 75 man-hours of labor, 50 tons of a certain raw material, 20 hours of machine time, and supervisory services of one very able production engineer for one week. But this does not tell the manager whether the operation is profitable or not unless he can assign monetary values to the physical quantities of outputs and inputs involved.

The assignment of monetary values to physical quantities of inputs may be very easy in some cases and very hard in others. Furthermore, different people or different groups may assign different values to the same input.

Economists might want to discuss production behavior of firms for a variety of reasons:

(1) to *describe* actual behavior of a firm;

(2) to *predict* how the firm's behavior will respond to specified changes in the conditions it faces;

(3) to *help* the firm make the best decisions it can in achieving its goals;

(4) to *evaluate* how well firms use scarce resources.

The same measure of cost need not be correct for all of these purposes. For example, if the firm happens to be misinformed about the value of some resource, it will behave according to that misinformation. In describing or predicting the firm's behavior, the economist should use the information the firm actually uses, even if he knows it to be based on misinformation. But in helping the firm to achieve its goals, the economist should substitute the correct information.

Economists have an explicit principle for defining costs for solving problems of the kind cited in (3) and (4) of the list above. If we assume that businessmen use the same principle and have the same information, the economist's definition will be appropriate for problems of types (1) and (2) as well. *We will make this assumption for the moment.* The consequences of this assumption being in error are discussed in Chapter 30 below.

Although the details of economic "costing" vary, they are governed by a common principle. The essential principle that economists use in assigning costs is sometimes called *user cost,* but is more commonly called *opportunity cost:*

The cost of using something in a particular venture is the benefit foregone (or opportunity lost) by not using it in its best alternative use.

An old Chinese merchants' proverb says: "Where there is no gain, the loss is obvious." The economic sense of this proverb is that the merchant who shows no gain has wasted his time—time that he could have used to produce profit in some other venture.

Since this "opportunity cost" doctrine plays a very central role in economic analysis and affects the significance that can be attached to economists' conclusions, let us consider a few examples of assigning opportunity cost that are somewhat removed from the production problem, yet may be relevant for decisions.

Example 1. Miss Anne Thrope doesn't like bankers so she keeps her life's savings of $10,000 hidden in her mattress. What does it cost her per year to dislike bankers? One answer might be that it is the loss of interest she would have earned if she had placed her money in a savings account at 4 percent ($400 per year) plus the added cost of the extra fire and theft insurance she carries on her house and belongings. This is the right answer if she regards the savings account as her best alternative.[1]

Example 2. George Bernard Shaw, upon reaching his ninetieth birthday, was asked how he liked being ninety. He is reputed to have said, "It's fine, when you consider the alternative."

Example 3. O. L. Tymer, a successful lawyer, complains that file clerks "are not what they used to be" and insists on doing his own filing. He is, in fact, able to do the job 30 percent faster than the best obtainable file clerk and at the same level of accuracy. Is this a sensible use of his time?

Example 4. Retired General William Russ, who is married to a very wealthy woman, has decided to contribute $5,000 to a political candidate he likes very much. His lawyer points out to him that since he is in the 50-percent tax bracket, and since political contributions are not deductible from his income, the real cost of his contribution is the same as giving an extra $10,000 to his favorite charity: the Gen. Russ Foundation. What is the opportunity cost of the political contribution?

Example 5. A very successful doctor complains that now that he is earning huge fees he can no longer afford to take a vacation trip to Europe. In what ways, if any, does it make sense to say that the cost of his trip depends upon his fees?

Example 6. A thirty-five-year-old bachelor is thinking about marrying at last. But, although he thinks Grace is a lovely girl, he

---

1. She could dislike bankers and still earn money on her savings by investing in government bonds, real estate, or stocks. But perhaps Miss Thrope dislikes governments, risk, and businessmen too.

figures that if he marries her he will give up the chance of wedded bliss with another girl he may meet next year. So he decides to wait a while. What additional information do you require to determine the opportunity cost of this decision?

The Measurement of Opportunity Cost by the Firm

In principle, measuring opportunity cost is easy. The firm must decide what factors of production it has used and assign to each a monetary value equal to what it has sacrificed in order to have the use of the factor. When we come to apply this principle to specific cases, however, some tough problems arise.

In the case of those factors of production that the firm hires, such as labor, there is no problem. The cost per unit is clearly known and, since payments are made explicitly, the cost will be deducted from the firm's revenues in assessing the profitability of a given line of production.

In the case of factors of production that the firm itself owns, the cost must also be assessed but, since no payment is made to anyone outside the firm, these costs are not so obvious. Such costs are called *imputed costs*. If the most profitable lines are to be discovered, the cost of these factors should be reckoned at their market prices. That such amounts do represent costs to the firm can be seen by the fact that the firm could earn a revenue by leasing to someone else such factors as it owns. If, for example, a firm uses $10,000 worth of its own money that could have been loaned out to someone else at 5 percent, yielding $500 per year, then this $500 should be deducted from the firm's revenue as the cost of funds used. If, to con-

tinue the example, the firm makes only $400 over all other costs, then we should say not that the firm made $400 but rather that it lost $100, for if it closed down completely and merely loaned out its capital to someone else, it could have earned $500.[2] Similarly, if the owner of a firm also acts as its manager, he should impute as costs to the firm a management fee equal to what he could obtain if he leased his services to some other firm. If the firm uses its own plant and equipment, it should charge as a cost a fee reflecting the market value of these services. (After all, the firm could cease operations and rent its plant and equipment to someone else.)

The most difficult problem of imputed costs concerns the evaluation of the service of *risk-taking*. Business enterprise is often a risky affair. Some businesses are more risky than others and someone must take the risk in each case. The risk of business is in fact borne by the owners and the risk that they take is that they may lose the money they have invested in the firm. The owners of the firm will not take these risks unless they receive a remuneration in return. They must expect to receive a return in excess of what they could have obtained by investing their money in a virtually riskless manner, say by buying a U.S. Government bond. In the sense in which we have used the term, risk-taking is a

2. Charging the market value of the capital is appropriate if the firm can obtain all the funds that it requires by borrowing. If, as is sometimes the case, this is not so, then the firm will place a high value on the funds that it does have. Such a firm must cost its capital by looking at the other ventures it might have undertaken, since its inability to raise all the capital it wants means that it will be unable to do all the things it wants.

factor of production. It is a service that must be provided if the firm is to carry on production and it must be paid for by the firm. If a firm does not yield a return sufficient to compensate for the risks involved, the firm will not be able to persuade people to contribute money to it in return for a part-ownership in the firm.

Raw materials, supplies, labor, use of buildings and machinery, use of capital, services of managers, and risk-taking, plus many others, are factors of production that are used in producing the firm's output. If they have alternative productive uses (and in general they always do), the firm must charge itself for their use if it wishes to determine whether it is making the most profitable use of the resources it controls or purchases.

Costs, Rents, and Profits

You have just learned that imputed charges for using certain factors of production, including capital, risk-taking, and managerial services not covered by salaries, are properly *costs* to the firm. *When valued by the opportunity-cost principle they are the amounts required to make the use of these factors in this venture precisely as attractive as in their best alternative use.*

If the firm is covering all its costs in the sense that we have defined costs, then it follows that the firm could not do better by using its resources in any other line of activity than the one currently being followed. Indeed, it would probably do worse in most other lines of activity; it certainly would do no better. Thus a situation in which revenues equal costs is not an unsatisfactory one—because all factors, hidden as well as visible, are being rewarded at least as well as in their *best* alternative uses. To reverse the Chinese proverb cited earlier, "Where there is no loss compared to the best alternative use of every factor, the gain is obvious."

If the firm is covering all its costs, it is doing as well as it could do in any other line of activity; it thus has no incentive to alter its behavior. Is it always the case that the firm receives revenues that just cover the costs? No. There are many reasons why the firm might earn less than enough to cover all costs, at least temporarily. If demand falls, for example, price will fall and a firm that was covering all costs may no longer be able to do so. This means that the firm could do better in some other line of activity and it will tend to abandon its present line. *When revenues in a particular line of activity are less than costs, it is a signal for resources to move out of that line of activity.*

The situation in which revenues exceed costs is a little more complex and we must first consider the various causes of such a situation and then inquire into the consequences in each case.

A common source of an excess of revenues over costs is a temporary shortage of output. An increase in demand can raise price; as a result, if revenues originally equaled cost, they will now exceed costs. Until such time as more factors are brought into the production of the product, the existing factors will be especially scarce and may earn what are called *quasi-rents*.[3] The existence of *quasi-*

3. A *rent* is any earning in excess of opportunity cost that will persist indefinitely. A *quasi-rent* is any earning in excess of opportunity cost that exists because of a temporary shortage and thus will not persist indefinitely. The historical explanation of why these particular words are assigned to these ideas is given in Chapter 34.

rents will mean that owners of factors of production will want to shift resources into the industry earning quasi-rents;[4] if they are free to do so the quasi-rents will gradually disappear. Quasi-rents thus play an important role in the allocation of resources among products. The larger the quasi-rent earned by a firm in producing a product, the stronger the signal that leads new resources to be channeled into this line of production. Conversely, as we have already seen, if opportunity costs exceed revenues, this is a signal for resources to shift from these lines of production to their best alternatives. (In this case we could say that there are negative quasi-rents.)

In some cases what appear to be quasi-rents may be long-lived or even permanent if the firm enjoying them can prevent new resources from shifting into its industry. The power to prevent such resource flows is called *monopoly power*. Excesses of revenues over costs of this sort are sometimes called *monopoly profits* or *monopoly rents*. These may persist indefinitely.

Revenues may also exceed (or fall short of) costs because of random fluctuations of one sort or another. Uncertainty is a feature of the real world, and anticipations are unevenly realized: Sales fall or rise, equipment breaks down, strikes occur, risks work out in unexpected ways, and so on. Persistent profits or losses tend to induce flows of resources, but very short-run fluctuations of a haphazard nature do not.

The final reason why firms can earn returns in excess of costs is that, in some circumstances, they can appropriate for themselves revenues resulting from the special ability of the factors of production they employ. There are numerous cases in which there exists a factor with specialized talent that is fully useful only in a single industry.

This is true of many professional athletes, actors, airline pilots, and even college professors; it is also true of some craftsmen such as glass-blowers, cabinet-makers, and computer-programmers. The services of such people will be worth more to one industry than to any other. Will their employers always pay them only the amount they could earn in the next best occupation? If there are many firms competing with each other in the industry, it is likely that this competition among firms for valuable talent will lead to bidding up the price to the full value of the service. In a situation in which there is only one firm that can use the services of a particular factor, the firm can keep for itself some of the excess value (i.e., rent) that the factor earns in this industry. For example, until Independent Television came along, the only firm that could use television announcers with a British accent was the British Broadcasting Corporation. The same holds true when various firms agree not to compete for the services of a factor. This often happens in professional baseball. How the rent attributable to the factor (perhaps as much as $200,000 per year in the case of Willie Mays) is divided between the firm and the owner of the factor is a matter of bargaining power, and we need not discuss it here. The point is that if the firm retains *any* of this excess value, it will appear as an excess of revenues over costs.

We define *profits* as the difference between revenues and opportunity costs, whatever the source of that difference. If profits are negative, we refer to them as *losses*. At any moment the profits of a firm may consist of many different things: the quasi-rents, the differences between revenues and costs caused by random fluctuations, monopoly profits, and rents appropriated from factors. Over a fairly long period of time,

---

4. Because, in any other use, their opportunity cost has risen.

many of these things tend to cancel out, or lead to their own corrections. Resources respond to the shifts both in demands and in costs that produce quasi-rents; random fluctuations average out; and technology often overcomes the special advantages and shortages that lead to rents. Monopoly power, if it can be maintained, is another matter. For this reason many economists have tended to regard profits that persist for very long periods of time and do not provide a self-correcting flow of resources into the industry as evidence of the existence of monopoly power.[5] Given a long enough period of time even monopoly profits may be eroded.[6]

DIFFERENT USES OF THE TERM PROFITS

We have defined profits to be the excess of revenues over opportunity costs, whatever the source of such excess. This is a technical and specialized definition of a word that is in everyday use. It is, therefore, a potential source of confusion to the student who runs into other uses of the same word.

The businessman defines profits as the excess of revenues over the costs with which his accountant provides him. The major differences are that, since the accountant does not include as costs charges for risk-taking and use of the owners' own capital, these items are recorded by the businessman as part of his profits. When the businessman says he needs profits of such and such an amount merely to break even, he is making sense within his definition. For his "profits" must be large enough to pay for those factors of production that he uses, but that the accounting profession does not recognize.

The income-tax authorities have yet another definition of profits, which is implicit in the thousands of rules as to what may be (and what may not be) included as a deduction from revenue in arriving at taxable income. In some cases, the taxing authorities allow more for cost than the accountant recommends; in other cases they allow less.

Some economists, while following the same definitions we use in substance, label as *normal profits* the imputed returns to capital and risk-taking just necessary to prevent the owners from withdrawing from the industry. These "normal profits" are, of course, what we have defined as the opportunity costs of risk-taking and capital, and these economists include them as costs to be covered, as do we. The difference is purely semantic: They speak of "total costs including normal profits"; we speak of "total costs."

It is important to be clear about different meanings of the term profits not only to avoid fruitless semantic arguments but also because a theory that predicts that certain behavior is a function of profits defined in one way will not necessarily predict behavior accurately given some other definition. For example, if the economist predicts that new firms will enter an industry whenever there are business profits, his prediction will frequently be wrong if he is working from the businessman's definition of profits. Our definition of profits is for many purposes the most useful, but the student who wishes to apply it to business behavior or to tax policy must be prepared to make the appropriate adjustments.

5. See, for example, J. S. Bain, "The Profit Rate as a Measure of Monopoly Power," *Quarterly Journal of Economics*, LV, February, 1941. In the article, Bain is concerned with "excess profits," that is, those above "normal profits." Our statement above speaks merely of profits, because we included "normal" profits in cost.
6. This is the hypothesis of Joseph Schumpeter, who described as "creative destruction" the process by which established positions in the economy are destroyed by such processes as the introduction of new products to replace old ones. See below, Chapter 20.

Cost to Whom?

Cost is the valuation placed upon the use of resources. Who should do the evaluating? In this chapter, we have looked at cost from the point of view of the producing firm. The firm sacrificed funds when it bought coal, or hired labor, or used up equipment. The economy as a whole, or *society* as it is often called, also sacrifices something: whatever the quantities of coal, labor, equipment, or capital could have produced if they were not used by that firm for that purpose. *Social cost* interests economists who want to study how an economy organizes its use of resources. Social cost may differ from private cost as measured by the firm in a number of ways. For example:

1. Firms may use resources they do not regard as scarce. They may discharge waste into the air (causing smog) or into rivers (causing pollution). Use of these resources — air and water — involves costs to society (smog is unpleasant and costly to get rid of, for example), even if it does not represent costs to the firm.

2. The cost to society of using a resource to make good X is the value of what it could have made of good Y (its next best use). The cost to the firm is what it must pay to bid the resource away from other firms that are also making good X. There is no reason why these two costs should be the same.[7]

3. Some goods and services that society values are not sold on any market. For example, the price of standing timber, which the firm engaged in lumbering will regard as the cost of a key raw material, will not reflect the value society attaches to the conservation of its forests. Put differently, the firm values the

forest for the trees, whereas society values the trees for the forest. The firm will consider the opportunity cost of using the trees for lumber against using them for other commercial purposes, but not for using them as a public park, since this use will not produce revenue for the firm. In other words, firms may have "best alternatives" different from society's.

Although there are many examples of the *differences* between social and private cost, there is a very large number of cases in which both firms and society *use the identical standard of valuation*—the prices set by the market. The firm regards the opportunity cost of purchasing a ton of coal for $5 as $5 because it must sacrifice $5 to acquire the coal. The social cost is also $5 if the market price of $5 reflects the value of the resources used to produce a ton of coal in alternative uses.

Social cost and private cost may sometimes differ and may sometimes be the same. The more they are the same, the greater the reliance that the members of society will place on the market mechanism to allocate resources among uses. Where private and social valuations are the same, private firms seeking to maximize private gains by making the best allocation of resources according to private valuations will also be allocating according to social valuations. The more private and social valuations differ, the greater will be the desire of the members of society to interfere with the private market mechanism through various devices of governmental regulation, operation, ownership, or control.

Two crucial questions of social policy are

7. Cases in which these costs will differ are analyzed in Appendix A to this chapter and in Chapter 43.

factual ones: Are there differences between private and social costs?[8] If there are how large are they? If there is a consensus that such differences exist and are large (as appears to be the case in the United States in many areas; for example, in defense, elementary education, conservation, and some aspects of recreation), governmental action to replace or interfere with private market determination of the resources to be devoted to these purposes may occur. Where differences generally appear nonexistent or small, the issue of public versus private provision is unlikely to arise. The activity is left to the market. The areas of major controversy (at any time) will be the ones where there is no consensus on the facts.[9]

It is perfectly clear that among countries at the same time, for given countries over time, and among political parties or factions, as well as among individuals, judgments about these facts differ as do opinions about the significance that should be placed upon them. To the extent that these disagreements rest upon the existence and size of the differences between social and private costs, they are subject to analysis by economists.

One further point: All actual economies are mixed economies in the sense that some functions are left to the market mechanism and some are heavily influenced by governmental policy. Although there may be some people who believe that unrestricted private enterprise is always the best way to have a service provided and some who believe that government action is always required to achieve satisfactory resource allocation, there is no evidence that any society has ever operated at either extreme. The serious debate in any generation and in any place is not about whether to have a mixed economy, but about where the line should be drawn.

Summary: The Significance of Opportunity Cost

1. The opportunity cost of using a resource is the value of that resource in its best alternative use.

2. If the opportunity cost of using a resource in one way is less than or equal to the gain from using the resource in this way, there is no superior way of using it.

3. A firm maximizing profits, defined as the difference between revenue and opportunity cost, is making the best allocation of the resources under its control, according to the firm's evaluation of its alternatives.

4. If *social* valuations of cost are the same as the *firm's* valuations, there is a sense in which this allocation can also be considered as best from the society's point of view.

5. Profits earned in some enterprise provide a signal that more resources should move into similar enterprises. Losses show that some resources have better employments elsewhere, and serve as a signal for them to move out of that enterprise.

8. As well as of such related judgments as concern the existence and magnitude of differences between private and social benefits. See Chapter 43.

9. Even total agreement on the facts would not resolve all policy issues, since people will and do disagree on for example, how large a discrepancy has to be before they want public policy to come into play. There is a wide range of views on the relative merits of private and public action in cases where other things are equal. Some abhor governmental action and would **pay** a substantial price to avoid it; others actively prefer public to private provision.

6. For these reasons, the opportunity-cost principle provides a crucial clue to the nature of the allocation of resources. Since this is a primary concern of economists, we find this concept of cost the best one to use. The word cost as used hereafter should always be understood to mean opportunity cost, either to the firm or to society.

QUESTIONS FOR DISCUSSION

1. How much is it costing you to attend college?

2. "Because our corporation had unusually large cash reserves, we chose the costless method of finance and invested in ourselves." Discuss the meaning of cost as used here. How does it differ from the definition of cost used in this chapter? Which definition is more useful to the profit-maximizing firm?

3. What rent does Elvis Presley earn as an entertainer? What rent does he earn as an employee of one particular entertainment organization? Does it help to know that he was a truck driver before he was discovered?

4. If a shortage of doctors drives up doctors' earnings, how long will it take for the quasi-rents to disappear (a) if there is free entry to medical school, and (b) if there is a great deal of restriction? How do policies regarding foreign-trained doctors affect the situation?

5. What point in this chapter is illustrated by the following quotations from the 1965 Report of the Council of Economic Advisors to the President? Are there solutions to these problems?

a. "The cost of air pollution is borne mainly by the community at large, rather than by those responsible for it."

b. "Although people value open spaces in urban areas, there is no market on which they can register their preferences."

APPENDIX A TO CHAPTER 17 DETERMINING PRIVATE OPPORTUNITY COST[1]

IN CHAPTER 17 WE DISCUSSED the opportunity-cost principle:

The cost of using a factor in a particular venture is the benefit foregone (or opportunity lost) by not using it in its best alternative use.

This can sometimes be a difficult concept to apply to a specific case. Let us see what happens when we do try to apply it.

Purchased Factors

Assigning costs is perhaps most straightforward for those factors that the firm buys on the market and uses up entirely during the period of production. Many raw-material and intermediate-product purchases fall into this category.[2] If a firm pays $5 per ton for coal delivered to its factory, it has sacrificed its claims to whatever else $5 can buy, to which

---

1. Appendix B, p. 204, presents a highly simplified example of a firm's operations in order both to acquaint you with the basic summary statements of the accountant and to relate these to the costs of production as measured by accountants and economists.

2. Where the sources of raw materials are owned by the firm, a different procedure for assigning costs is required.

we assign the monetary value $5.[3],[4]

Hired Factors

For hired factors of production, where the rental price is the full price, the situation is identical. Most labor services are hired, but typically the cost is more than the wages paid because employers usually contribute to social security, to pension funds, and to various kinds of unemployment and disability insurance. Frequently, there are other "fringe benefits" as well. The cost of these is measured by the extent of the firm's financial obligations to them, and they must be added to the direct wage in determining the opportunity cost of labor services used.

Owned Factors

The costs of using assets the firm owns, such as buildings, equipment, and machinery, consist of the cost of the capital tied up in them, and the "user charges" that should be made against them. The user charges, usually called depreciation, reflect the *imputed* charge for the loss in value of the asset because of its use in production. The economic theory of depreciation can be highly complex under certain circumstances (for example, in periods of inflation) and is beyond the scope of this book. But, since we are interested in opportunity costs, we must define depreciation to include the loss in value due to physical wear and tear *and* to obsolescence.[5] The actual measurement of depreciation is very difficult, except in those cases in which active "used-asset" markets exist. Accountants use various conventional methods of depreciation based upon historical costs.[6] While these are often useful approximations, they may in some cases seriously differ from the depreciation re-quired by the opportunity-cost principle. "Rectification" of accounting data is one of the practical problems faced by economists in empirical research on the business firm.

We illustrate the possible error involved in basing depreciation on historical costs in the following example: Suppose a firm, through its research and development department, discovers a new and improved process on which it acquires a patent that gives it exclusive rights to the process for 17 years. Let us say this process cost the firm $1,000 to develop. It is an asset of the firm. Although the patent has a legal life of 17 years, the firm estimates its useful life to be only one year because it knows other firms will develop similar processes in a year's time. What can the firm do with its patent in the year of its useful life, and what are the costs involved? See Table 1.

Clearly, the firm is fortunate.

---

3. It does not matter whether the firm pays cash for its purchases or charges them. The cost is charged in the period in which the factors are used up. Because there are lags between payment for factors and selling the product they are used to make, there is often an additional factor of production involved. This is the money tied up in the process of production. It is called "working capital" and its cost is discussed below.

4. In certain exceptional cases, opportunity cost will differ from purchase price even for purchased factors. For example, if in wartime the government both rations the quantity of the resource the firm may purchase and fixes its price, the firm might well value the resource more highly than its market price. In cases like this, black markets often exist in which the factor is sold and purchased illegally at a price above the fixed market price. We shall ignore exceptions of this kind.

5. Many students may think it wholly unreasonable that the buyer should be "charged" for using his purchase. Consider the man who buys a $3,000 automobile that he intends to use for six years. Why should he charge himself $1,000 depreciation during the first year just because the used-car market sells one-year-old used cars at one-third off new prices? After all, *he* does not intend to sell for six years. The answer is that one of the purchaser's alternatives is to buy a one-year-old car and operate it for five years. Indeed, that is the very position he is in after the first year. Whether he likes it or not he has paid $1,000 for the use of the car during the first year of its life.

6. There are a variety of approved methods, heavily influenced by the income-tax laws, which specify "permitted" techniques of depreciation for tax purposes. One purpose of the tax rules may be (as in the case of accelerated depreciation) to provide incentives for investment by permitting more rapid depreciation than is justified; thus these laws provide no assurance that the allowable depreciation is that depreciation which interests the economist when measuring opportunity cost. Many firms recognize this fact and keep two or more sets of books—one for tax purposes and one or more for internal review of their operations and reports to their stockholders.

The patent is a valuable asset and the firm can do two profitable things with it. The firm wishing to maximize its profits chooses alternative (a), and benefits to the extent of $10,000.

What is the opportunity cost of alternative (a)? The answer is $8,000, the benefits of the next *best* alternative, which is (b). This $8,000 bears no necessary relation to the cost of developing the patent. The profit from exclusive use of the patent is $2,000, the excess over opportunity cost. The rest of the profit is not a profit from production but a profit from research and development.[7] Notice that if the firm could have leased the patent in alternative (b) for $6,000 (other figures the same), it should charge itself $11,000 to use the patent exclusively, and would *lose* money in the economic sense. This means it has made the wrong decision; it should have adopted alternative (b). This example illustrates a point to which we shall return: Opportunity cost provides the clue to the best use of resources.

Consider next the cost to a firm of using a raw material that it owns rather than purchases. Steel companies own coal mines, iron ore deposits, and so on.[8] When the steel company "buys" a ton of iron ore from its ore-mining subsidiary what "price" should it "pay"? If there is an alternative source of iron ore from which the steel company could purchase (and/or

TABLE 1 **THE VALUATION OF ALTERNATIVE USES OF A PATENT**

Alternative	Direct increase in firm's profits from use of patent	License fees received	Total increase in profits of firm
(a) Use the patent exclusively in its own operations	$10,000	0	$10,000
(b) Use the patent, but also lease it to other firms	$ 5,000	$ 3,000	$ 8,000
(c) Lease exclusive rights to the patent to another firm	− $15,000	$10,000	− $ 5,000
(d) Do nothing with the patent	0	0	0

alternative buyers to whom the iron-ore subsidiary could sell), it should pay the market price, which is, say, $12 a ton. What difference does it make? Since the same group owns both the ore company and the steel company, the total combined profits will be the same if the "price" charged for the purely internal sale is $5 or $50. It makes a difference because the firm needs to know whether *each* of its operations is efficient. If the cost to it of producing ore is $20 a ton, it should be buying its ore at the market price, $12, not producing it.[9] Only if the cost of producing ore is less than the market price of ore should the company be producing ore. The market price of ore provides a test of the economic efficiency of the part of the com-

pany producing ore. This same price also provides a test of the efficiency of the part of the company that purchases and uses the ore. Consider the profits after all costs, except the cost of ore, from the amount of steel one ton of ore can make. If profits are more than $12, the firm is genuinely making a profit on its steel production. If profits are less than $12—say $8—the firm is losing money making steel: It is sacrificing a resource worth $12 to gain $8. It should devote fewer resources to steel production. This is true even if the firm is an exceptionally efficient ore producer and can produce ore at $5 a ton. The firm's choice is to use the ore in steel production (gain of $8 per ton of ore) or to sell the ore to other pro-

7. The research and development division might be viewed as having sold exclusive rights to the production department for $8,000, an amount that exceeds the cost of developing the patent by $7,000.

8. Students of industrial organization speak of such firms as being "vertically integrated"—that is, they operate in a series of industries in which the outputs of one become the inputs of the next.

9. Many firms recognize this fact and instruct their divisions to purchase parts or supplies outside of the company if they can do so more cheaply than from a subsidiary.

ducers (gain of $12 per ton of ore). Clearly, it would prefer to sell. Here again we see how opportunity cost provides the clue to the allocation of the firm's resources.

If there is no outside market price, the firm must impute one on the basis of the inputs into ore production. This may be difficult, but it is necessary to well-informed internal decision-making.[10]

The Cost of Capital

Determining the opportunity cost of capital—the funds tied up in long-term assets and in materials and supplies for current production—involves certain special problems. Suppose a firm is using $1 million of funds, raised as follows:

(1) $100,000 of bank credit, on which it pays interest at 5 percent;

(2) $300,000 of bonds, on which it pays interest at 4 percent;

(3) $600,000 of invested share capital, which represents the investment of its stockholders. Of this amount $500,000 was supplied in cash by stockholders when the stock was issued, and $100,000 represents

undistributed past profits that have been reinvested by the firm. The firm has no legal obligation to pay any return to the stockholders, although it normally does pay a dividend when there are profits.

The total legally required expenditures for interest are only $17,000 ($5,000 to the bank, $12,000 to the bondholders), or 1.7 percent of the total funds in use. You will readily see that this is not the cost of capital in any meaningful economic sense. But what *is* the cost?

The answer is implicit in the following argument, presented to the directors of the firm by the plant manager. The manager wishes to expand the plant by an addition that will cost $100,000, which he argues will cover all costs, except capital, and provide a profit of $6,000 per year. He argues that since this rate of return (6 percent) is greater than the cost of either bank credit or the money raised via the sale of the bonds, the investment is clearly worthwhile.

The plant manager is correct in his argument, *if* the firm can borrow as much additional money as it wants from the bank or if it can sell more bonds at 4 percent.[11] He is wrong if

the firm is limited in the amount of capital it can raise. Assume (for simplicity) that the firm is in a position to raise an additional $100,000, but that this amount is the total extra it can raise for any or all purposes over the next year. The opportunity cost of using this $100,000 is the best alternative project that it will not be able to undertake. It may well be that there are many competing demands for scarce funds: plant modernization, new product development, development of an overseas selling outlet, to name just a few. The cost of the proposed expansion is the lost opportunity to do these things.

Many business firms operate with rough cut-off rates of return, which are chosen to approximate the return on projects that the firm could undertake if it had sufficient funds. Empirical studies of certain American manufacturing industries suggest that the opportunity cost of capital is substantially in excess of bond rates, and may well be as high as 20 percent.[12] By this standard, the plant manager's proposal for plant expansion, which would earn 6 percent, does not seem attractive.

In general, many firms, in-

10. This example is suggestive of a wide range of real problems and actual practices. To name just two: Socialist economies, which substitute governmental decisions for market determination, have found it necessary to *create* "prices" for internal transactions in order to judge the efficiency of different components of their over-all production. See, for an introduction, Alec Nove, *The Soviet Economy* (Praeger, 1961). Many firms use sophisticated "standard costs" and budgets to evaluate and control the many small operations that add up to a process of production. See, for example, James S. Earley, "Business Budgeting and the Theory of the Firm," *Journal of Political Economy*, March, 1961.

11. Or if the firm can borrow money for the addition to the plant without limiting its general borrowing capacity for other purposes.

12. The fact that it is so high helps explain why many firms are anxious to retain and reinvest a major portion of their profits, and why many stockholders (who do not have similar personal investment opportunities) are willing to have corporations pay dividends that are substantially less than earnings. There are other considerations as well, including tax laws.

deed perhaps most, regard their total borrowing capacity as limited either because of their unwillingness to incur the fixed interest charges associated with loans or because bankers and other lenders set limits to the amount they will lend the firm. Because of this, *capital budgeting* is widely practiced.[13] This practice recognizes that the opportunity cost of using capital may well exceed the rate of interest at which the firm can borrow small or moderate amounts of money. Whether a firm should impute the same opportunity cost to all of its capital depends upon whether all of its capital expenditures are subject to the same general limit. In many cases, highly marketable assets, such as office buildings and inventories, can be mortgaged for a sizable fraction of their value, regardless of the over-all debt position of the firm. If this is the case, the capital invested in these assets has an opportunity cost equal to the rate at which the firm can borrow funds by these means.

The Cost of Management

Another important kind of imputed cost that sometimes arises concerns the services of the owner-manager. The firm should be charged a "cost" for these services equal to what the owner-manager could earn if he hired his services to some other firm.[14]

Risk-Taking

In saying that charges for such things as use of owned assets (like patents), returns on capital, and payments for services of owner-managers are properly *costs* to the firm, the economist is treating as cost many of the payments included by the accountant in the category of profits. This is true as well of one further factor of production: risk-taking. The investor demands a higher return on a risky venture than on a certain one because, in addition to having his capital used, he runs the risk of never getting it back. The rate of return he charges on a risky investment must be high enough to pay for this factor of production—his assuming the risks of the venture. In order to earn the required return on the total investment—the successful and the unsuccessful—the investor requires a greater return on the successful investments. Suppose in investing $100,000 in a class of risky ventures, the businessman expects $10,000 to be lost.[15] Suppose further he requires a 20 percent return on his total investment. In order to earn $20,000 profit and recover the $10,000 expected loss, he needs to earn $30,000 profit on the $90,000 of successful investment. This is a rate of return of $33\frac{1}{3}$ percent. He charges 20 percent for the use of the capital, $13\frac{1}{3}$ percent for the risk he takes.[16] Some forms of risk may be paid for directly —by purchasing insurance, for example. But risk-taking, if it is required, is a factor of production and thus has a cost in a society in which there is a demand for risk-takers.

13. Use of cut-off rates of return is one form of capital budgeting. Further discussion belongs to a specialized course, but note that overestimating opportunity costs of capital can be expensive. One large American firm built up huge cash balances because it could not find any investments that promised to pay it the 20 percent rate of return that its executives believed it should earn.

14. A very similar situation exists with respect to special talents of any sort that the firm may have under exclusive contract. To take one example, the San Francisco Giants have exclusive rights to the baseball services of Willie Mays, which services they can use, trade, or sell. The opportunity cost of using his services may differ from his salary.

15. Of course, he does not know *which* $10,000 will be lost. To keep the arithmetic simple, we assume that successful investments are liquidated at cost after one year.

16. The particular investor in fact may be either lucky or unlucky—he may lose none or all of his capital. If his assessment of the risk is correct, investors as a group in this kind of venture will on the average be unsuccessful 10 percent of the time. To take one example, drilling for oil wells in new areas in the United States shows a highly stable percentage of "dry holes"—about 89 percent. On the average, only one well in nine produces oil. You will readily see that oil exploration is a big gamble for the small operator who has capital enough to dig only one or two wells, but much less of a gamble for the big company that drills thousands of holes. But even the big company must have a high rate of return on its capital invested in the successful wells to cover the losses on the dry holes. The *actual* required rate of return is affected by the nature of the tax laws.

QUESTIONS FOR DISCUSSION

1. If a firm can borrow $10,000 at 6 percent per year to invest in a new machine that is expected to bring in a return of $1,000 a year, should it borrow the money?

2. What do you need to know in order to compare the cost of renting a plant with the cost of buying it outright?

3. An official of the team drilling for oil in the North Sea said in 1965, "Of course it's a risky business. If it wasn't, the rate of return wouldn't be so high." Explain this in terms of opportunity cost. What would happen if new methods of oil detection made the drilling of wells substantially less risky than it is now?

APPENDIX B TO CHAPTER 17 BALANCE SHEETS, INCOME STATEMENTS, AND COSTS OF PRODUCTION: TWO VIEWS

ACCOUNTING IS A MAJOR BRANCH of study in and of itself. Many students of economics will want to study accounting at some stage in their careers. It is not our intention to give a short course in accounting in this appendix, but rather to acquaint you with the kind of summary statements that are used by both economists and accountants. *Balance sheets* report the picture of a firm *at a moment in time*. They balance in the sense that they show the assets (or valuable things) owned by the firm on one side and the claims against those assets on the other side. *Income statements* do not refer to a moment in time but to *a period of time* (like a year), and report in summary fashion the flows of resources through the firm in the course of its operations. Balance sheets thus measure a stock, income statements a flow.

In order to illustrate what balance sheets and income statements are we shall treat the same example from two points of view: that of the accountant and that of the economist.

An Example

Late in 1964, Mr. James Maykby, the Second Vice-President of the Acme Artificial Flower Corporation (at a salary of $25,000 per year), decided he would go into business for himself. He quit his job and organized the Maykby Leaf Company. He purchased suitable plant and equipment for $80,000 and supplied himself with some raw materials and supplies. By December 31, 1964, he was in a position to start manufacturing. The funds for his enterprise were $40,000 raised as a bank loan on the factory (on which he is obligated to pay interest of $2,400 per year) and $55,000 of his own funds, which had

previously been invested in common stocks. He also owed $5,000 to certain firms that had provided him with supplies.

Maykby, who is a trained accountant, drew up a statement of his company's position as of December 31, 1964. (See Table A1, p. 205.)

Mr. Maykby showed this balance sheet to his brother-in-law, an economist, and was very pleased and surprised[1] to find that he agreed that this was a fair and accurate statement of the position of the company as it prepared to start operation.

During 1965 the company had a busy year, hiring factors, producing and selling goods, and so on. The following points summarize these activities of the twelve-month period:

1. The firm hired labor and purchased additional raw materials in the amount of $60,000, of which it still owed $10,000 at the end of the year.[2]

---

1. He usually finds that he and his brother-in-law disagree about everything.

2. In this example we will treat all purchased and hired factors in a single category.

TABLE A1 MAYKBY LEAF COMPANY, ACCOUNTANT'S BALANCE SHEET, DECEMBER 31, 1964

Assets		Liabilities and Equity	
Cash in bank	$ 5,000	Owed to suppliers	$ 5,000
Plant and equipment	80,000	Bank loan	40,000
Raw materials and supplies	15,000	Equity	55,000
Total assets	$100,000	Total liabilities and equity	$100,000

2. The firm manufactured artificial leaves and flowers whose sale value was $100,000. At year's end it had sold all of these, and still had on hand $15,000 worth of raw materials.

3. The firm paid off the $5,000 owed to suppliers at the beginning of the year.

4. At the very end of 1965, the company purchased a new machine for $5,000 and paid cash for it.

5. It paid the bank $2,400 interest on the loan.

6. Mr. Maykby paid himself $10,000, "instead of salary." (See Table A3.)

An Accountant's Balance Sheet and Income Statement

Taking account of all these things and also recognizing that he had depreciation on his plant and equipment,[3] he spent New Year's Day, 1966, preparing three financial reports. (See Tables A2, A3, and A4.)

These accounts reflect the operations of the firm as described above. The bookkeeping procedure by which these various activities are made to yield both the year-end balance sheet and the income statement need not concern you at this time, but you should notice several things.

First, note that some transactions affect the balance sheet but do not enter into the current income statement. For example, the purchase of a machine, which is an exchange of assets —cash for plant and equipment —and which will be entered as a cost in the income statements of some future periods as depreciation is charged; and the payment of past debts, which entered the income statements in the period in which the things purchased were used in production.[4]

Second, note that the net profit from operations increased the owner's equity since it was not "paid out" to him. A loss would have decreased his equity.

Third, note that the income statement, covering a year's operations, provides a link between the opening balance sheet (the assets and claims against assets at the beginning of the year) and the closing balance sheet.

Fourth, note that every change in a balance sheet between two dates can be accounted for by events that occurred during the year. (See the exhibits to the balance sheet, Table A3.)

After studying these records, Mr. Maykby feels that it has been a good year. The company has money in the bank, it has

TABLE A2 MAYKBY LEAF COMPANY, ACCOUNTANT'S BALANCE SHEET, DECEMBER 31, 1965

Cash in bank (See Exhibit 1)	$ 32,600	Owed to suppliers of factors (See Exhibit 4)	$ 10,000
Plant and equipment (See Exhibit 2)	73,000	Bank loan	40,000
Raw materials and supplies (See Exhibit 3)	15,000	Equity (See Exhibit 5)	70,600
Total assets	$120,600	Total liabilities and equity	$120,600

3. The tax people told him he could charge 15 percent of the cost of his equipment as depreciation during 1965, and he decided to use this amount in his own books as well. No depreciation was charged on the new machine.

4. Beginning students often have difficulty with the distinction between *cash* flows and *income* flows. If you do, analyze item by item the entries in Exhibit 1 (Table A3) and in Table A4, the income statement.

TABLE A3   **EXHIBITS TO BALANCE SHEET OF DECEMBER 31, 1965**

Exhibit 1.   Cash

Balance, January 1, 1965	$ 5,000	
+ Deposits		
Proceeds of sales of goods	100,000	$105,000
− Payments		
Payments to suppliers (1964 bills)	5,000	
Payments for labor and additional		
raw materials	50,000	
Salary of Mr. Maykby	10,000	
Purchase of new machine	5,000	
Interest payment to bank	2,400	72,400
Balance, December 31, 1965		$ 32,600

Exhibit 2.   Plant and Equipment

Balance, January 1, 1965	$ 80,000	
+ New machine purchased	5,000	$ 85,000
− Depreciation charged		12,000
Balance, December 31, 1965		$ 73,000

Exhibit 3.   Raw Materials and Supplies

On hand January 1, 1965	$ 15,000	
Purchases in 1965	60,000	$ 75,000
Used for production during 1965		60,000
On hand December 31, 1965		15,000

Exhibit 4.   Owed to Suppliers

Balance, January 1, 1965	$ 5,000	
New purchases, 1965	60,000	$ 65,000
Paid on old accounts	5,000	
Paid on new accounts	50,000	55,000
Balance, December 31, 1965		$ 10,000

Exhibit 5.   Equity

Original investment	$ 55,000	
Plus income earned during year	15,600	
(see income statement)		
Balance, December 31, 1965	$ 70,600	

shown a profit, and it was able to sell the goods it produced. He is bothered, however, by the fact that he and his wife have felt poorer than in past years. Probably the cost of living has gone up!

An Economist's Balance Sheet and Income Statement

When Maykby's brother-in-law reviews the December 31, 1965, balance sheet and the 1965 income statement he criticizes them in three respects. He says:

1. Mr. Maykby should have charged the company $25,000 for his services, since that is what he could have earned outside.

2. Maykby should have charged the company for the use of the $55,000 of his funds. He computes that had Maykby left these funds in the stock market he would have earned $5,500 in dividends and capital gains.

3. He tells Maykby that the depreciation figure is arbitrary. The plant and equipment purchased for $80,000 a year before now has a *market value* of only $62,000. (Assume he is correct about this fact.)

The brother-in-law prepared two *revised* statements. (See Tables A5 and A6 and the exhibit, Table A7.)

It is not hard for Mr. Maykby to understand the difference between the accounting profit of $15,600 and the reported economist's loss of $10,900. The difference of $26,500 is made up as follows:

Extra salary	$15,000
Imputed cost of capital	5,500
Extra depreciation	6,000
	$26,500

What Maykby does *not* understand is in what sense he lost $10,900 during the year. In order to explain this his brother-in-law prepared the report shown in Table A8.

Although Maykby spent the afternoon muttering to himself and telling his wife that his brother-in-law was not only totally lacking in any business sense but unpleasant as well, he was observed next morning at the public library asking the librarian whether there was a good "teach-yourself" book on economics. (We do not know her answer.)

Summary

We can make the following general observations after studying this example:

1. The *balance sheet* reports the assets and the claims against those assets at a moment in time. Balance sheets always balance because the equity of the owners is *by definition* the amount of the assets less the claims of the creditors of the company.

2. How large the "total assets" figure is depends upon the valuations placed upon them, and these can differ. In our example the accountant's plant and equipment figure, which was based upon purchase price less 15 percent for depreciation, differed from the economist's

5. Market value on January 1 less market value on December 31.

6. Because the bank loan is secured by the factory, its opportunity cost seems to the economist as properly measured by the interest payment.

TABLE A4   MAYKBY LEAF COMPANY, ACCOUNTANT'S INCOME STATEMENT FOR THE YEAR 1965

Sales		$100,000
Costs of operations		
Hired services and raw materials used	$ 60,000	
Depreciation	12,000	
Mr. Maykby	10,000	
Interest	2,400	84,400
Profit		$ 15,600

TABLE A5   MAYKBY LEAF COMPANY, ECONOMIST'S INCOME STATEMENT FOR THE YEAR 1965

Sales		$100,000
Cost of operations		
Hired services and raw materials	$ 60,000	
Depreciation[5]	18,000	
Interest to bank[6]	2,400	
Imputed cost of capital	5,500	
Services of Maykby	25,000	$110,900
Loss		$(10,900)

TABLE A6   MAYKBY LEAF COMPANY, ECONOMIST'S BALANCE SHEET, DECEMBER 31, 1965

Cash	$ 32,600	Owed to suppliers	$ 10,000
Plant and equipment	67,000	Bank loan	40,000
Raw materials, etc.	15,000	Equity (see Exhibit A)	64,600
	$114,600		$114,600

TABLE A7   EXHIBIT TO BALANCE SHEET, DECEMBER 31, 1965

Exhibit A. Equity of Mr. Maykby

Original investment		$55,000
New investment by Mr. Maykby:		
Salary not collected	$15,000	
Return on capital not collected	5,500	20,500
		$75,500
Less loss from operations		10,900
		$64,600

TABLE A8 **MAYKBY'S SITUATION BEFORE AND AFTER**

	(1) As Second Vice-President Acme Flower Company	(2) As Owner-Manager of Maykby Company	Difference (2) − (1)
Salary paid	$25,000	$10,000	− $15,000
Earnings on capital, invested in stocks	5,500		− 5,500
Assets owned	55,000 (Stocks)	64,600 (Equity in Maykby Co.)	+ 9,600
Net change			− $10,900

figure, which was based upon market value at the balance-sheet date. In a more realistic example,[7] the valuation problem arises over and over again —in the matter of inventories, patents, properties, and so forth, owned.

3. In order to avoid arbitrary, misleading, and even deliberately deceptive manipulation of accounts, accounting has developed certain normal and usual procedures of valuation. These may not in all cases reflect the economist's definition of the value of the resources.

4. The income statement reports the revenues and the costs that arise from the firm's use of inputs to produce outputs. It always covers a specified *period* of time. It also crucially involves the valuation problem: What is the value of the inputs used and outputs produced? Here again there are conventional accounting principles that may or may not be satisfactory for purposes of economic analysis.

5. The income statement of a firm may be important for several different purposes, and different principles of valuation may be required. For determining its income-tax liability, the firm must use the valuations specified as permissible by the tax authorities. For determining its comparative performance compared to other companies, or to itself in other periods, it must use a consistent set of procedures, whatever the principle that governs them. For determining whether it has made the best use of the resources under its control, it must use valuations based upon the alternative use of these resources. The economist's concept of opportunity cost is designed to do this job.

6. In general, it is the principles of valuation used and not the form of these statements that are important and that are decisive in interpreting the operations of the firm. Students of the firm who use the reported financial data as an aid to their analysis must be prepared to examine in detail whether the principles of valuation used are appropriate for their purpose and to adjust, correct, or recompute in cases where they are not appropriate.[8]

QUESTIONS FOR DISCUSSION

1. Is the following statement an hypothesis? Assets and claims against those assets (liabilities) are always equal to each other. What would you call it?

2. If Maykby had not been on speaking terms with his brother-in-law from the start, how might his decisions in the second year of his operations have differed from what you now expect them to be? What would have happened if he had received an offer for his business of $55,000 and a bid from his old company to return at a salary of $27,000 a year? Can we conclude that Maykby is irrational if he turns down both offers. What can we conclude?

7. Every student is urged to examine the balance sheet of an actual corporation.

8. Read again the discussion on this point in Chapter 17, p. 191. If Mr. Maykby acts on the basis of his analysis of his operations he may well *behave* differently than if he acts on his brother-in-law's. If the economist wishes to predict Maykby's future behavior, he must know the information on which Mr. Maykby will base his decisions, even if the economist feels sure the information is misleading Indeed, he may want to predict how the information will mislead.

Chapter **18** CHOOSING A TECHNIQUE OF PRODUCTION

ONE OF THE MAJOR PROBLEMS FACING THE firm is how its output should be produced. In trying to solve this problem, the managers of the firm take into account both the day-to-day operation of the firm and expectations about the future.

If the rate of sales has fallen off, should production be reduced correspondingly or should it be held at its old rate, with the unsold amounts being stored up against an anticipated rise in sales in the future? If production is to be reduced, how can this be accomplished most cheaply? Should one whole plant be closed down, or should all the plants be operated on short time?[1] If demand increases sharply and unexpectedly, how can more production be squeezed out of the existing facilities? It will take time to build new plants and, in the meantime, something must be done to meet the new demand. All of these matters concern how best to use the existing plant and equipment. They concern time periods too short to build new plants or to install more equipment. The decisions made will be implemented quickly: A plant can be shut down on a week's notice, overtime can be increased tomorrow, and new workers can be added to production as soon as they can be hired and trained.

More weighty decisions must be made when the managers consider a longer time horizon. Should the firm adopt a highly automated process that will greatly reduce its wage bill, even though it will have to borrow large sums of money to buy the equipment? Should it carry on instead with the same kind of techniques it is now using? Should it build new plants in an area where labor is plentiful—possibly even moving abroad where labor is both plentiful and cheap (but possibly not so efficient)—and adopt techniques that replace some of the more costly mechanized processes with labor? Should it tell the engineers who are designing its plant to worry only about making costs as low as possible when the plant is working to capacity, or should it tell them to worry also about making the plant as flexible as possible so that output can be varied over a wide range at a reasonable level of costs? These matters concern what the firm should do when it is changing or replacing its plant and equipment. Decisions on them may take a long time to implement.

---

1. If the firm chooses to close down one whole plant, and this plant is the major source of employment in a town, it may critically affect the fate of the people living in that town.

In the above cases the managers were making decisions from known possibilities. But large firms also have staffs working on research and development. The managers of these firms must decide how much money to make available to their research and development staff in the hope that they will come up with some wholly new and more efficient ways of doing things. But they must first decide in what areas the payoff for new developments will be largest and then direct their research staff to work in these areas. If, for example, a shortage of a particular labor skill or raw material is anticipated, the research staff can be told to try to find ways of economizing on that labor or raw material, or even eliminating it from the production process. It is difficult, of course, to anticipate particular labor shortages far in advance, but material shortages can more often be foreseen.

What all this adds up to is that the firm is constantly making decisions: Some that apply to today, some to tomorrow, and some to the far distant future. These decisions are made in an uncertain world, and the firm can never be sure that when a particular decision finally goes into effect the circumstances that gave rise to it will still make it an appropriate one. When making such decisions, a major concern of the firm is how it can raise the probability that the anticipated range of output will, when the time comes, be produced at the lowest possible cost.

Time Horizons for Decision-Making

In order to reduce these myriad decisions to manageable proportions, economists organize them into the three groups that we have already distinguished. We think of the firm as making decisions about (1) how best to employ its existing plant and equipment; (2) what new plant and equipment and production processes to select, given the framework of known technical possibilities; and (3) what to do about encouraging the invention of new techniques. Corresponding to these three groups of decisions we define three time periods: (1) the short run, which is a period of time over which decisions are restricted by the fact that certain factors of production—usually plant and equipment—cannot be increased in supply; (2) the long run, which is a period of time over which all factors of production can be varied but in which decisions are restricted by the existing state of knowledge of technical possibilities; (3) the very long run, which is a period of time over which decisions made now about such things as research and development can change the supply of available techniques. These three time periods are theoretical constructions. They abstract from the more complicated nature of real decisions and focus only on the key factor that restricts the range of choice in each set of decisions. Whether or not this theoretical abstraction is useful depends on whether or not it can be used to develop a theory that successfully predicts what choices firms will actually make in various real situations. We must now consider these three periods in more detail.

THE SHORT RUN

The *short run* is defined as the period of time over which the inputs of some factors cannot be varied. The most usual meaning is that a firm is committed to paying for the use of a specified quantity of *fixed factors* whether or not it needs them, and that it cannot get the use of more of this factor than it has on hand. This is the meaning we shall use. The factors that can be varied in the short run are called *variable factors*.

The factor that is fixed in the short run is usually an element of capital (such as plant and equipment), but it might be land, or the services of management, or even the supply of skilled salaried labor. What matters is that at least one significant factor should be fixed.

The short run does not correspond to a fixed number of months or years. In some industries it may extend over many years, in others it may be only a matter of months or even weeks. In the electric-power industry, for example, where it takes three or more years to acquire and install a steam-turbine generator, an unforeseen increase in demand will involve a long period during which the extra demand must be met as best as can be with the existing capital equipment. The other side of this coin is that, because this equipment has a very long life, a decrease in demand leaves the firm committed to all the costs of this equipment that do not vary with output. In the hydroelectric industry, the short run may extend over decades. At the other end of the scale, a machine shop can acquire new equipment (or sell existing equipment) in a matter of a few weeks, and thus the short run is correspondingly short: If there is an increase in demand, it will have to be met with the existing stock of capital for only a short time, after which it will be possible to adjust the stock of equipment to the level made desirable by the higher demand.[2]

THE LONG RUN

The *long run* is defined as the period long enough for the inputs of all factors of production to be varied, but not so long that the basic technology of production changes. Again, it does not correspond to a specific period of time, but varies among industries.

The special importance of the long run in production theory is that it corresponds to the situation facing the firm when it is *planning* to go into business; or to expand substantially the scale of its operations; or to branch out into new products or new areas; or to modernize, replace, or reorganize its method of production.

The *planning decisions* of the firm characteristically are made with fixed technical possibilities but with freedom to choose whatever factor proportions prove to be efficient. Once these planning decisions are carried out —once a plant is built, equipment purchased and installed, and so on—the firm has fixed factors and makes operating decisions in what we have called the short run.

THE VERY LONG RUN

Unlike the short and the long run, the very long run is concerned with situations in which the technological possibilities open to the firm are subject to change. A central observable characteristic of industrial society over the recent centuries has been the change in technology that leads to new and improved products and new and improved methods of production. These changes may be affected by what the firm itself does, particularly in its

---

2. The length of the short run is not fixed solely by technological factors. For example, if the machine shop can persuade its customers to wait for delivery, it need not *produce* under short-run conditions. (Of course, the *customers'* short run is now increased in length.) Further, the speed of delivery of new equipment may itself be influenced by the price the firm is willing to pay for the equipment.

programs of research and development. While decisions of this kind may clearly affect the techniques of production used (and hence the costs of production), they are of a different kind from the short-run and long-run deci-

sions. They are discussed in Chapter 20. For the remainder of this chapter and in the next, we ignore them and treat choice of techniques of production under the assumption of a constant technology.

The Production Function

The existing technology gives rise to a particular relation between inputs and outputs: If so much of each factor is used, so much output will be obtained. If the state of technology changes, a new relation will be established between inputs and outputs. The invention of superior techniques usually means that the same quantities of all factors will produce a larger output than before.

The technological relation between inputs and outputs is referred to in economics as the *production function*. We define this function as the specification of the relation between the physical quantities of all inputs used and the resulting quantity of output obtained.[3]

What does the production function look like in our three time periods? In the very long run, the production function itself changes since the same quantities of inputs produce different quantities of output.

In the long run, the production function describes the full set of choices open to the firm. It shows what each set of inputs (e.g., lots of a certain kind of expensive machine and a few skilled laborers, or lots of a less

expensive machine and quite a few unskilled laborers) will produce by way of outputs.

In the short run, the choices open to the firm are more restricted, since some of the factors are fixed and only some can be varied. The firm is interested in the relation between those inputs that can be varied and its output. This relation will, however, be influenced by the nature of the fixed factors with which the firm has to work. The relation between output and the quantity of labor and raw materials used will be different in a supermodern factory from what it is in a factory built twenty years ago.

Thus, if we say that in the short run production varies with the quantities of the variable factor, we must remember that the way in which it varies depends on the quantity and quality of the factors that are being held constant. It follows that there is a whole host of short-run production functions all derived from a single long-run function. Each short-run function describes how output changes as the variable inputs are changed given a particular set of fixed factors.

3. In the language of the appendix to Chapter 3, we can write $Q = Q(f_1, \ldots, f_n)$, where Q is the quantity produced of some good and f_1 to f_n are the quantities used of each of n factors of production. The basic concepts introduced in the remainder of this chapter are all summarized in functional notation in the appendix, p. 215.

The Cost Function

The profit-maximizing firm is interested in what it costs to produce its output. If the prices of factors of production are known, it can go directly from the production function to the cost function. If it knows how the quantity of each input varies as it varies output, and if it knows the cost of each input, then it knows immediately how the cost of production varies as output is varied.

The Firm's Set of Choices

The goal of the profit-maximizing firm in choosing a production technique will be to achieve a given level of output at the lowest possible cost. The principle involved in making this choice is thus simple and may be stated as follows:

For any specific anticipated output the firm chooses the least costly way of achieving that output from the alternatives open to it.

If there is a known stable required output rate, and if the costs of factors are known, this is all there is to it.

Our previous discussion of the choices actually facing a firm shows that the problem of achieving this goal is not an easy one. Indeed, the actual process of making the necessary decisions often uses a large amount of a scarce and expensive input: managerial skill. The problems involved may be illustrated by a few of the complications facing such decision-makers.

1. Every longer-run decision creates its own short runs, and the consequences for the short run may be important. For example, a highly automated operation that is efficient in producing a required monthly level of output may be both durable and inflexible. As a result, fluctuations in monthly production may be expensive;[1] the production technique that is best for monthly production of (say) 100 units may not be best for monthly production that *averages* 100 units per month. Thus the short-run relation of cost and output may influence the long-run decision.

2. The relevant factor prices that a firm must use in choosing a technique of production are future factor prices: those that will pertain when the factors are actually used. At the time the firm makes its decision, it will have to consider how current factor prices may change, due either to the firm's influence, or to events outside of its influence. To take one example, entry of a large firm into a small labor market ("because labor is plentiful and cheap") may itself make labor scarcer and more expensive because of the quantity of labor demanded by the firm, or

4. Variation in required output may arise because the demand for the product of the firm is seasonal in nature (the firm sells more bathing suits in June than in November), or because it is growing (it sells more toward the end of a five-year period than at the beginning), or because demand fluctuates in response to economy-wide factors over which the firm has no control.

because the entry of the new firm provides the incentive to a union to organize a previously unorganized market. Both of these have occurred to some extent in the move of the American cotton textile industry from New England to the South.

3. The firm in estimating its outputs may make errors in either direction, and the penalties it pays for those errors may be of different kinds. The firm that underestimates its future demands may sacrifice the opportunities to grow with its market; the firm that overestimates them may operate inefficiently (i.e., at high cost) because of its heavy fixed costs for commitments to unneeded resources.

Long-run and short-run decisions thus affect one another. Of crucial importance in these interrelations is the way in which costs vary in response to changes in output, in both the long and short runs.

Summary

1. One of the major problems facing the firm is the way in which its output should be produced.

2. The first aspect of this problem that the firm has to decide is how best to employ its existing plant and equipment. For purposes of making these decisions, plant and equipment are regarded as a fixed factor and other inputs as variable factors. Such decisions are made over the short run, which is defined as a period of time during which at least one significant input is fixed in supply to the firm.

3. The second aspect of the problem is the best size and organization of plant and equipment, given the planned output of the firm. For purposes of making these decisions, technological knowledge is regarded as a fixed factor and all other factors of production as variables. Such decisions are made over the long run, which is defined as a period of time long enough for all inputs—including plant and equipment—to be varied, but during which the state of technological knowledge is fixed.

4. The final set of decisions concerns advancing the state of knowledge by research and development. These decisions are made over the very long run, which is defined as a period of time during which significant changes in knowledge about productive techniques are possible.

5. The production function is the technological relation between physical units of inputs and physical units of outputs. If there is a specific cost per unit associated with each kind of input, we can derive a cost function from the production function.

6. We can say of the profit-maximizing firm that, for any anticipated output, it will choose, from the alternatives open to it, the least costly way of achieving the output.

QUESTIONS FOR DISCUSSION

1. To what time period do the following decisions of a newspaper belong?
  a. whether to hire an additional city-news reporter;
  b. whether to invest in equipment that will enable it to set up an office in a state 2,500 miles away and publish a national newspaper by transmitting copy from the main paper to the new branch;
  c. whether or not to ask IBM to investigate for

it the possibility of finding ways of setting type by computer;

d. whether or not to hire an additional linotype operator for the night shift;

e. whether or not to build a new printing plant in cooperation with another paper in the city that publishes at a different time of day;

f. whether or not to close down a branch 2,500 miles away;

g. whether or not to close down all its operations.

2. How long is the short run?

3. In what units does a production function measure inputs and outputs? What about a cost function?

4. How long is the short run likely to be in the rubber and the egg industries? Use the facts given on page 135 to determine your answer. How long was the long run in the rubber industry in 1941?

5. Why does the profit-maximizing firm choose the least costly way of producing any given output? Can you think of any objective that a non-profit-maximizing firm might have that would lead it to choose a method of production other than the least costly one?

† APPENDIX TO CHAPTER 18 THE PRODUCTION FUNCTION

IN THIS APPENDIX WE DESCRIBE in functional notation the relations discussed in Chapter 18. You do not have to read this appendix before proceeding, but anyone who masters this notation will find it helpful in clarifying the verbal discussion.

The firm is seen as facing a production function:

$$Q_i = Q_i(f_1, \ldots, f_n),$$

where Q_i is the output of the ith good and $f_1, \ldots, f_n$ are the quantities of n factors used as inputs. This function depends on the existing state of technology.

A change in the state of technology alters the relation between inputs and outputs, and gives a new long-run production function:

$$Q_i = Q_i^*(f_1, \ldots, f_n),$$

where Q_i^* represents a different relation from that represented by Q_i.

An infinite number of short-run production functions can be obtained; these are distinguished from each other by the particular inputs that are held constant and the level at which they are held constant.

Consider as an example a simple long-run production function in which

$$Q = 10\sqrt{X_1 X_2}.$$

If X_2 is the fixed factor, we can write

$$Q = K\sqrt{X_1},$$

where K is 10 times the square root of X_2. But the relation between Q and the variable factor is different depending on the level at which X_2 is held constant. Three examples for $X_2 = 1, 4,$ and 9 are given below.

$$Q = 10\sqrt{X_1}, \text{ for } X_2 = 1,$$

$$Q = 20\sqrt{X_1}, \text{ for } X_2 = 4,$$

$$Q = 30\sqrt{X_1}, \text{ for } X_2 = 9.$$

A similar procedure can be followed by holding X_1 constant and letting X_2 be the variable factor.

In general, if

$$Q = Q(X_1, X_2),$$

we can define one family of short-run functions by making X_2 the fixed factor and X_1 the variable factor:

$$Q = Q(X_1)\Big|_{X_2 = X_2^0}.$$

The functions of this family differ from each other according as the *level* at which X_2 is held constant differs (i.e., according to the value ascribed to X_2^0).

We can then define a second family of short-run functions by making X_1 the fixed factor and X_2 the variable one:

$$Q = Q(X_2)\Big|_{X_1 = X_1^0}.$$

The functions in this family differ from each other according as the level at which X_1 is held constant differs (i.e., according to the value ascribed to X_1^0).

The two families are distinguished from each other by the factor that is held fixed and the factor that is allowed to vary. In general, if

$$Q = Q(f_1, \ldots, f_i, \ldots, f_n),$$

we can define the families as follows:

$$Q = Q_i(f_1, \ldots, f_i) \, \bigg|_{\substack{f_{i+1} = f_{i+1}^0 \\ \vdots \\ f_n = f_n^0}}$$

By letting i range from 1 (one variable factor) to $n - 1$ (all but one factor variable) we define many families of short-run functions. (If $i = n$ we have the

unique long-run function in which nothing is held constant). Each family has an infinite number of short-run functions as members depending on the actual values ascribed to the fixed factors.

In subsequent chapters wherever a short-run function is used, you should notice which of the possible ones is actually being considered.

QUESTIONS FOR DISCUSSION

1. $Q = 4 \sqrt[3]{X_1 X_2}$, and X_1 is the fixed factor.

a. Write the general equation for Q in terms of X_2 and a constant, K. What does K equal?

b. How many possible short-run productions are there? Explain.

c. When X_1 is 1, 8, and 125, what are the short-run functions? What is the actual quantity of output in each of these cases if X_2 is 8?

2. $Q = Q(X_1, X_2, \ldots, X_9)$.

a. How many different short-run production functions are

there? (If you said eight, think again.)

b. How many different families of short-run production functions are there?

c. If $X_1 = 14$, but nothing else is fixed, what is the short-run production function?

Chapter 19   HOW COST VARIES WITH OUTPUT

WE HAVE DISCUSSED THE RELATION BETWEEN outputs and physical inputs and also the problem of assigning costs to physical inputs. We are now in a position to relate outputs to the cost of producing them. The material in this chapter is not easy, but it is extremely important; time devoted to serious study here will be amply repaid later.

The theory of costs is central to all of the problems considered in Parts II to VIII. The

direct problems with which we are concerned in this chapter are illustrated by the following ones: Why did Kaiser-Fraser find it impossible to break into the rapidly expanding auto industry after the war? Why has there not been a successful new entrant into the auto industry since 1925, in spite of the fact that between 1928 and 1965 the dollar value of auto sales expanded 434 percent?[1] Why is it that the cost per kilowatt hour of generating

1. The answer to these questions is related to the long-run costs of the auto industry.

electricity is highest in those hours of the day when output is at its maximum and is substantially lower during those hours when output is low, so that a typical kilowatt hour of electricity costs much more to generate at noon than it does at midnight?[2] Why is it that if the lumber industry were asked to increase output by 20 percent in three weeks' time the cost per board foot of the new output would be much more than the cost per board foot of the existing output, whereas if it were given more warning, and asked to increase output by 20 percent in two years' time, the cost per board foot of the new output would not be substantially higher and even might be less than the costs of existing output?[3]

Long-Run Cost Behavior: Fixed Factor Prices

How can a firm best produce various alternative volumes of output? Assume that sufficient time is allowed to elapse for the firm to make all of the adjustments that it requires. If the rate of output is low, the firm will have a small plant and will have its whole production process organized accordingly. If the rate of production is high, then the firm will have a large plant and will have all its organization geared to a large scale of production: The firm may have many separate plants producing its main product and may have subcontracted the production of some of the components of its product out to specialized firms. Whatever the actual organization, there will be some best method of organizing production for each given level of output and some corresponding level of costs. Costs could be higher if the best technique of production were not used, but they could never be lower than the costs associated with the best available technique.

Figure 1 is a graph of a long-run cost curve. The rate of output is measured on one axis and the cost per unit of output (i.e., total cost divided by the number of units) is measured on the other. In order to obtain a long-run, average, cost curve, we plot, against any given

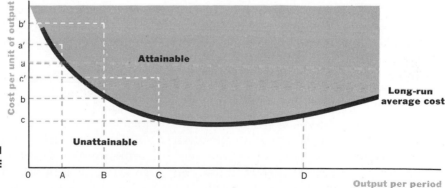

FIGURE 1 A LONG-RUN AVERAGE COST CURVE

2. The answer to this question is related to the short-run costs of the electricity industry.

3. The answer to this question concerns the relation between the short-run and the long-run costs of the lumber industry.

rate of output, say *OB*, the average cost that results from the selection of the lowest cost method of production, *Ob*, in this case. We do the same for each rate of output and, by joining the points, obtain the curve illustrated.

This curve is related to the long-run production function. You should be absolutely clear as to its meaning. There are several technically feasible ways of producing output *OB*; for the given factor prices there is one least-cost technique. The cost per unit using *that* technique is *Ob*. Levels of cost below *Ob* are not technically possible at that output; levels above *Ob* (such as *Ob'*), while possible, are not economically efficient. This is so also with points on the curve above *A, C, D*. The curve is the boundary between what is feasible and what is not feasible, given the production function and the costs of the factors of production.[4]

If, at any moment in time, the firm moves from output *OA* to output *OB*, it will *not* find its costs changing from *Oa* to *Ob*. The long-run cost curve shows alternative outputs, and to move from one point on this curve to another the firm must change its plant and equipment in order to achieve the lowest possible cost of production at the new level of output.

THE SHAPE OF THE LONG-RUN COST CURVE

The long-run cost curve in Figure 1 had to be given some shape in order to draw it. At this stage we regard the shape as arbitrary. What we must do now is to label the various possible shapes with the terms usually given to them. Figure 2 shows three stylized long-run cost curves for three different firms. Firm

A is what is called a *decreasing cost firm*. An expansion in production will, once sufficient time has elapsed for all desired adjustments to be made in the techniques of production, result in a reduction in costs per unit of output. Since money costs of factors are assumed constant, the fall in costs per unit must be because output increases faster than inputs as the scale of the firm's production expands. Such a firm is often said to enjoy *increasing returns to scale*. Firm B is what is called a *rising cost firm*. An expansion in production will, even after sufficient time has elapsed for all adjustments to be made, be accompanied by a rise in average costs per unit of output. Since costs per unit of inputs are constant, this rise in costs must be the result of an expansion in output less than in proportion to the expansion in inputs. Such a firm is often said to suffer *decreasing returns to scale*. Firm C is a *constant cost firm*. Its average costs per unit of output do not change as the scale of output changes. This means that output must be increasing exactly as fast as inputs are increased; the firm is said to be encountering *constant returns to scale*.

It is common in the literature of economics to refer to these three situations, increasing, constant, or decreasing long-run returns, as the *laws of returns*. One will often find writers speaking of a particular industry obeying the *law* of increasing long-run returns. Such a usage is misleading and is based on a misunderstanding of the concept of an hypothesis. What we have done is to label all possible cases. Such a division of the possibilities into three groups may or may not prove useful, but such a classificatory scheme covering all conceivable cases cannot be re-

---

4. Another boundary, or, as it is sometimes called, frontier, between what is possible and what is impossible was encountered in Chapter 1, see page 6.

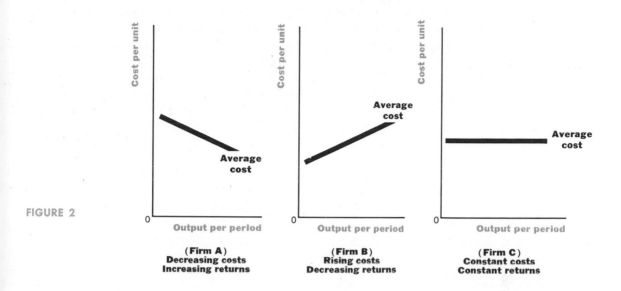

FIGURE 2

garded as a theory (much less a "law").
An investigation of the possibility of obtaining hypotheses about the behavior of

long-run costs is a difficult task that must be postponed. It is discussed in the appendix to this chapter.

Short-Run Cost Behavior: Fixed Factor Prices

Assume, first, that the firm has selected some size of plant and equipment and is producing at the appropriate point on its long-run cost curve. Say that the firm in Figure 1 is producing output OB at an average cost of Ob per unit. Now assume that the firm wishes to change its rate of output from OB before sufficient time elapses to change its plant and equipment. The firm is now in a short-run situation with plant and equipment as the fixed factors, and labor, management, materials, etc., as the variable factors. What will happen to costs as output is varied above or below OB while the size of plant remains unchanged at the size most appropriate to producing OB? The first thing we can say is

that the firm can never achieve a lower level of cost than that shown by the long-run cost curve. On the other hand, it may well do worse. The output OA can, for example, be produced at cost Oa when the size of plant and organization of production is adjusted to that output. If OA is produced with a plant adapted to output OB, costs may be higher, say Oa'. Similarly, if output OC is produced not by a plant most appropriate to that level, but by overworking a plant designed to produce at the rate OB, then costs may be Oc' rather than Oc.

We now introduce an empirical hypothesis about costs that is sufficient to guarantee the above results. We assume that for each level of production there is some best proportion in which to use the various factors. This proportion, which is often referred to as the *optimal factor combination,* is best in the sense that it results in a lower cost per unit of product than does any other factor proportion. We also assume that the further away the actual factor proportion is from the proportion optimal for that level of output, the higher the costs per unit. The optimal factor proportion need not be the same for each level of output. Indeed, when output is small, the optimal factor combination may be a lot of labor and not very much capital; when output is high, the optimal combination may be a lot of capital with relatively little labor.

> All that is necessary is that for each level of output there should be an optimal factor combination and that, as input proportions depart from this combination (for a given level of output), average costs per unit should increase.

It follows immediately that each point on the long-run cost curve must represent an optimal combination of factors. If it did not, then the same output could be produced more cheaply by using the optimal combination, and thus the original point could not have been on the curve.

It also follows that short-run costs will be above the long-run curve, except at the point representing the output for which the fixed factor was designed.

Figure 3 illustrates a firm with plant and equipment designed for output *OB*. What happens to costs when output is varied in the short run? As output is varied from *OB*, the factor combination must vary. Since some factors are constant, the variation of output brought about by varying some inputs neces-

sarily causes factor proportions to vary. As output departs from *OB*, factor proportions depart from the optimal level. Thus, short-run costs will rise above the long-run costs as shown in the figure. All this means is that the firm's unit costs will be higher if it is forced to produce an output with a plant designed for another output than they are if it can produce the output with a plant optimally designed for that level of output. Note that the short-run cost curve is tangent to (touches) the long-run curve at the level of output for which the fixed factor is appropriate and lies above it for all other levels of output.

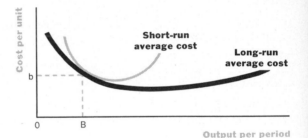

FIGURE 3   **A SHORT-RUN AVERAGE COST CURVE**

If we now repeat the whole process, assuming that the firm is fully adjusted to some different level of output and that it then has to vary output in the short run, we shall generate a new short-run cost curve. If we repeat this process for every level of output, we will find that every point on the long-run cost curve has associated with it a short-run cost curve that touches it at that point and that shows how costs vary as output is varied, holding some factors fixed at the level most appropriate to that output. This is illustrated in Figure 4.[5]

5. Each short-run curve touches the long-run curve at one point and lies above it everywhere else. We say the short-run curves are tangent to the long-run one. This has an important, though subtle, consequence. Two curves that are tangent at a point have the same slope at that point. If LRAC is decreasing where it is tangent to SRAC, then SRAC must also be decreasing. Thus the point where SRAC = LRAC need not be the

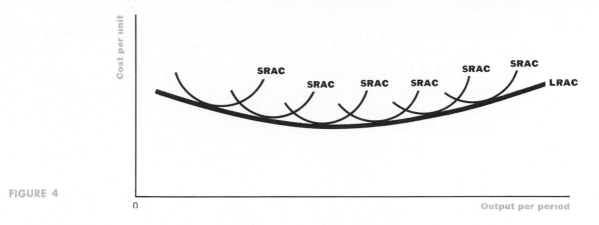

FIGURE 4

THE SHAPE OF THE
SHORT-RUN COST CURVE

The short-run cost curves that we have derived are U-shaped or saucer-shaped. This shape is a consequence of the hypothesis that we introduced on page 219. This hypothesis is often called the *law of variable proportions*, although, since it is an empirically testable assertion about the world, it would be better described as the *hypothesis of variable proportions*. Short-run variations in output are necessarily brought about by varying factor proportions. This hypothesis states that, for any level of output, an optimal factor proportion exists, and, the more this proportion is departed from, the higher average costs will be per unit.[6]

(continued)

minimum point of SRAC. Unless LRAC is horizontal at the point of tangency, it will not be tangent at the minimum point of SRAC. The economic sense of this rests upon the subtle distinction between the most efficient way to utilize a given plant, and the most efficient way to produce the amount of output required. It is the *second* that interests us as economists. If bigger plants can achieve lower costs per unit, we will gain by building a bigger plant and underutilizing it whenever the gains from using the bigger plant are big enough to offset the costs of being inefficient in our use of the plant. If there are *some* gains from building bigger plants (if LRAC is declining), there is always some underutilization that is justified. The student who is doubtful should ask himself whether he will learn more from a book whose every word he understands or the book that teaches him the most. They may be different. The student who is still troubled may take some comfort from the fact that less than thirty-five years ago one of the world's leading economic theorists, Jacob Viner, instructed his draftsman to draw the LRAC through the minimum points of the SRAC but "so as never to lie above" the SRAC. He reports of his draftsman, "He is a mathematician, however, not an economist, and he saw some mathematical objection to this procedure which I could not succeed in understanding. I could not persuade him to disregard his scruples as a craftsman and to follow my instructions, absurd though they might be."

6. The hypothesis is often stated as the *hypothesis of diminishing returns.* This is exactly the same relation looked at in another way. The hypothesis of diminishing returns states that if more and more of a variable factor is used in combination with a fixed factor, the amounts added to total production by successive increases in the variable factor will eventually begin to decline. The reason for this is that as the firm uses more and more of a variable factor with a given amount of a fixed factor it increasingly departs from the optimal combination of factors. This means that equal additions of the variable factor bring smaller and smaller increments of output or, what is the same thing, the cost of producing each additional unit of output must be rising.

Variations in Factor Prices

A rise in the price of any factor will shift all the cost curves—both short- and long-run—upward. If, other things being equal, one factor gets more expensive, then costs of all products that use anything at all of this factor must rise.

A rise in the price of one factor will also alter the optimal or least-cost factor proportions that underlie the long-run curve. If one factor gets more expensive, then this may be partially compensated for by using somewhat less of this factor and more of others that can be substituted for it. How much substitution occurs will depend on how much the price has risen and on the extent to which it is technically possible to substitute other factors. In general, however, we can say that a rise in the price of one factor will alter the optimal factor combination for each level of output and thus cause each point on the long-run curve to represent a lower proportion of this factor and a higher proportion of its substitutes.[7]

Average, Total, and Marginal Costs

So far we have confined ourselves to average costs when we talked about the costs of producing various levels of output. We can, however, look at costs in three distinct but related ways. We can look at (1) the total cost of producing some level of output, (2) the average cost, which is total cost divided by the number of units produced, or (3) the marginal cost, which is the difference between the total cost of producing that rate of output and the total cost of producing at a rate of one less unit per period. We must now consider these important concepts in detail.

1. *Total cost* means just what it says: the total cost of producing any given level of output. This total cost is conveniently divided into two parts, total fixed costs and total variable costs. *Fixed costs* are those costs that do not vary with output; they will be the same if output is one unit or one million units. The costs of any fixed factor will be a fixed cost: Since the factor cannot be varied the costs associated with it cannot be varied. Fixed costs are also often referred to as *overhead costs* or *unavoidable costs*. *Variable costs* are all those costs that vary directly with output, rising as more is produced and falling as less is produced. In our previous example, since labor was the variable factor of production, the wage bill would be a variable cost. Variable costs are often referred to as *direct costs*.†

7. See pages 178–179 on the principle of substitution.

† In symbols we may write:

$$TC = TFC + TVC$$
$$TFC = \overline{K}$$
$$TVC = w_i X_i,$$

where *TC* is total cost, *TFC* is total fixed cost, *TVC* is total variable cost, $\overline{K}$ is some constant amount, X_i is

2. *Average cost* is the total cost of producing any given output divided by the number of units produced so as to give the cost per unit. Average total cost may be divided into average fixed costs and average variable costs in just the same way as total costs were divided.†

We may note that while average *variable* costs may rise or fall as production is increased (depending upon whether output rises more rapidly or more slowly than average variable costs), it is clear that average fixed costs decline continuously as output increases. A doubling of output always leads to a halving of fixed costs per unit of output.

This is a process popularly known as "spreading one's overheads."

3. *Marginal (or incremental) cost* is the increase in total cost resulting from raising the rate of production by one unit.†† Since fixed costs do not vary with output, marginal fixed costs are always zero. Therefore marginal costs are necessarily marginal variable costs, and a change in fixed costs will leave marginal costs unaffected. The cost of producing a few more potatoes by farming a given amount of land more intensively is the same, whatever the rent paid for the fixed amount of land.†††

These three measures of cost are merely

(continued)

the quantity of the variable factor used, and w_i is the price per unit of this factor. Since fixed costs are constant and variable costs necessarily rise as output rises, total costs must rise with output or, to put the point more formally, TC is a function of total product and it varies directly with it: $TC = f(Q)$.

† In symbols:

$$ATC = \frac{TC}{Q} = \frac{TVC + TFC}{Q} = AVC + AFC$$

$$AVC = \frac{TVC}{Q}$$

$$AFC = \frac{TFC}{Q} = \frac{\overline{K}}{Q}.$$

†† In symbols:

$$MC_n = TC_n - TC_{n-1},$$

i.e., the marginal cost of the nth unit of output is the total cost of producing n units minus the total cost of producing $n-1$ (*i.e.*, one less) units of output. If we are producing a number of identical units of output, we cannot, of course, ascribe a separate (and different) cost to each unit. When we speak, therefore, of the marginal cost of the nth unit we mean nothing more than the change in total costs when the rate of production is increased from $n-1$ units to n units per period of time.

††† Only the simplest bit of algebra is necessary to prove this important theorem:

$$MC_n = TC_n - TC_{n-1}$$
$$= (TVC_n + TFC_n) - (TVC_{n-1} + TFC_{n-1}),$$

but

$$TFC_n = TFC_{n-1} = \overline{K};$$

therefore,

$$MC_n = (TVC_n + K) - (TVC_{n-1} + K)$$
$$= TVC_n - TVC_{n-1}.$$

Hence marginal costs are independent of the size of fixed costs.

different ways of looking at a single phenomenon, and they are mathematically interrelated.† Sometimes it is convenient to use one, and sometimes another.

The Relation of Marginal and Average Costs

Although we have studied only average costs in this chapter, we have noted that it is possible to move from one concept of cost to another. Figure 5 shows the relation of average and marginal costs for the short-run costs of a firm.

The relation between these two curves is a mathematical one and not a matter of economics. Although it is a purely formal relation, it is very important that you understand how these curves are related, since, when we come to use our theory of costs, we shall want to be able to use whichever of average or marginal costs happens to be more convenient in the particular circumstances. The average cost curve slopes downward as long as the marginal cost curve is below it; it makes no difference whether the marginal cost curve is itself sloping upward or downward.

When AC is declining, MC is below it. The

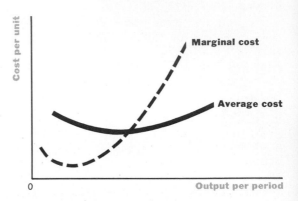

FIGURE 5 **THE RELATION OF AVERAGE COST AND MARGINAL COST**

common-sense interpretation is that, if the cost of an additional unit of output lowers the average cost, it must itself be less than the average cost. When average cost is rising, marginal cost is above it. This is because, if an additional unit is to raise average costs,

†

$$ATC = \frac{TC}{Q}; \text{ hence } TC = Q \cdot ATC;$$

$$MC = \frac{\Delta TC}{\Delta Q}, \text{ where } \Delta \text{ means "the change in."}$$

The term marginal cost should not be used unless the change is very, very small. For finite changes, the term incremental cost is preferred. Where the changes are infinitesimal, the differential calculus is required to express the concept accurately. In the calculus we define marginal cost as follows:

$$MC = \frac{dTC}{dQ},$$

which is read: "The derivative of total cost with respect to output" and which means the rate at which cost is changing as output changes. The concept of a derivative is familiar to the student in such an everyday notion as speed: to say one drives at 80 miles per hour is to say that the rate at which distance is covered (miles) with respect to time (hours) is 80, or $\text{Speed} = \dfrac{d\,\text{Distance}}{d\,\text{Time}}$.

its cost must be more than average cost. It follows from these two propositions that the marginal cost curve must cut the average cost curve at the lowest point on that curve. This is a virtually self-evident proposition, and a valuable one to remember.†

Summary

1. The cost of producing a commodity varies with the amount being produced. A short-run cost curve shows how costs vary with output when some inputs are fixed. A long-run cost curve shows how cost varies with output when all inputs can be varied.

2. A long-run cost curve shows the lowest attainable costs of producing each level of output on the assumption that all inputs can be adjusted to their optimal level for that output. Different points along this curve represent alternative outputs for which the firm must build different plants in order to achieve the lowest possible cost of production.

3. The long-run cost curve may slope upward, downward, or it may be horizontal. Situations of rising, falling, and constant long-run costs are sometimes referred to as the laws of returns, but they are nothing more than classifications of all possible cases.

4. For every level of output there is, by hypothesis, an optimal factor combination. In the short run, the inputs of some factors are fixed and thus, as production is varied by varying some inputs, the optimal factor combination is departed from. From this it follows that the short-run cost curve will be above the long-run one for every point except one—the output for which the fixed factor was designed.

5. A rise in the price of any factor of production will shift all cost curves upward and will also change the optimal factor combination for each level of output, with other factors being partially substituted for the factor whose price has risen.

6. The total cost of producing any output can be divided into fixed (or overhead) costs, which do not vary with output, and variable costs, which do. Average cost is total cost

† The propositions of this paragraph are easily proved using calculus.

Let

$$C = \text{average cost,}$$
$$Q = \text{quantity of output,}$$
$$MC = \frac{d(C \cdot Q)}{dQ} = Q\frac{dC}{dQ} + C.$$

$\frac{dC}{dQ}$ is the slope of the average cost curve. Since quantity of output (Q) is positive,

$$\frac{dC}{dQ} < 0 \text{ means } MC < C \qquad\qquad (1)$$

$$\frac{dC}{dQ} > 0 \text{ means } MC > C \qquad\qquad (2)$$

$$\frac{dC}{dQ} = 0 \text{ means } MC = C. \qquad\qquad (3)$$

Condition (3) is, of course, a necessary condition of minimum C, and proves that marginal cost is equal to average cost at its minimum point.

divided by the number of units produced; average fixed cost always falls as output rises; average variable cost falls for a while then rises (i.e., the average variable cost curve is U-shaped). Marginal cost is the cost of increasing the rate of output by one unit. Since marginal fixed costs are always zero, a change in fixed costs does not affect marginal cost. The marginal cost curve cuts the average cost curve at the lowest point of the average curve.

QUESTIONS FOR DISCUSSION

1. On page 217 of this chapter, we asked what might happen if the lumber industry were asked to increase output by 20 percent in three weeks or by 20 percent in three years. Can you explain this possibility now?

2. We mentioned that there has not been a successful new entrant into the automobile industry since the 1920s. What possible explanation can be found in this chapter? (Hint: What is the likely scale of production of any new entrant for several years?)

3. The firm's short-run cost curve can never be below its long-run curve. Why not? Is our statement a testable one?

4. If the salaries of university professors go up, what will happen to the cost curves of universities? What about optimal factor combinations?

5. Explain what "spreading one's overheads" means in terms of our vocabulary of costs.

6. If a firm's fixed costs rise while everything else remains unchanged, what happens to the firm's average total cost curve, its average variable cost curve, and its marginal cost curve?

7. If the marginal cost curve is below the average cost curve, is the average cost curve rising or falling? What if the marginal cost curve is above the average curve? Illustrate your answer with numerical examples.

APPENDIX TO CHAPTER 19 **LONG-RUN VARIATIONS IN OUTPUT**

SHORT-RUN VARIATIONS IN OUT-put necessarily involve *changing factor proportions* (progressively more of the variable factors being applied to the fixed factor), but long-run cost variations can occur with or without changes in factor proportions. If 100 units of output can be produced with 10 units of X_2 and 150 units of X_1 (in a two-factor situation), how might 200 units be produced? One way to produce them is to increase the quantities of both factors, *keeping proportions the same,* and follow the identical techniques that were used to produce 100 units. This is called *replication.* The firm can build two identical 100-unit plants and operate them both. These two plants would use 20 units of X_2 and 300 units of X_1 to produce 200 units of output. But the firm may be able to do better than this: Perhaps a specially designed 200-unit plant need not be twice as big and not use twice as much of factor X_1 to achieve twice the output.[1] Furthermore, perhaps a *change* in factor proportions may per-

1. This would arise if the increase in size allowed the use of more specialized (and hence more productive) capital and labor, so that doubling all inputs and reorganizing the production process more than doubled the output.

mit still greater gains in efficiency.

In Chapter 19 the sources of variation of cost with output were characterized simply as "economies or diseconomies of scale." In this appendix we shall use a more specialized vocabulary. We shall use the phrase *returns to cost* to describe the over-all effect of all sources of long-run variation of costs with output. Returns to cost are divided into three parts:

(1) *returns to scale*, in which factors are kept in constant proportion but varied in level;

(2) *returns to substitution*, in which factor proportions are varied at the same time the quantities of all factors are varied; and

(3) *pecuniary returns to cost*, in which induced factor price variations are included.

The first two of these components are purely physical phenomena and are defined by the production function. In discussing them, we assume that factor prices are fixed and are independent of the quantity of the factor used by the firm.

Returns to Scale

Suppose we can produce a specified output Q^* by using specified quantities of a series of inputs $X_1^*, X_2^*, \ldots, X_m^*$, where the asterisk denotes the fact that these are specific quantities. In other words, start from the specified value of the production function:

$$Q^* = f(X_1^*, X_2^*, \ldots, X_m^*). \ (1)$$

Now consider multiplying each

of the inputs by a fixed amount, λ. In general, output can be expected to change and we denote the proportion by which Q^* does change by α. Thus we may write

$$\alpha Q^* = f(\lambda X_1^*, \lambda X_2^*, \ldots, \lambda X_m^*), (2)$$

and we list the three possibilities as follows:

$$\alpha < \lambda$$
(decreasing returns to scale)

$$\alpha = \lambda$$
(constant returns to scale)

$$\alpha > \lambda$$
(increasing returns to scale).

Equation (1) says that the total output originally produced depends on the exact quantities of the factors actually used. Equation (2) describes a situation in which the initial quantities of the factors are all multiplied by the same amount (e.g., they are all doubled or halved for $\lambda = 2$ and $\lambda = 0.5$, respectively), while the total product changes by some proportion, α. In the next lines we attach a term to each of the logically possible outcomes of this event.

In order to go beyond a mere labeling of all possible cases it is necessary to offer hypotheses that say something about behavior. We start with two technological hypotheses.

The Hypothesis of Replication. If all identifiable factors of production are free to be varied, it is always possible to increase output by an integral multiple

λ *by increasing the quantity of every factor used by the same multiple* λ.[2]

This hypothesis is suggested by the definition of the long run; it is another way of saying that all factors that affect output can be identified and varied by the firm. In a world of identical chickens (and identical chicken feed, etc.), if one hen can produce one egg in one day, two hens can produce two eggs in one day, if they are provided with twice as much chicken feed (and twice as much of every other factor). Although there have been attempts to show that the hypothesis is incorrect, the evidence suggested in each case appears to us, on close examination, fallacious. A common kind of attempted refutation is of this sort: "A firm with ten identical plants may produce less than ten times as much output as a firm with one plant because the complexities of management increase." You should recognize that this is a false argument: It is implying (1) that the factor "management" is fixed; or (2) that management of a given quality is limited and the firm is substituting an inferior factor; or (3) that the management problems of the large operation are more than ten times as complex (and thus require more than ten times the mangement) as the small operation. The first two merely imply that the factor "high-quality management" is fixed and so are not refutations; the third implies that the firms are not profit-maximizers since they could al-

2. When we say an "integral multiple λ" we mean that λ is to be a whole number, or, as it is more usually called, an integer.

ways replicate by building ten identical independently functioning units.

From the hypothesis of replication it follows at once that there can never be *decreasing* returns to scale, for the hypothesis says that replication always permits at least constant returns to scale.[3] The hypothesis of replication does not rule out increasing returns to scale. Although it says that one can always double output by doubling all inputs, it does not say that one cannot do better.

Whether there can or cannot be increasing returns to scale depends upon whether factors are perfectly divisible, as the following hypothesis points out:

The Hypothesis of Perfect Divisibility. If all factors are free to be varied, it is always possible to decrease output by a multiple λ (0 < λ < 1) by decreasing the quantity of every factor used by the multiple λ.

This is a testable hypothesis about the possibility of dividing input into smaller and smaller units and about the effects of doing so. In some cases, the hypothesis is obviously wrong. Half a hen may very well produce no eggs because one hen is an *indivisible* quantity of hens. Whether a loom or a tractor or a blast furnace or an assembly line is perfectly divisible is an empirical matter, not a logical one.

The hypothesis of perfect divisibility is frequently rejected on empirical grounds. For most operations there is a minimum level of operation that is required to make certain factors efficiently usable. Whether this level is very low (as in the case of the whole chicken) or quite substantial (as in the case of a blast furnace) matters a good deal and is often used to define the point of *minimal efficient scale* of a process of production. Below this point proportionate reductions in factor quantities will lead to more than proportionate decreases in output.

The major source of imperfect divisibility has to do not with the physical characteristics of factors but with specialization in their use. Consider the butchering of livestock. To turn one steer into marketable cuts of beef one man with one knife must do about 100 distinct tasks. One hundred men with 100 identical knives *could* butcher 100 steers by each butchering one steer entirely (this is, of course, the hypothesis of replication). Or, each of 100 men could become very expert in one operation; by specializing in this operation and performing it over and over again on each steer, the 100 men could butcher 100 steers in less time than one man could butcher one steer.[4] Where does indivisibility come in? One could hire 100 specialists to butcher one steer *if* one could hire human services by the minute for the same rates as by the day, week, or year; this is, of course, impossible. It is not possible to duplicate this efficient organization of production on a small scale because it requires a rate of output sufficiently large that a man can work all day at a very specialized part of the whole process.

If factors were perfectly divisible, increasing returns to scale would be impossible.† Taken in conjunction with the hypothesis of replication, perfect divisibility implies constant returns to scale over all possible ranges of output.

If we do not have perfect divisibility of factors but we do have the possibility of replication, returns to scale may increase or be constant.

When considering a single *process* of production,[5] it is typi-

---

3. Since replication is limited to integral increases in output, this statement is correct for large enough increases in output, but may be incorrect for smaller increases. That is, one need never do worse than constant returns to scale if one doubles output; but for a 50 percent increase in output, replication by itself does not provide a technique of production. This is not an important qualification in the context in which we wish to talk about returns, and we shall ignore it.

4. Since output is always "per unit of time," this is an increase in output.

† Suppose the reverse. Suppose production at a rate of 100 units per week appeared to use less than twice as much of all inputs than were required to produce at a rate of 50 units per week. One available technique of producing 50 units would be to use the technique used to produce 100 units at half the level of use of each factor. Nothing excludes this possibility, and thus the initial situation could not have been a technologically efficient use of factors if factors were perfectly divisible.

5. What we now label as a *process* of production is the case that in practice corresponds to the "fixed-factor proportions" required to discuss returns to scale.

cally found that, owing to factor indivisibilities, there is some minimal efficient level of operation that is required in order to achieve the efficient use of the process. For some processes this level is very low; for others it is more substantial. (This variation of minimal efficient scales among processes is the source—as we shall see—of substantial returns to substitution.)

If returns to scale were the only source of variation of cost with long-run variations of output, we would expect long-run costs to exhibit a pattern such as that exhibited by the curves in Figure A1. Curve *xA* defines the variation of average cost with output of some process of production as the quantities of factors of production are increased in constant proportions. Output *Oa* is the minimal efficient scale of production of that process. Curve *zB* refers to a different process, and has a minimal efficient scale of production *Ob*. Each of these curves exhibits increasing returns to scale up to its point of minimal efficient scale, and constant returns to scale thereafter.

Returns to Substitution

Long-run costs may vary owing to changes in factor proportions as well as to changes in scale. This is easily seen in Figure A1, which presented scale cost curves for two different processes.[6] If the firm an-

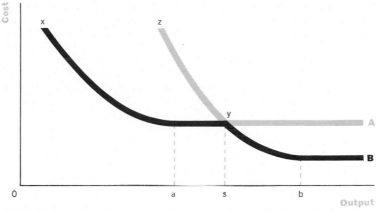

FIGURE A1

ticipated production at levels below *Os* (and was limited in its choices to these two processes), it would use process *A*. If output was to be at a rate in excess of *Os*, the firm would prefer process *B*. Over the whole range of output from zero to *Ob* the firm would achieve lowest costs by first using process *A* and then shifting from process *A* to process *B* at the point where the curves cross. (Output *Os*.) The dark curve *xyB* exhibits a pattern of variation different from either process curve. This pattern can occur whenever different processes have different minimal efficient scales owing to different effective indivisibilities.[7]

The following example illustrates the interaction of substitution with replication and indivisibilities: A man wishes to produce one shirt per day. He hires one girl with a needle and thread to do the job. Now

assume he wishes to raise his output to two, and then to three, shirts per day. He hires two, then three, girls, each with needles and each producing one shirt per day. In other words, he replicates, keeping factor proportions constant; he encounters constant returns to scale. If he wishes to produce four shirts per day, he finds it worthwhile to buy a sewing machine and hire one girl for four hours to produce four shirts. This method is more capital-using than the previous method in which each girl had as capital one needle; now one girl has a sewing machine. The manufacturer has thus changed factor proportions (and technologies); he encounters increasing returns to substitution. If he wishes to raise output to five, six, seven, and eight shirts, he hires his one girl for five, six, seven, and eight hours without buying a second machine.

6. Each process by definition used constant-factor proportions, but process A and process B must use factors in different proportions; if they did not, they would be the same processes and their cost curves would coincide.

7. To return to the livestock example, our 100 men might be equipped with more specialized equipment than 100 identical knives, in which case a different process, use of an electric bone saw, say, would be required. An electric bone saw, however, might well require a larger level of output to be efficiently used.

This indivisibility of the sewing machine leads him to encounter increasing returns to cost in the four-to-eight shirts per day range. If he wishes to raise output to sixteen, twenty-four, or thirty-two shirts per day, he buys two, three, or four sewing machines, each with an operator working eight hours. He is now encountering constant returns to scale by the process of replication. Once his output reaches fifty shirts per day, it pays him to buy a factory with machines for all the processes and to utilize it at 60 percent capacity. His ratio of labor to capital has now changed and he has encountered a factor-substitution effect. As his demand expands, he encounters increasing returns to cost as the factory approaches 100 percent capacity. After this, increases in output are obtained by building duplicate factories so that he is back in the range of constant returns.

Even the most casual observation of the differences in production technique used in large- and small-sized plants supports the existence of the differences in factor proportions that we are calling differences in processes. The reason is that large specialized machinery and equipment,

which uses a different ratio of labor to capital than does smaller, less specialized equipment, is useful only when the volume of output that the firm can sell justifies its use. Consider a few examples: The use of the assembly-line technique, body-stamping machinery, and multiple-boring engine block machines in automobile production make economic sense only if individual operations are to be repeated thousands of times. This substitution of mechanized equipment for labor, or for simpler tools, represents factor substitution. The use of elaborate harvesting equipment (which combines many individual tasks that might be done by hand and by tractor) makes economic sense on a big farm but not on a few acres. The continuous strip-rolling mill in steel production provides a highly efficient technique of producing flat steel, but only if the volume of production is such as to utilize the capital equipment on a nearly full-time basis.

Typically, the substitution involved is of capital for labor, and of complex machines for simpler ones.[8] Electronic devices can handle a very large volume of operations very quickly, but, unless the level of production

requires very large numbers of operations, it does not make sense to use these techniques.[9]

Increasing returns to substitution are possible if individual processes have points of minimal efficient scale at different levels of output.[†] Constant returns to substitution will result (according to the hypothesis of replication) when output exceeds the minimal efficient point of the lowest cost process. Decreasing returns to substitution are not possible for a profit-maximizing firm.[10]

Empirical Evidence on Returns to Scale and Substitution

Important empirical questions concern where and when increasing returns exist, how large these returns are, and over what ranges of output they occur. Many empirical studies have been made that attempt to measure the fraction of the total industry's market that a single plant requires in order to achieve approximately minimum efficient size.[11] By way of illustration, we cite the findings of a study by Joe S. Bain.[12] This study presents the following classification of a number of

---

8. Automation is a contemporary example of this kind of substitution. We shall discuss it in Chapter 20.

9 Even a moderate-sized electronic computer, which costs in excess of $1 million, can perform as many computations per hour as 100,000 women with desk calculators The substitution of electronic for manual computation may make sense for a large life-insurance company, but not for the local grocer or bookie.

† It can be proved that if every process exhibited perfect divisibility there would exist constant returns to substitution as well as to scale. This is left is an exercise for the student.

10. Except for in-between levels of output. See footnote 2 above. Common sense tells us that factor substitution is never *necessary* in the long run—the firm can expand by replication. Factor substitution is used if, but only if, it promises greater efficiency.

11. The concept of "minimal optimal plant-scale," as it is sometimes called, combines the effects of returns to scale and returns to substitution.

12. Bain, *Barriers to New Competition* (Harvard University Press, 1956), Chapter 3.

U.S. industries according to the size of plant required to achieve moderately efficient production:

1. Industries with very important plant-scale economies:[13] automobiles, typewriters.

2. Industries with moderately important plant-scale economies:[14] cement, farm machinery, rayon, steel.

3. Industries with relatively unimportant plant-scale economies:[15] canned fruits and vegetables, cigarettes, flour, liquor, meat packing, petroleum refining, soap, shoes, and tires and tubes.

Further sources of increasing returns may occur for the firm beyond the level of the plant. For example, a large enough firm may find it efficient to establish a nationwide organization for the sale or service of its product.

Evidence on these matters is important because, as we shall see later, the nature of costs in an industry has very important effects on such things as how easy it is for new firms to enter the industry, whether or not there is a tendency toward monopolization in the industry, and how easy it is for the industry to adapt rapidly to changes in demand.

Pecuniary Returns to Cost

As a firm or an industry expands its production, it requires increasing supplies of the factors it purchases. It will require increases in the production of the supplying industries, which must in turn adapt to the changes in demand they face. These changes may lead to changes in the prices the supplying industries charge; or, from the point of view of the purchasing firm, changes in the costs of its factors.

Such "external" returns to cost have been suggested as possible in either direction.

The Possibility of Increasing Pecuniary Returns. This possibility can arise when one industry, call it industry A, uses the output of another industry, call it B, as its own input. If the scale of industry A expands, it will demand more of B's product and B will expand as well. If B is subject to increasing returns to scale, its costs will fall and the price of its product will fall as well. Thus the price of A's input will fall so that A is subject to increasing pecuniary returns.

At least superficially this is an appealing and plausible possibility. Consider, for example, the great increase in large-scale agricultural production, which has vastly increased the demand for farm machinery. If the production of farm machinery is subject to increasing returns, the cost of production per machine will have decreased and the price paid by farmers may well have been reduced because of this.

Empirical evidence that this actually occurs (as distinct from the plausibility that it might occur) is difficult to find. The reason is that it requires long-run reorganizations of production in supplying industries, which take years to occur. Moreover, over such long periods many other influences also are operating to change factor prices.[16]

The Hypothesis of Eventually Decreasing Pecuniary Returns (Rising Supply Price). Increases in the volume of purchases from any industry will eventually cause scarcity of those factors that are heavily used by the supplying industry, and thus will lead to increases in supply prices.

Whether or not this is an empirically testable hypothesis is a matter of some debate among economists. It is possible to find some cases that do confirm the prediction of rising supply prices for expanding industries. For other industries no such effect is visible, but this does not prove that rising supply prices will not occur *eventually*. If the hypothesis is interpreted to mean there is the *possibility* of decreasing pecuniary returns, it may be regarded as demonstrable, and actually demonstrated. If the hypothesis is interpreted as eventually *requiring*

---

13. Industries where at least 10 percent of market capacity is required to achieve efficient production.
14. Industries where 5 percent to 10 percent of market capacity is required to achieve efficient production.
15. Industries where less than 5 percent of market capacity is required to achieve efficient production.
16. Note that it is only the *induced* changes in factor prices that we include as pecuniary returns to cost. Other changes in such prices, whether random or whether caused by factors other than growth in demand for the industry under study, are not included.

increasing pecuniary returns it can never be disproved empirically: For any case that does not show increasing supply prices, the proponents of the hypothesis will argue "we are *not yet* at the point where decreasing returns occur."

This proposition is the only proposition in the theory of long-run costs that permits in- *creasing long-run costs as a function of increases in production.*[17]

Conclusion

Considering all sources of possible long-run variation of cost with output, costs over any specified range may fall, be constant, or rise. A U-shaped long- run curve is thus *possible*, but it is not *necessary*. *Rising* long-run costs, if they occur, are due not to scale or substitution effects, but to increases in factor costs.

With respect to long-run cost curves, impressive evidence of a substantial range of decreasing costs exists, whereas such evidence as has been advanced for the existence of increasing costs to the firm is inconclusive.

QUESTIONS FOR DISCUSSION

1. What do we mean by the hypothesis of replication? Can you give examples from your own observations of industrial processes that have been replicated by single firms?

2. What do we mean by the hypothesis of perfect divisibility? Can you think of processes that are divisible? Can

you think of ones that are not?

3. Why is it easier to imagine cases of increasing returns to scale than cases of decreasing returns?

4. If Switzerland (population 5,810,000) decided to build her own auto industry to supply the home market under heavy

tariff protection, do you think she would be well advised to adopt the latest, most highly automated techniques available in America? Why or why not? If the population of Switzerland began to expand very rapidly, would the Swiss auto industry encounter increasing or decreasing returns to scale? Why?

Chapter **20** THE VERY LONG RUN

"BETTER THINGS FOR BETTER LIVING" IS THE slogan of a major American manufacturer; and it is a goal that most families share, and that most have achieved.

Products change in many ways. A 1966

Ford automobile is very different from a 1926 Ford automobile. Nylon stockings are very different from rayon or silk stockings. The fact that in our statistical series we treat any car as a car but a silk stocking as a different

---

17. Note that it rests upon the argument that, while the firm is free to vary its use of factors, society is limited in its supply of some factors.

product from a nylon stocking is of no real significance. Many of the important consumer products of today either did not exist a couple of generations ago or are so changed that their nominal connection with the "same" product produced in the past is meaningless.[1]

Productivity

There is no doubt whatever that over the last 20, 50, or 100 years, the standard of living of the typical family has increased enormously. Our great-grandfathers would have regarded our standard of living as something quite out of their world. And indeed it is. This is true of most industrialized countries in the world. A major source of this increase has been the increase in output per unit of input, which is called an increase in *productivity*.

Whether we should discuss the effect of productivity changes as part of the economic theory of supply depends upon whether producers' decisions affect the rate of change of productivity. If they do not (if, to put the matter more formally, productivity changes are *exogenous* to the firm's decisions), we can ignore them at this stage, just as we ignore other noneconomic elements of the environment that may shift cost curves about. If, however, they are *endogenous*, they must be included. To decide whether they are exogenous or endogenous requires attention to the sources of productivity increases.

If the nature of goods had not changed, and if factor prices had not changed, increased productivity could be easily represented by downward shifts in the cost curves of producing goods. We cannot, of course, in the very long run take these things as given.

Society has not concentrated solely on producing a *fixed list of goods* more and more cheaply. It has sought better quality products, new products to meet old—and new—needs, increased pay and increased leisure for workers, and so on.

For this reason it is appropriate to discuss the sources of the increases in productivity rather than to discuss mere changes in the levels of cost. Particular goods, whose output and cost per unit we can easily measure, are only one means of satisfying wants or needs. Ability to get a better product at the same cost may be more (or less) effective in increasing the user's satisfaction than getting the same product at lower cost. *But each is a means of getting more satisfaction of wants per unit of resources employed.* According to our definition of costs, each of the above is a lowering of the *costs* of want satisfaction. In the "very long run," products change; thus we must use the broader concept.

The magnitude of increases in productivity deserves some attention. The apparently modest rate of increase of output per man hour of labor of 2.5 percent per year leads to a doubling of output per man hour every 28 years. Productivity in the United States has increased at approximately this rate since the turn of the century.[2] Since World War II,

1. Measurement of output in a world of changing products is not impossible, but it is complex. Economic statisticians have developed some ingenious techniques for measuring output changes, but we do not discuss them in this volume.

2. We do not have reliable statistics for the nineteenth century, but the rate of increase surely was substantial.

productivity in Japan has increased at over 7 percent per year, representing a doubling in approximately 10 years of the output per man hour.[3]

SOURCES OF INCREASING PRODUCTIVITY

These long-run increases in efficiency are due to, and can be divided into, scale effects, substitution effects, increases in the quality of the inputs, changes in the known techniques of production, and improvements in product. Mere population growth, other things equal, will permit higher productivity if most products are subject to increasing returns to scale. Substitution of more and more capital for labor will, as the level of production expands, lead to greater productivity if there are increasing returns to substitution of capital. Better raw materials, better trained or educated labor, or better machines will increase productivity even if no changes in factor quantities or proportions take place. Better organization of production can alone account for increases in productivity. New ideas can raise efficiency by being applied to new products: Imagination can design a better mousetrap, with no increase in the quantity, quality, or proportions of factors.

But in practice these factors are intertwined.[4] All but the scale effects are related to the processes of invention and innovation that are continuously improving raw materials and machines, improving ways of combining factors, and improving the products they make.

The extent and importance of change is so basic to economic activity that it cannot safely be neglected. Consider, for example, changes in sources of energy in the United States within this century: Energy to plow fields, to turn machines, to move goods, to provide heat, and to transform natural resources is a major determinant of the productive power of an economy. In 1900, more than half of all energy requirements was supplied by men, horses, mules, and oxen. By 1960, animal and human power provided less than 10 percent of all energy; it has been increasingly replaced by such inanimate sources of power as coal, oil, gas, and water power. The over-all growth in inanimate fuels is exhibited in Figure 1. Total energy from these fuels increased fivefold over the first six decades of this century—an increase that is more than twice as large as the increase in population.

While this is, in itself, a major substitution of factors of production, it conceals even greater ones. In 1900, almost nine-tenths of energy from inanimate fuels came from coal. Today only one-quarter comes from coal. The rise in the use of petroleum and natural gas is shown in Figure 2. Today, 70 percent of

3. In using here output per unit of labor input, we are focusing on the efficiency of use of factors in terms of a single factor. The reason is twofold: First, labor time is relatively homogenous over time; second, and more important, we are a society of people and the use of people is of particular concern. But the student should note that a doubling of output per man hour is equivalent to a cut in half of costs only if factor proportions and prices remain constant. If capital is being substituted for labor, costs will be reduced by less than the increase in productivity per unit of labor. Total factor productivity in the United States has increased at an average rate of about 2 percent per year during this century.

4. Recent empirical work has attempted to separate some of these components. For example, John Kendrick, *Productivity Trends in the United States* (Princeton, N. J., 1961), has attempted to measure the changing quality of labor. Studies now under way are attempting to distinguish between mere substitution of capital for labor and changes in the quality of capital. These attempts are still in sufficiently experimental stages that their discussion is not appropriate in this volume.

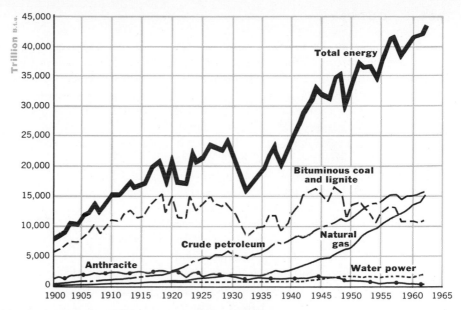

FIGURE 1   PRODUCTION OF MINERAL, FUEL, AND WATER POWER ENERGY, UNITED STATES, 1900–1962

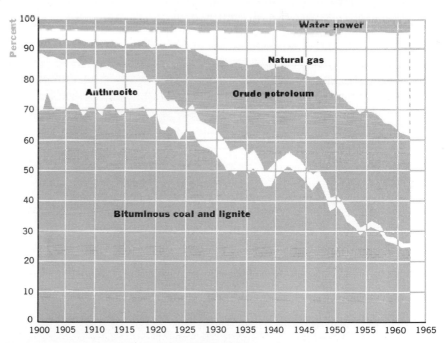

FIGURE 2   THE RISE IN THE USE OF NATURAL GAS AND PETROLEUM, UNITED STATES, 1900–1962

our energy comes from these sources. Six decades from now, atomic energy may be playing a dominant role as the process of energy substitution continues.

Nor do these aggregate figures do full justice to the changes that have occurred. The uses of individual fuels have also changed. The primary use of coal at the beginning of the century was to produce steam to drive steam engines. Today, coal is used primarily to generate electric power. Electrical energy production has increased almost tenfold since 1920. The uses of petroleum products have likewise changed and continue to change. Similar changes occur with respect to other inputs. Review the statistics from the Census of Manufacturers and you will see the declining relative importance of primary metals, lumber products, and textile mill products, and the corresponding increase in importance of transportation equipment, fabricated metal products, and machinery of all kinds. Within these categories are yet further changes. For example, the kind and quality of metals has changed. Steel replaces iron, and aluminum substitutes for steel, in a process of change that

makes a statistical category like "primary metals" seem unsatisfactory and obsolete.[5] Figure 3 illustrates this by showing percentage changes in the U.S. production of three kinds of metals since 1890.[6]

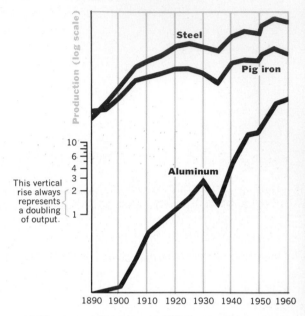

FIGURE 3   **PRODUCTION OF STEEL, PIG IRON, AND ALUMINUM, UNITED STATES, 1890–1960**

The Nature of Innovation

Innovation is defined as the introduction of a change into the production function. Innovation can work through changing the nature or quality of factors or of the product, or through changing the techniques by which factors are combined to produce outputs.

When an innovation occurs one may infer that someone has thought that it will be profitable to use some new knowledge. An innovation presupposes the existence of a new technique, but requires as well its introduction. Many discoveries (inventions),

5. The student working with census materials is repeatedly frustrated by the changes in definitions of products and industries used. However, changes in the definitions result from real changes and provide what is the most persuasive evidence of the changes that have occurred in the structure of both productive processes and the nature of products.

6. This kind of "logarithmic" chart focuses on the slope of the curves. The same vertical rise always represents the same percentage increase. See the scale on Figure 3. The three curves are given positions on the figure roughly representing their importance in dollar volume of output.

large and small, are made; many never become practicable. When an innovation persists for long periods, one may infer that it has proved profitable.

An important thing to recognize about innovation is the *cumulative* nature of the process. A useful invention is used; a useless one is discarded. Except where whole societies disappear, knowledge is seldom lost, and the state of technical knowledge improves or stays the same. It does not ordinarily recede. For this reason, the cumulative impact of many small innovations may be fully as large or larger than the occasional dramatic invention, such as the discovery of the steam engine, the cotton gin, or the sewing machine.[7]

Almost all of the sources of increased productivity are related to the process of innovation somewhere in society. Thus the question of whether productivity changes are exogenous or endogenous rests upon whether innovation is exogenous or endogenous. A number of hypotheses about the sources of invention have been offered:

1. *Invention is a random process.*

Some men are by nature both curious and clever. Thousands of attempts will be made to invent better ways of doing things. Many men will fail, and they remain nameless, but a few succeed. These are the Fultons, Edisons, Whitneys, and Fords. The successful inventions become a pool of potential innovations, and, when the climate is right, they are introduced into production.

2. *Invention is a response to the institutional framework.*

Things like the patent laws, the tax structure, or the organization of business enterprise stimulate or retard the process of invention. Invention, in this view, is not exogenous to society, but it does not respond primarily to economic variables, and it certainly is exogenous to the individual *firm*.

3. *Invention and innovation are the product of the inherent logic and momentum of science.*

Science has a logic and momentum of its own. There was a time for the discovery of the steam engine, the airplane, hybrid corn, the electron tube, and the rocket. Particular men are the instruments, not the causes, of scientific discovery. Had Edison never been born we would still have had, at about the same time, both the light bulb and the phonograph. According to this view, the present is the electronic age, and automation is the industrial form of introduction of electronic devices into production.

4. *Necessity is the mother of invention.*

Ignorance is only skin deep. With enough expenditure of funds, men can do anything —split the atom, conquer cancer, fly to Mars, or cultivate the desert. The pace and rate of invention depends upon how many resources are devoted to solving problems, and resources are devoted according to needs. A firm for which a certain factor is becoming scarce will discover ways to economize on using it, or will develop a more plentiful substitute for it. (For example, the scarcity of high-grade iron ore led to the development of ways of using low-grade ores.) In this view, automation is a response to expensive labor. The impetus for invention may thus come from within the firm. But it may also come from without: Governments may set priorities and do the research that leads to

7. None of these famous inventions sprang full blown from the mind of a primitive man, but rested upon the cumulative developments of others. For an excellent account of some famous inventions, see A. P. Usher, *A History of Mechanical Inventions* (rev. ed.; Harvard University Press, 1954).

major discoveries and innovations. Atomic energy, for example, is the result of the United Kingdom's and later of the United States' desire to develop superweapons during World War II. The space and missile programs are responsible for some current discoveries that have industrial applications as well.

5. *Profits are the spur.*

The profit motive not only leads men and firms to seize the best known methods, but to develop new ways to meet both old and new needs and wants. But profit opportunities are vitally connected to the economic climate and to economic circumstances.

Which of these hypotheses is correct? Very possibly all of them. They are not self-contradictory and the evidence for one cannot be regarded as disproving the others. The fact that some firms spend millions of dollars on research and development to overcome specific problems or invent new products does not negate the fact that Charles Martin Hall discovered, in the chemistry laboratories of Oberlin College, the technique that made aluminum possible. The fact that many patentable discoveries are given to the world does not prove that others are not motivated by the prospect of huge personal gain. And so on.

Whether invention is or is not exogenous requires more careful specification if it is to be a testable question. One may ask: Is endogenous invention a *sufficiently important* activity of firms that it deserves incorpora-

tion in the theory of firm behavior? To this the answer is given by the fact that private expenditures on research and development amounted to about $4 billion in 1960.[8] This is a magnitude of activity that needs incorporation into the body of the theory of the firm.[9]

Innovation, as distinct from invention, involves the introduction into use of new techniques, products, or processes. Even if invention were purely random, the process by which its fruits are utilized might be highly responsive to profits, sales, costs, and other economic variables.

Where do economists stand on the matters of invention and innovation? The consensus is that innovation is a process that requires economic analysis. Whether the stock of technical knowledge that exists at any moment in time is itself to be explained in economic terms is debated and must be regarded as an unsettled issue, but it is agreed that the rate at which what is known gets put into practice (the rate of innovation) does respond to economic incentives.

The reason why invention receives major attention in studies of long-term growth is very simple. Variations in efficiency that are possible by choice among *known* techniques and among alternative levels of output are limited in scope. We can, of course, never do better than a 100 percent utilization of what is currently known. Improvements by invention are potentially limitless. For this reason, the long-run struggle of men to get more from the limited resources of the world is

8.   To give this figure some meaning, these expenditures amounted in 1960 to roughly 15 percent of gross private investment in producers' durable goods. The "industry of discovery," as Sumner H. Slichter called it, has been increasing very rapidly. Total (government and private combined) research and development expenditures in the U.S. economy increased from $3.4 billion in 1953 to $7.2 billion by 1957. By 1962 the figure exceeded $10 billion.

9. The interested student is referred to "Technological Research as Related to the Growth and Stability of the Economy," *Proceedings of a Conference on Research and Development and Its Impact on the Economy* (Washington: USGPO, 1958).

critically linked to discovery. "Progress is our most important product" is the slogan of a large manufacturer. It is a noble thought.

Economics used to be known as the dismal science, but this designation has long since ceased to be applied. Why? Economics was thought dismal because its predictions were dismal. The basic prediction about the very long run put forward by classical economists was that the population of the world would continue to expand and that the pressure of more and more persons on the limited resources of the world would cause a decline in output per head.[10] The history of the world would be one of more and more people living less and less well, with the surplus of persons that could not be supported at all dying off by plague, famine, and pestilence. This prediction has been dramatically correct in some of the countries now called underdeveloped. It has, however, been falsified in all of the industrial countries. Why? On the one hand, because of voluntary restriction on population growth due to the wide acceptance of birth control, the birth rate was lowered so that, in spite of dramatic reductions in the death rate due to advances in medicine and hygiene, the population did not expand as rapidly as was foreseen by economists writing before the wide availability of birth-control techniques.[11] Second, pure knowledge and applied techniques based on it have expanded so rapidly during the last 150 years that man's ability to squeeze more out of his limited resources has expanded faster than the population has expanded. The race is a close one and should the rate at which the frontiers of knowledge are being pushed back fall below the rate of population increase, then economics may once again become the dismal science. In the meantime, output per person and standards of living have risen greatly in the last century and economics has had the task of explaining why things have gotten better and better rather than of explaining why things have gotten worse and worse.

The lot of those underdeveloped economies for which the dismal predictions of the classical economics proved correct is in many ways hard to understand. If the key to the performance of Europe and America is invention and innovation, why could not these inventions be copied and installed in underdeveloped countries, thus raising their living standards? Evidently, more than invention is required for innovation. What we have to do is to explain the slow pace of innovation given the vast stock of accumulated inventions. We shall examine these problems in Chapter 57.

The importance of the long-run struggle does not mean that efficient use of resources at a given time is unimportant. But it must be kept in focus. And there is always the *possibility* that efficient use of resources at one time may be in partial conflict with the most rapid rate of innovation.[12]

10. Because of the operation of the law of diminishing returns. See page 221, footnote 6.

11. This is meant as a positive statement of fact and not as a normative statement about whether this development was good or bad in an ethical sense.

12. Joseph Schumpeter's famous hypothesis that monopoly, which is thought to encourage some inefficiency in resource use (as we shall see in Chapter 26), might encourage innovation and thus promote long-term increased efficiency is based on such a potential conflict.

Summary

1. The standard of living of all industrialized countries has increased enormously in the past century. The rise in productivity (output per unit of input) in America has averaged between 2 and 2.5 percent over a long period of time.

2. The long-run increases in productivity are due to scale effects, substitution effects, increases in the quality of inputs, changes in the techniques of production, and improvements in products. All but scale effects are related to the process of invention, which is the discovery of new techniques, and innovation, which is the introduction of these into the production process.

3. A number of hypotheses about invention have been offered: Invention is a random process; invention is a response to the institutional framework; invention is the product of the inherent logic and momentum of science; invention is the child of necessity; invention is the spur of profits. These hypotheses do not necessarily contradict one another, for

there is no reason why invention should not respond to more than one influencing factor.

6. Economics used to be known as the dismal science because of the gloomy predictions about the very long run made by the classical economists. These predictions have been falsified for most Western countries. The classical economists did not foresee the voluntary restriction on population growth or the very rapid rate of invention and innovation that has occurred.

7. In underdeveloped countries where the gloomy classical predictions are close to being realized, the problem is to explain the slow rate of innovation from known techniques.

8. The problem of obtaining the most efficient use of resources at any one point of time is important, but in the long run it is much less important than increases in productivity. There is a possibility that the most efficient use at any moment of time may be in partial conflict with obtaining the most rapid growth of invention and innovation.

QUESTIONS FOR DISCUSSION

1. The average American is considered to be far healthier today than he was in the early 1900s. How could this improve efficiency? In which of the causes of long-run increases of efficiency would you classify this change?

2. In 1965, when announcing the start of the War on Poverty program, President Johnson said, "No country can make a better investment than to invest in its young people." In what way can this investment lead to greater long-run efficiency?

3. How many products can you think of that were not available when your parents were going to school?

4. To which of the sources of invention would

you attribute the following: color television, the cotton gin, nuclear power, penicillin, the assembly line, radar, the smashing of atoms, the nuclear bomb, the hula hoop, synthetic rubber, polio vaccine, the airplane, the moving picture, and the wheel? Are any of these attributable to more than one source?

5. Why was economics once called the dismal science? What happened in Western economies to falsify this prediction?

6. How do you define labor productivity? Does the fact that labor productivity is lower in Africa than in the United States mean that Africans are less industrious than Americans? What else might it mean?

MARKET
PRICE

Chapter **21** INTRODUCTION TO THE THEORY OF PRODUCT PRICING

IN PART II WE DEVELOPED AND APPLIED A theory of competitive markets based on the concepts of market demand and market supply. Market demand and market supply are aggregate concepts behind which lie the decisions of many individual households and firms. In Part III we went behind the demand curve to consider the behavior of individual households with respect to demand for commodities. In Part IV we went behind the market supply curve to consider the production and sales decisions of individual firms.

Although demand curves of individual households and cost curves of individual firms are the basic elements of the theory of product pricing, they are not themselves sufficient to provide a theory of price. We need hypotheses that tell us how these elements combine and interact and finally come together in a *market*. In the present chapter, we discuss the concept of a market, and, in subsequent chapters, we go on to develop the fundamental rules for the equilibrium of a profit-maximizing firm.

The Concept of a Market

From the point of view of a consumer, the market consists of those firms from which the consumer can buy a well-defined product; from the point of view of the producer, the market consists of those buyers to whom he can sell a single well-defined product (if the conditions of sale are sufficiently favorable).

For the purpose of introducing you to the theory of firm behavior, this definition of a market is adequate, even though it abstracts substantially from the complications of reality that we encounter when we come to apply and to test the predictions of our theory. Most of the predictions of the theory relate to a single market, but not to all markets taken together; therefore, it is important to be able to identify the market that we are dealing with. Indeed, economists have sometimes made substantial blunders by not correctly identifying the real-world market that most closely corresponded to the "market" of economic theory. For instance, it is sometimes argued that the market for cement in the United States must be characterized by intense competition among a large number of possible suppliers, since there are several thousand small firms producing cement in the country. Actually, however, the cost of transporting cement is so high that the market for one producer does not extend much beyond a 200-mile radius from his factory. Thus "the" U.S. cement market is best characterized as a large number of separate markets, each one of which contains only a very few suppliers—sometimes only one.

SOME COMPLICATIONS

The following examples will give you an idea of the complications that arise when one tries to make contact between the predictions of the theories we are about to develop and the actual data.

Consider first the retail food market in a city.[1] When the typical housewife says she is going to the food market she means she is going to one of the relatively few food stores in her neighborhood. Even if she lives in a city that has fifty supermarkets (to say nothing of other food stores), the market as she views it will probably consist of three or four stores, all of which are relatively close to her house. But is it true that only these few sellers constitute her sources of supply? If prices at the other end of town were much lower, might she not find it worthwhile to make the trip? How widespread a market area she *will* cover depends upon the prices that prevail. How widespread a market area she *might* cover depends upon the cost (in money, in time, and in inconvenience) of extending her range. Although the Berkeley, California, housewife might consider shopping for groceries in Oakland or even in San Francisco, she would certainly not go to Seattle or to Los Angeles to do her weekly shopping.

It is not coincidence that usually makes prices on the east side of town sufficiently similar to those on the west side that most housewives feel it is not worthwhile to make

1. The interested student is referred to Bob R. Holden, *The Structure of a Retail Market and the Market Behavior of Retail Units* (Prentice-Hall, 1960), for an interesting empirical study of a U.S. city with a population of about 50,000.

the trip across town. Rather, it is that the sellers on both sides of town realize that they are in the same market and that they would lose their customers if prices got too far out of line.

In determining the extent of a market, a visual presentation of the geographical spread of prices can sometimes be very helpful, as, for example, in the gasoline price war sketched in Figure 1. Prices in Dubuque, Iowa, where the war started, dropped 10¢ a gallon below the regular price. Within a week every service station within 20 miles had lowered its price by 10¢. In Cedar Rapids and in Davenport, Iowa (each about 75 miles away), prices fell by only 2¢; in Madison, Wisconsin, and Rockford, Illinois (each about 100 miles away), no effect was noticed. Clearly, this pattern provides some clues to the extent of the Dubuque gasoline market.[2]

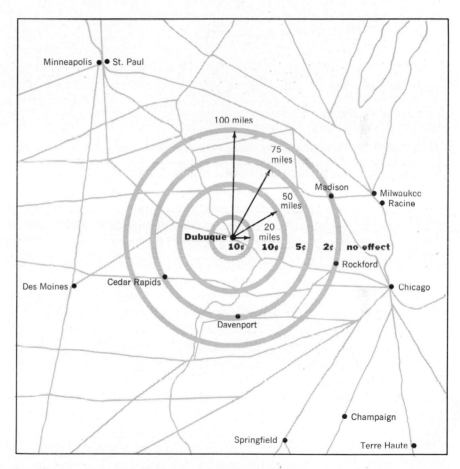

FIGURE 1

A GASOLINE
PRICE WAR

2. But ponder the following facts about the interest paid on savings and loan deposits. In the Midwest, in 1964, Savings and Loan Associations paid 4 percent interest compounded semiannually. On the West Coast, Savings and Loan Associations paid in excess of 4¾ percent compounded quarterly. All had identical insurance features, all paid the costs of banking by mail, and all reported that they had depositors from every state of the union. What may we conclude about the market?

We have observed so far that the definition of a market depends partly on the prices that prevail, partly upon whose point of view (buyer's or seller's) is being examined, and partly upon variables like distance. It also depends upon what the product is. The Champaign-Urbana housewife who would never think of going to Chicago for her groceries might well go there for her furniture.[3] And she might go to New York, San Francisco, Paris, or Mexico City for her vacation. Her stamp-collecting husband may receive catalogues and buy stamps from dealers all over the world.

To say, however, that a market depends partly on the product raises further problems. Is a product a car or is it a Chevrolet? For most car buyers, Fords and Chevrolets belong in the same market in the sense that they may be regarded as alternative ways of satisfying a buyer's wants. Whether the cheapest Chevrolet and a Cadillac should be regarded as belonging to the same market is doubtful, and a decision must depend on the purposes for which we are going to use our theory.[4]

A further problem in dealing with particular products is that even a well-defined product will have different market definitions for different buyers. Suppose, for example, that a firm wishes to borrow $100,000 for working capital. A small firm in Milwaukee may be limited to the banks in his city where the bankers know him; a large corporation in the same city may borrow from banks as far away as New York or Los Angeles.

The theory of product pricing abstracts from most of these difficulties by defining a market as the set of conditions under which exchange takes place and then by creating certain simplified kinds of markets that are distinguished from one another in specified ways. This enables us to develop hypotheses about the way in which behavior is affected by the type of market situation.

Why Does Market Structure Matter?

If a firm knows precisely *the demand curve it faces,* it would know the price it would receive for any level of sales, and thus it would know its potential revenues. If it also knows its costs, it can readily define the profits that correspond to any output and can choose that output which maximizes its profits.†

Let us assume that the firm does know its costs and that it also knows the *market demand curve* for the product it wishes to sell. Although it knows the total sales that all firms would make at each price, it does not know what its own sales would be. In other words, it does not know its *own* demand curve. In order to determine what this curve will be, the firm needs answers to the following questions: What fraction of the total

---

3. She may feel the choice is too limited at home. She may reason: "I don't do it very often so the cost is small over the life of the furniture." (To herself she may add: "Anyway I *like* to go to Chicago.")

4. They are, however, manufactured by the same firm. And each is treated as one car in statistics on automobile production.

† Put more formally, the firm's demand curve tells the firm what its total revenues (TR) are as a function of the quantity sold (Q). Its total cost curve (TC) gives the total costs as a function of quantity produced (P).

$$TR = f(Q)$$
$$TC = g(P)$$

If $P = Q$, then profits $(TR - TC) = f(Q) - g(Q)$. This says that profits are then a function of Q.

market demand will be met by sellers other than itself? If our firm changes its price, will its market share change? If so, in what way? If it reduces price by 10 percent, will other sellers leave their prices unchanged, or will they also reduce them? If they reduce them, will they do so by less than 10 percent, by exactly 10 percent, or by more than 10 percent? Quite obviously, each of the possible outcomes will have a different effect on the sales, and thus on the revenues and profits, of the firm.

The answers to questions of this kind will be different in different circumstances. For example, if there are only two large firms in an industry, each of them may be expected to pay more attention to the other than if there are 5,000 small firms. For another example, if two firms are producing absolutely identical products, we might expect different behavior than if they produced similar but somewhat different products. These two aspects of *market structure* (number of sellers and similarity of product) suggest the hypothesis that market behavior will be affected by market structure. (This is the central hypothesis of the branch of economics called industrial organization.) It is an hypothesis we shall examine in some detail in later chapters.

Dimensions of Market Structure

The following aspects of market structure may influence the behavior of sellers and buyers and may therefore influence the nature of market results:

1. the number and size distribution of sellers in the market;

2. the extent to which these sellers recognize that the actions of one of them will cause others to change their behavior;

3. the nature of the similarities and differences in the products of different sellers;

4. the nature, number, and size of purchasers;

5. the extent of knowledge of buyers and sellers about the prices of other transactions;

6. the ability of individual sellers to change market demand by advertising, by quality improvements, etc.; and

7. the ease with which new firms may enter the industry (*entry*) or existing firms may leave that same industry. (*exit*).

It would be possible to spend a good deal of time speculating how each of these dimensions might affect the behavior of an individual seller, but we shall not do so at this time. Notice, however, that taken together they create thousands of different sets of market conditions among which behavior *might* vary.[5] This represents, of course, far too many conditions for even an advanced theory, in part because of our inability to test such complicated hypotheses with a small amount of data. Instead, economists have focused on certain theoretical market types that represent selected kinds of market behavior that we hypothesize will be related to certain sets of market conditions. Two of these, *perfect competition* and *monopoly,* are discussed in Chapters 22 and 23 and are compared in Chapters 25 and 26.

5. For example, if each of these seven dimensions had only three different categories (e.g., small, medium, and large number of sellers), we would have $3^7 = 2,187$ different categories. This does not, of course, mean that all of these theoretical possibilities are equally interesting or empirically relevant.

Rules for the Profit-Maximizing Behavior of the Firm[6]

Since we have assumed that firms *desire* to maximize their profits, we must translate this desire into behavioral rules for the firm. These rules are important, for they form the foundation on which all profit-maximizing theory is erected.

Rule 1. *A firm should not produce at all if the total revenues from its product do not equal or exceed its total variable cost.*

The common sense behind this rule is that a firm always has the option of producing nothing. If it produces nothing, it will have an operating loss equal to its fixed costs. Unless actual production adds as much to revenue as it adds to cost, it will increase the loss of the firm.

Rule 2. *Assuming that it pays the firm to produce at all, it will be profitable for the firm to expand output whenever marginal revenue is greater than marginal cost, and to keep expanding output until marginal revenue equals marginal cost.*[7]

The common sense behind this rule is that any unit that adds more to revenue than it does to cost increases profits. As long as marginal cost is less than marginal revenue, increases in output will increase profits. Once the marginal cost of a unit exceeds its marginal revenue, that unit is decreasing the profits of the firm and should not be produced.

We now restate these two rules as three *necessary conditions* for the profit-maximizing behavior of the firm. (These conditions apply to a firm, no matter what type of market it operates in.)

1. *For a given output to be the profit-maximizing output, it is necessary that at that output MC = MR.*

2. *For a given output to be the profit-maximizing output, it is necessary that for slightly smaller outputs MR > MC, and that for slightly larger outputs MC > MR.*[8]

3. *For a given output to be the profit-maximizing output, it is necessary that at that output total revenue is equal to or greater than total*

---

6. The propositions of this section are essentially aspects of mathematics, not of economics, but they are necessary to our derivation of predictions about economic behavior. In the text we merely state and attempt to make plausible mathematical results that are proved in the appendix to this chapter.

7. The concepts of marginal revenue and marginal cost are used throughout the theory of the firm and it is therefore suggested that the student review these concepts in Chapter 10, pages 103–105, and Chapter 19, pages 222–225.

8. The graphical interpretation of these two conditions is that the profit-maximizing output occurs at a point where MC cuts MR from below. The student should satisfy himself why in the adjacent sketch only output OA is a possible position of maximum profit.

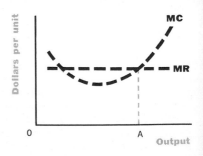

variable costs. Another way of putting this is that it is necessary that average revenue (price) be equal to or greater than average variable cost.

We want the theory of the firm in order to understand, explain, and predict a great deal of the market behavior in which we are interested. In order to do this, we must be willing to take the time to develop the necessary theoretical apparatus. This we do in Chapters 22 and 23. The student is asked to be patient and to work through these chapters. The payoff will begin in Chapter 25.

Summary

1. A market for a product is defined as follows: From the point of view of a consumer, the market consists of those firms from which the consumer could buy the product; from the point of view of the producer, the market consists of those buyers to whom he could sell the product.

2. Our theory abstracts from a number of complications: the factors that delineate a given market depend partly on the prices that prevail, partly on the point of view being examined, and partly on such factors as distance. Other complications include the fact that the area of a market for a product is partially dependent on the nature of that product, and that we may have difficulty in defining the product exactly; in fact, the same product may have different market definitions for different buyers.

3. A firm's production decisions are in-fluenced by its *own demand curve*, and not just its product's *market demand curve*. For this reason, we hypothesize that the firm's behavior is influenced by factors such as the number of sellers, which are aspects of what we call *market structure*.

4. Seven dimensions of market structure are listed on page 247. There are thousands of possibilities suggested by these categories. Because of this, economists have focused on certain selected sets of conditions, such as perfect competition and monopoly.

5. The hypothesis that firms desire to maximize their profits implies two rules of behavior: (a) that a firm should not produce at all if total revenue is less than total variable costs; and (b) that, if it does pay the firm to produce at all, it will be profitable to expand output until MR equals MC.

QUESTIONS FOR DISCUSSION

1. How do we define a market in this chapter? Compare this definition with our earlier "first approach" definition (see page 287). What real-world problems are we still abstracting from? Are such abstractions necessarily undesirable?

2. If New York City has a city sales tax while neighboring Westchester County has none, how do you predict this will affect sellers of toothpaste, gasoline, refrigerators, and mink coats in both localities, assuming all these items are

subject to New York's tax? Use the ideas we have discussed in the section on complications in the definition of a market. Do you think the magnitude of the tax matters?

3. Describe a hypothetical market along the lines of the seven categories listed on page 247. Can you think of any real-world market that approximates this? How does it differ?

4. From what we have said about perfect competition so far, what do you think are the descrip-

tions of it in each of the seven categories?

5. How would you describe the market for automobiles, university educations, retail gasoline, graded Macintosh apples, and IBM common stock, according to our seven categories? Are there any complications?

6. A ship-building yard recently submitted a tender for a new ocean liner at a price that the yard described as "substantially below cost." Why might the yard do such a thing?

†APPENDIX TO CHAPTER 21   MATHEMATICAL PROOF OF THE RULES FOR THE PROFIT-MAXIMIZING BEHAVIOR OF A FIRM

THIS APPENDIX PROVES, FOR THE student who is uneasy about common-sense arguments, the propositions we asserted on pages 248–249. The proofs illustrate clearly how a little bit of mathematics can settle some things once and for all:

Let $\pi_n = TR_n - TC_n$,

where π_n is the profit when n units are sold.

Let $\triangle \pi_n = \pi_n - \pi_{n-1}$,

where $\triangle \pi_n$ is the change in profit resulting from the sale of the nth unit.

If the firm is maximizing its profits by producing n units, it is necessary that the profits at output Q_n are at least as large as the profits at any other output. Consider three specific alternative outputs: 0, $n - 1$, $n + 1$. If the firm is maximizing its profits at output n, then:

$$\pi_n \geqq \pi_0 \qquad (1)$$
$$\pi_n \geqq \pi_{n-1} \qquad (2)$$
$$\pi_n \geqq \pi_{n+1} \qquad (3)$$

The first condition says that profits from producing must be

greater than profits from not producing. The second and third say that, if π_n is a maximum, a change of one unit in either direction cannot increase profits.

Rule 1. A profit-maximizing firm should not produce at all if the total revenues from its product do not equal or exceed its total variable cost.

Proof of Rule 1

From (1) above

$\pi_n \geqq \pi_0$, which can be rewritten
$$TR_n - TVC_n - TFC_n \geqq$$
$$TR_0 - TVC_0 - TFC_0. \quad (4)$$
But we note by definition that
$$TR_0 = 0, \qquad\qquad (a)$$
$$TVC_0 = 0, \qquad\qquad (b)$$
$TFC_n = TFC_0 = K$, where K is a constant. $\qquad\qquad (c)$
By substituting (a), (b), and (c) into (4), we get
$$TR_n - TVC_n \geqq 0,$$
from which we obtain
$$TR_n \geqq TVC_n.$$

This is the result desired.

On a per unit basis, it becomes

$$\frac{TR}{Q_n} \geqq \frac{TVC_n}{Q_n},$$

where Q_n is the number of units. Since $TR_n = Q_n p_n$, where p_n is the price when n units are sold, this may be rewritten

$$p_n \geqq AVC_n.$$

Rule 2. Assuming that it pays the firm to produce at all, it will be profitable for the firm to expand output whenever marginal revenue is greater than marginal cost, and to keep expanding output until MR = MC.

Proof of Rule 2

By definition,
$$\triangle \pi_n = \pi_n - \pi_{n-1}$$
$$= (TR_n - TC_n) -$$
$$(TR_{n-1} - TC_{n-1})$$
$$= (TR_n - TR_{n-1}) -$$
$$(TC_n - TC_{n-1})$$
$$\triangle \pi_n = MR_n - MC_n.$$

Now, if $MR_n - MC_n > 0$, it is possible to increase profit by increasing output; thus this situation does not represent profit-maximization. (More formally, it implies $\pi_{n+1} > \pi_n$, which violates (3) above.) Similarly if $MR_n - MC_n < 0$, it is possible to increase profit by decreasing output. (This inequality implies $\pi_{n-1} > \pi_n$, which violates (2) above.)

Hence, for maximum profits, $MR_n = MC_n$, in the neighborhood where $MR_{n-1} - MC_{n-1} > 0$.

Alternate Proof of Rule 2

Using elementary calculus, this result may be shown in a manner that sharpens the final conclusion:

$\pi_n = TR_n - TC_n$, each of which is a function of output

Q. To maximize π it is necessary that

$$\frac{d\pi}{dQ} = 0 \qquad (d)$$

$$\frac{d^2\pi}{dQ^2} < 0 \qquad (e)$$

$$\frac{d\pi}{dQ} = \frac{dTR}{dQ} - \frac{dTC}{dQ} = MR - MC.$$

From (d), a necessary condition of maximum π is $MR - MC = 0$, or $MR = MC$. For Q_n to maximize profits requires $MR_n = MC_n$. Now,

$$\frac{d^2\pi}{dQ^2} = \frac{dMR}{dQ} - \frac{dMC}{dQ}.$$

From (e), a necessary condition of maximum π is

$$\frac{dMR}{dQ} - \frac{dMC}{dQ} < 0,$$

which says that the slope of MC must be greater than the

slope of MR. Taken with the previous result it implies that, for Q_n to maximize π, $MR_n = MC_n$ at a point where MC cuts MR from below.

Summary

We have established the following three necessary conditions of Q_n maximizing profits:

$MR_n = MC_n$;

$TR_n \geqq TVC_n$;

marginal cost cuts marginal revenue from below at the point where $MR_n = MC_n$.

These are the conditions stated without proof in Chapter 21.

Note that these are general results that apply to all market structures.

Chapter **22** THE THEORY OF PERFECT COMPETITION

THE THEORY OF PERFECT COMPETITION IS built on two critical assumptions, one about the behavior of the individual firm and one about the nature of the industry in which it operates.

1. *The firm is assumed to act as if it can alter its rate of production and sales within any feasible range without this having any significant effect on the price of the product*

it sells. The firm can double or treble its sales or stop producing altogether without affecting this price. Thus the firm must passively accept whatever price happens to be ruling on the market. We say that the firm is a price-taker.

2. *The industry is assumed to be one in which any new firm is free to set up production if it so wishes and in which any existing*

firm is free to cease production and leave the industry if it so wishes. This means that existing firms cannot bar the entry of new *firms and that there are no legal prohibitions on entry or exit. We say that the industry displays freedom of entry and exit.*

The Firm's Demand Curve

Is it reasonable to think that a firm would ever regard itself as a price-taker? Consider, for example, the demands for the products of an automobile manufacturer and of a wheat farmer.

The automobile manufacturer will be aware of the fact that his own policies can influence the market for his product. He will know, for example, that if he makes a substantial increase in his price, his sales will fall off. He will also know that, if he lowers his price substantially, he will be able to sell more of his product. If he contemplates making a large increase in his production that is not in response to some known or anticipated rise in demand (i.e., a rightward shift in the demand curve for his product), he knows that he will have to reduce his price in order to sell the extra output. The manufacturer of automobiles is *not* a price-taker, although he cannot, of course, control both price and quantity in any way he wishes. The quantity that he is able to sell will depend on the price that he charges, but he does not have to accept passively whatever price is set by the market. In other words, the manufacturer of automobiles is faced with a downward-sloping demand curve for his product; he is able to determine *either* the price of his product *or* the quantity that he sells; he may fix his price, in which case the maximum quantity that he can sell is determined, or he may fix the quantity that he wishes to sell, in which

case the maximum price that he may charge is determined.

Now consider, by way of contrast, an individual producer of wheat. He will be one of a very large number of farmers all growing wheat; his own contribution to the total production of wheat will be but a very small drop in an extremely large bucket. The elasticity of demand for wheat is approximately 0.25.[1] This means that if the farmer did succeed in increasing the world supply of wheat by 1 percent he would bring down the world price by 4 percent. The farmer is, however, not interested in the relation between changes in *world* output and the price of wheat, but rather in the relation between changes in *his own* output and the price of wheat. Even very large percentage changes in his own output will represent only very small percentage changes in world output. The elasticity of the market demand for wheat is defined as

$$\eta_M = -\frac{\%\ \text{change in total quantity of wheat}}{\%\ \text{change in market price of wheat}},$$

where η_M stands for the elasticity of market demand for wheat.

Let us now introduce a new concept, the *firm's elasticity of demand*, which we define as

$$\eta_F = -\frac{\%\ \text{change in firm's production of wheat}}{\%\ \text{change in market price of wheat}},$$

1. Wilfred Malenbaum, *The World Wheat Economy: 1885–1939* (Harvard University Press, 1953).

Although the denominators of these two elasticities are the same, the numerators are not. Any change in one farmer's wheat production will represent a larger percentage change in his own production than it will in world production. Thus, in the case of the wheat farmer, η_F will be substantially larger than η_M.

To see this, let us roughly calculate the firm's elasticity of demand for a very large wheat farmer. We have noted that the elasticity of demand for wheat (η_M) has been estimated to be about 0.25. Total world production of wheat was approximately 200 million tons in 1964, and the output of a certain large Canadian wheat farm was 50,000 tons. Now suppose that this wheat farm increased its production by 20,000 tons, a 40 percent increase in its own production but an increase of only $\frac{1}{100}$ of 1 percent in world production. Exhibit 1 shows that this increase would lead to a decrease in the world price of $\frac{1}{25}$ of 1 percent (4¢ in $100), and give the firm an elasticity of demand of 1,000! This is a very high elasticity of demand. The farmer would have to increase his output 1,000 percent to bring about a 1 percent decrease in the price of wheat. Since the farmer is quite unable to vary his output this much, it is not surprising that he regards the price of wheat as being unaffected by any changes in output that he could conceivably make. Clearly, we

EXHIBIT 1　**CALCULATION OF A FIRM'S ELASTICITY OF DEMAND**

Given: $\eta_M = 0.25$

World output $= 200$ million tons

Firm's output increases from 50,000 to 70,000 tons

Step 1. Find the percentage change in world price:

$$\eta_M = -\frac{\text{percentage change in world output}}{\text{percentage change in world price}}$$

$$\text{Percentage change in world price} = -\frac{\text{Percentage change in world output}}{\eta_M}$$

$$= -\frac{1/100 \text{ of } 1\%}{0.25}$$

$$= -4/100 \text{ of } 1\%.$$

Step 2. Compute the firm's elasticity of demand:

$$\eta_F = -\frac{\text{percentage change in firm's output}}{\text{percentage change in world price}}$$

$$= -\frac{+40\%}{-4/100 \text{ of } 1\%} = +1,000$$

will not be far from the truth if we say that, for all practical purposes, one wheat farmer is unable to affect the world price. We therefore assume, with only a very slight simplification of reality, that the farmer is *totally* unable to influence the world price of wheat and is able to sell all that he could conceivably produce at the going world price.

> The individual wheat farmer is thus assumed to be faced with a perfectly elastic demand curve for his product. He is a price-taker.

The difference between the wheat farmer and the automobile producer is one of degree of *power* over the market. The wheat farmer, because he is an insignificant part of the whole market, has no power to influence the world price of wheat. On the other hand, the automobile manufacturer does have the power to influence the price of automobiles, because his own production represents a quite significant part of the total supply of automobiles.

One requirement for a perfectly competitive industry is that every firm have a *firm* elasticity of demand so high that it may neglect the influence that any change in its output might have on market price. Another way of saying this is that the firm acts as if the elasticity of demand for its product is infinite.

To see why this may be reasonable in the

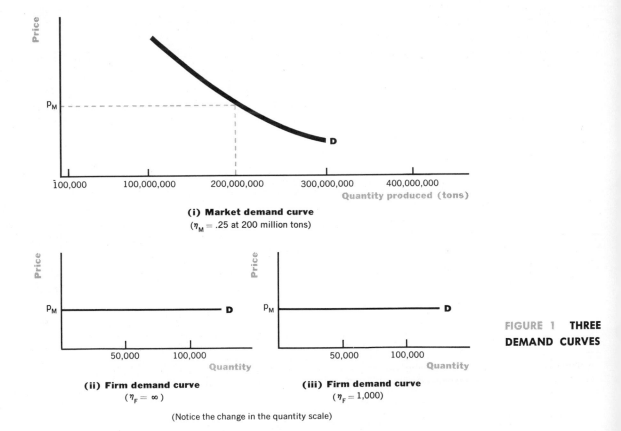

(i) Market demand curve
($\eta_M = .25$ at 200 million tons)

(ii) Firm demand curve
($\eta_F = \infty$)

(iii) Firm demand curve
($\eta_F = 1,000$)

(Notice the change in the quantity scale)

FIGURE 1   **THREE DEMAND CURVES**

case of the wheat farmer, examine Figure 1. The market demand curve for the product is downward sloping, indicating that, if there is an increase in the quantity supplied, the price will fall. The firm's demand curve is assumed to be perfectly elastic, because variations in its production *over the range that we need to consider for all practical purposes* will have such a small effect on price that the effect can safely be assumed to be zero. Of course, if the single producer increased his production by a vast amount, 1,000-fold, say, then this would cause a rather significant increase in supply and he would be unable to sell all he produced at the going price. The perfectly elastic curve does not mean that the producer could actually sell an infinite amount at the going price, but rather that the variations in production *that it will normally be practicable for him to make* will leave price virtually unaffected. Compare Figures 1(ii) and (iii). They are drawn to the correct scale, yet it is almost impossible to distinguish visually between the two demand curves.

A DIGRESSION: THE TRADITIONAL ASSUMPTIONS OF PERFECT COMPETITION

We have said that to establish "perfect competition" it is necessary that each firm regard itself as a price-taker. This is a subjective matter. But certain objective conditions may make this kind of assumption more plausible than would others. In particular, each firm is likely to assume it cannot affect its price if:

1. there is a very large number of sellers, no one of whom commands a large share of the total market;

2. the products of different sellers are identical, and buyers have no preference among sellers;

3. there are so many buyers that sellers and buyers do not establish personal relationships with one another; and

4. buyers are perfectly informed about the prices of different sellers.

These structural conditions are often stated as being the assumptions of perfect competition. But the model of perfect competition depends upon price-taking, whether it is produced by this set of structural conditions or by some other set. Although we shall not go into them now, there are other conditions that may also lead to price-taking behavior. The basic condition of behavior that is necessary for perfect competition is that firms should be price-takers. Thus, to define perfect competition in terms of the above four assumptions is too restrictive, since other assumptions will also give rise to price-taking.[2]

TOTAL, AVERAGE, AND MARGINAL REVENUE OF THE COMPETITIVE FIRM

Figure 2 shows revenue curves of the kinds developed in Chapter 10 for a price-taking firm.[3] Under conditions of perfect competition, the individual firm faces a perfectly

2. The significance of this point for testing the theory is very important; failure to appreciate it has occasioned much fruitless debate. In the real world, for example, large numbers of buyers are never perfectly informed. Does this mean that perfect competition is never applicable? The answer is No, provided that substantially less than perfect knowledge is still conducive to sellers behaving as price-takers. Put differently, the listed conditions may be *sufficient* for sellers to be price-takers, but they may not be *necessary*. If they are not necessary, an empirical study that shows that they do not exist does not by itself refute the theory.

3. Review Chapter 10, pages 103–105.

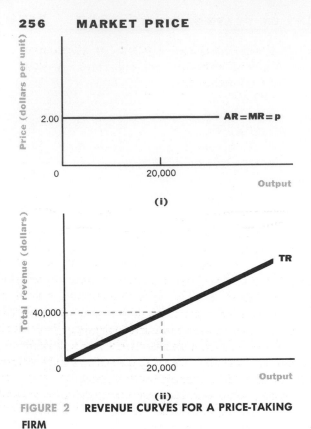

FIGURE 2   **REVENUE CURVES FOR A PRICE-TAKING FIRM**

elastic demand curve for its product and this determines the slope of the marginal revenue curve. If, for example, a farmer is faced with a perfectly elastic demand curve for wheat at a market price of $2 per bushel, each additional bushel he sells will bring in that amount. Thus the marginal revenue is $2, and the average revenue (total revenue divided by number of units sold) is also $2. In more general terms, we can say that, since the market price is unaffected by variations in the firm's output, it follows that the marginal revenue resulting from an increase in the volume of sales by one unit is constant and is equal to the average revenue. As illustrated in Figure 2, the demand curve, the average revenue curve, and the marginal revenue curve coincide in the same horizontal line, showing that price, average revenue, and marginal revenue all remain constant as output varies. Total revenue, of course, does vary with output; since price is constant, it follows that total revenue rises steadily as output rises.

Short-Run Equilibrium of the Competitive Firm

We saw in Chapter 21 that profit-maximization implies that marginal cost equals marginal revenue. Since, for the perfectly competitive firm, marginal revenue equals the market price, it follows that (if the firm maximizes profits) marginal cost will equal price.

This is illustrated in Figure 3. At output *Oa* the cost of making an extra unit is less than the revenue gained from selling that unit. It thus pays the firm to increase its

rate of production and, by so doing, to increase its profits by the difference between *MC* and *MR*. This relation holds for any point to the left of *Ob*, and the incentive to raise production is indicated by the arrow. At output *Oc*, on the other hand, the cost of making an extra unit exceeds the revenue gained from the sale of that unit. It thus pays the firm to reduce its rate of production and, by so doing, to increase its profits by the amount of the difference between *MC* and *MR*. This relation

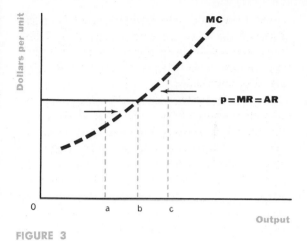

FIGURE 3

holds for any point to the right of Ob, and the incentive to lower production is indicated by the arrow. At output Ob the firm cannot increase profits either by raising or by lowering output. Output Ob is thus the rate of output for which profits are maximized. This is also the rate of output for which marginal costs equal marginal revenue. When the firm is maximizing profits, it has no incentive to change its output policy. Unless prices or costs change, the firm will stay put, since it is doing as well as it can do, given the situation it faces. We thus say that the firm is in *equilibrium*.

The Firm's Supply Curve

Figure 4 (i) shows a numerical example of a firm's marginal cost curve, together with four *alternative* demand curves: D_a if the market price were $2; D_b if the market price were $3; D_c if the market price were $4; and D_d if the market price were $5.

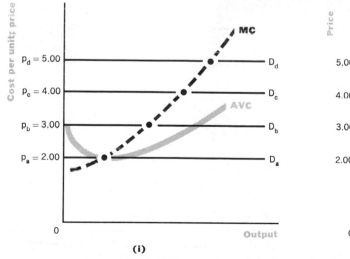

(i)

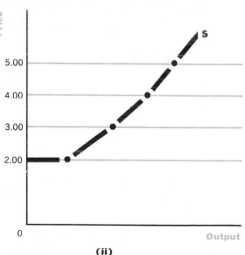

(ii)

FIGURE 4   **MARGINAL COST AND SUPPLY CURVES FOR A PRICE-TAKING FIRM**

The firm's marginal cost curve gives the marginal cost corresponding to each level of output. We desire a supply curve that gives the quantity the firm will supply at every price. For prices below *AVC* the firm will supply zero units (Rule 1). For prices above *AVC* the firm will equate price and marginal cost (Rule 2). From this it follows at once that:

In perfect competition the firm's marginal cost curve above AVC is its supply curve.

This proposition is so obvious that it sometimes causes difficulty to the student who is looking for something difficult and profound. If you are not absolutely certain that you understand the proposition, construct the firm's supply curve for yourself. Given perfect competition, profit-maximization, and the actual cost curve of Figure 4 (i), you can discover the output of the firm corresponding to any given market price. You can then plot the firm's supply curve on a graph of your own by relating market price to quantity produced by the firm. Once you have done this, you will see that the supply curve you have constructed is identical with the marginal cost curve in Figure 4 (i), above p_a.

In Figure 4 (ii), we have plotted such a supply curve for the firm. The points in this graph correspond point for point with those in Figure 4 (i).

The Short-Run Supply Curve for a Competitive Industry

Now that we have discovered how to find the supply curve for *each firm* in a competitive industry, we have to determine how to find the supply curve for the whole industry. To do this, we need to know the sum of the amounts supplied by each firm for any given price. Let us consider the simple numerical example illustrated in Figure 5. Firm A's supply curve is shown in the first diagram and Firm B's in the second. The problem is to construct an aggregate supply curve showing how the total supply of these two firms will vary with price (on the assumption that they are in a perfectly competitive industry). Below the price of $1, nothing is produced. Between $1 and $2, only Firm A produces, so the aggregate supply curve is identical with Firm A's curve. At a price of $3, Firm A produces 400 units and Firm B produces 300 units; the total production at $3 is 700 units. (Check the construction of this aggregate supply curve for a number of alternative prices.) For any given price the aggregate quantity is the sum of the two quantities produced by the two firms *at that price*. If there are hundreds of firms the process is the same: each firm's *MC* curve shows what the firm will produce at any given price, p. The industry supply curve relates the price p to the sum of the quantities produced by each firm.

Thus the supply curve for an industry is the horizontal sum of the supply curves of all the individual firms in the industry.[4]

In Part II we used short-run industry supply curves as part of our theory of price. We have now derived these curves for a competitive industry, and we have seen how they are related to the behavior of individual, profit-maximizing firms. An industry is said to be in *short-run equilibrium* when price is such that supply equals demand. This was dis-

4. Students who have committed this proposition to memory without fully understanding it sometimes get confused between the horizontal and vertical summation of curves. See Footnote 1 on page 156.

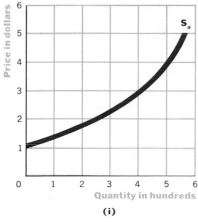

(i)

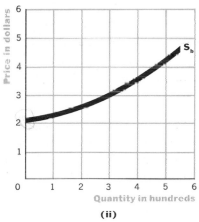

(ii)

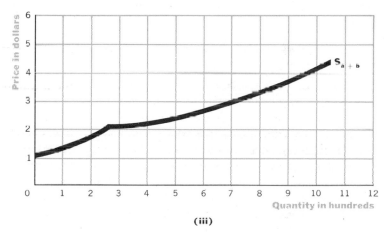

(iii)

FIGURE 5   **SUPPLY CURVE FOR A COMPETITIVE INDUSTRY**

PROFITS AND LOSSES IN THE SHORT RUN

We have shown that the firm is in short-run equilibrium at a rate of output for which its marginal cost equals its marginal revenue. Although we know from this that the firm is maximizing its profits, we do not know how large these profits are. It is one thing to know that a firm is doing as well as it can in the

cussed in Chapter 9 above. Figure 6 illustrates such an equilibrium.

We know that at price p_E the quantity supplied by each firm setting $p_E = MC$ will add up to the quantity OE. This is true by definition: We constructed the industry supply curve in such a way as to make it true. The industry is said to be in equilibrium when supply equals demand and thus when, for each firm, marginal cost equals price.

circumstances; it is quite another thing to know how well it is doing.

Figure 7 shows three possible positions for a firm in short-run equilibrium. In all cases, the firm is maximizing its profits at p_A by producing an output of Oq, but in case (i) the firm is making profits in excess of all costs; in case (ii) it is just covering all costs; and in case (iii) it is making losses. In case (iii) it might be better to say that the firm is minimizing its losses rather than maximizing its profits, but both statements mean the same thing: The firm is doing as well as it can do, given its costs and prices.[5]

All three of these positions represent possible short-run equilibrium positions for the profit-maximizing firm in perfect competition. They are all equally possible in the short run. But only one of them will persist in the long run. Which one?

Long-Run Equilibrium of the Competitive Firm and Industry

In the *long run*, the behavior of the firm will be the same—with one important exception. It would be the same in the sense that the firm would continue to adjust to the market price by producing where $p = MC$. But should price drop below *ATC* and remain there (below p_B in Figure 7), the firm would want to withdraw its resources from this industry. You will recall that total costs measured the returns on the best alternative use of the resources. When average revenue is below average cost in this industry, the firm

is not using its resources to maximum advantage. When it gets the chance, it will shift them. It gets this chance as its fixed factors, such as machines, gradually are used up. When they are used up, it will not replace them, and will gradually liquidate its investment and withdraw (or *exit*) from the industry. In the long run, the firm will remain in production only if price is at least equal to average *total* cost. Thus firms in situation (iii) will withdraw from the industry in the long run. As firms withdraw, the supply curve of the industry will shift to the left and prices will rise. Firms will continue to withdraw and prices will continue to rise until the firms remaining in the industry are able to cover all their costs—until, that is, they are in situation (ii).

Now, assume that, in the short-run equilibrium position, firms are in situation (i). The individual firms are making profits in excess of the returns available on the alternative use of the resources devoted to the industry. This fact will attract new investment into the industry in the form either of new firms entering the industry and/or of existing firms expanding their plants. The cases are not different. For simplicity we will illustrate for the case of new firms entering the industry.

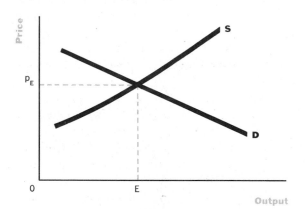

FIGURE 6   EQUILIBRIUM OF A COMPETITIVE INDUSTRY

---

5. In case (iii), we have drawn in the average variable cost curve as well, just to indicate that, in the short run, it pays the firm to stay in production. If price fell below p_Z, it would pay the firm to shut down production.

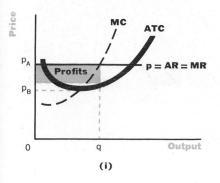
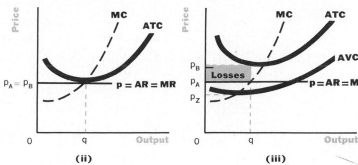

(i)   (ii)   (iii)

p_A is the price at which **P = MC**
p_B is the price at which **ATC is a minimum**
p_Z is the price at which **AVC is a minimum**

FIGURE 7   SHORT-RUN EQUILIBRIUM OF A COMPETITIVE FIRM

Suppose, in response to high profits for 100 existing firms, ten new firms enter an industry. Market demand, however, does not change, and the market supply curve that formerly added up the outputs of 100 firms now must add up the outputs of 110 firms. At any price, more will be supplied because there are more suppliers. But this shift in supply will mean that p_E in Figure 6 is no longer the equilibrium price. As Figure 8

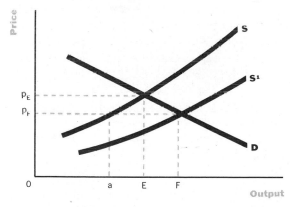

FIGURE 8   NEW ENTRANTS SHIFT THE SUPPLY CURVE

shows, for equilibrium, price will have to fall, and both new and old firms will have to adjust their output to this new price.

In Figure 8, we assume that the profits at p_E attract new entrants whose output shifts the supply curve to S^1. This causes price to fall to p_F. At this price *before* entry an amount equal to only Oa would have been produced. The extra output aF is supplied by the new productive capacity.

After the new entry has occurred, and market price has fallen to p_F, there are three possibilities:

1. At p_F the individual firms may still be earning profits in excess of total cost. (In terms of Figure 7, p_F may be above p_B.) There continues to be incentive for resources to enter the industry, and a further increase in supply and a fall in price are to be expected.

2. At p_F the individual firms may be suffering losses (p_F less than p_B). In this case, no new firms will wish to enter the industry, and existing firms will not wish to replace fixed equipment as it wears out. Ultimately, there will be exit from the industry, and the market supply curve will shift to the left.

3. At p_F there may be zero profits ($p_F = p_B = ATC$). In this case there is no incentive to enter or to exit.[6]

One feature of what we mean by long-run equilibrium is that the industry is neither expanding nor contracting for a given state of demand. Only the third of our three possibilities has this feature. From this it follows at once that, if there is freedom of entry and exit, existing firms in equilibrium must be at a position where $p = ATC$.

ECONOMIES OF SCALE

If the industry is to be in equilibrium, it is necessary that each firm should just be covering total costs when it is doing as well as it can with its existing plant. But this is not enough. If the firms are subject to economies of scale, they will be able to reduce their average costs of production by building larger plants; since they assume that they can sell all they want at the going price, they will see an expansion of the scale of their operations as necessarily increasing their profits. This is because price (= average revenue) does not fall, whereas average costs do. Thus firms will expand their scale of operations as long as they are in a perfectly competitive market and are subject to falling long-run costs. From this it follows that, in long-run equilibrium, each firm must be at a point where no further unexploited economies of scale remain within its grasp.

This is depicted geometrically in Figure 9, which shows three different sets of short-run cost curves. If the cost curves are those marked MC_1 and $SRAC_1$ (where long-run

costs are decreasing), it is apparent that the industry will not be in long-run equilibrium, even if price is p_a, because a firm can make profits by building a bigger plant. If the cost curves are those labeled MC_2 and $SRAC_2$ (where long-run costs are increasing), it is apparent that the industry will not be in long-run equilibrium, even if price is p_b, because a firm can make profits by building a smaller plant. Only if price is p^*, output is OE, and firms are operating plants with the cost curves MC^* and $SRAC^*$ will it be true that no firm can increase its profits by changing either its output or its scale of plant. Thus output OE with price p^* represents the long-run equilibrium situation for a competitive industry.

Given two assumptions, first that individual sellers are price-takers and, second, that there is freedom of entry and exit, the conditions of competitive equilibrium may be restated as follows:

1. Every firm produces where price equals marginal cost.

2. Every firm produces where price equals short-run average total cost.

3. Every firm produces where price equals long-run average total cost.

These three conditions are all met only at the minimum point of the long-run average cost curve, as illustrated at output OE in Figure 9.[7] The first condition results from the firms maximizing their profits for a given price. The second and third result from the incentives for new resources to enter into (or existing resources to exit from) the industry if they are not satisfied with the profits that they are earning.

---

6. Recall that we have included in total cost the wages of management, returns to capital, risk premiums, and all other payments to resources at the level of their best alternative use. (See Chapter 17.) Zero profits over opportunity cost implies no hardship to the firm.

7. If the long-run cost curve of a firm in a competitive industry does not have a minimum point, there is no competitive equilibrium. Whether long-run costs eventually increase is thus of paramount importance to theorists who depend upon the model of a perfectly competitive industry.

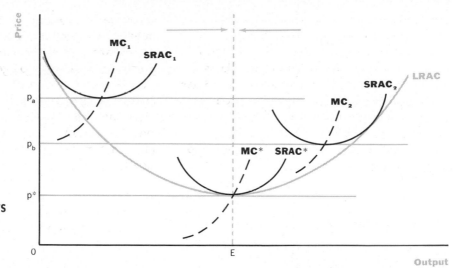

FIGURE 9   **THREE SETS OF SHORT-RUN COST CURVES**

Summary

1. The theory of perfect competition is an extremely simple and valuable theory as we shall see in Chapter 25, and, indeed, as we saw in Chapter 11. We should not, however, go overboard and think it solves all problems or applies in all situations. The theory is built on two critical assumptions: The firm is unable to have any significant effect on market price— (i.e., it is a *price-taker*); and the industry is one in which there is *freedom of entry and exit*.

2. The condition that every firm in a perfectly competitive industry is a price-taker means that every firm has a *firm elasticity of demand* so high that it is rational for the firm to neglect the influence any change in its output may have on the market price.

3. It follows from the condition that the firm's own demand curve is perfectly elastic in perfect competition that price equals marginal revenue equals average revenue.

4. For the profit-maximizing, perfectly competitive firm, marginal cost will equal price in equilibrium.

5. In perfect competition, a firm's supply curve is its marginal cost curve, above its average variable cost curve.

6. In the long run, firms have the option to enter or leave a perfectly competitive industry. Only if price equals average total cost will there exist no incentive to do so. In this case, the industry will be neither expanding nor contracting; we say that it is in equilibrium.

7. If, over the relevant range, costs are always decreasing, there can be no competitive equilibrium. In long-run equilibrium, each firm must be at a point where no further unexploited economies of scale remain within its grasp.

8. The conditions of long-run competitive equilibrium may be restated as follows: Every firm produces where price equals marginal cost, short-run average total cost, and long-run average total cost. These three conditions

are met together only at the minimum point of the long-run average cost curve.

9. Three limitations to the usefulness of this extremely simple and valuable theory should be noted: (a) If an industry is subject to decreasing costs over the entire relevant range of output, there is no competitive equi-librium. (b) If the scale of the firm required to achieve minimal long-run cost is large enough that the firm has an appreciable share of the market, the assumption that the firm will be a price-taker breaks down. (c) The theory is a static one that explains equilib-rium positions only.

QUESTIONS FOR DISCUSSION

1. State and explain the two critical assump-tions of the theory of perfect competition.

2. If, in the steel industry, there is not a large number of producers, does it follow that the steel industry is not perfectly competitive?

3. "Perfect competition implies that marginal cost will invariably equal price." Explain why you agree or disagree.

4. Draw two hypothetical cost curves and sum them, explaining the process.

5. Draw supply and demand curves illustrating what will happen if, in a perfectly competitive industry, firms are not covering their total costs. Draw a diagram showing what will happen to firms remaining in the industry.

6. Why do we say that perfect competition and decreasing costs (over the entire relevant out-put) are incompatible in long-run equilibrium? If we observed an industry with many firms, each one of which had unexploited economies of scale, would you conclude that the industry was not perfectly competitive? Would your answer be affected by the added information that (a) the industry was not growing in size, or (b) the industry was growing in size?

Chapter **23** THE THEORY OF MONOPOLY

IN CHAPTER 22, WE DEVELOPED A THEORY OF the behavior of a firm and industry under conditions of perfect competition. In this chapter, we deal with a second, very differ-ent type of market structure, *monopoly*.

The word monopoly comes from the Greek words *monos* and *polein*, which mean "alone to sell." It is convenient for the present dis-cussion to think of monopoly as the situation in which an entire industry is supplied by a single seller. We shall call this seller the *monopolist*. Further on in the chapter, we will define monopoly in a less restrictive way. (See pages 270–271.)

The Monopolist's Demand Curve

Since the monopolistic firm is the only producer of a particular product, its demand curve is identical with the demand curve for its product. The elasticity of the firm's demand and the elasticity of market demand are one and the same thing. The market demand curve, which shows the aggregate quantity that buyers will take for every price, also shows the quantity that the monopolist will be able to sell at every price that he sets. If we assume that the monopolist sets a single price and supplies all buyers who wish to purchase at that price,[1] we can readily deduce his average and marginal revenue curves. Since price is identical with average revenue, the market demand curve for the product is the average revenue curve of the monopolist. (Review the discussion of revenue curves on pages 103–105.)

Look at Figure 1. Buyers will demand, in aggregate, quantity OA if price is p_a. From the seller's point of view, p_a is the average revenue received per unit when OA units are sold. Thus the seller receives total revenues of $OA \cdot p_a$ (the shaded area $O\,p_a\,a\,A$).

In perfect competition, average and marginal revenue curves are identical, but this is not the case in a monopoly. Since the monopolist knows that if he changes his rate of sales he will have to change his price, he must take into account the effect on his price of a change in output.

Suppose the monopolist could sell 100 units per month at $2 per unit; to sell 101 units per month, however, he must reduce the

price per unit to $1.99. Total revenue for 100 units is $200 per month; for 101 units it is $200.99 per month. The marginal revenue of the 101st unit is 99¢, which is considerably less than its price. This 99¢ represents the $1.99 the monopolist received for the

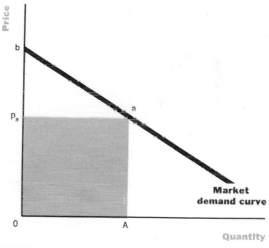

FIGURE 1

101st unit *minus* the 1¢ he lost on *each* of the first 100 units when he lowered the price from $2 to $1.99. The price reduction is included because the monopolist had to make it in order to sell an extra unit per month.

Suppose his sales are at the rate of n units per month (at output OA on Figure 2) and that he now considers raising his rate of sales by one unit to $n + 1$ units per month (at point

---

1. This is an important assumption that we shall make throughout this chapter. In Chapter 24, we shall consider *price discrimination*, which means that the seller charges different prices to different buyers.

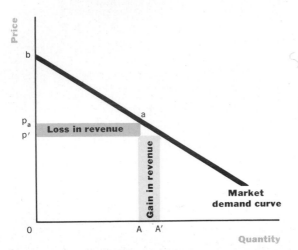

FIGURE 2   **THE EFFECT OF AN INCREASE IN SALES**

OA'). Figure 2 shows the effect of this increase graphically. In order to sell $n + 1$ units, he must lower his price from p_a to p'. The effect on his revenue is twofold: By selling the extra unit he gains p' dollars (the lightly shaded area), but, by having to lower the price from p_a to p', he sacrifices $(p_a - p')$ dollars on *each* of the first OA units (the darkly shaded area). The *net* change in total revenue (which we call marginal revenue) is p' *minus OA* $(p_a - p')$, and is therefore *less than p'*.†

For a downward-sloping demand curve, the marginal revenue resulting from the sale of any given unit will be less than the price obtained for that unit. Figure 3 plots both the monopolist's demand curve and his marginal revenue curve. The curve D shows the price corresponding to any given rate of output; the curve MR shows the marginal revenue

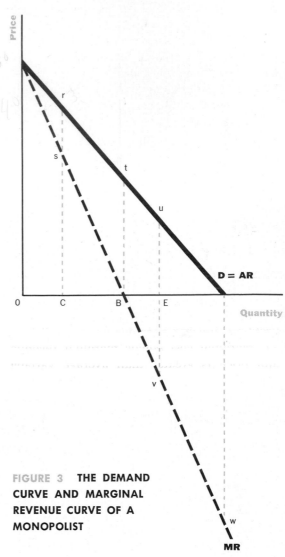

FIGURE 3   **THE DEMAND CURVE AND MARGINAL REVENUE CURVE OF A MONOPOLIST**

corresponding to the same rate of output. Thus, for example, the price obtained when OC units are sold is Cr, while the marginal

---

† Formally, $MR = p' - [(p_a - p')n]$, where n is the number of units sold. If the demand curve is downward sloping, the expression in brackets is positive, and therefore $MR < p'$. Since both MR and p' refer to the same unit (the $n + 1$st), we have shown quite generally that given a declining demand curve $MR_n < p_n$.

revenue resulting from a rise in sales from $OC - 1$ units to OC units is only Cs. The price obtained when OB units are sold is Bt, but the increase in revenue when sales go from $OB - 1$ units to OB units is nothing at all! (This is, of course, perfectly possible: 4 units can be sold for $10 each, but a cut in price to $8 may be necessary to raise sales to 5 units.) When OE units are sold, the price is Eu, but the change in total revenue resulting from the sale of one more unit is negative and equal to Ev, so that total revenue is decreased by the sale of one more unit! (That an increase in sales could reduce revenue should not be surprising; if a given percentage fall in price is met by a smaller percentage rise in sales, total revenue earned will decline. This corresponds to elasticity of demand less than 1.)

Equilibrium Under Monopoly

To illustrate graphically the determination of the profit-maximizing output, we must bring together the cost curves and the demand curve. This is done in Figure 4. In the figure, output OA meets the several conditions for profit maximizing behavior given in Chapter 21. Marginal cost equals marginal revenue, and price is greater than average variable cost.

The aggregate amount of profits is represented by the shaded rectangle (the area $ab \cdot OA$). To see that this *is* the profit-maximizing output (or, alternatively, that p_a is the profit-maximizing price), compare output OA with outputs OA' and OA''.

If the firm produces at some rate of output less than OA, say OA' in Figure 4, then marginal cost is less than marginal revenue. This means that if the rate of output is increased by one unit, the extra unit adds more to gross revenue than to cost, and so will increase profits (by fg in this case). *If profits are to be maximized, the rate of output should be increased whenever marginal cost is less than marginal revenue.* If, on the other hand, the firm produces more than OA, say OA'', then marginal cost exceeds marginal revenue.

The last unit produced adds more to cost than it does to revenue; clearly, the production and sale of the last unit causes a reduction in total profits (by hk in this case). *If profits are to be maximized, output should be reduced whenever marginal cost exceeds marginal revenue.*

It is a common mistake to think that a monopolist who is not maximizing profits must be making losses. At output OA, where $MC = MR$, total profits are as large as possible. But for the whole range of quantities from OA to OB, profits are *positive,* since average revenue is greater than average total cost. Consider again quantity OA'', where MC is greater than MR. Additional units are *reducing* total profits, but these profits do not disappear altogether until output OB. Indeed, it is not until output surpasses the rate of OC units per period that price falls below *average variable cost,* thus making the seller worse off than he would be if he were not producing at all. The monopolist might be *willing* to produce OA'' or OB rather than not produce at all, but he is not faced with that choice, and (assuming he is a profit-maximizer) he prefers OA to any other level of output.

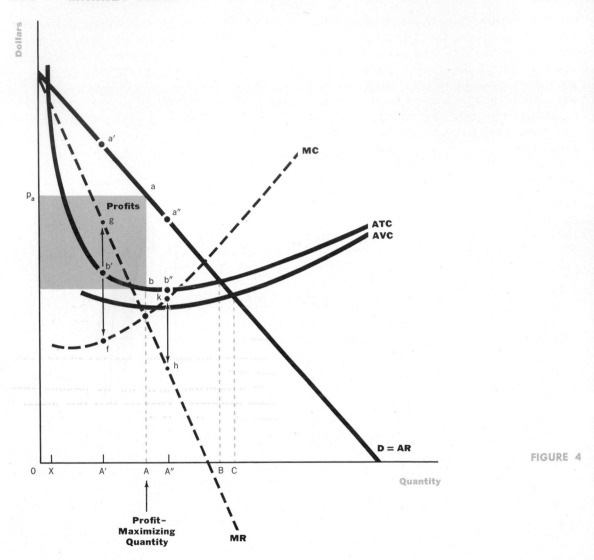

FIGURE 4

FIRM AND INDUSTRY, SHORT AND LONG RUN

A monopolist, as we have defined him, is the only producer in an industry. There is thus no need to have a separate theory of the firm and the industry, as was necessary with perfect competition. The monopolist *is* the industry.

In a monopolized industry, as in a perfectly competitive industry, profits provide an incentive for new firms to enter the industry. If the monopoly is to persist in the long run, other firms must be discouraged from entering the industry. There must be, in technical terms, *barriers to entry*. These may take several forms: Patent laws may create and perpetuate monopolies by conferring on the patent holder the sole right to produce a particular commodity. The government may grant a firm a charter or a franchise that prohibits competition by law. Monopolies may also arise because of economies of scale. The established firm that can produce at a lower cost than any new, and necessarily small, competitor may retain a monopoly through a cost advantage. A monopoly may also be perpetuated by force, or by threat: Potential competitors can be intimidated by threats ranging from sabotage to a price war in which the established monopoly has sufficient financial resources to ensure victory.

Because there is no entry into a monopolistic industry, the profits of a monopolist may persist over time. In perfect competition, the long run differed from the short run because of the process of entry. In monopoly, where entry is prevented, the long-run equilibrium is no different from the short-run equilibrium.

The Nature and Extent of Monopoly Power

Our monopolist looked at the demand curve facing his firm, and at his cost curves, and selected the price-quantity combination that maximized his profits. The price he selected turned out to be the *market* price of the industry at equilibrium, and the quantity he intended to supply was the quantity demanded at equilibrium. We assumed that his demand curve was the industry demand curve and that no other seller, present or potential, threatened his position as the sole supplier.

In what way does this description of a monopolist differ from the situation of *any* producer who faces a downward-sloping demand curve? Such a producer would also choose the price-quantity combination (where $MR = MC$) that maximized his profits. *But this price might turn out not to be the long-run equilibrium price*, because his choice of a particular price-quantity combination might itself lead to changes in the behavior of others that would *shift* his demand curve. We saw earlier that a demand curve represents the relationship between price and quantity when all other things remain unchanged. But the very act of choosing a price may lead to changes that are assumed not to occur when demand curves are drawn. Such changes will lead to a shift in the *ceteris paribus* demand curve.

Consider an example. The Coca-Cola Company is the sole producer of Coca-Cola and faces a demand curve for its product that slopes downward. Suppose that this demand curve shows that, if the Coca-Cola Company cuts the price of its product by 20 percent and if all other soft-drink suppliers keep *their* prices at their present level, the Coca-Cola Company will experience a 50 percent increase in sales, which would result in some (unspecified) increase in profits. Since Coca-Cola is unquestionably free to cut its price by 20 percent, why does it not do so? The answer is that if it did, it strongly suspects that *ceteris paribus* will not hold—that its very action of reducing prices will lead other sellers to reduce *their* prices. If they do, Coca-Cola's demand curve will shift to the left, and its sales may end up increasing not by 50 percent but (perhaps) only by 10 percent. In such an event, profits would decrease rather than increase.

Shifts in the demand curve of a seller as a result of the seller's pricing decisions have two main sources. The first (illustrated in the Coca-Cola example) is the reactions of sellers of those other products that substitute to some extent for the product of our seller. The second is the *entry* of new sellers who succeed in capturing part of the sales that the seller included in "his" demand curve. Shifts of either of these kinds threaten the monopoly power of the seller, and will reduce the profits the seller would have received if they had not occurred.

Is it not possible to imagine a firm without any competition whatsoever? A firm may have a complete monopoly of a particular *product,* but every product has some substitutes for the *services* it provides.

Some products have fairly close substitutes, and even a single seller producing such a product will have rivals for his customers' expenditure. Not only will his demand be relatively elastic, but new entrants into closely allied fields may shift his demand curve. Even if there is no very close substitute for his product at any moment, high profits may induce rivals to develop a close substitute to cut into his market.

Monopoly power exists when a firm is at least to some extent insulated from loss of customers to other sellers. Since no firm is perfectly insulated from all other products or for all time, *perfect* monopoly power does not exist. But the extent of shifts in a seller's demand curve due to other producers' actions is a *quantitative* variable: In some cases, such shifts may be very minor; in others, they may be very large. Thus, the *degree of monopoly power* may vary and it is useful to think of it as a variable.

In general, the extent of monopoly power will be greater, the smaller the shifts in demand caused by the reactions of sellers of other products and the smaller the shifts in demand caused by the entry of new sellers. How large these shifts will be depends upon a great variety of other variables, which will be considered in Chapters 28 and 29.

It is well to note at this point that a single seller is neither sufficient for, nor necessary to, monopoly power. The Coca-Cola example demonstrated that it is not sufficient. It is not necessary, because two sellers (who are not faced by the threat of entry) could agree between themselves to set a common price and to share the market. Their behavior would be no different than if they were a single seller.

How Do We Measure Monopoly Power?

Our theory predicts that behavior in monopolistic markets will differ from behavior in perfectly competitive markets. If we are to test this theory, we must be able to give some idea of the extent of monopoly power in various markets. Also, it is often felt by government agencies (acting on behalf of the people) that uncontrolled monopoly power is undesirable. These governmental agencies must know where monopoly power exists if they are to control or eliminate it. For both of these reasons, and for others as well, it becomes important to measure the extent of monopoly power in various markets. This is not an easy thing to do.

Several measures of monopoly power have

been suggested.[2] Ideally, one would like to compare the prices, outputs, and profits of firms in any industry with what prices, outputs, and profits would be if all firms were under unified (monopoly) control and were fully insulated from entry. But this hypothetical comparison does not lend itself to measurement.

In practice, two alternative measures are widely used. The first of these is the *concentration ratio*. A concentration ratio shows the fraction of total market sales controlled by the largest group of sellers. Common types of concentration ratios cite the share of total industry sales of the largest four or eight firms.[3] Whether concentration ratios measure effective monopoly power is a matter of some debate among economists. Clearly, market share is one measure of the potential power to control supply and set price. The inclusion in concentration ratios of the market shares of several firms rests upon the possibility that large firms will adopt a common price-output policy that is no different from one they would adopt if they were in fact under unified management.[4] Concentration ratios measure

actual exercise of monopoly power only if this "possibility" occurs. High concentration ratios may be necessary for the exercise of monopoly power, but they are not sufficient.[5] It is, nevertheless, interesting to know where potential monopoly power does exist.

The second approach to measuring the extent of monopoly is to examine profits. If profits are and remain "high,"[6] so goes the logic of this measure, it is indirect evidence that neither rivalry among sellers nor entry of new firms prevents existing firms from pricing as if they are monopolists.

While neither of these measures is ideal, each is of some value and each is widely used. In fact, concentration ratios and high profit rates are themselves correlated.[7] Because of this, alternative classifications of industries, according to their *degree* of monopoly power measured in these two ways, do not differ from each other very much. Because monopoly power is measurable, and in spite of some difficult problems of measurement, the theory of monopoly is often very useful to both economists and policy-makers, and it is widely used by them.

---

2. Two of the most famous early discussions are A. P. Lerner, "The Concept of Monopoly and the Measurement of Monopoly Power," *Review of Economic Studies*, I (1933–1934), 157–175; and Joe S. Bain, "The Profit Rate as a Measure of Monopoly Power," *Quarterly Journal of Economics*, February, 1941, pp. 271–293.

3. In Chapter 27, we present some concentration ratios for U.S. industries.

4. Such behavior might occur in various ways. The most common suggestion is that they are in *tacit collusion*.

5. We will discuss this point more fully in Chapter 29.

6. By "high" profits the economist means returns sufficiently in excess of all opportunity costs that potential new entrants desire to enter the industry. For empirical applications this will usually be taken to mean rates of return that are substantially higher than the average of all industries having roughly the same degree of risk.

7. The classic study is by Joe S. Bain, "Relation of the Profit Rate to Industry Concentration," *Quarterly Journal of Economics*, August, 1951, pp. 297–304.

Summary

1. *Monopoly* is defined initially as the situation in which an entire industry is supplied by a single seller, called a *monopolist*.

2. The monopolist's *own demand curve* is thus identical with the *market demand curve* for the product. The market demand curve is the monopolist's average revenue curve. The marginal revenue resulting from the sale of another unit by a monopolist will always be less than the price obtained for that unit.

3. The profit-maximizing monopolist will produce where marginal revenue equals marginal cost.

4. The presence of profits in a monopolized industry provides the same incentive to entry as it does in perfect competition. Therefore, for the monopoly to persist in the long run, there must be blockaded entry. This can be aided by patent laws, charters, grants or franchises, or by economies of scale.

5. Complete absence of competition can never be achieved. Every monopolist will find that there exist some substitutes for his product that are outside his control; in the long run, totally new products may be developed to compete with his. Monopoly power exists when a firm is to some extent insulated from loss of custom to other sellers; the degree of monopoly power may best be thought of as a quantitative variable.

6. Two of the most widely used measures of the degree of monopoly power are the *concentration ratio*, which shows the fraction of the sales of an industry controlled by a group of the largest sellers, and the *comparison of profits* in one industry with those earned in other industries. These measures are highly intercorrelated.

QUESTIONS FOR DISCUSSION

1. Explain why a profit-maximizing monopolist's marginal cost will be less than his price. Think of an alternative assumption about the monopolist's objective (i.e., that he tries to do something other than maximize profits) that would not lead to this prediction.

2. It is sometimes asserted that "monopolies are creatures of the state." What do you think is meant by this, and to what extent do you agree?

3. In what way can we say that "no firm is a complete monopoly"? Is this at odds with the statement that many firms have some degree of monopoly power?

4. In 1940, a study estimated, a 100,000 ton alumina plant would have unit costs 20 percent higher than those of a 500,000 ton plant. Two tons of alumina make one ton of aluminum, so that the larger plant would have an output sufficient to make 250,000 tons of aluminum. Until 1942, the annual aluminum consumption of the entire United States economy was less than 250,000 tons. In addition, there were fairly high tariffs on imported aluminum. Comment on these facts and their relevance for the probable market structure of the American aluminum industry at the time. What effect might the removal of tariffs on imported aluminum have had?

5. Since there is, by law, only one telephone system, could it, if it were not regulated, maximize profits by setting very high prices? How would it set prices, and what information would you want to have if you were to advise the company on the most profitable price to set?

Chapter **24** PRICE DISCRIMINATION

RAW MILK IS OFTEN SOLD AT ONE PRICE IF IT is to go into fluid milk, but at a lower price if it is to be used to make ice cream or cheese. Doctors, lawyers, and business consultants sometimes charge rates for their services that vary according to the incomes of their clients. Movie theaters charge lower admission prices for children. Railroads charge different rates per ton mile for different kinds of products. Manufacturers often sell their product abroad at a lower price than at home. Electric companies sell electricity more cheaply for industrial use than for home use. State universities charge out-of-state students higher tuition.

Such price differences could never persist under perfect competition. Yet many of the examples we have quoted have existed for decades. Persistent price differences clearly require the exercise of some monopoly power, since the seller is exerting some influence over the price at which his product is sold. Why should a seller want to sell some units of his output at a price well below the price that he gets for other units? Why, in other words, does he practice *price discrimination*?

Price discrimination occurs when a producer sells a specific commodity to different buyers at two or more different prices, *for reasons not associated with differences in cost.*[1] The theory of price discrimination is sufficiently complicated that a thorough discussion had best be left for a more advanced course.[2] But since price discrimination of some sort occurs in a very large fraction of all markets, often with the approval of public authorities, it is important to understand the phenomenon.

Why Price Discrimination Pays

Why does persistent price discrimination occur? It occurs because different buyers may be willing to pay different amounts for the same commodity, and it may be profitable for the seller to take advantage of this willingness. Look at the demand curve in Fig-

1. Thus quantity discounts, differences between wholesale and retail prices, and prices that vary with the time of day or the season of the year are not generally considered price discrimination. The latter are not usually discriminatory, because the same physical product sold at a different time is a different product, if the time of purchase is important to the purchaser. A long-distance phone call placed after 8 P.M. costs less than the same call placed at 3 P.M. But it is not the same service, as any businessman knows.

2. The interested student will find the topic discussed in any good intermediate price-theory text. See, for one example, Joe S. Bain, *Price Theory* (Henry Holt, 1953), Chapter 9.

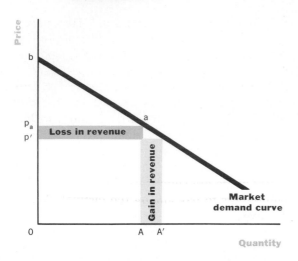

FIGURE 1   THE EFFECT OF AN INCREASE IN SALES

ure 1. Think of it as a market demand curve for a market containing individual buyers, each of whom wishes to buy one unit, and each of whom has indicated the price he is prepared to pay for it. Suppose a single price, p_a, is charged. We predict that the quantity OA will be sold because the buyers of each of the OA units are willing to pay at least p_a per unit. Although one buyer was willing to pay only p_a, all of the other buyers were willing to pay more. They have benefited because the price was limited to p_a.[3] If the seller could negotiate with each buyer individually, he might be able to charge some buyers more than p_a. In fact, by charging each person the maximum that person is prepared to pay, the seller could greatly increase his profits. To sell the $n + 1$th unit, the seller had to lower the single price from p_a to p'. Marginal revenue was less than the new price charged because of the effect that the reduction in price had on the revenues from the first n units, a reduction that was not necessary to sell them (since they were already being sold at the higher price). If the seller had been able to sell the $n + 1$st unit at p' without reducing the price on the first n units (if, in other words, he had been able to discriminate), he would have profited thereby.

When Is Price Discrimination Possible?

The conditions under which a seller can succeed in charging discriminatory prices are, first, that he can control the supply of the product in the sense of controlling what is offered to a particular buyer, and, second, that he can prevent the resale of the commodity from one buyer to another. However much the local butcher would like to charge the banker's wife twice as much for hamburger as he charges the taxi driver, he cannot succeed in doing so. Madame Banker can always go into the supermarket for her meat, where her husband's occupation is not known. Even if the butcher and the supermarket agreed to charge her twice as much, the banker could hire the taxi driver to do his shopping for him. The surgeon, on the other hand, may succeed in discriminating (if all reputable surgeons will do the same) because it will not do the banker much good to hire the taxi driver to have his operations for him.

The first of the two conditions—control over supply—is the feature that makes price discrimination an aspect of the theory of

3. The area under the demand curve above the line p_a (= the area $p_a ba$) is sometimes called *consumers' surplus*. It represents the amount consumers would have been willing to pay, unit by unit, for the quantity *OA, above the amount they actually paid* at the fixed price p_a.

monopoly. Monopoly power in some form is necessary to (but not sufficient for) price discrimination. Competition among sellers for customers leads to a single price at (or near) the level dictated by the costs of production.

The second of the two conditions—ability to prevent resale—tends to be associated with the character of the product or the ability to classify buyers into readily identifiable groups. Services are less easily resold than commodities; goods that require installation by the manufacturer (like heavy equipment) are less easily resold than are movable commodi-

ties (like household appliances).[4] Transportation costs, tariff barriers, or import quotas serve to separate classes of buyers geographically and may make discrimination possible.

To summarize, price discrimination will be both profitable and possible where the supplier(s) can control the amount and distribution of supply, where the buyers can be separated into classes among which resale is either impossible or very costly,[5] and where there are significant differences in the willingness to pay among the distinct classes of buyers.[6]

The Positive Effects of Price Discrimination

The positive consequences of price discrimination are summarized in the following two propositions, which we state and make intuitively plausible, but do not prove:

1. For any given level of output the best system of discriminatory prices will provide higher[7] total revenue to the firm (and thus also higher average revenue) than the best single price.

This should be intuitively obvious at once. If it is not, review the first pages of this chapter.[8]

2. Output under monopolistic discrimination will generally be larger than under single-price monopoly.

To see this quickly, look again at the discussion of Figure 1. Marginal revenue will tend to be higher, given the possibility of price

---

4. An interesting example of nonresalability occurs in the case of plate glass. Small pieces sell much more cheaply per square foot than bigger pieces, but the person who needs a 6' x 10' plate window cannot use four pieces, each of which is 3' x 5'.

5. The discussion of this paragraph relates directly to discrimination among *classes of buyers*. Discrimination among *units of output* follows similar rules. Thus the tenth unit purchased by a given buyer in a given month can be sold at a different (higher *or* lower) price than the fifth unit *only* if the seller can keep track of who buys what. This can be done by the seller of electricity through his meter readings, or by the magazine publisher, who can distinguish between renewals and new subscriptions. The owner of a car-wash establishment and the manufacturer of aspirin find it more difficult, although by such devices as coupons or "one-cent" sales, they too can determine which unit is being purchased.

6. "Willingness to pay" is reflected in the demand curves. The fact that demand curves slope downward shows that some units could always be sold at a higher price if sellers are permitted to deviate from a single price.

7. A more careful statement would say "higher than or equal to" in order to recognize the possibility that the best single price may be the best system of prices in a given situation.

8. We are saying here that the removal of a constraint (the limitation to a single price) upon a seller will never worsen his situation, and will generally permit him to improve it.

discrimination, because the lower price the producer must charge in order to sell an additional unit will not apply to all previous units salable. The common sense of this is as follows: The monopolist who must charge a single price produces less than the perfectly competitive industry, because he is aware that by producing and selling more he drives down the price against himself. Price discrimination allows him to avoid this disincentive. To the extent that he can sell his output in separate blocks, he can sell another block without spoiling the market for the block already being sold. In the case of *perfect* price discrimination, where every unit of output is sold at a different price, his output would be the same as the output of a perfectly competitive industry.[9]

The predicted combination of higher average revenue and higher output does not in itself have any *normative* significance. We cannot say that price discrimination is per se better or worse than any other scheme of pricing. It will often lead to a different distribution of output as well as to a different level of output; it will typically lead to a different distribution of income. The particular patterns will depend upon more facts than we have introduced. Having specified the differences, men can debate their desirability. Economic analysis can describe consequences, but it cannot finally evaluate them.

The Normative Aspects of Price Discrimination

This foregoing discussion may not satisfy the student who is aware that price discrimination has a bad reputation among economists and lawyers as well as among laymen. The very word "discrimination" has odious connotations. The Robinson-Patman Act makes certain kinds of price discrimination illegal. Much of the impetus for railroad regulation came from the outraged cries of farmers and their organizations that they were being discriminated against and forced into bankruptcy by the railroads.

Whether an individual judges price discrimination to be an "evil" depends upon the details of the case, as well as upon his value judgments. Consider the following examples:

Example 1. A very large oil refiner agrees to ship his product to a market on a given railroad, only if the railroad gives his company a secret rebate on the transportation cost and does not give a similar concession to rival refiners. The railroad agrees, and is thus charging discriminatory prices. This rebate gives the oil company a cost advantage that it uses to drive its rivals out of business or to force them into a merger on dictated terms. (John D. Rockefeller used similar tactics in forming the original Standard Oil Trust.)

Example 2. When the Aluminum Company of America (ALCOA) had a virtual monopoly

9. If each unit can be sold at a separate price, the seller does nothing to spoil the market for previous units by selling an additional unit. The marginal revenue of selling an additional unit is the price of that unit. Thus, the demand curve becomes the marginal revenue curve, and the monopolist reaches equilibrium at a point at which the price (in this case, marginal revenue) equals marginal cost. This is also the point of competitive equilibrium. Under perfect price discrimination, as under perfect competition, $p = MR$: Thus, in both cases, profit-maximization leads to the output where $p = MC$.

on the production of aluminum ingots, it sold both the raw ingots and fabricated products (such as aluminum cable) made from the ingots. At one time, ALCOA sold cable at a price 20 percent below the price it charged for ingots, although of course the cable price was above its cost of producing cable. It did so because users of cable could substitute copper cable, but many users of ingot had no substitute for aluminum. In return for its "bargain price" for cable, ALCOA made the purchasers of cable agree to use it only for transmission purposes. (Without such an agreement, any demander of aluminum might have bought cable and melted it down.)

Example 3. Three manufacturers of heavy equipment operate in an industry in which orders are given on the basis of sealed bids. The manufacturers do not wish to compete with each other, so they decide in advance which of them shall make the low bid at whatever price he feels the buyer can afford to pay. The other manufacturers agree to submit higher bids. (Allegations of this sort of monopolistic price discrimination were made in the 1960 indictments against manufacturers of electrical equipment.)

Example 4. A product that a number of people want has the cost and demand structure pictured in Figure 2. There is no single price at which a producing firm can cover total costs. However, if the firm is allowed to charge discriminatory prices, it will be willing to produce output OA, and it will make a profit.[10] (Electrical-utilities companies are often said to operate under these conditions.)

Example 5. In the United Kingdom, railways are not allowed to discriminate among passengers. To prevent discrimination, the regulatory authority has established a fixed

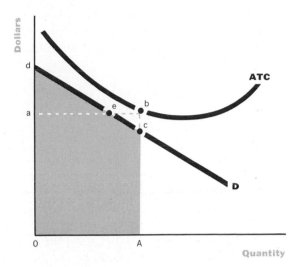

FIGURE 2

passenger fare per mile traveled. Some branch lines have been forced to shut down because they could not cover their costs at the national rates. Passengers along these branch lines are irate at the abandonment of service because they value the service and are prepared to pay the rate that is required to make a profit.

Example 6. The government decides to offer elementary-school education to all children. The cost per child is estimated at $500 per child per year. Instead of charging tuition to each child's parents, the government chooses to make the school free and to raise the money by a school tax that is proportional to the value of the houses of the people who live in the community, whether or not they have children.

Each of these examples, as well as those at the beginning of this chapter, involves price discrimination. We suspect that there are few readers who would regard them all as equally

10. Given perfect discrimination, total revenue would be the shaded area $OdcA$, whereas total costs are $OabA$. As long as the triangle ade is larger than ebc, there are profits.

good or bad. The point we wish to stress is twofold: First, the consequences of price discrimination can differ in many ways from case to case. And, second, no matter what any individual's values are, he is almost bound to evaluate the individual cases differently.

Price Discrimination: Systematic and Unsystematic

Everything that we have discussed in this chapter has been concerned with systematic and persistent price discrimination. Another sort of price discrimination is frequently found: Any seller who occasionally gives a favorite customer a few cents off, or shades his price to land a new account, is engaged in price discrimination. If these practices are used infrequently, they are called *unsystematic discrimination*. Such discrimination is not really part of the price structure and we have ignored it in this chapter. This does not mean that it is unimportant—indeed, unsystematic price discrimination plays a very real role in the dynamic process by which prices do change in response to changed conditions of supply and demand. Systematic price discrimination most often consists in classifying buyers according to their age, location, industry, income, and so forth, or according to the use they intend to make of the product, and in charging different prices for the different "classes" of buyers. It may also take other forms, such as charging an individual more for the first unit he buys than for subsequent units, or vice versa, or by setting an "all or nothing price" on a specified quantity of the product that is different for different quantities of the product.

The causes and consequences of systematic and unsystematic price discrimination are very different. Control legislation will, however, generally be unable to distinguish between them and will hit at both. If legislation is motivated solely by a desire to attack systematic discrimination, it may have unforeseen and possibly undesired effects on unsystematic discrimination.[11]

Summary

1. Price discrimination occurs when different units of the same commodity are sold for different prices, for reasons not associated with differences in costs. Different buyers may be charged different prices or the same buyer may be charged different prices on different units of the commodity he buys.

2. The conditions under which a seller can succeed in charging discriminatory prices are, first, that he can control the supply of the product offered to particular buyers, and, second, that he can prevent the resale of the commodity from one buyer to another. It is the condition of control over supply that

---

11. If unsystematic price discrimination is important for the working of competition, prohibiting it may aid the maintenance of monopoly power.

makes price discrimination an aspect of the theory of monopoly. It is the second condition that tends to be associated with characteristics of the product or the ability to classify buyers into readily identifiable groups.

3. Commodities that lend themselves to price discrimination include services rather than goods, equipment requiring installation by the manufacturer, and commodities whose buyers can be separated geographically by transport costs or international trade barriers.

4. Two predictions about price discrimina-

tion are (a) for any given level of output the best system of discriminatory prices will provide higher total revenue to the firm than the best single price, and (b) output under monopolistic discrimination will be larger than under a single-price monopoly.

5. The consequences of price discrimination can differ in many ways from case to case. Any individual is almost certain to evaluate the individual cases differently, according to his personal set of values.

QUESTIONS FOR DISCUSSION

1. In the nineteenth century, it was not uncommon for American railroads to charge farmers more for a "short haul" of their produce along a given line than for a "long haul." Explain why it might be possible and profitable for railroads to do this.

2. What motive and assumption might prompt theaters in a college town to give discounts to students?

3. A great deal of protest is often aroused over the practice of "dumping," whereby a manufacturer sells some of his output abroad at prices substantially lower than those prevailing in his home market. Why is such a practice possible, and why may the producer find it desirable? What are the general consequences of such practices, and who do you think might lose and who gain?

4. IBM used to give a substantial "educational discount" to universities purchasing its com-

puters for academic work. What might lead the corporation to choose to abandon this practice, other than legal restrictions?

5. Does the schedule of airline rates to Europe, higher in the summer than in the winter, represent price discrimination? What additional information would you like to have before deciding? What about charging children under twelve half-fare?

6. Electricity companies commonly charge each consumer a lower rate the more he consumes ($X\phi$ for the first A kilowatts consumed, $Y\phi$ for the next B kilowatts, etc.). Why is this form of price discrimination possible? Why is it profitable?

7. Is the automobile insurance companies' practice of charging as much as triple the standard rate for unmarried males under twenty-five an example of price discrimination as we have discussed it here? Indicate any additional information you might like to have.

Chapter 25 MONOPOLY AND COMPETITION:
IMPLICATIONS ABOUT BEHAVIOR

IN CHAPTERS 22 AND 23 WE PRESENTED TWO opposite theories of market structure, perfect competition and monopoly. Until roughly 1930, economists analyzed pricing decisions and discussed economic policy almost entirely in terms of these two theories. Today, some able economists continue to do so, but most feel that a more varied set of market structures is required in order to make reasonably accurate predictions about the behavior of firms and markets. The central points of disagreement between these groups are discussed in Chapters 27, 28, and 29. Before we can discuss them intelligently we have to know how far our two theories of competition and monopoly can take us. This chapter discusses some of the implications of the theories of competition and monopoly for the *market behavior* of firms. Chapter 26 considers the extent to which conclusions can be reached about the quality of the *market performance*

under the two kinds of market structure.

These comparisons are important historically in understanding the development of modern economic theory; they are also important in their own right: Many of the insights of economics into the workings of the price system and many of the testable hypotheses about pricing decisions come directly from the theories of perfect competition and monopoly. Moreover, more complicated market structures are elaborations, rather than replacements, of the simpler ones.

In this chapter, we are concerned with deriving certain implications of the theories of competition and monopoly. For the present, we shall treat them purely as logical implications of the formal theories developed in Chapters 22 and 23. They may also be viewed as hypotheses about the real world, and in subsequent chapters we shall treat them as such.

Effects of a Rise in Demand: Competition[1]

Figure 1 shows the cost and demand conditions for a single firm (i), and for a whole industry (ii), under perfect competition.

When the demand curve is D_1, both the individual firm and the industry are in equilibrium at price Op_1. (If you have any doubts

1. After studying this section, analyze the case of a *fall* in the demand for the product of a competitive industry.

about this, review Chapter 22.) There is no incentive for any firm to change its output, nor is there incentive for entry or exit of firms.

Now assume that the market demand curve in Figure 1 shifts from D_1 to D_2. This demand shift causes a shortage of the product to develop. This shortage causes the price to rise and firms to increase output. In the short run, the market price rises to Op_2, at which price the total industry supply is equal to the total demand for the product. At price Op_2 the individual firm that we are considering will produce Oq_2 units and the total production of all firms will be OQ_2. Our firm will be making profits on each unit equal to the difference between the price per unit and the average cost per unit ($q_2h - q_2i = hi$). Thus the firm's total profit is equal to the area of the rectangle $hijp_1$.

These then are the predictions about the short-run effects of a rise in demand:

1. *Price will rise.*
2. *There will be an increase in the quantity supplied by each firm and hence by the industry.*
3. *Each firm will now be earning profits over opportunity costs.*

The long-run effects follow from prediction 3. Since firms are now making profits, this industry becomes an attractive one in which to invest. New firms will enter the industry, and existing firms will tend to expand. Thus, there will be an increase in supply that will tend to bring the price below the previously established short-run equilibrium level p_2. As we saw in Chapter 22, supply will increase and price will fall until the profits are eliminated and there is no longer any incentive for new firms to enter the industry or existing firms to expand. Whether the long-run equilibrium price is above, equal to, or below the original price will depend upon the shape of the long-run supply curve. Figure 2 illustrates the three possibilities.

In each case, D_1 is the original demand curve and p_1 is the equilibrium price at which each existing firm in the competitive industry

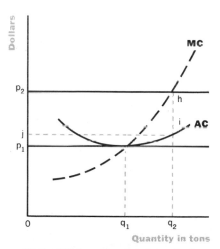

(i) **Equilibrium of a firm in perfect competition**

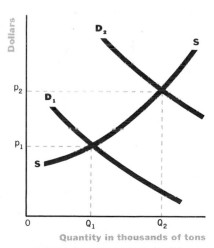

(ii) **Equilibrium of a perfectly competitive industry**

FIGURE 1

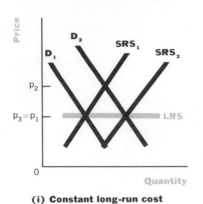

(i) Constant long-run cost

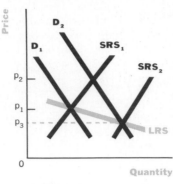

(ii) Falling long-run costs

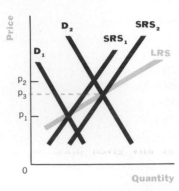

(iii) Rising long-run costs

FIGURE 2

is covering its cost. (See Figure 7 (ii) on page 261 above.) SRS_1 represents the short-run supply curve.[2] In response to the shift in the demand curve to D_2, short-run price rises to p_2. In response to the profits earned at p_2, new firms enter the industry and the supply curve shifts to the right. The new equilibrium price is p_3. LRS is the long-run supply curve.

Why does equilibrium price change? Suppose that the industry incurs increasing costs as it expands. Cost curves rise as the industry grows and, were price to fall to its original level, there would be losses. The expansion

of the industry under the incentive of profits will stop before price returns to its original level. The long-run supply curve of the industry will, in this case, be upward-sloping.

Thus the long-run consequences of a rise in demand are as follows:[3]

1. *The scale of industry will expand.*
2. *Profits will eventually return to zero.*
3. *Price will be above, below, or equal to its original level according as the industry is one of increasing, decreasing, or constant costs.*

Effects of a Rise in Demand: Monopoly[4]

The first and most important point to notice is that in monopoly, in contrast to perfect competition, there is no single relation between price and quantity supplied. In perfect competition, we knew the industry short-run

supply curve as soon as we knew the marginal cost curves of the individual firms. This was because the profit-maximizing firms equated marginal cost to price so that, given marginal costs, we knew exactly how much would be

2. Recall that this supply curve is the sum of the marginal cost curves of all the firms in the industry.

3. Beware of this wording, which is almost universally employed. What it means is that *these are the propositions that have been shown to be implied by our assumptions.*(Whether or not the propositions conform with real-world observations is a matter for empirical testing.)

4. Again, we leave as an exercise the case of a fall in demand.

produced at any price. A profit-maximizing monopolist (or indeed any profit-maximizing firm facing a downward-sloping demand curve) will equate marginal cost to marginal revenue, *not* to price. Under these conditions it is possible for different demand conditions to give rise to the same output but to different prices. In order to know the amount produced at any given price, we need to know the demand curve as well as the marginal cost curve.

The proposition that there is no unique relation between price and output when a firm faces a downward-sloping demand curve is illustrated in Figure 3. In Figure 3 (i), we see alternate demand curves that lead to the same output but different prices. In Figure 3 (ii), we see demand curves that lead to the same price but different outputs. Because of the fact that there is no unique supply curve for a monopolist, the conclusion we reached in the case of competition—that a rise in demand would lead to an increase in the quantity produced and sold—can no longer be made. In general, we can make only the very weak prediction that both quantity and price will not fall in response to a rise in demand.[5] Any other outcome is possible. Figure 4 illustrates two possible outcomes: (i) illustrates a case in which output rises and price falls, and (ii) illustrates a case in which both price and output rise.[6] (Draw a graph illustrating a case in which price rises and output falls.) In the diagram D_1, p_1, and q_1 refer to the initial situation before the rise in demand, and D_2, p_2, and q_2 to the situation after the rise.

The reason for this very limited ability to predict is that when demand rises, the elas-

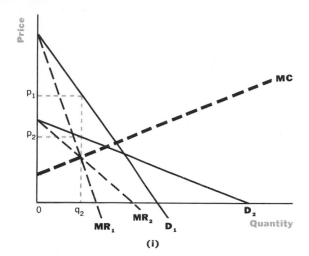

(i)

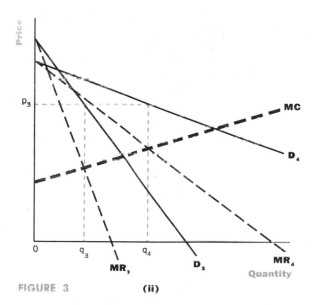

FIGURE 3   (ii)

ticity of demand may change. If demand becomes more elastic, it may pay the monopolist to lower his price and increase his sales. If

---

5. This prediction is so weak as to be trivial. It is really a part of the definition of an increase in demand, for if the demand curve shifts to the right, it is impossible to find any point on the new curve where *both* price and quantity are less than they were on the original curve.

6. Note that to say that several outcomes are all logically possible does not say anything about how likely the alternative outcomes are to occur. This is an empirical matter, not a logical one.

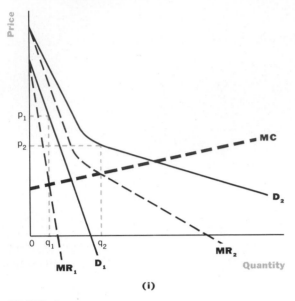

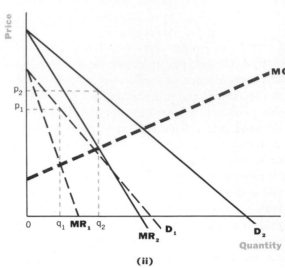

FIGURE 4

demand becomes less elastic, it may pay him to raise his price and reduce his output.

At this level of generality, we are left with the conclusion that a rise in demand for a monopolist can cause both his price and his output to rise, but that it is possible for either his price or his output to fall. In applying the theory of the firm, it is important to have some more definite prediction about the effect of a change in demand on a monopolist's price-output policy, and we here briefly mention how you might proceed with a fuller investigation of the theoretical model: Using mathematical tools, you would seek to determine precisely what changes in elasticity of demand would have to accompany a rightward shift

in the demand curve if either price or output were to fall. Having determined this, you might then appeal to empirical evidence for particular commodities to see if it appears at all likely that such combinations of shifts in curves and changes in elasticity might occur. Or, you might go directly to empirical evidence to determine what price and output changes have in fact accompanied changes in demand. If you found, for example, that increases in demand were always accompanied by increases in both price and output, you could take this to be the normal real-world case, with the other cases as possible, but unlikely, exceptions.

Elasticity of Demand at Equilibrium

In a competitive industry, equilibrium occurs where the industry supply curve (which is the sum of the marginal cost curves of the firms that compose the industry) cuts the demand curve. The elasticity of the market demand curve at the equilibrium price may be anything from zero to infinity. In the case of monopoly, however, equilibrium occurs at the level of output at which the marginal cost curve cuts the marginal revenue curve. Since marginal costs are almost always greater than zero,[7] it follows that marginal revenue must also be greater than zero at the equilibrium point. But if marginal revenue is greater than zero, it implies that the elasticity of demand is greater than one.[8] Thus, a profit-maximizing monopolist will always move to some point on his demand curve at which elasticity exceeds one; if he finds himself momentarily at a point at which demand is inelastic, it will obviously pay him to reduce output, thus increasing his total receipts and reducing his total costs, hence increasing his total profits. Thus, while it is quite possible for a competitive industry to be in equilibrium in a position in which a reduction in output would result in an increase in consumers' *expenditure* on the product, such a situation is not possible for a profit-maximizing monopolist.

This fact provides some insight into the grievances of producers who are forced by competition to operate where the demand curve is inelastic. The most notable examples are found in the field of agriculture. Farmers' cooperatives try to control supply and limit production in order to raise prices and raise the revenue yield from their products. The much-publicized "holding actions" of the National Farmers' Organization are a similar example of trying to raise price by limiting output in a situation in which demand is inelastic.

PRODUCERS' COOPERATIVES[9]

The theory of competitive price says that the market will come into equilibrium at the point at which the quantity demanded equals the quantity supplied, and that there is no restriction whatever on the elasticity of demand at the point of equilibrium. It is an observed fact that many agricultural commodities have inelastic demands in the neighborhood of equilibrium.

What does the theory predict about a competitive market that is in equilibrium at a point at which demand is inelastic? Note first that in competition individual farmers will act as price-takers; their behavior will be

---

7. Negative marginal costs are an oddity, but some examples have been found. One of these is the marginal cost to a radio or television station of selling a block of time to a sponsor, the program being provided by the sponsor. The station not only receives revenue, but is relieved of the obligation to provide a program and thus of some direct costs.

8. If the elasticity of demand is less than one, a 1 percent increase in sales will be met by a fall in the price of *more than* 1 percent; hence, total receipts will fall and marginal revenue (the change in total revenue resulting from selling a little more) will be negative.

9. Cooperatives exist for many purposes. We are concerned in this section only with those of their activities that are designed to raise members' incomes by output restriction.

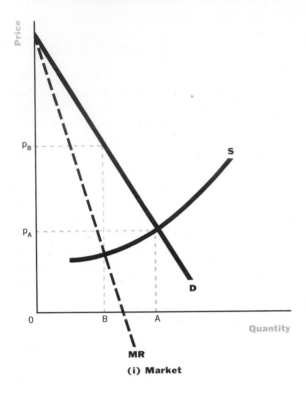

(i) Market

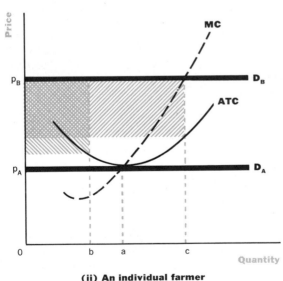

(ii) An individual farmer

FIGURE 5

the same whatever the elasticity of market demand at the point of equilibrium. This is because there is no point in any one of them cutting back on his output, since any one of them faces a perfectly elastic demand for his own product. If he did reduce his output, he would leave price unaffected and so would merely reduce his income as his output fell. The first prediction of our theory is that *there are gains to be had if all farmers can act together.* The common sense behind this prediction is that if all farmers form a producers' co-op and each agrees to cut production by establishing quotas for every member's output, then the total supply will be affected, price will rise by more than the fall in output, and all the farmers will be better off. (Since their gross revenue is up and their costs down because they are producing less, their profits must be up.) Second, the theory predicts that, *once output has been restricted by the co-op, any one farmer will have the incentive to increase his output and the producers' co-op will, therefore, tend to exhibit unstable behavior.* The common sense behind this prediction is as follows: The co-op raises prices by cutting production. If any one farmer could raise his output, his own actions would not affect the price, and his income would rise, since he could go back to selling his pre-co-op output at the post-co-op prices. Thus, unless the co-op is very carefully policed and has the power to enforce its quota restrictions on everyone's output, there will be a tendency for members to begin to violate quotas once prices have been raised. Furthermore, the co-op must have power over all producers, not merely over its members; otherwise a producer can avoid the quota restriction merely by leaving the co-op.

Let us examine these predictions more closely with the assistance of Figure 5. Figure 5 (i) represents the market conditions of supply and demand; Figure 5 (ii) represents the conditions of demand and cost for an individual farmer. Before the co-op is formed, let us suppose that the market is in competitive equilibrium at price p_A and output OA (where $D = S$), and the individual farmer is producing output Oa, and just covering costs. The co-op is formed in order to allow producers to exert a monopolistic influence on the market. By persuading each farmer to reduce his output, it reduces market output to OB (where $MR = S$) and achieves the price p_B. Our farmer in Figure 5 (ii) has a quota of Ob, but even though he has reduced his output he has improved his position: He is now earning profits in the amount shown by the area on the figure in which the lines rise to the left. This demonstrates our first prediction:

Every farmer will be better off if a co-op is formed and succeeds in raising price to p_B than if no co-op is formed and price remains at p_A.

But, once price is raised to p_B, the individual farmer would like to increase his output because price is greater than marginal cost. Left to himself, he would like to increase his output to Oc, and earn the profits shown in (ii) by the area in which the lines rise to the right. This profit is necessarily greater than the profit he earns by producing Ob.[10] This leads to our second prediction:

Every co-op member can increase his profits by violating his output quota, providing the other members do not violate theirs.

These two predictions highlight the dilemma of the attempts of the producers' co-op to raise farm income: Every farmer is better off if the co-op is formed and is effective. But he is even better off if everyone else plays ball, but he does not. Yet if everyone cheats (or stays out of the co-op), all will be worse off. Thus we are led to the summary prediction:

Producers' co-ops formed to exploit inelastic demands in competitive industries will be able to raise producers' incomes, provided they are able to enforce strictly quotas on the outputs of all producers. Such co-ops will, however, exhibit unstable tendencies, for it will always be in the interest of any single member to raise his output. If many producers do so, the co-op will collapse and all producers will lose.

The history of schemes to raise farm incomes by limiting crops bears ample testimony to the empirical applicability of this prediction. Crop restriction breaks down and prices fall as individuals exceed their quotas. The great bitterness and occasional violence that is sometimes exhibited by members of crop-restriction schemes against nonmembers (or members who cheat) is readily understandable.

Changes in Costs: Their Effect on Price and Quantity

A fall in costs, both in perfect competition and in monopoly, leads to a rise in output and a fall in price. Consider the case of an invention that lowers the unit variable cost of production by X percent. Such an invention reduces marginal costs, since it now costs

10. The reason is that at Ob, price was greater than marginal cost. See Chapter 21, pages 248–249, if you **do not understand this.**

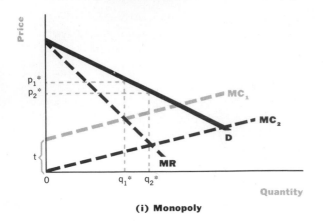

(i) Monopoly

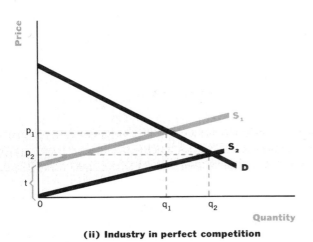

(ii) Industry in perfect competition

FIGURE 6 **EFFECT ON PRICE OF A REDUCTION IN MARGINAL COST**

less than it did previously to produce any unit of output. In a competitive industry, the fact that each firm's marginal cost curve shifts downward means that the industry supply curve (which is the sum of the marginal cost curves) also shifts downward: As a result of the invention, any given output will be pro-

duced at a lower price than before, while any given price will call forth a higher output. Thus the cost-saving invention lowers price and raises output. Draw a diagram illustrating this conclusion.

In a monopoly, the marginal cost curve also shifts downward; thus, it is obvious that the marginal cost and the marginal revenue curves will now intersect at a higher level of output than they did previously. Since the demand curve is unchanged, it follows that the price must fall. We conclude that it is a prediction both of the theory of competition, and of the theory of monopoly, that a fall in costs will cause an increase in output and a reduction in price. Thus, the benefit from any fall in costs will be to some extent passed on to consumers in terms of lower prices in the cases of both competition and monopoly.

But while prices will fall in both cases, they will not usually fall to the same degree, as Figure 6 illustrates. The demand curve is the same in both (i) and (ii), and the marginal cost curve for the monopolist (i) is identical with the supply curve of the competitive industry (ii). The monopolist equating MR and MC_1 is led to the price p_1^*. The competitive industry equating demand and supply is led to the price p_1. The dark lines MC_2 and S_2 reflect the effect of an equal reduction in costs in the two cases, and lead to the new prices p_2^* and p_2. *Notice that the amount of the price change is greater in the competitive case than in the monopolistic one.* The reason is that the monopolist is guided by the marginal revenue curve, which is steeper than the demand curve: The same vertical fall in marginal costs leads to a lesser increase in quantity and thus a lesser fall in price.

Our prediction is that, *other things being equal, prices and quantities will change less in monopoly than in competition in response to a change in marginal costs.*

Taxes: Their Effect on Price and Output[11]

There are many kinds of taxes. We shall here consider only three of them: a tax that is a fixed amount per unit produced; a tax that is a fixed amount; and a tax that is a fixed percentage of profits. We shall call the first kind a per unit tax, the second kind a lump-sum tax, and the third kind a profits tax.[12]

PER UNIT TAX

A per unit tax increases the cost of producing each unit by the amount of the tax. The marginal cost curve of every firm shifts vertically upward by the amount of the tax. In perfect competition, this means that the industry supply curve shifts upward by the amount of the tax.

Figure 6, with a little reinterpretation, illustrates this case. Suppose that MC_2 and S_2 reflect the cost and supply conditions (under monopoly and perfect competition respectively) before the tax. A tax of $\$t$ per unit is imposed, and the curves shift to MC_1 and S_1. It is immediately evident that in both cases such a tax will lead to an increase in price and a decrease in output. As we have drawn the diagram, the increase in price is less than the amount of the tax, even in the case of perfect competition. Is this necessarily the case?

The answer is No. In perfect competition, whether the price effect of a per unit tax is less than, equal to, or greater than the amount of the tax depends upon the shape of the supply curve. If the supply curve is rising,

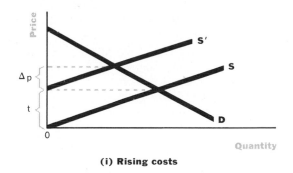

(i) Rising costs

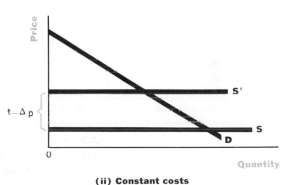

(ii) Constant costs

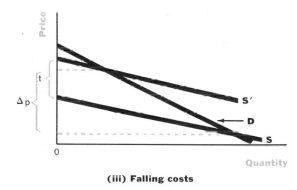

(iii) Falling costs

FIGURE 7

11. A subsidy is a negative tax. We shall discuss the tax case, and leave extension to subsidies as an exercise for the student.

12. As an exercise, extend the analysis to a further type of tax—a tax that is a fixed percentage of the price. Such a tax is called an ad valorem tax.

price will increase by less than the amount of the tax; if the supply curve is horizontal, the price rise will be equal to the amount of the tax; if the supply curve is declining, the increase in price will be greater than the amount of the tax. Figure 7 illustrates these three cases. In (i), (ii), and (iii), the imposition of a tax of $t per unit shifts the supply curve S up vertically to S', and leads to a change in price of $\triangle p$.[13]

In competition, *in the short run*, since costs are rising, prices will increase by less than the tax; in the long run, this need not be the case, as we have just seen.[14]

LUMP-SUM TAX

Consider now the effect of a lump-sum tax. Such taxes increase the fixed costs of the firm but do not increase marginal costs. The short-run effect on price and output of a change in fixed costs is zero, both in perfect competition and in monopoly. Since both marginal costs and marginal revenues remain unchanged, the profit-maximizing level of output cannot be affected. Hence we deduce the implication that a lump-sum tax leaves price and output unchanged in the short run.[15]

In the long run, the tax has no effect on a monopolist's price and output. Assuming that the monopolist was previously making profits, then the tax merely reduces the level of these profits. But, since the monopolist was making as much money as he possibly could before the tax, there is nothing that he can do to shift any of the tax burden onto his cus-

tomers. (Of course, if the lump-sum tax was so large that, even at the profit-maximizing level of output, profits were reduced to less than zero, the monopolist would cease production in the long run.)

In the case of perfect competition, we would expect the tax to affect price and output in the long run. If the industry was in equilibrium with zero profits before the tax was instituted, then the tax would lead to losses. Although nothing would happen in the short run to price and output, equipment would not be replaced as it wore out. Thus, in the long run, the industry would contract, and price would rise until the whole tax had been passed on to consumers and the firms remaining in the industry were again covering costs.

PROFITS TAX

It is usually stated that a percentage tax on the profits of a profit-maximizing firm will not affect either the price or the quantity produced. The sense in which this is correct is easily seen. Suppose one price-quantity combination (say p^*, q^*), gives the firm higher profits (without considering taxes) than any other. If the government imposes a 20 percent profits tax, the firm will have only 80 percent as much after-tax profit as it had before; *this will be true for each possible level of output*. Therefore p^*, q^* will still be the profit-maximizing output. This is illustrated in Figure 8. This standard prediction of economic theory is subject to very important

---

13. This case was analyzed in greater detail in Chapter 11. If you have any difficulty with the present argument, reread pages 119–123.

14. In the monopoly case, it is also possible for the price change to be greater than the amount of the tax, but the condition is not a simple one and we shall not present it. With a horizontal marginal cost curve, the monopolist's price change will be less than the amount of a per unit tax.

15. Unless the tax is so high that it causes the producers simply to abandon the business at once. Because of this, a lump-sum tax is a little bit different from a fixed cost in that it can be avoided by quitting the industry.

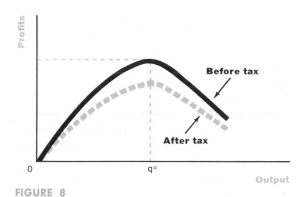

Profits

Before tax

After tax

0   q*

Output

FIGURE 8

reservations. For it to be correct, the tax must be on the "pure" profits that the economist defines after all costs have been covered.

In fact, taxes on profits usually apply to a different definition of profits.[16] Various kinds of imputed costs, such as returns on the owner's capital, risk premiums, imputed wages of the owner-managers, etc., are included in profits as defined for tax purposes. Other imputed costs, such as allowable depreciation, may be more generous than opportunity cost. If so, "profits before taxes" include payments for certain factors and possibly subsidies for other factors. In reality, a tax on "profits" is a tax on payments to the factors that are to be paid out of what the tax authorities call profits. Such taxes on

the use of factors of production will affect price and quantity. Suppose that all costs, except risk premiums, are included in costs as defined by the taxing authorities. A certain risky industry requires, say, a 5 percent return on its capital to make owners willing to invest in the industry. Suppose the industry is earning 6 percent on its investment before taxes. A 50 percent profits tax will reduce the return to risk below the point that makes investment attractive, and resources will leave the industry. Obviously, price and output changes will occur.[17] As firms leave the industry and as supply decreases, prices will rise until the remaining firms can earn a sufficient level of profit so that they are once again compensated for the risks involved.

Economists who fail to realize this difference between the taxes levied on "pure profits" and "profits taxes" will make predictions about the real world that do not in fact follow from their own theory. The theory predicts that a tax on "pure profits" will have no effect on the monopolists' price and output policy, but that a tax on "profits" as they are defined by the taxing authorities will have a definite effect on these decisions. Beware when the same term is given one meaning by economists and another meaning by the general public or by government officials.

The Price of Haircuts

So far in this chapter we have derived testable predictions from the simple models of perfect competition and monopoly. We have also seen how they provide a framework

for incorporating factual information: For example, knowing something about the shape of a long-run supply curve leads us to make a more specific prediction about price response

16. See Chapter 17, page 196.

17. In a somewhat similar fashion, a profits tax levied on short-run profits may reduce the size of the transitory gains from a price change or an innovation and thus affect the willingness of the firms to innovate or reduce prices.

than would be possible without such information. In general, it is true that the more detailed information one puts into a theory, the more specific predictions one gets out of it. If, for example, we know the elasticity of demand and how the demand curve is shifting over time, the theory can be made to yield a large number of predictions.

In order to see what the theory yields when more specific information is fed into it, consider as an example the efforts of all the barbers in a particular city to avoid the rigors of competition. Assume there are a very large number of barber shops and that there is freedom of entry into barbering in the sense that anyone who obtains a stated set of qualifications can set up as a barber. Assume that the going price for haircuts is $1, and that at this price all barbers feel their income is too low. The barbers hold a meeting and decide to form a trade association. They reach agreement on the following points: first, that all barbers in the city must join the association and abide by its rules; second, that any new barbers who meet certain professional qualifications will be required to join the association before they will be allowed to practice their trade; and, third, that the association will recommend a price for haircuts that no barber shall undercut.

The barbers intend to raise the price of haircuts in order to raise their income. You are called in as a consulting economist to advise them as to the probable success of their plan. What do you predict?

The first thing you need to know is whether the organization is strong enough to enforce its minimum price on members and to prevent barbers from operating outside of the organization. If it is not this strong, you will predict that their plan will not succeed in raising its price above the market level. But suppose that you are persuaded that the organization does have the requisite strength to enforce a price rise to, say, $2.[18] What are your predictions about the consequences of the price increase?

Clearly, you now need to distinguish between the short- and the long-run effects of this increase in the price of haircuts. In the short run, the number of barbers is fixed. Thus, in the short run, the answer is simple enough: It all depends on the elasticity of the demand for haircuts. If the demand elasticity is less than one, total expenditure on haircuts will rise and so, therefore, will the incomes of barbers; if demand elasticity exceeds one, the barbers' incomes will fall. Now you need some empirical knowledge about the elasticity of demand for haircuts. If you were actually advising the barbers' organization, you might be lucky enough to be able to refer to a full-scale econometric study of the demand for haircuts. However, it is unlikely, in the case of haircuts, that such a study is available. Thus you will probably have to try to gain some idea of demand elasticity by studying the effects of changes in haircut prices either at other times or in other places.[19]

18. Actually the barbers intend to raise the price in four stages over the course of two years in order not to shock their customers.

19. Such a study has to avoid the pitfall of "other things not equal." For example, the price of men's haircuts in England is less than one-half as much as the price in the United States after making allowance for differences in real purchasing power. Yet Englishmen wear their hair longer, and possibly have fewer haircuts per year than Americans. This is a difference in tastes that would destroy the comparison of price elasticity: These are not two observations on the same demand curve. A further difference is that in most London barbershops relatively few customers buy only a haircut—many buy a

When you propose making such a study, one of the leaders of the organization (who took a course in economics at his Barbers' College) tells you not to waste your time, because, he says, "Haircuts are a necessity since no one goes without them. Therefore the demand is almost perfectly inelastic." You reject this argument for two main reasons: First, because you realize that the time between haircuts is by no means fixed. Thus an increase in the average period between haircuts from two weeks to three weeks would represent a 50 percent fall in demand. If such a change were occasioned by, say, a 25 percent rise in price, the elasticity of demand over this range would be 2.0. Second, you reject the argument because you realize that people can have their hair cut elsewhere than in a barber shop. The sale of hair clippers for home use has grown into a big industry in America, and this growth is probably due to the sharp rise in the price of haircuts.

Let us suppose, however, that, on the basis of the best available evidence, you estimate the elasticity of demand over the relevant price range to be 0.4. You then predict that barbers will be successful in raising incomes in the short run: A 100 percent rise in price will be met by a 40 percent fall in business, so that the total revenue of the typical barber would rise by about 20 percent.† In predicting the consequences, you would also want to estimate the length of the short run for this industry.

Now what about the long run? If barbers were just covering costs before the price change, they will now be earning profits. Barbering will become an attractive trade relative to others requiring equal skill and training, and there will be a flow of barbers into the industry. As the number of barbers rises, the same amount of business must be shared out among more and more barbers, so that the typical barber will find a steady decrease in the amount of business he does. His profits will thus decrease.[20] This movement will continue until barbers are earning just normal incomes, at which time the attraction for new entrants will subside. The industry will settle down in a new position of long-run equilibrium in which individual barbers make incomes only as large as they did before the price rise. There will be more barbers than in the original situation, but each barber will be working for a smaller fraction of the day and will be idle for a larger fraction. (The industry will have *excess capacity*.)[21] The report that you finally present will say: "You may succeed in the short run (if demand is sufficiently inelastic), but your plan is bound to be self-defeating in the long run unless you are able to prevent the entry of new barbers."

The general moral of the story is that, if

---

shampoo, a massage, or other extras because the price of haircuts alone is so low. In other words, the typical "product" purchased in barbershops is different in the two countries.

† Revenue = $p \times q$. At $p = \$1$, revenue = $1 \times q$. At $p = \$2$, revenue = $2 \times (q - 0.4q) = 1.20q$.

20. Profits may also be squeezed from another direction. With fewer customers coming their way, the barbers may compete against each other for the limited number of customers. Since the association does not allow them to compete through price cuts, they can only compete in service. They may spruce up their shops, offer their customers expensive magazines to browse through, and so forth. This kind of competition, however, will raise operating costs. It takes us out of the simple prototypes of perfect competition and monopoly and into the area of monopolistic competition. See Chapter 28.

21. Barbers may prefer this situation: They have more leisure. But we are talking about the effect on their income, not on their leisure.

you cannot control entry, you cannot succeed in keeping earnings above the competitive level in the long run. If price competition is ruled out, then profits will be driven down by the entry of new firms and the resulting creation of excess capacity. Producers' associations that are successful in keeping earnings up are those that are successful in restricting entry.[22]

Monopoly and Competition: A Final Statement

In this chapter, we have developed a number of quite general predictions of the simple theories of the firm and industry in competition and monopoly. We have also illustrated the use of the theory in yielding predictions after certain specific information has been added to its general assumptions. It is fashionable these days among many professional economists to emphasize the inadequacies and the failures of the theory of the firm under perfect competition or monopoly. Such shortcomings, real though they are, should not be allowed to obscure the fact that this theory is an outstanding intellectual achievement. The theory of perfect competition shows, in a quite general way, how a large number of separate profit-maximizing firms can produce, with no conscious coordination, an equilibrium that depends only on the "technical data" of demand and costs. The theory ignores individual attitudes and eccentricities of producers and a host of other factors, and it shows how an equilibrium follows solely from the conditions of costs and demand. The analysis extends, with appropriate changes, to the theory of monopoly and to cases that are a direct mixture of these two theories.

As well as providing some general insight into the possible workings of the price system, the theory provides a series of predictions, or testable hypotheses, about how firms and industries will react to various changes in the data. Some of these predictions have been developed in the present chapter. Generally, the more information we start with, the richer the set of predictions that can be derived from the theory. If we knew (or assumed) no facts, we could deduce no consequences; for, in spite of occasional appearances to the contrary, economic theory is unable to produce something out of nothing. Out of ignorance comes only ignorance. If we knew (or assumed) only one thing—for example, that firms maximize profits—we could deduce only this one thing. We need to know at least two things before we can begin to deduce any further consequences of these facts. Generally, the more facts we know (or assume we know), the more likely it is that we shall be able to deduce interesting and possibly unsuspected consequences from them.

22. Whether barbers in the United States do succeed in limiting entry is debatable. Of the 48 continental states, 47 have licensing laws. Some of these set standards that appear to be much higher than what might be regarded as minimum standards. Clearly, it is *possible* to set standards at a level that would effectively limit entry. See Simon Rottenberg, "The Economics of Occupational Licensing" (*Special Conference Series, No. 14*), National Bureau of Economic Research (Princeton University Press, 1962). See, especially, "Postscript on Barber Licensing in Illinois," pp. 14–20.

The theories of perfect competition and monopoly assume a quite modest degree of knowledge about the real world, and the testable implications that can be shown to follow from them are on a correspondingly modest scale. But they are by no means negligible.

TABLE 1 THE PREDICTED EFFECTS OF VARIOUS TAXES

Type of Tax	Monopoly		Competition	
	Short run	Long run	Short run	Long run
A per unit tax	Price rises by less than the amount of the tax and part of the tax is passed on to the consumer.	Same as short run.	Price rises by less than the tax. Output falls and part of the tax is passed on to the consumer.	Price rises by more than, less than, or the same as the tax, depending on the slope of the long-run supply curve. All of the tax is passed on to the consumer.
A lump-sum tax	No effect unless post-tax revenues are less than TVC, in which case the monopolist ceases production. All of the tax is borne by the producer.	No effect unless post-tax revenues exceed TVC, but are less than TVC and TFC, in which case the monopolist ceases production in the long run. All of the tax is borne by the producer.	Same as in monopoly.	Scale of the industry contracts, and price rises until revenue again equals total cost. All of the tax is passed on to the consumer.
A tax on profits as defined by the economist. (Revenues in excess of all opportunity costs.)	No effect on price and output. All of the tax is borne by the monopolist.	No effect on price and output. All of the tax is borne by the monopolist.	No effect on price and output. All of the tax is borne by the firms.	No effect because the tax is zero in long-run equilibrium.
A tax on profits as defined by the authorities. (Includes some opportunity costs.)	Effects in the same direction as a per unit tax, since this is also a tax on cost.			

Summary

1. We are concerned to develop predictions about observable events from the theories of monopoly and competition.

2. The predicted effects of a rise in demand for a product of a competitive industry are as follows: In the short run, price will rise, there will be an increase in the quantity supplied by each firm, and each firm will earn revenues in excess of total opportunity costs; in the long run, the scale of the industry will expand, output will rise, price will fall, and profits will return to zero.

3. Because a monopolist does not have a supply curve that associates each price with a unique output (see Figure 3, page 283), it is not possible to predict that a rise in demand will always cause both price and output to rise. If elasticity of demand changes sufficiently, it is possible for a rise in demand to be accompanied by a reduction in either price or output (but not both).

4. The theory predicts that it is possible for a competitive industry to be in equilibrium when the demand curve is inelastic at the prevailing market price, but that this is not possible for a monopolistic firm.

5. Producers' co-ops formed to exploit inelastic demands in competitive industries will always be able to raise producers' incomes, provided they are able strictly to enforce quotas on the outputs of all producers. Such co-ops will, however, exhibit unstable tendencies, for it will always be in the interests of any single producer to raise his output. If many producers do so, the co-op will collapse, and all producers will lose.

6. The theory predicts that, other things being equal, prices and outputs will change less in monopoly than in competition in response to a change in marginal costs.

7. The predicted effects of various taxes are given in Table 1 on page 295.

8. The theories have been developed on very general assumptions, such as the assumption that demand curves slope downward; they yield general predictions about the *direction* of changes. The theories give more specific predictions when more specific data are available (e.g., the demand curve for a particular product slopes downward with a slope of -2).

QUESTIONS FOR DISCUSSION

1. Particularly good weather produces an unusually high demand for bathing suits *this* summer. What will happen in the bathing-suit industry this summer? Give the textbook prediction and try to explain it in common-sense terms. Meteorologists think that the climate has changed slightly and that we can expect summers to be generally drier and sunnier. What will happen in the bathing-suit industry now?

2. Since profit-maximizing monopolists will always choose to operate on the elastic portion of their demand curve, does this imply that the most profitable industries to monopolize are ones with highly elastic demand curves?

3. In 1965, many federal excise taxes were removed or sharply reduced. President Johnson stated that he wanted the American consumer

to be the full beneficiary of the tax cut and assigned several investigators to verify that he was—i.e., verify that prices were reduced by the full amount of the tax. Comment on the President's theory of the behavior of the economy implied by his action.

4. "A government policy that increases the costs of all firms is unfair because it is easier for monopolists who set their own prices to pass on cost increases to the consumer than it is for perfect competitors whose prices are given." Comment on this assertion, ignoring the normative issues.

5. France is occasionally beset by "artichoke wars." When good weather produces a bumper crop, prices fall sharply and angry farmers from Brittany storm into Paris, even barricading the streets with artichokes in protest. Assuming that not many artichokes are used up in pelting the citizenry of Paris, what would you say to the farmers if called upon to advise them? You are expected to be honest with them, and to explain the difficulties as well as the advantages of your plan.

Chapter 26 MONOPOLY VERSUS COMPETITION: IMPLICATIONS ABOUT PERFORMANCE

MONOPOLY HAS BEEN REGARDED WITH suspicion for a long time. It is often held that modern economic theory has *proved* that monopoly is a system whereby the powerful producer exploits the consumer, whereas the competitive system always works to the consumer's advantage. Indeed, Adam Smith, the founder of classical economics, developed, in *The Wealth of Nations,* a ringing attack on monopolies and monopolists. Since that time, most economists have advocated free competition and criticized monopoly. In this chapter, we shall consider the classical case against monopoly and then go on to see what else can be said about monopoly and competition on the basis of positive economics.

The Case Against Monopoly

The classical case against monopoly is to a great extent based on a single proposition: If a perfectly competitive industry should be monopolized, *and the cost curves of all productive units be unaffected by this change,* the price will rise and the quantity produced

will fall. Thus, given identical cost and demand conditions, monopoly leads to a lower
output and a higher price than does perfect
competition. This proposition follows from
the theories of competition and monopoly, as
you can verify by looking at Figure 1. In this
figure, the demand curve that faces the competitive industry is labeled D. The curve
labeled MC is the horizontal sum of the margi-

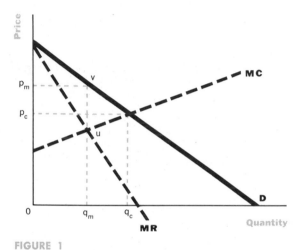

FIGURE 1

nal cost curves of the firms, and, as we have
seen, is the supply curve. The competitive
price and output are Op_c and Oq_c, respectively.

Now assume that this industry is monopolized as a result of a single firm buying out
all the individual producers. Further assume
that each plant's cost curve is unaffected by
this change. In other words, assume that
neither economies nor diseconomies result
from the coordinated planning of production
by a single decision unit. This means that
the marginal costs will be the same to the
monopolist as to the competitive industry:
The competitive industry's supply curve will
be the monopolist's marginal cost curve. But

the monopolist who seeks to maximize profits
will equate marginal costs not to price but
to marginal revenue. We now draw a marginal
revenue curve on Figure 1. This curve will lie
below the demand curve at every level of output. The output of the industry now falls from
Oq_c to Oq_m and price rises from Op_c to Op_m.
Our argument may be summarized as follows:

1. In perfect competition, marginal cost
equals price.

2. In monopoly, marginal cost equals marginal revenue.

3. For any given output, marginal revenue
is less than price as long as the demand curve
is downward-sloping.

4. Therefore, at the perfectly competitive
output, marginal revenue is less than marginal cost.

5. Since the marginal revenue curve slopes
downward, and the marginal cost curve slopes
upward, these two can only be equated by
reducing output below the perfectly competitive level.

6. Since the demand curve slopes downward, the lower level of output will necessarily be associated with a higher price.

The proposition that we just proved has a
strong common-sense appeal. In perfect competition, no one firm is big enough to affect
the price of the product by varying its production. Every firm, therefore, fixes its production at the most profitable level on the
assumption that the market price is given.
When the industry is monopolized, it becomes
possible to drive price up by restricting output, and this is what we have shown will
happen. What may not be obvious from a
purely common-sense argument is that, whatever the cost conditions, it will *always* pay
the monopolist to restrict output below, and
to raise price above, the perfectly competitive
level, *as long as the market demand curve is
downward sloping.*

The Case for Competition

If prices are higher and output lower under monopoly as compared with competition, are we justified in saying that one price-output situation is *in any sense* better, or more nearly optimal, than the other? The classical economists, in their case against monopoly, argued that perfect competition led, *in equilibrium*, to a use of resources that was, in a clearly defined sense, the "best" one.[1] They regarded competition as leading to a *more efficient allocation of resources* than monopoly. (Throughout this discussion, remember that we are assuming that the costs of production are not affected by the form of market organization.)

Their argument went as follows:

1. In perfect competition, equilibrium price is forced down to the lowest possible level—that of minimum average total cost.[2]

2. Because the costs reflect the alternative opportunities for the use of resources, there can be no better use of any of the resources.

3. In a monopoly, on the other hand, revenues will typically exceed costs and provide a signal for resources to move into the industry. But monopoly, by preventing entry, prevents both low prices and the best use of resources. These resources must seek second-best employment elsewhere in the economy.

4. In perfect competition, marginal cost equals price. Marginal cost shows the cost of producing the last unit of the commodity actually produced, and the price indicates what consumers are prepared to pay for the last unit of the commodity purchased (as shown in Figure 2).[3] It follows that consumers are prepared to pay, for the last unit they actually purchase, an amount exactly equal to the cost of producing that last unit.

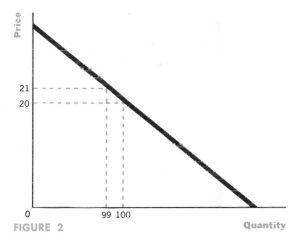

FIGURE 2

---

1. We cannot go into detail here, for the subject of *welfare economics*, which is concerned with identifying the conditions under which (and the cases in which) one situation is better than another, is best left to a more advanced course.

2. See Chapter 22, especially pages 260–262. The long-run average cost cure reflects the lowest unit cost of producing any output, and competition forces price down to the minimum point on this curve.

3. Look at the individual demand curve in Figure 2. When the market price is 20¢, the individual buys 100 units. If the price is 21¢, he buys only 99 units. As the price rises he buys fewer units. If the market price settles at 20¢, he will buy 100 units; thus he gets all but the last unit at a price less than he would be prepared to pay for them. (He is prepared, for example, to pay 21¢ each to get 99 units.) Thus, assuming his demand curve to be downward-sloping, the price measures what he is prepared to pay for the last unit he purchases; he would be prepared to pay more than the current price in order to obtain all but the last unit (which is why he would continue to buy them at higher prices); to obtain additional units, he is only prepared to pay an amount less than the market price (which is why he does not at present buy these additional units).

5. In a monopoly, price exceeds marginal cost. From this it follows that consumers pay, for the last unit they actually purchase, an amount greater than what it actually costs to produce it. Furthermore, consumers would be prepared to buy further units for an amount greater than the cost of producing these units. (Consumers are not allowed to purchase these extra units, because the monopolist restricts output in order to maximize his profits.) In Figure 1, for example, the marginal cost at the monopolist's equilibrium is $q_m u$ and price is $q_m v$; consumers are prepared to pay uv more for another unit than it actually costs to produce that unit. They are also willing to buy at a price in excess of the marginal costs of production a total of $q_m q_c$ units more than they are permitted to buy.

There is a strong intuitive appeal in the idea that consumers will in some sense be "better off" when production is pushed to the level at which marginal cost equals price than when it is held at a level at which marginal cost is less than price. It can in fact be shown, and it is a well-known proposition in welfare economics, that when marginal costs equal price in all lines of production, an optimal situation will occur *in the sense that it will be impossible to make some consumers better off without simultaneously making others worse off.* On the other hand, if, in some industries, marginal costs are less than prices, this will result in a suboptimal situation *in the sense that it will be possible to make all consumers better off simultaneously by changing some prices and outputs in the economy.*

Is Monopoly Really Evil?

On the basis of the preceding analysis, it is tempting to conclude that economics has *proved* that monopoly is evil, that it exploits the consumer, and that it should be condemned and stamped out whenever possible. It is extremely important for you to realize, however, that nothing in positive economics allows us to speak of monopoly as an evil, even if the considerations discussed above were the only ones (which they are not) and even if they had been thoroughly tested and found to conform with real-world observations. Positive economics seeks to establish propositions about the real world. If our economics is done well, we shall be able to say with some confidence that, if an industry is monopolized, certain changes will occur in price and output. *But there is absolutely nothing in positive economics that allows us*

to draw the conclusion that such changes are either good or bad. Positive economics at the very best tells us the consequences of our actions: Whether or not we like these consequences is a subjective matter. We can be in complete agreement about the consequences and yet disagree irreconcilably about whether they are desirable or undesirable, good or evil.

It *is* a prediction of the simple theory of monopoly and competition that, *providing demands and costs are unaffected*, price will be higher and output lower when an industry is monopolized than when it is competitive. Which of these situations we prefer, and whether our margin of preference is sufficient to justify incurring any substantial costs by moving from one to the other, are matters that involve value judgments and that take us, therefore, beyond the scope of positive economics.

The classical economists accepted not only the assumption that led to the prediction of output restriction under monopoly, they also accepted as *goals* those things that competition led to. These goals were accepted because to fulfill them would in turn satisfy certain more basic values, such as the sovereignty of the consumer, the dispersion of power, and efficiency. They regarded monopoly, which produced different results, as bad.

POLICY IMPLICATIONS OF ACCEPTING THE CLASSICAL POSITION

The belief that competition produced ideal results and monopoly nonideal ones led at once to the notion of prohibiting *by law* the practice of monopoly. *Antitrust laws*, perhaps the first manifestation of the classical down-with-monopolies policy, make attempts to monopolize and conspiracies in restraint of trade illegal and give the courts the power to stop such practices, as well as to dissolve a monopoly into a larger number of independent companies, if they deem it necessary. (We

discuss antitrust policy further in Chapter 43.)

A second policy—*public-utility regulation*—grew out of the classical economists' belief that, in some fields (for example, in transportation and public utilities), competition was impossible. These fields were regarded as areas of "natural monopoly"—as exceptions to the classical assumption that market organization does not affect levels of cost. The cost advantage in having one railroad between two points rather than fifty railroads (or one water company in a city, or one telephone company in a country) is evident. But, said the classical economists, a natural monopoly, one in which a single seller is able to operate more efficiently than if he were subject to competition, cannot be allowed to maximize profits by charging any price it will. Public-utility regulation gives, to appropriate public authorities, control over the price and quantity of service provided by a natural monopoly; prices are geared to provide only a "fair" return on capital. The principle behind the policy is to regulate a natural monopoly in such a way as to secure the price, output, and profit results that competition would produce, were it able to operate efficiently.[4]

Costs and Efficiency Under Monopoly and Competition

The basic proposition that monopoly leads to higher price and lower output than does competition depends on the assumption that costs are unaffected when an industry is monopolized. If any savings are effected by combining numerous competing groups into a

single integrated operation, then the costs of producing any given level of output will be lower than they were previously. If this cost reduction does occur, then it is possible for output to be raised and price to be lowered as a result of the monopolization of a per-

---

4. The details as to how this is done and the many difficulties in the area of public-utility regulation are left to a course in that field.

fectly competitive industry. Such a situation is illustrated in Figure 3. The competitive equilibrium price is Op_c and quantity is Oq_c. If the industry were monopolized and costs unaffected, production would be cut back to Oq_m', and price would rise to Op_m'. If, however, the integration of the industry into a single unit causes economies in costs, then the

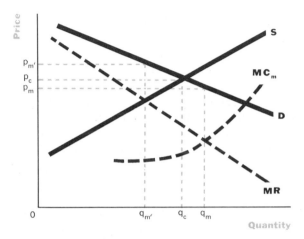

FIGURE 3   THE EFFECTS OF A MONOPOLY THAT IS MORE EFFICIENT THAN A LARGE NUMBER OF COMPETING FIRMS

marginal cost curve will shift downward. If it shifts to MC_m, then production rises to Oq_m and price falls to Op_m. This shows that the monopolization of an industry, combined with a sufficiently large consequent increase in efficiency, can result in a fall in price and a rise in quantity produced, as compared to the competitive industry.[5]

Of course, it is also possible that the monopolization of an industry may reduce the

efficiency of production and so shift the marginal cost curve upward. In this case, monopolization will, *a fortiori,* raise price and lower output as compared to the competitive industry. Draw a diagram showing the effects on price and output of a monopolization that caused costs to rise above those ruling under competition.

It is sometimes argued that monopolization will lower costs because wasteful duplication will be eliminated, and because economies of scale will result from, for example, establishing one coordinated management body for the industry. On the other hand, it is often argued that competition forces the individual firm to be efficient because the firm will not survive unless it keeps its costs as low as its competitors', whereas inefficiency is more common under monopoly because, although inefficiency may reduce profits, it will not result in bankrupting the monopolistic firm.

We cannot predict the effects on price and output of monopolizing a competitive industry unless we know the effect of this change on the industry's costs. If, for example, monopolization usually results in large cost savings, then it may be that monopolization usually results in a fall in price and an increase in output. If, on the other hand, monopolization usually either leaves costs more or less unchanged or increases them, then it will cause a rise in price and a fall in output. This is as far as our theory can take us; it can predict what empirical magnitudes are important, but, until we have some evidence of the effects of monopolization on an industry's cost structure, we cannot predict the effect that monopolization will have on price and output.

---

5. You should be able to show that, if the elasticity of demand were less than one at the competitive price, the monopolist would reduce output and raise price, no matter how large the reduction in his costs.

THE INCENTIVE TO INNOVATE

Does our theory predict anything further about the relative incentive, under monopoly and under competition, to keep costs down by being efficient or to reduce costs by introducing new innovations? As far as profits are concerned, both the monopolist and the perfect competitor have an incentive to reduce costs. A monopolist can always increase his profits if he can reduce his costs. We saw in Chapter 25 (pp. 287–288) that a cost reduction will cause the monopolist to produce more, to sell at a lower price, and to thus increase his profits. Furthermore, since he is able to prevent the entry of new firms into his industry, these additional profits will persist into the long run. Thus, from the standpoint of maximizing his profits, the monopolist has both a short- and a long-run incentive to reduce his costs.

The firm in perfect competition has the same incentive in the short run, but not in the long run. In the short run, a reduction in costs will allow the firm that was just covering costs to earn profits. In the long run, other firms will be attracted into the industry by these profits. Existing firms will copy the cost-saving innovation, new firms will enter the industry using the new techniques, and the profits of the innovator will eventually disappear. The effectiveness of profits as an incentive to reduce costs for a firm in competition will depend on the magnitude of the extra profits and the length of time over which they persist. If, for example, it only takes a few months for existing firms and new entrants to copy and install the new invention, then the original firm's profits will be above normal for only a very short time, and the extra profits actually earned may not be sufficient to compensate for the risks and the costs of developing the new innovation. In such cases, the direct incentive to innovate would be absent from a competitive industry.[6] On the other hand, if it takes several years for other firms to copy and install the cost-saving innovation, then the profits earned over these years by the innovating firm might be more than sufficient to compensate for all costs and risks, and yield a handsome profit as well. In this case, the incentive to innovate is present in a competitive industry.

Evidently, the key issue that we are faced with is the extent to which market organization affects the rate of innovation. Reread pages 236–239 at this point.

The greatest opponent of the classical position on monopoly was the distinguished Austrian (and later American) economist, Joseph A. Schumpeter.[7] His argument in brief was that only the incentive of profits led men to take the great risks of innovation and that monopoly power was much more important than competition in providing the climate under which innovation occurred. The short-run profits of the monopolist provided the incentive for other men to find *their* special advantage. He called the process of one monopoly being replaced by another the *process of creative destruction*. Speaking of the large firm with monopoly power, he said:

6. Some economists in the classical tradition have argued that indirectly the incentive remains: A firm that does not innovate as rapidly as possible runs the risk of being scooped by another firm. If this happens, the first firm will suffer short-term losses that it can ill afford. If this risk is smaller than the risks of trying to innovate, however, the firm will take it. Also, the easier it is to copy an innovation, the less the potential profit, and by the same token, the less the potential losses from not innovating.

7. His most famous book is *The Theory of Economic Development* (English ed.; Harvard University Press, 1934). The beginning student is referred to the lucid but less technical *Capitalism, Socialism, and Democracy* (3d ed.; Harper & Bros., 1950). Both works are available in paperback.

What we have got to accept is that it has come to be the most powerful engine of that progress and in particular of the long-run expansion of total output not only in spite of, but to a considerable extent through, this strategy which looks so restrictive when viewed in the individual case and from the individual point of time. In this respect, perfect competition is not only impossible but inferior, and has no title to being set up as a model of ideal efficiency. It is hence a mistake to base the theory of government regulation of industry on the principle that big business should be made to work as the respective industry would work in perfect competition.[8]

Economists of the classical view were not unaware of this consideration and they usually supported *patent laws*. Patent laws represent an attempt to lengthen the short-run period during which the innovating firm can earn supernormal profits as a reward for its innovation. Once the patent expires, other firms can copy the innovation and, when they do so, production will expand until profits fall to normal. There is little doubt that, were there no patent laws, many innovations could be copied with greater speed than at present, and that the original innovators would not earn as much extra revenue to compensate them for the costs and risks of development. On the other hand, patents can be imitated, so their real advantage to the small firm should not be exaggerated. Indeed, it has been argued that patents are of greater advantage to the monopolist who has the resources to develop, patent, and "keep on the shelf" processes that might enable a potential competitor to challenge his position.[9]

The monopolist has another possible advantage over the competitive firm in the process of innovation in that funds for research and development are more readily available to him. Tax laws that permit him to write off business expenses may make research and development a relatively cheap endeavor. Suppose that this year a monopolist expects to make $2 million profit on which he will have to pay taxes of approximately $1 million. If he spends the $2 million on research and development, however, he will show no profits for tax purposes this year, and will save $1 million in taxes. In effect, he can get $2 million worth of research for only $1 million dollars. His successes will lead to future profits, and will strengthen his position as a monopolist. Of course, in later years he will have to pay taxes on the profits he earns, unless he reinvests them.

There is thus no reason why cost conditions should be predicted to be the same for a monopolistic industry and a competitive one. Although it has been hypothesized that the monopolist may be in the stronger position when it comes to the incentive and means to innovate, the reverse may also be argued: that a firm has a stronger incentive to innovate if it is in a competitive industry. A monopolist who does not innovate may be missing larger profits, but at least he will have some profits. But, so goes the argument, if the competitive firm does not innovate, its competitors may do so, and it may find itself in a position in which it cannot even keep up with its competitors, thus incurring bankruptcy and liquidation.

If you are tempted to choose one side or the other in this debate, remember that, although theory is useful in posing alternative

8. Schumpeter, *Capitalism, Socialism, and Democracy*, p. 106.

9. This charge was a basic element in the antitrust case against the United Shoe Machinery Corporation in 1957. This company had a virtual monopoly on shoe-making machinery in the U.S. It leased its machines to shoe manufacturers. The company had a huge array of patents, which, it was charged, it simply held to prevent competitors from developing their own machines.

possibilities, estimating the effects of monopoly and competition on efficiency and innovation is an empirical matter that can be achieved only by an appeal to real-world observations. This appeal can be made only after the question has been stated in a manner sufficiently precise so that it is capable of being answered.

An Example of the Decline and Fall of a Patent Monopoly: Ball-Point Pens[10]

In 1945, Milton Reynolds acquired a patent on a new type of pen that used a ball bearing in place of a conventional point, He formed the Reynolds International Pen Company, capitalized at $26,000, and began production on October 6, 1945.

The Reynolds pen was introduced with a good deal of fanfare by Gimbels, who guaranteed that the pen would write for two years without refilling. The price was set at $12.50 (the maximum price allowed by the wartime Office of Price Administration). Gimbels sold 10,000 pens on October 29, 1945, the first day they were on sale. In the early stages of production, the cost of production was estimated to be around 80¢ per pen.

The Reynolds International Pen Company quickly expanded production. By early 1946, it employed more than 800 people in its factory and was producing 30,000 pens per day. By March, 1946, it had $3 million in the bank. Demand was intense.

Macy's, Gimbels' traditional rival, introduced an imported ball-point pen from South America. Its price was $19.98 (production costs unknown).

The heavy sales quickly elicited a response from other pen manufacturers. Eversharp in-troduced its first model in April, at $15. In July, 1946, *Fortune* reported that Schaeffer was planning to put out a pen at $15, and Eversharp announced its plans to produce a "retractable" model priced at $25. Reynolds introduced a new model, but kept the price at $12.50. Costs were estimated at 60¢ per pen.

The first signs of trouble emerged. The Ball-point Pen Company of Hollywood (disregarding a patent infringement suit) put a $9.95 model on the market, and a manufacturer named David Kahn announced plans to introduce a pen selling for less than $3. *Fortune* reported fear of an impending price war in view of the growing number of manufacturers and the low cost of production. In October, Reynolds introduced a new model, priced at $3.85, that cost about 30¢ to produce.

By Christmas, 1946, approximately 100 manufacturers were in production, some of them selling pens for as little as $2.98. By February, 1947, Gimbels was selling a ball-point pen made by the Continental Pen Company for 98¢. Reynold's introduced a new model priced to sell at $1.69, but Gimbels sold it for 88¢ in a price war with Macy's. Reynolds felt betrayed by Gimbels. Reynolds introduced a new model listed at 98¢. By this

---

10. A fascinating and highly readable account of some aspects of the ball-point case is Thomas Whiteside's "Where Are They Now?," *The New Yorker*, February 17, 1951. Our discussion leans heavily on Mr. Whiteside's article.

time ball-point pens had become economy items rather than luxury items, but still were highly profitable.

In mid-1948, ball-point pens were selling for as little as 39¢, and costing about 10¢ to produce. In 1951, prices of 25¢ were common. In 1965, there was a wide variety of models and prices, ranging from 11¢ to $2.95, and the market appeared stable, orderly, and only moderately profitable. Ball-point pens were no passing fad, as every reader of this book knows. Their introduction has fundamentally changed the writing-implement industry in America and in the world.

The ball-point pen example has interested observers in many fields. Lawyers have been concerned about the ease with which patent rights were circumvented. Psychologists have noted the enormous appeal of a new product even at prices that seemed very high. Advertising men have regarded it as a classic case of clever promotion.

From the point of view of economic theory, it illustrates several things:

1. that a monopoly (in this case a patent monopoly) can in the short run charge prices not remotely equal to costs and earn enormous profits;

2. that entry of new firms (even in the face of obstacles) will often occur in response to high profits;

3. that where it does occur, entry will in time drive prices down to a level more nearly equal to the costs of production and distribution; and

4. that the lag between an original monopoly and its subsequent erosion by entry may nevertheless be long enough that the profits to the innovator, as well as to some of the imitators, may be very large indeed. (It is estimated that Reynolds earned profits as high as $500,000 *in a single month*—or about 20 times its original investment.)

Different observers might stress different aspects of the evidence sketched in this example. Some would see it as an example of power of competition in stimulating production of a desired commodity and ultimately making it available at low cost to the consumer. Others would see it as evidence of the ability of monopoly to exploit the gullible public. Still others would see it as an example of the great incentive that capitalism provides to the successful innovator (or promoter) to find and introduce a new product. All would be, to a degree, right.

Summary

On the basis of positive economics, it is easy to show that if costs are not affected and if the nature of the product is not affected by whether production is conducted in a monopolized industry or a competitive one, then price will be higher and output lower under monopoly than under competition. We have briefly examined one of these "ifs"—that costs are unaffected—and found that there are theoret-

ical reasons why costs might well be different *because of* the form of organization. Similar arguments showing that the variety and quality of product produced may differ can also be made, but we will not do so here.[11] It is sufficient for our purposes to have shown that, even in terms of the effect on price and quantity, no unambiguous prediction emerges from the theory. On many crucial points, we have

11. An example that bears on this issue is developed in Chapter 29 below.

no accepted theory at all, and, on other points, existing theory has been inadequately tested. It is obviously necessary to keep an open mind on the subject and to admit that, on the basis of existing theory, it is impossible to make out an overwhelming case for the specific ways in which market results of monopoly will differ from those of competition. Everyone will have his own guess, hunch, or prejudice on the subject—often based on bits of personal experience. But, as economists, we are interested in carefully documented, objective evidence; and on these grounds a great deal remains to be discovered, even at an elementary level, about the comparison of the effects of monopoly with those of competition.

As to the normative side, we cannot expect economics to decide whether one form of market organization is better than another until the *goals* we are seeking to achieve have been specified. Everyone will have his own views on this normative issue. Economists as a group (just as doctors or plumbers as groups) may have a majority opinion as to what appropriate goals are, but this opinion is a value judgment, not a scientific fact.

QUESTIONS FOR DISCUSSION

1. "The patent laws should be revised so as to prevent monopolistic abuse of the patent grant without destroying the incentive to innovate." Suppose you had to propose such a reformulation. What would you want your new law to provide for and what information might you want first?

2. State the classic case against monopoly as provided in this chapter. Is it sufficient to convince you of the value of antitrust laws? What other considerations pro and con occur to you?

3. Have you noticed anything over the years with regard to the advertising of ball-point pens?

4. Two economists (Armen Alchian and Ruben Kessel) have advanced a case for the proposi-tion that monopolists choose to satisfy more of their nonpecuniary aims than do perfect competitors. (Discrimination in hiring is included as one of the nonpecuniary motives.) One of the reasons for this behavior might be that monopolists cannot risk adopting complete profit-maximizing behavior for fear of arousing the wrath of the Attorney General. Alchian and Kessel suggest several possible tests for their theory. Can you think of any?

5. Would the case against monopoly be stronger or weaker in a society in which there was not, and could not be, any technological innovation, or in a society in which innovation and change were a large source of a rise in living standards from generation to generation?

Chapter **27** MONOPOLY AND COMPETITION IN AMERICA

IN THE FOUR PRECEDING CHAPTERS WE HAVE dealt with two basic theories, perfect competition and monopoly. Do these two theories provide a sufficient basis for the predictions that we wish to make about price and market behavior in the real economy? Forty years ago, most economists would have said Yes; today, most would say No, although the matter is still subject to debate. Those who say No must reply in the negative to *all three* of the following questions:

1. Do the abstractions of competition and monopoly adequately describe the forms of market organization found in the real world?

2. Are actual forms of market organization, however different in many ways from these abstractions, sufficiently similar in their behavior that we can approximate their behavior by using models of either perfect competition or monopoly to represent them?

3. Are more complicated forms of market organization, which are analytically different from either competition or monopoly, readily understood as simple mixtures of these two kinds of market organization?

If the answer to the first question were Yes, the predictions of Chapters 25 and 26 would apply immediately to the real world. If the answer is No, we could not conclude that they do not apply; instead we must move to the second question. It is the business of science to abstract from reality, and it might well be that descriptively unrealistic models were analytically adequate to make predictions that were confirmed by observations. Even if the second question is answered negatively—if there are situations in which the predictions of neither perfect competition nor monopoly are confirmed—it may be that we can analyze a situation that is, say, monopolistic in such and such ways, but competitive in all others.[1]

The first question is discussed in this chapter. The second and third questions concern predictive accuracy, and are deferred until Chapters 28 and 29. The reason is that ac-

1. Consider an analogy. Can a dry martini (three parts gin, one part dry vermouth in a popular recipe) be fully analyzed if one understands the chemical properties of gin and of vermouth? This is an empirical matter that depends upon whether mixing them together produces (on the one hand) an averaging of their properties or (on the other hand) a chemical interaction that makes the mixture different from the average of its parts. Every student of chemistry knows that some mixtures blend and that others produce reactions.

curacy in prediction is relative: Almost any theory predicts some things correctly, and no theory is always correct. Since science is concerned with being as nearly correct as possible, the real test of a theory is how well it performs in relation to competing theories. In Chapters 28 and 29, we introduce competing theories and compare them with the theories of perfect competition and monopoly.

Structure of the American Economy[2]

At first glance, it is relatively easy to divide American industries into two broad groups, those with a very large number of relatively small firms and those with a very few relatively large firms. The first group includes most agricultural production, most services (barbers, lawyers, plumbers, television repairmen, etc.), most trade (stores, gas stations, wholesalers, etc.), most mining industries (especially coal), most of construction, and many other individual industries. Somewhere between 40 percent and 50 percent of the national product of the economy comes from sectors of the economy that are predominantly characterized by a large number of small firms.

About an equal percentage of national product arises in the second group, which is characterized by a few very large firms. (About 12 percent of national product originates in the government rather than the private sector.) Indeed, the names of these firms are part of the average citizen's vocabulary. In this category fall most of transportation (e.g., the Pennsylvania Railroad, the New York Central, the Santa Fe, United Airlines, American Airlines, TWA, Greyhound); communi-

cations (AT&T, NBC, CBS, Western Union); public utilities (American Electric Power, Consolidated Edison); and much of the largest sector of the American economy, manufacturing.

These two broad groups do not, when examined more closely, fit the models of competition and monopoly. Indeed, it is extraordinarily difficult to find more than isolated examples of industries for which either perfect competition or monopoly provide reasonable descriptions.

The essential aspects of competition are that firms act as price-takers and that free entry and exit of firms force price to the level of minimum average cost. Agriculture in most ways seems to fit fairly well. The individual farmer is clearly a price-taker, entry into farming is easy, and exit is possible though not really very rapid. Agricultural prices in the U.S., however, are not left to the workings of the competitive market alone, but are heavily influenced by governmental policies. The coal industry, often cited as competitive, is plagued by the very severe problem of the difficulty of exit of firms. In the retail trades and services, most firms think

---

2. This is, of course, a subject on which many books have been written. One of the best is Leonard W. Weiss, *Economics and American Industry* (John Wiley, 1961). Somewhat more advanced but within range of the undergraduate is Joe S. Bain, *Industrial Organization* (John Wiley, 1959). In this section we present only a very few highlights.

they have some influence over prices—the local grocer (or supermarket or discount house or department store) not only considers his "weekend specials" (or "sales") crucial to his success, but spends a good deal of money advertising his prices. The competitive model does quite well in describing some industries whose major business is exchange rather than production. The New York Stock Exchange is a notable example, and commodity exchanges are very similar. But, all in all, the competitive model does not *describe* very much of the American economy. Whether it explains more behavior than it describes will be discussed at a later point.

Examples of pure monopoly are almost as hard to find. The essential aspects of monopoly are that the monopolist can act as if the market demand curve is substantially the same as his own demand curve and that he is protected from new entry. In transportation and public utilities, it is not hard to find examples of monopolies, but these are precisely the natural monopolies where public regulation of prices occurs. Telephone and telegraph rates are reviewed and approved by the Federal Communications Commission, railroad rates by the Interstate Commerce Commission, and rates of electric power producers by various state and local regulatory commissions.

Examples of nearly perfect monopoly out-side of the regulated areas are few. The Aluminum Company of America (ALCOA) was the sole producer of primary aluminum in the United States from 1893 until World War II.[3] Even during this period, however, some aluminum was imported from Canada and some aluminum scrap was reprocessed, thus giving ALCOA less than complete control over supply. Nevertheless, ALCOA and a few other companies have all been reasonably accurately described as monopolies.[4]

The great bulk of the unregulated "large firm" sector of the economy fits a different mold, as Tables 1 and 2 point out.

Table 1 presents concentration ratios showing the market share of the *four* largest firms in thirty major manufacturing industries for 1954. All but one of these industries had shipments in excess of $1 billion in 1954. Together they accounted for about 40 percent of the value of shipments in manufacturing. (The dollar values will have changed since 1954, but the concentration ratios will not have changed very much.) Few of these industries are adequately described by either of the models described so far. The competitive model conceivably fits the three or four industries at the bottom of the list, but even here there are doubts.[5] At the other end of the scale, in both aluminum and automobiles, the very high concentration is achieved by three or four firms in apparently vigorous rivalry with one

3. The need for aluminum during World War II led the government to build up aluminum capacity. The postwar disposal of this capacity played a major role in the entry of Reynolds Aluminum and Kaiser Metals as new producers.

4. The United Shoe Machinery Company had a monopoly on certain types of shoe machinery until antitrust decrees limited its exercise of monopoly power. The National Cash Register Company, the International Nickel Company, the Climax Molybdenum Company, and IBM all had at one time or another control over more than 90 percent of the output of the industries in which they operated.

5. Style considerations play some role in women's clothing, and many manufacturers think of themselves as having some control over price. Sawmills and commercial printing establishments, while very numerous nationally, operate in small regional and local markets in which there is a small number of sellers in direct rivalry with one another, none of whom regards himself as a price-taker.

Primary aluminum	99
Passenger cars, knocked down or assembled	98
Cigarettes	82
Tin cans and other tinware	80
Synthetic fibers	79
Tires and inner tubes	78
Tractors	67
Aircraft	55
Hot rolled sheet and strip	53
Copper rolling and drawing	52
Electric motors and generators	48
Plastic materials	45
Meat-packing products	39
Flour and meal	38
Farm machinery, except tractors	36
Petroleum refining	32
Footwear, except rubber	30
Pulp	29
Canned fruits and vegetables	28
Beer and ale	27
Fluid milk	21
Paper and paper board	19
Bread and related products	19
Newspapers	19
Machine tools	18
Cotton broad-woven fabrics	17
Commercial printing	9
Sawmills and planing mills	6
Dresses, unit price	5
Women's suits, coats, and skirts	3

[a] The concentration ratios given here show the share of the four leading firms in total shipments of the products of the industry in question. Total shipments include quantities shipped by firms that produce that product only incidentally, as well as by those that make it their main business.

SOURCE: *Concentration in American Industry*, Report of the Subcommittee on Antitrust and Monopoly, Committee of the Judiciary, U.S. Senate, 85th Cong., 1st Sess., 1957, Table 37.

another. That these firms have appreciable market power is undoubted; that they may be described by our monopoly model is more questionable. The dominant pattern, which we shall call *oligopoly*, is that in which firms have enough market power that they may not be regarded as price-takers (as in perfect competition), but are subject to enough rivalry that they cannot consider the market demand curve as their own. Further, in most of these cases, entry is neither perfectly easy nor wholly blockaded.[6] A second pattern, which we shall call *monopolistic competition*, deals with cases in which, despite relatively easy conditions of entry, product differences give the firms some feeling that they can have something to say about prices.

Table 2 shows the distribution of all 434 manufacturing industries covered by the 1954 Census of Manufacturers according to the four-firm concentration ratios. These data lend further support to the importance of intermediate categories in the American economy. More than 50 percent of all shipments originate in industries in which the four largest firms control between one quarter and three-quarters of the total. Further, most of the industries that are in the least concentrated class turn out upon examination to be poorly represented by the perfectly competitive model (although that is not shown in the table).

In summary, then, the answer to the first question is negative: The models of perfect competition and monopoly do not adequately describe the industrial structure of the United States economy. We must now look to the second question.

6. An example of the difficulty of entering an oligopolistic industry is the unsuccessful attempt of Henry Kaiser to become established as an automobile manufacturer. Kaiser-Frazer entered the industry in 1945, suffered staggering losses, and quietly withdrew.

TABLE 2 THE NUMBER AND IMPORTANCE OF MANUFACTURING INDUSTRIES WITH VARIOUS
DEGREES OF CONCENTRATION, 1954

Concentration ratio (percent)[a]	Number of industries listed by the census	Total value of shipments, 1954 (billions of dollars)	Percentage of total shipments of all manufacturing industries
75–100	40	16.4	7.8
50– 75	101	35.2	16.7
25– 50	157	74.5	35.3
0– 25	136	84.7	40.2
TOTAL	434	210.8	100.0

[a] Market share of the four largest firms.
SOURCE: *Concentration in American Industry,* Report of the Subcommittee on Antitrust and Monopoly, Committee on the Judiciary, U.S. Senate, 85th Cong., 1st Sess., 1957, Table 17.

Summary

1. It is argued that the abstractions of competition and monopoly do not adequately describe the forms of market organization found in the United States.

2. We cannot be sure, however, that alternative models will explain the real-world behavior we observe any better than do the simple models of monopoly and competition. In order to see whether or not this is the case, we shall examine in the next chapters the theories of two different market forms: *oligopoly* and *monopolistic competition.*

QUESTIONS FOR DISCUSSION

1. Is it sufficient to dismiss the abstractions of the previous chapters because of the lack of "realism" of their assumptions? Why or why not?

2. Entry into and exit from farming are both possible; there are as many individual sellers as you could possibly want; and products are homogeneous and easily graded. Why then do we say that the behavior of American farming in the 1950s and 1960s is not the best example of perfectly competitive behavior?

3. What is the mold into which most non-regulated large-firm industries fit?

Chapter **28** COMPETITION AMONG THE MANY: MONOPOLISTIC COMPETITION VERSUS PERFECT COMPETITION

"THERE'S A DRUGSTORE ON EVERY CORNER." So goes a key line in the play *Brother Rat*. This is only a slight exaggeration in many big cities where there are more drugstores than are required to meet the needs of the population. Most of these stores could handle more business than they get. On the shelves of each drugstore are a half-dozen or more brands of aspirin, each of which is identical to all the others, except for the label, the package, and the price. Most cities and most highways have many more gas stations than are needed to provide all the cars on the highway with fast and effective service. Walk into almost any supermarket and count the number of different brands of toilet paper. Notice that, although price, packaging, and quality differ, every brand is selected by at least some customers.

These phenomena, as well as the very large role played in American life by advertising and "salesmanship," have led many economists to seek a theoretical model for markets that are characterized by a large number of firms selling similar but differentiated products, with much effort devoted to *nonprice competition*.[1] The theory of *monopolistic competition* is just such a model. In the first section of this chapter, we consider the theory; in the second section, we compare its predictions with those of the theory of perfect competition.

The Theory of Monopolistic Competition

Consider an industry in which there are a large number of producers with free entry into and exit from the industry, but in which each producer sells a differentiated product —a product that varies somewhat from those sold by his competitors. In the soup industry,

1. Nonprice competition means competition in product quality, labeling, advertising, and so forth.

for example, there might be a large number of competing firms selling rather similar but by no means identical products. Each soup differs in physical composition from competing products; each has a different packaging, and, as the advertisers say, each has a different brand image from its competitors. Such an industry is said to be *monopolistically competitive* (or *imperfectly competitive*). The terms monopolistic competition and imperfect competition describe a situation similar to perfect competition, with the single important difference that each producer sells a product somewhat different from the product sold by his competitors.

The fact that the product is differentiated between firms means that each firm does not face a perfectly elastic demand curve for its products. If we were to construct a demand curve for a soup firm showing how much it can sell at various prices, we would have to draw it *on the assumption that competing firms would not vary their prices*. If the firm should raise its price, it would lose customers to its competitors, but it would not lose all of its customers, because it would not make the mistake of raising the price more than slightly above those of its competitors. Many people prefer a particular soup *for* its differences and will continue to prefer it even though it becomes somewhat more expensive. As it raises its prices above those of similar products, the firm can expect, however, that fewer and fewer customers will persist in buying this good. On the other hand, if it lowers its price to a level below that charged by its competitors, the firm can expect to attract customers. Remember, however, that we observe that not everyone is attracted by a small price differential. Thus the firm will be faced with a downward-sloping demand curve for its product. Generally, the less differentiated the product is from its competi-

tors, the more elastic this curve will be. (If there is no differentiation, the demand curve will be perfectly elastic, because, if the firm raises its price even slightly above the price of the competing products, it will lose all of its customers, whereas, if it decreases its price even slightly below those of its competitors, it will attract *all* of the competitors' customers.)

In Figure 1, we depict a firm with a downward-sloping, but rather elastic, demand curve for its product. On the basis of the theory outlined in Chapter 19, the firm is as-

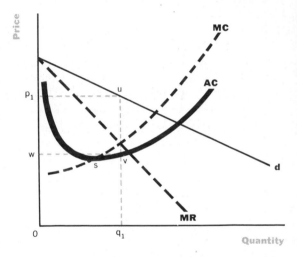

FIGURE 1   THE SHORT-RUN EQUILIBRIUM OF A FIRM IN MONOPOLISTIC COMPETITION

sumed to have a U-shaped, short-run cost curve. The short-run equilibrium of the firm is exactly the same as that of a monopolist. The firm is not a passive price-taker; it may juggle price and quantity until profits are maximized, at output Oq_1 and price Op_1 in the figure.

What about the long-run equilibrium of the industry? The firm that we have shown in Figure 1 is earning profits $(= p_1uvw)$; there-

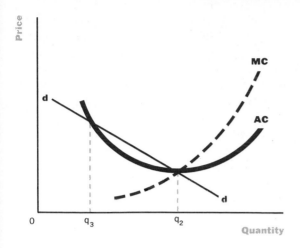

FIGURE 2

curve shifts to the position indicated in Figure 2, in which the average revenue curve intersects the average total cost curve at the point of lowest average cost. Will this do? Surely, if the firm produces output at Oq_2, it will just cover costs. But, if it restricts output below Oq_2, it will increase average revenue more than average costs and, hence, will move into a range of output at which profits can be earned. In Figure 2, zero profits are earned at outputs Oq_2 and Oq_3, but profits are earned at any output between these levels. We have not yet found an equilibrium in which the profit-maximizing firm will be earning only normal profits.

If we are in the situation shown in Figure 2, a new firm will be able to earn profits, and expansion of the industry will continue. The

fore, if this firm is typical of the others in the industry, there will be an incentive for new firms to enter the industry. As more firms enter, the total demand for the product must be shared among this larger number of firms so that each can expect to have a smaller share of the market. At any given price, each firm can expect to sell less than it could before the influx of new firms. Thus, the demand curve for the firm's product will shift to the left. This movement will continue for as long as there are profits. Profits provide an attraction for new firms to enter, and the industry will continue to expand.

Before reading further, make a genuine effort to see if you can discover for yourself the final equilibrium position. Start from Figure 1 and observe that, as new firms enter the industry, the demand curve (d) facing our one firm will shift to the left. Also observe that this will continue until there are no further profits. What will be the position of the final equilibrium?

Assume, to begin with, that the demand

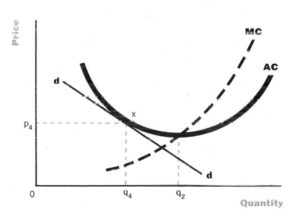

FIGURE 3   **THE LONG-RUN EQUILIBRIUM OF A FIRM IN MONOPOLISTIC COMPETITION**

final position will be that indicated in Figure 3. The average revenue curve touches the average cost curve at only one point, point x corresponding to quantity Oq_4 and price Op_4. The average revenue curve is *tangent* to the average cost curve at point x. When output is at Oq_4, normal profits are just being earned, since average revenue equals average total costs. At any other level of output, profits would be negative, since average revenue is less than average total cost.[2]

A zero-profit equilibrium is possible, we see, under conditions of monopolistic competition, in spite of the fact that the individual firm is faced with a downward-sloping demand curve. Each firm is forced into a position in which it has *excess capacity*. The firm in Figure 3 could expand its output from Oq_4 to Oq_2 and reduce average costs, but it does not make use of this productive capacity because to do so would be to reduce average revenue even more than average costs. If the demand curve *cuts* the average total cost curve, as in Figure 2, it is always possible to make profits by producing in the range over which the demand curve lies above the cost curve. An equilibrium in which only normal profits are possible requires that the demand curve should just be tangent to the average total cost curve; this, in turn, implies that in equilibrium the firm will have some unused capacity (equal to q_4q_2 in Figure 3).

WHAT DOES THE THEORY PREDICT?

The theory we have developed rests upon four assumptions:

1. Firms maximize profits.
2. Firms make price and output decisions

on the basis of downward-sloping *ceteris paribus* demand curves that neglect the effect of a price change by the firm on the prices of other sellers.

3. The demand curves are downward-sloping because of the fact that the products are differentiated.[3]

4. There is free entry and exit of firms.

The implications of this theory, which we shall treat as hypotheses about the way some markets behave, differ from those of perfect competition in two respects: The first implication is that:

1. *The equilibrium output of the firm occurs at an output less than the one at which average total cost is a minimum. (This is known technically as the excess-capacity theorem.)*

This implication follows directly from the assumptions of the theory. Free entry pushes firms to the point at which the demand curve is tangent to the average total cost curve. But, if the demand curve slopes downward, such a tangency must, mathematically, be in the declining portion of the curve.†

Potentially, this is one of the most important insights in the whole theory of the firm. It says that a long-run normal-profit equilibrium can occur even though each firm is like a monopolist in the sense of having a downward-sloping demand curve. It will occur because so many firms, attracted by profits,

---

2. Although the marginal revenue curve has not been drawn in the figure, it is clear that the MR curve must equal the MC curve at output Oq_4.

3. Buyers are supposed to think in such terms as: "I *prefer* Del Monte peaches"; "I *trust* Mr. Green, even if he is a bit more expensive"; and "Isn't that the brand Rock Hudson uses?"

† Proof: Two curves that are tangent have the same slope at the point of tangency. But the demand curve slopes downward by assumption; therefore, average total cost must also slope downward.

will enter the industry that the individual firms will be unable to utilize all of the capacity at their command.[4] The theory predicts that industries in monopolistic competition will exhibit a continual tendency toward excess capacity. It also predicts that prices will be higher than they would have been under perfect competition, and that price will be greater than marginal cost. These are real differences between the theories of perfect competition and monopolistic competition. If one is interested in making predictions about tendencies for capacity utilization, the theories need to be tested in order to establish which one of them provides more accurate predictions about the real world.

Although literally dozens of well-known articles both attacking and defending this theorem on *a priori* grounds exist, we do not know of even one article reporting an empirical attempt to test these predictions. (We shall suggest a reason soon.)

The second implication is that:

2. *It may pay the monopolistically competitive firm to engage in nonprice competition of a kind that it would not pay it to use in perfect competition.*

To see that this is an implication of the theory, recall that a firm in perfect competition can sell as much as it wants to at the going price and that it regards itself as a price-taker. Therefore, it does not pay it to spend money to increase the amount it can sell. But, in monopolistic competition, expenditures on product differentiation, product quality, or advertising can change the slope or shift to the right the demand curve of the seller. Expenditures on advertising and other forms of nonprice competition may increase short-run profits.[5] We are thus led to the prediction that *industries characterized by the conditions of monopolistic competition will be found to engage in nonprice competition, whereas those in perfect competition will not.*

The Great Debate

A great debate exists between the devotees and critics of the theory of monopolistic competition. The devotees call the theory a "revolution" of major importance; the critics say: "In the general case, [the theory does not help us to] make a single statement about the economic events in the world we sought to analyze."[6]

The student may find it hard to understand why such a debate exists. After all, he will say, the two theories make different predictions. Surely, one or the other must predict

---

4. The example of the barbers discussed on pages 291–294 had exactly this result.

5. It can be formally shown that there is a connection between the elasticity of a firm's demand curve and the profit-maximizing amounts of advertising, product differentiation, and quality improvement. Thus it will pay the firm to engage in these activities if it can affect the elasticity of the demand curve in certain ways. These propositions are proved in R. Dorfman and P. O. Steiner, "Optimal Advertising and Optimal Quality," *American Economic Review,* December, 1954.

6. The first quotation is from Robert L. Bishop, "Monopolistic Competition After Thirty Years: The Impact on General Theory," *American Economic Review*, May, 1964, p. 33. The second is from George Stigler, *Five Lectures on Economic Problems* (Longmans, Green, 1948), p. 18.

more accurately. It is a legitimate point. Part of the trouble is that it is difficult to get the two sides to agree on a fair test. An imaginary dialogue between them might run this way:

S: "I defend the theory of perfect competition. I am interested in such things as how a change in demand, or costs, or taxes will affect the behavior of the industry. Both theories lead me to the same predictions. Therefore, I am content to use the theory of perfect competition."

B: "That may be, but I am interested in the presence of excess capacity in an industry. I can find cases of excess capacity; therefore I am not satisfied with perfect competition."

S: "How do you measure excess capacity anyway? How do you know you are not observing disequilibrium?"

B: "Consider the case of the barbers [see above, pp. 291–294], who everyone knows have excess capacity."

S: "A good case, indeed! But it is not monopolistic competition. It is a clear case of a perfectly competitive industry that changed when the barbers started to act like monopolists. The case of the barbers is a case of monopoly with free entry, and we do not need a new theory to explain that. The barbers *knew* that they could not neglect the price adjustments of other barbers; therefore they got together and fixed prices."

B: "All right. Explain then why there are so many brands of aspirin."

S: "Because people are just not correctly informed; they do not all know that all aspirin is the same. If people are ignorant or misin-

formed, we cannot predict their behavior perfectly with either theory."

B: "Does not the great amount of advertising impress you at all?"

S: "It depresses me; it doesn't impress me. Most of it is done by automobile companies, cigarette companies, soap companies, and so on, each of which has very few sellers and all of which fit neither perfect nor monopolistically competitive theories."

B: "Name me a perfectly competitive industry."

S: "Name me a monopolistically competitive industry."

There are two points in this imaginary dialogue that deserve emphasis. To see the first one, consider a popular example of monopolistic competition: the market for soaps and detergents. Among the well-known brands are Ivory, Dash, Joy, Comet, Cascade, Camay, Lava, Duz, Tide, Cheer, Dreft, Oxydol, Spic 'n' Span, and Zest. Surely this is impressive differentiation—and the fact that most of the names are familiar to the reader is impressive evidence of the advertising on their behalf.[7] On first glance, this might appear to be a perfect example of monopolistic competition. But, *every one* of the products named above is manufactured by a single company, Procter and Gamble, which alone accounts for more than half of the national sales of soaps, cleansers, and detergents.[8] Will Procter and Gamble really believe that if it lowers its prices Lever Brothers will not lower its? Does the soap industry exhibit only normal profits and have free entry? The answers

---

7. The radio and television serials whose commercials extol their virtues are, after all, called soap operas.

8. The three-firm concentration ratio exceeds 80 percent. We owe this illustration to J. W. Markham's article in the *American Economic Review,* May, 1964, p. 54. His point is that the multiproduct *firm* is not the multiproduct industry of monopolistic competition, and that we may well require a different theory to explain its behavior.

are negative. The fact that the theory of monopolistic competition is consistent with nonprice competition does not mean that the presence of nonprice competition is due to monopolistically competitive behavior.[9]

The above example also suggests the second point we wish to emphasize: Since neither monopolistic nor perfect competition is designed to explain all market structures, neither theory can be refuted by demonstrating that it does not apply in a particular situation.

It is not possible to resolve this debate in this book. So meager has been the empirical testing of the predictions of these theories that the case for one as against the other cannot be said to be established. They may both be useful, in different cases. They may indeed be in conflict on some issues; and if they are, then they are in principle testable.[10] But testing will require more effort than has so far been expended on it. Some economists, feeling that this debate will never be resolved, combine the two theories into what may be called *atomistic competition*, a theory whose central assumptions are, first, that sellers always perceive their demand curve to be much flatter than it really is (because they neglect parallel actions of other sellers), and, second, that there is free entry and exit. This theory embraces both perfect and monopolistic competition.

MONOPOLISTIC COMPETITION AFTER THIRTY YEARS

Monopolistic competition, as a theory, is more than thirty years old.[11] Its survival over so long a period cannot be explained by the number of tested and confirmed predictions, for there are few of them so far.

Whatever may be the outcome of the debate on the predictive value of monopolistic competition, there can be little doubt that it has contributed two important things to the development of the subject: At the time that it was first developed, perfect competition was under severe attack because of the lack of realism of its assumptions. The theory of monopolistic competition recognized the facts of product differentiation, the ability of firms to influence prices, and advertising. By incorporating all of these new assumptions into a new theory, economists were encouraged to consider the question of their effect on the operation of the price system. Also, by showing that such dramatic changes in the assumptions might not affect the predictions of the theory, economists have become a little more sceptical of attacks based solely on assertions that the assumptions of their theories are unrealistic.[12]

The second major contribution of the theory is that many economists have been profoundly influenced by it. It has served to call attention to the potential importance of

---

9. We have met this point of logic before. In general, the point is that if *A* is a sufficient reason for the existence of *B*, the observation that *B* exists does not imply that *A* must exist, since there may be sufficient reasons for *B's* existence that do not include *A*. See pages 255–256.

10. G. C. Archibald has made a strong case that monopolistic competition does not produce any predictions that conflict with the predictions of perfect competition that we are likely to be able to test. See his "Chamberlin *versus* Chicago," *Review of Economic Studies,* October, 1961. This article can be read only by advanced students because of the mathematical techniques used to develop the argument.

11. The two basic books on the subject were first published in 1933, one on each side of the Atlantic: E. H. Chamberlin, *The Theory of Monopolistic Competition* (Harvard University Press, 1933); and Joan Robinson, *The Economics of Imperfect Competition* (Macmillan, 1933).

12. See pages 19–24.

the extent to which the sellers recognize that they are interdependent, the extent to which entry is free, and the nature of the product. These things were freed, by the theory of monopolistic competition, from the polar models of monopoly and competition. This has led to the development of other impor-

tant models that we shall discuss in Chapter 29.

The major impact of the theory of monopolistic competition has been in changing the way economists think about problems of market behavior. This impact has been particularly noticeable in the field of oligopoly.

Summary

1. The theory of monopolistic competition is meant to apply to those markets that are characterized by a large number of firms selling similar but differentiated products, with much effort devoted to nonprice competition.

2. The theory is based on four assumptions: firms seek to maximize profits; they make price and output decisions on the basis of downward-sloping demand curves; they face these downward-sloping curves in spite of having numerous competitors because their products are somewhat differentiated from those of all other competitors; there is freedom of entry and exit.

3. The implications of this theory differ from those of perfect competition in two major respects. The first important implication is that the equilibrium of the firm occurs at an output less than the one at which aver-

age total cost is a minimum. (This is called the excess-capacity theorem.) From this it follows immediately that the monopolistically competitive price will exceed marginal cost and will also exceed the competitive price. The second important implication is that it may pay the monopolistically competitive firm to engage in forms of nonprice competition that it would not pay a perfectly competitive firm to use.

4. There has been a great deal of debate in the past thirty years over the relative applicability of the two models. Part of the difficulty in deciding between the two views lies in getting each side to agree on what constitutes a fair test. Another point is that, since neither model is meant to apply to all market structures, neither can be rejected as being inapplicable just because we find a case to which it does not apply.

QUESTIONS FOR DISCUSSION

1. In many states "fair trade" laws allow manufacturers to set prices below which their goods may not be sold. Most of the goods sold by drugstores come under fair-trade agreements where such agreements are allowed. Entry into the retail drug industry is rather free. What do you predict about the amount of idle time, the

amount of business per store, and the propensity to engage in nonprice competition (such as free delivery) in fair-trade as opposed to non-fair-trade states?

2. Continue the dialogue between *B* and *S* on page 318, assuming that we have found more

excess capacity in the drugstores in fair-trade states as opposed to non-fair-trade states.

3. Some people claim that small grocery stores are an example of firms in a situation of monopolistic competition; others claim that they are firms in a perpetually "sick" though perfectly competitive industry. The latter contend that people habitually overestimate their chances of success in the industry. How might you go about deciding between these two theories?

4. As a further example of the grocery-store dispute, set up a model of the acting profession along the lines suggested for grocery stores. (You must, of course, include *all* actors, not just the stars.)

5. Has the discussion of the theory of monopolistic competition changed your opinion of the theory of perfect competition?

6. In what ways is the retail filling-station industry monopolistically competitive and in what ways is it perfectly competitive? Can you think of any of the predictions of either theory that would be refuted by the behavior of the firms in this industry?

Chapter **29** COMPETITION AMONG THE FEW: OLIGOPOLY VERSUS MONOPOLY

THE WORD OLIGOPOLY COMES FROM THE Greek and means, in rough translation, "few sellers." Oligopoly is often described as "competition among the few."[1] The basic behavioral assumption about oligopoly is that the firms in an oligopolistic industry recognize that they are interdependent. They recognize that anything they do will probably lead to a reaction by *rival* sellers. Rival is the key word. Monopolists, on the other hand, have no close rivals.[2] Although firms in either perfect or monopolistic competition recognize

that other sellers exist, they do not engage in any personal rivalry with them. The oligopolistic firm's policy depends on how it *thinks* its rivals will react to its moves, and the outcome of the firm's policy depends on how they *do* react. In oligopoly, there is no simple set of cost and demand conditions for the equilibrium either of the firm or of the small group of firms that constitute the industry. Neither is there a set of simple predictions about how the firms will react, either individually or collectively, to various

---

1. This is the title of one of the leading treatises on the subject, by William Fellner (Alfred Knopf, 1949).
2. All firms are in a sense rivals in competing for consumers' limited expenditures. When a monopolist changes his price, however, there are no other sellers to react. Thus, the monopolist's *ceteris paribus* demand curve is his actual demand curve.

changes in terms, costs, and demand. Everything depends on the policy one firm pursues, on the policies its rivals pursue, on how each reacts to the others' changes, and on how each *thinks* the others will react.

It is often said that, under these circumstances, price and output are *indeterminate*. Such a statement is misleading, for price and output do, of course, get determined somehow. What is meant by the statement is that, under oligopoly, we need more information than we do under other market forms before we can make any specific predictions about price and output behavior, for this behavior depends on or varies with the strategies adopted by the competitors.

Theories of Oligopoly

How do we go about developing a theory of oligopoly? One way is to *assume* that individual sellers behave in a particular way and to see what follows from the assumption. Economists have done a good bit of this, from 1838 to the present.[3] But the number of possible sets of assumptions about actions, reactions, and repercussions is so great that there can be no hope of exhaustively analyzing all of them.[4] There is no single formal theory of oligopoly; instead there are many proposed special cases.[5]

An alternative to specifying special cases, deducing the behavioral consequences of each, and hoping that they turn out to predict real-world behavior is to attempt to state directly testable predictions about market behavior. Modern oligopoly theory does just this. It does not consist of a large body of formal predictions derived from a well-specified theory, but of a series of propositions out of which, someday, we hope to construct a fully defined theory. The theory of oligopoly is in transition: We have rejected a number of very simple models and are searching for the elements that will produce a more complex theory. Although we cannot enter into a detailed discussion of these elements in this book, we can mention a few of the specific predictions that have been suggested in order to convey some of their flavor.

THE HYPOTHESIS OF QUALIFIED JOINT PROFIT-MAXIMIZATION

The hypothesis of qualified joint profit-maximization may be stated as follows:

Firms that recognize that they are in rivalry with one another will be motivated by two opposing forces, one moving them toward a set of policies that maximize the combined

3. A. A. Cournot, in 1838, made the first known attack on the duopoly (two-sellers) problem. He had each seller always assume that his rival would not change his price. The rival always did, of course. (This sort of quaintness pervades the early attempts to deal with oligopoly.)

4. For a review of the literature and some of the special cases, the student who goes on in economics should consult Fellner, *op cit.*, Chapters II and III.

5. The modern development of the *theory of games,* which is a study of rational strategies in small-group situations, promises to provide an analytical structure suitable for handling a number of cases. *But an analytical technique is only as fruitful as the real-world information it analyzes.* Thus even the most powerful new techniques will be empty without empirical knowledge of how firms do behave in relevant small-group situations. For an entertaining general introduction to game theory, see J. D. Williams, *The Compleat Strategyst* (McGraw-Hill, 1954).

profits of the existing group of sellers. (These are called joint profits.) The other set of tendencies move them away from the joint profit-maximizing position. Both sets of tendencies are associated with observable characteristics of firms, markets, and products, and thus we can make predictions about market behavior on the basis of these characteristics.

This hypothesis explicitly recognizes that the actions of the rivals affect the size of the "pie" as well as its division among them. This is, of course, not surprising, since the group must face a downward-sloping demand curve and, unless the elasticity of this market curve just happens to be unity, total revenue earned by the group will vary as their collective pricing policies vary. If the firms behave as a single firm, they can act as a monopolist and adopt the policy that will maximize their joint profits. If the firms depart from monopoly behavior, they will reduce their joint profits. But it may pay one firm to depart from the joint profit-maximizing position if, by so doing, it can increase its share of the profits. If a firm adopts such a strategy in order to raise its share of the profits, it must balance what it expects to gain by securing a larger *share* against what it expects to lose because there will be a smaller total to go around among all firms. The hypothesis says that there are forces operating on the individual firm that lead it to alter its behavior *toward* the joint profit-maximizing position and other forces that lead it to alter its behavior *away from* the

joint profit-maximizing position. To make the hypothesis testable, we must specify which forces push the firm in which direction.[6]

A few of the hypotheses that have been advanced as explaining and predicting the strengths of the tendencies toward and away from joint profit-maximizing are as follows:

1. The industry will tend to be closer to the joint profit-maximizing position, the greater the degree of *mutual recognition of interdependence*. Mutual recognition of interdependence will tend, other things being equal, to be greater, the smaller the number of sellers, the more nearly equal the sellers are in market shares and in methods of production, and the more nearly identical the products of the sellers.

2. The industry will tend to be closer to the joint profit-maximizing position, the easier it is for firms to reach *tacit agreement.*[7] The ability to reach and abide by tacit agreements will be greater, other things being equal, in a market in which the price that maximizes joint profits is stable or rising rather than falling (since it is easier to get orderly agreements on maintaining or raising prices than on reducing them); the less the degree of uncertainty attached to the firm's estimates of future demands, costs, and other relevant factors; in an industry with a dominant firm rather than in an industry without one; and among firms with similar expectations of the future than among firms with widely differing expectations.

3. The industry will tend to be closer to the joint profit-maximizing position, the greater the *barriers to entry*. This is because

---

6. Notice that if the hypothesis were correct it would explain why the theory of monopoly is not sufficient to predict the market behavior of oligopolies. Monopoly theory predicts full joint profit-maximizing and it cannot predict the extent of departures from it.

7. Tacit agreement is one term for the process by which firms may come to common policies without explicit discussion. Other terms for the same process are *tacit collusion, quasi-agreement, conscious parallel action,* and *implicit coordination.*

stronger barriers to entry give the existing firms more scope to exploit their monopolistic position. Such barriers will tend to be greater, other things being equal, the greater the economies of scale, the greater the brand-name advertising in the past, and the greater the technical complexities of production.

These are only a few of the possible hypotheses concerning the forces moving firms toward or away from the joint profit-maximizing position. Oligopolistic competition can have many aspects other than price competition, and we give below two hypotheses about nonprice competition.

1. Nonprice competition will tend to be more vigorous, the greater the limitation on price competition. The argument here is that firms may well tacitly agree to avoid price cutting in order to avoid expensive and potentially explosive price wars, but that the basic rivalry of the sellers for customers will seek other outlets as firms seek to maintain or improve their market positions.

A price war is a situation in which each of two or more sellers attempts to undersell the other. A classic example occurred in the late 1930s when Macy's announced that it would sell liquor at 6 percent less than a certain rival, and the rival announced that it would meet any price Macy's charged. Before the war was over, prices had fallen to less than 25 percent of their original prices (well below costs) and the rival had gone out of the liquor business. Lines outside of the stores were so long that they caused major traffic problems.

2. Advertising will tend to be greater, the weaker the other barriers to entry of new firms. The argument here is that advertising itself may give an established firm an advantage over potential entrants that is very possibly a crucial deterrent to entry. This possible motive for advertising is greater, the greater the threat of entry.

Some of these hypotheses have been tested, others have not been. But all are subject to empirical testing. When our testing has proceeded to a point where we are reasonably sure which hypotheses are confirmed and which are rejected, it will be much easier to create a comprehensive theory that yields the confirmed ones.

Do We Need a Theory of Oligopoly?

Do the above hypotheses about oligopolistic behavior lead to different predictions about market behavior than the theory of monopoly? Consider three examples.

I. CIGARETTES

The American cigarette industry is one of the most highly concentrated of manufacturing industries. It has three dominant firms: the American Tobacco Company, R. J. Reynolds, and Liggett & Myers. If we were to analyze it using the theory of monopoly, we would predict that the cigarette companies would avoid competing with each other either in buying tobacco or in setting the price of cigarettes. We would also predict substantial profits to persist for many years. These things *have* happened. In an antitrust suit against these three companies, it was shown that they conspired to purchase tobacco in auctions without bidding against each other, and that they followed a uniform high-price policy (high relative to cost) in the finished product.[8]

The profits of these cigarette companies were and remain well above the average for all manufacturing industries. In these respects the theory of monopoly predicts well. But there are other characteristics of the industry that are readily observable and that are not predicted by the theory. The most notable is the enormous expenditure on advertising by each of the companies in every advertising medium. Such expenditure raises costs and lowers profits. It has two aspects: First, it represents intense nonprice competition among the existing sellers who recognize that it does not pay to compete by price cutting, and, second, it represents an attempt to raise barriers against potential competitors. The high cost of establishing a new brand name represents a really substantial barrier to entry. The theory of oligopoly predicts that advertising will occur for these reasons.[9] The theory of monopoly does not predict that it will.[10]

2. STEAM TURBINE GENERATORS

Three electrical manufacturers, General Electric, Westinghouse, and Allis-Chalmers, produce more than 95 percent of all the steam turbine generators in the United States. These three firms were indicted in June, 1960, and charged with having held a series of meetings beginning at least as early as June, 1957, for the purpose of agreeing on prices and sharing the market among themselves. Subsequently each of the firms pleaded guilty. Do we need a theory of oligopoly to explain this behavior, or is the theory of monopoly sufficient? Certainly, the behavior as charged in the indictments is fully consistent with the theory of monopoly. For the period from July, 1957, to May, 1958, the conspiracy apparently succeeded in producing something very close to joint profit-maximizing behavior. Midway in 1958, however, prices fell very drastically in response to a number of factors, and vigorous price competition developed among the sellers.[11] All attempts to stop the price cutting were in vain. Behavior had ceased to be monopolistic. In analyzing the market behavior in this industry, the monopoly model would have led to accurate predictions for one period and to very poor predictions in another period. Simple models that predict with accuracy under some circum-

---

8. A dramatic (and monopolistic) episode occurred in June, 1931, when, in the depths of the Depression and in the face of the lowest tobacco-leaf prices in a quarter of a century, the three big cigarette companies (which then controlled 90 percent of the market between them) all raised their prices. The policy proved spectacularly unsuccessful. Smokers shifted in large numbers to cheaper brands and ultimately prices fell well below the May, 1931, level as the big three tried to regain their market shares. (They have not since achieved as large a share as they held in May, 1931.)

9. Concern over entry on the part of the existing cigarette manufacturers is marked, because there appear to be very few cost or technological advantages for the existing sellers. The plant needed is very small, and cost curves are flat. Thus a small new entrant could produce as cheaply as a large established firm.

10. Some kinds of advertising are consistent with monopoly theory: If a monopolist, through advertising, can change consumers' preferences toward his product in such a way as to shift the demand curve to the right, or make it more inelastic, he may increase revenues by more than the cost of the advertising. But such advertising is product-oriented advertising ("Smoke!"), not brand-name advertising ("Winston tastes good . . ."). It certainly would not pay a monopolist to advertise two of his brands in competition with each other.

11. Among the factors were the threat by the TVA to ask for foreign bids on a turbine generator it required, a slackening of demand, and rumors of antitrust prosecution. Some interesting aspects of the conspiracy are reported in Richard A. Smith, "The Incredible Electrical Conspiracy," *Fortune*, April and May, 1961.

stances but not under others are useful if we know, or can define, the situations in which they will work and those in which they will not work. *But defining these situations is precisely the purpose of more complex or elaborate theories.* For example, if the theory of oligopoly were to tell us that the monopoly model will work well for steam turbine generators in periods of strong demand, but will not work when firms develop excess capacity, it would be useful in itself and would also increase the usefulness of monopoly theory.

3. PRODUCT VARIETY: THE RANGE OF CHOICE

It is sometimes argued that the greater the number of competitors, the greater the opportunity for an individual consumer to have a choice of kind and quality of product. One very interesting case in which oligopoly tends to provide *less* product variety than is provided by either monopoly or atomistic competition is that of radio and television programming. It is important because it suggests that oligopoly is not a mere mixture of competition and monopoly.[12]

Consider a case in which there are two potential television audiences; one group, comprising 80 percent of the total audience, wishes to see a Western; the other group, comprising 20 percent, wishes to see a concert of chamber music. Assume that each individual television station seeks to maximize its own viewing audience.[13] If there is only one station, this station will produce a Western. If a second competing station opens up,

its most profitable policy will be to produce a similar Western on the grounds that having half of the 80 percent audience is still better than having all of the 20 percent audience. A third station would also prefer a third of the large audience to all of the small one. In fact, four stations would be needed before one of the stations could get as large an audience by producing a concert as by providing another Western. Thus, rivalry between two or three stations would tend to produce two or three almost identical Westerns, each competing for its share of the large audience.

A monopoly controlling two stations would not, however, pursue this policy. In order to maximize its total viewing audience, it would produce a Western on one channel and a chamber-music concert on the other. The monopoly might spend more money on preparing the program for the larger audience, but it would not spend money to produce a similar program on its second channel. The optimal policy for its second channel would be to go after the other 20 percent of potential listeners so that, between the two channels, the monopoly would have the largest possible audience. In each case, the individual firm tries to maximize its own viewing audience, but, when there are two competing stations, they both go after the same large audience, ignoring the minority group, whereas, when there are two stations owned by one monopoly, they go after both audiences, one for each station. Under these circumstances, oligopolistic rivalry produces a uniformity of product that ignores the desires of the minority,

12. It thus suggests a negative answer to the third question posed on page 308. This case is discussed at length in P. O. Steiner, "Program Patterns and Preferences and the Workability of Competition in Radio Broadcasting," *Quarterly Journal of Economics,* May, 1952; and P. O. Steiner, "Monopoly and Competition in Television: Some Policy Issues," *The Manchester School,* May, 1961.

13. Also assume that two stations producing the same type of program will share the audience equally.

whereas monopoly produces a varied product catering to the desires of both the majority and the minority groups. Rivalry in producing Westerns may lead the oligopolistic firms to produce a better Western than the monopoly would have produced. Of course, with enough stations, both programs would be produced.

This theory was tested against the experience of British radio, which is a three-station monopoly, and British television, which was (at the time) based on competition between two stations, each taking as its criterion of success its own viewing audience.[14] It was found that the three stations of the monopolized radio produced very little similarity between the products offered at any one time, whereas the two stations of British television produced almost identical programs for a great deal of the time. Thus, at a randomly selected time of the day, the radio listener was likely to have two or three varied possibilities open to him, whereas the television viewer was likely to be forced to choose between two almost identical programs.

There seems little doubt that, in predicting the market behavior of industries characterized by small numbers of large firms, both the theory of atomistic competition and the theory of monopoly are inadequate much of the time. The need for hypotheses of oligopolistic behavior is established. At this point in the development of economics, only a few hypotheses about oligopolistic behavior have been tested.

The theories of perfect competition, monopoly, and monopolistic competition, as well as the variety of hypotheses about oligopoly, all remain viable, in the sense that none has generally refuted any of the others. Each one has a range of problems over which it may be regarded as having something to predict, but in each case this range is less than the whole of market behavior that is observed and about which an economist would like to be able to make predictions. Perhaps someday we will have a unified and tested theory of the market behavior of firms applicable to all possible situations. We do not have it today.

Summary

1. The basic assumption of the theory of oligopoly is that the firms in an industry recognize to some substantial extent that they are interdependent and that anything they do will probably lead to a reaction by rival sellers.

2. There is no simple set of predictions about the outcome of oligopolistic situations: Everything depends on the strategies adopted by the various rivals. Therefore, instead of a single theory there are many proposed special cases.

3. One very general hypothesis is the hypothesis of qualified joint profit-maximization, which says that firms that recognize that they are rivals will be motivated by two sets of opposing forces, one set moving toward joint profit-maximization and the other moving away from it. Among the factors that may predict a tendency toward joint

14. There are now three channels.

profit-maximization are greater mutual recognition of interdependence, greater facility of tacit agreement, and greater barriers to entry.

4. Nonprice competition may persist in oligopoly. One hypothesis says that nonprice competition will be more vigorous, the greater the restrictions on price competition. This hypothesis also predicts that advertising will tend to be greatest when other barriers to entry are weakest.

5. Many of the predictions made by oligopolistic theory differ from those made by monopolistic theory. One prediction is that oligopoly may produce less variety in broadcasting than is produced by monopoly.

QUESTIONS FOR DISCUSSION

1. In 1949, the vice-president of the McGraw-Hill Book Company wrote, in an article in the *American Economic Review,* that, if there were only two firms in an industry, and if they were of the "hard-driving, fiercely independent type . . . [that] has played such a large part in the industrial development of the U.S.A., two of them would be enough to create a ruggedly competitive situation." Are two competitors sufficient to guarantee nonmonopolistic behavior? Discuss this argument.

2. Why is there no single simple theory of oligopoly?

3. "One aim of government policy should be to eliminate product differentiation." How do you think this assertion should be answered?

4. It is often claimed that oligopolistic prices are sticky (i.e., that they do not adjust rapidly to market changes). Why do you think this claim is made? How would you go about testing it?

5. A number of steel companies were recently indicted by the government for price collusion. Some economists feel that, although the companies may ostensibly fix a uniform price, they in fact "cheat" by using such devices as charging for 100 tons and shipping 110. With what theory would you explain this behavior?

6. Name five industries that you would use to test any theory of oligopoly. Name five that you feel would not provide a reasonable test. How do you distinguish between the two groups?

Chapter **30** CRITICISMS AND TESTS OF THE THEORY OF THE FIRM

IN PREVIOUS CHAPTERS, WE DEVELOPED A number of testable implications of the theory of the firm. In many cases, if a particular implication is refuted,[1] only a minor change in the basic theory is needed to make it once again consistent with the facts. We might, for example, discover that firms do not always close down when they are unable to cover their variable costs of production. Such a discovery would refute the theory of short-run profit-maximization as we have presented it, but only relatively minor changes in the theory might be required in order to make it consistent with the new facts. In other cases, however, economists have claimed to have made empirical observations that strike at the very core of the theory of the firm. If these refutations were substantiated, we would either have to make very drastic amendments in our theory or we would have to abandon it completely.

The following three assumptions about the behavior of firms have been criticized:

1. the assumption that the decision-makers have access to and use the information that economic theory assumes they use (see pages 191–192);

2. the assumption that we can abstract from the individuals that make the decisions for the firm and the kind of organization in which they work (see page 174); and

3. the assumption that decision-makers strive to maximize profits (see pages 175–176).

These assumptions are interrelated, for all concern the profit-maximizing behavior of the firm. We shall, however, treat the criticisms of them separately. Before we do so, we digress for a moment to consider different approaches to evaluating our theory. We do so because in some actual cases the data that have been used do not provide evidence relevant to our theory.

Approaches to Testing the Theory

Each of the following three approaches has often been used in criticizing and testing the theory of the firm:

1. *Formulate an alternative (and competing) theory that predicts different market results.* Given an alternative theory, one can

---

1. The decision to regard a theory as refuted is a problem in statistical decision-making that was discussed in detail in Chapter 4, pages 49–50.

discover the areas in which the two theories make conflicting predictions and choose between the two theories on the basis of which comes closer to predicting what actually is observed to happen. We might hypothesize, for example, that firms choose to maximize their sales rather than their profits, and we would then have two competing theories. This is a satisfactory way of testing two theories.

2. *Observe decision-makers to see if they behave as the theory predicts they will behave.* We might observe, for example, how a certain executive makes a certain decision: what records he consults, what questions he asks, and so on. Or we might create a laboratory situation and give "subjects" a chance to make decisions, then record and analyze their decisions.

Although this approach may give rise to new theories, it does not by itself provide a test of an existing theory, since it does not tell us whether the procedure actually employed by the decision-maker really makes any difference in his decision.[2]

If, for example, an executive systematically discusses proposed price changes with his sales manager and his lawyer, but rarely with his cost accountant, it may *suggest* the hypothesis that demand and antitrust considerations loom larger in his mind than cost conditions, but it does not *demonstrate* that these things play a more important role than cost in pricing decisions.[3]

3. *Ask decision-makers how they make decisions.* Replies to questions can again *suggest* hypotheses about behavior, but they can never *refute* them. This point has often been over-looked. Suppose we are concerned with what motivates businessmen, and we ask a sample of them whether their sole motivation is to maximize profits. You should not be too surprised to learn that most of them reply in the negative. They seek, they say, to charge a fair price, to make only a reasonable profit, and generally to conduct their affairs in a manner conducive to the social good. Asking people what they do and why they do it may well provide some interesting hunches and suggest hypotheses about behavior for further testing. If you have always taken it for granted that businessmen are motivated by profit, and inquiry shows that they deny it, you may become sufficiently suspicious to check your ideas further. *But their denial can never prove that your original idea was wrong.* A denial might mean (1) that they were lying; (2) that they spoke what they thought was the truth, but were not actually aware of their own motives; or (3) that they were in fact not motivated by profit. How are we to judge which of these possibilities is the correct one? One needs only a nodding acquaintance with elementary psychology to realize that we are not likely to discover very much about human motivation by asking a person what motivates him. Generally, he will have either no idea at all of his motivations or only a pleasantly acceptable rationalization of them.

Direct questioning at best (assuming the subject *tries* to be scrupulously honest) tells us what the person questioned *thinks* he is doing. Such information may be interesting, but it can never refute an hypothesis about what the person actually is doing. To refute

---

2. One executive was systematically observed to telephone his wife and inquire whether there was a letter from their married daughter before every meeting of his investment board. A theory that ignores such behavior is not deficient in explaining that executive's investment decisions.

3. The executive may be an expert on cost conditions, or he may need less time to acquaint himself with cost data than with demand data, or his cost accountant may provide him with lucid memos, whereas his sales manager can only communicate orally. There is a host of other possibilities.

such an hypothesis, we must observe what he does, not ask him what he does.

The technique of direct questioning is, nevertheless, not without value. It can definitely refute an hypothesis about what people *think* they do. It can make us sceptical about an hypothesis about what people actually do, and so lead us to make direct tests of this hypothesis. And it can suggest the formulation of some new hypothesis about what people actually do. *What it cannot do is to provide evidence either in favor of, or against, an hypothesis about what, in fact, people do.*

Criticism 1: Firms Do Not Have Adequate Information

One group of critics says that the profit-maximizing theory will prove inadequate because businessmen, however hard they may try, *cannot* reach decisions the way the theory predicts. Most businessmen have never heard of the terms marginal cost and marginal revenue. Therefore, these critics argue, since the theory assumes that businessmen equate marginal cost and marginal revenue, and since empirical observations show that businessmen have never heard of marginal cost and marginal revenue, the theory is refuted, because businessmen cannot employ concepts of which they are ignorant.

The observation that businessmen do not use the terms marginal costs and marginal revenue would refute the theory that businessmen make decisions by calculating marginal values and consciously equating them. But it does not refute the theory that businessmen make decisions in such a way as to maximize profits. The economic theorist uses the mathematical concepts of marginal cost and marginal revenue to discover what will happen as long as, by one means or another—by guess, hunch, clairvoyance, luck, or good judgment—the businessman does approximately succeed in maximizing his profits. The constructs of the theory of the firm are, in other words, merely tools employed by the economist to discover the consequences of certain behavior patterns. They are not meant to describe *how* the businessman reaches his decisions.[4] If the businessman wants to maximize his profits, then the theory of profit-maximization allows us to predict how the businessman will react to certain changes—e.g., the introduction of a tax. This prediction is independent of the thought process by which the businessman actually reaches his decision.

A similar argument stems from the observation that businessmen do not calculate down to single units with such a nice degree of accuracy as is assumed. In presenting the theory of the firm to elementary students, the economist usually states that the businessman will carry on production until the cost of producing the very last unit is just equal to the revenue gained from its sale. In doing so, he is stating in verbal terms the mathematical conditions for the maximization of profits. The observation that businessmen do not calculate down to single units is not of

---

4. A famous analogy concerns how one might analyze whether it is safe for a driver to pass a truck on a two-lane road. The analyst must consider the driver's speed, the truck's speed, the driver's ability to accelerate, the possibility of an oncoming car, its speed and distance, weather conditions, etc. But the *driver* (unlike the analyst) need not solve a mathematical equation to make his decision. And yet, if the driver and the analyst are competent, both will reach the same decision.

itself relevant as a test of the theory. Marginal analysis allows us to predict how the businessman will respond to certain changes in the data; if he is maximizing his profits, he will be observed to respond in this way, even though he calculates in a much cruder fashion than does the mathematician.

More sophisticated critics point out that the information available to the producer is simply not adequate to permit him to reach the decisions that the economist predicts he will make. This argument generally takes one of three forms: that the businessman is the victim of his accountants, and bases decisions on accounting concepts, which differ from economic ones;[5] that the natural lag between accumulating and processing data is such that important decisions must be made on fragmentary and partially out-of-date information; and that, because acquiring full economic information is costly, firms cannot afford to acquire as much information as economists assume them to have.[6]

THE HYPOTHESIS OF FULL-COST PRICING

Out of these lines of criticism has come the hypothesis of *full-cost pricing*, which was originally suggested by businessmen's answers to questions on how they set prices.

This hypothesis explicitly denies that businessmen will charge the price that will maximize their profits. According to the full-cost hypothesis, businessmen use available data to compute full costs per unit (variable costs plus overhead) and add to this a conventional markup; price is set at this figure and sales are determined by what the market will absorb at that price.[7] The full-cost hypothesis portrays the businessman as a rather conservative creature, a prisoner of his habits and his accounting records, instead of the alert profit-seeker of traditional theory.[8] You can easily verify by drawing diagrams that the two theories, full-cost and profit-maximization, give different predictions.

Although full-cost theory has occasioned considerable heated argument, no generally accepted authoritative test of it exists. Insofar as the theory is made to rest on the inadequacy of accounting records, it has been effectively refuted by showing that modern accounting procedures do not limit firms to the use of average costs.[9] But the belief that the theory is appropriate for some firms cannot be refuted either by showing that firms are not forced to be full-costers by modern accounting methods or by showing that some firms do not choose to follow full-cost methods.

The fact that some economists continue to take the theory of full-cost pricing seriously, whereas others dismiss it as not even worth

5. Review Appendix B to Chapter 17.

6. The growing importance of business consultants and of economic-research departments within firms suggests that firms may not always have been successful in maximizing profits and that they are making serious efforts to improve performance in this direction.

7. The theory may also be regarded as an attack on the *desire* of businessmen to maximize profits. A paper by R. L. Hall and C. J. Hitch, "Price Theory and Business Behaviour," *Oxford Economic Papers*, May, 1939, generated a long debate that is well summarized in R. A. Gordon, "Short-Period Price Determination in Theory and Practice," *American Economic Review*, June, 1948.

8. Many economists believe that the full-cost theorists discovered the rule of thumb by which day-to-day decisions are made within the firm, but that the critical decision of what the markup should be is made periodically by management at a high level with profit-maximization as an important objective.

9. See, for example, James S. Earley, "Recent Developments in Cost Accounting and the 'Marginal Analysis'," *Journal of Political Economy*, June, 1955.

testing, is cogent argument for subjecting every theory to empirical tests, no matter how little confidence one has in it. So long as theories are judged on the basis of casual and private observation, there will be disagreement. If, however, the choice between the two theories is as clear as most economists seem to think, a carefully documented set of tests should settle the matter once and for all.

The procedure for testing is clear enough: Determine as many as possible of the predictions made by both the full-cost and the profit-maximizing theories; take those cases in which the two theories predict different reactions to the same event (e.g., that a rise in demand will lead to a rise in price—profit-maximization; that a rise in demand will leave price unchanged—full-cost); and confront these predictions with empirical evidence to see if one is contradicted by the facts and the other consistent with them. Such a task is, of course, easier outlined than accomplished, but it is interesting, in view of the heated controversy over this theory, that so few attempts have been made to test it systematically.[10]

Criticism 2: Decisions Depend on Who Makes Them

A major attack on the theory of the firm as we have developed it comes from a group of economists whose central concern is with what is called *organization theory*.[11] In terms borrowed from social psychology, they argue that in big organizations decisions are made after much discussion by groups and committees and that the structure of the *process* affects the *substance* of the decisions. Their central conviction is that different decisions will result from different kinds of organizations, even if all else is unchanged.

Although it has proved easier for organization theorists to express their central point of view than to formulate specific testable hypotheses, they have formulated a number of the latter. One is that a large and diffuse organization finds it necessary to develop standard operating procedures to help it in making decisions. These decision rules arise as a compromise among competing points of view and, once adopted, are changed only reluctantly. One prediction following from this hypothesis is that the procedures used may be nonoptimal and will persist for long periods of time, despite changes in conditions affecting the firm. For either reason, profits will not be maximized. Another prediction is that this procedure will lead large firms to adopt conservative policies and avoid large risks. Smaller firms will take bigger risks.

Hypotheses like these are very hard to test. Proponents of organization theory feel that the evidence supports them; critics feel that they are undemonstrated. It is our view that at the present time the evidence is inconclusive. By this we do not mean to reject the attack of the organization theorists; rather we reserve judgment until a sharper statement of conflicting predictions is made and until such predictions are more fully tested.

10. Such evidence as there is seems to go against the full-cost theory. See particularly L. Rostas, "Productivity, Prices, and Distribution in Selected British Industries," *NIESR Occasional Paper II* (Cambridge University Press, 1948). The evidence is quite strong that markups do not stay constant over time.

11. The interested reader is referred to R. M. Cyert and J. G. March, *A Behavioral Theory of the Firm* (Prentice-Hall, 1963).

Criticism 3: Firms Do Not Seek To Maximize Profits

A third kind of criticism, often made by the same critics, is as follows: Businessmen do not seek to maximize profits at all. Of course, they must make *some* profits or they will go out of business. But once some minimum level of profits has been achieved, they pursue totally different goals. The actions necessary to achieve these other goals are substantially different from those necessary to achieve profit-maximization. For this reason, all the deductions based on the assumption of profit-maximization will be at variance with the facts, except in those cases in which the actions necessary to achieve the goals actually being pursued happen, by chance, to coincide with the actions necessary for profit-maximization.

This is stronger than saying that firms are prevented from achieving maximum profits by the lack of information available to businessmen or by the organization's structure. This hypothesis states that businessmen do not *wish* to maximize profits.

SATISFICING

Organization theorists have criticized the profit-maximizing model and suggested an alternative that they call *satisficing*. Professor Herbert Simon says, "We must expect the firm's goals to be not maximizing profits but attaining a certain level or rate of profit, holding a certain share of the market or a certain level of sales."[12] According to this theory, firms will strive very hard to achieve certain

minimum (or "target") levels of profits, but, having achieved them, they will not strive aggressively to further improve their position. This means that the firm could come to rest in a large number of situations rather than in only one unique situation (the profit-maximizing one). In the language of economic theory, we say that equilibrium is not unique.

To test the satisficing theory, one must specify the "targets" of the firm. This has not been done carefully enough to permit us to specify the precise areas of conflict between satisficing and profit-maximizing theory. Until we know precisely what predictions of the two theories are in conflict with each other, we do not know to what extent the theories differ and thus we cannot test them to see which is more consistent without empirical observations.

The satisficing theory is potentially an important alternative to the profit-maximizing theory. Perhaps Simon exaggerates when he says, "The satisficing model vitiates all the conclusions about resource allocation that are derivable from the maximizing model when perfect competition is assumed,"[13] but very probably it does lead to differences in expected behavior. One case that is cited by proponents of satisficing is that, immediately after World War II, prices of new cars were lower than prices of used cars. As viewed by the proponents of satisficing, manufacturers of automobiles were satisfied with (even possibly embarrassed by) their high profits and

---

12. H. A. Simon, "Theories of Decision-Making in Economics," *American Economic Review*, June, 1959, p. 263.

13. *Ibid.*, p. 265.

were content not to take advantage of the excess demand to increase profits. As is so often the case, however, there are other possible explanations of this behavior, including fear of antitrust action.

SALES-MAXIMIZATION

Another theory recently put forward is that firms seek to maximize not their profits but their sales revenue. Firms, it is assumed, wish to be as large as possible and, faced with a choice between profits and sales, would choose to increase their sales rather than their profits.[14]

The basic argument offered to make this theory seem plausible is a modern version of the separation of management and ownership.[15] In the giant corporation, the managers need to make some minimum level of profits to keep the shareholders satisfied; after that they are free to seek growth unhampered by profit considerations. This is a sensible policy on the part of management, so the argument runs, because salary, power, and prestige all vary with the size of a firm as well as with its profits; generally, the manager of a large, normally profitable corporation will earn a salary considerably higher than that earned by the manager of a small but highly profitable corporation. Thus we may assume that firms seek to maximize their sales revenue, subject to some minimum-profit constraint. This theory is a genuine alternative to the theory of profit-maximization, because it leads to different predictions.[16] It has not yet been carefully tested, however.

LONG-RUN PROFIT-MAXIMIZATION

In order to take account of various criticisms of the assumption of profit-maximization, some economists modify profit-maximization to mean "long-run profit-maximization." In this view, for example, sales-maximization is long-run profit-maximization. Sales are the key to growth, and growth to future profits. Thus, maximizing current sales is the correct long-run policy for maximizing profits. In much the same way, the "long-run" approach can be used to explain other facts that are disturbing to believers in short-run profit-maximization. Why, for example, did automobile companies in 1946 keep prices down? They did so in order to keep the "good will" of automobile buyers, a policy worthwhile in terms of long-run profits. Or, for another example, a firm may be right to avoid risky ventures, even if they promise large short-run profits, because the surest way to long-run profits is to survive in the short run. Long-run profitability requires survival, and survival requires caution.

Is long-run profit-maximization the answer? There is little doubt that when the theory of short-run maximization in a perfectly competitive market is applied to a market in which each producer sets his own

14. See W. J. Baumol, *Business Behavior, Value, and Growth* (Macmillan, 1959).

15. See Chapter 16. Basically, that hypothesis suggests that managers have the power to pursue their own goals, whatever they might be, rather than the goals of the stockholders. No specific alternatives were discussed.

16. For example: A firm with substantial monopoly power will tend to charge a price where the elasticity of demand is unity (sales-maximizing theory) or where it is greater than unity (profit-maximizing theory). Observations of industries where elasticity of demand tends to be consistently above unity, but in which the firms continue to earn profits above the required minimum, cast doubt upon the sales-maximizing hypothesis.

price, extensive modifications in the theory must be made. In particular, prices can and do change daily in perfectly competitive markets, but they cannot and do not in markets in which the producer sets his own price. Thus, for these latter markets, we cannot say that the producer maximizes profits from day to day as costs and demands change. We must specify a realistic period over which he makes his decision. This might lead us to say: "The producer does not change price from day to day to maximize profits in the short run; rather he makes decisions over a long period and seeks to maximize his profits in the long run." It is, however, exceptionally difficult to give such a long-run theory any testable content. If we are not careful, we may find ourselves rationalizing, whenever we find a firm not maximizing profits, by saying merely that it was maximizing over *some other time period* than the one we were considering. Unless we work out our theory carefully and include in it a means of identifying the long-run period over which profits are supposed to be maximized, we will have a universal *untestable* alibi for all refutations of profit-maximizing theory. If this happens, then our theory becomes consistent with absolutely any behavior on the part of businessmen and becomes, as a result, totally uninteresting.

Summary

The theories of full-cost pricing, satisficing, and sales-maximization compete with the theory of short-run profit-maximization. As yet, however, none of them has provided a body of evidence sufficient to lead us to accept it over the others or to reject the theory of profit-maximization.

There is one further possibility: These theories may be complementary rather than competing. It may well be that no one motive is dominant. The firm may have several strong motives—profits, security, growth, etc. —so that any theory that concentrates on only one of these will, sooner or later, be refuted. If this is so, it will be necessary to develop a much more complex theory of the firm than any of those outlined here.

We may have conveyed in this chapter the image of conventional theory embattled, with its proponents beating off attackers right and left. In a sense, this image is correct; in a broader sense, it is misleading. Each of the criticisms arises from the frustration that comes from trying to apply the concepts of the economist to the world of the businessman. When one cannot easily bring theory into contact with the data generated by firms, it is hard both to apply the theory and to test it. The most damaging charge against the theory of profit-maximization may be that it is *nonoperational,* which means that it cannot be applied to the real world.

Whether this charge is or is not generally valid, it has had a profound effect on contemporary work in economics. Models of firm behavior in production, in pricing, and in other forms of market interaction, are increasingly being restated in more specific terms, and in terms that make predictions on the basis of available data. For example, questions about how to produce are being reformulated in terms of choice among processes that are well defined in a production-engineering sense. There are many other examples. The main result has been an attempt to state narrower, more specific, and more readily testable propositions about firm behavior. This is not a subject for an elementary book at this stage in the development of economics. Within a decade this should have changed.

QUESTIONS FOR DISCUSSION

1. What approaches, satisfactory and unsatisfactory, have been used to criticize the theory of the firm? What is the potential value of each?

2. If you found seven gas stations along a road, all selling brands of regular gasoline at the same price, would you regard this as evidence of perfect competition, collusion, or what?

3. What alternatives do we have, at the moment, to the hypothesis of profit-maximization? Examine the predictions of each in a hypothetical situation, such as a rise in demand.

4. The hypothesis of long-run profit-maximization has a weakness. What is it and what attempts might be made to overcome it?

5. Comment on the following quotation: "And, of course, garment manufacturers must compete incessantly or go out of business. They do not gang up to fix production or prices. None dominates the market. Their marginal costs often equal —and sometimes exceed—their prices." (*Fortune*, June, 1952.)

6. "Economists are not strictly enough compelled to reduce metaphysical concepts to falsifiable terms, and cannot compel each other to agree to what has been falsified. So economics limps along, with one foot in untested hypotheses and the other in untestable slogans." (Joan Robinson, *Economic Philosophy* [Aldine, 1962]). How well do you think this describes this chapter? What solutions are there?

7. If you are particularly convinced by one of the theories mentioned in this chapter, how might you try to make the theory most convincing to others?

DISTRIBUTION

Chapter **31** DISTRIBUTION:

A GENERAL VIEW

FOR BETTER OR FOR WORSE, ANY SOCIETY'S output gets distributed somehow. What determines the distribution? Income takes many forms: wages and salaries, rental income from property, interest, and profits, to name the major ones. Table 1 shows the distribution of income in the United States, by major types, for 1964. This so-called *functional distribution of income* is the income paid to factors of production, rather than the income received by persons who provide the factor services. A single individual may receive incomes of several sorts—from his labor, from the use of his savings, from the rental of property he owns, and from his investments in shares of stock. The amount of his

TABLE 1   **FUNCTIONAL DISTRIBUTION OF INCOME IN THE UNITED STATES, 1964**

Type of income	Billions of dollars	Percentage of total
Wages and salaries	362	70.8
Corporate profits	58	11.3
Proprietors' income	52	10.2
Interest	27	5.2
Rental income	12	2.4
TOTAL	511	100.0

SOURCE: *Survey of Current Business*, May, 1965.

income is merely the sum of his income from each source.

   Much of the theory of distribution that

we discuss in this part is concerned with the functional distribution of income. But economists are also interested in the equality or inequality in the distribution of income among persons and families. Many economic policies are designed to modify income distribution.

TABLE 2   **INCOME OF AMERICAN FAMILIES, 1964**[a]

Income class	Percentage of families
Less than $2,000	10
2,000–3,999	16
4,000–5,999	18
6,000–7,999	20
8,000–9,999	14
10,000–14,999	16
15,000 or more	6

[a] The Census definition of family excludes single persons not living in families.
SOURCE: *Current Population Reports*, Series P-60, No. 44, May, 1965.

The basic facts about the distribution of income are given in Tables 2 and 3. Table 2 shows the distribution of American families by income level. Everyone knows that some families are richer than others and that some families are very poor indeed. Median family income in 1964 was about $6,500, but more than a quarter of American families lived on less than $4,000. Table 3 focuses on this inequality: The 20 percent of the population at the bottom of the income scale receive only 5 percent of the nation's income; the 20 percent at the top receive 42 percent of it. Economists want to know why.

It is tempting to give superficial explanations of differences in income. People often say: "A man is paid what he's worth." But the economist must ask: "Worth what to whom?" "What gives him his value?" His wife, his mother-in-law, and his employer may all give different answers. Sometimes people say: "Men earn according to their ability." But note that incomes are distributed in a very much more unequal fashion than any *measured* index of ability, be it I.Q., physical strength, typing skill, or the quality of the books one writes. In what sense is Willie Mays twenty times as able as the promising new rookie? He gets paid twenty times as much. In what sense is a truck driver more able than a schoolteacher? In what sense is a football coach more able than a wrestling coach?

If answers couched in terms of worth and ability are easily refuted, so are answers like "It's all a matter of luck," or "It's just the system." We are concerned now with discovering whether or not the theories of economics provide explanations of the distribution of income that are more satisfactory than

TABLE 3   **INEQUALITY IN INCOME DISTRIBUTION, 1963**

Group in population	Percentage of income
Lowest 20 percent	5
Lowest 40 percent	17
Lowest 60 percent	34
Lowest 80 percent	58
Lowest 95 percent	84
Lowest 100 percent	100

SOURCE: *Current Population Reports*, Series P-60, No. 43, September, 1964.

the ones mentioned above. The predictions of economics, and the hypotheses they come from, rest upon theories we have already studied. In this chapter, we present a general survey of the theory of distribution, which we will develop in detail in subsequent chapters.

Factor Prices and Factor Income

Every element of income has, in a purely arithmetical sense, two components: the quantity of the income-earning service that is provided, and the price per unit paid for it. The amount a man earns in wages depends upon the number of hours he works and the hourly wage he receives. The amount a group of men (say, union members) earns depends

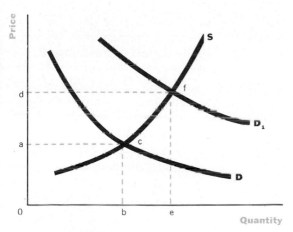

FIGURE 1   **DETERMINATION OF FACTOR INCOME IN A COMPETITIVE MARKET**

upon how many of them there are and how much each earns. The amount of dividends a stockholder receives depends upon the number of shares of stock he owns and the dividends that each share pays.

Since factor prices are one of the two elements that determine factor income (and hence the amount of the national product that the owner of the factor is able to command), we need a theory of factor prices. This, in turn, is just a special case of the

theory of price and involves little that is not already familiar.

Our price theory states that the competitive market price of any commodity or factor is determined by demand and supply. Figure 1 shows the demand and supply curves for some factor of production. The equilibrium price is Oa; quantity is Ob. The total income earned by the factor is $Oacb$. If we now assume that the prices of all other factors of production, the prices of all goods, and the level of national income are given and constant, then fluctuations in $Oacb$ will cause fluctuations in the money earnings of the factor, in the relative earnings (compared to other factors), and in the share of national income going to the factor. Assume, for example, that the demand curve for the factor in question rises from D to D_1. The money price of the factor will now rise from Oa to Od, and the relative price of the factor from Oa/w to Od/w, where w is the (given) price of some other factor. The total earnings rise from $Oacb$ to $Odfe$ and, if the total income of the whole economy remains constant at Y, then the share of income going to this factor rises from $Oacb/Y$ to $Odfe/Y$. Thus the problem of distribution in a competitive market boils down to a question of the determinants of the demand and supply of factors of production. However, our interest in distribution is not limited to competitive markets. Since the factor we want to study may not be exchanged in a competitive market, there is an additional problem: We have to determine the effect of the various departures from a competitive market caused by monopolistic organizations, government action, unions, and so forth.

Demand for a Factor Is a Derived Demand

In considering the demand for a factor of production, the most important thing to remember is that consumers do not want factors (land, labor, raw materials, machines, etc.) for themselves, but rather for their ability to help to produce other goods that *are* wanted. The only use for pig feed is to help to produce pork. If there is no consumer demand for pork, then there will be no demand for pig feed;[1] if there is a large demand for pork, then there will be a large demand for pig feed. If a rise in the price of pork causes a great reduction in its demand, then there will be a great reduction in the demand for pig feed; if a rise in the price of pork causes only a small fall off in its demand, then there will only be a small fall off in the demand for pig feed. Clearly, the demand for a factor of production depends on the demand for the consumption goods that it helps to make. The demand for the factor is *derived* from the demand for the consumption good; in the terminology of the economist, the demand for a factor of production is a *derived demand*. Typically, one factor will be used in making many goods, not just one. Steel is used in dozens of industries, as are the services of carpenters. The total demand for a factor will be the sum of the derived demands for it in each productive activity.

WHAT DETERMINES DEMAND FOR A FACTOR?

What determines the quantity of a factor that producers will wish to purchase? Eco-

nomic theory contains three main hypotheses about the determinants of demands for a factor.

1. The quantity of a factor that producers demand will depend upon the level of demand for the commodities that the factor is used to make.

The greater the demand for a product, the greater the derived demand for the factors that make it. Examples leap to the mind. The demand for computer programmers is strong and is growing as the use of large-scale electronic computers spreads through industry. The demand for college professors increases as the number of students going to college increases. The demand for coal miners and coal-digging equipment declines as the demand for coal decreases. It follows at once that factors that are relatively heavily used in industries with high income elasticities of demand will find that the demand for their services will have high income elasticity. Indeed, anything that increases demand for a commodity—population changes, changes in tastes, etc.—will increase the demand for the factors required to make it.

2. The quantity of a factor that producers will demand depends upon the price of the factor relative to the prices of other factors.

The reasons are familiar ones. Since producers can substitute one factor for another, a rise in the relative price of one factor will, *ceteris paribus*, lead producers to substitute relatively cheaper factors for it. The rise in

1. Except, of course, by pigs.

the cost of labor has led to the development of more and more labor-saving machinery in manufacturing, in agriculture, and elsewhere. In countries where labor is cheap, more labor-intensive methods of production are used than in countries where labor is expensive.

There are, of course, cases in which factors are complementary. If the cost of computers goes down, we expect the demand for operators of computers to rise, even though the relative price of computer operators rises. This is because it takes operators to run computers. In the short run, at least, computer operators are a complementary factor to computers. In the long run, substitutions may occur if computers are invented that reduce the number of operators required to do a given job.

3. The quantity of a factor demanded will depend upon the productivity of the factor.

The greater the productivity of a factor, *ceteris paribus*, the greater the quantity of the factor that will be demanded. This proposition is not so simple as it appears, and the main discussion of it is deferred to a later chapter. On the surface it is clear enough: If some factor suddenly becomes more productive, it becomes more useful, and the demand for it should rise. Very often, however, changes in the productivity of one factor (say, labor) will be associated with changes in the same direction in the productivity of another factor (say, machines). In this case, *ceteris paribus* does not hold. If labor productivity increases, but machine productivity increases even more, will more or less labor be used? We will answer this question later on.

To summarize, we hypothesize that the demand for a factor is a function of the level of demand for the product it makes, the price of the factor, the prices of other factors of production, and the productivity of the factor.

Following our now-familiar procedure (review Chapter 7 if it is not familiar), we draw a demand curve to examine the variation of the quantity of a factor with respect to its price, all other things held constant. Curve D in Figure 1 is such a demand curve. Variations in the other things lead to shifts in the demand curve, such as the shift from D to D_1 in the figure.

ELASTICITY OF FACTOR DEMAND

What determines the elasticity of demand for a factor?

1. The elasticity of demand for a factor varies directly with the elasticity of demand for the final product.

A rise in the price of a factor of production will raise the cost of producing the final product and will cause an increase in the price of the product. If the price rise causes a large reduction in demand (i.e., the demand is very elastic), then there will be a large reduction in the quantity of the factor now needed. If, on the other hand, the price rise causes only a small reduction in the demand for the final good (i.e., the demand is inelastic), then there will be only a small reduction in the quantity of the factor now required. To summarize, the rise in the price of the factor causes a rise in the price of the final good; the rise in the price of the final good causes a reduction in the quantity demanded, the amount of the reduction depending on the elasticity of demand for the final good; and the reduction in demand, and hence in production, causes a reduction in the demand for the factor. Thus, the more elastic the demand for the final good, the more elastic will be the demand for the factors that go to make it.

2. *The smaller the cost of a given factor as a proportion of the total cost of the final good, the more inelastic the demand for the factor.*

Consider now two factors: Factor *A* makes up 50 percent of the total cost of commodity *X*, whereas factor *B* makes up only 10 percent. A 10 percent increase in the price of factor *A* would raise the cost of producing *X* by 5 percent, whereas a 10 percent increase in the price of factor *B* would raise the cost of *X* by only 1 percent. Thus, a 10 percent increase in factor *A*'s price would occasion a larger increase in the price of *X*, hence a larger reduction in demand, first for *X* and then for *A*, than would a 10 percent increase in the price of factor *B*. In general, the smaller the proportion of total costs of producing *X* that are made up by the cost of one factor, the more inelastic will be the demand for that factor. This illustrates the importance of being unimportant.

3. *The demand for a factor will be more elastic, the easier it is to substitute some other factor for it in production.*

When the price of some factor rises, that factor becomes more expensive relative to all other factors. There will be a tendency for firms to save on costs by using less of the now more expensive factor and more of the other factors. How easy it is to substitute one for another depends on the technical conditions of production. It is important to emphasize that it is very easy to underestimate the degree to which factors can be substituted for one another in the production of some commodity. It is fairly obvious that a bushel of wheat can be produced by combining land either with a lot of labor and a little capital, or

with a little labor and a lot of capital. When he comes to manufactured goods, however, the student often tends to think in terms of using inputs in pretty fixed proportions. Casual observation of an industry over time will show just how factor proportions can be varied to produce a given product. There is, for example, a case in which glass and steel turn out to be good substitutes for each other: In automobile manufacture, one can be substituted for the other over a wide range merely by varying the dimensions of the windows.

It is easy enough to answer the factual questions implied by the above analysis when one is considering one industry's demand for some factor, but it is much more difficult when one is considering the total demand for the factor in all industries. Steel plays a relatively small role in residential construction (though even wooden houses need steel nails), but a very large one in ship construction. Clearly, the demand for ships will be more important than the demand for houses in influencing the elasticity of demand for steel.

This analysis gives some idea of the determinants of the elasticity of demand for a factor of production. It is easy enough to understand and to commit to memory these general principles. It is also easy, however, to forget to apply them. In countries where a high proportion of imports are raw materials, one frequently hears it said: "These imports are *absolute necessities*, for without them factories would grind to a halt; therefore the demand for them will be completely inelastic." Anyone who would make such a statement has forgotten the principles of derived demand.[2] What would be the effect of an increase in the price of an imported raw material that is a major cost in the production

---

2. What the person may mean is that *some* minimum amount of the basic raw materials is essential. But this is a very different statement from the one quoted.

of a commodity with a fairly elastic demand? Clearly, it is wrong to assume, even as a first approximation, that the elasticity of demand for every imported raw material is zero.

Supply of Factors

What causes variations in the total supply of a factor of production to the *whole economy*? This is a very difficult question, in part because the several factors of production are so different from one another. Labor, in particular, is very different from other factors of production. We are a society of men, not of machines. The supply of engineers is very much affected by the educational policies of the nation's colleges. The over-all supply of labor depends not only on the size and age distribution of the population, but also on those customs and institutions of a society that determine when children should leave school and enter the labor force and when retirement should take place. The supply of coal is determined by a wholly different set of considerations, and the supply of machines by yet a different one. (We discuss the determinants of the total supply of particular factors in Chapter 33.)

The adjustments of supply to changes in the conditions of particular industries are easier to deal with. *The supply of a factor to one particular industry is predicted to depend on the price paid by that industry relative to the price paid by other industries that operate in the same factor market.*[3]

Supplies of the factor can be expected to move between industries, leaving those offering lower earnings and moving to those offering higher earnings. Similar movements of factors may occur between geographical areas, although in the case of labor, as we shall see, the movement may be very slow.

The hypothesis that supply will be an increasing function of the price of the factor leads to a rising supply curve, such as the one depicted in Figure 1.

Distribution Theory and Resource Allocation

Factor prices play an important role in the distribution of the national product. In a competitive factor market, factor prices will be determined by the joint forces of demand and supply. Since the demand for factors is a derived demand, the theory of factor prices provides a direct link between the allocation of resources (factors) and the demand for goods and services. The link depends upon the movement of factors between occupations and industries (and areas of the country as well) in response to differences in factor prices. Distribution theory, which is primarily a theory about the relative earnings of factors in different uses, is a key part of the theory of the allocation of scarce factors between alternative uses.

3. See Chapter 21 for a discussion of the problems of defining a market. With minor modifications, this discussion applies to factor markets as well as to product markets.

Summary

1. The quantity of labor demanded is a *derived demand,* and the theory predicts that it depends on the level of demand for the commodity that the factor is used to make, the relative price of that factor, and the productivity of the factor.

2. The elasticity of demand for a factor varies directly with the elasticity of demand for the final product, the cost of the factor as a proportion of total cost, and the ease of substitution of other factors for it.

3. The theory of factor prices provides a direct link between the allocation of resources and the distribution of income.

QUESTIONS FOR DISCUSSION

1. What is the functional distribution of income? What common categories have we divided it into?

2. What will happen to the elasticity of automobile manufacturers' demand for steel when the elasticity of demand for automobiles falls? What will happen to the market elasticity of demand for steel?

3. What does our hypothesis predict will happen to the elasticity of demand for printers with the invention of computer processes for setting type?

4. What hypothesis leads us to predict a rising supply curve in an individual industry? What complications are there in considering the supply of, say, labor to the whole economy?

Chapter **32** THE DEMAND FOR FACTORS: MARGINAL PRODUCTIVITY THEORY

THIS CHAPTER IS PRINCIPALLY CONCERNED with establishing the proposition that the demand curve for a factor is downward sloping.

The *marginal productivity theory* provides the basis for this proposition, provided we assume that firms are profit-maximizers. The reason we *derive* this proposition, rather than treating it as an original hypothesis to be tested, is that we are eager to preserve the link that derived demand provides between pricing of factors and pricing of products.

Profit-Maximization: Another View

In Part V, we considered the conditions for maximizing profits in the short run. When one factor was fixed (usually capital) while another factor was allowed to vary, we saw that the profit-maximizing firm would increase its output to the level at which the last unit produced added just as much to costs as it did to revenue or, in technical language, until marginal cost equaled marginal revenue. Another way of stating this is to say that the firm will increase production up to the point at which the last unit of the variable factor employed adds just as much to revenue as it does to costs. Just as it is true that all profit-maximizing firms, whether they are selling under conditions of perfect competition, monopolistic competition, oligopoly, or monopoly, produce to the point at which marginal costs equal marginal revenue, so it is true that all profit-maximizing firms will hire units of the variable factor up to the point at which the marginal cost of the factor (i.e., the addition to the total cost resulting from the employment of one more unit) equals the marginal revenue produced by the factor. Since we have already used the term marginal revenue to refer to the change in revenue resulting when the rate of sales is increased by one unit, we shall use another term, *marginal revenue product* (MRP), to refer to the change in revenue caused by the sale of the product contributed by *an additional unit of*

the variable factor. It is true, therefore, of all profit-maximizing firms that, in equilibrium:

the marginal cost of the variable factor =
the marginal revenue product of that factor   (1)

If the firm is unable to influence the price of the variable factor by buying more or less of it (i.e., if the firm is a price-taker when *buying* factors), then the marginal cost of the factor is merely its price. The cost, for example, of obtaining an extra man on the payroll is the wage that must be paid to that man. We may now state the condition of (1) above in the following form:

$$w = MRP, \qquad (2)$$

where w is the price of the factor.

This statement is sometimes called the *marginal productivity theory of distribution*. Let us be clear about what it says and where it came from. It is merely an *implication* of two assumptions: first, that the firm is a profit-maximizer, and, second, that the firm *buys* its factors in markets in which it is a price-taker.[1] The firm hires factors up to the point at which $w = MRP$ because it is profitable to do so. In the form we have stated it, this implication is not an hypothesis about market behavior. It is merely an alternative statement about the equilibrium condition for a firm under the two conditions assumed.

---

1. Note that the second assumption says nothing about the firm's behavior in the market where it *sells* its product. The firm can equally well be a monopolist or a perfect competitor.

The Demand for a Factor as a Derived Demand

It is necessary for our theory of distribution to have a downward-sloping demand curve for factors of production. We can, in fact, deduce this result on the basis of what has gone before.

To begin with, assume that we know the marginal revenue product of a factor. Condition (2) allows us to derive the demand curve for the factor immediately. In Figure 1, we show a hypothetical marginal revenue product curve for a variable factor of produc-

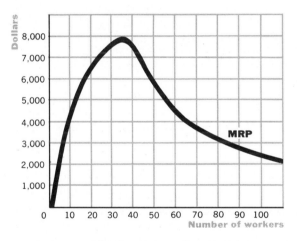

FIGURE 1   A MARGINAL REVENUE PRODUCT CURVE FOR A FACTOR

tion. Condition (2) states that the profit-maximizing firm will employ additional units of the factor up to the point at which the marginal revenue product equals the price of the factor. If, for example, the price were $6,000 per year, then it would be most profitable to employ 50 workers.[2] The curve in Figure 2 shows the quantity of labor employed at each price of labor. Such a curve can be derived from Figure 1 by picking various prices of the variable factor and reading off the amount used from the marginal revenue product curve.

Note that this curve is identical with the downward-sloping portion of the marginal revenue product curve in Figure 1. The curve in Figure 2 relates the price of the variable factor to the quantity employed; hence, it is the demand curve for the variable factor. We hypothesize, therefore, that:

The downward-sloping part of the marginal revenue product curve of a factor is the firm's demand curve for that factor.

To show that the *market* demand curve for the factor declines, we must show first that the demand curves for the factor of individual firms slope downward. This is equiva-

---

2. A price of $6,000 per year is equal to MRP at *two* levels of employment: 15 and 50. Recall the similar problem in connection with marginal cost. (Chapter 21.) Evidently, having 15 workers is a point of minimum profit: Each of the first 15 workers contributes less to the value of the product than $6,000. Every additional worker between 15 and 50 adds more to the value of the product, but, after 50, the workers would again contribute less than their wage. There is no point in employing a fifty-first worker: He would add only $5,900 to the value of the product but would add $6,000 (his wage) to costs. Why does not a similar argument apply to the fourteenth worker or the first? The reason is that you cannot have a twentieth if you do not have a first or a fourteenth. The condition for maximum profits given in (1) is only one of the necessary and sufficient conditions for profit-maximization. It is also necessary that MRP cut MC from above. (See Footnote 8 in Chapter 21 for the parallel requirement for marginal costs.) In (2) this means that MRP must be declining for the intersection with the factor price to be a position of maximum profit.

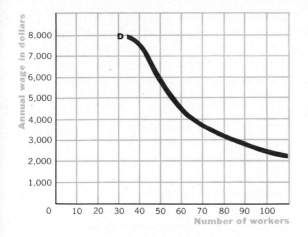

FIGURE 2 DERIVED DEMAND FOR A FACTOR

lent to showing that the *MRP* has a declining section. (See Footnote 2 above.)

WHY DOES THE DEMAND CURVE DECLINE?

Marginal revenue product may be thought of as depending on two things: (1) the physical increase in output that an additional unit of the variable factor makes possible, (2) multiplied by the value to the producer of that extra output. The first of these is called marginal physical product (MPP); the second is the by-now familiar concept of marginal revenue.

In symbols:

$$MRP = MPP \times MR. \qquad (3)$$

In Footnote 6 in Chapter 19, we introduced the hypothesis of diminishing returns. From this hypothesis it follows at once that MPP has a declining section over some range of output. (Reread Footnote 6 in Chapter 19 at this time.) If *MR* is constant (as it is in perfect competition), *MRP* has the same shape as *MPP* and must thus also decline. If *MR* declines as output increases (as it does in monopoly and in any other situation in which the product demand curve declines), then *MRP* must decline even more sharply.† Thus we have shown that the hypothesis of diminishing returns implies diminishing *MRP*.

MARKET DEMAND

In the appendix to Chapter 13, we learned how to aggregate the demands of individual households to get a market demand curve for a product. In precisely the same fashion, we may aggregate the firm's demand curve for a factor to obtain a market demand curve for the factor. (There is only one complication, which we consider in the next paragraph.) If all firms have downward-sloping demand curves, the market demand curve necessarily also declines. Therefore, unless there is something in the aggregation process that changes the individual firm's demand curves, we can extend our deduction about downward-sloping demand curves for the firm to the market curve for a factor.

The complication in aggregation is as follows: If, in response to a decrease in the price of a factor, all firms increase their use of the

---

† This clumsy verbal argument can be replaced by an easy proof:

$$MR = f(Q)$$
$$MPP = g(Q)$$
$$MRP = MPP \times MR = f(Q) \cdot g(Q).$$

By the hypothesis of diminishing returns, there is a level of output beyond which $g(Q)$ declines. Hence, unless $f(Q)$ rises, *MRP* will also decline. But $f(Q)$ is constant or declining for all market structures we identify. Therefore, *MRP* must have a declining section.

factor and increase output, the market price of their product will fall (as a consequence of the increase in supply in the final product market). This, in turn, changes the value of *MRP*. See condition (3) above. We assert (without providing the proof) that this will increase the steepness of the market demand curve for the factor (compared to the aggregate *ceteris paribus* curve) but that the curve will continue to be downward sloping.

Summary

What is often (misleadingly) called the marginal productivity theory of distribution is the proposition that a firm will hire factors up to the point at which the marginal revenue product is equal to the price of the factor.

This proposition is a logical implication of two assumptions: that firms are profit-maximizers, and that they purchase factors in a competitive market.

It follows from these assumptions that the downward-sloping portion of the marginal revenue product curve is the firm's demand curve for the factor. The assumption of diminishing returns assures that the firm's demand curve is downward sloping for the factor, which is sufficient to assure that the market demand curve for the factor also declines.

QUESTIONS FOR DISCUSSION

1. What influences the demand for steelworkers? How would this be affected by a rise in the price of steel, according to our hypotheses?

2. What assumption is sufficient to guarantee us that the marginal revenue product curve slopes downward? How useful is it to know that it slopes downward eventually?

3. "It is necessary for our theory of distribution to have a downward-sloping demand curve for factors of production." (Page 350.) What do we need to know about the actual shape of the demand curve?

4. What assumptions do we need to derive the downward-sloping factor demand curve?

5. Assume that in the textile industry, which approximates a perfectly competitive industry, there is a rise in the price of unprocessed cotton. Trace verbally and diagrammatically the reaction of the firms in the industry to this change, and show the final result on the demand for the cotton.

Chapter **33** THE SUPPLY OF FACTORS

IF WE CONTINUE TO USE PETROLEUM AT THE same rate that we did in 1965, we shall have used up all the proved reserves of oil in the United States by 1984. There is enough coal in the United States to last for more than 5,000 years, at present rates of consumption.

Yet we continue year by year to substitute oil for coal. Is this madness? When we use our natural resources are we depriving our grandchildren of their basis for a good life? Should we not conserve our wasting resources by using as few of them as possible?

The Total Supply of Factors

Are the total supplies of factors fixed, in any meaningful sense? Many people think they are, and, at first glance, this is intuitively plausible. After all, there is only so much land in the world, or in the United States, or in New York City. There is an upper limit to the number of workers; there is only so much coal, oil, copper, and iron ore in the earth. These considerations do indeed put absolute maximums upon the supplies of any factor. But, in virtually every case, we are not near these upper limits, and the problem of changes in the total effective supply of land, or labor, or natural resources, or capital deserves discussion.

LABOR

By the total supply of labor we mean the total number of hours of work that the popu-

lation is willing to supply. This quantity, which is often called the supply of effort, is a function of three things: the size of the population, the proportion of the population willing to work, and the number of hours worked by each individual. What are the determinants of each of these things? Populations vary in size, and these variations may be influenced to some extent by economic factors. There is some evidence that the birth rate is higher in good times than in bad. You may have found it hard to get into college, in part because you were born in the postwar baby boom. Much of the variation in population is, however, not explained successfully by economists, and, for Western countries, we must accept that the total population varies for reasons that are at the moment largely unexplained.[1] The proportion of the population entering the labor market, the

1. In some underdeveloped areas, the population varies directly with the food supply and the quantity and quality of medical services.

labor force, as it is called, varies considerably in response to variations in the demand for labor. Generally, a rise in the demand for labor, and an accompanying rise in the earnings of labor, will lead to an increase in the proportion of the population willing to work. Women and elderly people are inclined to enter the labor force when the demand for labor is high. The dramatic increase in the proportions of married women and persons over sixty-five who joined the labor force during World War II is a case in point. Variations in the number of hours people are willing to work have resulted in a substantial *reduction* in the supply of labor over a long period of time. Generally, a rise in real wages, such as has occurred in most Western countries over the last two centuries, leads people to consume more goods *and also to consume more leisure.* This means that people will be willing to work fewer hours per week, a fact that, unless offset by a rise either in total population or in the proportion of the population in the labor force, will lead to a decline in the supply of labor. Workers are in the position of trading their leisure for goods; by giving up leisure (i.e., by working), they obtain money and, hence, goods. A rise in the wage rate means that there is a change in the relative price of goods and leisure. Goods become cheaper relative to leisure, since each hour worked results in more goods than before, and each hour of leisure consumed is at the cost of more goods foregone. This is illustrated in Figure 1. Leisure is measured on the vertical axis and the money value of goods consumed on the horizontal axis. Each individual starts with 24 hours of his own time. If the wage rate is $2 per hour, he can have 24 hours of leisure and no goods, or $48 worth of goods and no leisure (much less any sleep), or any combination of goods and leisure indicated by points on *budget line A.* Assume, first, that he chooses the position in-

dicated by point *x,* so that he consumes 14 hours of leisure and trades the other 10 (at $2 per hour) for $20 worth of goods. Now assume that the wage rate doubles to, say, $4 per hour. He can now have any combination of goods and leisure indicated by points on budget line *B.* If he continues to work for

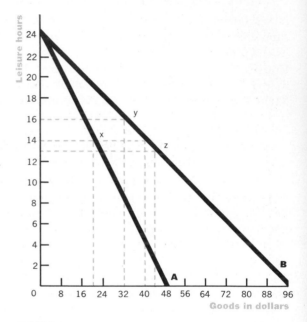

FIGURE 1

10 hours per day, he gets $40 worth of goods, but there is nothing to stop him from moving to a point above and to the right of *x,* in which case he can have more goods *and* more leisure. If, for example, he moves to the position indicated by *y,* he will have an extra 2 hours of leisure and an extra $12 worth of goods. On the other hand, the extra income that can be obtained *per unit of leisure sacrificed* might make him more willing to give up leisure to get goods. He might, for example,

move to point z and work one more hour, getting $44 worth of goods.[2]

Do increases in wages cause people to work fewer hours or more hours? Examples of both have been observed. Attempts to increase the supply of effort offered by coal miners in postwar Britain have consistently been thwarted, for the miners have wished to take out part of their increased real income by consuming more leisure. They can do this without departing from the agreed-upon workweek merely by increasing their absenteeism. On the other hand, overtime pay (at time and a half) appears still to be a very effective inducement to persuade people to work more hours.

TAXES AND THE SUPPLY OF EFFORT

Many people believe that today's high income taxes tend to reduce the supply of effort by reducing the incentive for people to work. People complain, and always have complained about high taxes. They protest that working is not worthwhile because of the crushing tax burdens that workers have to shoulder. Such systematic, objective evidence as exists on this subject suggests, however, that high taxes do not reduce the supply of effort. One economist studied a high-income, highly tax-sensitive group, but found no general disincentive effect of the high tax rates (including high marginal rates) over the period studied.[3] Also the long-run historical evidence of all countries demonstrates that, as people get richer (i.e., as their reward per hour's effort rises), they wish to work fewer rather than more hours, which leads us to suspect that, as the reward for effort falls (as taxes rise), they will wish to work more hours. We must conclude that such evidence as exists goes against the commonly held view that a lowering of the existing level of taxes, and hence an increase in the net reward per hour worked, would increase the supply of effort in the economy.

LAND

If by land we mean the total area of dry land, then the supply of land in a country is, in this definition, pretty well fixed. A rise in the earnings of land cannot result in much of an increase in the supply of land, unless we can drain land that is at present covered with water. The traditional assumption in economics is that the supply of land is absolutely inelastic. However, if by land we understand all the fertile land available for cultivation, then the supply of land is subject to large fluctuations. Considerable care and effort is required to sustain the productive power of land and, if the return to land is low, the fertility of the land may be destroyed within a short period of time. On the other hand, a high return to land may make worthwhile irrigation, drainage, and fertilization schemes that can greatly increase the supply of arable land.[4]

---

2. The movement from his original position on A to his new position on B is the result of an *income effect* and a *substitution effect*. When the wage rate rises, the substitution effect works to increase the supply of labor, because giving up leisure to get goods is now a more profitable occupation than before. The income effect works to decrease the supply of labor (i.e., increase the consumption of leisure), because the person can consume more of everything, including leisure. Whether the rise in wages causes a rise or a fall in the number of hours people will wish to work depends on the relative strengths of these two effects.

3. George F. Break, "Income Taxes and Incentives To Work: An Empirical Study, Great Britain, 1955–56," *American Economic Review,* September, 1957.

4. It is common practice, following David Ricardo, to define land as the *original and inexhaustible powers of the soil*. But dust bowls were a phenomenon unknown to Ricardo, who did not know either that the deserts of North Africa were once fertile plains. Clearly, the fertility of land is not inexhaustible.

There is no value in debating which is "real" land: the total land area or the total supply of arable land. The magnitude we are interested in depends on the problem at hand. For most problems in economics, however, it is the total supply of cultivable land that is relevant. If we are interested, for example, in the effect of land taxes on the prices of agricultural goods, then it is of no help to be told that the total land area of a country is fixed; what we need to know is the effect of such taxes on the supply of cultivable land. The total supply of cultivable land is by no means perfectly inelastic; it can be expanded greatly by irrigation and other forms of reclamation and it can be contracted drastically and rapidly—as many farmers have found to their sorrow—by neglecting the principles of soil conservation.

NATURAL RESOURCES

Men often worry—usually too late—about exhausting natural resources. As we said at the beginning of this chapter, the proved oil reserves in the United States will not last another twenty years at current rates of production. But this was also true in 1920! And in 1935! The apparent paradox is resolved by the fact that every year we discover about as much oil as we produce. As long as oil remains valuable, it pays to find more of it. If the cost of finding oil becomes too high, the supplies that it is economically feasible to find will indeed be exhausted—at those prices. But, in that event, prices will surely rise (unless we discover a cheaper fuel or a cheaper method of finding and producing oil). But even if technology remains unchanged, an increase in the price of oil of as much as 35 percent will make it economically worthwhile to process the vast quantities of heretofore unexploited shale oil.

Our fathers heard the same story about iron ore that they heard about oil. They were told that the great Mesabi Range in Minnesota would be exhausted by 1975. It was effectively exhausted by 1965! And yet we still produce steel, mainly because we have discovered ways to use low-grade iron ores, once thought worth less than nothing (because they had to be dug through to get to the richer ores). The known supplies of coal appear to be inexhaustible at the current rate of use.

Although natural resources can indeed be exhausted, the problem of actual exhaustion rarely arises. By ingenuity, by substitution of other factors, and by other means, resources have generally been expandable as needed. Perhaps the best example of this is the United States experience with rubber during World War II. Cut off from all the world's supplies of natural rubber, the chemical industries produced synthetic rubber in a period much shorter than would have been required to grow new rubber trees! To be sure, the price was higher and the quality less good.

But let us not be overconfident. Man's ability to find more of any given resource, or to find a substitute to do the job, is impressive in case after case. But he has had reverses as well. The destruction of the forests of Great Britain and the extinction of some species of fish and wildlife should serve as warning. Pollution of the water and the atmosphere goes on, and could become disastrous. As with land, natural resources are neither inexhaustible nor rigidly limited.

CAPITAL

Capital is a man-made factor of production. The supply of capital in a country consists of the stock of existing machines, plant, equipment, etc. This capital is used up in the course of production and the supply is thus diminished by the amount that wears out each year. On the other hand, the stock of capital is added to each year by the production of new capital goods, the expenditure on which is called *investment expenditure*. New machines replace ones that wear out (although the new ones will rarely be physically identical with the machines they are "replacing"). The total amount of money spent on machines for all purposes is called *gross investment*. Money spent on machines that are not replacing worn-out ones, and that therefore represent net additions to the stock of capital, is called *net investment*.

The supply of capital has been observed to increase considerably over time in all modern countries. The volume of net investment determines the rate of increase of the capital stock. There is considerable evidence that net additions to the stock of capital vary considerably over the trade cycle, being low in periods of slump and high in periods of boom. Taking the long view, however, and ignoring cyclical fluctuations, there has been a fairly steady tendency for the stock of capital to increase over a very long period of time. The theory of investment, which we shall develop in subsequent sections of this book, is thus a theory of changes in the stock of capital.

The only limit to the possible growth of the capital stock is the willingness of people to divert resources from consumption to investment.

The Supply of Factors to Particular Uses

The problem of allocating factors of production among uses is an extremely general one. Even if all factors had only one use, it would still be necessary to allocate them among competing firms in the same industry. As it is, factors have many uses; a given piece of land can be used to grow a variety of crops, and it can also be subdivided for a housing development. A machinist in Detroit can work in a variety of automobile plants, or in a dozen other industries, or even in the physics laboratories at Ann Arbor. Money can be invested in government bonds, or in IBM stock, or in a find-it-yourself uranium-prospecting kit. Factors must be allocated among different industries and they must also be allocated among different firms in the same industry.

If the owners of these factors are mainly concerned with making as much money as they can, they will move their factor to that use at which it earns the most money; this movement out of one use into another will continue until the earnings of a factor in each of its various possible uses are the same. Since owners of factors take other things besides money into account—things like risk, convenience, and a good climate—factors will be moved among uses until there is no *net advantage* in further movement, allowing for both the monetary and nonmonetary advantages of different uses.

THE HYPOTHESIS OF EQUAL NET ADVANTAGE

The hypothesis of equal net advantage may be stated as follows:

Owners of factors will choose that use of their factors that produces the greatest net advantage to themselves. Net advantage includes both pecuniary and nonpecuniary elements.

This hypothesis plays the same role in the theory of distribution as the hypothesis that firms seek to maximize profits plays in the theory of production. The significant prediction that it leads to is that factors of production will be allocated among various uses in such a way that they receive the same net return in each use. What is wrong with this hypothesis as it stands?

The trouble with it is that, unless we can measure nonmonetary advantage, it is irrefutable. Suppose we observe that a mechanic is working in Ann Arbor for $1,000 a year less than he could make in Detroit. Is this evidence against the hypothesis, or does it merely mean that the nonmonetary benefits of living in Ann Arbor (or of not living in Detroit) are worth $1,000 to him? A moment's thought will make it clear that any conceivable observation could be rationalized to fit the hypothesis. ("John would rather starve as a lawyer than work for his father.")

To restore the hypothesis to the point where it can be refuted—and thus to the point where it can be useful to us—we must do one of two things: We must define in a measurable way the nonmonetary benefits that we believe are important to choices. Or we must make an assumption about the relative stability of monetary and nonmonetary advantages. The first alternative is generally regarded as impossible, unless we assume that the hypothesis is correct. It used to be said, for example, that faculty members at the University of Wisconsin paid $1,000 a year for the privilege of living on the shores of Lake Mendota. The story is still told, but, with recent salary trends in mind, the figure has been upped to $2,000. We know of no way to estimate the value of Lake Mendota to the residents of Madison; we can only observe that they appear to be willing to pay so many dollars to live there. But imputing a value in this way gives us no basis for testing the hypothesis.

The second alternative—to make an assumption about the relative stability of monetary and nonmonetary advantages—is more feasible. If, for example, we assume that the differences in nonmonetary advantages between two uses of a factor remain constant over time, we can predict that variations in monetary advantages will widen or narrow the gap and that some resources will flow in response to the change. To return to Lake Mendota, when salary differentials were $1,000, some people refused to join the University of Wisconsin faculty. If we assume that Lake Mendota's value is stable, then a widening salary differential between the University of Wisconsin and other universities would lead us to predict (1) that some people, formerly content, would now leave the university to take higher paying jobs elsewhere, and (2) that the university would have more trouble recruiting new people.

It is not necessary, of course, to make the strong assumption that nonpecuniary advantages are constant. Instead, we can assume that they change, but more slowly than pecuniary ones. In this case, we can still extract predictions about behavior.[5] This weaker assumption leads us to the following fundamental prediction:

Any change _in the relative size of the rate of pay between two uses of a factor will lead owners of factors to increase the quantity they wish to supply to the use in which the relative pay has increased, and decrease the quantity they wish to supply to the use in which it has decreased._

---

5. It would be sufficient to assume that pecuniary and nonpecuniary advantages are independent of each other. See Chapter 4. But this is an assumption that is likely to prove incorrect.

This prediction implies the necessity for a rising supply curve for a factor in any particular use. Such a supply curve (like all supply curves) can shift in response to changes in other variables. One of these is the size of the nonmonetary benefits.

Factor Mobility (Elasticity of Supply)

Does our hypothesis that factor-owners want to respond to changes in what they can earn from their factors mean that even small changes in offered rates of remuneration lead to large movements of factors, and thus to very elastic factor supplies? The answer depends upon *factor mobility*, the ease with which factors can move between uses.

Factor mobility, or immobility, is an important aspect of how well resources respond to the signals that indicate where factors are wanted. If a factor is highly mobile in the sense that the alert owners of this factor will quickly shift from use A to use B in response to a small change in factor price, then supply will be highly elastic. If, on the other hand, a factor-owner is "locked in" to some use and cannot respond quickly, the supply will tend to be inelastic, even though the owner may genuinely wish to take advantage of the higher prices offered elsewhere. Factor mobility is dependent on the speed with which factors will respond. The barriers to mobility vary substantially from factor to factor.

MOBILITY OF LAND

Land, which is physically the least mobile of all factors, is paradoxically one of the most mobile in an economic sense. Consider agricultural land. Within a year at most, one crop can be harvested and a totally different crop planted. A farm on the outskirts of a growing city can be sold for subdivision and development on very short notice. Once land is built upon, as urban land usually is, its mobility is much reduced. One can convert a site on which a hotel has been built into an office building (and many of New York's famous old hotels are being razed for just that purpose), but it takes a very large differential in the value of land use to make it worthwhile. When does it pay to tear down an existing structure that still has years of physically useful life in it? When the value of the land in the new use exceeds the value in the old one plus the costs of removing the old structure. (The larger this "plus," the more immobile the factor will be.)

MOBILITY OF CAPITAL

Most capital equipment, once constructed, is pretty immobile. A great deal of machinery is utterly specific; once built, it must either be used for the purpose for which it was designed, or else not used at all. This is, of course, not true of all pieces of capital equipment—a shed, for example, may be used for a large number of purposes—but much capital equipment is extremely immobile among uses during its physical lifetime. It is the immobility of capital equipment that makes exit of firms from declining industries a slow and difficult process.

In popular discussion, sums of money are often referred to as capital. Money represents a claim on resources. A firm or a household that has accumulated money savings can spend these on anything that it desires. It can buy beer or machines and, by so doing, will direct the nation's resources to the production of beer or machinery. Also, the firm or household can lend its money to other firms or households and thereby allow the borrowers to determine what the nation's resources will be used to produce.

Money itself is not a factor of production. But it represents a claim to the goods and services produced by factors, and the way in which the claim is exercised influences the allocation of factors of production among alternative users. Money itself is highly mobile. An owner who planned to use it for one purpose can change his mind at the last moment and use it for another. The long-term mobility of capital equipment comes about through the mobility of money. During the life of a piece of capital, the firm may lay aside depreciation funds that allow it to replace the capital good when it wears out. If conditions of demand and cost have not changed, the firm may spend the money to replace the worn-out piece of equipment with an identical one. The firm may, however, do many other things with these funds: It may buy a newly designed machine to produce the same goods; it may buy machines to produce totally different goods; or it may lend the money to some other firm for the latter's uses. In this way, the long-run allocation of a country's stock of capital among various uses changes.

MOBILITY OF LABOR

Labor is unique as a factor in one most important way: Nonmonetary considerations play a larger role in the mobility of labor than in the mobility of any other factor, because the resource involved and the owner of it are inseparable. People may be both satisfied with or frustrated by the kind of work they do, where they do it, the people they do it with, and the social status of their occupations.

Many organizations, private and public, adopt policies that affect their personnel and impede their mobility as workers. When labor unions negotiate seniority rights for their members, they protect the old employee from being laid off in a cutback of production, but they also make him very reluctant to change jobs. When an employer provides his employees with a pension plan, the employees may not want to forfeit this fringe benefit by changing jobs. When states provide compensation to unemployed residents, these residents may be reluctant to leave the state, even to find work.

Although labor is in substantial degree influenced by nonwage considerations, we should still expect, according to the fundamental hypothesis of factor supply, that labor would respond to changes in the wage structure. But we must be careful. If doctors' earnings go up and farmers' earnings go down, would farmers move into medicine? No, for it is not easy for a farmer to become a doctor (or for that matter for a doctor to become a farmer). The very visible barriers between various occupations have led some economists to speak of labor as consisting of a series of *noncompeting groups* and to explain differential pay between occupations as the consequence. Since, as we all know, the sons of many farmers become doctors, the notion of real walls between various occupations does not seem a very adequate explanation of the immobility of labor. And not all occupational shifts are as difficult as that between medicine and farming.

The key to understanding labor mobility is *time*. In the short run, it is very difficult for people to shift occupations. It is not hard for a secretary to shift from one company to another, and it is not hard to persuade her to take a job in New York instead of in Jersey City, but it will be difficult for her to become an editor or a fashion model in a short period of time. There are two considerations here: ability and training. Lack of either will stratify some people and make certain kinds of mobility difficult for them.

Over long periods, labor mobility between occupations is very great indeed. In assessing the mobility of labor, it is important to remember that the labor force is not static. At one end, young people enter the labor force from school, and at the other end, exit from retirement or death. The turnover in the labor force, due to these causes, is something on the order of 3 or 4 percent per year. Thus, even if no one ever changed jobs, it would be possible to reallocate 3 or 4 percent of the labor force annually merely by redirecting new entrants to jobs other than the ones left vacant by persons leaving the labor force. Over a period of twenty years, a totally different occupational distribution could appear without a single individual ever changing his job. The role of education in adapting people to needed jobs is very great. Since children spend much of their first twenty years in school, it is possible to achieve large increases in the supply of any desired labor skill within a decade or so. Sputnik made the world aware of the notable success of the Soviet Union in increasing its supply of scientists in a very short period of time.

Various studies have been made to determine the amount of mobility shown by labor in moving from job to job and place to place. In times of heavy depression, mobility from place to place is very low. Labor is understandably reluctant to move from areas with, say, 20 percent unemployment into areas with, say, 10 percent unemployment, even though the chances of finding a job in the latter areas may be higher than in the former ones.[6] In periods of more or less full employment, there appears to be some evidence that differentials in wages between areas and occupations do reflect relative scarcities and that labor does tend to some extent to move from low-wage sectors of the economy to high-wage ones; there seems to be even stronger evidence, however, that labor is more attracted by the chance of obtaining a job than by the wage rate actually paid for that job.

Mobility appears to be somewhat higher in the United States than in many European countries, but the same reluctance to move in the face of unemployment is found.[7] Approximately 1 million American families move to a different city each year. (This is, of course, the basis for the moving industry.)

By way of contrast, studies of labor mobility over the generations, or *social stratification* as the sociologists call it, indicate impressive mobility. The data show, in a nutshell, that while it pays to have a successful father (successful in the sense of being a member of one of the occupations at the high end of the scale), it is not necessary to becoming successful one's self. Education is the key to an individual's earning a high income and, *by the same token*, to expanding supplies of factors in those occupations for which there is the greatest demand for services.

To sum up, labor is much more mobile in the long run than in the short run. Over a given time period, it is more mobile between jobs in the same location and occupation than between different locations (where movement of

---

6. See H. W. Robinson, "The Response of Labour to Economic Incentives," in *Oxford Studies in the Price Mechanism,* ed. T. Wilson and P. W. S. Andrews (Clarendon Press, 1951).

7. See Gladys Palmer, *et al., The Reluctant Job Changer* (University of Pennsylvania Press, 1962).

the family is a deterrent) or different occupations (where lack of skills is a deterrent).

MAN-MADE BARRIERS TO LABOR MOBILITY

Among the many institutions that man has introduced that limit factor mobility, we have already mentioned private pension schemes, eligibility requirements for unemployment compensation, and seniority provisions in collective-bargaining agreements.

There are other barriers as well: *Licensing* is required in dozens of trades and professions. Barbers, electricians, doctors, and, in some places, even peddlers must have licenses. There is, of course, a perfectly legitimate reason for requiring licenses in cases where the public must be protected against the incompetent or the quack or the nuisance. But licensing can also have the effect of limiting supply. The fact that medicine has long been the highest paid occupation (average income about $25,000 per year in 1965) and that doctors have long been in short supply is a result of the difficulties in getting into

medical schools, the long internship and residency requirements, the rules concerning certification, and so forth. It is at least possible that doctors' earnings are high because the barriers to entry into the profession prevent even long-run increases in the proportion of the population being admitted to medical practice. Whether such barriers as exist are required by the standards of the profession or are designed to keep the supply limited (and the earnings high) is a matter open to debate.

Unions may impose barriers to labor mobility. The "closed shop," for example, which requires all employees of a plant or a trade to be a member of a particular union, gives unions the power to limit the supply of labor that they represent.[8]

Racial prejudice, and other arbitrary attitudes, also limit the mobility of labor.

How important barriers of each of these kinds are, singly and in aggregate, is an empirical matter and the evidence is not conclusive.

Summary

1. The labor force is defined as that part of the populace working or looking for work. The size of the labor force varies considerably in response to variations in the demand for labor. Attempts to increase the total supply of labor by increasing the wage rate could result in a decrease in supply instead. Such evidence as we have suggests that the common belief that high taxes reduce the supply of effort is not substantiated.

2. For most economic problems, it is cul-

tivable land, and not total land area, that matters. While the latter may be fixed, the former is not. As with land, natural resources are neither inexhaustable nor rigidly fixed.

3. Net investment, which is gross investment in capital goods minus the funds spent replacing capital that has worn out, is observed to vary considerably over the trade cycle, but there has been a tendency for the stock of capital to rise in the long run.

4. The hypothesis of equal net advantage

8. Closed-shop practices were very sharply curtailed by the Taft-Hartley Act of 1947.

states that owners of factors will choose that use of their factors that produces the greatest net advantage to themselves. Net advantage includes both pecuniary and nonpecuniary elements. As it stands, this hypothesis is irrefutable, but we can reformulate it in a number of ways that make it meaningful. See the discussion on page 358. This leads us to the fundamental hypothesis of factor supply: Any change in the relative size of the rate of remuneration between two uses of a factor will lead owners of a factor to increase the quantity they wish to supply to the use in which the relative pay has increased, and decrease the quantity they wish to supply to the use in which it has decreased. This leads us

to predict a rising supply curve for a factor in any particular use.

5. Agricultural land, though physically immobile, is economically mobile. It can move with a fair amount of ease from one use to the next. Urban land is far less mobile. Capital equipment is quite immobile, and it is this that makes the exit of firms from declining industries a difficult process.

6. The discussion of labor mobility is summarized on page 361. There are also manmade barriers to labor mobility, such as private pension schemes, eligibility requirements for unemployment compensation, job seniority, licensing, "closed shops," and prejudice.

QUESTIONS FOR DISCUSSION

1. "If the picture of the profit-maximizing businessman hiring and firing labor to keep his costs down is imperfect, the idea of workers always on the lookout for higher pay and ready to move to better jobs is worse." In what way does our theory differ from this?

2. "Recent empirical studies have shown that workers simply do not behave according to the assumptions of economic theory. Workers have strong attachments to particular geographical localities, to occupations, even to specific jobs, often without regard to the economic advantage of such attachments." Is this contrary to "economic theory"? What difficulty is presented by the inclusion of such factors in our theory?

3. Use Figure 1 to show what would happen if, instead of a doubling of the wage rate, the worker received an increase to only $3.00 an hour with, however, an overtime bonus of an extra $3.00 for every hour worked after eight hours. What choice has he under each system

that he does not have under the other? Assume, again, that he is free to work any number of hours he chooses.

4. "The analysis surrounding Figure 1 is obviously unrealistic, and therefore useless, since we know that no one is physically capable of sacrificing all 24 hours of his leisure in order to work." Does this undoubtedly correct observation that people must take time out at least to sleep vitiate any of the analysis? Can you amend the figure to show the choice available to the individual if he is physically incapable of sacrificing more than 16 hours of his leisure?

5. What natural and man-made barriers to labor mobility have been mentioned in this chapter? Can you think of any others?

6. Arrange the following factors in what you regard as their order of decreasing mobility: a wheat farm, a doctor, a Boeing 909 belonging to Pan American Airways, the Empire State Building, and the land the Empire State Building is on.

Chapter **34** THE PRICING OF FACTORS IN COMPETITIVE MARKETS

WE HAVE NOW DEVELOPED THEORIES BOTH OF the demand for, and the supply of factors of production. This is all we need to develop a theory of the pricing of factors on a free market. Given that factor prices are free to vary, prices and quantities employed will tend to the point at which supply equals demand. Furthermore, shifts in either the demand for, or the supply of factors will have the effects on prices, quantities, and factor incomes predicted by normal price theory.

The theory of factor prices is an absolutely general one. If one is concerned with labor, one should interpret factor prices to mean wages; if one is thinking about land, factor prices should be interpreted to mean rent, and so on. We shall start by assuming that factors are bought and sold on a competitive market by a large number of buyers and sellers. In Chapter 35, we will look at the effect of introducing monopolistic elements into the markets for factors.

Money, Real, and Relative Prices

Changes both in relative factor prices and in the share of national income going to a factor are likely to be brought about through changes in the *money prices* of a factor; but the mere knowledge that the money price of a given factor has risen tells us very little about what has happened either to the position of the factor relative to another factor, or relative to the whole national income. If we wish to inquire into relative prices we need to know how the money prices of at least two factors have changed, for only then will we be able to say that the price of one factor

has increased or decreased relative to the price of another factor. If we wish to know what has happened to the share of the national income going to some factor, then we must know its money income and the money value of total national income. Only if money national income and all other money prices are constant can variations in the money prices of one factor give us direct information about the factor's relative price and its share in the national income. In partial equilibrium analysis, we assume that total income and all other prices remain constant. In this case, therefore, a variation in the money price of a factor causes a simultaneous variation both in its relative price (compared to any other single factor) and in the share of the national income going to the factor.

Relative Prices Under Competition

Consider the prices of a number of closely related factors, such as different kinds of labor.

If all these factors were identical, then all factor prices would tend toward the same level. Factors would tend to move from low-price occupations to high-price ones. The supply of factors would diminish in occupations in which prices were low, and the resulting shortage would tend to force prices up; the supply of factors would increase in occupations in which prices were high, and the resulting surplus would force factor prices

down. The movement would continue until there were no further incentives to transfer, i.e., until factor prices were equalized. This equality would be established whatever the states of demand in the various industries. Equal factor prices do not mean that all industries use equal amounts of a factor. Figure 1 illustrates two industries with very different demands for a certain factor. Given these conditions of demand, most of the factor would flow into the industry pictured in Figure 1(ii).

Causes of differences in factor prices are

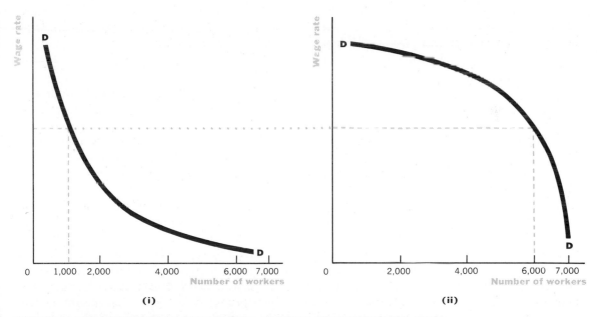

(i)   (ii)

FIGURE 1   THE ALLOCATION OF WORKERS BETWEEN TWO INDUSTRIES WITH DIFFERING DEMAND CURVES

of two sorts, dynamic (or disequilibrium) ones, and static (or equilibrium) ones. The dynamic differences are ones associated with various changes, such as the rise of one industry and the decline of another. Such differentials set up movements in factor supplies, and these movements will themselves act to remove the differentials. The differences in prices may persist for a long time, but there is a tendency for them to be reduced and, in equilibrium, they will be eliminated.

If there were a rise in the demand for product A and a fall in demand for product B, there would be an increase in the (derived) demand for factors in industry A and a decrease in the (derived) demand for factors in industry B. Factor prices would go up in A and down in B. This is an example of a dynamic change in relative prices, for the changes themselves will cause factors to move from industry B to industry A, and this movement will cause the price differentials to lessen and eventually to disappear. How long this process takes depends on how easily factors move from one industry to the other— that is, on the extent of factor mobility. Some factors, particularly labor, may be relatively immobile in the short run, and thus dynamic differentials might last for some time, even if all factors were identical and even if there were no man-made barriers to movement.

Equilibrium-price differences, on the other hand, are ones that would persist in a state of equilibrium without there being any tendency for them to be removed by the competitive forces of the market. Equilibrium differentials in factor prices are related to differences in the factors themselves (e.g., land of different fertilities, or labor of different abilities) or to different nonmonetary advantages of different factor employments. *Ceteris paribus*, a job with high nonmonetary rewards will have a

lower equilibrium wage rate than a job with low nonmonetary rewards. Thus, it is often possible, for example, to pay people in academic and research jobs less than they would be able to earn in the world of commerce and industry, because there are substantial nonmonetary advantages attached to the former compared with the latter. If labor were paid the same in both jobs, then it would move out of industry and into academic employment. Excess demand for labor in industry and excess supply in universities would then cause industrial wages to rise relative to academic ones until the movement of labor ceased.

Equilibrium differentials may also be caused by differences among factors. There is, for example, a shortage of persons able and willing to do skilled jobs. Thus, in equilibrium, the skilled worker earns more than the unskilled worker; no movement from unskilled to skilled jobs eliminates this differential, because it is difficult for most unskilled workers to become skilled ones. It is important to realize that the high pay of the skilled man relative to the unskilled one merely reflects relative demand and supply conditions for these two types of labor. There is nothing in the nature of competitive markets that ensures that the skilled worker always gets high pay just because he is skilled. If, for example, the demand for skilled workers fell off so much that, even though the supply was small, there was a glut of such workers, their wages would come down. On the other hand, if there were a change in education so that unskilled workers could now acquire skills, the wages of skilled workers would fall relative to those of unskilled workers. History is replete with examples of particular groups of skilled workers who have lost their privileged position when there was a change in the supply of or the demand for their services. Many people feel that it is both unjust and incomprehensible that, since World War II, truck drivers and coal miners have made more money than have schoolteachers. Whatever the justice of the matter, it is certainly not incomprehensible. A rise in the supply of schoolteachers relative to the demand for their services and a decline in the supply of truck drivers and coal miners relative to the demand for their services will, according to the normal workings of the market, raise the earnings of truck drivers and coal miners relative to those of schoolteachers.

Costs and Rents

In Chapter 17, we encountered the notion of economic rent, which was the difference between the value of the factor in its best use and its value in its next best alternative use. We now want to consider the concept again, but from the point of view not of the individual firm but of society. Let us regard the total payment to a factor as being made up of two parts: the amount paid to a factor that is just enough to keep it from transferring to another use (which we shall call *transfer earnings*) and the remainder, which we shall continue to call *economic rent*.

We care about this distinction for two reasons: First, a change in a factor's earnings that decreases its transfer earnings will induce factor supplies to shift to other uses, whereas a decrease in its rent will not. (How much of the salary of a Supreme Court Justice or of the President of the United States is transfer earnings? Would a reduction in pay lead them to seek other employments? Compare them to postal clerks.) Thus, policies that are designed to lead to resource shifts must have an effect on transfer earnings. And we care about it, second, because the incidence of different kinds of taxes, a matter that has interested economists for generations, depends crucially upon the distinction between transfer earnings and rents.

ECONOMIC RENT: HISTORY OF THE CONCEPT

The present concept of rent arose out of a policy controversy. In the early part of the nineteenth century, when English economics was in its infancy, there was a controversy about the high price of corn (the generic term for all grains). The high price was causing great hardship, since grain was a primary source of food. Some people argued that corn had a high price because the landlords were charging very high rents to corn farmers. In order to meet these high rents, the price that farmers charged for their corn had to be raised to a high level also. Thus, it was argued, the price of corn was high because the rents of agricultural land were high. Those who held this view advocated restricting the power of the landlords and somehow forcing them to behave reasonably. Other people, including David Ricardo, one of the great figures of English classical economics, held that the situation was exactly the reverse: The price of corn was high, they said, because there was a shortage of corn caused by the Napoleonic Wars. Because corn had a high price, there was keen competition among farmers to obtain land, and this competition bid up the rents of corn land. If the price of corn were to fall so that corn-growing became less profitable, then the demand for land would fall, and the price paid for the use of land (i.e., its rent) would fall as well. Those holding this view advocated removing the tariff so that imported corn could come into the country, thus increasing the supply and bringing the price down. Ricardo's argument involves the idea we have met before of *derived demand*. Landlords, Ricardo was saying, cannot charge any price they want for land; the prices they get will depend on demand and supply.

The argument was elaborated by considering land to have only one use, the growing of corn. The supply of land was regarded as given and virtually unchangeable—i.e., land was in perfectly inelastic supply and land-owners would prefer to rent out their land for some return rather than to leave it idle. Nothing had to be paid to prevent land from transferring to a use other than growing corn because it had no other use, and no self-respecting landowner would leave his land idle as long as he could obtain some return, no matter how small, by renting it out. Therefore, so went the argument, all of the payment to land, i.e., rent, is a surplus over and above what is necessary to keep the land in its present use. Given the fixed supply of land, the price will depend on the demand for land, which is itself a function of the price of corn.

Rent, which was the term for the payment for the use of land, thus became the term for a surplus payment to a factor over and above what was necessary to keep it in its present use. Subsequently, two facts were realized: First, factors of production other than land often earn a surplus over and above what is necessary to keep them in their present use. Movie stars, for example, are in very short and pretty well-fixed supply and their possible earnings in other occupations are proba-

bly quite moderate. But, because there is a huge demand for their services, they may receive payments greatly in excess of what is needed to keep them from transferring to other occupations. Second, it was realized that land itself often had many alternative uses, and, from the point of view of any one use, part of the payment made to land would necessarily have to be paid to keep it in its present use. Thus, it appeared that all factors of production were pretty much the same; part of the payment made to them would be a payment necessary to keep them from transferring to other uses and part would be a surplus over and above what was necessary to keep them in their present use. This surplus came to be called economic rent.

RENT: ECONOMIC AND OTHERWISE

The term economic rent is most unfortunate. The adjective economic is often dropped and the economist may speak of rent when he means economic rent—thus causing confusion between the surplus concept and the payment made for hiring land and buildings. When the tenant speaks of the high rent he pays to his landlord, most of what he refers to is a transfer payment and only some is an economic rent. It is usually clear from the context whether the term rent is meant to indicate a surplus above transfer earnings (the economist's usage) or the total payment for hiring land or buildings (the common usage). Guard against confusion. If you are asked on an examination to discuss the effects of a 10 percent tax on all apartment rents in New York, you may be tempted to apply the concept of economic rent to the rent of apartments. But you should not. The land has alternative uses. If apartments become less profitable, apartment builders will not be able to outbid other potential users of the land and fewer apartments will be built. As the supply diminishes, rentals (in the everyday sense) will rise and some of the tax will be passed on to the tenants. Compare this result with the case in which the land has only one use so that all the rent paid is economic rent.

Economic Rent and Transfer Earnings

In most cases, the actual earnings of a factor of production will be a composite of transfer earnings and economic rent: It is possible, however, to imagine a case in which

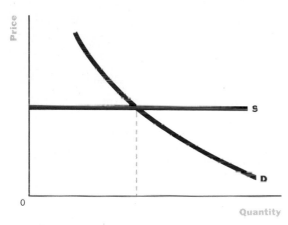

FIGURE 2

all earnings are either transfer earnings or economic rent. Consider some individual firm or some industry faced with a perfectly elastic supply curve of a factor of production; it will be able to obtain all that it wants at the going price, but, if it does not pay this price, it will not obtain any quantity of the factor. In such a case, which is illustrated in Figure 2, the whole price paid to the factor represents transfer earnings: The amount that is actually paid must be paid to prevent the factor from transferring to another use.

What about a factor that is fixed in supply

and has only one use? This factor is in perfectly inelastic supply: The amount offered for sale will be the same whatever the price. (See Figure 3.) The whole of the price paid to the factor is an economic rent, because, if a lower price were paid, the factor would not transfer to an alternative use. You might think that, in such a case as this, the factor would not command any price, but you would be wrong. The price, as in all other free-market cases, is determined by demand and supply. The fixed quantity available is, in the example

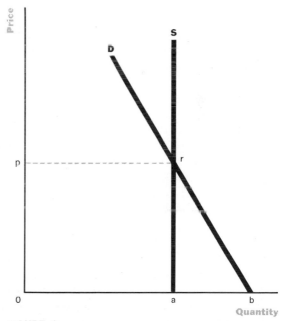

FIGURE 3

illustrated in Figure 3, the amount *Oa;* if the price were zero, however, the amount demanded would be *Ob.* Thus, at a price of zero, there would be excess demand for the factor, and competition among buyers would force the price upward until it reached *Op* and the excess demand disappeared. The equilibrium price paid to the factor is *Op,* and the quantity employed is *Oa;* hence, total factor income is indicated by the area of the rectangle *Opra.*

Figure 4 shows an upward-sloping supply curve of a factor of production. Given the demand curve, *D,* the equilibrium price would be *Op* and the equilibrium employment *Og;* total factor earnings would be *Opzg.* If *Og* units of the factor are to be attracted into the industry, and if a single price must be paid, then it is necessary to pay the price *Op.* However, all but the last unit (i.e., the *Ogth,* which might, say, be the 15,000th) would be prepared to remain in the industry for a price less than *Op.* In fact, *Oa* of these units would be prepared to remain if the price were

as low as *Or.* If the price rose from *Or* to *Os,* an additional *ab* units would be attracted into the industry; if the price rose by a further *st* units, an additional *bc* units would enter the industry. Clearly, for any unit that we care to pick, the point on the supply curve corresponding to it shows the minimum price that must be paid in order to keep that unit in the industry (i.e., its transfer earnings). Equally clearly, if the supply curve slopes upward, all previous units have lower transfer earnings. Consider, for example, the *Odth* unit (possibly the 10,000th). The transfer earnings of this unit are *Ou;* if any less is paid, this unit will not be supplied, and if any more is paid, it is a rent—a payment in excess of what is necessary to keep the factor in its present use.

We could repeat the same argument for every point; we could show, for example, that the transfer earnings of the *Oath* unit are *Or,* of the *Obth* unit *Os,* and of the *Octh* unit *Ot.* Repetition of this argument for every unit

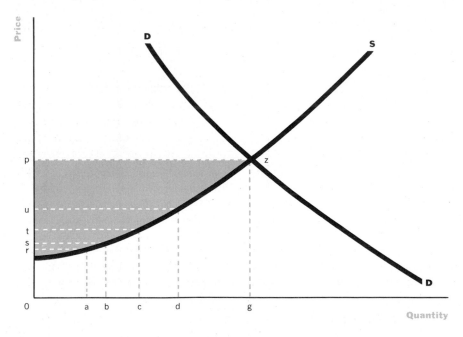

FIGURE 4

from the first to the Ogth shows that the total transfer earnings of the Og units is the white area *below* the supply curve. Since the total payment made is the rectangle $Opzg$, it follows that the economic rent earned by the factor is the shaded area *above* the supply curve and below the line pz.

The following example illustrates why a rising supply curve involves rents: If universities increase the salaries paid to professors of economics in order to attract additional economists into university teaching (and away from industry and government), those economists who are persuaded to shift into university teaching will be receiving only transfer earnings. But those economists who were already content to be university professors will find their salaries have increased as well, and this increase will be a rent to them. Figures 2, 3, and 4 suggest the following important conclusion:

The more elastic the supply curve, the less the amount of the payment to factors that is a rent and the more that is a transfer earning.

KINDS OF TRANSFERS

How much of a given payment to a factor is an economic rent and how much is a transfer earning depends on what sort of transfer we are considering.

If we consider the transfer of a factor from one firm to another within a single industry for which the supply of the factor should be highly elastic, then pretty well all of the factor's earnings will be transfer earnings. If the firm in question did not pay the factor the going price, then the factor would transfer to another firm in the same industry. If we are

considering the transfer of a factor from one industry to another, then part of the payment may be a transfer earning and part an economic rent, since mobility will be less and thus the supply curve less elastic. We cannot point to a given factor, a laborer, say, and assert that of his income of $6,000, $5,000 is a transfer earning and $1,000 a rent, for it all depends on what transfer we are considering.

This discussion also highlights the point we encountered in Chapter 17: A cost to the firm may be a rent to society. The National Broadcasting Company regards the enormous amount it pays Jack Benny as a cost, since it is necessary to keep him broadcasting for them instead of for CBS or ABC.[1] But society, which is only concerned that he *is* broadcasting, regards much of this payment as a rent, since he could be paid less and would still go on broadcasting. This is a difficult point, and we spell it out below for labor and for land.

ECONOMIC RENT AND TRANSFER EARNINGS IN THE PAYMENT TO LABOR

Since labor is able to move from job to job, something must be paid to keep a given unit of labor in its present use; this payment is a transfer earning to labor. The amount that has to be paid to keep labor in its present use depends upon what the use is. Let us say, for example, that carpenters receive $30 for working a normal 8-hour day. A single small construction firm will have to pay carpenters $30 per day or no carpenter will work for it. To that one firm, the whole $30 is a transfer payment; if the whole $30 were not paid, the carpenters would not work for that firm. But

---

1. He has in fact shifted several times in his thirty-nine years.

consider what would happen if the whole construction industry were forced to reduce the wages offered to carpenters. In this case, carpenters could not move to other construction firms to get more money. If they do not like the wages offered, they will have to move to another industry. If the best they can do elsewhere is $25 per day, then they will not begin to leave the construction industry until wages in that industry fall below $25. In this case, the transfer earnings of carpenters in construction are $25 and, when they were receiving $30 (presumably because there was a heavy demand for their services), the additional $5 was an economic rent from the point of view of the construction industry. What would happen if there was a decline in the demand for carpenters in all industries? The carpenter, if he did not like the wages, would have to move to another occupation: In other words he must cease to be a carpenter. If no carpenter was induced to do this until the wage fell to $20, then $20 would be the transfer earnings for carpenters in general. The wage of $20 must be paid to persuade carpenters to remain carpenters. The moral of this story is as follows: The amount of any given payment that represents transfer earnings and the amount that represents economic rent depends on what sort of a transfer we are considering: one from firm to firm, one from industry to industry, one from occupation to occupation, or one from area to area.

An important policy implication of the distinction between rents and transfer earnings concerns the effectiveness of wage increases on supply. For example, if the United States wants more physicists, should it subsidize physicists' salaries? In the long run, such a

policy may well have an effect upon supply. It may influence schoolboys uncertain about whether to become engineers or physicists to become physicists. But it will also mean that a great deal of money will have to be spent on extra payments to people who are already physicists. And these payments will be economic rents, since existing physicists have demonstrated that they are prepared to be physicists at their old salaries. Although some may have been considering transferring to another occupation, such movements are not common.[2] An alternative policy, which may produce more physicists per dollar, is to subsidize scholarships and fellowships for students who will train to become physicists. The National Science Foundation and the Atomic Energy Commission do precisely this. In the same way, baseball teams and movie studios provide training schools. If the supply curve is quite inelastic, an increase in the quantity supplied may be more easily achieved by shifting the supply curve to the right than by moving along it.

ECONOMIC RENT AND TRANSFER EARNINGS IN THE PAYMENT TO LAND

The formal analysis here is identical to that given in the case of labor. How much of the payment made to a given piece of land is a transfer payment depends upon the nature of the transfer. Consider, first, the case of an individual wheat farmer. He must pay the going price for land in order to prevent the land from being transferred to another wheat farmer. From his point of view, therefore, the whole of the payment that he makes for the

---

2. The problem is different where international mobility is high—as it is with physicists. One of the reasons for the considerable migration of trained physicists of all ages from Britain to the United States is very much higher monetary rewards to be earned in the U.S. compared with the U.K. Clearly, many British physicists are being paid less than their transfer earnings and the result is a steady one-way flow from Britain to America. This flow is called the "brain drain" in the British press.

land is a transfer payment. What about a particular industry that uses land? In order to secure land for, say, wheat production, the industry must pay at least as much for the land as it could earn when put to other uses. From the point of view of the wheat industry, that part of the payment made for land that is equal to what it could earn in its next most remunerative use is a transfer payment. If that much is not paid, then the land will in fact be transferred to the alternative use. If, however, land particularly suitable for wheat-growing is scarce relative to the demand for it, then the actual payment for the use of this land may be above the transfer payment; any additional payment is an economic rent. Assume, for example, that farmers will pay up to $50 per acre to use land for the crop most remunerative after wheat. Now wheat farmers must offer $50 to secure the land. But it may be that the price of wheat is such that the profits of wheat-growing are very high when only $50 per acre is paid for the land. A large number of farmers will wish to hire land at this price in order to grow wheat. The demand for wheat land will exceed its supply. Competition will bid up the rent offered until the demand is equal to the supply. The rental finally established might be, say, $60 per acre. In this case, from the point of view of the wheat industry as a whole, $50 is transfer earnings and the remaining $10 is economic rent. If the price of wheat falls and, as a result, the demand for wheat land falls, then the rent paid for wheat land will also fall. This will continue until the rent offered falls to $50 and then land will begin to be transferred out of wheat into other uses. As this transfer continues, the supply of wheat diminishes and the price of

wheat rises. The process will continue until the price of wheat has risen enough to allow the remaining wheat farmers to pay the $50 transfer cost necessary to keep the land out of other uses.

Land is very mobile between agricultural uses because the location is usually of little importance. In the case of urban uses, however, location of the land is critical. If there is a shortage of land in central Los Angeles, such land as is available will command a high price but, no matter what the price paid, this will not cause land in rural areas to move into downtown Los Angeles.

The high payments made to urban land are largely economic rents. The land is scarce relative to the demand for it and it commands a price very much above what it could earn in agricultural uses. The payment it receives is thus well in excess of what is necessary to prevent it from transferring from urban uses back to agricultural uses.

From the point of view of one particular type of urban use, however, high rents are a transfer payment that must be paid to keep the land from transferring to other urban uses. Motion-picture theaters, for example, provide but a small portion of the total demand for land in central New York; if there were no movies at all, rentals of land would be about what they are now. Thus the industry faces a perfectly elastic supply of land in central New York, and the whole of the price that it pays for its land is a transfer payment that must be paid to keep the land from transferring to other uses.[3]

A DIGRESSION: THE VALUE OF ASSETS

Consider, for example, two pieces of land of equal size, one growing wheat and return-

---

3. A classic examination question of two decades ago was: Discuss the view that the price of theater seats is high in central New York because the price of land is high. The question should be answered in the affirmative, not the negative, as examiners often seem to expect. The confusion is between transfer from urban to rural uses and transfer from one urban to another urban use.

ing, after costs, a profit of $1,000 per annum; the other growing oats and returning, after all costs, a profit of $500 per annum. Assuming that the second piece of land is as good as the first, the person farming it would be likely to transfer it from oats to wheat production. Assume, however, that this cannot be done—that the first piece of land is suitable only for growing wheat and that the second piece is suitable only for growing oats. Under these circumstances, the first piece of land is clearly worth twice as much as the second piece of land. If, for example, the two pieces were offered for sale at prices of $10,000 and $7,500, no one would buy the second piece in preference to the first one. Ten thousand dollars invested in buying the first piece of land yields $1,000 per year, whereas three-quarters as much money, i.e., $7,500, invested in the second piece yields only half as much income, i.e., $500 per year. Clearly, the first piece of land is a better investment than the second one, and no one would be prepared to buy the second piece. If, however, the first piece were offered for $10,000 and the second piece for $5,000, then both pieces would represent equally good investments. The rate of return per dollar invested would then be the same for each piece of land.

When people buy an asset—a piece of land, a government bond, a common stock—they are investing their money in return for some expected yield. Self-interest on the part of investors ensures that the relative prices of various assets will reflect their relative earning powers. If one asset brings an income twice as big as that brought by another asset, *ceteris paribus*, the one asset will command twice the price of that commanded by the other asset. If this is the case, then a dollar invested in either asset will bring the same rate of return. Were this not the case, a dollar invested in one asset would bring a higher return than a dollar invested in the other and all investors would prefer one asset to the other.

This comparison between assets can best be made by expressing the return on each asset as a percentage of the purchase price. In the above example, the annual earnings are 10 percent of the purchase price; anyone buying either piece of land would have an annual income equal to 10 percent of his investment.

Now, assume that the general rate of return that can be made on investments of a given degree of risk is X percent. In this case, the price of any single asset of a comparable degree of risk will be determined in the market, so that it also yields a return of X percent. If the price were lower, everyone would rush to buy this asset rather than the others that yield X percent; if the price were higher, no one would wish to buy this particular asset when all others yielded X percent.

Assume, for example, that the going rate of return is 5 percent. A particular asset yielding a net income of $200 per year indefinitely would command a price of $4,000. If the price were less, say, $2,000, the earnings would be in excess of 5 percent; in fact, they would be 10 percent, and everyone would rush to buy this asset. The competition among potential purchasers would push up the price. If the price were higher than $4,000, say $8,000, then the yield would be less than 5 percent—in fact, 2.5 percent in this case—and no one would wish to purchase the asset and its price would have to fall.

The price of an asset is directly related to its earning capacity. If there is competition among purchasers of assets, asset prices will tend to be set at levels that yield equal rates of return.

The above discussion of the pricing of assets can be applied to one problem that is extremely important in subsequent parts of this book. A bond is evidence of debt. It usually takes the form of a piece of paper recording a promise to repay the sum of money originally borrowed (the principal) at some future date, and to pay a stated sum of money each year in the interim (the interest on the loan). A stylized picture of such a bond is presented here:

Harper & Row, Publishers
promises to pay to
the Bearer

$1000
in 1975

and, on the first of January each
year until 1975, to pay

$50

Assume that I loan $1,000 to Harper & Row by purchasing this bond at a time when the market rate of interest is 5 percent. Now assume that a few years later the market rate of interest rises to 10 percent so that firms issuing new bonds similar to the one illustrated will have to offer $100 per year by way of interest payment. Now, if I should wish to sell my existing $1,000 bond, paying $50 interest per year, I will be unable to obtain $1,000 for it. Since investors can purchase a new bond yielding 10 percent, no one will purchase my bonds for $1,000, as this will yield them only 5 percent. Thus a purchaser would offer me a price sufficiently below $1,000 so that he would receive 10 percent on his investment.

A rise in the current rate of interest entails a fall in the market price of all existing bonds, the fall being sufficient so that a purchaser of an existing bond will receive the same return on his investment as he could receive by buying a new bond. Thus the current rate of interest on new loans and the market price of existing bonds vary inversely with each other.

LAND RENTS, LAND VALUES, AND LAND TAXES

The relation between the earnings of land and the value of land is just a special case of how the value of assets is determined. Quite clearly, the larger the yield that can be obtained for any given piece of land, the higher the rent (in the everyday sense of the word) that can be obtained for the land's services, and the higher the price that can be obtained from selling the land. The sale value of a piece of land is therefore directly related to the rent that can be asked for the land; both of these reflect the same thing, earning power. A tax on land values and a tax on the payments for the use of land are thus taxes on precisely the same thing. Most actual land taxes are based upon the assessed value of land. Who pays them? If the same tax rate is applied to all uses of land, the relative profitability of different uses will be unaffected and thus there will be no effects on the allocation of land among uses. Land will not be forced out of use because land that is very unprofitable will command little rent and so pay little tax. Thus there will be no change in the supply of goods that are produced with the aid of land, and, since there is no change in supply, there can be no change in prices. *The tax cannot be passed on to consumers.* Farmers will be willing to pay just as much (and no more) as they would have offered previously for the use of land. Agricultural prices and rents will be unchanged and the whole of the tax will be borne by the landlord. The net rents earned by landlords will fall by the full amount of the tax, and land values will fall correspondingly (because land is now a less attractive investment relative to, say, bonds than it was previously).

This argument depends on the assumption that the supply of land is completely inelastic. If the total supply of land to all uses does not respond to the tax on rentals, then the tax cannot be shifted by landlords. We have already warned against the assumption that the total supply of arable land is necessarily fixed in supply. Some taxes on land might discourage long-run conservation policies, so that the total supply of cultivable land would diminish. If this were true, the prices of agricultural commodities would rise and part of the effect of the tax would be passed on to the consumers of agricultural produce.

THE SINGLE-TAX MOVEMENT

Taxation of land values has had enormous appeal both intellectually and politically. The peak of its appeal was eighty years ago. The "single-tax movement" of which Henry George (1839–1897), a printer by trade,[4] was the guiding genius, caught the imagination of hundreds of thousands of people. The policy was to tax away the "unearned increment" that accrued to landowners. What was the appeal?

The total supply of land in a country tends to be pretty well fixed. As both population and incomes rise, there will be an increase in the demand for land. This rise in demand will cause an increase in the rents, and, since values depend on what can be earned, it will also cause an increase in the values of land.[5] Thus the owners of land gain from the natural progress of society without their having to contribute anything.

We cannot, on the basis of positive economics, make a moral judgment on this situation. It is sufficient to point out that many people have been incensed at this "unearned increment" and, watching the huge fortunes accruing to landlords in a rapidly growing society, they have proposed various measures for removing this "unearned wealth" from the landowner.

It should be noted that the normative issue here is not necessarily one of the "rich landowner" versus the "poor worker." Many landowners (farmers and owners of family residences) may be relatively poor, whereas a millionaire may invest in certain assets whose values do not rise automatically with the progress of society.

The less emotive, but more enduring appeal of taxes on land values arises from the fact that economic rent can be taxed away without affecting the allocation of resources.

---

4. George ran for Mayor of New York City in 1886, and very nearly won. He campaigned on the issue of the single tax. His book *Progress and Poverty* (Appleton, 1880) is probably the all-time best seller on an economic issue.

5. This was the prediction of the classical economists, particularly David Ricardo. The prediction has proved correct in the case of urban land, but has been falsified in the case of agricultural land. The prediction follows from a concentration on the *demand* for land. In the case of urban land, the supply is fixed (since it depends critically on location) and the growth of the economy does lead to a large rise in the value of this land. In the case of agricultural land, there has indeed been an increased demand for the produce of land, but there has been an even greater increase in the productivity of land, thus the value of the land has not tended to rise as predicted.

Thus, for someone who does not wish to interfere with the allocation resulting from the free play of the market, the taxation of economic rent is attractive.[6] It should be noted, however, that economic rent is not unique to landlords; it accrues to the owners of any factor that is fixed in supply and that faces a rising demand. If there is, for example, a fixed supply of first-class opera singers in the country, then they will gain in exactly the same way as landlords do when the society becomes richer and the demand for operas increases without there being any corresponding increase in the supply of singers.

ECONOMIC RENT AND TRANSFER EARNINGS IN THE PAYMENT TO CAPITAL

If a piece of capital equipment has several uses, then the analysis of the previous section can be repeated for the case of the machine. Many machines, however, once they are constructed, are utterly specific, having only one use. In this case, any income that is made from the operation of the machine is in the nature of a rent. Assume, for example, that when a machine is installed it is expected to earn $500 per year in excess of all its operating costs. If the demand for the product now falls off so that the machine can earn only $200, it will still be worthwhile operating rather than discarding. Assuming the machine to have only one use, we can say that all of the return is an economic rent because the machine would still have been allocated to its present use—it has no other—as long as it yielded even $1 above its operating costs.[7] Thus, *once the machine has been installed*, any net income that it earns is a rent (i.e., a payment not necessary to keep it in its present use). However, the machine will in time wear out and it will not be replaced unless it is expected to earn a return over its lifetime sufficient to make it a good investment for its owner. Thus, over the long run, some of the revenue earned by the machine is like a transfer earning; if the payment is not made, the machine will not continue to be allocated to that use in the long run. In any one year, however, the income earned can sink to zero without affecting the allocation of existing machines to different uses in the economy.

In this case, whether a payment made to a factor is an economic rent or a transfer earning depends on the time span under consideration. In the short run all of the income of a machine is in the nature of a rent, while in the long run at least some of it is in the nature of a transfer payment. Factor payments which are economic rents in the short run and transfer payments in the long run are what we earlier called quasi-rents. (See page 194.)

---

6. We must be careful not to forget the meaning of our terms. The statement in the text refers to *economic rent* as described; it does *not* refer to the payment actually made by tenants to landlords. What is called rent in the world is partly an economic rent and partly a return on capital invested by the landowner. The policy implications of the statement in the text depend on being able to identify *economic rent* in practice. At best, this is a very difficult thing to do; at worst, it may be quite impossible.

7. This is, in a different set of words, the same thing we discovered in Chapter 21: that fixed costs play no role in determining *short-run* profit-maximizing behavior of the firm.

Summary

1. Under competitive conditions, if all factors were identical, all factor prices would tend toward the same level. Causes of differences in factor prices in a nonhomogeneous world are either dynamic ones that exist only in disequilibrium situations or static ones that persist in equilibrium situations.

2. We regard the total payment to a factor as made up of two parts: *transfer earnings,* which are just enough to keep the factor from transferring to another use, and the remainder, which we call *economic rent.* Changes in transfer earnings have allocative results, whereas changes in rents do not.

3. A rising supply curve involves rents to all units of the factor, except the last unit to be employed. The flatter the supply curve, the less the amount of the payment to factors that is a rent and the more that is a transfer earning.

4. How much of a given payment to a factor is an economic rent and how much is a transfer earning depends on what sort of transfer we are considering.

5. If the supply curve is quite inelastic, an increase in the quantity supplied may be more easily achieved by shifting the supply curve to the right than by moving along it.

6. A rise in the current rate of interest entails a fall in the market price of all existing bonds, the fall being sufficient so that a purchaser of an existing bond will receive the same return on this investment over its lifetime as he could receive by buying a new bond.

7. The current rate of interest on new loans and the market price of existing bonds vary inversely with each other.

8. A tax on economic rent, such as a tax on all land, will have no allocative effects.

9. The payment to a capital good is an economic rent in the short run (called a quasirent) and a transfer payment in the long run.

QUESTIONS FOR DISCUSSION

1. What might explain the change in differential wages between white-collar workers and manual workers in this century? How would this differ from an explanation of changes in the farm-worker–urban-worker wage ratio?

2. Hotels report that these days they often have to pay the kitchen help more than they pay the front-desk people. Why?

3. "Broadway tickets are expensive because stars are highly paid." "Stars are highly paid because Broadway tickets are so expensive." Do you agree with either or with both of these statements?

4. Under what labor-market conditions might a firm offer a bonus to all employees who brought in a new worker, or spend a fair amount advertising new jobs?

5. For what reasons might a school system be able to pay women less than men, despite no prejudice, rational or irrational, against women?

6. What would be the effect of a tax of 10 percent on all the land in the United States? On downtown Los Angeles land only? On land in all cities with a population of more than 500,000?

7. What would be the effect on the wages of carpenters of (a) a rise in the price of houses; (b) a fall in the wages of bricklayers due to a rise in the supply of bricklayers? Clue: In answering (a), ask yourself why the price of houses rose.

Chapter 35 LABOR UNIONS, COLLECTIVE BARGAINING, AND THE DETERMINATION OF WAGES

WHY DO AUTOMOBILE WORKERS GET THE SAME pay for the same work, no matter where they work in the United States? Why do carpenters get different wages in different locations? Why do coal miners, who work in a declining industry, get higher rates of pay than equally skilled workers in many expanding industries? How does a worker in a plant employing 5,000 men "ask for a raise"? How does he let his employer know that he would be glad to trade so many cents per hour in wages for a better pension scheme? Why do strikes occur?

The competitive theory of factor price determination, which has been the subject of the last four chapters, yields enormously useful predictions about factor prices, factor movements, and the distribution of income, many of which have been tested and confirmed. Indeed, for the pricing of many non-human factors, there is little need to discard or to modify the competitive model. Much of what we observe about labor markets is also consistent with the theory. But not all of it is.

Labor is in many ways the exceptional factor of production. The factors that govern a man's working conditions and pay are vitally important to himself and to his family. When employees and employers negotiate over the price to be paid to the factor of production called labor, they are negotiating over something that is vital to most households. It is not surprising that people are sometimes prepared to fight over such negotiations. Factors other than material advantage enter into the relationship between employer and employee, for it is a relation between people to whom qualities such as loyalty, fairness, appreciation, and justice are at least as important as productivity. And attitudes about these qualities can vitally affect productivity.

Labor unions, employers' associations, and the institutions and customs governing collective bargaining are features of the real world that have developed in response to the exceptional conditions governing the bargaining between free men about the terms on which one will work for another. If these institutions are important determinants of what happens, it must be because the nature of the institutions influences the wages and working conditions that are finally agreed upon.

Theoretical Models of Factor Markets[1]

It is often useful to approach the complexities of the world by examining extreme cases. In this section, we look at four of these.

1. MANY BUYERS, MANY SELLERS (COMPETITION)

Suppose there are so many employers hiring labor and so many employees providing it that no single employee or employer can exert any appreciable influence on the wage rate. This is a situation in which the competitive theory of wage determination, outlined in the previous chapters and illustrated graphically in Figure 1(i), applies. The equilibrium wage is w_1. At that point, the demand for laborers and the supply of laborers are equal at q_1.

2. ONE SELLER, MANY BUYERS (MONOPOLY)

Suppose there is a single labor monopolist who controls the entire supply of some kind of labor. The cost to him of supplying different quantities of labor is assumed to be a rising function of the quantities supplied. The curve S in Figure 1(ii) reflects the marginal cost to him of supplying different quantities of labor. He is in precisely the position of the monopolist we studied in Chapter 23. Knowing that the demand curve for labor slopes downward, he will restrict the quantity supplied to the point at which the *marginal revenue* from the last unit of labor he provides is equal to the marginal cost of supplying it. In terms of Figure 1(ii), he chooses to supply the quantity q_2 at the wage rate w_2.

Wages are higher than in the competitive case, and the quantity of labor supplied is less. (If you do not understand this result, reread Chapter 23.) The labor union, as we shall see, may be an instrument for exercising monopoly in factor markets.

3. ONE BUYER, MANY SELLERS (MONOPSONY)

Suppose that a monopsonist, the sole employer of labor in a certain town, can offer any wage rate he chooses. The laborers can either work for him or seek employment elsewhere. The supply curve shows how much labor he will get at any given wage. In Figure 1(iii), D is the monopsonist's demand for labor based upon his *MRP*.

For any given quantity that is purchased, the supply curve shows the price per unit that must be paid; to the monopsonist, this is the *average cost curve* of the factor (average cost of a factor = total cost/number of units purchased = price per unit of the factor). But the marginal cost of employing extra units of the factor must exceed the average cost. If, for example, 100 units are employed at $1.50 per hour, then total cost is $150 and average cost per unit is $1.50. If 101 units are employed and the factor price is driven up to $1.60, then total cost becomes $161.60; the average cost per laborer is $1.60, but the total cost has increased by $11.60 as a result of hiring one more laborer. The marginal cost of obtaining an extra laborer will exceed the wage paid, because the increased wage rate necessary to attract him must also be paid to

---

1. The following theories apply to any factor, but we shall discuss them in the context of labor because the conditions assumed are most often found with labor.

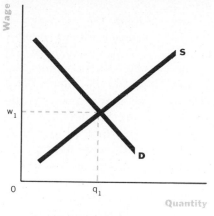

**(i) Many buyers, many sellers
(competition)**

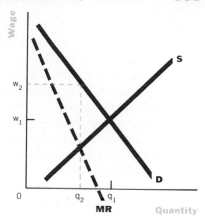

**(ii) One seller, many buyers
(monopoly)**

FIGURE 1   **FOUR
KINDS OF FACTOR
MARKETS**

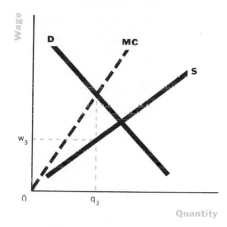

**(iii) One buyer, many sellers
(monopsony)**

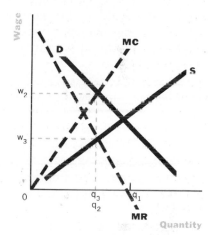

**(iv) One buyer, one seller
(bilateral monopoly)**

all the laborers already employed. Thus, in Figure 1(iii), we can draw a marginal cost curve for labor that will lie above the average cost curve. The demand curve is the marginal revenue product curve and the curve just derived is the marginal cost curve. The profit-maximizing monopsonist will equate marginal cost of labor with its marginal revenue product; in other words, he will go on hiring labor until the last unit increases total costs by as much as it increases total revenue. The equilibrium employment will be q_3 and the

wage rate w_3. From the above discussion we have derived the following prediction:

Monopsonistic conditions in the factor market will result in a lower level of employment and a lower wage rate than would rule when the factor is purchased under competitive conditions.

The reason for this is that the monopsonist purchaser is aware that, by trying to purchase more of the factor, he is driving up the price against himself. He will, therefore, stop short of the point that is reached when the factor is purchased by many different firms, no one of which can exert an influence on its price.

If we compare factor monopoly, in Figure 1(ii), with factor monopsony, in Figure 1(iii), we see that wages under monopoly will be higher than under monopsony (Ow_2 compared to Ow_3). We can make no comparative prediction about the level of employment. In either case, employment will be less than under competitive conditions. (We have drawn the diagram so that Oq_2 is the same as Oq_3, but by varying the shapes of the demand and supply curves you can alter this result.) The wage rates differ in the two cases because, in the monopoly case, the seller of labor is in a position to restrict the supply to Oq_2 and, thus, to receive the wage Ow_2 that purchasers will pay to hire that quantity of labor; in the monopsony case, the buyer will hire only quantity Oq_3 of labor, and the supply curve shows that he can get this quantity by offering the low wage Ow_3. We predict that:

Monopsonistic conditions in the factor market will result in a lower wage rate than would rule under monopolistic conditions.

4. ONE BUYER, ONE SELLER (BILATERAL MONOPOLY)

In bilateral monopoly, a monopolist sells to a monopsonist. The monopolist wants to supply Oq_2 at wage rate Ow_2. The monopsonist wants to supply Oq_3 at wage rate Ow_3. If both are stubborn to the point where neither will yield a penny, no labor will be bought or sold, but this is not a likely result. Instead, we may expect the buyer and seller to bargain. Suppose (to keep things simple), they agree first on a quantity of labor to be used, represented in Figure 1(iv) as $Oq_2 = Oq_3$. The supplier will not accept any wage below Ow_3. The demander will not pay any wage above Ow_2. But for any wage between these limits each of them is better off than if they did not strike a bargain. Our theory leads to the following prediction:

The wage rate in bilateral monopoly will be somewhere in between the monopoly wage rate and the monopsony wage rate, but the theory does not predict where it will be.

Given our present theory, the wage rate is "indeterminate" within a specified interval. To predict more precisely where the wage rate will be set would require a further theory. Such a theory might be based upon such things as the bargaining skill of the monopolist and the monopsonist, on the resources of each to "hold out" until the other gives in, on the presence of third parties who might mediate or arbitrate the disagreement, and so on. Such matters are left to a more advanced course.

Competition, Monopoly, Monopsony, or Bilateral Monopoly: Which Pattern Exists Today?

Monopoly and monopsony in the sense of a single seller or buyer are very rare indeed. Even the large firm with thousands of workers is not likely to be the only employer to whom the workers may turn. We shall, as we did with monopoly in product markets, speak of monopoly power and monopsony power as matters of degree, and be particularly concerned with *relative* strengths of buyers and sellers.

The answer to the question of which pattern exists today is: "All four, depending upon where you look." Approximately 18 million Americans belong to a labor union today. This is roughly one-fourth of the total labor force. Are you impressed with how many, or how few? It is six times as many as in 1933. But, it also means that three-quarters of the labor force is not organized. In some sectors of the economy, such as agriculture, there is no labor organization to speak of, and among white-collar workers union membership is very slight. The market for agricultural labor and for clerical workers is reasonably close to that of the competitive model. In many of the service trades, and in much of the South, employers are dealing with unorganized work-ers, and the situation is closest to that of the monopsony model—with the important modification that there is a minimum wage. In some industries, especially the building trades, garment trades, coal mining, stevedoring, and truck driving, unions are very strong, and employers are very weak. The balance of power lies on the union side, and the situation is close to that of monopoly. For a vast sector, including most of manufacturing, and transport, strong unions are opposed by strong employers or employers' associations and the conditions of bilateral monopoly apply. In these circumstances, collective bargaining becomes all important.

Because there is so much variety in the form of labor markets, there is no single pattern of wage determination. A detailed discussion of patterns of bargaining and wage determination must be left to a more specialized course.

The Vocabulary of Labor Economics

The vocabulary we use in this chapter comes partly from theoretical economics ("monopoly," "monopsony," etc.) and partly from labor economics ("employers' association," "collective bargaining," etc). These latter terms are usually self-explanatory, but occasionally they are not, so that a slight digression on terminology is required.

I. POTENTIAL MONOPSONISTS: FIRMS AND EMPLOYERS' ASSOCIATIONS

We have encountered the term *firm* many times before. The large firm has some degree of monopsony power just by virtue of its size and the number of employees with which it deals. It recognizes that its actions affect the wage rate, especially the rates received by those kinds of labor that are in some way limited to the industry in which the firm operates. This limitation will result when one large firm's need for this kind of labor represents a large fraction of the total demand for it. The U.S. Steel Corporation exercises enormous monopsony power in its dealings with steelworkers, because it represents a large share of the demand for the special talent required for the making of iron and steel.

Employers' associations are groups of employers who band together for the purpose of adopting a common policy in labor negotiations. If all steel companies offer the same terms, they exercise more monopsony power than any one can exercise on its own. The steelworker who does not wish to accept the common conditions has no alternative but to seek work in another industry, and he is likely to be much less well-equipped for work in a different industry. Formal employers' associations, which appoint official bargaining representatives, exist on a local level in many industries today, including the hotel, restaurant, newspaper printing, and construction industries. There are regional or national associations today in the garment maufacturing, hosiery, textile, coal mining, and furniture maufacturing industries, among others.

At least as important as formal associations are informal ones in which the several firms in an industry follow the lead set by a key firm. The *industry-wide pattern* characterizes many manufacturing industries today. The automobile industry, for example, achieves nation-wide agreement with its workers without the formal apparatus of an employers' association.

2. POTENTIAL MONOPOLISTS: UNIONS

No one bothers to define unions any more, perhaps because every one knows what they are, or perhaps because a union is so many things: a social club, an educational instrument, a political club, one more source of withholding money from a worker's pay, a bargaining agent for an individual worker, and, to some, a way of life. For the purposes of our discussion of labor markets, a *union* (or *trade union*, or *labor union*) is an association of individual workers that speaks for them in negotiations with their employers.

Craft unions and *industrial unions*. Unions today have two different principles of organization: the *craft* (or trade) union, in which workers with a common set of skills are

joined in a common association, no matter where or for whom they work. The craft principle of organization was and is the hallmark of the American Federation of Labor (AFL). Until the 1930s, virtually all unions were organized along craft lines, and for good reason, as we shall see. The *industrial union* is organized along industry lines: All workers in a given plant or a given industry are collected into a single union, whatever their skills. This is the pattern developed by the member unions of the Congress of Industrial Organization (CIO). Among the prominent industrial unions are the United Auto Workers and the Steel Workers.

The two principles of unionism conflict. Should a carpenter employed in the steel industry be represented by the carpenters' union or the steelworkers' union? Disputes over which union shall have the right to *organize* (i.e., bring into their union) a particular group of workers are known as *jurisdictional disputes*. They have led to prolonged, bitter, and bloody battles of union against union.

Local unions, national (or *international*)[2] *unions, federations*. American unions, whether craft or industrial, operate at three levels. The important level for most of the *economic* functions of the union is the national level. The national officers do the bargaining, set the policies, and set the tone. Individual workers, however, belong to a local, to which they pay dues (a part of which goes to the national) in much the same way that local chapters of political parties provide the focus and the "home" of the members of the national parties. There are about 200 national unions, which have over 75,000 locals. The local for a craft union is geographical—the Chicago chapter of the carpenters, say. The local for an indus-

2. Most unions became international as soon as they acquired a Canadian local.

trial union is a plant or a company—the Ford local of the United Automobile Workers, say.

The *federation* is a loose organization of national unions. Today there is one federation, the AFL–CIO. Prior to 1955 the AFL and CIO were two separate organizations. The federation has little real power, but serves an important role as spokesman for organized labor. Its function in recent years has been political; it has thrown its support behind certain candidates, testified before Congress, and so on.

3. KINDS OF BARGAINING ARRANGEMENTS: OPEN, CLOSED, AND UNION SHOPS

In an *open shop*, a union represents its members, but does not have exclusive bargaining jurisdiction for all the workers of its kind. Membership in the union is not a condition of getting or keeping a job. Unions feel that this represents an impossible situation. If, on the one hand, the employer accedes to union demands, the nonmembers achieve the benefits of the union without paying dues or sharing the risks or responsibilities. If, on the other hand, the employer chooses to fight the union, he can run his plant with the non-union members, thus weakening the power of the union members in the fight.

In a *closed shop*, only union members may be employed and the union controls its membership however it sees fit. Employers tend to regard this as an unwarranted limitation on their right to choose their employees.

In a *union shop*, the employer may hire anyone he chooses, but every employee must join the union within a specified period.

4. WEAPONS OF CONFLICT: STRIKES, PICKET LINES, BOYCOTTS, STRIKE-BREAKERS, LOCK-OUTS, BLACK LISTS

The *strike* is the union's ultimate weapon. It consists in the concerted refusal to work of the members of the union. It is the strike or the threat of a strike that backs up the union's demands in the bargaining process. Workers on strike are, of course, off the payroll, and many unions set aside a portion of the dues collected to have a fund for paying striking workers. *Picket lines* are made up of striking workers who parade before the entrance to their plant or firm. One of their objectives is to get public opinion on their side; another is to force a total shut-down in the plant's operation. Other union members will not, by long convention, "cross" a picket line. This means that if bricklayers strike against a construction firm, carpenters will not work on the project although they may have no grievance against the firm, nor will any teamster deliver supplies to a picketed site. Pickets represent an enormous increase in the bargaining power of a small union. (Much of the bitterness against jurisdictional disputes arises from the fact that an employer may be unable to settle with either union without facing a picket line from the other union.) A *boycott* is an organized attempt to persuade customers to refrain from purchasing the goods or services of a firm whose employees are on strike.

The *lock-out* is the employer's equivalent of the strike. By closing his plant, he locks out the workers until such time as the dispute is settled. *Strikebreakers* (*scabs*) are workers who are brought in by management to operate the plant while the union is on strike. A *black list* is an employers' list of workers who have been discharged for union activities.

5. COLLECTIVE BARGAINING

This term is used to describe the whole process by which unions and employers (or their representatives) arrive at and enforce agreement.

The Evolution of the Modern Union[3]

When representatives of the United Auto Workers sit down this year with representatives of the Ford Motor Company to discuss wages, contributions to pension funds, number and length of holidays, and other issues, they are engaged in what has been termed *mature collective bargaining*. At the end of the negotiations, the newspapers show the smiling representatives shaking hands, and each of the 300,000 workers in the Ford plants then knows the conditions under which he will work for the next year or so. Should an employee have a grievance at any time, he reports it to his union representative (called a shop steward), and a carefully designed procedure is set in motion to settle the dispute.

Unionism today is both stable and accepted. It was not always so. As recently as thirty years ago unions were fighting for their lives, and union organizers and members were risking theirs.[4] Why the change and how did it come about?

THE URGE TO ORGANIZE

Trade unionism had its origin in the pitifully low standard of living of the average nineteenth-century worker and his family. Much of the explanation of the low standard of living throughout the world lay in the small size of the national product relative to the population. Even in the wealthiest countries, an absolutely equal division of national wealth among all families in 1850 would have left them all in poverty by our present standards.

Poverty had existed for centuries. It was accentuated, however, by the twin processes of urbanization and industrialization. The man who was moderately content working his land usually became restive and discontented when he moved into a grimy, smoky, nineteenth-century city, took employment in a sweatshop or a factory, and settled with his family in a crowded, unsanitary tenement. The focus of his resentment was his employer.

The employer set the wages, and the wages were low. The boss was often arbitrary and seldom sympathetic. And the boss himself was usually conspicuously better off. The unhappy worker had, of course, the right of all free men to quit his job—and starve. If he grumbled or protested, he could be fired, and worse still black-listed, which meant no one else would hire him.

Out of these conditions, and other real or imagined grievances of the working man, came the full range of radical political movements from revolutionary socialism, which today we call Marxist Communism, to Fabian socialism, which tried to effect change gradually through existing political systems. Out of the same conditions came also the char-

---

3. This is a fascinating subject, and there are hundreds of books on it. For an able introduction, the student is referred to M. W. Reder, *Labor in a Growing Economy* (John Wiley, 1957). For a lively account, see R. R. R. Brooks, *When Labor Organizes* (Yale University Press, 1937), *Unions of Their Own Choosing* (Yale University Press, 1939), and *As Steel Goes* (Yale University Press, 1940).

4. If you ask a fifty-year-old American how he feels about unions, you will usually find that he feels strongly one way or another. If you ask someone under thirty, he will usually think it an odd question and will probably reply, "Oh, they are mostly all right, I guess."

acteristically American form of collective action, the *bread-and-butter* trade union.[5] Why this form of collective action, and not the others, took hold in America is a matter that historians still debate, but it need not concern us.

The American worker perceived that ten or a hundred men acting together had more influence than one acting alone, and he dreamed of the day when all the workers would stand solid[6] against the employer. The union was the organization that would provide a basis for confronting the monopsony power of employers with the collective power of the workers. But it was easier for the worker to see where the solution to his problems lay than to achieve this solution. Organizations of workers would hurt the employer, and the employer did not sit by idly. He too knew that in union there was strength. "Agitators" who tried to organize other workers were fired and black listed, and in some cases beaten and killed.

REQUIREMENTS OF A SUCCESSFUL UNION

In order to realize the dream, it was necessary, first, for the unions to gain effective control over the supply of labor, and, second, to have the financial resources to outlast the employer in a struggle of strength. There was no "right" to organize; the unions had to force the employers to do business with them.

The first unions were unions of the highly skilled, for obvious reasons: Organize the unskilled or the semiskilled and the employer could find replacements for them; they were streaming into the country as immigrants, and into the city from the farm. But the skilled workers—the coopers, the bootmakers, the shipwrights—were another matter. There were few of them, and they controlled the access to their trade by controlling the conditions of apprenticeship. The original unions were in effect closed shops: One had to belong to the union to hold a job, and the union set the rules of admission. But control of supply was only half the battle. Most employers detested unions and regarded them as an infringement of their rights. (Many still do: The goal of the so-called right-to-work movement is the right to work without belonging to a union. It is mainly a movement of employers rather than employees.) Employers in general opposed unionization and fought it with great bitterness.

Such success as unions had was in occupations both small and strategic. The costs of giving in to such a union were relatively small compared to the costs of a protracted strike.[7] Even in such cases unions had their ups and downs. When employment was full and business booming, the cost of being fired for joining a union was not so great, for there were other jobs. During periods of depression and unemployment, however, the risks were greater. The individual worker knew that other unemployed members of his trade would be there to take his job if he caused trouble.

---

5. The goals of bread-and-butter or business unionism are higher wages, better working conditions, and so on, rather than social and political reform.

6. The word solidarity figures importantly in the literature and songs of the labor movement.

7. The point is important. If a certain group of key workers accounts for only 5 percent of the total labor cost, giving them a 10 percent increase in wages increases total costs by only 0.5 percent. See page 346 on the relation between the elasticity of demand and the importance of the factor in the total costs of production.

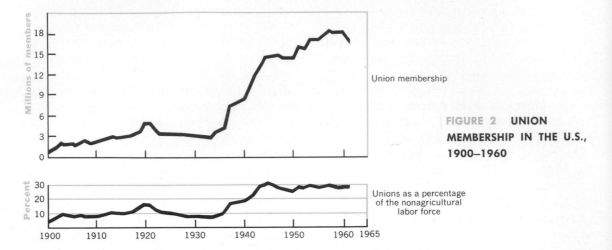

FIGURE 2   **UNION
MEMBERSHIP IN THE U.S.,
1900–1960**

Membership in trade unions until the late 1930s showed a very clear cyclical pattern, rising in good times and falling in bad.

THE BEGINNINGS: 1870–1933

The American Federation of Labor, founded in 1886 under the guiding genius of Samuel Gompers, an English immigrant and a cigarmaker, was totally committed to organizing the skilled trades, to pursuing bread-and-butter issues, and to restricting labor supply. This was where the union had a chance to survive. It is no coincidence that Gompers, although himself an immigrant, led the AFL in vigorous opposition to further immigration: Restriction of supply was the key to preserving union power.

For the unskilled, the prospects of unionization were bleak: It was impossible to control supply. The hope of the unskilled worker lay in political reform, in socialism, in cooperatives, or in revolution. The Knights of Labor, organized in 1869, had 700,000 members in 1886 and was a focal point of this feeling. But the political climate was hostile, and the Knights collapsed in the depression of 1887.

The AFL continued its steady growth among the skilled. In 1900, it had 3 percent of the labor force (almost a million members) and by 1920 it had 5 million members, 12 percent of the labor force. See Figure 2.

By 1922, in the face of depression and the strong antilabor attitude of government and business alike, union membership had declined to 4 million members and, by 1933, after a decade of gradual decline, to less than 3 million, or about 6 percent of the labor force.

THE NEW DEAL: 1933–1945

The dramatic effect of the New Deal is illustrated in Figure 2. What happened? First, the monstrousness of the Great Depression created a climate of public opinion openly hostile to big business. Second, the Wagner Act (1935), known as labor's Magna Charta, guaranteed the *right* of workers to organize and to elect, by secret ballot, an exclusive bargaining agent by majority vote of the employees. And, third, the unskilled were organized in industrial unions. The Wagner Act provided the means to control the supply of labor, even unskilled labor. The great industrial unions in steel and in automobiles, following the leadership of John L. Lewis of the United Mine Workers, organized, split from the conservative AFL, formed the CIO, and struck for recognition. Using tactics thought to be illegal (for example, the sit-down strike, where employees sat down in the plants and thus prevented employers from operating with strikebreakers), the CIO won recognition, and members. It doubtless benefited from an atmosphere of public opinion in which there was no disposition on the part of the government or the courts to try to stop them. The Supreme Court decision upholding the legality of the Wagner Act ratified their victory. In short, the unions won—by force, by violence, and finally by law—the recognition that was required to convert monopsony into bilateral monopoly.

AFTER THE WAR

The New Deal period, and its legislation, was frankly and avowedly pro-labor. The country as a whole recognized that labor had been the underdog and sought to redress the balance. By the end of World War II, the attitude had changed, for several reasons, including the increasing number and changing character of strikes. The long series of strikes during the organizing period were undertaken to compel employers to recognize and deal with unions and were received with a good deal of sympathy. But the jurisdictional strikes between rival AFL and CIO unions were less comprehensible to public and employer alike. And the aggressive tactics of some unions, most notably the United Mine Workers, particularly in the immediate prewar and war periods, added to the alienation. Immediately after the war, work stoppages soared in number, as Figure 3 makes clear.[8] The Taft-Hartley Act (1948), regarded by the unions at the time as violently antilabor, appears now to have been in the main a sober piece of legislation that corrected some of the excesses encouraged by the New Deal legislation. Among many other provisions, unfair labor practices on the part of unions as well as management were defined and prohibited; use of the closed shop was much limited; and the

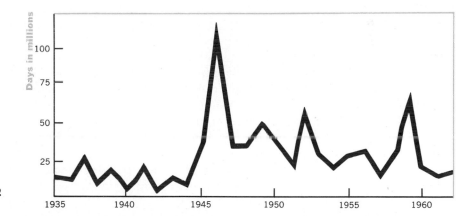

FIGURE 3 **DAYS LOST BY STRIKES IN THE U.S., 1935–1962**

8. In percentage terms, even at their peak in 1946, the days lost in strikes were less than 1.5 percent of the total days worked. But a strike is headline news, and the 1 percent of negotiations that break down get widespread attention.

ability to strike under circumstances that "imperil the national health and safety" was subject to an eighty-day cooling-off period. The most controversial feature of the act was the encouragement it gave to states to pass right-to-work laws. In 1965, President Johnson urged that this provision be repealed, and repeal seems likely.

Since 1950, unions have continued to grow, but that growth has now tapered off, and the percentage of the labor force in unions has declined somewhat. The important develop- ment of the most recent period is the stabil- izing of union-management relations in in- dustry after industry. Strikes still occur, and always will, for they are a key part of the poker game of collective bargaining. But strikes are now overwhelmingly directed to- ward specific issues and negotiations, rather than for recognition or jurisdiction, and the violence and passions of a generation ago are largely gone. The present era is described by some as that of mature, responsible, and peaceful collective bargaining.

Who Controls Unions and for What Ends?

Union constitutions are extremely demo- cratic documents. All members have one vote, officers are elected by the vote of the member- ship, the rights of individual workers are fully protected, and so on. In practice, how- ever, the relation between the members of a union and its national officers is closer to that of the relationship between stockholders and managers of a giant corporation than to that of the American people and their government. The office of union president was contested in less than 20 percent of cases between 1900 and 1948, and the percentage has gone down since then.[9] Unions, though democratic, tend toward one-party democracy in the vast major- ity of cases. Union leaders are true profes- sionals whose main business is to run the union, whereas the main business of the union member is to earn his living in his job. The typical union member's indifference is under- standable: He is paying dues that permit the union to pay generous salaries to union leaders to look out for his interests—and as long as the leadership "delivers," all goes well. But delivers what, and to whom?

WAGES VERSUS EMPLOYMENT

How is an increase in the wage rate se- cured? The union leader has substantial power in determining the wage rate, but he knows that the firm's demand curve for labor is downward-sloping, as in Figure 4. If the wage rate is raised from Ow_1 to Ow_2, the level of employment will fall from Oq_1 to Oq_2; there are union members who would like to work at this wage, but who cannot find employ- ment. The excess supply of labor is q_2q_3. The members of the union who remain employed will be much better off, but those who lose their jobs will not be. Should the union strive to maximize the total earnings of the group that remains employed, or the total employ- ment of its present members? In the United

---

9. There are occasional successful challenges to union leadership, just as in the corporation there are successful proxy fights. A recent example is the unseating of David MacDonald of the Steel Workers, news that made the front pages all over the nation.

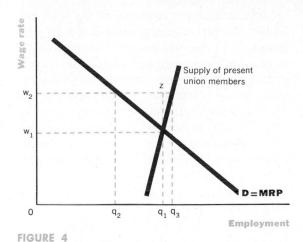

FIGURE 4

Mine Workers Union, a high-wage strategy has been followed for many years, and both employment and union membership have fallen. The hypothesis that this has been the conscious strategy of John L. Lewis, leader of the mine workers for half a century, has been advanced, and it is certainly consistent with the facts. In longshoring, the union has achieved high wages, but it rations the available jobs among its members [10] In the garment trades, on the other hand, the demand for labor is relatively elastic and the major unions have accepted lower wages than they could have achieved in order to protect the employment of their members. The problem is particularly acute today in the automobile industry, where production is booming, but where more than 8 percent of the current members of the UAW are unable to find work. High wages have led to the installation of more and more labor-saving equipment. Walter Reuther, president of the UAW, has been pushing hard to negotiate a guaranteed an-

nual wage. In other words, he has been attempting to negotiate both a wage rate and a volume of employment.

This is represented in terms of point z in Figure 4. The demand curve shows for each wage rate the amount of labor the employer would like to hire. But he may prefer to hire some other amount rather than to go without labor altogether. When wages are Ow_1 and employment is Oq_1, the union might offer the employers the alternative of employing Oq_1 labor at a wage of Ow_2 or of facing a strike. If the employer accepts the former alternative, then he will move to point z, *which is off his demand curve.* In this case, the union raises the per capita wages and total real earnings of its members without causing any reduction in employment. The union's success in pursuing such a policy will probably depend on the size of the profits in the industry and the willingness of the employer to go along with the union.

WAGES VERSUS FRINGE BENEFITS

Newspapers usually report the settlement of a contract negotiation in such terms as: "The package settlement of 20¢ per hour was approved late yesterday. Of this, 12¢ was in wages, 4¢ in increased contributions to the union's welfare and pension fund, and the remainder in other fringe benefits, including increased holidays and sick leave."

The most important figure to the employer is the size of the total package—20¢ in this case—for contributions to pension funds add to his costs in just the same way as payments in the form of wages. But there are advantages to the employer in giving indirect, or fringe,

---

10. The "shape-up" is the relevant institution. Longshoremen appear on the docks and are either assigned to jobs for the day or are sent home. The opportunities for favoritism and graft in such a scheme were well documented in the film *On the Waterfront.*

benefits that may lead him to grant more than he otherwise would. One advantage is that the real cost of fringe benefits per hour is often difficult to estimate. Although the union may claim it has gotten 8¢ worth, the employer may really believe it will come to less. A second advantage is that some forms of fringe benefits (such as pension funds) tend to bind the worker more closely to the company, and thus decrease the "turnover rate" among his employees.[11] Finally, some forms of payments (such as pay to workers who are laid off during seasonal slumps, etc.) may be easier to justify to stockholders or to other employers.[12]

From the employees' point of view, fringe benefits also have some appeal. Many of them are not taxable as current income. Pension funds and the like allow employees to provide for their future and that of their family.

Most important, for both union and employer, fringe benefits provide scope for bargaining. A union official may have promised his members not to take less than 15¢, and the employer's representatives may have assured their directors that they would stand firm at 10¢. In the negotiation, they may agree on 9¢ in wage increases and 7¢ in fringe benefits. Both negotiators may claim success, whereas either would feel reluctant to accept a straight 12½¢ wage increase.

By and large, the union's choice between wages and fringe benefits comes from the union's leadership, not from the rank and file, but strong feelings on the subject do influence policies. Union members will accept decisions on these matters from their leaders that they would not accept if such decisions originated with their employers.

Leadership Control: Corruption and Communism

The fact that union leadership is not subject to close control by union membership raises the possibility that the leadership will use the union for its own purposes. This is a threat in any organization with a well-entrenched leadership.

In the vast majority of cases, union leadership has worked for union purposes, but opportunities for graft and corruption exist, and the increase in the size of union funds has heightened them. Since the war, scandals of major proportions have been unearthed in

the teamsters' and longshoremen's unions by Congressional investigators. The Landrum-Griffin Act (1959), violently opposed by all of labor, was passed in an effort to control the excesses. Whether this legislation was necessary or sufficient to cure the problems it dealt with is a matter of much debate, and we cannot discuss it here. There is no evidence that corruption is any greater in unions than it is in corporations or in governments.

Are American unions Communist-infiltrated? It is often charged that Communist

---

11. If an employee loses part of his benefits by changing jobs his mobility is decreased. From the employer's point of view this is an advantage.

12. The face-saving aspects should not be taken lightly. Fringe benefits began to be important during World War II when the War Labor Board was bent on a policy of wage stabilization. Having forbade direct wage increases, the Board used fringe benefits to "save" its popular though unenforceable policy.

workers were and are attracted to the labor movement, but this is hardly surprising. Workers of all political persuasions join unions. American unionism has been aware of the Communist threat and has fought it both bitterly and successfully. In a handful of unions, out of 200, Communists did succeed in achieving control. The Furriers, the United Electrical Workers, and the West Coast Longshoremen, among others, were expelled from the Federation in 1949 and 1950 because of their Communist affiliations.

One of the unique characteristics of the American labor movement as distinct from its British and European counterparts has been its consistent rejection of ideological in favor of bread-and-butter causes. How much of this is due to the strong personality of its early leaders, particularly Gompers, and how much to the special character of American society we do not know. But Communism, like other radical and political causes before it, has found little welcome in the unions.

Unions and the Level of Wages

Union members believe that unions can and do raise wages. But do they really? Surprisingly, this is one of the most debated and unsettled questions in all of economics, despite the fact that a great deal of empirical work has been done on the subject. We cannot settle the issue here, but we can discuss why it arises at all.

Let us first consider a union that represents the workers in an industry *that is but a very small section of the whole community*. The union can attempt to raise wages by creating a shortage of labor. Such a supply-curve shift can be accomplished in a number of ways, but the most usual way is by restricting entry into the industry. Long periods of apprenticeship, costly training programs, high entrance fees, or stringent qualifications will all tend to reduce the supply of labor in an industry and, hence, to increase the earnings of those who remain in the industry. Early craft unions worked on this principle and, whatever their actual intention, most modern professional organizations, such as those of the medical, legal, and teaching professions, have a similar effect. The union controls the

supply of labor and then accepts the wages and employment determined by the market. It does not necessarily have to indulge in collective bargaining.

The second means of raising wages open to the union is to bargain for a wage above the competitive level and take the consequences in terms of reduced employment opportunities. The third method is to try to bargain about both price and quantity and thereby to force the employer to move to some point *off his demand curve*.

So far, we have considered what a single union *that is small in relation to the whole economy* can do to raise wages. This italicized clause is the key to being able to use demand and supply curves, the tools of *partial equilibrium analysis*. Beware of generalizing the conclusions reached above to the economy as a whole. If we asked whether unions can raise the real wage rate of *all* workers in the country, we would have to know the effects of the wage increase on the cost of production, on the price of commodities, and on the incomes of all members of society. This would take us into the realm of *general equilibrium analysis*, which we are not yet able to discuss.[13] The reason we must proceed with care is that, if wage increases lead either to price increases or cuts in employment, the real purchasing power of labor as a whole may not be increased. In fact, there is no generally accepted, well-worked-out theory that would allow us to deal with this important question.

If labor as a whole is to gain relative to other groups, its share of the total of national income must grow. The fact is, however, that the share of income going to labor is remarkably stable over time, and that the great growth in union membership since the 1930s has not been accompanied by an increase in labor's share. What does this prove about the influence of unions? We are not sure.

Of course, as we have seen, everyone is not unionized. Do union members do better than workers in unorganized industries? Again, the evidence is inconclusive. Workers in many nonunion trades have achieved larger *percentage* increases in pay than union members since 1933. But, of course, what unions achieve affects labor markets and laborers in other industries as well. Albert Rees of the University of Chicago, one of the leading students of the influence of unionism on wages, concluded, "I would say that perhaps a third of the trade unions have raised the wages of their members by 15 to 20 per cent above what they might be in a non-union situation, another third by 5 per cent to 10 per cent, and the remaining third, not at all."[14]

It is generally believed that, since World War II, there has been a narrowing of wage differentials for various grades of labor and that the unions have had something to do with this. There are two extreme views about the influence of unions. The first is that unions have complete power over wage differentials; wage differentials are, according to this view, a function of union choice. The second view is that unions exert no effective influence on wage differentials; in spite of collective bargaining, relative wages come out to be pretty well what they would be in a freely competitive market. It is important to realize that each of these views constitutes an hypothesis that can be subjected to empirical test. That the conditions of demand and supply exert some influence on relative wages, independent of the wishes of unions, has been pretty conclusively established. What has not really been established is how much independent influence unions are able to exert on the structure of relative wages.

Unions and Economic Life: A Final Statement

If we are uncertain about precisely how and how much unions have affected the wages of their members, there is little dispute over some other facts. Unions have clearly been a vehicle for improving both the working conditions and the dignity of the working man. They have brought a very substantial equality of bargaining power to labor and management and in many cases they have brought order and stability to the process of collective bar-

---

13. We will introduce the topic in Chapter 42, but by and large it cannot be discussed thoroughly in an elementary text.
14. Albert Rees, *Wage Inflation* (National Industrial Conference Board, 1957).

gaining. Modern labor-management relations make the "class struggle" between the worker and the capitalist seem mild indeed, and dire predictions of an eventual armed conflict seem quaint and unreal.

Summary

1. Four possible extremes of factor markets are: (1) many buyers, many sellers (competition); (2) one seller, many buyers (monopoly); (2) one buyer, many sellers (monopsony); and (4) one seller, one buyer (bilateral monopoly). All four of these extremes are illustrated in Figure 1, page 381.

2. Standard price theory predicts that the wage rate will be higher and the quantity of labor supplied lower in the monopolistic case as compared with the competitive case.

3. Another prediction is that monopsonistic conditions in the factor market will result in a lower level of employment and a lower wage rate than would rule when labor is purchased under competitive conditions.

4. The theory also predicts that the wage rate in bilateral monopoly will be somewhere between the monopoly wage rate and the monopsony rate, but the theory does not predict where it will be within these limits.

5. All four patterns exist in the American labor market.

6. An employers' association is a group of employers who band together for the purpose of adopting a common policy in labor negotiations.

7. A union is an association of workers that speaks for the workers in negotiations with their employers. Unions are subdivided into craft unions and industrial unions.

8. In general, individual union members belong to a local union to which they pay dues (part of which goes to the national union), and a national or international union which is an organization comprised of local unions. A federation is a loose organization of national unions; today, there is one federation, the AFL-CIO, which was formed in 1955 from the previously separate AFL and CIO federations.

9. Three kinds of bargaining arrangements are the "open shop," where, though a union represents its members, union membership is not a condition of getting or keeping a job; the "closed shop," where only workers who are already union members may be employed; and the "union shop," where the employer is free to hire as he chooses, but where all new employees must join the recognized union within a specified period.

10. The strike is the ultimate weapon of the union. It is the concerted refusal to work on the part of the members of the union. Picket lines are parades before the entrance to plants whose workers are on strike, making the implied request to outsiders to support their efforts. A boycott is an organized attempt to persuade customers to refrain from purchasing the products of a firm whose employees are on strike. The lock-out is the employers' equivalent of a strike. Strikebreakers are workers brought in to operate a plant while the union is on strike. A black list is an employers' list of workers who have been discharged for union activities.

11. The whole process by which unions and employers arrive at and enforce agreement is called collective bargaining.

12. A union may often face the issue of whether it should strive to maximize the

total earnings of the group or the total employment of its present members. It may at times be possible for a union to bargain an employer off his demand curve and negotiate both wages and employment. The union must also decide whether to press for wages or for fringe benefits.

13. The evidence so far is inconclusive as to the effect of unions on labor's return as a whole and as to their effect on the wages of organized workers as opposed to unorganized ones. One other undecided question concerns the impact of unions on the structure of relative wages.

QUESTIONS FOR DISCUSSION

1. Use the theoretical models of factor markets to rank the following according to the probable magnitude of the equilibrium wage rate and the quantity of employment: (a) In a fairly isolated town, there is a large number of small candy manufacturers. The workers in these plants have no union. (b) A union is organized that almost all the workers join. (c) After a few years, the union disbands due to lack of interest. At the same time, a large outside firm buys up most of the small candy plants, hires the former owners as managers, and operates all the plants as one firm. (d) A large national union comes to town and reorganizes the union. (If you have any doubts as to the ranking, do not hesitate to state them explicitly.)

2. Write three hypothetical clauses in three different collective-bargaining agreements establishing a union shop, a closed shop, and an open shop.

3. What, in general, is the difference in organizational principle between former AFL unions and former CIO unions?

4. What economic problem does the union face in using its bargaining power to further its aims?

5. In 1965, President Johnson urged that the section of the Taft-Hartley Act that allows states to pass right-to-work laws be repealed. Who do you think stands to gain by repeal, and what,

precisely, does it mean? Comment on the following quotation from *Newsweek* magazine: "There is plenty of evidence to show that right-to-work laws are a major lure to runaway companies (firms that leave the North for new facilities in the South and Midwest), says one insider." How would you go about testing this view?

6. "The labor of a human being is not a commodity or article of commerce," states the Clayton Anti-Trust Act. The purpose of this was to secure for unions some measure of exemption from legal action. What do you think about this?

7. Trace what is generally called the "ebb and flow" of unionism in America from the 1870s on. What do you think has characterized the general aims of American unions throughout the years?

8. It is frequently charged that "big labor" (the leaders of the large national unions) now have more in common with management than with their union members. Why might this change have occurred? How might you test the validity of the charge?

9. It is often claimed that to become a plumber's apprentice in many big cities, you must be a plumber's son or, at least, a nephew of a plumber. Show the implications of this, using a simple supply and demand diagram. Does this mean that there are unemployed plumbers? If not, what does it mean?

Chapter **36** INTEREST AND THE RETURN ON CAPITAL

WHY ARE INTEREST RATES DIFFERENT WHEN buying a house than when buying a car? Why do bonds of different companies pay different rates of interest? What is the difference between interest and profits? Why do people borrow to buy instead of saving to buy? How do firms decide how much to borrow? Are interest and profits elements in incomes only in a capitalist society or do they exist in socialist economies too? What real role do they play in the economy? What gives rise to them?

In this chapter we are concerned with the payments made for the use of money capital. Such payments are called *interest* if made to the creditors of a firm, but they are called *dividends* or *profits* if paid to the owners of a firm. In discussing the functional distribution of income, a common distinction is made between rents, profits, and interest payments, all of which may be, in part or in whole, payments for the use of someone's funds. Beware of the fallacy that there is one true division in the national income. Distinctions between different payments are man-made. They are made when it is convenient to do so, and are not made when it is not convenient. It makes sense to ask if a certain distinction is useful;

it does not make sense to ask if it is the correct one.

Interest, as we shall use the term in this chapter, is a payment for the use of money. An *interest rate* of 6 percent means that one must pay 6¢ for the use of one dollar of money for one year. The interest rate is the price of using money for one year, *and then returning it*. One does not buy money; one hires its services, and the interest rate is the price paid for those services.

If you borrow money from your bank to buy a house, a car, or a washing machine, you will have to pay interest for the use of this money. You will also have to arrange to pay the money back, either in installments or in a lump sum. The interest that you pay each year is likely to be somewhere between 4 percent and 20 percent of the amount of money that you borrow. If a firm borrows money from the public by selling its bonds, it will have to pay interest on this loan. Most bonds state the rate of interest that will be paid each year for as long as the loan is outstanding. If a firm uses its own capital, the economist will *impute* an interest payment to that capital equal to the opportunity cost of the funds.

Why Pay for the Use of Money? The Demand for Loanable Funds

The demand for loanable funds comes from households, from firms, and from the government. Since each borrows for different reasons, we shall consider each separately.

1. HOUSEHOLDS

People wish to borrow money for consumption and for investment. They are prepared to borrow it at interest because they prefer to have a certain quantity of goods now rather than to save now and buy later. This is sometimes called impatience, but it is more than that. A young couple that had to save the full price of a house would probably not have enough money saved until they were ready to retire. Furthermore, many people have an expectation of a rising level of income over their lifetime and they are glad to buy now, when they are relatively poor, and pay later, when they are wealthier. *Time preference* for present consumption very clearly exists. Individuals, we observe, spend part of their income to hire now money they must pay back later. Total outstanding debt of U.S. households in 1963 was about $250 billion dollars, or more than $1,000 for every person in the country. Most of this, $180 billion, was owed on housing, but more than

$50 billion of it was for consumer credit. Charge accounts amounted to about $6 billion.[1] In addition, credit cards extend the amount of credit outstanding. Some individuals borrow money for investment or speculative purposes. Buying stock and bonds "on margin" involves borrowing money from a broker (at a specified rate of interest) in order to buy securities that the purchaser hopes will more than pay him back for the use of his funds and the costs of the borrowed funds. It is generally believed (and there is some evidence to support the belief) that households' demand curve for funds is downward sloping: The amount of money households borrow increases as the rate of interest falls.[2]

2. FIRMS

The biggest private demand for loanable funds comes from firms that borrow because they expect an investment in capital goods to yield a return over the cost of the capital. When capital is used, production can be greater than when it is not used, even when allowance is made for the labor and resources consumed in making the capital. This extra return is called the *productivity of capital*.

---

1. Are charge accounts free? Unlike loans from banks or finance companies, no specific interest charge is made on them. But who pays for the "loan" of funds for a month and for the costs of record-keeping, collection, and bad debts? The seller must either borrow the money to meet his payments for raw materials, and so forth, tie up his own capital in them, or pass the credit back to his supplier. *Someone* is advancing credit and thus incurring costs, and someone must pay. The obvious choice is the customer, who pays in higher prices.

2. We make such a guarded statement because some of the motives for borrowing reflect expectations about prices of goods. If one expects the prices of cars (or stocks) to rise, one may rush to buy now even though interest rates are high. We shall assume for the remainder of this chapter that the price level is constant, so that variations in the money rate of interest represent real variations in the incomes of lenders.

The demand for funds by businesses is a derived demand, just as the demand for labor is a derived demand. Let us examine it more closely. Consider first a single investment opportunity. Let us say a firm can invest $1,000 in a machine that will last for 10 years and will produce output that it can sell for $300 per year for each of the 10 years. The firm estimates the total costs (for wages, raw materials, and depreciation), excluding only the opportunity cost of capital, at $180 per year. It thus estimates a profit (or a return on its investment) of $120 per year. The productivity of this investment is said to be 12 percent per year. ($120 is 12 percent of $1,000.) The firm would like to borrow (i.e., demand) $1,000 of money capital at rates of less than 12 percent in order to purchase this machine.

At any one time, however, the firm has many investment opportunities, some better than others: A few may promise rates of return of 40 or 50 percent; some may promise only 3 or 4 percent; and some will involve negative rates of return. If the firm knew the whole set of its investment opportunities, and the rate of return on each, it could prepare a schedule of the amount of dollars it could invest at various rates of return. Such a schedule is given in Table 1. The first two columns show the number of dollars a firm can invest at each of a series of different rates of return. The cumulative schedule of these amounts, shown in the third column, is the *marginal productivity of capital* (MPC) schedule for this firm. For example, if the firm had $40,000 to invest, its MPC would be 10 percent: The best it could do (with the investment opportunities listed) would be to invest $5,000 in projects yielding 30 percent,

$20,000 in projects yielding 20 percent, and $15,000 in projects yielding 10 percent. The last or marginal dollar would earn a return of only 10 percent.[3]

TABLE 1   **HYPOTHETICAL SCHEDULE OF PRODUCTIVITY OF CAPITAL FOR A FIRM**

Rate of return (in percentages)	Number of dollars that can earn this amount	Marginal productivity of capital (number of dollars that can earn this amount or more)
30%	5,000	5,000
20	20,000	25,000
10	15,000	40,000
5	30,000	70,000
1	150,000	220,000

These values of the marginal productivity schedule are plotted on Figure 1. For a firm with a larger number of investment opportunities, or for an industry, or a whole economy,

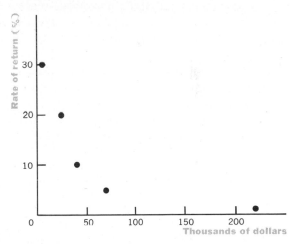

FIGURE 1

---

3. Verify that the *average* return on $40,000 would be 17.5 percent. The average return will be above the marginal return.

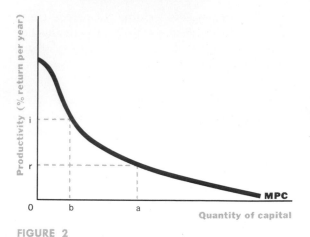

FIGURE 2

we could replace the individual dots by a curve that represents the whole cumulative listing of investment opportunities, as we have done in Figure 2. The curve in Figure 2 tells us, for example, that *Oa* dollars of investment have an MPC of *Or* percent per year. This means that each of the *Oa* dollars has a productivity of *Or* percent *or more*.

Would it be worthwhile borrowing money in order to purchase a capital good? It would depend, of course, on the productivity of the particular investment and the rate of interest that must be paid on the loan. If the rate of interest is very high, then there will be only a few projects for which it will be profitable to borrow money—those that have a rate of productivity greater than the rate of interest. At a rate of interest of *Oi*, only *Ob* dollars worth of capital would pay a rate of return over their cost. If the rate of interest falls, less productive projects will yield a re-

turn over and above the interest charges on money borrowed to institute them. At very low interest rates, it will be profitable to borrow money for all sorts of projects that yield only a low return over other costs. *Thus the MPC schedule represents the demand for loanable funds by businesses.*[4] Notice that, although we are talking about the demand for money, its productivity is based upon the use of the real capital—the factory or the machine—that it will purchase.

3. GOVERNMENTS

State and local governments borrow funds to build highways and schools and to undertake long-term investment projects. Any government has only two sources of revenue, taxes and borrowing, and most local and state governments borrow to finance their long-term investment projects. Although the amount of money state and local governments need will depend upon such factors as the growth in their population, there is ample evidence that their demand curve for funds is downward sloping: More is borrowed when the interest rates are low.

The federal government also borrows money, sometimes in very large amounts, as in World War II, to finance capital improvements, defense expenditures, and so on. The federal government's choice between borrowing and taxing is, however, often based on considerations other than the cost of funds. As we shall see in Chapter 58, governments sometimes borrow in order to run a deficit (spending more than they collect) for the purpose of combating depressions.

---

4. The MPC declines by definition; we list projects in decreasing order of their rate of return. The MPC schedule is the demand curve for capital only if we assume that firms are profit-maximizers and that they are certain about the yield from each individual investment. If they are uncertain about the yield, as will almost always be the case, they may require a margin over the expected return in order to compensate them for the risks involved. In this case the demand curve for capital will be to the left of the MPC schedule and in equilibrium the return on capital will exceed the rate of interest.

Thus we cannot assume that the federal government's demand for loanable funds is downward sloping.

Many empirical studies have been made of the demand for funds and they leave us in little doubt that, taking all sources together, they lead to a downward-sloping demand curve plotted against the rate of interest.[5]

Who Lends Money? The Supply of Loanable Funds

Money is offered for loan by firms and households that have funds that they do not require for current expenditure. If one has surplus funds on hand, it pays to loan them out, providing that the rate of interest offered more than covers any possible risk that the loan might not be repaid. Funds are provided by the savings both of households and firms. *But this is only part of the story.* Banks have a great deal to do with the supply of loanable funds. Not only are they the channel by which a good part of the savings of individuals and firms is loaned to those who wish to borrow, but, as we shall see in Part X, banks actually can create and destroy money. Further, the central authorities, both the Federal Reserve System and the U.S. Treasury, exercise a great deal of control over the supply of loanable funds.

"The" Interest Rate: The Price of Loanable Funds

We have said that the rate of interest is the price paid for borrowing money. We have also argued that there will be a downward-sloping demand curve for money to borrow plotted against the rate of interest, and also that there is a supply of money to borrow. It would seem a very natural thing to say next that the price of loanable funds is determined by the demand for, and the supply of, such funds. However, a simple supply-and-demand analysis is not adequate, for several reasons.

First, the rate of interest is not free to fluctuate sufficiently so as always to bring about an equality between the demand for loanable funds and the supply. To take one example, banks fix the rates of interest that they charge on loans with many considerations in mind. They are reluctant to change these rates every time changes occur in the demand for money to borrow. If there is an excess demand for loanable funds, then the banks often ration the available supply of funds among their customers according to such criteria as the credit rating of the borrower, how long the banker has known him, the size of business done, and the persuasiveness of the customer, rather than by raising the rate of interest. *Credit rationing* is commonly found in lending institutions in most Western countries.

Second, evidence suggests that although the demand for loanable funds is influenced

---

5. Net borrowing by the federal government (except during wars) is not a large enough fraction of total borrowing to reverse the tendency, even if it were completely different in its pattern.

by the rate of interest, it is also influenced by many other factors, such as the general level of demand in the economy and changes in this demand. When we draw a demand curve, we assume that factors affecting demand other than the rate of interest remain constant. In fact, this is observed not to be the case: The other things are observed to change continuously and to exert a major influence on the demand for loanable funds. This means that our demand curve will be continuously shifting about due to changes in these other things.

Third, a large part of the business demand for and supply of funds does not enter the market at all but represents rather the plowing-back of business profits. Funds may be locked in to a given large corporation both by virtue of the income-tax laws and by virtue of any differences between the motives of the managers of a corporation and the motives of its stockholders.

Fourth, the federal government (and related agencies) affects *both sides* of the money market. It is a large borrower (through its sales of government bonds) and it is also the chief influence on the size of the money supply. Governments commonly use their influence to affect the rate of interest for purposes of public policy.[6]

But however the interest rate is set, it will have an important effect on the share of national income going to lenders of funds and on the allocation of resources among competing uses.

INTEREST RATES AND THE INCOMES OF THE LENDERS

The great bulk of outstanding loans on which interest is paid represents loans made in the past, whereas loans made within the current year represent a small proportion of total loans outstanding. The interest rate payable on a loan is usually (although not always) fixed at the time when the loan is originally made. Thus fluctuations in the current price of loanable funds affect the *income* only of those suppliers of funds who are currently making new loans. The total income of all suppliers of loanable funds is arrived at by multiplying the volume of outstanding loans made in each past year by the market rate of interest ruling in the same year, and adding up these amounts.

Fluctuations in interest rates affect the *wealth* of all lenders of funds. (Reread pages 374–375 at this time.) If the interest rate rises from 5 percent to 6 percent, the owner of a $1,000, 5 percent bond will still receive his $50 each year, but the market value of his bond will fall.[7]

The incomes of suppliers of funds who have purchased equities rather than bonds will vary according to the dividend policies of the corporations they own, and their wealth will vary with the prices of their shares. But these are complicated matters in which many more factors than the rate of interest come to bear. There is no simple relation between the welfare of lenders of funds and the rate of interest.

6. Because there is a very large stock of government bonds outstanding, the central authorities can, by choosing to buy or sell such bonds, drive their prices up or down (and thus push interest rates down or up). They can also, through regulatory powers, affect the behavior of commercial banks. See Chapter 53.

7. Exactly how far it will fall depends upon the redemption date of the bond. For a perpetual bond, the price would fall to $833.33 (6 percent of which is $50); if the bond is redeemable tomorrow, however, its price would fall below $1,000 by only a few pennies.

INTEREST RATES AND THE ALLOCATIVE MECHANISM

Funds for investment are scarce at most times.[8] These funds represent command over resources that can be used for constructing capital goods. There is thus, as with all scarce factors, the problem of allocating them between a large number of competing uses. A freely fluctuating rate of interest determined by the demand for, and supply of, loanable funds, would provide one way of doing this. If capital were scarce, interest rates would be high, and if it were plentiful, rates would be low. A high rate would mean that only projects with a high productivity would obtain funds, whereas a low rate would allow low-productivity projects to obtain funds. If the rate of interest were set so as to equate the demand and supply of funds, this would ensure that the projects yielding the highest money return would always be the ones undertaken first. If there were not enough of such projects to exhaust the supply of funds, then the supply would exceed the demand, the rate would fall, and less remunerative projects could obtain funds. If, on the other hand, there were, at the current rate of interest, more projects yielding a positive return over interest charges than there were funds available, then demand for funds would exceed supply, the rate of interest would rise, and the less remunerative projects would be squeezed out. Allocating scarce funds by means of interest rates thus means that it is always the most remunerative projects that obtain the funds.

If the interest rate is determined by the central authorities (instead of by the free market), precisely the same process would take place if the central authorities at the same time controlled the supply of funds in such a way as to equate demand and supply at that interest rate. Setting rates (with no control over supply) is similar to controlling prices (discussed in Chapter 11). An artificially low rate of interest will create a problem of rationing and possibly a black market in funds. An artificially high rate of interest will find loanable funds accumulating with no borrowers. To control the volume of loans involves managing both their price and their quantity.

It is, of course, not necessary to let the market allocate funds. In fact, banks do not usually allocate loanable funds in this manner; more often, they charge a customary interest rate and then ration the available supply of credit among their customers. This means that projects that cannot yield a return as high as the going interest rate will not get money, since no one will want to borrow money to undertake them. Thus there is some allocation according to relative profitability. All projects that yield a return in excess of the going rate of interest, however, will be able to make a profit, and if demand for funds exceeds supply, some other allocation principle will have to be adopted by the lenders of funds. If, for example, lending institutions allocate most of their funds to their oldest customers, and hardly any to new ones, this will not necessarily mean that the projects yielding the highest returns will get the money. We may call this the allocation of funds according to lenders' preferences. A number of Congressional hearings have been held to try to determine if new and small businesses have been discriminated against in such allocations.

In a system in which the current rate of

---

8. At other times, for example, during severe depressions, loanable funds may be in excess supply.

interest does bear some relation to the general scarcity or abundance of investment funds, but where current demand and supply are equated by credit rationing, we have a mixture of allocation by profitability and allocation by lenders' preferences. As loanable funds become abundant, the rate of interest will fall and more projects will be able to compete for the scarce capital, but the ones that are successful out of those profitable enough to be able to compete will be determined by lenders' preferences. This mixed system is the one found in many Western countries.

Another means of allocating scarce capital is by government edict. The central government could establish its own set of priorities according as it judged various investments to further the national interest, and it could then allocate the scarce funds first to the top-priority project, then to the second-priority one, and so on down the list, until the funds were exhausted.

A mixed system would be one in which the government allocated some of the available capital to projects that it judged to be in the social interest, independent of their financial profitability, and let the remaining funds go to the highest bidder and thus to the financially most remunerative projects.

In centrally planned economies, it is impossible for one central planning body to make all the decisions about the allocation of investment funds. Usually, the central planners make decisions on broad matters of policy, and much of the detailed—but often quite important—decision-making is decentralized. Decision-makers require some guide as to what investments are worth making and what investments are too unremunerative, given the general supply of capital in the whole country; this guide often takes the form of some sort of a rate of interest (often called by another name). If the decentralized decision-makers are told that their investments must yield a return over and above an interest charge on the capital used, then this ensures that the more remunerative investments will take precedence over the less remunerative ones. If the state ensures that prices of goods and factors of production reflect its own valuation of their relative importance, then this investment procedure ensures that the most important projects will be undertaken first. The difference between such a system and the Western market system is, thus, not in the existence of an interest rate, for one exists in both kinds of societies, but in the absence of a class of people who receive the interest payment in return for making available their privately owned capital, and in the way in which different projects are valued (according to market prices or according to state-administered prices).

INTEREST RATES IN EVALUATING ALTERNATIVES

In the foregoing section, we discussed interest rates in terms of the actual allocations of funds. Interest rates are also used to evaluate and compare projects that yield benefits over a different period of time. To

TABLE 2

Profits at end of year	Project A	Project B
1	$100	—
2	100	—
3	100	—
4	100	—
5	100	—
6	—	—
7	—	—
8	—	$700

take a simple example, suppose a firm can choose between the two projects in Table 2. Project A will provide profits of $100 a year for each of 5 years, a total payoff of $500. Project B will pay nothing at all until 8 years have passed, but then will pay $700. Which project is better, and how much should the firm be prepared to pay for the better project? Answers to both questions depend upon the interest rate.

I. PRESENT VALUE (P.V.)

How much would you pay someone *now* in return for his promise to pay you $100 in 10 years, assuming you are absolutely sure he will pay you? It is obvious that you would pay him less than $100. But how much less? Let us answer an easier question first: How much would you pay today for a promise to pay you $100 one year from today, if the rate of interest paid by savings banks is 4 percent? If you put $100 into a savings bank you could take out $104 in one year. The *present value* of that $104 next year is $100 now. The present value of $100 next year (if the interest rate is 4 percent) is:

$$\frac{100}{1.04} = 96.15,$$

because $96.15 put in a savings account that pays 4 percent will be worth $100 after 1 year. If the interest rate were 6 percent, the present value of $100 one year hence would be

$$\frac{100}{1.06} = \$94.34.$$

In general, P.V. of X dollars 1 year hence at an interest rate of i percent per year is

$$P.V. = \frac{X}{(1 + i)}.$$

One hundred dollars 2 years hence would have a present value (at 4 percent) of

$$\frac{100.00}{(1.04)(1.04)} = 92.46$$

because $92.46 put in a savings bank now would be worth $100 in 2 years. In general, we may write, for the present value of X dollars after t years at 1 percent

$$P.V. = \frac{X}{(1 + i)^t}.$$

We see from this that the present value of a given sum will be smaller the farther away the payment date and the higher the rate of interest.

The answer to how much you would pay for $100 in 10 years depends upon the interest rate. At 4 percent

$$P.V. = \frac{100}{(1.04)^{10}} = \$67.56.$$

The simple formula permits us to compute the present value of any time stream of payments. In practice, one usually uses specially prepared tables to avoid the necessity of doing the calculations.

2. THE EXAMPLE ONCE MORE

Table 3 gives the present values of the two projects at three different interest rates.[9] It is clear that at either 4 percent or 6 percent Project B is more valuable than Project A, but that at 8 percent Project A is more valuable. And in each case the present value tells what the project is worth to the firm. Suppose

---

9. The present value of Project A is the sum of the present values of 5 different payments of $100 each. Tables of interest make it easy to find the P.V. by giving the P.V. of an annuity of $1 per year for t years. In this case, t is 5.

the firm can buy either or both projects for $425 each. If the interest rate is 4 percent, both projects are worth buying: The present value is worth more than the present outlay. At 6 percent, only Project B is worthwhile, and at 8 percent neither is worthwhile.

TABLE 3   **PRESENT VALUES OF INCOME STREAMS IN TABLE 2**

Interest or discount rate (in percentages)	Project A	Project B
4%	$445.18	$511.48
6	421.24	439.19
8	399.27	378.19

Let us summarize the important features of this example:

1. If money can earn interest, promises of money in the future are worth less than their nominal value. The greater the rate of interest, the less the present value of a given sum in the future. The farther away the payoff, the less the present value.

2. The *relative* attractiveness of different projects will change, depending upon the interest rate.

Specifically, projects that do not pay off for a long time become increasingly less attractive the higher the interest rate. (The reason is clear: The opportunity cost of giving up the use of money for a long time is higher, the higher the interest rate that it could be earning.) Thus the interest rate has an effect in terms of allocating funds over time. High interest rates discourage long-lived projects with benefits far in the future.

3. CHOOSING THE INTEREST RATE TO USE IN COMPUTING PRESENT VALUE[10]

If a firm can borrow as much money as it likes at r percent per year, it should *discount* at r percent per year. But in every case, the firm should discount at the opportunity cost of the funds it uses. (See Appendix A to Chapter 17 for a fuller discussion.)

The Structure of Interest Rates

We have spoken heretofore of *the* interest rate, but it is readily apparent that at any one moment of time there are many different interest rates. Today, although you may receive an interest rate of about 4.5 percent on deposits at a savings and loan association, you will have to pay 6 percent to borrow from the same savings and loan association to buy a house. Interest rates on consumer-install-ment credit of 12 percent and 16 percent are common. A small firm pays a higher interest rate than a giant corporation on funds it borrows from banks. Different government bonds pay different rates of interest, depending upon the length of the period for which the bond runs. Corporation bonds tend to pay interest at a higher rate than government bonds, and there is much variation among

10. We limit discussion to profit-maximizing firms. Discount rates may also be used by the government in allocating its funds, but somewhat different considerations apply. There are many difficult problems here —for example, what rate of discount should the government of India use in evaluating a dam or a steel plant? We must leave such questions to more advanced courses.

bonds of different companies. Since money is extremely mobile, why do such great differences exist? Why doesn't the flow of funds between different uses diminish these differences?

The answer is that the quoted interest rates involve more than merely the "rental fee" on the use of money. Different loans differ with respect to their riskiness, their liquidity, and the costs involved in processing them and collecting them. Each of these things must be paid for, and the interest payments include them.

A few years ago, bonds of a Brazilian tin-mining company were selling at a price that made their interest rate more than 10 percent per year; at the same time, U.S. Government bonds of the same duration were paying 4 percent. But investors did not sell their government bonds and rush to buy the mining bonds. They were sure of the ability of the U.S. Government to pay both the interest and the principal on their bonds, but they were less sure about the Brazilian tin-mining company's ability to pay. In fact, they were afraid that the government of Brazil would seize the company and repudiate the bonds. In other words, part of the high interest rate was a risk premium. U.S. corporation bonds generally have higher interest rates than government bonds because they have a greater degree of risk. Even a little bit of risk can make a big difference in an interest rate. Suppppose the rate of interest is 4 percent on a U.S. Government bond that is considered to be free of risk.[11] Suppose the bonds of a particular company are considered quite safe,

but that there is a small chance—say 1 in 50—that the company might be forced to repudiate its bonds during the year. Investors would want at least 2 percent as a risk premium on their investment. The combination of the 4 percent "risk-free" rate and the 2 percent risk premium add up to 6 percent, half again as much interest as on the government bond. Differences in risk to the lender account for some of the differences in interest rates or loans for different purposes. The risk involved is that of collecting the principal. "Secured loans," where the borrower pledges an asset as collateral, tend to have lower interest rates than unsecured loans, other things being equal. Loans, or mortgages, secured by houses tend to have lower interest rates than loans secured by automobiles, in part because it is harder to run away with a house than a car.

The term (duration) of a loan may likewise affect its price. The same bank will usually pay a higher rate of interest on a certificate of deposit (which cannot be redeemed for one year) than for a straight savings account (which legally may be redeemed in thirty days but which can in fact be withdrawn in a matter of minutes). Yet many savers prefer savings accounts, because they want to be able to withdraw their money on short notice: They value *liquidity*. Cash, the most liquid of all forms of holding money, earns a zero interest rate. The real liquidity of a loan, whether it be a note or a bond, is not always to be judged by its redemption date. If you own a ten-year bond, you can get your money tomorrow by selling the bond on a bond

11. The United States Government is considered so stable by investors that its obligations are usually thought to have no chance of being repudiated. This was, of course, not always so. During the Civil War, both the Confederate States and the Union issued bonds that were regarded as having high degrees of risk. One way to judge public opinion about the way the war was going is to compare the yields of the two kinds of bonds at different times during the war.

market. But liquidity here involves both costs (the fee paid to the broker who sells it) and risk (the bond may not be worth its face value tomorrow, although it will be ten years from now). In general, the shorter the term of a loan, the more liquid it is and, other things being equal, the lower the interest rates.

Finally, there is the matter of the costs to the lender of processing and collecting a loan. It is almost as cheap (in actual numbers of dollars) for a bank to lend United Airlines $1 million that the airline agrees to pay back with interest after 1 year as it is for the same bank to lend you $1,600 to buy a new car on an installment loan that you agree to pay back in 24 equal installments.[12] The

difference in the cost *per dollar* of each loan is enormous. The bank may very well make less profit per dollar on a $1,600 loan at 12 percent per year than on a $1 million loan at 4 percent per year. In general, the bigger the loan and the fewer the payments, the less the cost per dollar of servicing the loan.[13]

Differences in interest rates are, for all of these reasons, akin to the nonpecuniary returns to labor we discussed in Chapter 33. A perfectly working capital market would equate the *net advantage* of different kinds of loans; since interest rates are only one part of the net advantage to the lender, there is every reason to expect a structure of interest rates among loans of different kinds.

Actual Versus Nominal Interest Rates: A Digression[14]

One of the reasons, not mentioned above, for differences in interest rates is that people may be totally unaware of what they are paying for the use of money. This may partly be due to their not caring: If they buy a car and are told the payments will be $65 per month for 36 months, they may be content never to know how much they borrowed or what rate of interest they are paying. Often people do

care, but they never bother to figure out what rate of interest they are paying. Suppose you wish to borrow $1,200 for one year, and you have heard that the interest rate is 6 percent per year. You go to your bank and say, "Give me $1,200 now and I will pay back $1,272 one year from today." The banker looks troubled and says he would be glad to lend you the money, but would you mind paying $106 a

---

12. Just consider the number of bookkeeping entries required in each case. In addition to this, it is much easier, and thus less costly, to find out about United Airlines' credit rating than it is to find out about yours.

13. Why then do banks and finance companies urge frequent installments? They worry that if you do not pay regularly you will not have the money when the loan comes due. They worry less about United Airlines. If they are good bankers, they consider the possibility in either case.

14. In one sense, this section is a digression designed to clear up very widespread confusions about what real interest rates are. In another sense, it is not a digression. So far as our theories assume that people react to interest rates, what matters is what people believe the interest rate to be. If they behave on misinformation, predictions about what they will do will be different from what they would be if they have correct information. It is clearly irrational for people to borrow money at 75 percent or 100 percent per year if they can borrow for much less. But some do so when they borrow from loan sharks. Are we to conclude that these people are irrational and that we cannot therefore predict anything about their behavior? Or are we to assume that they are acting rationally but are grotesquely misinformed? If the latter, we would be able to predict the effects on their behavior of a campaign to educate them.

month instead? You are good at arithmetic, so you know that $106 \times 12 = 1,272$. You agree to his plan. You find out later that you have agreed to pay interest at the rate of about 12 percent per year instead of 6 percent! The key difference is that, in your proposal, you had the use of the full $1,200 for the whole year, whereas, in his proposal, you had it all for only one month. After the first monthly payment of $106 (of which $6 was the correct interest charge for 1 month at 6 percent per year), you had the use of only $1,100 for the second month. (If you pay $6 to use $1,100 for one month you will be paying at the rate of over 6.5 percent per year.) Jump to the last month and suppose you still owe $100. If you pay $6 to use $100 for one month you are paying interest at the rate of 6 percent *a month* or 72 percent a year. Without going into the actuarial details, the banker's proposal involves your having an average

loan of $600 a month for 12 months; the $72 interest you pay comes to 12 percent of this amount.

Another popular scheme is to deduct the interest in advance. Instead of lending you $1,200 the bank gives you $1,128 ($1,200 less the 6 percent interest for 1 year) and you pay back $100 per month for 12 months. You will end up paying a little more than 12¾ percent. (It is higher than in the previous case, because, although you paid $72 in both cases, you only borrowed $1,128 in this case instead of $1,200.)

Finally, in response to your desire for $1,200, the bank might ask you for the $72 interest, plus a "carrying charge" of $28. They will give you $1,100 to be paid back in 12 monthly installments of $100 each. You will be paying interest at the rate of over 19 percent per year.[15]

Profits: Once Again

As you learned in Chapter 17, what the businessman calls profits includes many things. One of these is the rate of return on the owner's investment that is necessary to keep the funds in the industry. In Chapter 34 we called such a payment a transfer earning. This in turn is what we are in this chapter treating as an interest rate, and its level must include an adjustment for risk. But, as we have seen, profits may vary for reasons other than risk and the use of the owner's capital.

Profits are generally associated with the dynamic factors of change and uncertainty.

We have seen in our study of the theory of the firm how shifts in demand give rise to profits and to losses. A rise in demand will make an industry abnormally profitable and, until the industry has expanded, high profits will be earned. A fall in demand will make an industry less than normally profitable so that, until the industry has contracted, low or negative profits will be earned. Changes in costs should also be mentioned. If a firm introduces new cost-saving methods, then its profits will increase; the same thing will happen if the firm produces a new product that is preferred

15. In no area in American commerce is there such a plethora of misinformed buyers as in the retail market for money. The practices described above are indulged in not only by loan sharks but by reputable banks and finance companies as well.

by consumers to existing products. We have called such changes innovations. Successful innovations are undoubtedly a source of profits, and we (along with Professor Schumpeter, whose writings emphasize this) may regard profits as an incentive to make, and as a reward for making, successful innovations.

We have seen throughout the theory of the firm how variations in profits signal shifts in demand and costs and thus act as an incentive or disincentive to investment in a particular industry. Profits thus fulfill a function in the free-market system of resource allocation. Relative profitabilities signal the relative attractiveness of investment in various lines. Highly profitable investment opportunities give rise to the demand for investment funds. The interest rate then, insofar as it does reflect demand and supply for funds, serves to choke off the demand for funds at the available supply, leaving those projects that yield a "profit" (in the businessman's sense) higher than the rate of interest to be undertaken, and those that yield a "profit" less than this rate to go undone.

It is only those profits that do not succeed in inducing flows of investment that serve no allocative function. The classical opposition to monopoly and to monopoly profits rested in part upon those profits existing, but not inducing the resource flows that would eliminate them.

The Share of Interest and Profits in the National Income

The share of interest and of profits in the national income has remained remarkably constant over time. We have no satisfactory theory of this share, and we can do little to explain past behavior of it; nor do we have a body of predictions about the effect on this share of occurrences such as the rise of unions, wage freezes, profits taxes, price controls, etc. There is a great deal of basic research that needs to be done by students of this subject. We do have a considerable body of systematic observations of how the share of profits and interest in the national income varies from one economy to another, and within economies from one time period to another. Perhaps from these observations we will one day have a satisfactory theory. Perhaps one of you will propose the hypothesis, or make the measurements, that will enlighten us.

Summary

1. Interest, as we use the term in this chapter, is a payment for the use of money. The interest rate is the price of using money for one year and then returning the money.

2. Households borrow because of time preference and sometimes for investment and speculation. The biggest private demand for loanable funds comes from firms that borrow because they expect an investment in capital goods to yield a return over the cost of borrowing the money. The total demand for money to borrow is believed to be downward sloping when plotted against the rate of interest.

3. Fluctuations in the current price of loanable funds affect the interest income of only those suppliers of funds who are currently making new loans, but these fluctuations affect the wealth of all lenders of funds.

4. There is a number of alternative systems of allocating funds. One system, which is commonly found in Western countries today, is a mixed system in which funds are allocated partly on the basis of the profitability of their proposed use and partly on the basis of lender's preferences.

5. If money can earn interest, promises to pay money in the future are worth less than their nominal value. The greater the rate of interest and the farther away the payoff, the less the present value of the promise.

6. Rather than there being one interest rate, there is a structure of rates. Rates depend on, among other things, the riskiness, term, and liquidity of a loan, and the cost to the lender of processing and collecting it.

7. One of the things that the businessman calls profits is the rate of return on the owner's investment necessary to keep the funds in the industry. We treat this as an interest rate, and by profits we understand revenues in excess of total opportunity costs. It is only those profits that do not succeed in inducing flows of investment that serve no allocative function.

8. As yet, we have no generally accepted hypothesis to answer the question of what determines the share of interest and profits in the national income.

QUESTIONS FOR DISCUSSION

1. For what purposes might you borrow? What types of consumer credit can you name?

2. Why do businessmen borrow?

3. With high interest rates prevailing in 1965, the Bank of England still urged British banks to restrict loans to importers and to favor exporters. What would the effects of this have been on the loanable-funds market as opposed to a situation where, for example, the bank used its available weapons to raise the interest rate yet further?

4. Marxist theory denies the existence of an interest rate in Marxist societies. What would you expect to find if you queried Russian local authorities on their method of allocating the funds available to them?

5. In 1965, Dun and Bradstreet, the influential raters of corporate credit, downgraded New York City bonds one notch from a formerly excellent category. On the next bond issue, a week later, the city found itself having to pay 0.5 percent more in interest than before. Explain this. Would this change have any effect on people who had bought New York City bonds in the past?

Chapter **37** CRITICISMS AND TESTS OF THE THEORY OF DISTRIBUTION

IN PREVIOUS CHAPTERS, WE DEVELOPED THE traditional theory of distribution in a number of different contexts. In this chapter, we first summarize the theory and then go on to consider various criticisms and tests that have been put forward from time to time.

The Theory Restated

The theory of distribution asserts that factor pricing can be explained by demand and supply. The whole of distribution theory is based on only two or three basic hypotheses about behavior.

Factor supply is determined, in the theory, according to the principle of net advantage. When, taking pecuniary and nonpecuniary rewards into account, differentials exist in the wages offered to factors, factors will move among uses, among industries, and among places in such a way as to equalize the net advantages to the owners of factors. Because there are impediments to the mobility of factors, there may be lags in the response of factors to changes in relative prices. Thus the elasticity of supply will depend upon what factor is being discussed and what time horizon is being considered.

The demand for a factor is a derived demand, depending on the marginal physical productivity of a factor and the demand con-ditions for the commodity made by the factor. The addition to revenue caused by employing another unit of some variable factor depends on the addition to physical output contributed by that factor and the change in total revenue when the rate of sales is increased by this amount. The curve that displays this information is called the marginal revenue product curve of the factor. As long as the *factor* is purchased under competitive conditions, and as long as firms are maximizing short-run profits, the marginal revenue product curve of a factor is the firm's demand curve for that factor. This is true whether the product is sold under conditions of perfect competition, imperfect competition, or monopoly. In equilibrium, each type of factor will be paid a wage equal to its marginal revenue product.

A firm that is not equating the marginal revenue products of each of its factors with that factor's price is not maximizing its profits. On the other hand, if the firm is maximizing its profits, then it is necessarily equating each factor price to the corresponding marginal revenue product. The theory thus stands or falls with the theory of profit maximization. It is merely an implication of profit maximization, and the only reason for spelling it out in detail is that this may help us to develop interesting and useful hypotheses about the effects of various changes in the economy on the markets for factors of production.

When one thinks of all the heated arguments over the theory, of all the passionate denunciations and defenses that it has occasioned, it is surprising to observe how few predictions it makes and how uncontroversial most of them are. The theory predicts that demand for factors depends on, and varies with, the demand for the products made by the factor. This was undoubtedly a great discovery when it was first put forward; now, however, it is almost a platitude. The theory also asserts that the technical conditions of production will influence the demand for a factor. The theory predicts that, assuming the supply curve of the factor has not shifted, changes in the factor price must reflect changes in the demand for the commodities made by the factor. On the supply side, the theory predicts that movement of resources between firms and between industries will occur in response to changes in factor prices. It is very hard to quarrel with any of these predictions; in fact, they seem so obvious as to be trite. They are, nevertheless, important and often arise in practical issues of policy.

Marginal productivity theory explains the demand for factors of production; it constitutes half of the traditional theory of distribution. The other half is the theory of supply, which asserts that factors will move between occupations in search of the highest net advantage. It is the marginal-productivity half of the theory that has been subject to most criticism and about which there exist so many misconceptions. Much of the controversy is due to misconceptions. We shall now consider a representative set of these.[1]

Six Common Misconceptions

1. *The theory assumes perfect competition in all markets.* This is simply not correct. The relationship between the marginal physical product and the marginal revenue product will be altered if the degree of competition alters, but the marginal revenue product curve is the demand curve for the factor in perfect competition, imperfect competition, and monopoly. Competition is assumed in the factor market, not in the product market.

2. *The theory assumes full employment.* Marginal productivity by itself is a theory of the *demand* for factors of production; it says nothing about the supply of factors. Unemployment is a relation between the demand for, and the supply of, factors of production. Clearly, therefore, the marginal productivity theory predicts nothing, one way or the other, about unemployment.

3. *The theory assumes that the amount and value of the marginal product of a factor is known to the entrepreneur.* The theory as-

1. This particular set is taken from F. C. Benham, *Economics: A General Introduction* (6th ed.; London: Pitman, 1960).

sumes no such thing! Critics argue that the firm will not pay any factor the value of its marginal product, because the firm will generally have no idea what that marginal product is and would be unable to calculate this magnitude even if it tried. This criticism is irrelevant. It has already been pointed out that payment according to marginal revenue product occurs *automatically* whenever the firm is maximizing its profits. It does not matter *how* the firm succeeds in maximizing profits—by guess, hunch, luck, clairvoyance, skill, good judgment, or calculating marginal quantities. As long as profits are maximized, factors will be getting the value of their marginal products. The theory does not purport to describe how businessmen calculate; it merely predicts how they will react to various situations on the assumption that they are maximizing profits.

4. *Since the theory predicts that all factors will receive a wage equal to their marginal revenue product, the theory denies the possibility of exploitation of factors by their employers.* The theory is a theory about *competitive* factor markets: All employers are assumed to be wage-takers. They can choose how much of a factor to employ, but no one of them can influence the wage. If labor were free, it would pay an employer to take on labor until its marginal revenue product had fallen to zero. If labor costs $2.00 per hour, it will pay the employer to add laborers until the marginal revenue product is $2.00 per hour. If the employer stops short of this point —say, by using labor in a quantity such that the marginal revenue product is $2.50—then the employer is paying workers less than the value of their marginal product. Whether or not this constitutes "exploitation" of the workers is debatable; there is no doubt, however, that it constitutes exploitation of the employer by the employer! As long as the wage

is less than the value of the marginal product, the employer can increase his own profits by hiring more labor.

The theory *assumes* profit maximization; it then *deduces* that the wage will be equal to the value of the marginal product. Labor can be paid less than its marginal revenue product in the case of monopsony. Indeed, this is a prediction of the theory of monopsony; it is not a refutation of the theory of competitive factor markets.

5. *The theory is inhuman because it treats human labor in the same way as it treats a ton of coal or a wagonload of fertilizer.* One must be careful to distinguish one's emotional reaction to a procedure that treats human and nonhuman factors alike from one's evaluation of it in terms of positive economics. Anyone who accepts this criticism must explain carefully why separate theories of the pricing of human and nonhuman factors are needed. He must also show that his "human" theory makes predictions that differ from those made by the marginal productivity theory. The marginal productivity theory is only a theory of the *demand* for a factor. It predicts only what employers would like to buy. It predicts that employers' desired purchases of labor (and all other factors) depend on the wage rate, the technical conditions of production, and the demand for the product made by labor. *Supply* conditions may differ between human and nonhuman factors, but these differences are accommodated within the theory. No evidence has yet been gathered to indicate that it is necessary to have separate theories of the *demand* for human and nonhuman factors of production.

6. *The theory assumes that the price per unit of a factor will be the same in every industry in which it is employed.* This is incorrect. The theory does not *assume* it. As we have seen, the theory *predicts* that labor

will move between industries until *net* advantage is equalized. There is nothing in the theory that prevents it from accommodating unequal payments in various industries due to such factors as a lack of mobility of labor between industries, nonpecuniary considerations, or the existence of disequilibrium in a market in which the adjustment mechanism works only slowly.

Marginal Productivity and Justice

We have seen that it is a condition of equilibrium in the marginal productivity theory applied to a world of perfectly competitive factor markets that all factors receive a payment equal to the values of their marginal products. Some supporters of the theory of marginal productivity have held that not only was the theory correct, but that it satisfied the canons of justice,[2] i.e., that it gave rise to a just distribution of the national product, because factors were rewarded according to the value of their contributions to the national product. Many critics of the levels of wages that prevailed reacted with passion against a theory that was claimed to justify them.

It is beyond the scope of a book on positive economics to enter into normative questions of what constitutes a just distribution of income. It is, however, worth getting the facts straight. According to the marginal productivity theory, each laborer (or each unit of any other factor) does *not* receive the value of what he personally contributes to production. He receives, instead, the value of what one more laborer would add to production if all other factors were held constant. If 1 million similar laborers are employed, then each of the 1 million receives as income an amount equal to the extra product that would have been contributed by the millionth laborer if he had been hired while capital and all other factors had remained unchanged. Whether or not such a distribution of the national product is regarded as just, one cannot say that each unit of a factor receives as income the value of *its own* contribution to production. Indeed, where many factors cooperate in production, it is generally impossible to divide total production into the amounts contributed by each factor of production.[3]

Do Market Conditions Determine Factor Earnings?

FACTORS OTHER THAN LABOR

Most nonhuman factors are sold on competitive markets. The theory predicts that changes in the earnings of these factors will be associated with changes in market conditions. The overwhelming preponderance of evidence supports this prediction of the theory. Consider some examples:

2. One of the most famous exponents of this view was the American economist John Bates Clark.
3. Which one of your two eyes gives you three-dimensional vision? The second one, of course.

I. RAW MATERIALS

A dramatic example was provided during the Korean War when a rapid increase in the demand for many strategic materials sent their prices soaring to the extent that the incomes earned by their owners soared as well. The prices of copper, tin, rubber, and hundreds of other materials fluctuated in response to changes in the demand for these products.

2. LAND VALUES

Land in the heart of growing cities is clearly fixed in supply, and values rise steadily in response to increasing demand for it.[4] The value of the land itself even makes it worthwhile to destroy durable buildings to convert land to more productive uses.[5] The skyscraper is a monument to the high value of urban land. In many smaller cities, the change in tastes from shopping downtown to shopping in outlying shopping centers has lessened the demand for land downtown and influenced relative land prices. The increase in the price of land on the periphery of every growing city is a visible example of the workings of the market.

Agricultural land appears at first glance to provide counterevidence. The classical economists predicted 150 years ago that, as population and the demand for agricultural products grew, the price of the fixed supply of land would rise enormously.[6] The price of agricultural land, however, has *not* sky-

rocketed. Although the demand for agricultural produce did expand in the predicted fashion because of the rise in population, the productivity of agricultural land has increased in quite unexpected ways due to the invention of the vast range of machines and techniques that now characterize modern agriculture. The prediction was falsified, not because the price of agricultural land is not determined by market forces, but rather because some of the market forces were incorrectly foreseen.

3. TAXICAB MEDALLIONS

The supply of New York taxicabs is rigidly controlled by a licensing system, and the number of cabs is kept well below what it would be in a free-market situation.[7] The medallion, which confers the right to operate a cab, acquires a scarcity value (presently about $26,000); its market price is predicted by the theory of rent, one aspect of which is the pricing of factors in perfectly inelastic supply. As the demand for services of taxicabs rises due to increases in population and average incomes, the price of medallions rises correspondingly, so that new entrants earn only normal profits. If fares are increased and the demand proves inelastic, so that gross income from operating a cab rises, the price of the medallion rises correspondingly. The fare increase thus amounts to a free gift to the current holders of medallions; it does nothing to raise the net incomes of cab oper-

---

4. A friend of ours is fond of saying: "Nobody buys land any more; its price is much too high because everybody wants it."

5. Many of New York's old and favorite hotels have been pulled down in response to the intense demand for high-rise office buildings.

6. They were writing in, and thinking about, Britain and Europe. But similar predictions were made about post-frontier America.

7. Restricting the number of cabs makes sense if cabs impose a cost on the community (congestion, etc.) that is not borne by the operators, or, in others words, if the social cost of operating the cab exceeds the private cost. (See Chapter 17.)

ators newly entering the industry.

Possible examples would fill endless pages, but the point should now be clear: The prices and earnings of nonhuman factors are very successfully predicted by the theory of factor pricing in competitive markets.

LABOR

When we try to apply our theory to labor, we encounter two important sets of complications: First, labor markets are a mixture of competitive and noncompetitive elements, the proportions of the mixture differing from market to market; and, second, labor being the human factor of production, nonmonetary considerations loom large in its incentive patterns. These complications make labor economics one of the most difficult fields of economics. They also make the question posed in the heading of this section hard to answer. Monopolistic elements and nonmonetary rewards, both difficult to measure, require careful specification if the theory that labor earnings respond to market prices is to be testable. Nevertheless, we do have a mass of evidence to go on. We do have cases in which a strong union—one able to bargain effectively and to restrict entry of labor into the field—has caused wages to rise well above the competitive level. The West Coast longshoremen could never have hoped to obtain their present privileged position were it not for the extremely effective operations of Harry Bridges, president of the union. When Bridges was mobbed in San Francisco in Spring, 1964, by unemployed laborers wanting jobs as longshoremen, we were given impressive evidence that, if entry could not be restricted, the high earnings of longshoremen could not be long maintained. Many other similar cases have been documented. Unions can and do succeed in raising wages and incomes when they operate in small sections of the whole economy; the high earnings do attract others to enter the occupation or industry; and the privileged position can be maintained only if entry can be effectively restricted.

Earnings do then respond, at least to some extent, to monopoly power. Do they respond to normal fluctuations of demand and supply? Here the evidence is mixed. The competitive theory predicts that a decline in the demand for some product will cause a decline in the derived demand for the factors that make the product, a decline in their income, and the exit of factors to other uses. Cases come easily to mind. With the advent of the motor car, many skilled carriage-makers found the demand for their services declining rapidly. Earnings fell, and many in the older age brackets found that they had been earning substantial rents for their scarce, but highly specific, skill. These men were forced to suffer large income cuts when they moved to other industries. Many silent-screen stars who found their voices unsuitable for the talkies suffered disastrous cuts in income and fell into oblivion when the demand for silent films disappeared. A similar but less dramatic fate hit many radio personalities who were unable to make the transition to television and had to compete in the greatly reduced market for radio talent. Much earlier, the same fate met those vaudeville stars whose talents did not project on to the flat, flickering screen of the early silent movies. How soon will television entertainers, who have enormous incomes due to the high demand for their services, go the same way when a yet newer entertainment medium sweeps away the present one?

College professors are an example of a group currently enjoying gains as a result of changes in labor markets. The relative earnings of a college professor today are much higher than they were twenty years ago. This is particularly so at the starting end of the scale where intense competition for the scarce supply of good students who have just obtained Ph.D.'s forces up their price to levels that would have seemed princely only fifteen years ago.[8] Furthermore, the relative earnings of different kinds of professors reflect the relative strengths of the demands for their services in nonacademic fields. Engineers, chemists, and economists are all in heavy demand by nonacademic organizations, and their incomes relative to those of their colleagues in less favored fields reflect their comparatively high transfer earnings. Nor is this an isolated example. Why, if you have the talent, can you make a lot of money writing copy for an advertising agency on Madison Avenue, whereas, if you have the talent, you will not make a lot of money writing books of poetry? Not because any economic dictator or group of philosophers has decided that advertising is more valuable than poetry, but because in the American economy there is a large demand for advertising and only a tiny demand for poetry. A full citing of all such evidence would cover many pages, and it would all point to the conclusion that earnings of factors do very often respond to changes in market forces.

On the other hand, not only can monopoly elements raise incomes above their competitive levels, but they can also prevent incomes from falling and reflecting decreases in demand. Of course, if the demand disappears more or less overnight (as it did in the case of silent-movie stars), there is nothing any

union can do to maintain incomes. But the story may be different if, as is more usually the case, demand shrinks steadily over a few decades. Once-thriving industries, the railroad and coal-mining industries, have faded to pale shadows of their former selves. Year by year, the level of employment in these industries shrinks in response to declining demand. (See Table 1.) How does this relocation of labor out of declining industries occur? The competitive theory predicts low incomes for labor in these two industries, exit of the most mobile factors under this forceful disincentive, and hard times for the least mobile who decide to stay it out. But, in fact, the wages of coal miners and railroad employees have remained some of the highest in the whole industrial field. On the other hand, the predicted exit has occurred. Employment in coal mining fell from over 400,000 in 1947 to 121,000 in 1963, while employment on the railroads fell from over 1.3 million to under .7 million in the same period. What has happened is that powerful unions in each case have been able to prevent wages from falling, but the decline of job opportunities has discouraged the young from entering these industries. As workers left the industries due to retirement, ill health, or death, they were not replaced.[9]

By way of summary, it seems clear that the competitive theory does help to explain the relative earnings of different groups of labor; clearly, however, a strong dose of monopoly theory must be added if we hope to explain much of what we see.

There is a debate as to how much of the

8. The new professors do not necessarily consider their salaries princely. There is no evidence that increases in standards of living between generations increase the happiness of successive generations.

9. We cannot suppress the conjecture that the "restrictive behavior" of unions in these cases has led to a more orderly, humane, and civilized phasing out than would have occurred had the adjustment been left to a free market, in which case those who remained in the industry, and who were needed by it, would all have suffered depressed conditions in order that the disincentive could operate on those who did leave and on those who might otherwise have entered.

TABLE 1   **EMPLOYMENT AND HOURLY WAGES IN RAILWAY AND COAL INDUSTRIES (SELECTED YEARS)**

| | Employment in Thousands | | Hourly Wages in Dollars | | |
| | Class I railroads, all employees | Bituminous coal, production workers | Class I railroads | Bituminous coal | All U.S. manu-facturing |
Year					
1927	1,737	554	.61	.73	.55
1937	1,115	471	.68	.83	.62
1947	1,352	411	1.19	1.58	1.22
1955	1,057	205	2.12	2.72	1.95
1963	679	121	2.76	3.15	2.46

SOURCE: "Employment and Earnings Statistics for the United States," *Bureau of Labor Statistics, Bulletin 1312–2;* and *Historical Statistics of the United States.*

behavior of labor markets can be explained by economics. Some argue that one must use one's knowledge of political science, sociology, or even psychiatry to understand the labor leaders. What makes Walter, Dave, and Harry run? We cannot resolve this debate. To do so would require clearly specified predictions of alternative theories and careful testing of the differences among these predictions. We understand the present state of the evidence to be that economic explanations and economic forces do determine, within limits, the behavior of factors, so that there is no need to abandon such explanations and seek totally different ones. *Within these limits,* there is room for much additional explanation, and economists should welcome theories from wherever they can get them. Debates about conflicting theories, each of which is logically consistent, can be resolved only by a proper attention to the facts. The view that we have expressed in this paragraph rests upon the present state of the evidence and is subject to refutation.

Do Factors Move in Response to Changes in Earnings?

In the previous section we saw that earnings do tend to change in response to demand and supply conditions. Changes in earnings are signals whose purpose is to attract resources into lines of production in which they are more needed and out of lines in which they are less needed.

In the case of nonhuman factors, there is strong evidence that the theory is able to predict the actual course of events with reasonable accuracy. Land is transferred from one crop to another in response to changes in the relative profitabilities of the crops. Land on the edge of town is transferred from rural to urban uses as soon as it can earn substantially more as a building site than as a corn field. Materials and capital goods move from use to use in response to changes in earnings in these uses. Little more needs to be said here; the most casual observation will show the allocative system working pretty much as described by the theory.

Again, the complications come with labor. Countless studies of labor mobility have been made, but they do not point to a simple answer to the question of whether factors move in response to monetary incentives. On the one hand, it is clear that the great migration of Americans to the West Coast during World War II was induced by expanding employment opportunities and soaring wages in the shipyards and aircraft factories of California. On the other hand, why were the depressed areas of Appalachia not depopulated ten years ago when the coal mines began to shut down? At the risk of grossly simplifying a complex situation, we hazard the statement that the existing evidence is consistent with the following hypotheses: 1. There exists a fairly mobile component in any group. This mobile component tends to consist of the youngest, the most adaptable, and often the most intelligent members of the group. 2. This mobile group can be attracted from one area, occupation, or industry to another by relatively small changes in economic incentives. 3. Providing the pattern of demand for resources does not shift too fast, most of the necessary reallocation can be accomplished by movements of this mobile group.[10] As we go beyond these very mobile persons, we get into ranges of lower and lower mobility until, at the very bottom, we find persons who are virtually completely immobile. The most immobile are the very old, those with capital sunk in nonmarketable assets, the timid, the weak, and those who receive high nonmonetary rewards in their present occupation or locations. For them to shift is difficult; in extreme cases, only the

threat of starvation will motivate them.[11] Thus, it may be relatively easy to create a substantial inflow of workers into an expanding industry, or some outflow of workers from a depressed industry, occupation, or area by a relatively small shift in earnings. Such outflows from depressed areas such as Appalachia and parts of New England, the Maritime Provinces of Canada, Sicily and southern Italy, the Highlands of Scotland, declining areas of northeast England, and rural parts of central France have been observed over long periods of time.

Although it is relatively easy to get *some* outmigration, it is difficult to get large transfers in a short period of time. When demand falls rapidly, pockets of poverty tend to develop. In each of the geographic areas mentioned above, labor has been leaving, but poverty has increased. The reason is that the rate of exit has been slower than the rate of decline of the economic opportunities in the area. Indeed, the exit itself causes further decline, for, when a family migrates, both the supply of labor and the demand for labor decline. This is because all the locally provided goods and services that the family consumed before they migrated now suffer a reduction in demand.

One of the main functions of inequalities in earnings is to signal labor to reallocate. It is sometimes asserted that if this signal is removed, government compulsion would be the only allocative device available. This assertion is not correct.

An alternative signal, still largely within the free-market mechanism, is to keep the earnings of the employed from varying, but

---

10. Of course, the same individual need not move over and over again. The group is constantly replaced by new entrants into the labor force.

11. Even this may not be enough. Some people believe, rightly or wrongly, that they will starve even if they move.

to let unemployment rates vary. This is roughly what has happened in the coal-mining industry. The mechanism we have been studying for reallocating labor from industry A to industry B in the face of a shift in demand is a rise in earnings in B and a fall in A. But what if wage rates in A and B are fixed by powerful unions or by government decree? Unemployment will develop in A, and severe shortages will develop in B. Even though there is no difference in the earnings of labor in A and B, the chance of obtaining a job is much higher in B than in A. This may well induce new entrants into the labor force to train for B rather than A, and it may induce some unsuccessful applicants for jobs in A to transfer to B.

Thus it is possible to imagine allocative signals other than earnings differentials and government compulsion. The question is now an empirical one: To what extent does labor respond to earnings differentials and to what extent to other signals? One recent study suggests that the regional movement of labor responds more to relative regional unemployment rates than it does to relative earnings.[12]

On the other hand, the unemployment in Appalachia seems to be fully as ineffective as wage differentials in inducing sufficient movement, and there is some evidence that farm unemployment does not drive people off the farms as rapidly as the decline in the demand for farm labor requires.[13]

Recently, nonmarket-oriented policies have increased in popularity with the U.S. authorities, apparently in the belief that no set of changes in market signals will suffice to secure the necessary movement of labor within an acceptable time period. The federal government has given retraining a prominent role in its distressed-area programs. The Area Redevelopment Act of 1961, the Manpower Development and Training Act (1962), and the War on Poverty Program of 1964 all include retraining schemes. Hundreds of millions of dollars are now being devoted to such retraining, the costs of which range from $500 to $1,300 per worker retrained.[14] But such strides as have been made are minute relative to the need: By 1964 only 44,000 workers had completed retraining—about 1 percent of the number then unemployed.

The Functional Distribution of Income

We have referred several times to the problem of how national income is distributed into such broad aggregates as wages, rent, interest, and profits. Table 2 shows the percentage distribution of the national income since 1900. The behavior of functional shares of income over time has sometimes been taken to refute the theory of distribution we

12. An article by B. A. Corry will be published in *Economica* in 1966.

13. A song popular soon after the end of World War I asked the question, "How're you going to keep them down on the farm after they've seen Paree?" This suggests that information about and direct experience of alternatives may be more influential than the mere existence of these alternatives.

14. For an evaluation of the programs, see G. Somers and E. Stromsdorfer, "A Benefit-Cost Analysis of Manpower Retraining," *American Economic Review*, May, 1965. The authors conclude that the benefits exceed the costs.

TABLE 2   **DISTRIBUTIVE SHARES IN U.S. NATIONAL INCOME, 1900–1957, IN PERCENTAGES**

Period	Employee compensation	Entrepreneurial income	Corporate profits	Interest	Rent	Total
1900–1909	55.0	23.6	6.8	5.5	9.1	100
1905–1914	55.2	22.9	6.9	5.8	9.1	100
1910–1919	53.2	24.2	9.7	5.2	7.7	100
1915–1924	57.2	21.0	8.9	5.3	7.6	100
1920–1929	60.5	17.6	8.2	6.2	7.6	100
1925–1934	63.0	15.8	6.4	8.1	6.6	100
1929–1938	66.6	15.5	4.3	8.9	4.6	100
1930–1939	66.8	15.0	4.9	8.2	5.0	100
1934–1943	65.1	16.5	9.1	6.0	3.3	100
1939–1948	64.6	17.2	11.9	3.1	3.3	100
1944–1953	65.6	16.4	12.6	2.1	3.4	100
1949–1957	67.1	13.9	12.8	2.7	3.4	100

SOURCE: I. B. Kravis, "Relative Income Shares in Fact and Theory," *American Economic Review*, December, 1959.

have studied. *But, the traditional distribution theory cannot be refuted by any observed time path in the distribution of income, because it makes no prediction about the distribution of income.*

In order to make predictions about aggregate factor incomes, we would need to know the elasticities of demand and supply of all factors of production, which in turn would require a knowledge of the elasticities of demand for all products (from which factor demands are derived). Traditional distribution theory is a market theory. Questions about the distribution of income between, say, the total wage bill and total profits cannot be answered until we have a complete theory explaining the demand for factors and the prices prevailing in *all* the markets in the economy. We are a very long way from having such a general theory at this time. With our present state of knowledge, the traditional theory provides no predictions about the effect on functional distribution of such changes as shifts in total factor supplies,

taxes on one factor, the rise of unions, etc. We must, at the moment, admit defeat; we cannot deal at all with this important class of problems.

A number of notable attempts have been made to side-step this somewhat gloomy conclusion. These attempts have taken the form of aggregate theories of distribution that attempt to explain distribution without reference to the detailed workings of individual markets. The best-known attempts along these lines are those of M. Kalecki and N. Kaldor. Kalecki attempted to explain distribution between wages and profits in terms of the *degree of monopoly*. His theory is open to many criticisms, but some economists regard it as having pointed the way to a theory specifically designed to explain and predict distribution phenomena without requiring a complete theory of the interrelations among all markets.

Kaldor has been developing his theory over a number of years. It is probably fair to say that it is not yet fully worked out and that it has certainly not been subjected to anything like a critical test.[15] It is basically an attempt to explain distribution between wages and profits in terms of a *macro* theory of national income instead of in terms of a *micro* theory of relative prices. The general macro theory on which Kaldor based his own theory will be studied in Part IX.

Summary

We conclude that the traditional theory of distribution makes a number of predictions about factor prices in particular markets. There is ample evidence confirming many of these predictions and, even if the theory should be discarded because it was empirically refuted in other spheres, these predictions would need to be implicit in the theory that succeeded it. Also, we conclude that the marginal productivity theory of the demand for factors of production is merely an extension of the profit-maximizing theory of the firm and that it stands or falls with profit-maximizing theory. Finally, we conclude that, in the absence of much more empirical knowledge than we have at present, the traditional theory does *not* provide us with a testable theory of the distribution of the national product into such large aggregates as profits and wages. Probably the most serious criticism of the theory is that it has no predictions to offer at all with respect to a number of interesting questions in the field of distribution. The extraordinary difficulty in testing the theory, even when people are determined to make the most of it, suggests that it does not easily yield a large number of testable predictions in this sphere.[16]

QUESTIONS FOR DISCUSSION

1. Why do we say that the long controversy about the marginal productivity theory is, in many ways, a tempest in a teapot? What common misconceptions help to stir up the tempest?

2. Is marginal productivity theory a complete theory of distribution? If not, what is it? What is the standard theory of distribution?

3. Where do we find that our theory has the most predictive power? If we could collect more cases, would we succeed in proving the theory?

4. What do we mean by saying that the marginal productivity theory stands or falls with the theory of profit-maximization?

5. Of what value in testing our theory of distribution is a questionnaire that asks businessmen what they would do in response to a rise in wages?

6. "But a worker might consider the benefits of a job's working conditions adequate to accept exploitation—i.e., being paid less than his marginal value product. Marginal productivity theory does not allow for this." Comment fully on all the issues raised by this statement.

15. For a summary of various theories of distribution together with some empirical evidence relating to each (including a test of Kaldor's theory), the advanced student should consult M. Reder, "Alternative Theories of Labor's Share," in *The Allocation of Economic Resources: Essays in Honor of B. Haley,* ed. M. Abramovitz and others (Stanford University Press, 1959).

16. See, for example, J. L. Stein, "The Predictive Accuracy of the Marginal Productivity Theory of Wages," *Review of Economic Studies,* June, 1958, and G. C. Archibald, "Testing Marginal Productivity Theory," *Review of Economic Studies,* February, 1959.

INTERNATIONAL TRADE

Chapter **38** EXCHANGE RATES

IN PART VII, WE CONSIDER THE COMPLICA-tions that arise because of trade between nations. Production and consumption require exchange between households and firms. If countries were self-sufficient, their firms producing all that was required to satisfy the wants of their households, our present picture of the markets in the economy would be complete. Countries, however, are not self-sufficient: Households in one country buy goods produced by firms located in other countries, and firms in one country produce goods that they sell to households in other countries. *International trade* gives rise to many problems. In this chapter, we consider the complications introduced because different countries use different currencies; in

Chapter 39, we shall ask a more fundamental question: Is there anything to be gained from trade between nations? In Chapter 40, we go on to consider the pros and cons of interfering with the flow of international trade.

The United States is closer to being self-sufficient than most nations. Large and diversified countries usually tend to have more interregional trade and less international trade. If Europe were united politically into a single country, much of what now appears as foreign trade would become interregional trade within the borders of the "United States of Europe." If, on the other hand, the United States of America were split up into half a dozen different countries, each with a different currency, international trade would be very important to each of these "countries." As long as these six American "countries" adopted a free-trade policy, trade would go on much as it does today, but it would take the form of international trade and require the exchange of one currency for another.

A Word of Warning

In common speech, and indeed in what follows here, it is convenient to speak of *nations* as trading various commodities. This convenient anthropomorphic form of expression should not mislead the student into thinking that all, or even the majority of, decisions about trade are actually made by governments. In most countries, governments do play *some* role in foreign trade; but, in market economies, *most* of the decisions are made by individual households and firms. Firms may think they see an opportunity of selling goods abroad, and they may arrange to have these goods exported; other firms may think they see an opportunity of selling foreign goods in the home market and arrange to have these goods imported. If households find the goods attractive and purchase them, the venture will be successful; if they do not, then the goods will remain unsold and will no longer be imported. Governments may, of course, try to influence this process; they may put subsidies on exports, seeking to encourage foreign sales of domestically produced

goods by making their prices more attractive; they may put tariffs on imports, seeking to discourage domestic sales of foreign-produced goods by making their prices less attractive. But in free-market economies, foreign trade, just like domestic trade, occurs as a result of independent decisions made by firms and households, decisions that are coordinated—more or less effectively—by the price system.

The major complication in foreign trade is that different countries use different currencies. The currency of one country, while generally acceptable within the bounds of that one country, will not be acceptable to the firms and households of another country. If, for example, an importer in India wishes to purchase American goods, he cannot pay for them in rupees; he has to obtain dollars first. *In general, trade between nations can occur only if it is possible to exchange the currency of one nation for that of another.* What is the mechanism for exchanging currencies? What are the consequences of the need to exchange currencies?

What Is an Exchange Rate?

The exchange rate between two currencies is nothing more than the rate at which these two currencies exchange for each other; it is thus the price of one currency in terms of an-

other. If, for example, the exchange rate between British pounds sterling and U.S. dollars is £1 = $2.82, then one pound will exchange for two dollars and eighty-two cents or one dollar will exchange for 7s. 1d.[1] Thus, if a holder of sterling gives up £1, he will receive $2.82 in exchange, whereas if a holder of dollars gives up $1, he will get 7s. 1d. in return.

Exchange rates arise because the (paper) currency of one country is not an acceptable medium of exchange in another country. They arise because it is necessary, in the course of international trade, to trade the currency of one country for that of another. If a U.S. manufacturer sells goods abroad, he wishes to receive dollars in exchange: Rupees, yen, or pounds sterling are of little use to him, for he cannot pay his workers or purchase materials or pay dividends to his shareholders in these currencies; for all of these purposes the only acceptable currency is U.S. dollars. If a manufacturer sells goods abroad, he will accept payment in other currencies only if he knows that he can exchange them for dollars.

The British importer of American goods requires dollars in order to purchase these goods from the American manufacturer. When he buys these dollars, he will offer pounds in exchange for them. Thus the British importer is a *demander* of dollars and a *supplier* of pounds. The American importer, on the other hand, requires pounds in order to purchase goods from the British manufacturer. When he buys pounds, he offers dollars in exchange. He is, therefore, a demander of pounds and a supplier of dollars. This gives us all the conditions that we need for the determination of a price. Some people are trying to trade pounds for dollars, and others are trying to trade dollars for pounds.

The Balance of Payments

THE BALANCE OF DESIRED PAYMENTS

If, at the current rate of exchange, the demand for dollars exceeds the supply, it follows that holders of sterling are trying to make more payments in dollars than holders of dollars wish to make in sterling. In other words, *desired* payments between the two countries are not in balance. If the total volume of payments that holders of sterling wish to make to America is equal to the total volume of payments that holders of dollars wish to make to Britain, the demand for dollars will equal the supply, and the demand for sterling will equal its supply. Desired payments between the two countries will be equal. Finally, if the amount that holders of dollars wish to pay to Britain exceeds the amount that holders of sterling wish to pay to America, then the demand for sterling will exceed the supply, and the demand for dollars will be less than the supply. Again, desired payments between the two countries will not

1. One pound sterling is made up of 20 shillings (20s.), and one shilling is made up of 12 pennies (12d.). This is, in many ways, a cumbersome system. It has the one great advantage, however, that the basic number, 12, is a much more flexible number than the basic number of the decimal system, 10. Ten is divisible only by 2 and 5, so that the only fractions that come out to be whole numbers are ½ and ⅕. Twelve, on the other hand, is divisible by 2, 3, 4, and 6, so that ½, ⅓, ¼, and ⅙ all come out as whole numbers. It is a considerable convenience to be able to divide the monetary unit into such frequently encountered fractions as ½, ⅓, and ¼ without encountering recurring decimals (as in the case of ⅓ of a dollar).

be in balance. Thus, to say that there is dis-equilibrium in the foreign-exchange market (i.e., demand for foreign currency does not equal supply) is the same thing as saying that the desired payments between the two countries are not equal.

THE BALANCE OF ACTUAL PAYMENTS

In order to know what is happening to the course of international trade, governments keep track of the actual payments between countries. The record of such payments is called the *balance of payments*. Although it is quite possible for holders of sterling to want to purchase more dollars in exchange for pounds than holders of dollars want to sell in exchange for pounds, it is not possible for sterling holders actually to buy more dollars than someone sells. Every dollar that is bought must be sold by someone, and every dollar that is sold must be bought by someone.† Since the dollars actually bought must be equal to the dollars actually sold, the payments actually made between countries must be in balance, even though desired payments may not be.

The *balance-of-payments accounts* record the reasons for which payments are made. Thus, we can tell what volume of payments was made by foreigners to Americans for the purchase of American goods, the use of American services—shipping, insurance, etc.—the lending of money to American households, firms, or governments, or the investment of money in the ownership of firms in America. The accounts also tell what volume of payments was made by Americans to foreigners for the purchase of foreign goods, the use of foreign services, the lending of

money to foreign households, firms, or governments, or the investment of money in the ownership of firms located abroad. Any item that gives rise to a purchase of foreign currency is recorded as a debit item on the accounts, and any item that gives rise to a sale of foreign currency (and a purchase of dollars) is recorded as a credit item.

Although the total number of dollars bought on the foreign-exchange market must equal the total number sold, this is not true if we look at purchases and sales for a particular purpose. It is quite possible, for example, that a larger number of dollars were sold for the purpose of obtaining foreign currency to import, say, foreign cars than were bought for the purpose of buying U.S. cars for export to other countries. In such a case, we would say that the U.S. had a balance-of-payments deficit on the "car account," by which we would mean that the value of the U.S. imports of cars exceeded the value of its exports of cars, or, in other words, the number of dollars sold because of car imports exceeded the number of dollars bought because of car exports. For most general purposes, we are not interested in the balance of payments for single commodities but only for larger classes of transactions.

The most important division in the balance-of-payments accounts is between *current account* and *capital account*. The balance of payments on current account includes all payments made because of current purchases of goods and services. There is no automatic reason why current-account payments should balance. It is quite possible for more dollars to be sold in order to purchase our imports than were bought in order to purchase our exports. If so, the dollars must have come from somewhere, and the excess of sales over

---

† In symbols, $S_\$ \equiv P_\$$ and $S_\pounds \equiv P_\pounds$, where S is sales and P is purchases.

purchases on current account must be exactly matched by an excess of purchases over sales on the capital account.

The capital account records transactions for everything other than what is recorded in the current account. The main items are capital transfers and sales from or purchases of stocks of gold and foreign exchange. When a U.S. citizen wishes to invest abroad, he must obtain the currency of the relevant foreign country; he must sell dollars and purchase foreign currency. This is recorded as a deficit item in the balance of payments, since the transaction uses dollars.

We may think of the balance-of-payments accounts in a variety of ways. We have already seen that:

| Sales of foreign currency and purchases of domestic currency | = | Purchases of foreign currency and sales of domestic currency. |

If we look instead at the transactions that lead to these exchanges of currency, we obtain:

| All exports of goods and services plus all capital imports | = | All imports of goods and services plus all capital exports. |

If we now divide these transactions into two major divisions, we obtain:

	Credits	Debits
Current account		
A. Exports of goods and services		C. Imports of goods and services
Capital account		
B. Imports of capital		D. Exports of capital

The fact that $A + B$ is necessarily equal to $C + D$ shows that a deficit on one account must be matched by an exactly opposite surplus on the other account.

Now assume that in a given year the value of U.S. imports exceeds the value of U.S. exports, considering all current-account transactions. The foreign currency necessary to finance the imports that were in excess of exports had to come from somewhere, and, clearly, it could not come from people selling foreign currency for U.S. dollars in order to buy U.S. goods and services. The money must have been lent by someone or else provided out of the government's reserves of gold and foreign exchange. If foreigners are investing funds in the U.S., they will be selling foreign currency and buying U.S. currency in order to be able to buy stocks and bonds issued by U.S. firms. Such foreign lending can provide the foreign exchange necessary to allow the U.S. to have an excess of imports over exports. The other possibility is that the U.S. central authorities have reduced their holding of foreign currency or gold by selling some to persons wishing to purchase foreign goods and accepting dollars in return.

A deficit on current account must be matched by a surplus on capital account, which means either borrowing from abroad or reducing the foreign exchange and gold held by the domestic central authorities.

What about a surplus on current account? This means that the value of exports exceeds the value of imports. This means that foreigners will not have been able to obtain all the U.S. dollars they needed to buy U.S. goods from U.S. sources eager to supply dollars in return for foreign currency in order to buy foreign goods. The excess of exports over imports could only have been paid for if foreigners obtained dollars from other sources. Again there are two main possibilities: U.S. dollars may be provided by U.S. investors eager to obtain foreign currency so that they can buy foreign stocks and bonds. In this case the excess of exports over imports is balanced by U.S. loans abroad. The other possibility is that foreign governments may have reduced their holdings of U.S. dollars by selling these to persons wishing to buy U.S. goods and accepting their own domestic currency in exchange.

A surplus on current account must be matched by a deficit on capital account, which means either lending abroad or running down the reserves of gold and foreign exchange held by the foreign central authorities.

THE MAKE-UP OF THE CURRENT ACCOUNT

The current account is usually subdivided into the trade in *visibles* and *invisibles*. Visibles refer to goods, i.e., to all those things, such as cars, wood pulp, aluminum, coffee, and iron ore, that we can see and touch when they cross international borders. Invisibles refer to services, to all those things we cannot see or touch, such as insurance and freight haulage. When a U.S. firm insures a shipment of goods consigned to Australia with Lloyds of London, the firm consumes a British export just as surely as if it purchased and used a British-made automobile or sent its president on a vacation to Scotland. Payment for the insurance services and for the automobile and the vacation must be made in pounds—and thus each is a U.S. import and a British export.

THE MAKE-UP OF THE CAPITAL ACCOUNT

The capital account records all foreign-capital movements. If U.S. investors invest abroad, they must supply U.S. dollars and demand foreign currency. A U.S. investment abroad thus contributes toward a foreign-exchange deficit because it uses foreign currency. An investment in the U.S. from a for-

eign source contributes to a surplus on capital account.

Capital movements can be divided into long-term capital movements, short-term movements, and changes in the exchange reserves. Long-term capital represents genuine international investment. Why do such international capital movements occur? Allowing for risk and other such factors, investors will seek to invest where the return is highest. Just as capital moves from industry to industry within one country in search of its most productive uses, so would we expect capital to move from country to country in search of the highest rates of return. Such capital movements mean that the households and firms of one country are investing in the industry of another country, and they show up as long-term capital movements in the payment accounts.

Short-term capital holdings arise in many ways. The mere fact of international trade forces traders to hold money balances. Traders' receipts and expenditures are not perfectly synchronized, and they necessarily hold balances, because they must be able to pay their bills when they fall due. It usually does not matter where in the world such funds are held. The funds can thus be moved from one currency to another in response to small changes in incentives or because of real or imaginary fears of all sorts. The large quantity of these funds is a potential source of international instability, because a sudden rush of short-term capital out of one currency into another can cause violent shifts in demands and supplies for foreign currency.

The final element in the capital account is changes in gold and foreign-exchange reserves held by central authorities. Central authorities of most countries hold supplies of gold and foreign exchange in order that they may intervene in the foreign-exchange market for a wide variety of purposes. Gold (being universally acceptable at a fixed price) is immediately transferable into any foreign currency that may be required. If a country has a payments deficit on all other counts (i.e., if it uses more foreign currency than it obtains), this deficit must be made up by an equivalent reduction in its reserves of gold and foreign exchange. In America, the reserves are mainly held in the form of gold, and a balance-of-payments deficit on all other items shows up as an export of gold (i.e., a reduction in the gold stock).

When we add up all the uses to which foreign currency is put and all the sources from which it came, these two amounts are necessarily equal, since the foreign currency that goes to any use must have come from somewhere. The over-all accounts on all international payments are thus necessarily in balance. When we speak of a balance-of-payments deficit, we mean the balance on some part of the accounts. Usually the term refers to the balance excluding changes in the reserves held by the central authorities. A balance-of-payments deficit thus means that the reserves of the central authorities were being run down by exactly the amount of the deficit.

Table 1 shows the U.S. balance-of-payments accounts for 1963. The U.S. had a balance-of-payment surplus on current account, indicating that the value of exports exceeded the value of imports. This has been the case for every year since the war. The U.S., in recent times, has been a current-account surplus country. The table also shows that the U.S. was a large exporter of capital. On balance, U.S. firms and households lent much more abroad than they borrowed from abroad. This gives the U.S. a deficit on long-term capital account that exceeds her surplus

TABLE 1   **U.S. BALANCE OF PAYMENTS, 1963, IN BILLIONS OF DOLLARS**[a]

Current account		
Exports of goods and services	+32.0	
Imports of goods and services	−26.3	
Balance on current account		+5.7

Capital account		
Imports of foreign capital and repayment of U.S. loans	+0.9	
U.S. private capital exports[b]	−5.1	
U.S. government capital exports[c]	−3.8	
Balance on capital account		−8.0

Balance of payments on recorded transactions		−2.3
Balance of payments on unrecorded transactions		−0.3
BALANCE OF PAYMENTS		−2.6

Balanced by:

Decreases in monetary reserve assets[d]		0.4
Increases in foreign holdings of liquid dollar assets[e]		2.2
		2.6

a Items that lead to an inflow of dollars are indicated by a plus sign; those that lead to an outflow of dollars are indicated by a minus sign.
b Includes remittances and pensions to persons abroad.
c Includes grants.
d Includes gold, convertible currencies, and International Monetary Fund position.
e Includes short-term official and banking liabilities and foreign holdings of U.S. Government bonds.
SOURCE: *Economic Report of the President*, 1965, Table B–79.

on current account. The funds invested abroad in excess of the current-account surplus came partly from short-term borrowing from foreign sources and partly from a reduction in the U.S.'s gold reserves.

The Meaning of Exchange Rates

How is the price at which one currency trades for another set? The theory we shall develop applies to all international trade and to all exchange rates, but, for the sake of expositional simplicity, we shall discuss only two countries, Britain and America, and only the rate of exchange between their two currencies. Since one currency is traded for another on the foreign-exchange market, it follows that a demand for dollars implies a supply of pounds, whereas an offer (supply) of dollars implies a need (demand) for pounds. If, at an exchange rate of £1 = $2.82, a British importer demands $5.64, he must be offering £2; if an American importer offers $5.64, he must be demanding £2. For this reason, we can deal either with the demand for and the supply of dollars, or with the demand for and the supply of pounds sterling; we do not need to consider both. We shall conduct the argument in terms of dollars.

The demand for dollars arises because holders of sterling wish to make payments in dollars; the demand for dollars thus arises from exports of American goods to Britain and from the movement of investment funds from Britain to the United States.

Dollars are offered in exchange for sterling because holders of dollars wish to make payments in sterling. The supply of dollars arises, therefore, on account of American imports from Britain and the movement of investment funds from America to Britain.

PRICE CHANGES CAUSED BY EXCHANGE-RATE CHANGES

A British manufacturer wants to receive a certain payment for his goods in pounds sterling. It follows that the dollar price at which these goods must be sold in America depends upon the exchange rate between pounds and dollars. If the manufacturer wishes to obtain £1 each for his goods, then the goods must sell in America (ignoring the cost of transport) for $3 when the exchange rate is £1 = $3, for $2 when the rate is £1 = $2, and for $4 when the rate is £1 = $4. An American manufacturer wishes to be paid a certain number of dollars when he sells his goods. It follows that the pound price for which these goods must be sold in Britain depends on the rate of exchange between sterling and dollars. If, for example, the rate of exchange goes from £1 = $2 to £1 = $1, then the dollar price of British exports to America must fall, whereas the sterling price of American exports to Britain must rise. In general, a rise in the value of the pound vis-à-vis the dollar raises the dollar price of British exports to America and lowers the sterling price of British imports from America. A fall in the value of the pound has the reverse effect.

The Demand and Supply Curves for Dollars

If Americans have an elastic demand for British goods and the British also have an elastic demand for American goods, a cut in the price of the goods that either country exports will cause a more than proportional rise in their sales so that total spending on these goods will rise. This is the simplest and probably the most empirically relevant case to analyze. Other cases can be studied, but they are more complex.

In Figure 1 we plot the price of dollars (measured in shillings) on the vertical axis and the quantity of dollars on the horizontal

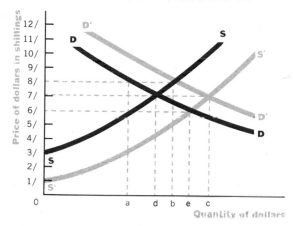

one. As we move down the vertical scale, the dollar is becoming cheaper (i.e., it is worth fewer shillings), and we say that the value of the dollar is depreciating on the exchange market. As we move upward, the dollar is becoming dearer, and we say that the dollar is appreciating on the market.

What is the shape of the demand curve for dollars? As the dollar is depreciated in value

the sterling price of U.S. exports falls. The British will buy more of the cheaper U.S. goods and will require more dollars for this purpose.[2] The demand for dollars will rise. If the dollar rises in value, the price of U.S. exports rises in terms of foreign currency. The British will buy fewer U.S. goods and will thus need fewer U.S. dollars. The demand for dollars will fall.

The demand curve for dollars on the foreign-exchange market is downward sloping when plotted against the sterling price of dollars.

What about the supply curve of dollars? When the dollar is depreciated, the price of British exports to the U.S. rises. Americans will buy fewer of the now more expensive British goods and will spend fewer dollars on them. The amount of dollars being offered in exchange for pounds sterling in order to pay for these imports thus falls off. The supply of dollars is reduced. When the dollar is appreciated, British exports to the U.S. become cheaper, more will be sold, and more dollars will be spent on them. Thus, more dollars will be offered in exchange for pounds in order to obtain this foreign exchange. The supply of dollars will rise.

The supply curve of dollars on the foreign-exchange market is upward sloping when plotted against the sterling price of dollars.

2. Here, and in the next paragraph, the assumption of elastic demand is crucial. If demand for foreign goods were inelastic, the physical quantity would still change as described, but the values would not. It is the values that matter in determining the amount of dollars demanded and supplied on the foreign-exchange market.

What Determines the Equilibrium Exchange Rate?

Assume that the current price of dollars is too low, in the sense that at this exchange rate the demand for dollars exceeds the supply. In other words, desired payments are not in balance, for desired payments to the U.S. by holders of sterling exceed desired payments to Britain by holders of dollars. Dollars will be in scarce supply; some people who require dollars to make payments to America will be unable to obtain them, and the price of dollars will be bid up. The value of the dollar vis-à-vis the pound will appreciate, or, which is the same thing, the value of the pound vis-à-vis the dollar will depreciate. As the price of dollars rises, the sterling price of American exports to Britain rises, and the demand for U.S. dollars to buy these goods falls off. On the other hand, as the dollar price of British exports to America falls, a larger quantity will be sold, and the supply of U.S. dollars will rise. Thus this rise in the price of the dollar reduces the quantity demanded and increases the quantity supplied. Where the two curves intersect, demand equals supply and the exchange rate is in equilibrium. In Figure 1, the equilibrium exchange rate is at $1 = 7s. 1d., which is, to the nearest cent, £1 = $2.82. What happens if the price of dollars is too high? The demand for dollars will fall short of the supply. With the dollar in excess supply, some people who wish to convert dollars into pounds will be unable to do so. The price of dollars will fall, fewer dollars will be supplied, more will be demanded, and an equilibrium will be re-established.

What will be the effect on the exchange rate of various changes in the data?

A CHANGE IN TASTES

What will be the effect of a change in tastes whereby the British preference for American goods increases? At each sterling price charged in the British market, more U.S. goods will be demanded than previously. Thus, at each exchange rate, more U.S. dollars will be demanded (in order to pay for these goods). Thus the demand curve for dollars will shift to the right, say to D' in Figure 1. At the original exchange rate of 7s. 1d. per dollar, demand exceeds supply. The price of dollars will rise until a new equilibrium is reached; in the figure, this new equilibrium is at 8s. to the dollar (i.e., £1 = $2.50). We thus conclude that an increased preference on the part of British consumers for American goods will lead to an appreciation in the value of the dollar (a depreciation in the value of the pound). Work out the effect of an increased preference of American consumers for British goods.

A FALL IN THE DOMESTIC SUPPLY PRICE OF EXPORTS

Assume that the domestic price of U.S. goods falls. This means that at any given exchange rate the sterling price of U.S. exports will fall. What will this do to the exchange rate? Can you work out the answer before reading on? If the dollar price of U.S. exports falls by X percent, then at each exchange rate the sterling price of these goods will also fall by X percent. If, as we have assumed, the British demand for U.S. goods is elastic, the quantity demanded will increase by more than X percent. Thus a fall in the dollar price of U.S. exports will shift the demand for dollars to the right. We conclude that the sterling price of dollars will rise. In other words, the dollar will appreciate and the pound will depreciate in value.[3]

A CHANGE IN THE PRICE LEVEL OF ONE COUNTRY

What will happen if there is inflation in the U.S.? The dollar price of U.S. goods will rise. American goods will become more expensive in the U.K., and the demand for dollars will diminish. British exports to America will have an unchanged dollar price, whereas the price of American goods sold at home will have increased. Thus British goods will be more attractive compared to American goods (because they have become *relatively cheaper*) and more British goods will be bought in America. Thus, at any given exchange rate, the demand for pounds, and, hence, the supply of dollars, will be increased. The demand curve for dollars shifts to the left and the supply curve shifts to the right, so that the equilibrium price of dollars must fall. We conclude, therefore, that an American inflation leads to a depreciation in the value of the dollar (an appreciation in the value of the pound).

AN EQUAL PERCENTAGE CHANGE IN THE PRICE LEVEL IN BOTH COUNTRIES

What if there is a 10 percent inflation in both the U.S. and the U.K.? In this case, the sterling prices of British goods and the dollar prices of U.S. goods both rise by 10 percent. At any given exchange rate, therefore, the dollar prices of British goods and the sterling prices of American goods will also rise by 10 percent. Thus, the relative prices of imports and domestically produced goods will be unchanged in both countries. There is now no reason to expect any change in either country's demand for imports at the original exchange rate, so that the inflations in the two countries leave the equilibrium exchange rate unchanged. The argument of this and the previous section can easily be combined to establish the following important conclusion:

If the price level of one country is rising faster (falling slower) than that of another country, the equilibrium value of its currency will be falling relative to that of the second country.

Fixed Exchange Rates

We have been concerned so far with the effect of various changes on the equilibrium rate of exchange. If exchange rates are left free to be determined by the forces of demand and supply, our analysis provides predictions about what happens to actual exchange rates. This was the case, for example, with the rate of exchange between the Canadian and American dollars until May, 1962, because the value of the Canadian dollar was allowed to

3. Opposite results occur if the British have an inelastic demand for American goods.

fluctuate on the free market according to the demand for and the supply of such dollars. Such an exchange rate is called a *fluctuating exchange rate*. On the other hand, the rate of exchange between most currencies today, including the rate between the British pound and the U.S. dollar, is fixed, within very narrow limits, by government decree. In this case fluctuations in the demand for and supply of dollars vis-à-vis pounds cannot affect, except within very narrow limits, the actual exchange rate, but, according to our hypothesis, they do change the magnitude of the excess demand for, or supply of, dollars.

Assume that, in Figure 1, the demand for dollars is *DD*, that the supply is *SS*, and that the exchange rate is fixed by decree at 8*s.* per dollar (i.e., £1 = $2.50). At this rate, the demand for dollars is *Oa* and the supply is *Ob*. There is an excess supply of dollars, a potential balance-of-payments deficit of *ab* dollars. If the U.S. Government does not intervene, some demanders of pounds will be able to obtain them and others will not; a black market is likely to develop with the available pounds commanding a clandestine price far in excess of $2.50 per pound. In order to prevent this, the U.S. Government may step in and ration the available supply of pounds. All persons wishing to convert dollars into pounds are forced to do so through the government, and the available supply of pounds is then rationed out according to priorities established by the government.

How is a fixed exchange rate successfully maintained? First, if the rate to be maintained is not near the free-market equilibrium rate, then *controls* of various sorts must be introduced to shift the demand curve for foreign currency until it intersects the supply curve at a rate very near the controlled one. This can be done by restricting foreign travel, bringing home servicemen's families, prohib-

iting certain kinds of imports, and restricting, by license and quota, the quantity of other kinds of imports. Second, short-run fluctuations in demand and supply must be canceled out by *government sales and purchases of foreign exchange.*

Short-run fluctuations in the demand for and supply of foreign exchange must inevitably occur. For example, imports and exports are subject to seasonal and random fluctuation, and short-term capital movements constantly occur in response to such factors as differences in short-term interest rates between the various financial centers of the world. In the face of these unavoidable and uncontrollable short-term fluctuations, the central authorities can hold a fixed exchange rate only by entering the market and buying and selling as is required to stabilize the price.

As long as the exchange rate the central authorities are trying to maintain is one that equates demand and supply on average, the policy can be successful. Sometimes the authorities will be buying and at other times they will be selling, and, although their reserves will fluctuate, they will maintain a constant average level. If, however, there is a permanent shift in one of the curves due to some change such as an inflation in one country, then it will be very difficult to maintain the fixed rate. If, for example, the supply of dollars shifts to the right because there is a long-term increase in the desire of Americans to invest abroad, the equilibrium price of the dollar in terms of foreign currency must fall. If the central authorities try to maintain the old rate, they will have to buy dollars and supply gold and foreign exchange more or less continuously. This policy can only be continued as long as the reserves of gold and foreign exchange last. Should reserves appear to be approaching exhaustion, there are two possible solutions: Either restrictions can be introduced on imports and foreign lending in an attempt to shift the supply curve back to the left, or the dollar can be depreciated until the new controlled rate is the one that equals demand with the increased supply.

In terms of Figure 1, we can imagine a fixed rate at 7s. 1d. to the dollar with demand and supply curves at DD and SS. Now assume a rise in the supply of dollars to S'S' as a result of a capital outflow from the U.S. If the outflow continues, reserves will run down at the rate of de per period as long as the old rate is maintained. Once the reserves are near exhaustion, the authorities have the option either of trying to shift the supply curve back to SS by curtailing foreign spending, or of devaluing the dollar to a rate around 6s. to the dollar ($3.33 to the pound).

The explanation of fixed and fluctuating exchange rates provides an example of a successful application of the theory of the determination of price by demand and supply to one very important market. We shall see, in Chapter 41, that there is much empirical evidence confirming the predictions of the theory when applied to the foreign-exchange market.

Fixed Versus Fluctuating Exchange Rates

Why bother with all this apparatus of control? Why not let the rate be set on a free market so that demand and supply can always be brought into equilibrium by suitable and automatic changes in exchange rates?

A long debate has raged among economists about the relative merits of fixed versus fluctuating exchange rates. No general conclusion has been reached, and the whole debate has been more notable, with a few major exceptions, for the passions involved than for the objectivity used in assessing empirical evidence. Contrary to the contentions of some of the protagonists, neither free nor fluctuating rates will lead to disaster, for both policies have been successfully maintained at one time or another by several countries.

The debate is too complex to go into here. By and large, the supporters of fixed rates believe that the stability of such rates is conducive to trade. The advocates of fluctuating rates believe that these rates would not fluctuate enough to upset trade, that speculative capital movements would reduce short-term fluctuations, and that the simplest way to maintain international equilibrium is to allow relative prices of the exports of all countries to change as conditions of demand, supply, and price change. These relative price changes of internationally traded goods can be effected by changes in the exchange rates.

EXCHANGE RATES AND NATIONAL PRIDE

It is interesting, sociologically and psychologically, that the value of exchange rates often becomes an important symbol of national pride. If Americans are to understand some of the actions of foreign governments, they must understand that great symbolic value is often attached to the price of one's currency on the foreign market. During much of the 1950s, for example, the Canadian dollar sold on the market for around $1.03 U.S. The fact that the Canadian dollar was worth more than the U.S. dollar was a source of great satisfaction to many Canadians.

The economist does not seek to explain this phenomenon, but he can wonder at it. There can be no doubt that there are circumstances when the rise in the value of a country's currency would be taken as a good sign. There are other circumstances in which such a change would be symptomatic of undesirable domestic circumstances. For example, a major domestic depression or deflation could easily lead to a rise in the external value of a country's currency. On the other hand, major technical innovations that reduced domestic costs and prices might lead to a fall in the exchange rate if foreign demands were inelastic. It is not obvious that this should

cause a loss of national prestige. A large inflow of foreign capital, leading to a transfer abroad of the control of one's industries, would cause an appreciation of the exchange rate. It is not obvious that such a move is a cause for national congratulation in all circumstances. It was certainly peculiar for some Canadians during the 1950s to point with great pride to their high exchange rate and to point with grave concern to the inflow of foreign capital that caused the high rate! Exchange rates can appreciate or depreciate for many different reasons, and to take the price of one's currency per se as a symbol of national pride is to commit oneself in advance to being proud of a great rag bag of varied events.

Summary

1. Because the currency of one country is not an acceptable medium of exchange in another country, it must be possible to trade the currency of one country for that of another if there is to be international trade.

2. Foreigners who wish to buy American goods will be suppliers of foreign currency and demanders of dollars, whereas Americans who wish to buy foreign goods will be demanders of foreign currency and suppliers of dollars.

3. Equilibrium on the foreign-exchange market occurs when the amount of foreign currency that some people desire to sell is equal to the amount that others desire to buy. When this occurs, we say that desired payments are in balance.

4. Since the amount of currency bought is necessarily equal to the amount sold, actual payments are always in balance.

5. The balance-of-payments accounts are

records of actual payments between countries. The accounts are broken down into various categories, the most important division being between *current account* and *capital account*. The current account includes payments for all other purposes. The primary items are imports and exports of capital and changes in the stocks of gold and foreign exchange.

6. A deficit on current account must be matched by a surplus on capital account, which means either borrowing from abroad or reducing the foreign exchange and gold held by the domestic central authorities. The reverse is true for a surplus on current account.

7. Capital movements can be divided into long-term movements, short-term movements, and changes in the exchange reserves. Long-term movements represent genuine international investment. Short-term movements arise from many sources and are a potential

source of international instability. Changes in gold and foreign-exchange reserves occur when all other transactions are not in balance. The expression *balance-of-payments deficit* or *reserve* usually refers to the balance on all items other than gold and exchange reserves.

8. The free-market exchange of dollars and pounds is an example of the familiar theory of price determination in competitive markets. The application of this theory allows us to predict the results of such things as changes in tastes, changes in the domestic supply price of exports, and changes in domestic price levels.

9. Exchange rates left to be determined by a free market are called *fluctuating exchange rates*. The most common type of rate prevailing today is a fixed rate that is maintained within very narrow limits by the market operations of central authorities. If the rate to be maintained is not near the free-market rate, controls must be introduced to limit the average level of demand to that of the available supply. Even when this is done, short-term fluctuations in demand and supply will have to be compensated for by sales and purchases made by the central authorities.

QUESTIONS FOR DISCUSSION

1. What do the following people demand and supply in the foreign-exchange market?
a an American importer of English antiques;
b. a London businessman who wishes to invest on the New York Stock Exchange;
c. a Swiss banker who holds pounds as a reserve currency for international payments and believes that the pound will be devalued;
d. an American couple vacationing in Scotland;
e. a German importer of American-made refrigerators that are transported in Norwegian ships and insured with Lloyds of London;
f. an American company that wishes to use its accumulated profits to establish branch plants in Canada and France;
g. American firms located in Canada and France that need to pay interest to bondholders who are residents of the United States.

2. What does it mean to say that Britain has a serious balance-of-payments deficit on current account, that Germany has a current-account surplus, and that the United States has a deficit on capital account?

3. If exchange rates are fixed at an equilibrium level for all countries, and if prices in France subsequently rise much more rapidly than prices in all other countries, what do you expect to happen?

4. In 1964 and 1965, the U.S. Government tried to persuade businessmen not to invest abroad. President Johnson stated that he was fairly pleased with the response. What do you infer about the American balance of payments in those years?

5. In Great Britain, the state subsidizes graduate students by making large grants to universities and directing them to charge minimal fees to graduate students. Large numbers of foreign graduate students come to Britain each year to study at such famous institutes as the London School of Economics. What effect does the present policy have on the British balance of payments? What effect would there be on the balance of payments if fees were raised to cover costs, and if British nationals were given government grants to meet such costs?

APPENDIX TO CHAPTER 38 MORE ABOUT EXCHANGE RATES

IN THIS APPENDIX WE CONSIDER briefly three problems: (1) exchange reserves and exchange rates under a fixed rate of exchange; (2) short-term capital movements; and (3) long-term capital movements.

Managing Fixed Exchange Rates

Figure A1 shows free-market demand and supply curves for dollars. Assume that the British Government fixes the exchange rate between the limits of 7s. and 7s. 2d. to the dollar and restricts demand, through an *exchange control* system of rationing and prohibitions, to the curve D′D′. Certain goods will be allowed to be imported

without limit, others will be subject to a quota restriction setting the maximum amount of imports, and other goods will be prohibited from being imported altogether. By these means, the central authorities keep the demand for dollars lower than it otherwise would be. Even this restricted demand will, however, be subject to seasonal, cyclical, and other fluctuations.

Having restricted demand by the means outlined above, the authorities then control the exchange rate in the following fashion: All transactions go through the central agency, which buys and sells dollars. At the price 7s 2d. to the dollar, they offer to sell dollars, for permitted purposes, in un-

limited amounts; at the price of 7s. per dollar, they enter the market and buy dollars in unlimited amounts. If purchases equal sales, the authority's reserves of dollars will be unchanged; if purchases do not equal sales, these reserves will change.

1. If the demand curve cuts the supply curve in the range 7s. to 7s. 2d., then the authorities need not touch their exchange reserves. The amount of dollars being supplied for pounds will be equal to the amount of dollars being demanded in exchange for pounds.

2. If the demand curve shifts to D″D″, then the authorities must sell dollars to the extent of rs in order to prevent the price of dollars from rising above 7s. 2d. These dollars must be removed from the exchange reserves.

3. If the demand curve shifts to D‴D‴, the central authorities must buy dollars to the extent of tu and add them to its exchange reserves in order to prevent the price of dollars from falling below 7s.

If the authorities have restricted demand sufficiently so that *on the average* the demand and supply curves intersect in the range 7s. to 7s. 2d., then the exchange reserves will be relatively stable with the authorities buying dollars when the demand is abnormally high and selling them when the demand is abnormally low. In the for-

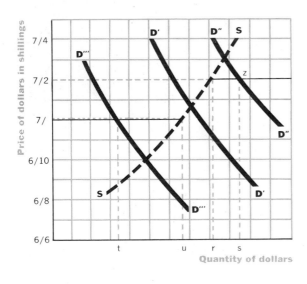

FIGURE A1

A FIXED EXCHANGE RATE

mer case, the reserves will rise, and in the latter case, they will fall; but over a long time their average level will be stable.

If the central authorities have guessed wrong, the exchange reserves will rise or fall more or less continuously. Say that the average level of demand is $D''D''$ with fluctuations on either side of this level. Then the average drain on exchange reserves will be rs per period; sometimes it will be more and sometimes less, and occasionally when demand is extremely low, reserves will be added to. *This situation cannot continue indefinitely.* Eventually, if nothing is done, reserves will fall to zero and the controlled price will have to be abandoned. The authorities have two possibilities: They can change the controlled price so that the band of permissible prices straddles the intersection of the curves at their normal level. In other words, they can devalue the pound. Or, they can try to shift the curves so that the intersection is in the band 7s. to 7s. 2d. They can take further steps to restrict demand for dollars: They can impose import quotas and foreign-travel restrictions, or they can increase the supply of dollars by encouraging exports.

The *actual* balance-of-payments surpluses, or deficits, reported in the press are the quantities we have just indicated: the difference between current expenditure of dollars and current earnings of them, i.e., the changes in the *reserves* held by the central authorities.

This must be sharply distinguished from the potential balance-of-payments surplus or deficit, which is the difference between the demand for and the supply of dollars as they would be if everyone were free to buy and sell dollars without government restriction.

Capital Movements on a Free Market

What about the exchange of currencies for the purpose of making loans abroad rather than for the purpose of purchasing foreign goods? Assume that investors in America wish to loan money in Britain, possibly to British firms. The British will require pounds, and the Americans will, therefore, have to purchase pounds on the foreign-exchange market.[1] Such a transaction entails a rise in the demand for pounds, which, in a free market, will bid up their price. A transfer of funds from country A to country B will tend to appreciate B's currency and depreciate A's.

MOVEMENTS OF SHORT-TERM CAPITAL

A temporary deficit in the balance of payments may be alleviated by attracting short-term capital into the country. Assume that, in Figure A1, the demand for dollars is $D''D''$ so that the British suffer a deficit in their balance of payments of rs per period. Now assume that this high demand is only a temporary one, but that the

central authorities wish neither to put on additional restrictions nor to let reserves run down by rs. What else can they do? They can raise the rate of interest they are willing to pay for short-term loans (loans of a few days' to a few months' duration) and attract short-term capital. There is a great deal of money available to traders for short time periods. These traders do not need the money now, but they will require it shortly. If someone is prepared to pay for the use of this money for a short period, then this is better from their point of view than leaving it idle. If the central authorities raise the rate of interest for short-term loans, people holding dollars will wish to obtain pounds in order to lend them out at the high British rates. Thus the supply of dollars shifts to the right. If it cuts the demand curve at z, then the inflow of short-term cash, rs, just covers the deficit on current account, and the exchange reserves are not run down. *Provided the government guessed correctly* that the demand was *abnormally high*, the policy will work. If the demand now falls to an abnormally low level, say $D'''D'''$, the government can buy tu dollars and add them to its exchange reserves. It can then lower short-term rates of interest so that people who have lent money in Britain would now prefer to lend it in, say, New York. There will be a demand on the part of these investors to turn pounds into dollars. The

---

1. This is, in effect, what happens. The actual transfer will be accomplished through one of several different institutional channels.

government can now sell *tu* dollars per period to these investors.

Thus short-term deficits in the balance of payments can be covered by attracting short-term capital into a country, but this policy will only be successful if an equivalent short-term surplus develops so that the capital can again be transferred out of the country.

MOVEMENTS OF LONG-TERM CAPITAL

Long-term capital is capital lent for long periods of time; anything from a few to twenty or more years is common. Such capital is used by governments and firms for long-range investment projects that normally increase, either directly or indirectly, the productive capacity of the economy. Often people in wealthy countries where savings are high will be prepared to invest funds in less well-developed countries where savings are not high enough to finance a high rate of investment. Money by itself does not build or produce things; only productive resources can do this. When a saver lends his money to an entrepreneur in his own country, the saver is electing not to exercise his claim to the output of the country's resources and is transferring this claim to the entrepreneur. When the latter spends the money on investment, he is directing the productive services of the country toward the manufacture of capital goods and away from the manufacture of the goods they would have made if the saver had spent all his income. Thus, lending means transferring the claim to the productive services of the country from the lender's use to that of the borrower. *International lending has the same effect.* If a person in country B lends money to an entrepreneur in country A, then the claim to the output of country B's resources is transferred to a citizen of country A. *All of the ensuing financial transactions are merely means of making this claim effective.* Assume that an individual in B saves pounds and wishes to buy the bonds sold by a firm in A. Then, in effect, it will be necessary for the saver in B to purchase dollars to purchase the bonds in country A. This means that someone else must have sold dollars and taken pounds in exchange. The simplest case arises when the firm in A wishes to buy machinery from B. The lender in B buys dollars and then uses them to buy bonds in A. The firm in A then uses the dollars to buy pounds and the pounds to buy machines. In the exchange market, there is a rise in the demand for dollars arising from the saver in B and a rise in the demand for pounds (supply of dollars) on the part of the firm in A. Looking at the "real" flows of production rather than the money flows, we see that the lending from B to A entails a flow of B's production, the machines in this case, from B to A. In general, lending from B to A entails a flow of goods from B to A (either directly, or via third countries, if we consider trade between many countries). The common-sense reason is that borrowing represents nothing more than a transfer of claims to the output of productive resources from the lender to the borrower. The income of an individual in A gives him a claim on the output *of his own country*; if he lends to an individual in country B, he is giving the borrower his claim *on A's output.*

It follows that international lending and borrowing affects the demands for, and supplies of, currency in the foreign-exchange market. In terms of the analysis in Chapter 38, lending from B to A entails a rise in the demand for dollars. This will, among other things, raise the price of dollars. We must conclude, therefore, that a transfer of capital from one country to another tends to appreciate the exchange value of the currency of the borrowing country and to depreciate the exchange value of the currency of the lending country.

QUESTIONS FOR DISCUSSION

1. What are the options open to a country that is trying to maintain an exchange rate if it fixes a value on its currency that is higher than the free-market value? Describe the intended effects of the alternatives diagrammatically.

2. What would be the effect on the U.S.–Vietnam balance of payments of a heavy transfer of dollar capital into Vietnam?

3. Why was the Canadian dollar worth more on the foreign-exchange market than the U.S. dollar throughout most of the 1950s? What effect would this have on employment in Canadian industries whose main market was in the United States?

4. In Chapter 53, you will learn how the central authorities can create unlimited supplies of their own currency, although they cannot create supplies of foreign currency. Would it be easier for the authorities to hold the exchange rate above its equilibrium value by appropriate selling and purchasing policies, or to hold it below its equilibrium value?

Chapter **39** THE GAINS FROM TRADE

IN THE LAST CHAPTER, WE DISCUSSED THE mechanics of trade—what commodities are traded and how they are paid for. In this chapter, we raise a much more fundamental question: Is there any advantage in trade between nations?

The foundations of modern economics were laid by men intimately concerned with the problems of foreign trade. Two of the earliest schools of European economists, the Physiocrats and the Mercantilists, took strong and divergent stands on the value of foreign trade. Economists in eighteenth-century France were responsible for major reforms in the government machinery for regulating both internal and foreign trade. The great eighteenth-century English philosopher and economist, David Hume, who was one of the first to work out the modern theory of the price system as a control mechanism, developed his theory mainly in terms of prices in foreign trade.[1] Adam Smith and David Ricardo, the two English economists who developed to its full height the classical theory of the functioning of the economy, were greatly concerned with problems of trade. Smith, writing in 1776, developed a ringing attack on government intervention in foreign trade and was personally responsible for many reforms in the branch of the British civil service concerned with the control of trade. Ricardo, writing in 1817, developed the basic theory of the gains from trade that is still maintained today. The repeal of the Corn Laws, and the transformation of Britain in the mid-nineteenth century from a country of high tariffs to one of complete free trade, was to some extent the result of agitation by the economists whose theories of the gains from trade led naturally to a condemnation of all tariffs. The question of just how valuable foreign trade is continues to be debated today.

---

1. There is very little in Chapters 6 and 9 that would have been strange to Hume. With great theoretical insight, he perceived how a price system worked and stated its basic principles.

How Important Is International Trade Today?

In the United States today, foreign trade accounts for 6 percent of the national income. Given a few years in which to invent synthetic substitutes for a few key imported raw materials, much of the existing foreign trade could be eliminated without much noticeable effect on the standards of living of U.S. citizens. What then accounted for the early economists' great concern with trade?

At other times and at other places, trade has been, and is, extremely important. Today, trade looms large in the incomes of many countries: 25 percent of the national income of the U.K. is accounted for by foreign trade; 21 percent in Canada; 11 percent in Japan; and 26 percent in Sweden. The loss of their foreign trade would have a serious effect on the standards of living in these countries. Similarly, in the eighteenth and nineteenth centuries, the rapidly developing industrial economies of Europe owed a great deal to trade both for the imports of raw materials and foodstuff and for the export of goods manufactured at home.

Although foreign trade is not of great importance in its total effect on the U.S. economy, it is very important to particular industries. Large quantities of certain materials—petroleum, bauxite, coffee, iron ore, lumber, and newsprint—are imported. The loss of these supplies would cause serious difficulties to some industries, and substitute products would have to be developed, possibly at very high cost. On the other hand, the existence of certain domestic industries—the ones producing bicycles, watches, clocks, and textiles, for instance—has been threatened from time to time by foreign competition, indicating that even if the existence of foreign

trade is not critically important to the country as a whole, it does affect particular sectors of it in important ways. If a domestic industry is threatened by foreign competition, the question arises: Should low-priced foreign imports be kept out of the country, or would the country be better off if industries unable to compete with foreign products were allowed to disappear? This question is hotly debated from time to time in Congress, and it is not surprising that we should want to know what light economics can shed on it.

TABLE 1   **PERCENTAGE OF TRADE WITH THE UNITED STATES, 1963**

Country	Percentage of exports to U.S.	Percentage of imports from U.S
U.K.	9.1	8.6
Germany	6.8	8.4
France	5.3	7.7
Italy	9.7	11.5
Netherlands	4.2	12.7
Denmark	6.6	6.9
Sweden	5.7	7.5
Austria	3.9	2.7
Portugal	11.3	7.7
Japan	27.6	25.3
Australia	11.4	17.6
New Zealand	18.9	7.9
Brazil	40.0	25.4
Canada	59.3	67.9
Ireland	7.8	5.4
Ghana	18.7	5.8
Nigeria	7.5	6.4
Venezuela	32.9	42.5
Thailand	8.4	15.8
Mexico	60.2	66.6
Philippines	49.1	46.9

SOURCE: Calculated from the *Statistical Abstract of the U.S.*, 1964, Table 1229; and from *International Financial Statistics*, June, 1965, pp. 34–35.

Although imports may not be critically important to the U.S. economy, these imports are the exports of other countries and, in some cases, they are very important to these other countries. In Canada, for example, 59 percent of total exports go to the U.S. A change in U.S. commercial policy that caused but a small ripple in the U.S. economy could cause a tidal wave in the Canadian one. One of the reasons why some other countries are so sensitive to changes in U.S. policy is that

it has a vital effect on them; they fear that, since it does not have such a vital effect on the U.S., policy changes may sometimes be made for frivolous reasons. It is unpleasant to be in the position of having your own welfare affected by decisions that do not matter much one way or the other to the person making them. Table 1 shows the importance of trade with the U.S. to the economies of some other countries.

The Gains From Trade Between Individuals

Economists early recognized that the principles governing the gains from trade applied equally well to foreign trade as to domestic trade. Governments tended to regard the two aspects of trade in very different lights, but economists were prominent in the fight to recognize that the causes and consequences of international trade were merely an extension of the principles explaining domestic trade. Some of these ideas were developed quite early, but it was not until the mid-nineteenth century that the English economist John Stuart Mill advanced a theory that showed satisfactorily how international trade could be governed by exactly the same principles as those governing domestic trade.

From time immemorial, human beings have lived in groups; even in the earliest societies, individuals tended to specialize in particular tasks rather than being utterly self-sufficient. Once an individual specialized in doing one thing, the range of goods that he required had to be obtained by trading most of what he produced for a little of what each of his neighbors produced. Why is such a system superior to one in which each person makes himself self-sufficient by satisfying all

of his needs by his own production? The answer is that people trading may have either *absolute advantages* or *comparative advantages* over each other. When they have absolute advantages, their gains from trade are obvious. When they have *comparative advantages* over each other, without absolute advantage, the basis of the gain from trade is less obvious but equally important.

In order to study the gains from trade among individuals, we shall consider a simplified example involving two persons, Peter and Paul, and two commodities, fish and deer. This simple example contains everything that is of importance to the problem. The same principles operate in a world of many people and many commodities.

ABSOLUTE ADVANTAGE

Assume that Peter and Paul have different capabilities. Peter can catch 6 fish for each hour that he spends fishing and he can kill 3 deer for each hour that he spends hunting. Paul can catch 8 fish for each hour that he spends fishing and he can kill 2 deer for each hour that he spends hunting. Clearly, Peter is a better hunter than Paul, and Paul is a better fisherman than Peter. If both insist on being totally self-sufficient, they will have to divide their time between hunting and fishing: Peter will be spending some time doing badly what Paul can do well, and vice versa. They realize, however, that they could produce more meat and more fish between them, and so could both be better off, if Peter spent more of his time hunting and Paul spent more of his time fishing. We say that Peter *specializes* in producing deer, and Paul *specializes* in producing fish. This is shown in Exhibit 1.

EXHIBIT 1

	Peter	Paul
Fish caught per hour	6	8
Deer killed per hour	3	2

Peter is a better hunter than Paul.
Paul is a better fisherman than Peter.

	Output per 10-Hour Day with Each Person's Time Divided Equally Between Hunting and Fishing		
	Peter	Paul	Total
Fish	30	40	70
Deer	15	10	25

	Output per 10-Hour Day with Peter Working 6 Hours as a Hunter and Paul 6 Hours as a Fisherman			
	Peter	Paul	Total	Gain
Fish	24	48	72	+2
Deer	18	8	26	+1

For each extra hour that Peter devotes to hunting rather than fishing and that Paul devotes to fishing rather than hunting, their joint output rises by 1 deer and 2 fish. Can we account for their gains in terms of the concept of opportunity cost? Every time Peter spends an extra hour hunting, he kills 3

deer and sacrifices the 6 fish he would have caught had he gone fishing. The opportunity cost of deer when Peter kills them is 2 fish per deer. Every time Paul spends an extra hour hunting, he kills only 2 deer and he sacrifices 8 fish. The opportunity cost of deer when Paul kills them is 4 fish per deer. Paul is a high (opportunity) cost producer of deer; thus the community (Peter and Paul) is better off in terms of fish foregone when Peter kills deer than when Paul does.

Now look at the same facts the other way around. Every time Peter spends an extra hour fishing, he catches 6 fish and sacrifices the 3 deer he would have killed if he had gone hunting instead. The opportunity cost of fish when Peter catches them is ½ deer per fish. Every time Paul spends an extra hour fishing instead of hunting, he catches 8 fish and sacrifices 2 deer. The opportunity cost of fish when Paul catches them is ¼ deer per fish. Paul is a low (opportunity) cost producer of fish; thus the community is better off in terms of deer foregone when Paul catches fish than when Peter does. This is summarized in Exhibit 2.

EXHIBIT 2

Opportunity Costs of Fish and Deer[a]	When Obtained by	
	Peter	Paul
Cost per fish caught, in terms of deer not killed	½ deer	¼ deer
Cost per deer killed, in terms of fish not caught	2 fish	4 fish

[a] Calculated from data in Exhibit 1.

We may now summarize our argument as follows:

1. One individual has *an absolute advantage* over the other in the production of some commodity, if, for a given amount of effort,

he can produce more of that commodity than can the other individual for the same amount of effort.

2. If there are two individuals and two commodities and each has an absolute advantage over the other in the production of one of the commodities, then the total production of both commodities can always be increased if each individual devotes more of his time to producing the commodity in which he has an absolute advantage.

3. If people specialize in producing commodities in which they have an absolute advantage, they will produce a smaller range of commodities than they desire to consume, and trade will be necessary if their desires for consumption goods are to be satisfied. *Production is increased by specialization, and specialization necessitates trade.*

4. In the above example, Paul had an absolute advantage in the production of fish, and Peter had absolute advantage in the production of deer. Total production of deer and fish went up when Paul spent more of his time catching fish and Peter more of his time killing deer. If they are to consume a balanced diet of fish and meat, it will now be necessary for them to trade with each other, Peter supplying deer to Paul and Paul supplying fish to Peter.

COMPARATIVE ADVANTAGE

We now alter our previous example to make Peter not only a better hunter than Paul, but also a better fisherman. This is shown in Exhibit 3.

Would Peter now be well-advised to make himself self-sufficient? If he can both hunt and fish better than Paul, surely he can only lose if he gets involved in any joint action with Paul. The answer is No, and the student who can discover why before reading on will have

EXHIBIT 3

	Peter	Paul	Peter's output ÷ Paul's output
Fish caught per hour	6	4	1.5
Deer killed per hour	3	1	3.0

Peter is a better fisherman than Paul.
Peter is a better hunter than Paul.

discovered for himself the principle of comparative advantage first enunciated by Ricardo 150 years ago.

First, notice that, although Peter is better than Paul at both hunting and fishing, his margin of advantage is different in the two cases. He is three times as good as Paul at hunting, but only 1.5 times as good as Paul at fishing. If we compare Peter's advantage over Paul across the two commodities, we find his greater advantage is in hunting. We say Peter has an absolute advantage over Paul in both fishing and hunting, but that his comparative advantage lies in hunting.

Now look at the same facts in a different way by calculating the opportunity costs of fish in terms of deer and deer in terms of fish for both Peter and Paul. The method of calculation was described in the previous section, so we only need to summarize the results here. See Exhibit 4.

EXHIBIT 4

Opportunity Costs of Fish and Deer[a]	When Obtained by	
	Peter	Paul
Cost per fish caught, in terms of deer not killed	½ deer	¼ deer
Cost per deer killed, in terms of fish not caught	2 fish	4 fish

[a] Calculated from data in Exhibit 3.

Exhibit 4 is the same as Exhibit 2, even though Exhibit 4 is based on a situation in which Peter is a better fisherman than Paul. The reason is simply that opportunity cost is a relative concept. When we moved from the first to the second example, we cut Paul's efficiency as a fisherman in half, but we also cut his efficiency as a hunter in half. Thus we did not affect the number of fish he sacrificed per deer killed or the number of deer he sacrificed per fish caught.[2]

The argument is now exactly the same as that based on Exhibit 2. (Reread the paragraph immediately preceding Exhibit 2.) It appears from this that Peter and Paul can once again do better by specializing than by being self-sufficient; to check that this is really so we carry out the calculations shown in Exhibit 5.

Clearly, Peter and Paul can both be better off, since their joint production of both fish and deer can be increased if each specializes in the production of the commodity in which he has a comparative advantage. Specialization will then require trade, for, if each is to have a balanced diet of fish and meat, Peter will have to supply deer to Paul and Paul will have to supply fish to Peter. *Peter gains by specializing in hunting, in which he has a comparative advantage, and by obtaining his fish by trading with Paul, even though he is*

EXHIBIT 5

Output per 10-Hour Day with Each Person's Time Divided Equally Between Hunting and Fishing[a]

	Peter	Paul	Total
Fish	30	20	50
Deer	15	5	20

Output per 10-Hour Day if Peter Spends 6 Hours Hunting While Paul Spends 7 Hours Fishing

	Peter	Paul	Total	Gain
Fish	24	28	52	+2
Deer	18	3	21	+1

[a] Calculated from data in Exhibit 3.

better at fishing than Paul is.

The discussion may be summarized as follows:

1. One individual has a comparative advantage over another in the production of one commodity if his opportunity cost of producing the commodity is lower than is that of the second individual.

2. If there are two individuals and two commodities and if one has a comparative advantage in the production of the first commodity, the other individual must have a comparative advantage in the production of the other commodity.†

2. In Exhibits 2 and 4, Paul's entry in row (1) is

$$\frac{\text{number of deer killed per hour}}{\text{number of fish caught per hour}}.$$

His entry in row (2) is the reciprocal of this:

$$\frac{\text{number of fish caught per hour}}{\text{number of deer killed per hour}}.$$

Neither of these ratios will be affected if *both* denominator and numerator are multiplied by the same amount, λ.

† Let X's refer to outputs per unit of input (say per hour's labor) and let subscripts refer to commodities 1 and 2 and superscripts refer to individuals I and II. Then

$$\frac{X_1^I}{X_2^I} > \frac{X_1^{II}}{X_2^{II}} \text{ implies } \frac{X_2^I}{X_1^I} < \frac{X_2^{II}}{X_1^{II}}.$$

3. If there are two individuals and two commodities and each has a comparative advantage in one commodity and if each individual is producing some of each commodity, then total production of both commodities can always be increased if each individual produces more of the commodity in which he has a comparative advantage.†

4. The gains from trade depend only on the existence of comparative advantage; it makes no difference if each individual has an absolute advantage in one commodity (Exhibit 1) or if one individual has an absolute advantage in both (Exhibit 3).

WHAT IF THERE IS NO COMPARATIVE ADVANTAGE?

Finally, alter the example as in Exhibit 6.

Here, for purposes of illustration, we have two cases for Paul (one in which he is better than Peter at hunting and fishing, and one in which he is worse than Peter at both). Demonstrate (1) that, in this case, both Peter and Paul have the same opportunity costs of producing fish and deer; (2) that neither has

a comparative advantage over the other in producing either deer or fish; and (3) that if we start with Peter and Paul both producing fish and deer, there is no gain to be had in having them specialize. They are just as well off to be self-sufficient.

OTHER SOURCES OF THE GAINS FROM TRADE

So far we have considered differences in opportunity costs as a source of the gains from trade. Other sources are possible and we may mention the most important of these. If there are economies of scale, then output per unit of input may rise when specialization occurs. In all the examples so far, we have assumed that the efficiency of Peter and Paul as fishermen and hunters was given and independent of how much fishing and hunting they did. It may be that when Peter takes to hunting full time and Paul to fishing, they will each develop special skills and become more efficient in their single task than they were when they were each trying to be both fisherman and hunter. If costs per unit of out-

EXHIBIT 6

	Peter	Paul I	Paul II	Output per hour of Peter / Output per hour of Paul I	II
Fish caught per hour	6	4	12	$1\frac{1}{2}$	$\frac{1}{2}$
Deer killed per hour	3	2	6	$1\frac{1}{2}$	$\frac{1}{2}$

† So far, we have only given an example. A simple algebraic proof follows: For individual I, the opportunity cost of $1Y$ is aX, whereas for individual II it is bX. Assume that $a > b$. It follows that the opportunity cost of $1X$ is $1/a$ for I and $1/b$ for II and that $1/a < 1/b$. Thus I has a comparative advantage in producing X, and II has a comparative advantage in producing Y. If I produces one less Y, he gains aX, and if II produces one more Y, he loses bX. As a result, production of Y is unchanged and production of X changes by $aX - bX = X(a - b)$, which is positive, since $a > b$. The increase in X depends on the magnitude of the differences in the opportunity cost of producing X.

put fall as the scale of output rises, then this will be a further source of gain from specialization. This may be an important source, but it is additional to the gain coming from differ-

ences in opportunity cost, which gain occurs even though costs per unit are unchanged as the scale of output changes.

The Gains From Trade Between Nations

The argument given in the previous section is an absolutely general one. We can replace fish and deer by agricultural products and manufactured products, or any other products we care to mention; and we can replace Peter and Paul by two cities, two states, two regions of one country, or two countries. Whenever two areas have different opportunity costs, then it pays the inhabitants of these areas to specialize the area in the direction of its comparative advantage.

We say a nation has a comparative advantage in the production of some commodity X when its opportunity cost of producing X (measured in terms of foregone output of some other commodity Y) is lower than that of another nation. When we have many nations and many countries, it becomes a bit more difficult to determine who has the comparative advantage in which commodities, but it is, nonetheless, still true that total world production will always be higher if nations specialize in suitable directions than if each tries to be self-sufficient.

RICH LANDS, POOR LANDS

Probably the most important and least obvious application of this idea of comparative advantage is the following: Just because one

country can produce everything more efficiently than another country, it does not follow that her best policy is to remain self-sufficient. Indeed, as long as the country's margin of superiority over other countries is different in different commodities, then world production can be increased if each country specializes in the commodities in which it has a comparative advantage and imports other commodities from other countries.[3] Efficient countries have as much to gain from world trade as have inefficient ones, and they all can gain by trading with each other.

A popular belief based on the erroneous proposition that rich countries cannot gain by trading with poor countries is that high-wage countries such as the U.S. can only lose if they permit trade with low-wage countries such as Japan. "Surely, the products of Oriental sweatshops will drive our products from the market, and the high U.S. standard of living will be dragged down to that of the impoverished Orient." Persuasive arguments of this sort have, through the years, swayed many voters. Before considering them carefully, stop and think what the argument would imply if we took it out of the international level and down to a local one—where the same principles govern the gains from trade. Is it really impossible for a rich

---

3. Strictly speaking, all that is shown by the theory given here is that specialization raises world production. It can also be shown that, on the assumption of competitive markets, trade can never make any country worse off than it would be if it were self-sufficient.

man to gain from trading with a poor man? Would the local millionaire be better off if he did all his own planting, gardening, and cooking? No one believes that a rich man cannot gain from trading with those who are less rich. But why then must a rich group of people lose from trading with a poor group? "Well," you say, "the poor group will price their goods too cheaply." Does anyone believe that the housewife loses from buying in a discount house or a supermarket, just because they sell at a lower price than the old-fashioned corner store? She gains if she can buy the same goods at a lower price. If the Japanese pay low wages and sell their goods cheaply, then *their labor suffers*, but we gain, because we obtain goods at a low cost in terms of the goods that we must export in return. The cheaper our imports are, the better off we are in terms of the goods and services available for domestic consumption.

Stated in more formal terms, the argument is that the gains from trade depend on comparative, not absolute, advantages. World production is higher when any two areas, say the U.S. and Japan, specialize in the goods for which they have a comparative advantage than when they try to be self-sufficient. The only remaining possibility is that one country will undersell the other in all lines of production and thus appropriate all, or more than all, of the gains for herself, leaving the other country no better, or even worse off, than if she had remained self-sufficient. The clue to why this cannot happen is found in Chapter 38.

Let us assume, for example, that trade exists between the United States and Japan and that, at the present rate of exchange between dollars and yen, the Japanese can undersell the United States in all commodities. Everyone will want to buy Japanese goods and thus everyone will need yen. No one will want to buy U.S. goods and thus no one will need dollars. On the foreign-exchange market, there will be a big demand for yen and no demand for dollars. In a free market, the dollar will depreciate in value and the yen will appreciate. As this happens, the prices of U.S. exports will fall, whereas the prices of Japanese exports will rise. This will continue until some U.S. goods become cheaper than their Japanese equivalents. When this happens, the U.S. will begin to sell goods to Japan and to buy fewer goods from her. The dollar will continue to depreciate until demand and supply are equated, or until, ignoring capital movements, the demand for exports equals the demand for imports.

Equality of demand and supply on the foreign-exchange market ensures that trade is in both directions and that the value of what a country imports is equal to the value of what it exports.

If the exchange rate had been fixed by government decree, then the rate would have had to be changed until the free-market result was obtained, or else all trade would have to cease between the two countries because no yen could be obtained to purchase the desired imports.

Imports can be obtained only by spending the currency of the country that makes the imports. This currency can be obtained only by exporting goods and services or by borrowing. Thus, lending and borrowing aside, imports must equal exports. All trade must be in two directions. We can buy only if we can also sell. Thus trade cannot hurt a country by causing it to import without exporting. Trade, then, always provides scope for international specialization with each country producing and exporting those goods for which it has a comparative advantage.

The paragraph above is a simple prediction of the theory of foreign trade. In centuries of experience, no observations have been made that conflict with this theory. The question of the magnitude of the gains from trade will be considered in the next chapter.

Summary

1. We say that one individual has an absolute advantage over another if he can produce more of a commodity than can the other individual for the same amount of effort.

2. We say that one individual has a comparative advantage over another in the production of one commodity if his opportunity cost of producing the commodity is lower than that of the second individual. If there are two individuals and two commodities, and if one has a comparative advantage in the production of one commodity, the other individual *must* have a comparative advantage in the production of the other commodity.

3. The theory of the gains from trade makes a number of predictions, the most important of which are listed in the following three points:

4. Total production of both commodities can always be increased if each individual increases his production of the commodity in which he has a comparative advantage. The gains from trade depend only on the existence of comparative advantage.

5. The same analysis applies to nations as to commodities. When we have many nations and commodities, the concept of comparative advantage becomes more difficult to define. But this can be done, and it still follows that total world production will be higher if nations specialize in suitable directions than if each tries to be self-sufficient.

6. Efficient and rich countries can gain from world trade in just the same way as can inefficient and poor ones.

QUESTIONS FOR DISCUSSION

1. The citizens of underdeveloped Atlantis can weave two feet of cloth an hour or gather one basket of coconuts. Is there any point in their approaching the republic of Mu, whose inhabitants can weave three feet of cloth or gather two baskets of coconuts in the same period of time, and offering to trade? After all, they are inferior on both counts. A visiting economist advises the Atlantans to try. What possible opposition speeches do you imagine will be heard in the Senate in the capital of Mu? Appraise the validity of a few different arguments.

2. It is generally agreed that America has a comparative disadvantage in the production of bicycles compared with British and European producers. If the present high tariffs on the importation of foreign bicycles were removed, what do you think would happen (a) to the average standard of living of U.S. citizens, and (b) to the average standard of living of people now employed in the U.S. bicycle industry?

3. If the European Common Market caused such a rise in efficiency that the price of every good

manufactured in Germany, France, and Italy fell below the prices of the same good manufactured in the U.S., what do you think would happen? Would Americans gain or lose because of this?

4. Suppose, after 1865, the United States had become two separate countries divided by tariff barriers. What predictions would you make about the 1965 standard of living compared to what it is in America today?

5. Suppose each of the American states was a separate country. If free trade were permitted among these "countries," would you expect a different pattern of production to exist than the one that does exist? If one of these countries, Illinois, say, prohibited all trade, what would be the effect on Illinois and on the other 49 countries? Suppose all 50 countries prohibited all trade. What would be the result?

Chapter **40** TARIFFS AND THE GAINS FROM TRADE

IN CHAPTER 39, WE SHOWED HOW THE classical theory of the gains from trade points to specialization according to comparative advantage as the souce of the gains from trade, with the possibility of exploiting economies of scale as an added source. In this chapter, we first consider the theory of the gains from trade as a positive hypothesis about the real world, and then go on to consider the case for interfering with free trade through tariffs.

We have demonstrated that where opportunity costs differ between countries some degree of specialization with some consequent amount of trade will raise world standards of living. There is abundant evidence to show that such cost differences do occur and that potential gains from trade do exist. Today, no one seriously advocates complete self-sufficiency, but some people do advocate increasing or diminishing the quantity of trade that we now have. This, as we shall see, is a more difficult issue to settle than the issue of whether we should have any trade at all.

It has sometimes been held that it is impossible for trade between any two parties to be to the mutual advantage of both. According to this view, one trading partner must always reap his gain at the expense of the other. The principle of comparative costs, which shows that it is possible for both parties to gain from trade, even if one of them is more efficient than the other in all lines of production, completely refutes the *exploitation doctrine of trade*. Seen in this light, comparative costs is to be viewed as a *possibility theorem*. It shows that, if opportunity-cost ratios differ in two countries, specialization and the accompanying trade make it possible to produce more of all commodities, and thus make it possible for both parties to get more goods as a result of trade than they could get in its absence. Thus the answer to the question: "Is it *possible* for trade to be mutually advantageous?" is an emphatic Yes; the answer to the question: "Is trade *in fact* mutually advantageous?" is quite another matter.

Free Trade Versus Prohibitive Tariffs

The theory of the gains from trade through the exploitation of differences in comparative costs may be looked at not only as a possibility theorem, but as a positive hypothesis about the real world.[1] As a positive hypothesis about the real world, the theory of comparative costs predicts that, in the real world, there will be gains from trade in the sense of increased world production, and that no country will lose from trade in the sense of having less to consume than it could have if it were self-sufficient. This general theory has not been extensively tested, mainly because it has long been believed to be self-evident. If asked to support it with empirical evidence, most economists would probably point to the widely differing cost conditions in certain countries, the most dramatic being those associated with climate. It would undoubtedly be possible, by using greenhouses, to grow oranges, cotton, and a whole host of imported raw materials and foodstuffs in Norway or to grow coffee in the United States. But the cost in terms of other commodities foregone would be prodigious, because these artificial means of production require lavish inputs of factors of production. It would likewise be possible for a tropical country currently producing foodstuffs to set up industries to produce all the types of manufactured products that it consumes. The cost, in terms of resources used, for a small country without natural advantages in industrial production, could be very heavy. It thus appears that there is a large gain to both countries in having specialization and trade. The real output and consumption of both sets of countries would be very much lower if each had to produce domestically all the goods that it consumed.

Thus, almost all economists would agree, the most casual observation reveals such major cost differences among countries that no one could doubt that there are gains from trade. Careful empirical measurement might put an actual numerical value on it, but it is inconceivable that it could refute the general hypothesis that production and consumption in the world, and in each major trading country, is higher with trade than it would be if all countries were forced to be utterly self-sufficient.

Free Trade Versus the Level of Tariffs Existing Today

It is quite a jump from the proposition that "Some trade is better (because it increases production) than no trade" to the proposition that "A bit more trade than we have at present is better than a bit less trade." Yet most arguments about commercial policy involve

---

1. The theory is often presented as if it were a general law that cannot be challenged on any grounds. It is unassailable only in the sense, that it undoubtedly follows logically for certain postulates. But in this sense, any theory to which the rules of logic have been correctly applied is unassailable. Like any other interesting theory, it is open to testing and to possible refutation. After all, any one of a half-dozen postulates on which it is based might prove to be empirically false.

the latter sort of proposition, not the former. Most actual policy disagreements concern the relative merits of free trade versus controlled trade with tariffs on the order of, say, 10, 20, or 30 percent. Such tariffs would not cut out imports of bananas, coffee, sugar, diamonds, iron ore, or any of the commodities in whose production America would be really ineffi-cient. Yet these are just the commodities that defenders of free trade use as examples when the doctrine of the gains from trade is chal-lenged. If we accept the hypothesis that some trade is better than no trade, we are not necessarily committed to accepting the hypothesis that free trade is better than con-trolled trade with, say, 20 percent tariffs.

Let us, then, compare a position of free trade with one of, say, 20 percent ad valorem tariffs on all imports. This is a simplified ver-sion of the sort of argument that really does take place over commercial policy, for tariffs are seldom advocated to protect industries that are violently inefficient compared to for-eign industries; they are usually advocated to protect industries that can very nearly com-pete, but not quite.

Let us predict, as comparative cost theory does, that there will be gains when we move from a position of 20 percent tariffs to one of free trade. If we have any doubt as to the empirical correctness of this prediction, we must look beyond the examples of bananas and sugar, for 20 percent tariffs will still allow trade in these goods. In fact, there can now be no adequate substitute for a care-ful empirical test of this hypothesis. But, in the absence of such a test, can we gain any idea of the possibility that the hypothesis is false? We can indeed get some idea of what

is involved by changing some of the assump-tions of the theory in ways that seem relevant and seeing what then happens to the predic-tion about the gains from trade. Let us take a few examples.

The theory is based on an assumption of competition that ensures that relative prices will reflect real opportunity costs. If the de-gree of competition differs between different industries, relative prices will not reflect comparative costs. Under these circum-stances, free trade may force countries to specialize in goods in which they have a com-parative disadvantage. In such circum-stances, trade will reduce world output. The conclusion that there are gains from trade is thus sensitive to variations in the assumption about the relation between relative prices and relative costs.

The theory is also based on the assumption that the existence of trade does not affect domestic production possibilities. The re-moval of a 20 percent tariff might create trade with a neighboring country, but labor unions might oppose this policy and express their discontent in strikes and slow-downs that would permanently lower output per man-hour. Under such circumstances, trade might reduce the total output of the two countries.[2]

The theory is based on the assumption of full employment. Most people would agree that free trade would not be worth having if its price were massive unemployment. But what if free trade led only to a slightly higher average level of unemployment than a situa-tion of 20 percent tariffs? If it did, then every-thing would depend on the *magnitude* of the gains resulting from resource reallocation under free trade. If, for example, free trade

2. There is no point in saying this does not upset the theory on the grounds that, if workers could be made to work as hard after trade as they did before, all would be well. We know already that, if all the con-ditions assumed by the theory are fulfilled, there will be a gain from trade. What we want to know, if we are to give policy advice in the real world, is "Are the conditions, in fact, fulfilled?"

led to a reallocation of resources that was 0.5 percent more efficient than one resulting from 20 percent tariffs, but led simultaneously to an average level of unemployment 1 percent higher than the one occurring with 20 percent tariffs, then free trade would bring losses rather than gains. We conclude, therefore, that the assumption that free trade *will* bring gains depends critically upon the assumptions that productivity per man-hour is not lowered and the level of unemployment is not raised by the removal of tariffs. At present, we have very little empirical evidence relating to either of these conditions. It is critical, therefore, that we know the order of magnitude of the potential gains from free trade; if these gains are small, they could be wiped out by a small real-world deviation from one of the many assumptions.

Our argument in the previous paragraphs did not refute the hypothesis that there are gains from free trade as compared with, say, 20 percent tariffs. Such an hypothesis can only be refuted by measurement and testing. In the absence of careful tests, such arguments as we have presented can cast doubt on the idea that the hypothesis is self-evidently true. The argument shows that the hypothesis is not self-evident; that its truth depends on a large number of circumstances about which we can by no means be certain without careful measurement.

We must conclude that the proposition, "Some trade is better than no trade" might be accepted as self-evident on the basis of very casual observation, but that the proposition, "Free trade is better than some trade (with, say, 20 percent tariffs)" is by no means self-evident and need not be accepted in the absence of careful empirical tests.

The Common Market: How Large Are the Gains?

Shortly after World War II, the movement toward a European Common Market began. The six Common Market countries, France, Germany, Italy, Holland, Belgium, and Luxembourg, were to remove all tariffs on trade with each other. As controversy developed about the advantages and disadvantages of such a union, and about the cost to other countries of staying out or the gains from coming in, economists set out to try to measure the gains from such a union. There have been three notable empirical measurements: Professor P. J. Verdoorn estimated the gain to the six European Common Market countries to be something on the order of the $\frac{1}{20}$ of 1 percent of their national incomes! Professor Harry Johnson estimated the maximum cost to Britain of staying out of the Common Market to be equal to approximately 1 percent of her national income. Professor W. Welmesfelder estimated the gain to Germany from major tariff reductions in the years 1956–1957 to be on the order of less than 1 percent of German national income.[3]

These measures came as a surprise to those convinced free traders who believed the loss

3. These studies are not suitable for the elementary student. For the best account of Verdoorn's work, see T. Scitovsky, *Economic Theory and Western European Integration* (Allen and Unwin, 1958). See also H. G. Johnson, "The Gains from Freer Trade: An Estimate," *Manchester School,* March, 1958; and W. Welmesfelder, "The Short-Run Effects of the Lowering of Import Duties in Germany," *Economic Journal,* March, 1960. There are reasons to believe that Welmesfelder's figure is a large overestimate.

from existing tariffs to be large. There are, however, good general reasons for believing that the orders of magnitude obtained in these three studies are the right ones. Typical European tariffs on manufactured goods are on the order of 20 percent. This means that industries from 1 to 20 percent less efficient than foreign competitors will be protected by these tariffs. If the costs of different industries are spread out evenly, then some tariff-protected industries would be 20 percent less efficient than foreign competitors, but others would be only 1 percent less efficient, and their average inefficiency would be on the order of half the tariff rate, which is 10 percent less efficient than foreign competitors. Typically, not much more than 10 percent of a country's resources would be devoted to producing behind tariff walls. This means that 10 percent of a country's resources would be producing 10 percent less efficiently than if there were no tariffs, which makes a reduc-

tion in national income of something on the order of 1 percent.

We must conclude that, on the best available evidence, the maximum gains from the extra trade resulting from removing 20 percent tariffs is on the order of 1 percent of national income. When one considers the violent feelings and passionate controversies over the difference between a policy of free trade and one of 10, 20, or 30 percent tariffs, it is understandable why many people were surprised at this figure when it was produced. This figure is itself important, because one would view the use of tariffs for "noneconomic" reasons in quite a different way if the cost of these tariffs were a once-and-for-all reduction of 1 percent in the national income rather than, say, a 10 percent reduction.[4] There is, indeed, a world of difference between merely establishing the direction of change and in actually measuring its magnitude.[5]

The Case for Tariffs

We shall now consider some of the common arguments used in favor of tariff protection.

ARGUMENT 1: "MUTUALLY ADVANTAGEOUS TRADE IS IMPOSSIBLE"

Since we have already shown this proposition to be wrong, it is not surprising that the arguments based on it all contain crude fallacies. Consider, for example, the argument that runs: "If I buy a foreign good, I have the good and the foreigner has the money, whereas if I buy the same good locally, I have the good and our country has the money too; therefore we are better off." The reader is left to provide his own retort to this argument. Recall the discussion in Chapter 39.

Probably the most subtle argument that

4. Some economists give the impression that the losses from tariffs would be large when they say that it may be necessary to become partially self-sufficient in certain lines of activity *at great cost* because of fear of future wars. The attempt to imply that the cost will be great is unwarranted in the light of present evidence.

5. This is not to say that the gains from European union are necessarily small; it does say that the gains resulting from a reallocation of resources according to comparative advantage are small. For a discussion of the other possible sources of gain, see R. G. Lipsey, "The Theory of Customs Unions: A General Survey," *Economic Journal*, September, 1960.

comes under this heading asserts that it is impossible for a rich, high-wage country to trade profitably with a poor, low-wage country. It is argued that the low-wage country will undersell the high-wage one; that unemployment will ensue; and that the standard of living of the high-wage country will be sacrificed. We considered this argument earlier in this chapter and saw why it was misleading. Reread pages 452–453, if you cannot refute the argument.

ARGUMENT 2: "LIVING STANDARDS WILL BE HIGHER WITH TARIFFS THAN WITH FREE TRADE"

Most of the common arguments in this group are concerned with single countries.[6] One argument concerns the effects of trade on employment. The classical argument for the gains from trade assumes full employment. If it were true that a free-trade country had a higher average level of unemployment (perhaps because of wider cyclical movements in unemployment) than a country levying tariffs, then it is possible that the loss in production through unused resources would more than offset the gain through a more efficient allocation of resources. No detailed studies have been made of the effect of trade on employment over any long period of time; in the absence of any evidence one way or the other, no verdict can be rendered on this possibility.

Another argument says that, if a country produces a significant portion of the world output of some commodity, it will be able to exploit its monopoly position by interfering with the free flow of trade. By buying less from abroad and selling less as a result, world prices will be affected and the country concerned can appropriate for itself a larger share of total world production than it would obtain if all prices were set on competitive markets. If other countries follow a fairly passive policy, then one country may be able to reap quite substantial monopoly gains. If, however, several countries all try to do the same thing, then a battle of move and countermove may ensue until, at the end, everyone may be worse off than they were under free trade.

Probably the most important argument under this heading is the one relating to economies of scale, which is usually referred to as the *infant-industry* case for tariffs. If an industry has large economies of scale, then costs and prices must be high when the industry is small, but they will fall as the industry grows. In such an industry, the country first in the field has a tremendous advantage over latecomers. A newly developing country may find that its industries are unable to compete in the early stages of their development against established foreign rivals. A tariff may protect these industries from foreign competition while they grow up. Once they are large enough, they will be able to produce as cheaply as can foreign rivals and thus be able to stand on their own feet without tariff support.

This has always been recognized as a theoretically sound pro-tariff argument. Most standard textbooks, however, wind up their discussion of it with some statement such as the following: "In practice, these industries

---

6. It is not difficult, however, to invent circumstances that apply to the world, although whether or not these circumstances are found in the real world is, of course, an empirical matter.

never admit to growing up and, even when they are full-grown adults, they cling to their tariff protection; the *infant-industry* argument, although valid theoretically, is thus to be rejected in practice."

But is it true that such tariffs are seldom removed? This is certainly part of the folklore of tariffs, but we are not aware of any careful study of this alleged fact. Notable illustrative examples spring to mind, of course, but in order to determine if it is true, we would have to compare the tariff levels existing in the infant industries with the general level of tariffs ruling in the country both when the infants were really infants and again after they had grown up. Only then could we say with any confidence that there was no tendency to remove the tariffs after the infants matured.[7] Second, it is not at all clear, even if this alleged fact is true, that this is a sufficient reason for avoiding such tariffs. If the economies of scale are realized, then the real costs of production are reduced and resources are freed for other uses. *Whether or not the tariff remains*, a cost saving has been effected. The existence of the tariff may protect the grown-up industry from foreign competition and allow it to charge a higher price than it otherwise could. Thus, if the tariff is not removed, all factors in the industry may earn more than they otherwise would. In other words, the continuation of the tariff may redistribute income in favor of factors employed in the protected industry to the cost of the rest of the country. It is quite possible, however, if there are sufficiently large economies of scale, that everyone in the country will have a higher income than if the industry had never been protected in the first place. Other cases are also possible, but the point is that it does not necessarily follow that there is a loss to the country just because the tariff is not removed as compared with a situation in which the tariff was not put on at all.

ARGUMENT 3: "TARIFFS ARE REQUIRED TO ACHIEVE AND ENCOURAGE GOALS OTHER THAN THE MAXIMIZATION OF OUTPUT"

Gains from trade, in the classical analysis, stem from increases in production. It is quite possible for someone to accept the classical prediction about output and yet rationally oppose free trade because of his concern with policy objectives other than production and consumption.

Comparative costs might dictate, for example, that a country should specialize in the production of a few primary products. The central authorities might decide, however, that there are distinct social advantages to having a more diverse economy—one that would give citizens a wider range of occupations in which to develop their talents. The social and psychological gains from having a diverse economy might more than compensate, the authorities decide, for a reduction in living standards to a level, say, 5 percent below what they could be with free trade.

Another possibility concerns fluctuations in the prices of certain primary goods. Com-

---

7. This kind of comparison is needed because it is not sufficient just to show that the industries keep some tariff protection even after they grow up; instead, we need to show that they keep higher protection than we would have expected them to obtain if they could not have availed themselves of the infant-industry argument.

parative advantage might dictate that a country should specialize in the production of one or two primary commodities that are subject to wide price fluctuations. This would mean that the incomes of the producers would also be subject to wide fluctuations. Because problems of a widely fluctuating national income can be serious, even though the average level of income over a long period is high, the central authorities may decide to sacrifice some income in order to reduce such fluctuations.[8] They could encourage the expansion of several stable industries that are protected by tariffs. (They realize also that specialization in one or two products leaves a country highly vulnerable to shifts in demand due to changes in tastes or technological innovations that make some materials expendable.)

Many Canadians are passionately concerned with maintaining a separate nation with traditions that differ from those of the United States. Many of these Canadians believe that the tariff helps them to do this, and they are fully prepared to accept a 5 or 10 percent cut in living standards in order to maintain this independence. As many Canadian economists have argued, Canadians may be mistaken in believing that the tariff helps them in preserving independence from the United States. The main point, however, is that there is nothing irrational in their being willing to accept substantial costs in order to obtain objectives other than the maximizing of living standards. There are many policy goals other than maximizing national income. Although most people would agree that, *ceteris paribus*, they prefer more income to less, the economist cannot pronounce as irrational anyone who chooses to sacrifice some income in order to achieve other goals.

The job of the positive economist is to point out what the actual cost in income might be.

Although one can think of many cases, particularly with the older countries of the British Commonwealth, such as Canada, Australia, and New Zealand, where a tariff policy was pursued after a rational assessment of the approximate cost, one cannot help feeling that, as often as not, high tariff policies are pursued for rather flimsy objectives of national prestige with very little idea of the actual costs involved. One of the reasons why many economists feel so strongly about free trade is probably that they react against the arguments and motives of politicians advocating high tariffs. Many of the anti-free-trade arguments contain crude fallacies, and many of the motives for advocating tariffs are, to say the least, suspect. (The fact that many of the arguments used by tariff advocates are incorrect does nothing to prove the correctness of the free-trade arguments. We must never forget that the failure of an argument for some case does *nothing* to prove the contrary case.)

Our main concern in this chapter has been not to argue a case for or against free trade, but to investigate what can be said about trade and tariffs on the basis of positive economics. As in all other realms, positive economics investigates the consequences of certain actions: It cannot say which goals one ought to pursue. Whether or not free trade is better than a tariff policy depends on the policy goals that one is trying to attain, the magnitude of the gains under a free-trade policy as compared to the gains under a tariff policy, and on the extent to which the policy adopted prohibits the attainment of goals other than the maximizing of consumption.

8. Just as many firms decide to diversify their outputs so as not to have all their eggs in one basket.

Summary

1. The principle of comparative costs, viewed as a *possibility theorem,* provides a refutation of the exploitation doctrine of trade by showing that trade can be advantageous to all parties; it is, however, quite another matter to know if trade is *in fact* advantageous to all trading parties.

2. Most economists would accept the proposition that some trade is better (in the sense of increasing production) than no trade, a proposition established by the most casual observation of existing cost differences. But the proposition that a little more trade than we have at present is better than a little less trade is not so easily established, although this is what current policy debates are about.

3. The conclusion that there are gains from trade is sensitive to variations in the assumptions that relative prices will reflect real opportunity costs, that trade does not affect domestic production possibilities, and that there is full employment. We conclude that the proposition that free trade is better than some trade is by no means self-evident.

4. From studies of the gains that might result from the lowering of tariff barriers within the European Economic Community, we must conclude that, on the best available evidence, the maximum gains from the extra trade resulting from removing 20 percent tariffs is on the order of 1 percent of national income.

5. Many arrangements have been advanced in favor of tariffs. Those based on the proposition that mutually advantageous trade is impossible all contain fallacies. Those that depend on ways in which one country can make itself better off at the expense of its trading partners cannot be rejected as being inconsistent. Other arguments depend on having goals of policy other than making production and consumption as high as possible, and there is nothing in economics that can lead to a rejection of tariffs as an instrument for achieving such policies.

QUESTIONS FOR DISCUSSION

1. Turn again to the questions at the end of Chapter 39. Would you change any of your answers?

2. When France established a tariff on chickens, which seriously hurt American exporters, the United States set up a tariff on brandy. Discuss the reasoning and the gains and losses from such moves.

3. What do you think Stephen Enke of the RAND Corporation meant when he said, in a Congressional committee paper, that "many arguments for protection come wrapped in the flag"?

4. What can an economist do to advise Canadians who feel it is worth something to remain independent of the United States, and who regard the tariff as a way of doing this?

5. It is sometimes argued that producers of primary products have special needs for tariff protection. Can you think of any reasons why this might be so?

6. American shipping lines receive very large government subsidies. Without these subsidies, they would probably give way completely to competition from such countries as Norway, Britain, and Greece. What does this say about American comparative advantage in shipping? Who gains and who loses if the British, Norwegian, and Greek governments subsidize their own shipping lines, and if U.S. importers and exporters rely exclusively on shipping from these countries? Who gains from, and who pays for, the U.S. subsidies?

7. Practically every major country in the world has an international airline. Is this predicted by the theory of comparative advantage? The great majority of these lines run at a loss and exist only because they receive heavy government subsidies. What reasons could there be for interfering in this way with the operation of comparative advantage? If one country decides not to operate an airline, is it better off if the governments of other countries subsidize their own airlines, or if they leave them to cover costs by their own efforts?

Chapter **41** INTERNATIONAL ECONOMIC EXPERIENCE

THE WORLD INTO WHICH YOUR GRANDFATHERS were born differed radically from the world we know today. It was a world with a large volume of international trade largely unobstructed by tariffs; it was a world in which the British Navy policed the seas and guaranteed the free flow of world trade; it was a world in which the universal acceptance of the gold standard guaranteed the complete convertibility of one currency into another and, hence, the ability of merchants to buy and sell where they wanted, unimpeded by governmental intervention. It was a world largely without passports—a world in which people could cross many international frontiers as easily as

they now pass from one U.S. state to another. It was a world in which there was very nearly a free international movement of goods and factors—a world we are now inclined to regard as nothing more than the economist's mental construct. That world is gone forever.

Today, international trade is restricted and controlled by tariffs and quotas. Today, the American Navy patrols the seas, but more in relation to the political battle between the East and the West than to ensuring that everyone conforms to the rules of the game of free trade. Today, the gold standard is known to most people only as something that existed in the "good old days." Today, most currencies are not freely convertible one into another. Today, most governments operate a scheme of exchange controls that restricts the ability of merchants to buy and sell any-where they want, even if they are prepared to pay all existing taxes and tariffs. What happened, and does it matter that it did happen?

Achieving Equilibrium in the Balance of Payments

Before we consider what happened and why, we need to know how equilibrium in international payments is established. We analyzed this problem in Chapter 38; here, we need only draw together the relevant points.

Establishing equilibrium in international payments in a free-market world requires that changes be made in the relative prices of goods produced by different countries. A country with a payments deficit must increase its exports and reduce its imports. These changes are accomplished if the goods produced by the deficit country fall in price so that imports become relatively expensive and exports become relatively cheap on the world market. On the other hand, a country with a payments surplus must reduce its exports and increase its imports. These changes are accomplished if the goods produced by the surplus country rise in price so that imports become relatively cheap and exports become relatively expensive on the international market.

Basically, there are two ways in which these relative price changes can be effected: Exchange rates can be varied, or domestic price levels can be varied. A deficit country must either allow its exchange rate to depreciate or its domestic price level to fall; a surplus country must either allow its exchange rate to appreciate or its domestic price level to rise.

We studied fluctuating rates in detail in Chapter 38. Under a system of fluctuating rates, changes in the relative prices of each country's imports and exports are accomplished by varying the exchange rates; there is no need to change domestic price levels. If exchange rates are determined by the forces of demand and supply on a free market, then surplus countries will automatically have appreciating exchange rates and deficit countries will automatically have depreciating ones.

Under the gold standard, exchange rates were fixed, and changes in the relative prices of a country's imports and exports were accomplished by changing the domestic price levels. If, under the gold standard, a country had a persistent tendency for imports to exceed exports, it was necessary that the country's price level be reduced. A fall in the domestic price level would mean a fall in the prices of all goods produced in that country, both those for domestic consumption and those for export. A fall in the domestic price level would thus mean that imports, whose prices would not have changed, would become relatively less attractive than domestically produced goods, while exports, whose prices would have fallen, would become relatively more attractive in foreign markets. These changes would tend to encourage exports and discourage imports and so restore equilibrium in the balance of payments. The gold standard required price-level adjustments and it also provided an automatic mechanism for accomplishing them. We do not need to go into the details here, but the essential links in the mechanism were: (1) a deficit country would lose gold; (2) the loss of gold would cause a contraction in the quantity of money in the country; and (3) a fall in the quantity of money would cause a fall in the price level.[1]

The Gold Standard

Although the detailed workings of the gold standard are now only of historical interest, a few features provide important contrasts to the present system.[2]

The gold standard was not *designed*. Like the price system, it just happened. It arose out of the general acceptance of gold as the commodity to be used as money.[3] In most countries, paper currency was freely convertible into gold at a fixed rate; the currency was little more than receipts for gold, and it circulated because paper was more convenient to use than metal.

Rates of exchange between the standard units of currency of various countries were fixed by their values in terms of the standard unit, gold. In 1914, the U.S. dollar was convertible into 0.053 standard ounces of gold, while the British pound sterling was convertible into 0.257 standard ounces. This meant that the pound was worth 4.86 times as much as the dollar in terms of gold, thus making one pound worth $4.86 U.S.[4] There was nothing good or bad nor was there any cause for national pride or shame in the fact that the pound sterling was worth more than the dollar. The British had simply chosen to make their basic unit, the pound, contain a larger amount of gold than was contained in the American basic unit, the dollar. If the British had made their basic monetary unit the shilling (there are twenty shillings in a pound), the American basic unit would have been worth more than the British one, since the shilling was worth just over 24¢.

As long as all countries were on the gold standard, a person in any one country could be sure of being able to make payments to a person in any other country. If he was unable to buy or sell the relevant currencies on the

1. This last link between the quantity of money and the price level is provided by the quantity theory, which is described in detail in Chapter 55.

2. If you read Chapter 52 on the nature and history of money at this point, the present chapter will seem easier.

3. The use of gold was not exclusive. Some countries used a silver standard, and frictions sometimes developed because of this. In the United States, bimetallism (the official use of both gold and silver as money) had many exponents in the latter half of the nineteenth century. The most eloquent spokesman for the free coinage of silver was William Jennings Bryan, three times a candidate for the Presidency. He is perhaps best remembered for his famous oratory, which included the ringing line, "You shall not crucify mankind upon a cross of gold."

4. In practice, the exchange rate did fluctuate within narrow limits set by the cost of shipping gold. If it cost 2¢ to ship $4.86 worth of gold from New York to London, it would be worth buying pounds in New York as long as their price did not rise above $4.88. At $4.87 to the pound, an American who wished to pay a bill in London would still buy pounds. At $4.89, it would pay him to convert his dollars into gold (at $4.86 per pound) and ship the gold (at 2¢ per pound's worth), making the total cost of paying his bill $4.88 per pound rather than $4.89 if he purchased sterling. Thus no one would buy sterling at a price in excess of $4.88. A similar argument for the British trader wishing to obtain U.S. funds establishes that the rate cannot fall below $4.84. The values at which it paid to ship gold were known as *gold points*.

foreign-exchange market, he need only convert the currency he held into gold and then ship the gold.

The century between the end of the Napoleonic Wars and the beginning of World War I was the heyday of the gold standard; during this relatively trouble-free period, the automatic mechanism seemed to work well. Subsequent research has shown, however, that the gold standard worked well during the period mainly because it was not called on to do much work. Trade flowed between nations in large and rapidly expanding volume, and it is probable that existing price levels were never far from the equilibrium ones. No major trading country found itself with a serious and persistent balance-of-payments deficit and so no major country was called upon to restore equilibrium through a large change in its domestic price level.[5]

In the 1920s and 1930s, the gold standard was called on to do a major job. It failed utterly, and it was abandoned. How did this come about? During World War I, most belligerent countries had suspended convertibility of currency (i.e., they went off the gold standard). Most European countries suffered major inflations, but the degree of inflation differed from country to country. After the war, countries returned to the gold standard (i.e., they restored convertibility of their currencies into gold). For reasons of prestige, some insisted on returning at the prewar rates. This meant that some countries' goods were overpriced and other countries' goods were underpriced. Deficits and surpluses in the balance of payments inevitably appeared, and the adjustment mechanism required that price levels should change in each of the countries in order to restore equilibrium. Price levels changed very slowly, however, and after five years had passed, equilibrium price levels had not yet been attained.[6]

The 1930s: Period of Experimentation

With the abandonment of the gold standard, the exchange rates were left to be determined by the free market. The way in which demand for and supply of foreign exchange determines exchange rates on a free market has already been described in Chapter 38.

Various experiments were tried with both fixed and fluctuating rates. Often rates would be allowed to fluctuate on the free market until they had reached what looked like equilibrium, and the rate would then be fixed at that level.

5. Inevitably, there were short-run fluctuations and these were ironed out by movements of short-run capital in response to changes in interest rates. Interest rates tended to rise in deficit countries and this tended to attract sufficient short-run capital to cover any balance-of-payments deficit, providing the deficit was short-lived. The way in which this is accomplished was spelled out in the appendix to Chapter 38.

6. The failure of the mechanism of price-level changes to work quickly has often been attributed to the growth of price and wage rigidities in the twentieth century. The student who consults some of the standard works on the subject will no doubt encounter this explanation. Recent research has shown, however, that the flexibility of the price and wage levels in the 1920s was no less than in the nineteenth century. Thus the success of the gold standard in the nineteenth century is not to be attributed to the fact that the mechanism worked well, but that it did not have to work at all. See A. W. Phillips, "The Relation Between the Level of Unemployment and the Role of Change of Money Wage Rates in the United Kingdom from 1862 to 1958," *Economica*, November, 1958, pp. 283–299; and R. G. Lipsey, "Can There Be a Valid Theory of Wages?," *The Advancement of Science*, July, 1962, pp. 105–112.

The period of experimentation coincided with the Great Depression of the 1930s. Trade was everywhere being reduced due both to rising unemployment and falling demand and to the increasing uncertainty and doubt about the future of international markets. Furthermore, this was a period during which many established ideas about the gains from trade were challenged, and many old-fashioned, long-discarded ideas on the desirability of exporting and the undesirability of importing were revived. In the terrible period of mass unemployment of the 1930s, governments began to cast around for any measure, no matter how extreme, that might alleviate matters. One superficially plausible way of doing this was to cut back on imports and to produce the goods domestically. Prejudice against foreigners is a potent force in most countries, and the idea that one's troubles are due to an influx of cheap imports from abroad has a strong appeal to the electorate everywhere in the world. As a result, most countries in the 1930s sought to reduce imports and to encourage exports in an effort to lower unemployment. If one country managed to reduce its imports, then its unemployment might be reduced because people would be put to work producing goods at home to replace goods formerly imported. But this country's imports are the exports of other countries. These other countries would find their exports falling and unemployment rising as a consequence. The world level of unemployment would not be reduced, for the first country's success in cutting unemployment would cause an increase in unemployment in other countries. These other countries would then retaliate by reducing their own imports and

trying to lower their unemployment by producing the goods at home. This would affect the first country, which would now find its exports falling and unemployment rising as a result. The net effect of such measures was to decrease the volume of trade, and thus to sacrifice the gains from trade without raising employment, since the simultaneous attempts of all countries to cut imports without suffering a comparable cut in exports was bound to be self-defeating.[7]

The policy of discouraging imports and encouraging exports can be achieved through two main sets of tools. The first set is composed of taxes, tariffs, subsidies, and quotas. For example, a policy of tariffs on imports and subsidies on exports will tend to discourage imports and encourage exports. The second policy is that of devaluation. We have already observed that both policies will work *only as long as* other countries remain passive. Consider what happens in the case of devaluations. If a country with 10 percent of its labor force unemployed devalues its currency, two effects can be expected: First, exports should rise, and, second, domestic consumers should buy fewer imports and more domestically produced goods. Both of these changes have the effect of lowering the amount of unemployment in the country. If other countries do nothing, the policy succeeds. But the policy will have raised the volume of unemployment in these other countries, since their exports to the devaluing country will be reduced. If other countries try to restore their positions, they will devalue their currencies as well. If all countries devalue their currencies in the same proportion, they will all be right back where they started,

---

7. This policy is considered further in Chapter 50. The problem was that total world demand was too low to employ all the world's productive resources. The attempt of all countries simultaneously to gain a larger fraction of this inadequate demand was bound to be self-defeating.

with no change in the relative prices of goods from any country and, hence, no change from the original situation.[8] A situation in which all countries devalue their currencies in an attempt to gain a competitive advantage over one another is called a situation of *competitive devaluations.*

Changes in exchange rates can be made for two quite different reasons. The first reason is to try to cut domestic unemployment by reducing imports (and thus necessarily raising foreign unemployment) in the manner analyzed above. We have seen that such attempts are self-defeating when they are made by everyone. The second reason is a desire to find an equilibrium position in international payments. If everyone changes exchange rates with the second reason in mind, the policy may well succeed. Economic theory predicts that (1) under quite general conditions, an equilibrium will exist, and that (2) the approach to the equilibrium will be signaled by a reduction in excess demands and excess supplies. Thus, the search for equilibrium through changes in exchange rates need not be self-defeating.

WERE THE 1930S A FAIR TEST OF FLEXIBLE EXCHANGES?

The changes in exchange rates in the 1930s served to discredit flexible exchanges as a means of reaching international equilibrium. It is important to remember, however, that the experiment was conducted under very unfavorable circumstances. In the uncertain and depressed circumstances of the time, the volume of trade was bound to be adversely affected. Whatever system was in existence at the time was likely to become associated with bad times and international uncertainty, even if there was no causal connection between the system and the circumstances.

Without doubt, changes in exchange rates were effectively and correctly discredited as a means of getting all nations out of the slump. When everyone played with more or less equal skill at the game, the resulting competitive devaluations brought no gain to anyone. Undoubtedly, this experience has made *any* use of flexible exchange rates seem dubious. A widespread fear of competitive devaluations persists to this day, and, whenever anyone suggests changes in exchange rates as a means of achieving international equilibrium, others often bring forward the evidence that changes in exchange rates failed to reduce world unemployment in the 1930s and produced only futile rounds of competitive devaluations. The 1930s, however, was a period of particularly extreme conditions. Such conditions do not characterize every disequilibrium in international economic affairs.

8. Under a paper-currency system, a simultaneous devaluation of all currencies has no effect. If, however, the devaluations are accomplished by raising the price of gold, as they must be under a gold standard, then the sole effect is to enrich the gold producers of the world in proportion to the devaluations.

The Postwar Period

In order to achieve a system of orderly exchange rates that would be conducive to the free flow of trade, representatives of the Allied nations met at Bretton Woods, New Hampshire, in 1944 to agree on a system of exchange rates for the postwar world. The one lesson that everyone thought they had learned from the 1930s was that a system either of freely fluctuating exchange rates or of fixed rates with easily accomplished devaluations was the road to disaster in international affairs.

THE INTERNATIONAL MONETARY FUND

What emerged from the Bretton Woods conference was the organization called the International Monetary Fund (also referred to as the IMF or the Fund). The Fund was designed to guarantee the maintenance of fixed exchange rates in the face of short-term fluctuations, and to guarantee that changes in exchange rates would occur only in the face of long-term, persistent deficits or surpluses in the balance of payments and that when such changes did occur they would not spark off a series of competitive devaluations.

Members of the IMF agree to keep a fixed exchange rate between their currencies and the currencies of all other countries. They agree that they will make major changes in this rate (i.e., changes in excess of 10 percent) only in the face of a persistent balance-of-payments disequilibrium and only after consultation with the officials of the Fund. In order to help governments to maintain fixed

rates in the face of temporary fluctuations in imports and exports or speculative movements of short-term capital, the Fund is prepared to lend foreign exchange to members in need of it. A member country that borrows gold or dollars can use it to support its exchange rate by selling these and buying its own currency. Later it hopes to sell its own currency and buy back the gold or dollars in order to repay the loan.[9] The capital for such loans is subscribed by member countries partly in terms of gold and partly in terms of their own currencies.

Without doubt, the operation of the IMF has helped many countries out of temporary balance-of-payments problems that might otherwise have ended in devaluations. There is also no question that the Fund has been a powerful force in favor of maintaining fixed rates of exchange. To economists who think fixed exchange rates are the best system, this appears as an advantage; to those who think fixed rates (with the necessity of restoring equilibrium by changing domestic price levels) is a cumbersome system, it appears as a disadvantage. This is not to say that changes in exchange rates have not occurred. Member countries have changed exchange rates more or less when it suited them and often without prior notice to, let alone consultation with, the Fund.

THE INTERNATIONAL BANK FOR RECONSTRUCTION AND DEVELOPMENT

The other major world financial institution emerging from the conference at Bretton

9. The way in which this works was described in the appendix to Chapter 38.

Woods was the International Bank for Reconstruction and Development (also referred to as the IBRD or the Bank). The Bank was designed to solve the problem of long-term capital movements. There are three ways in which this can be done. The Bank has funds of its own that it can loan to needy countries for development purposes. More important, the Bank can underwrite loans made by developing countries from other sources. Because the Bank has considerable expertise and inside knowledge, its guarantee that a borrower is reasonably sound may make it possible for a developing country to raise loans where otherwise it could not do so. In the process of doing this, the Bank can send investigating missions to the countries concerned and can issue authoritative reports on these countries. Finally, the Bank can itself borrow money in member countries in order to finance its loans.

There is little doubt that the Bank has been a success, although it has been accused of being too conservative in its loan-granting policies. Recently, two new institutions have been established in order to meet the demand for the more risky type of loan. The International Finance Corporation (IFC) is empowered to make loans directly to individual firms and not, like the Bank, only through governmental organizations. The International Development Association (IDA) deals with governments, but makes loans on rather riskier projects than does the IBRD.

These postwar organizations represent a really notable achievement in the field of international cooperation. When one compares them with the ineffectual attempts at cooperation fostered by the League of Nations after World War I, one realizes that, in a very short time, we have come a very long way in the field of international economic cooperation.

THE GENERAL AGREEMENT ON TARIFFS AND TRADE (GATT)

One of the most notable achievements of the postwar world in moving back from the high-water mark of protectionism achieved in the 1930s was the General Agreement on Tariffs and Trade. Under this agreement, GATT countries get together periodically to negotiate bilaterally on mutually advantageous cuts in tariffs. They agree in advance that any tariff cuts negotiated in this way will be extended to all member countries. Some significant tariff reductions have been effected by the member countries, but the total results have fallen far short of the hopes of the founders. Nonetheless, the agreements under GATT have probably prevented nations from solving various short-term problems by increasing tariffs. Although tariffs are not as low as free traders might wish, it is probable that, without this imaginative attempt at postwar cooperation, they would have been higher than they now are.

THE EUROPEAN ECONOMIC COMMUNITY

In 1945, Europe seemed on the verge of famine and collapse. The war-devastated countries were ready to forget their narrow-minded nationalism of the past and engage in a joint effort to meet their common crisis of insufficient food, shelter, and fuel. In 1947, America came forward with the Marshall Plan, which gave U.S. aid and encouragement to the devastated continent. Less than a decade later, the nations of Western Europe were no longer in need of any form of economic aid. Indeed, they were achieving rates of economic growth well above that of the United States, and were on the move toward an economic union that may possibly be the first step in an eventual political union.

The European nations solved the immediate postwar balance-of-payments problems among themselves by an ingenious arrangement called the European Payments Union (EPU). At the same time, they removed national boundaries insofar as these affected the movement of coal, iron, and steel. This required that the cooperating countries harmonize their coal, iron, and steel tax and subsidization policies and adopt a common tariff policy against the outside world. The successes in achieving these goals were critical, since the moves were test cases for the possibility of achieving a completely tariff-free single market on all goods in Europe. The Community is now leading a satisfactory, if not altogether untroubled, existence. Tariff reductions are now being made according to a schedule that will eliminate all tariffs on manufactured goods within the Community by 1970. If the progress continues, Western Europe will be, before the end of the century, a single economic community with a free movement of goods, labor, and capital among the six member countries, Germany, Italy, France, Holland, Belgium, and Luxembourg.

Supporters of the Community suffered a great setback in 1963 when, after months of negotiations, France vetoed Great Britain's application to enter the Community. Nonetheless, the results have been impressive, and there are many who hope, and more than a few who believe, that after economic union has been achieved political union will inevitably follow.

In 1965, a serious crisis developed over agriculture. We saw in Chapter 11 that governments intervene in agricultural markets in many ways and for many purposes. The problems of harmonizing agricultural policies have proved more difficult than those of harmonizing industrial policies. The French have proved even less willing to compromise than they have in the past, and there are many who believe that, as the inevitable loss of some national sovereignty to the higher European Economic Community draws near, the French Government is becoming increasingly reluctant to let the Community go forward. Whatever the reasons, there is no question that the Community is entering a critical phase of its existence. By 1970, it should be possible to see if it will be allowed to develop more or less as originally planned, or if its development will be severely curtailed.

International Payments: Current Problems

The present system of foreign exchange has three basic characteristics. First, currencies are convertible into each other at fixed rates of exchange with only a minimum of interference and restriction by central authorities. Second, balances that arise out of international payments are settled by gold flows between the central authorities of each country. Third, in some, but not all, countries, gold can be bought and sold freely on the open market, the price being maintained by the action of the central authorities in the U.S. This means that the currency of any country can in fact be converted into gold. Gold cannot be bought freely by private citizens in the U.S., but if a holder of dollars wishes gold, he merely buys pounds and then purchases gold on the free market in London.

This means that the British central authorities will accumulate dollars that they may eventually use to purchase gold from the U.S. authorities.

We discussed the problems of maintaining a fixed exchange rate in Chapter 38. Basically, the central authorities stand prepared to support the price of their own currency by buying it themselves whenever necessary and supplying foreign exchange in return. This means that reserves of foreign exchange must be held by these authorities. Normally, the reserves are held in two forms, gold and certain key *reserve currencies,* mainly the U.S. dollar and the British pound. Central authorities are prepared to hold reserves in the form of dollars and pounds because they are satisfied that these currencies will be convertible into any required currency or into gold at a fixed price on demand.

The problems of having one's currency used as a reserve currency are many. Two of the most important are discussed below. First, a constraint is put on the central authorities that makes it difficult for them to devalue the currency in order to adjust the balance of payments. If a country has a persistent balance-of-payments deficit due to the overvaluing of its currency, it may need to correct the situation by devaluation.[10] If other countries are holding their reserves in the form of this country's currency (or claims of any sort valued in this country's currency), the devaluation will lower the value of these reserves in proportion to the devaluation. If, for example, the British pound is devalued by 10 percent, then the dollar or gold value of the sterling reserves held in London by the Indian central authorities falls by 10 percent. If the U.S. central authorities devalue the dollar by 10 percent, then the gold value of the dollar reserves held by the French central authorities falls by 10 percent. Thus the devaluation of a key currency is more serious than is the devaluation of some other currency, such as the German mark, which is not held in large quantities as part of the foreign-exchange reserves of any country. Second, a key currency can be put under heavy pressure because of speculations over other currencies. For example, throughout the mid-1950s, Germany ran a persistent balance-of-payments surplus; in 1957, the belief spread that the German central authorities were going to correct this situation by raising the exchange value of the mark. This led to a speculative move to buy marks, which could be sold again at a substantial profit if the revaluation did occur. This meant that people holding reserves in dollars and sterling attempted to transfer these into marks. Since large volumes of sterling were held, there was a large volume of sales of sterling, and the British central authorities were hard put to maintain the value of sterling under this heavy selling.[11] Thus we see that the central authorities of a country whose currency is a reserve currency need to have access to very large reserves in case there is a sudden desire on the part of others to transfer their exchange holdings into some other currency, even if only for a short time.

ADJUSTING TO SHORT-TERM DISEQUILIBRIA

One of the most serious problems arising out of the present system of international payments is how to maintain fixed exchange rates in the face of short-term fluctuations

10. The only other thing that it can do is to restrict purchases of foreign exchange by some exchange-control scheme.

11. The American authorities held such large gold reserves that they could not be embarrassed by any *temporary* move to sell dollars.

in the balance of payments both on current account (caused by short-term fluctuations in imports and exports) and on capital account (caused by speculative movements of short-term capital). We have seen that, in order to stabilize the exchange value of one's currency, the central authorities buy or sell foreign exchange when the price threatens to move outside of predetermined narrow limits. In order to be able to operate this policy successfully, the central authorities need to have adequate stocks of gold or reserve currencies. These foreign-exchange reserves must be adequate to meet any temporary excess demand for foreign exchange due to an excess of imports over exports or to an outward movement of capital.

One of the major drawbacks of this system is that speculative movements of capital tend to accentuate any imbalance on current account and thus to make the system less stable than it otherwise would be. If some temporary increase in imports or decrease in exports makes the demand for foreign currency unduly large and if this temporary fluctuation persists a little longer than usual, reserves will be run down to a level lower than is usual. Once reserves get so low that people begin to suspect that the authorities will be unable to support the existing exchange rate, a speculative flight of capital out of the currency will occur. People with money to hold will want to obtain some other currency whose value seems more secure, and people who plan to buy the suspect currency will postpone their purchases wherever possible in the hope of getting the currency cheaper after the devaluation. These quite natural speculative movements increase the drain of foreign-exchange reserves and may force a devaluation that might otherwise not have been required.

One does not, of course, need to cry panic whenever one country loses some of its re-serves. This is what reserves are for. Their function is to offset imbalances arising in abnormal situations. Serious problems arise only when the reserves threaten to be exhausted before a temporary balance-of-payments fluctuation is reversed. Or, to be more precise, serious problems arise when individuals *think* reserves are about to be exhausted, for, once they think this, a speculative flight will develop that can easily exhaust the remaining reserves.

In order to be able to weather short-term fluctuations, central authorities need adequate stocks of foreign-exchange reserves in the form of gold and key currencies. Many countries have been getting along with very small reserves. They have thus found themselves in situations in which quite small fluctuations in demand for, or supply of, foreign exchange could cause a crisis by draining away too high a proportion of total reserves.

How can the countries of the world solve this problem of "international liquidity"? One cause of the problem is the fact that a very high proportion of the world's gold reserves are held in America. The U.S. central authorities have gold reserves far in excess of what they need to meet any short-term fluctuation in the U.S. balance of payments. For this reason, the U.S. payments deficit in the last decade, although troublesome to U.S. authorities, has been a good thing for the world, since the loss of (excessive) U.S. reserves of gold has meant an addition to the (inadequate) reserves of other countries.

The International Monetary Fund produced a great increase in liquidity by pooling the contributions of member nations and making these available to members who are in temporary balance-of-payments difficulties. But international liquidity is still judged by many to be inadequate, and recently there has been a great deal of thinking about what can be done to alleviate the problem. Probably the best-known plan for accomplishing this end is the *Triffin Plan,* named after its author, Professor Robert Triffin of Yale University.

The Triffin Plan is closely related to the proposals that were made by John Maynard Keynes for an International Clearing Union —proposals that were largely rejected when the IMF was established. The Triffin Plan proposes to convert the IMF into a world central bank.[12] The principal features of the plan are as follows: Each member country's reserves would include deposits at the IMF denominated in terms of a new unit of account. A minimum demand for these deposits would be created by requiring all countries to hold 20 percent of their official reserves in this form. The initial supply of deposits would be created by converting 20 percent of members' existing reserves—mainly in gold, dollars, and sterling—into the new deposits and by a further deposit of all sterling and dollar balances remaining in official reserves. Intermember payments would normally be made in terms of IMF deposits. (Under the Keynes plan this was the only way that deposits could be used, but the Triffin Plan allows for the conversion of deposits into the member's national currency or, at the Fund's option, into gold.) To ensure that the growing demands of world trade could be met, the IMF could increase its deposits by buying gold or, through loans (at its own discretion) and buying and selling securities, by acquiring further amounts of member countries' currencies. The size of the annual increase in deposits is agreed upon in advance, and increases in excess of the agreed level would require qualified majority votes. This provision was to meet one of the main criticisms of the Keynes plan—i.e., that it was inflationary. As long as, say, a two-thirds majority of countries have to agree on an increase over and above the normal average increase, it is hoped

that the likelihood of irresponsible inflationary action would be rendered minimal.

ADJUSTING TO LONG-TERM DISEQUILIBRIA

Fixed exchange rates also pose a problem of how to adjust to long-run changes in trading relations. The domestic price levels (and hence the export prices) of the various trading countries change for many reasons internal to the countries concerned. If all price levels do not move in line with each other, the rates of exchange that will equilibrate foreign payments must constantly be changing. In general, the equilibrium value of the currency of countries whose price level is rising fastest will be falling, while the equilibrium value of the currency of countries whose price level is rising slowest will be rising. (See Chapter 38, p. 437.)

In a system of fixed exchange rates where the equilibrium rates are changing continuously but the actual rates are not, we must expect a situation of more or less continuous payments disequilibria. These disequilibria will be linked together, because the very act of one country solving its disequilibrium is likely to cause a disequilibrium in some other country. This prediction has indeed been borne out by the postwar experience.

The ten years after World War II were unique in that the whole world tended to be in a balance-of-payments deficit to the U.S., which was in a position of chronic surplus. This "dollar shortage" was a result of the war, which left the United States as one of the few suppliers of manufactured goods still able to produce at a high rate. Europe, with her industries in ruins, needed goods for current consumption as well as capital goods to rebuild her consumption-goods industries. But until more goods could be produced in Europe,

12. For a full description of central banks, see Chapter 53.

there was little to export in return for the much-needed imports. For ten years, the dollar problem dominated the international-payments position. Countries just could not earn enough dollars through sales to the U.S. to pay for all the goods they wanted to buy from the U.S. The problem went on for so long that some economists thought it was endemic— that it would be with us forever.

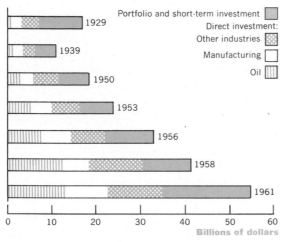

FIGURE 1 TOTAL U.S. PRIVATE INVESTMENT ABROAD

No sooner had other countries got used to accepting the dollar shortage as a fact of life than it ended! During the 1950s, productive capacity grew at a phenomenal rate in Europe and, as it did, the ability to sell to the U.S. grew and the need to buy from the U.S. shrank. At the same time, U.S. investment abroad rose at a very rapid rate, as Figure 1 indicates. As a result of both of these developments, the nations of the world one by one found themselves no longer in a chronic payments deficit to the U.S.

The dollar problem was hardly solved when the problem arose of the U.S. gold drain. In-

stead of having a chronic surplus, the U.S. began to have a chronic deficit on the balance of payments. We have already mentioned that this was not disastrous in the short run. A redistribution of the world's gold stock helped the liquidity position of other countries without doing any real harm to the U.S. The gold drain could not, of course, go on forever, and, unless things changed of their own accord, something would have to be done. In fact, mild restrictions were placed on tourist expenditure abroad (by cutting the value of goods a tourist could bring back duty free), and considerable reductions were made in the volume of overseas military and aid expenditures.

In attempting to solve its balance-of-payments problems, the U.S. did not, nor could it be expected to, discriminate among countries. This means, however, that as the U.S. moves back into a payments equilibrium by reducing foreign expenditure and increasing foreign receipts, those countries that were in the smallest surplus position will be pushed into a deficit: The disequilibrium, in other words, is merely transferred abroad. The severe foreign-exchange problems of some European countries, particularly Britain during 1964 and 1965, were partly the direct result of the changes that reduced the deficit in the U.S. balance of payments. Indeed, as long as the world is, for better or for worse, committed to fixed rates of exchange, and as long as the fixed rates are not the equilibrium ones (and as long as price levels are constantly changing at different rates in different countries for reasons unrelated to the balance of payments, we cannot expect any fixed set of rates to remain the equilibrium ones for any long period of time), we must expect a permanent balance-of-payments problem to exist and to be passed around from country to country. As soon as one country solves its problem, another will inherit it. When this inheritor cuts imports or expands exports to solve its problem, some other country will find its imports rising and its exports falling and it will move into a period of deficit.

Fixed Versus Fluctuating Rates

To what extent are all the problems described above the result of having fixed exchange rates? Would not the "problem" of international liquidity disappear if exchange rates were left to be determined on a free market? Why, in a market society, where most people accept the case for leaving prices and quantities free to be determined by demand and supply, do we feel that this one price should be rigidly controlled by the central authorities? Advocates of free-exchange rates argue that the whole set of postwar problems, such as shortage of reserves and restrictions on trade caused by chronic imbalances in payments, are of our own making and would disappear overnight if we only abandoned the arbitrary government control of this one key market—the market for foreign exchange. If the free market were allowed to operate, then, when a country's currency turned out to be overvalued, the value would be reduced automatically by the forces of the free market. The value would continue to fall until the equilibrium exchange rate was achieved. No exchange reserves would be needed, since governments would not be trying to restrict movements in exchange rates. There would be no problem of international liquidity. It is also argued that the activities of speculators would tend to stabilize the rate of exchange. If there was a temporary rise in imports, demand for foreign exchange would rise and the price of foreign exchange would rise. If speculators saw this change to be temporary, they would sell the expensive foreign exchange and buy the cheap domestic currency. Thus the change in demand on the part of speculators would be in the opposite direction from the change in demand on the part of importers, and the former would partially offset the effects of the latter.

The opponents of free-market rates reply that the fluctuations in exchange rates would add greatly to the uncertainty of persons engaged in international trade and would greatly lower the volume of trade as a result.[13]

The next step in the argument, the student might expect, would be to cite evidence. Although numerous works exist arguing the case one way or the other on intuitive grounds, there has been little significant work attempting to assess the argument quantitatively. All business is subject to numerous risks, and we do not have any careful study of how significant would be the added risks of the possibility of fluctuations in the exchange rates. To know this, we would need to know by how much we expected the rate to fluctuate from week to week and how the uncertainty involved compared to the other uncertainties of business. The student who consults a series of standard textbooks and

13. Others argue that international elasticities are so low that the free market would not work (see Chapter 38, page 435, footnote 2). Recent empirical research does not lend much support to this view.

specialized works on the subject will find many of the authors taking a variety of strong and mutually inconsistent positions on this problem. Some dismiss free rates as a product of the diseased imagination of the theorist, and others accept them as the obvious cure to the world's problems. The only thing that the whole debate seems to illustrate is that the less that is known, the greater is the certainty with which people hold to particular views about what is and is not correct. Not all of them can be right.

There is one bit of evidence: Canada adopted a fluctuating rate for the decade 1952–1962. Opponents of free rates are quick to argue that the experience of one country is not relevant to what would happen if the whole world were on a free-market system.[14] What the experience did show was, first, that the day-to-day fluctuations in a free-market exchange rate could be very small—indeed, they might be no larger than they are when the rate is pegged within narrow limits, and, second, that the uncertainties introduced by the fluctuations actually occurring did not have a sufficient disincentive effect on trade as to be observable.

The next thing the student might well ask is: "If we regard the evidence as inconclusive and if fluctuating rates seem to have worked once, why do we not experiment with them again? The worst that could happen would be that the experiment would fail, in which case we would be forced back to the present system." This is a very hard question to answer. Individuals and governmental organizations are noticeably reluctant to experiment in economic matters. The rational case against experimentation would have to show that the losses during the few years necessary for the experiment (two or three) would be so large if it did not work as to overweigh the possible gains over the indefinite future if it did work. So far, however, no one has even tried to guess what these losses might be.

In our view, the evidence does not allow one to take a strong stand on the superiority of fixed rates over fluctuating ones, or vice versa. There is, however, fairly general agreement among the policy-makers of the world that fixed rates are superior, and there is little doubt that the present system will be continued in the indefinite future. The assessment of whether or not the system is a good one or a very bad one will probably have to wait for the researches of future generations of economists who can be more detached in studying it than can those who are already committed to a specific answer.

The world of international economic relations is in some ways a topsy-turvy one. It is a world that awaits someone who will do for it what Keynes did for domestic unemployment: remove forever the necessity of accepting crises as inevitable and beyond the power of governments to solve for once and for all.

---

14.   The economist should immediately ask, "Why?" If we dismissed evidence merely because it came from a different time or place, we would admit no evidence whatsoever. Evidence can only be dismissed as irrelevant if our theory specifies that, under certain conditions, one result will occur and that, under other conditions, another result will occur and if the evidence can be shown to have been generated by the wrong set of conditions.

Summary

1. Restoring equilibrium in international payments in a free-market world requires a change in the relative prices of the goods sold by various countries. There are two basic ways to effect this change: through changes in exchange rates, or through changes in domestic price levels. The system of fluctuating rates, which we studied in Chapter 38, would bring about equilibrium in the first way; the gold standard was supposed to work in the second way.

2. In the period after World War I, the gold standard failed and was abandoned. In the period prior to World War II, fluctuating exchange rates were experimented with. After the war, the one lesson that everyone thought was to be drawn from the 1930s was that a system of either freely fluctuating exchange rates or of fixed rates with easily accomplished devaluations was the road to disaster. The Allied nations met in 1944 to discuss a new system, and from their meeting came the International Monetary Fund, which was designed to guarantee the maintenance of fixed exchange rates in the face of short-term fluctuations. They also set up the International Bank for Reconstruction and Development, which was designed to solve the problem of long-term capital movements.

3. A further attempt at postwar cooperation was GATT, the General Agreement on Tariffs and Trade, which was an agreement that mutually advantageous cuts in tariffs negotiated between any two member countries would be extended to all member countries.

4. One of the most outstanding moves in the period since the war has been that toward a united Europe and the establishment of the European Economic Community.

5. The present system of fixed exchange rates means that the central authorities must stand prepared to support the price of their own currency. Reserves for this support are normally held in gold and certain "key currencies," mainly the dollar and the pound. The authorities of a country whose currency is a reserve currency need to have access to very large reserves.

6. Although the establishment of the IMF produced a great increase in international liquidity by pooling the contributions of member nations and making these available to members who are in temporary difficulties, there is still a problem of insufficient international liquidity. Perhaps the best-known plan for overcoming this is the Triffin Plan.

7. There is also the problem of adjusting to long-term disequilibria. At the start of the postwar period, there was a dollar shortage, because America had a persistent payments surplus. This then changed to a situation in which America faced a chronic payments deficit, which aided other countries. The U.S., however, will eventually move toward balance (the gold drain cannot go on forever); when it does, other countries will suffer. We will find, in a system of fixed rates, that balance-of-payments problems move from one country to another.

8. There has been a long controversy over how many present problems could be solved, and how many would be aggravated, by moving to a system of fluctuating exchange rates. It appears that sufficient evidence does not exist to enable us to settle this issue at the present time.

QUESTIONS FOR DISCUSSION

1. What institutions of international cooperation came out of the conferences at the end of World War II? Why did countries want to set up these organizations?

2. Why is Britain more susceptible to the effects of expectations and rumors about its foreign exchange than is, say, France?

3. What is the Triffin Plan, and what problems is it intended to help solve?

4. "After World War II, the Allies, at Bretton Woods, set up an International Fund, which is a bank, and an International Bank, which is a fund." What is the purpose of the two organizations? Does the quotation describe what happened?

5. One hears a great deal about the "Kennedy Round" of negotiations, which members of GATT participate in. What is the organization? What is its purpose? What are the members negotiating?

6. Explain the economics behind the following *New York Times* headlines:
a. "U.S. Repayments Problem Remains Serious Despite Gains"
b. "Import Duty Rise Pressed in India"
c. "Yugoslavians say 'Ouch' over Devaluation"
d. "France Boycotts First Day of Common Market Negotiations"

7. What are the principal objections to fluctuating exchange rates? What evidence do we have?

8. The great majority of American economists support the European Economic Community, yet about 50 percent of British economists were opposed to Britain's application to enter. Can you think of any sensible reasons, economic or otherwise, for this strong opposition to what seems such an obviously desirable attempt to reap the advantages of the gains from trade?

THE MARKET ECONOMY AS A WHOLE

Chapter 42 THE NOTION OF GENERAL
EQUILIBRIUM: INTERACTIONS AMONG MARKETS

WHY IS IT THAT, WHEN A NEW FIRM DECIDES to start operating, it finds enough labor for its needs? Why is it that, when a man relocates for a new job, he eventually finds suitable housing? Why is it that, when the space program is accelerated, all the countless requirements—including even the increased production of minerals and other strategic materials—are met? These questions should sound familiar, for we have been discussing them (or ones like them) throughout this book. But heretofore we have treated individual markets as if they were functioning more or less in isolation. This was, of course,

a very great simplification. The economy does not consist of a series of self-contained markets functioning in isolation. It is to be viewed instead as an interlocking system in which anything happening in one market will greatly affect other markets, and could, potentially, affect every other market in the economy. This interaction is represented pictorially in Figure 1. We start by considering some *sector* of the economy—possibly the market for cabbages or for carpenters or for bicycles—and we call this sector A. If there is some change in sector A, this will cause changes in the rest of the economy,

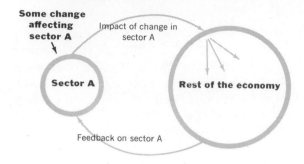

FIGURE 1

and these changes will in turn *reflect back* on sector *A*, causing further changes in that sector. Let us assume, for example, that the initial change in sector *A* is a fall in the supply of cabbages. This will cause an increase in their price and a fall in the quantity bought. The rise in the price of cabbages will cause other demands to change; in general, we would expect to find an increase in the demand for goods that are close substitutes for cabbages and a decrease in the demand for goods that are complementary with cabbages. As a result, the prices of all these other goods will change. These are the induced changes in the rest of the economy. The original demand curve for cabbages, which we used to derive our prediction, was based on the assumption that all other prices were given. Now, however, prices of substitutes for cabbages have risen and this will cause a *shift* in our original demand curve for cabbages. This is the *reflection back* (or, technically, *feedback*) of the induced changes in the rest of the economy on to the original sector.

The Distinction Between Partial and General Equilibrium Analysis

The basic assumption of *partial equilibrium analysis* is that the feedbacks on a sector are small enough that they may be neglected. *General equilibrium analysis,* on the other hand, explicitly allows for such feedbacks.

All partial equilibrium analyses are based on the assumption of *ceteris paribus*. Strictly interpreted, the assumption is that all other things in the economy are unaffected by any changes in the sector under consideration (sector *A*). This assumption is always violated to some extent, for anything that happens in one sector must cause changes in some other sectors. What matters is that the changes induced throughout the rest of the economy are sufficiently small and diffuse so that the effects they in turn have on sector *A* can safely be ignored. There is no simple rule telling us when partial analysis can safely be employed. The final test is in whether or not the predictions of partial theory are refuted by the facts.

Partial equilibrium analysis is useful because economists have found that for many kinds of decisions the external effects are relatively small, and the feedbacks negligible. As a first approximation, we may say that the smaller the sector under consideration, the more likely it is that feedbacks will prove to be negligible. Let a hotel chain raise its prices for rooms, and the principle effects will be those that can be predicted by assuming the chain to have a stable, downward-sloping demand curve for the rooms that it rents. Of course, those people who do pay the higher prices for rooms in hotels run by this chain will have less money for other things, and, assuming the demand for hotel rooms to be inelastic, some other industries will find that their sales fall off a bit, which may lead their employees and owners to travel less, and thus to decrease (i.e., shift to the left) the demand for hotel accommodations. It is probable that these particular feedbacks will be negligible.

There are also many instances when the feedbacks are large; to neglect them in these cases will invite serious error. If the steel industry raises its prices, the costs in most U.S. manufacturing industries will rise, and the chain of repercussion may very well feed back in a nonnegligible way on the demand for steel.

Figure 2 summarizes this discussion. In

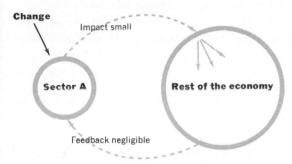

case (i) Partial equilibrium analysis is possible

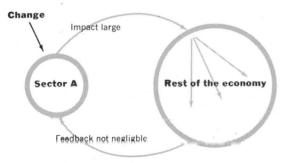

case (ii) General equilibrium analysis is necessary

FIGURE 2

the case pictured in Figure 2 (i), the initial change affects sector A, but there are only small impacts on the rest of the economy and the feedback is negligible. Partial equilibrium analysis is adequate. In Figure 2 (ii), the same initial change has a larger secondary effect on the rest of the economy, and the induced feedback to sector A cannot safely be ignored.[1]

Economists are interested in general equilibrium analysis because they want to understand how the economy functions as a whole. To do this, it is necessary to examine the way changes in one sector are absorbed and accommodated. So far we have studied the causes and consequences of disequilibria in particular markets, but we have not faced the question of whether or not there exists a general equilibrium of the whole economy at which point all markets could simultaneously be in a position in which demand equals supply. There is a difference between what is possible in one market and what is possible in the whole economy. If, for example, you suddenly decide that you want a new car, it is a simple matter (provided you have the money) to go out and buy it. But everybody cannot do what anybody can do, even if each one is equally able. If a million others like you simultaneously decide that they want a new car, most of them will be disappointed. First, they will find that all the salesmen are busy. Then they will find that the price has risen— dealers will be offering lower trade-ins or lower discounts. Some potential buyers will be told that they will have to wait weeks or months or even years for delivery.[2] All of this is only one part of the story. Although an economy may respond in the short run to

1. Indeed, this feedback may lead to a second cycle; it induces a further change in sector *A* and then in the rest of the economy, which again causes feedbacks, etc.
2. In 1946 and 1947, waits of ten to eighteen months for delivery were common.

changes in demand of this kind only by raising price and rationing goods, in the longer run it will make an attempt to produce more cars. But if more resources are used to produce cars, less of something else must be produced (unless more resources can be obtained). How do the necessary changes come about? Whose decisions contribute to them? Does the final result provide an allocation of resources that is in some sense satisfactory? If so, does the adjustment occur in a quick and orderly way? These are some of the big questions for the study of which general equilibrium analysis is necessary.

Generality Versus Comprehensiveness

A so-called general theory looks at the full set of interactions among a specified set of variables that are believed to interact with one another; a so-called partial theory neglects some of the interactions. If one wants to talk about all the prices in the economy, and all the outputs, a general equilibrium theory is very complex indeed.[3] But a theory can also be general and embrace only a very few variables. For example, consider the following general equilibrium theory:

1. The demand for peanuts depends upon the price of peanuts and the price of crackerjacks.

2. The demand for crackerjacks depends upon the price of crackerjacks and the price of peanuts.

3. The supply of peanuts depends upon the price of peanuts and the price of crackerjacks.

4. The supply of crackerjacks depends upon the price of crackerjacks and the price of peanuts.

5. The demand for peanuts must equal the supply of peanuts at equilibrium.

6. The demand for crackerjacks must equal the supply of crackerjacks at equilibrium.

This is a general equilibrium theory: Each of the six variables (two prices, two quantities demanded, and two quantities supplied) depends directly or indirectly upon each of the other five.† But this theory is not very *comprehensive*, because it neglects entirely lots of other things that might affect these variables—such as the price of cashew nuts. By way of contrast, the following theory is a partial theory:

The demand for peanuts is a function of the price of peanuts, the price of crackerjacks, the price of cashew nuts, and the price of admission to baseball games.

---

3. The great classic by Leon Walras, *Elements of Pure Economics*, is of this kind. The English translation of the definitive edition is by William Jaffe (Richard D. Irwin, 1954). The first edition of the original was published in 1874.

† Using the subscript 1 to designate peanuts and the subscript 2 to designate crackerjacks, and the letters D, S, and p to represent quantity demand, quantity supplied, and price, respectively, we may write our theory as a system of six equations:

$$D_1 = D_1\,(p_1, p_2) \qquad (1) \qquad\qquad S_2 = S_2\,(p_1, p_2) \qquad (4)$$
$$D_2 = D_2\,(p_1, p_2) \qquad (2) \qquad\qquad D_1 = S_1 \qquad (5)$$
$$S_1 = S_1\,(p_1, p_2) \qquad (3) \qquad\qquad D_2 = S_2 \qquad (6)$$

This is a system of simultaneous equations, with six equations and six unknowns. The general equilibrium values of the variables are those that satisfy all six of the equations at the same time.

It is partial because it does not allow for interactions and feedbacks; it is, however, more comprehensive in that it allows more variables to enter into the determination of the demand for peanuts.†

Is Generality a Virtue?

Generality is not in itself a virtue. It is sometimes asserted that "everything depends on everything else." For example, it may be said that the quantity demanded of any one commodity depends on the price of that commodity and on the prices of *all* other commodities. Consider what such a statement might mean. First, it might be an hypothesis about the world, in which case it is open to testing. Second, it might mean that everything could conceivably depend on everything else, in which case it is trite. Third, it might mean that everything is *known* to depend on everything else, in which case it is wrong, for, whether or not this is true, it certainly has not been established conclusively.

Consider (for the last time) the demand for peanuts. We might say that the demand for peanuts is a function of each of 285 different variables. This would be a very comprehensive theory. If, in addition, we said that each of these 285 other variables depended upon each other and upon the demand for peanuts, we would have a general theory as well. In practice, such theories will prove to be useless because we will not be able (within the foreseeable future) to obtain sufficient empirical knowledge of *the way in which* the demand for any good is influenced by the prices of most other goods. Conceptually, it is often useful to start from theories that remind us that the economy is complex and that, conceivably, anything might be influenced by anything else, but we must then observe that, in practice, most of the influences are likely to be negligible. Consider, for example, the effect on the demand for peanuts of a change in the price of cotton shirts.

In constructing a theory that will have empirical content, and thus will be useful in the real world, we start by removing *most* of the variables from a thoroughly general and comprehensive theory. Conceivably, every price in the economy might influence peanut demand, but, so the theory will run, only two or three (or possibly six or eight) prices really matter; the effects of the others are negligible and can be ignored. Now the theorist will go on to build a theory based on these simplifying assumptions and to test it against real-world observations. On the other hand, a theory that says that everything influences everything else will be so general that all it is likely to predict (in the absence of a truly vast amount of empirical knowledge) is that "anything can happen." A theory that picks out a few possible relations as the critical ones will not cover all conceivable cases, but it may work in dealing with the cases that actually occur.

There is no virtue in an uncritical application of the view that "general equilibrium is better than partial equilibrium and the

---

† Here we are specifying as our theory $D_1 = D_1 (p_1, p_2, p_3, p_4)$. Comparing this with equation (1) in the previous footnote, you will notice that this is a more comprehensive theory of demand for peanuts, but it is not a general equilibrium system. If p_1 changes, it directly changes D_1, but we neglect any indirect effect a change in p_1 may have on D_1, via its effect on p_2, p_3, or p_4.

more general the better." Usefulness and applicability come from the selection of the salient features and the most important relations. Refusing to make such a selection means refusing to make one's theory applicable to real-world situations.

This does not mean that general equilibrium analysis is useless. Indeed, for some problems, it is essential: The interactions are too large to be ignored. But it is usefulness and applicability, not generality, that is the basis for choosing a theory.

Interactions Within the Economy: An Example

In the period 1962–1964, the demand for automobiles in the U.S. expanded rapidly. As automobile manufacturers responded to increases in demand by increasing production, they required more steel, more tires, more chrome, and so on. Thus, demands increased for the products of many industries, and, as these industries expanded production, the demands increased for the goods and services that these industries use in production. For a time, increased production could be met by the existing capacity. But the expansion in demand was large and was believed to be long-lasting; thus it led producers to make plans to invest in new capacity. As part of the response to this rise in demand, the Chrysler Corporation decided to build a huge new assembly plant in Belvidere, Illinois. From the vantage point of 1965, let us consider some of the further repercussions of this decision.

Belvidere is a small town of 11,000 in the northwest corner of Illinois, 70 miles from Chicago and 40 miles from Rockford (population 160,000). The new assembly plant will require 5,000 workers. These workers, with their families, represent roughly 15,000 people. Where is the labor to come from? Neither Rockford nor Belvidere has any sig-

nificant number of unemployed workers; both are classified as labor-tight areas. But the Chrysler Corporation does not appear to be worried about getting its required labor force. Its optimism here probably results from the fact that it is introducing a wage rate that is substantially above the one prevailing in the area.[4]

Some of the new plant's workers will come from more distant areas, in response to the availability of well-paying jobs. These workers will require housing that is not now available, and they will add enough to the population of Rockford and Belvidere to make more food stores, more barbershops, and more movie theaters necessary. Will they be forthcoming? Chrysler assumes they will. The extra people represent extra business opportunities, and possible profits, and it is expected that someone will find it worthwhile to provide the needed facilities. Indeed, some of this expansion is occurring in *anticipation* of the shortages that will develop with the sudden population increase. Other required expansions will come only after the shortages develop. Present indications are that the supply of housing is one of them. As shortages develop, present landlords will raise rents and make higher profits, and others will be

---

4. Its wage rate is the national rate for automobile workers, since it and all the other automobile manufacturers engage in company-wide bargaining with the United Automobile Workers.

encouraged to cash in on the good opportunity by building houses to rent or to sell. This discussion has concerned only those goods and services provided privately. But the new plant will also mean that Belvidere will need more policemen, more schoolrooms, and more teachers. The impetus for providing schools, for example, will come, in response to overcrowded classes, from school boards that will try to persuade the city councils to issue bonds or to spend tax revenue on new schools and new teachers.[5]

On the other hand, some of the labor for staffing the new plant will come from the existing population of the area. Men will quit lower paying jobs in Rockford and Belvidere and commute to the new plant from their old homes, thereby increasing the demand for gasoline, tires, and automobiles. Their former employers will have to raise the wages they pay or they will lose some of their labor force. But this will increase their costs. Some may go out of business or move to lower wage areas; others will survive, but probably will end up producing less at higher prices. They may look for ways to improve their operations. For some others, the increased spending that the new plant brings

to the community may offset the increases in cost. And so on. There is virtually no end to the number of further steps one can enumerate in the chain of repercussions.

So far we have shown that this one decision made by the Chrysler Corporation will have major consequences in many other markets. In terms of Figure 2, we have shown the top arrow to be as drawn in Figure 2 (ii), rather than as in Figure 2 (i). To show that we have a genuine general equilibrium problem, we must also show that the changes in these other markets will reflect back on automobile markets in significant ways. This is a difficult thing to do, and we could not even guess at the feedback effect without a very detailed specification of all the effects we have been outlining. Certainly, some local automobile markets will be greatly affected. Although automobile sales in Belvidere will rise considerably, migration of workers from other areas may lower sales in these other areas. An increase in national automobile sales could also occur if the increase in employment in the automobile industry brings more employees into the income range at which they will buy a new automobile, rather than a secondhand one.

Interactions and the Functioning of the Economy

The changes we have predicted (in the Belvidere example and in general) occur because of the responses of individuals and firms to certain signals that serve to induce resource flows: changes in prices, wages, and profits. Adaptations to the initial shift take

place without being consciously coordinated by some single central authority. When shortages develop, prices and profits rise, and profit-seeking entrepreneurs are led to produce more of the goods in short supply. When surpluses occur, profits fall, and supply is

---

5. It is curious that most cities and states look forward to the increase in the tax receipts that new development will provide, but fail to anticipate the expanded services that *they* will need to provide. There is no substantial empirical evidence to indicate that industrial development ends up by lowering tax rates.

voluntarily contracted. The price system produces a series of automatic signals, and a large number of different decision-making units (firms and households) do, in fact, coordinate their efforts.

The price system was not consciously created. With a price system, it is not necessary to foresee and to coordinate all necessary changes: Such changes occur automatically as a result of the separate decisions made by a large number of individuals, each seeking his own private profit, but all responding to changes in demands and prices.

Once you have grasped this idea, beware of jumping to the conclusion that the price system has been shown to be the *best* system of regulating the economy; beware of equating the word automatic, which we have used, with the phrase "perfectly functioning," which we have not used. It is easy enough to control the heat in your house by means of an automatic thermostatic control, but it is also possible to have such a badly designed or imperfectly functioning system that the heat control you actually achieve is worse

than you would have had by stoking up and damping down by hand. To observe that the price system functions automatically, i.e., without conscious centralized coordination, does not tell us how well it functions. In the case of the "cobweb" (see pages 138–141), we saw how the automatic working of the price system can produce violent fluctuations in price and output. The theory of the price system is the subject of a large part of this book; the problem of assessing the *efficiency* of this automatic system, particularly in comparison with the efficiency of other systems, is a most important problem that belongs to a more advanced course in economics.

All of the above has suggested the type of interactions that occur in an economy, and the existence of a mechanism that leads to flows of resources to meet changed conditions. It does not really answer the hard questions: "Does an equilibrium set of values exist?" "What are the properties of general equilibrium solutions?" "What is the process by which a system moves when out of equilibrium?" To answer these requires more mathematical tools than most beginning students have and thus must be left to a more advanced course.[6]

Empirical Knowledge About General Equilibrium

The theory of general equilibrium consists in statements such as: "It can be proved that if such and such conditions exist in the economy, an equilibrium will exist toward which the economy will move; if nothing else changes, the economy will eventually reach this equilibrium." Propositions of this sort are

mathematical deductions; if the mathematics is sound, the propositions cannot be disproved.

In evaluating whether such a theory is helpful in understanding the real world, there are two difficulties: first, the "such and such conditions" almost surely will not be found

---

6. Since general equilibrium analysis involves interactions among sectors, it involves systems of simultaneous equations. The problems of solving large sets of equations may prove formidable.

to exist exactly. Second, other things do not stay constant long enough to permit us to observe whether shortages and surpluses eventually disappear. Does this mean that the theory is empty? It is, in this form; but it can be made testable.

Suppose we advance the hypothesis that the U.S. economy in 1966 possesses a general equilibrium toward which it is moving. Whether or not such an equilibrium exists is a question of fact that observation cannot easily answer: We observe that there *are* shortages and surpluses, but this only demonstrates that we are not in a position of equilibrium, and it tells us neither that equilibrium is impossible nor that it is possible. Moreover, we cannot wait five years to see if the U.S. economy reaches equilibrium, because many things will change in five years and each change will set up its own chain of repercussions.

One of the simplest ways to provide some test of the hypothesis is to assume that a general equilibrium exists and to attempt to deduce the equilibrium values of things that we *can* measure. If our assumption is valid, and if our hypothesis is correct, we can predict the directions in which actual magnitudes will be changing. For example, we might predict that labor will move from the farms and coal-mining regions to the areas of labor shortage. If we observe no such movements, our hypothesis is refuted. In fact, we do observe such movements, but at rates that are rather slow, and this leaves us in some doubt about the validity of our hypothesis.

This approach is quite limited in the information it provides about the workings of the economy; in recent decades a number of more ambitious approaches have been tried.

The most famous formulation of a general equilibrium system suitable for empirical testing is Professor W. Leontief's.[7] His pioneering work on the structure of the American economy has resulted in empirical measurements of the interrelations in the economy. These measurements allow us to predict the effects throughout the economy of changes in any one sector. The theoretical structure of *input-output models* (as they are called) is based on many simplifications. The basic unit is a broadly defined *industry* (or sector) that is assumed to use both labor and the products of other industries. It is assumed that industries use their inputs in fixed proportions. This assuming away of the possibility of factor substitutability (see Chapter 18) is done in order to focus on the adjustments among sectors and the nature of equilibrium solutions. Actual interrelations are measured and then used to predict the outcome of various changes in the economy. Performance of *input-output* models in predicting the behavior of market economics has been moderately satisfactory over short periods of time. Over longer periods, the absence of factor substitution causes considerable difficulties.

Input-output analysis (and its generalizations)[8] has become an important part of empirical economics, particularly in answering such questions as, "If we attempt to expand output of military and space products at such and such a rate, where will bottlenecks develop?" And, "What is the maximum output, given present techniques and patterns of use, that we can achieve with existing known quantities of factors?"

Input-output measures, when applied to

7. See Wassily W. Leontief, *The Structure of the American Economy* (2d ed.; Oxford University Press, 1951).
8. These generalizations are called mathematical programming.

some of the problems of both underdeveloped and planned economies, prove to be extremely valuable. In planning, it is desirable to be able to foresee all the major effects of certain measures. An *input-output table* of the actual interrelations thus becomes an important piece of apparatus for the central planner.

Another relatively new approach to measuring the behavior of complex general equilibrium systems is to use *simulation models*.[9] In essence, the approach builds an artificial and simplified representation or model of an economy in much the same way as aeronautical engineers build wind tunnels to simulate the atmosphere. Experiments can then be performed on the model. In economics, simulation models have used water in pipes and electric currents in wires to simulate the flows of goods and services, as well as the stock of goods. With the development of large-scale computers, very elaborate models can be represented electronically. Hypotheses about how individual units behave can be placed into the memory of a computer, and the economist can observe how large numbers of simulated households and firms interact in the simulated markets. (The behavior of markets is also governed by rules programmed into the computer.) The results of such interactions over time become outputs of the machine. Experiments can be performed on the system: For example, the economist can increase "taxes" and trace out the effects of the increase month by month over many "years." Since months of actual time can be simulated in a few seconds on a computer, the economist will be able to run many experiments (for example, he can try out *different* tax policies) and compare the results of each. This approach is in its infancy, and it is too early to evaluate its success.

A Final Word

There is no doubt that the millions of households and firms in an economy are interrelated and that their decisions, individually small, impinge upon one another through the market mechanism. Neither the theory of general equilibrium nor the empirical measurements of the nature or process of adjustments is anywhere near satisfactory. But it is clear that the economy does adjust, sometimes imperfectly, often slowly, to changing demands upon it. An enormous part of the adjustment process is handled by the price system, which no one planned and which is (by and large) unregulated. To say we do not understand the price system nearly well enough does not mean that we do not have a good idea of the way it works, the speed with which it works, the places where it appears to be least satisfactory, and the places where it appears to do very well. Some of our dissatisfaction with the workings of the price system have led policymakers, even in the most market-oriented of economies, to adopt policies that interfere

9. The interested student will find an excellent and nontechnical survey of this field in the paper by Guy H. Orcutt, "Simulation of Economic Systems," *American Economic Review*, December, 1960.

with the free working of markets. Some of the great efficiencies of the price system have led policy-makers in economies where every-

one is ideologically committed to planning to introduce pricing schemes to guide a large part of the decision-making process.

Summary

1. Anything that happens in one market will have effects on some other markets in the economy. Changes in these other markets will then feed back into the original market.

2. The basic assumption of partial equilibrium analysis is that the feedbacks in a sector are small enough that they may be neglected. General equilibrium analysis is designed to take account of such interrelationships between markets. Generality does not imply comprehensiveness; and generality is not, by itself, a virtue. It is usefulness and applicability that count.

3. The price system was not consciously created. With a price system, it is not necessary to foresee and to coordinate all necessary changes in various markets; such changes occur automatically as a result of the separate decisions made by a large number of individuals each seeking his own private profit, but

all responding to changes in demands and prices. To observe that the price system functions automatically does *not* tell us how well it functions.

4. It is often very difficult to test general equilibrium theories about the workings of the economy. In recent years, a number of ambitious approaches have been tried. The most famous is the *input-output analysis* of Professor Wassily Leontief. Its major drawback for longer-run predictions is that it assumes that factor inputs to industries are in fixed proportions. Nevertheless, it is an extremely valuable tool, particularly for short-run uses. One other approach is *simulation*. With the development of large-scale computers, very elaborate models can be represented electronically; but it is too early to evaluate the success of this approach.

QUESTIONS FOR DISCUSSION

1. What is the basic difference between partial and general equilibrium analysis? How do we know which one is right?

2. In the following cases, state whether you think feedback can be ignored, cannot be ignored, or whether you think the matter is in doubt:

a. A single small plumbing union obtains a wage rise for its members.

b. Steel companies meet secretly to fix prices.

c. A minimum wage is set by a small union for the firms with which it negotiates.

d. Congress passes a law raising the national minimum wage and extending its coverage.

e. The general wage rate is cut in order to persuade employers to hire more labor during a time of heavy unemployment. (Hint: What will this do to demands for goods and services?)

f. A decline in attendance at minor league baseball games reduces greatly the demand for peanuts.

3. If the Belvidere plant was to be established in a fully planned economy (in which all decisions

were made by the central authorities), what effects would the planners have to foresee? How would this process differ from what happens in a free-market economy?

4. There have been many headlines lately of the following sort: "Poland To Try Profit Incentives,"

"Russian Managers To Have More Initiative," "Czechs Use Profits as Guides." What do you think is the economic rationale for this?

5. What assumption of input-output analysis makes it difficult to use for long-range forecasting?

Chapter **43** MICROECONOMIC POLICY

THERE ARE TWO CARICATURES OF THE AMERI-can economy. In one, America is pictured as the last stronghold of free enterprise with millions of Americans racing in a mad and brutal chase for the almighty dollar. In the other, American businessmen, workers, and farmers are pictured as slowly strangling in a web of red tape spun by a spider called government regulation. Neither is realistic. It is true that many aspects of economic life, perhaps more than in most other countries, are determined, in America, by the operation of a free-market system. Here, private preferences, expressed through private markets and impinging upon private profit-seeking enterprises, determine what is produced, how it is produced, and how the product is shared. But even casual observation, and assuredly a close look, makes it clear that public policies and public decisions play a large role too. Not only do we have laws that restrict what people and firms may do, but we have

taxes and subsidies that affect choices, and large amounts of public expenditures that are not market determined and that lead to a very different "bill of goods" and a different distribution of national product from what would exist in a system that relied entirely upon private markets.

In this chapter, we are concerned with the nature, form, purpose, and effect of various public—i.e., governmental—activities that impinge upon the unrestricted workings of the free-market system. We are particularly concerned at this time with policies that affect the distribution of resources among uses, and the distribution of income among people, rather than those that have as their primary concern the over-all level, stability, and growth of national output. We shall start by reviewing the economics we studied in Parts II to VII to see why there is a need for, or a desire for, public intervention in markets.

Why Not Laissez Faire?[1]

If motivation can be judged by behavior, it is clear that a majority of Americans believe that an unrestricted, unmodified private-enterprise system is not the best of all possible worlds. What led free and rational men to reach this judgment? In trying to answer this question, do not make the error of assuming that what is, is exactly what should be. Social policies and social judgments evolve and change. In a society that elects its policy-makers at regular intervals, however, the majority view on the amount and type of government interference that is desirable will have some considerable influence on the interference that actually occurs.

There are several reasons for interfering with the free market.

1. MARKET IMPERFECTIONS

Markets use "signals," such as prices and profits, to allocate scarce resources among competing uses. These signals induce resources to move from uses for which effective demand is lower to uses for which the effective demand is higher. If factors are relatively immobile, however, the supply of factors will tend to be inelastic in the short run, and even large increases in the price offered for scarce factors may induce only small movements of such factors. As we saw in Chapters 33 and 34, if theoretical physicists are in short supply, their pay will rise, and an increase in the pay of existing theoretical physicists may ultimately lead to an increase in the total supply of physicists (for example, by persuading students who

had planned to become economists or engineers to go into physics instead). But such increases in pay may have only a small effect on supply for several years, in view of the training required to become a physicist. Meanwhile, existing theoretical physicists will earn high salaries, and will command a larger share of national income than they otherwise would. It may well be that public policy can bring about an increase in the supply of theoretical physicists more quickly and more cheaply than when the unhampered market does the job. The government might, for example, provide very generous scholarships and fellowships to encourage students to take degrees in physics. Since World War II, the Atomic Energy Commission and the National Science Foundation have done precisely this.

Factors may be immobile for reasons other than time lags required for education. For example, unemployed workers may be uninformed about job opportunities or inadequately trained to take jobs that are available; agencies such as the U.S. Employment Service can increase the speed with which such workers can find jobs by collecting data on what kinds of jobs are available in what places and informing unemployed workers about them. Special programs of retraining are also provided by some governmental units. Factors may often be reluctant to move from one location to another because of the heavy moving expenses, or the difficulties in finding housing, or racial prejudice in hiring. Public policies may lessen these imperfections by giving subsidies for expenses incurred in mov-

1. *Laissez faire* means literally "let do." A *laissez-faire* economic policy implies the absence of governmental interference with private decisions.

ing from one job to another, by building public housing (or subsidizing private housing) in areas that have labor shortages, and by compelling (in any of a variety of ways) "fair employment" practices with respect to minority groups.

Another kind of market imperfection is ignorance. Signals cannot work if they cannot be read. Providing market information, or enforcing a requirement that others provide it, is a major activity of many government agencies that makes markets work better. These activities range from requiring food manufacturers to identify the contents and the net weight of their product to the government inspection and grading of meat, grains, and other agricultural products. The Securities and Exchange Commission requires that companies offering securities to the public make no misleading claims. The Bureau of Labor Statistics and the Agricultural Marketing Service provide much basic information about labor and agricultural markets.

Monopoly power may create market imperfections by preventing resources from moving in response to market signals. Here, barriers to entry rather than inelastic supply frustrate the flow of resources. Antimonopoly policy is discussed at length later in this chapter.

2. DIFFERENCES BETWEEN INDIVIDUAL AND COLLECTIVE VALUES

We discussed the difference between private and social costs at some length in Chapter 17, and we saw that, where the differences were large, there was a strong case for public interference with free markets. California has recently required that antismog devices be attached to the exhausts of all automobiles, presumably because the people of California (through their elected representatives) attach a higher cost to a polluted atmosphere than the costs individual drivers or automobile manufacturers are willing to pay to avoid pollution. (Reread pages 197–198 at this time.)

Another kind of divergence between private and social values arises when individual actions have what are called *third-party effects*. If individuals A and B both want to make a certain exchange, is it their business and theirs alone? It depends upon the exchange. If A owns a building lot in a residential area (on which he intends to build a house in five years) and decides to "get some money out of it" in the meantime by leasing it to a farmer to pasture his goats, or to a carnival operator to run his side shows, the neighbors may well object. Zoning laws are designed to regulate activities that may have third-party effects. For another example, a person with a contagious disease who is unwilling to purchase medical care jeopardizes the health of others; public-health measures, however, interfere with his right to purchase only the quantity of medical care he desires. Much of the case for public education rests upon the advantages to you of having other people's children educated.

Social and private values may differ regarding the nature of the service provided. Public schools are probably not necessary; if they were abolished, a private-school system would be established. Does this mean that public schools *should* be abolished? In publicly owned schools, elected school boards determine the curriculum and decide on other matters of policy; in private schools, the owners, the teachers, or the parents make the decisions. Public schools may be better or worse than private schools, but they are likely to be different, particularly because persons other than parents, teachers, and owners influence their policy. There is thus nothing irrational in deciding to have publicly supported schools, even though the free market could provide a similar but not identical product. Virtually all American state and local governments must agree, for virtually all have opted for a system of public education.

3. COLLECTIVE CONSUMPTION GOODS

Certain goods or services, if they provide benefits to anyone, necessarily provide them to a large group of people. Such goods are called *collective consumption goods*. National defense is a prime example of a collective consumption good. If we have an adequate defense establishment, it protects us all. It protects you, even if you do not care to "buy" any of it; it costs just as much in present-day America to provide defense for 150 million people as it would to provide it for 250 million people. The quantity of national defense provided must be decided collectively, and there is no market where you can buy more of it and your neighbor less. Once you have agreed with him (and the rest of us) on a compromise quantity, there is no market where you can be made to pay for your share of the good. The government acquires the funds to pay for it by a compulsory scheme (taxation).

There are many other examples. The beautification of a city provides a service to all residents and visitors. A levee that protects a city from a flood is a collective consumption good. So is a hurricane-warning system. In general, market systems cannot compel payment for a collective good, since there is no way to prevent a person from receiving the services of the good if he refuses to pay for it.[2] Only governments, through their power to tax, can compel payments by all.

4. THE COSTS OF COLLECTING REVENUE

The power to tax enables governments to compel citizens to pay for collective consumption goods. Private concerns have no such power, and for this reason no private concern finds it worthwhile to provide such goods. There are similar problems with respect to some goods and services that are not strictly collectively consumed. For example, suppose motorists in a big city are willing—even eager—to pay to have a high-speed freeway system leading into and out of town. Suppose that there are enough people willing to pay 2¢ a mile to cover the costs of building such a road system, but that different groups of them want to use different sections of the system. A private company would find it profitable to build and operate the road if it could collect 2¢ a mile from everybody willing to pay that much. But, if it must build a toll house at every entrance and exit to the road in order to collect this money, the costs of the system would be vastly increased and the venture might very likely seem an unprofitable one. Intraurban freeways with many access points and many short-journey travelers are often unsuitable for private ventures, because the cost of collecting tolls is too high. It is no accident that virtually all toll roads are interurban roads where relatively few access points are needed and where the average journey is a long one.

To take another example, suppose the privately owned Skunk Power and Light Com-

2. The demand for a collective consumption good is the *vertical* sum of the demand curves of all individuals for the good. Compare this result with that discussed on page 156, and especially with footnote 1 on that page. The reason for the difference is that you and we can consume the *same* unit of a collective consumption good. If you are willing to pay $10 for it, and we are willing to pay $7, together we are willing to pay $17.

pany decides to build a dam across the Muskrat River in order to produce hydroelectric power to sell on the market. Its engineers and economists determine the best height of the dam to be 80 feet.[3] When these tentative plans are announced, someone realizes that if the SP&L Company builds a 100-foot dam instead of an 80-foot dam it will create a beautiful lake in back of the dam, provide an emergency water supply for nearby communities, and provide flood control for 200 miles downstream. Suppose the beneficiaries of these extras are prepared to pay for them once they exist. The SP&L Company realizes, however, that it has no effective means of charging for them.[4] It decides therefore to build the smaller dam. If benefits are not marketable, it is very likely that private producers will not be motivated to provide them. The very large role of the federal government in multipurpose water-resource projects is often explained to a great extent by the fact that it alone has a mechanism for financing such projects.

To take one more example, suppose every citizen of a given city is willing to pay ½ of 1 percent of his annual income in return for a civic auditorium, but that any flat admission price to the auditorium would not cover the costs. A scheme of price discrimination according to income would, however, repay all costs. There is no mechanism by which the private company can discriminate among buyers of tickets, because it cannot prevent resale. A government, however, with its power to tax incomes, could readily finance the project.

5. COMPASSION

A free-market system rewards certain groups and penalizes others. The workings of the market may be stern, even cruel; consequently, it may seem humane to intervene. Should unproductive farmers be starved off the farm? Should men be forced to bear the full burden of their misfortune, if, through no fault of their own, they lose their jobs? Indeed, even if they lose their jobs through their own fault, should they and their families have to bear the whole burden, which may include starvation? Should the ill and aged be thrown on the mercy of their families? Should small businessmen have to compete with the chain store and the discount house?

A great many government policies are concerned with modifying the distribution of income that results from such things as where one starts, how able one is, how lucky one is, and how one fares in the free-market world. Men have long debated the principles of social justice and have come up with many diverse philosophies, often capsuled in such slogans as "To each according to his need"; "To each according to his ability"; "To each according to his luck"; "The lion's share should go to the lion"; "Equality"; "Survival of the fittest"; and so on. In fact, no society has ever chosen one single principle above all others, and for this reason people often judge the distribution of income that the market produces to be less than ideal.

The range of governmental activities designed to redistribute income is enormous.

---

3. At this height, the company will maximize its profits.

4. Consider the lake. The higher dam will flood certain lands but create valuable shoreline property. The owners of this property will gain if the lake front is on their property. Suppose the SP&L Company said to these people: "After we create this lake you should pay us $X per year because of the increase in the value of your property." And suppose the typical owner answered: "Look, you're flooding my south forty acres and you want *me* to pay you? I'll sue." Governments, on the other hand, have means whereby they can acquire land, and where, if land values rise, recover their costs through land taxes.

The graduated income tax, in which the proportion of one's income paid as a tax rises steeply as one's income rises, is, of course, a major policy of this kind, and we shall discuss it in detail later in this chapter. Direct public expenditures, such as payments to the needy aged (Old-Age Assistance), and government-supported social-insurance schemes (Social Security), have as their main purpose the alleviation of financial hardship among those groups most disadvantaged by the market economy. The Economic Opportunities Act of 1964 represents a new addition to the field. Minimum-wage legislation may succeed in raising incomes of some of those at the lower end of the income scale, although, as we have seen, it may also make unemployable some people who could have found jobs at wages below the legal minimum. Most of our basic agricultural policy of price supports can best be understood as an attempt to raise the incomes of those who work with the land. (Maintaining and raising farmers' incomes also has important effects on the functioning of the economy, but the main motivation for these policies seems to come from a special concern for the well-being of the small farmer.) Small business is given preferential treatment in many ways and is subsidized to some extent in its struggle to survive in an economy of giant corporations. A special agency, the Small Business Administration, is its guardian. Many states have enacted "fair trade" laws that limit the ability of larger firms, discount houses, or chain stores to undersell the small businessman.[5] The McGuire Act (1951) exempts price-fixing under such laws from being prosecuted under the Sherman Anti-Trust Act (1890).

In the discussion above, we noted some of the reasons why people acting through their government may wish to achieve a different quantity, quality, and distribution of goods than the free market provides. This is the case against *laissez faire*. But members of a society may have other goals as well. One of these is a belief in the individual's freedom to act on his own and to make his own decisions. As we saw in Chapter 5, multiple goals often involve conflicts, and conflicts require choices. When and where and to what extent to interfere with the free-market system usually involves decisions as to whether a certain specific objective is worth the loss of individual freedom that is required to achieve it.

Major Policy Tools

The government has **three** main tools to affect the nature of what goods are produced and how they are distributed: rule-making, taxation, and public expenditures.

I. RULE-MAKING

Rules in a multitude of forms require, or prohibit, certain activities. Rules require people to send their children to school and to have

---

5. Ironically, these laws—and such others as the Robinson-Patman Act (1936), which was concerned nominally with price discrimination, but actually with limiting the ability of chain stores to undersell independent retailers—are classified as antitrust laws. Actually, they are designed to protect competitors from the rigors of competition, not from the behavior of monopolists.

them inoculated against smallpox and diphtheria; rules prohibit people from selling or using certain narcotics and from colluding in the pricing of commodities. We will examine in detail on pages 501–506 one very important form of policy-by-rules: antitrust policy. Rules affect other areas as well, especially transportation, utilities, and communications.

2. TAXATION

The nature of taxes and subsidies can affect both what is produced and the distribution of income. Differences in the way taxes are raised can redistribute income and change the relative prices and profits in different industries.

3. PUBLIC EXPENDITURES

Public expenditures can be used to produce goods that the market leaves unproduced, to increase the income of some groups in the population, and to change the signals to which households and firms respond.

These different kinds of tools, which we will examine at length in the later parts of this chapter, provide *alternative means* for achieving given policy objectives. Let us illustrate this by a hypothetical example.

DIFFERENT TOOLS AS ALTERNATIVES

Suppose the federal government decides that it is important to the national security to utilize more petroleum from Canada and less from the countries of the Middle East. (Since this is a hypothetical example, we shall not discuss whether the objective is sensible, although in every real case such a discussion is required.)

This objective might be achieved by rules —by, say, imposing import quotas on Middle Eastern oil. Although this policy would certainly reduce imports of Middle Eastern oil, there is no guarantee that it would increase Canadian imports. If it did not (if oil users turned to Venezuela or Texas for the petroleum they needed), it might become necessary to limit imports from all foreign places other than Canada and to place quotas on oil producers within the U.S. Although it may not be easy to achieve the goal by such methods, it would certainly be possible to do so.

Different rules might be used instead. The government might require all government agencies and all those private firms holding government contracts to purchase their oil through importers licensed only to import from Canada.

Alternatively, the government might attempt to induce (rather than require) the use of Canadian oil by any of a number of devices that made it more profitable to do so. One such device might be to subsidize importers of Canadian oil by agreeing to pay them X cents for each barrel imported. Alternatively, it might reduce the tariff on Canadian oil. Instead (or in addition), the government might increase tariffs on non-Canadian imports and place additional taxes on domestic producers. Yet another way for structuring incentives in favor of Canadian oil would be to subsidize the building of a huge pipeline for transporting Canadian oil to the refining and distribution centers in America. The reduction in transportation costs would make it profitable to substitute Canadian oil for oil from other countries.

Finally, the government itself might buy and import large quantities of Canadian petroleum and sell it on the market at prices that assured its use.

Any of a series of policy forms can achieve a desired objective. Each has very different side effects, and thus they may individually appear better or worse in terms of the other objectives of public policy. The central problem in choosing a public policy was discussed in Chapter 5: to choose that one among the feasible alternatives that appears most nearly to satisfy the many goals of the policy-makers. This is never easy, and it occasions major

policy debates that are often as heated as the debates about whether to do anything at all.

We cannot pursue the general problem of policy selection further at this time.[6] We now look in more detail at the specifics of microeconomic policy in the United States.

PUBLIC POLICY TOWARD MONOPOLY: ANTITRUST POLICY

The theory of monopoly, which we discussed at some length in Chapters 23 to 26, leads to two principal predictions: (1) Where monopoly power exists in an industry, it will lead to a restriction on the flows of resources into the industry and thus to the employment of fewer resources in the industry than would be used under competitive conditions. (2) Because of this, monopolists will be able to earn profits in excess of opportunity costs and will command a larger share of the national income than they would under conditions of competition. In short, monopoly power may alter the allocation of resources and the distribution of income.

A third aspect of monopoly, its effect on long-run costs, was discussed in Chapter 20, but no clear prediction emerged from the theory.

By and large, economists have regarded monopolistic restrictions on resource flows as adverse on the grounds that they hinder the efficient use of resources. Because those with monopoly power are usually relatively well off, any redistribution of income toward the monopolist also conflicts with the public's desire for more equality in income distribu-

tion. Whenever large firms have acquired sizable shares of the output of major industries, they have usually become objects of public concern, and the clamor for the government to "do something" about monopoly has been loud. Antitrust policy has been aimed at such firms. Before discussing antitrust policies, their aim, and their effectiveness, let us note several things:

1. Monopoly power when exercised by those who are relatively poor, rather than relatively rich, has frequently been supported rather than opposed by the government. For example, the efforts of farmers to increase farm income have not only been condoned by public policy, but they have been actively promoted by public policies of crop restriction, price supports, and generally favorable treatment of producers' cooperatives. For another example, the efforts of labor unions to achieve some degree of monopoly power over the supply of labor was actively supported by those public policies that encouraged the growth of unions.

2. Noneconomic motives for dealing with the "monopoly problem" also exist. Principal among these is the distrust of power. Many

---

6. The interested student is referred to Kenneth E. Boulding, *Principles of Economic Policy* (Prentice-Hall, 1958), for a lively and extended discussion.

people especially fear the political influence of those with substantial *economic* power.[7]

3. The role of big business, even monopoly, in promoting dynamical advances, as argued by Professor Schumpeter (see Chapter 20), has many adherents, but is largely ignored by public policies in America.

4. An important distinction in economic theory between the monopoly power of a firm on the one hand, and the size of a firm on the other, is frequently blurred in political discussions. Put differently, the distinction between oligopoly and monopoly (discussed in Chapter 29) is little evident in public attitudes toward big business.

Monopolistic power may be achieved in many ways:[8] (1) by firms conspiring among themselves (*colluding*) to restrict output, raise prices, or otherwise fail to compete with one another; (2) by firms adopting practices "in restraint of trade," such as contracts that bind a purchaser to buy all of his supplies from a single seller (this is a form of what is called a "requirements contract");

(3) by a firm employing "predatory" practices against rival sellers in an effort to force them into bankruptcy, "good behavior," or merger; (4) by a merger of existing firms into a single dominant firm; and (5) by one firm acquiring control of other firms by purchasing their stock or by acquiring their physical assets.

The basic tool of antitrust policy is a series of laws that seek to make illegal practices that lead to monopoly. Such practices may be either criminal or civil offenses. In criminal law, a firm found guilty may be fined, or its officers may be fined and/or sentenced to jail. If found liable under civil law, the firm may be required by the court to conform to the decision of the court by abandoning certain practices, and it may be forced to dissolve itself into a number of separate companies under procedures approved by the court. In the legal phrase, a firm found guilty of violating the law must "cleanse itself" of its guilt in a manner prescribed by the court.

Who Makes Our Antitrust Policies?[9]

Antitrust laws prohibit certain forms of activity. Since they are laws, they are enforced in the courts, and the enforcement follows the usual legal procedures by which charges are brought (typically by the Antitrust Division of the Department of Justice).

A trial is held and a judgment reached, and, in most of the more important cases, appeals occur that eventually reach the Supreme Court.

The over-all effect of antitrust policy at any time rests upon three things: (1) the nature

---

7. The hypothesis that big business wields enormous political power, and thus threatens the open society, is forcefully, if sometimes crudely, presented in many places. See, for example, Robert A. Brady, *Business as a System of Power* (Columbia University Press, 1943).

8. In the subsequent discussion, we neglect what the classical economists called "natural monopoly," in which, in the words of the Supreme Court, a firm finds monopoly "thrust upon it" either by its natural efficiency as a single producer or by successful innovation.

9. The interested student has a wide range of books to choose from in pursuing this topic. One of the standard texts is C. Wilcox, *Public Policies Toward Business* (Richard Irwin, 1955).

of the laws themselves; (2) the courts' attitude toward the law and their interpretation of it; and (3) the vigor with which prosecutions are brought by the Justice Department. All three have changed over time, and therefore the over-all antitrust climate has changed. Let us examine each briefly.

PRINCIPAL LAWS PROMOTING COMPETITION

The Sherman Anti-Trust Act (1890) was the first of the major pieces of legislation that arose in response to the great growth in the size of firms during the last half of the nineteenth century. Section 1 of the act declared illegal every contract, combination, or conspiracy in restraint of trade. Section 2 made it illegal to monopolize or to attempt to monopolize. It also made illegal conspiracies or combinations that resulted in monopolization. Although the language of the Sherman Act was strong, it was also vague, and it was to be some time before the courts were able to define the act's scope more specifically.

The Clayton Act (1914), in an attempt to be more precise, identified certain practices as illegal "where the effect may be substantially to lessen competition." Among these practices were acquiring shares of stock in a competing firm, discriminatory price cutting, and tying contracts.[10] The Clayton Act specifically exempted labor from the antitrust provisions. Although the Clayton Act made it illegal to take over control of another firm by purchasing its stock, it neglected to prohibit taking over control by purchasing the firm's plant and equipment. Although it dealt with the trust, or "loose-knit," combination of competitors, it neglected the merger, or "close-knit" combination.

The Federal Trade Commission Act (1914) created an independent commission to police unfair and predatory practices. Although initially the FTC had substantial powers to issue "cease and desist orders" without being subject to judicial review, the Supreme Court denied this power in 1919. The Commission remains an important agency in the antitrust field, but the act is not important for its additions to the legislative provisions of the Sherman and Clayton Acts.

The Celler-Kefauver Antimerger Act (1950) applied to asset acquisitions the same provisions as had previously applied only to acquisitions of stock, thus correcting the omission of the Clayton Act.

TRENDS OF JUDICIAL INTERPRETATION

The first important series of antitrust prosecutions occurred at the beginning of the twentieth century. Two decisions of major importance were issued in 1911 when, in forcing the Standard Oil Company and the American Tobacco Company to divest themselves of a large share of their holdings of other companies, the Supreme Court enunciated the "rule of reason." Not all trusts, but only *unreasonable* combinations in restraint of trade, merited conviction under the Sherman Act. The rule of reason received a narrow interpretation in the famous U.S. Steel case (1920), in which the court found that the company had not violated the law, even though it found that the organizers of the company had intended to monopolize the industry, and even though the company had at an earlier time conspired to fix prices. The court held that U.S. Steel had not succeeded in *achieving* a monopoly (indeed, its attempts

10. A tying contract requires a buyer to purchase other items in order to purchase the item he wants.

at price fixing proved it!). The fact that it was a big company that controlled half the industry and had potential monopoly power was, the court ruled, beside the point. The decision said in part, "The law does not make mere size an offense. It . . . requires overt acts."

The U.S. Steel decision, together with some similar ones,[11] and the highly business-oriented attitude of the 1920s ushered in a quarter of a century in which the antitrust laws were virtually unenforceable, so far as attacks on the structure of heavily concentrated industries were concerned.

A sharp break in this situation occurred in a series of cases prosecuted in the late 1930s and decided after World War II. The most notable was the Aluminum Company of America case (1945), which reversed the Steel decision and appeared to make size per se an offense.[12] Although subsequent decisions somewhat modified the strongly anti-big-business position of the ALCOA case, there is a consensus among economists and lawyers that, in the postwar period, it became possible to use the antitrust laws against highly concentrated oligopolistic industries. Since the war, a number of major decisions have been decided in favor of the government.

The disposition of the present (1965) Supreme Court seems at least as sympathetic to a vigorous application of the laws as any prior one. Even though the government is winning its cases today, the decisions are often close, and the court may once again swing toward a more pro-business position at any time.

PERIODS OF VIGOROUS PROSECUTION BY THE JUSTICE DEPARTMENT

Courts, whatever their predilections, decide only those cases that come before them. Whether to prosecute and which cases to choose is decided by the Antitrust Division, which in turn reflects the attitude of the President and his party.

When the Sherman Act was passed in 1890, it was adopted with little discussion and attracted remarkably little attention. It was not until President Theodore Roosevelt succeeded McKinley in the White House that "trust-busting" became an activity of any note. Roosevelt, the hero of San Juan Hill, tried to storm the hill of big business. It was he who, in 1903, set up the Antitrust Division in the Justice Department, and it was his Administration that initiated the series of major prosecutions that led to the Standard Oil, Tobacco, and Steel decisions. The decisions of the Supreme Court on these and related cases, as well as a sharply conservative turn in the climate of economic opinion, took the steam out of antitrust, and few major antitrust prosecutions were commenced for almost twenty-five years, from 1912 to 1937.

Students are often puzzled by the antitrust policies during the early years of the New Deal. In fact, President Franklin Roosevelt's first Administration (1933–1937) was so concerned with stemming the Great Depression that it fostered, under the National Recovery Administration, industry councils that were encouraged to fix prices, limit outputs, and

---

11. The most notable was the International Harvester Case (1927), in which the court held that not only was the mere size of a corporation not an offense. Neither, "however impressive [was] the existence of unexerted power on its part."

12. Prosecution was started in 1937 when Thurman Arnold was made head of the Antitrust Division of the Justice Department.

try to restore stability to demoralized markets. No Administration before or since has given such encouragement to policies in restraint of trade!

The appointment of Thurman Arnold in 1937 to the leadership of the Antitrust Division marked the beginning of a most vigorous period of antitrust activity. The Justice Department, no doubt partly because of a very marked change in the composition of the Supreme Court, attempted to bring cases that would reopen issues that had been foreclosed by the rule of reason. The fruits of this activity have already been mentioned in the ALCOA and related decisions.

Antitrust policy was pushed to the sidelines by the overriding problems of World War II, the postwar readjustment, and the Korean War, and did not begin to re-emerge until the 1950s. Antitrust has been pursued with some energy under the Administrations of Presidents Eisenhower, Kennedy, and Johnson.

The Success of Antitrust Policy

Many students of the subject feel that antitrust laws have proved remarkably ineffective in counteracting bigness and the concentration of market power in the U.S. It should be noted, however, that, although the Sherman Act is seventy-five years old, the combination of reasonably permissive (from the government's point of view) interpretation by the courts and reasonably active governmental activity has been present for only the last fifteen years. *Antitrust is, in this sense, in its early development.* Although it is an empirically valid conclusion that, as of today, the antitrust laws have been more effective in limiting and preventing certain predatory practices of big business than they have in restructuring the U.S. economy, their potential impact is not known, for it has never been well tested. Economists are not in general agreement as to whether the structure of American industry has been influenced very much by the antitrust legislation. American industry is highly concentrated (see Chapter 27), but empirical studies show no tendency for the concentration either to increase or to decrease very drastically. Would the pattern be very different if on the one hand there had been no antitrust laws, or if on the other there had been a half-century of vigorous enforcement of the laws? We do not know for sure. Some evidence is contained in a comparison of the British and American experiences.

ANTITRUST IN GREAT BRITAIN

Until 1948, Britain had no antimonopoly legislation of any kind, yet the extent of concentration in British industry was no greater than in the United States. So far as the *structure* of industry is concerned, this fact is consistent with the hypothesis that antitrust laws have not made enormous differences.

With respect to industry practices, the evidence is different. The Monopolies and Restrictive Practices Act (1948; strengthened in 1953) established a commission to investigate and report on monopoly practices against the public interest. Between 1948 and 1956, twenty-two such reports were made that led to negotiated agreements between the government and the industries involved over the abandonment of the objectionable practices. The general effect on the behavior of British industry was small. Importantly, however, the reports of the commission led to the identification of types of restrictive practices (of kinds outlawed in the U.S. since the Sherman Act) and eventually to the Restrictive Trade Practices Act (1956). This act required firms to register all restrictive agreements with an appropriate agency and, if challenged, to prove that these agreements did not adversely affect competition. By 1960, over 2,000 such agreements had been registered, and more than 500 were voluntarily abandoned. The mere requirement of registration probably serves to prevent the use of extreme forms of restrictive agreements. Most of the practices abandoned or successfully challenged by the government are of the kinds that have effectively been controlled in the U.S. by antitrust legislation.

The British experience suggests, though it does not prove, that our antitrust laws have been more nearly successful in inhibiting restrictive practices than in altering the basic structure of the economy.

TAX STRUCTURE AS A TOOL OF MICROECONOMIC POLICY

In 1963, the federal, state, and local governments collected approximately $168 billion in taxes—approximately one-quarter of the value of goods and services produced. They spent somewhat more. We are not concerned here with the *level* of these taxes, or with the relation of total tax revenue to total government expenditures. These important matters are discussed in Chapter 51. We are concerned, rather, with the *structure* of the taxes, for the way in which taxes are levied can exert a very great influence on both the distribution of income and the allocation of resources between uses.

Table 1 supplies basic data about the source of tax revenues in 1963.

Since one-third of these taxes are on personal income and almost one-half are on either personal or corporate income, and since "everybody knows" that income taxes take more from the rich man than the poor man, it will seem obvious that the tax structure is a weapon of great potential power for

TABLE 1   **FEDERAL, STATE, AND LOCAL TAX RECEIPTS IN 1963, IN BILLIONS OF DOLLARS**

Kind of tax	Federal government	State and local	Total
Personal income and related	52	3	55
Corporation income and profit taxes	23	2	25
Excise and sales taxes	16	14	30
Property taxes	—	20	20
Social security and related	23	—	23
License fees and other	—	15	15
TOTALS	114	54	168

SOURCE: *Economic Report of the President,* 1965.

redistributing income from the rich to the poor, but we shall see in a moment that this power has not in fact been used. Approximately $45 billion of taxes are either excise taxes, sales taxes, license fees, or related taxes that fall more heavily on some commodities than on others. As we saw in Chapters 11 and 25, taxes in this form have some effect on prices; for this reason, we expect the pattern of taxes to have a substantial effect on the allocation of resources among uses. There is much evidence on the effect of particular taxes on the allocation of resources to particular markets. We do not, however, have sufficient knowledge to assess the total effect of the whole tax system on the economy, and we are thus as yet unable to answer such questions as, "How different would the allocation of resources and the distribution of income be if all taxes were removed?"

Taxes and the Distribution of Income

"Equity" and "equality" are tricky words, but important concepts. To "tax people equally" might mean several things. It might mean that each person should pay the same tax, which would be very hard on the unemployed worker and very easy on the movie star. It might mean that each should pay the same proportion of his income, say a flat 25 percent, whether he is rich or poor, or whether he is a bachelor, a laborer with eight children, or an old man who is blind and who suffers from a disease that requires heavy use of expensive drugs. It might mean that each should pay an amount of tax such that everybody's income after taxes is the same. Or it might mean none of these. Instead of dealing in "equality," which is vague, we shall discuss the distributional effects of taxes, using the following technical definitions:

A tax is called proportional *if it takes amounts of money from people in direct proportion to their income. A tax is called* regressive *if it takes a larger percentage of income from people the lower their income. A tax is called* progressive *if it takes a larger percentage of income from people the larger their income.*

The words proportional, progressive, and regressive are treated as positive terms. Nothing in our definition implies that one is better than another. It is usually not too difficult to classify individual taxes as proportional, progressive, or regressive.

In structure, the personal income tax of the federal government is highly progressive, as Table 2 shows. Because of the special definitions given to taxable income, it is much less strongly progressive than the table suggests, but it is, nevertheless, progressive in effect as well as in structure. A fixed tax (per person) is certain to be regressive, because people's incomes vary, and any fixed amount is thus a larger portion of a low income than of a large one. A sales tax or an excise tax will tax people according to the proportion of their income they spend on the taxed items. If two people each spend the same proportion of their income on a certain commodity that is subject to a sales or an excise tax, the tax will be proportional in its effects on them. If the tax is on a commodity (such as food) that takes a larger proportion of the income of the lower income families, it will be regressive; if it is on a commodity (such as jewelry) on which the rich spend a larger proportion of their income than the

TABLE 2 **AMOUNT OF FEDERAL INCOME TAX TO BE PAID AT DIFFERENT INCOME LEVELS BY A CHILDLESS COUPLE, 1965**

Net income before exemptions (but after all deductions) (1)	Personal income tax (2)	Average tax rate, percent [=(2)÷(1)] (3)	Marginal tax rate (=tax on extra dollar) (4)
Less than $1,200	0	0	0
2,000	112	5.6	14
3,000	260	8.7	15
4,000	418	10.5	16
5,000	586	11.7	17
10,000	1,556	15.6	22
20,000	4,044	20.2	28
50,000	16,460	32.9	50
100,000	44,460	44.5	60
200,000	109,972	55	69
400,000	250,140	62.5	70
1,000,000	670,140	67.0	70
10,000,000	6,970,140	69.7	70

poor, it will be progressive. To determine the effect of an excise tax on the distribution of income, one must know the proportion of their income that people with different incomes spend on the taxed commodities. The answer is not always obvious: Is a tax on the value of owned homes, such as the property tax, regressive or progressive?[13] Is the corporate profits tax, which is a flat percentage (about 50 percent of corporate income), regressive or progressive?[14]

As to the over-all regressivity or progressivity of the tax system, examine Table 3, which reports one study of this problem. According to this study, the over-all tax pattern is nearly proportional. The departure from strict proportionality is in the direction of slight regressivity, except at the upper end of the income scale.[15]

These data are based upon the combined effect of all taxes: state, local, and federal. There is no doubt that, taking only federal taxes, they tend to be somewhat progressive. State and local taxes are clearly regressive. If the purpose of our tax structure has been to be neutral with respect to the over-all income distribution, it has been a success. If its purpose has been to be an instrument of general redistribution from rich to poor, it has not been a success.

13. Studies show that such taxes are highly regressive.

14. Studies show that it is regressive as among owners of shares in companies, but progressive as between shareholders and nonshareholders.

15. These data have been challenged. Richard A. Musgrave believes that he has evidence of slight but steady progressivity throughout the range $2,000 to $10,000. See his "The Incidence of the Tax Structure and Its Effects on Consumption," in *Federal Tax Policy for Economic Growth and Stability* (U.S. Government Printing Office, 1955). A statistician would say that there is insufficient evidence to reject the hypothesis that taxes are, over-all, proportional.

TABLE 3 EFFECTIVE TAX BURDENS
BY INCOME LEVELS[a]

Family income level	Tax burden as percentage of income
Under $2,000	28
2,000 – 3,999	26
4,000 – 5,999	26
6,000 – 7,999	26
8,000 – 9,999	24
10,000 – 14,999	24
Over 15,000	36
Average for all	27

[a] Estimates are for 1958.
SOURCE: *Allocation of the Tax Burden by Income Class* (New York: The Tax Foundation, 1960).

The tax system distinguishes among households not only according to the size of household income, but also according to a host of other characteristics, such as size of family, age, occupation, and source of income. The tax system undoubtedly does redistribute income among households when they are classified by some of these other characteristics. We cannot go into detail here, but let us note two examples of why a de-

tailed look might lead us to modify this conclusion. First, income taxes provide a concession to families with large numbers of children in the sense that they are allowed exemptions that lower their taxes. But it is unlikely that the tax saving would make the tax burden per person lighter for a large family than for a small one. A sales tax on food tends to fall more heavily on a large family than a small one. Over-all, it almost surely does not "pay" (in the sense of tax burden) to have a large family, although it does "pay" (in the same sense) to have a wife. Aggregate statistics also conceal the fact that two individuals with identical total incomes and identical family sizes may pay very different proportions of their income in taxes if their incomes come from different sources. Income from royalties in oil wells are taxed more lightly than income from royalties on books. Profits from the sale of assets (called capital gains) are taxed more lightly than wages and salaries. Dividends are taxed more lightly than interest income. And so on.

To understand these differences (and others like them), we must examine the effects of the tax structure, and thus of the tax policy that has led to that structure, on incentives and market signals.

The Structure of Taxes and the Goods the Economy Produces

Resources move, in a market economy, in response to changes in the *relative* prices of different goods and factors and in response to the relative profitability of different industries. A *neutral* tax is defined as one that does not change the structure of relative prices and profits and thus does not change any of the signals to which resources are supposed to respond. It is perfectly clear that the

American tax system is not in any sense neutral. It would be surprising if it were! A society may wish to allocate resources in a way different from the way the market allocates them, and many societies use taxes toward that end.

One way in which tax structure affects resource allocation is through the deductions allowed on the personal income tax. An allowable deduction is an expenditure that may be deducted from income before computing the amount of taxes payable. Consider a wealthy man in the 50 percent marginal tax bracket (see Table 2). Every $100 he spends on an item that is tax deductible costs him $50 in after-tax income. Every $100 he spends on items that are not tax deductible costs him $100 in after-tax income. Contributions to charitable and educational institutions are tax deductible, as are interest payments on a mortgage. Contributions to political parties are not, nor is rent paid on a home. The effect of these laws is to *restructure incentives* by making the relative cost of giving to educational institutions less than the cost of giving to political parties, and the "price" of owning a home relatively less than the price of renting one. If our theory of the effect of changes in relative prices on demand is correct, the deduction system should lead people to contribute more to colleges and less to political parties than they would in a free-market situation; similarly, they should be motivated to invest more money in owner-occupied housing and less in rental housing, and so on. If the *intention* of the policy is to shift incentives in this way, our theory predicts that it will be successful.[16]

Corporate tax nonneutralities work out in a similar fashion. The "investment credit" provides special tax relief for firms that are engaging in new investment. Income received from the production of minerals is also given favorable tax treatment. Income from mineral production is taxed less heavily than income from manufacturing because so-called depletion provisions allow a mineral producer to deduct from his income amounts that often exceed the costs actually involved. Because of this, other things being equal, explorers and producers of minerals earn greater profits after taxes than they otherwise would have, which leads more people to invest relatively more in these activities and less in others. Depletion provisions, particularly in oil and gas, are often regarded as "give-aways" or as tax loopholes designed to benefit the rich. Although these designations may be accurate, they also indicate that Congress, in establishing them, intended to provide special incentives for the exploration for and production of minerals because of its concern that the market, left to its own devices, would provide too little of these things. Empirical studies leave no doubt that the depletion provisions have increased investment in this area. If this was a definite public goal, we are closer to it than we would have been without the provisions.[17] If it was not a definite goal, the change in resource allocation may be regarded as costly. The heated debate about depletion allowances thus rests in major part on a debate about the goals of policy.

Excise and sales taxes raise the relative prices of taxed commodities. Commodities such as cigarettes, alcoholic beverages, and gasoline are taxed particularly heavily. As we saw in the discussion of tax incidence in Chapter 11, excise and sales taxes will have some effect on prices. Depending upon the elasticity of demand, this effect will, in turn, create varying effects on the quantities consumed. It is not clear whether taxes of these kinds are *intended* to curtail consumption or merely to raise revenue. The more inelastic the demand for a product, the less

16. We are not saying that this is the best way to achieve this objective. Reread Chapter 5, especially pages 57–59.

17. Again, we should not rest there. Perhaps there is a more efficient way to achieve the objective, etc.

the curtailment of consumption and the greater the revenue yield. At this stage you should have no difficulty in spotting the fallacy in the following argument: "A tax on cigarettes is a wonderful tax; not only will it cause most people to give up smoking, but it will yield lots of revenue as well."

The quantitative extent to which tax policies that affect the relative prices of goods in the private sector actually change the pattern of goods and services produced is not really known. It is clear that many prices are higher than they would otherwise be, and that some are lower. On the basis of our theory, we are led to predict that this leads to less production and consumption of the former commodities and more of the latter, but the question of *how different* the bill of goods is, is an empirical question that requires, but has not received, extended study. Nor is

it clear whether such effects as have occurred are intended consequences of a policy designed to achieve them, or are incidental side effects of policies designed to achieve other ends. For example, in response to a growing state budget for education and other public goods, the state of Wisconsin imposed a *selective* sales tax. It is clear that the legislators intended to tax appliances and exempt food, but it is less clear that they decided to do this because the residents of the state bought too many appliances and too little food. Nor is it likely that in taxing golf shoes but not tennis shoes the legislators intended to express a preference for tennis.

We end this section by reminding the student of the possible importance of taxes on the incentives to work; these were discussed on page 355.

PUBLIC EXPENDITURES: EFFECT ON MICROECONOMIC POLICY

Total public expenditure of approximately $170 billion can, like government taxes, have a great bearing on the nature of the goods produced and on the distribution of income. Table 4 shows the main categories of such expenditures.

The government's main influence on the use of resources is in providing those goods and services that it is assumed are desired and desirable but that the market by itself would fail to provide. Foremost among these (in volume of expenditure) are defense and defense-related activities of the federal government; but expenditures on education,

roads, conservation, and urban redevelopment are similar in character. In these activities, the government is acting like a firm, using factors of production to produce outputs. Unlike the firm, the outputs are provided without charge in most cases.[18] By and large, these outputs are of collective consumption goods, or of goods with strong third-party effects, or of services whose benefits are not marketable. Expenditures of this kind exceed $110 billion per year, about half of it for defense. Is this a great deal or is it not enough? The appropriate division of the resources of society between public goods

---

18. Some services, such as the postal service, charge fees, but such cases are exceptional.

TABLE 4   **GOVERNMENT EXPENDITURES, 1963, IN BILLIONS OF DOLLARS**[a]

Federal government	
Defense	55
Purchases of goods and services other than defense	10
Transfer payments	
to persons	28
to foreign governments (net)	1
Interest on debt	8
Subsidies	4
	106
State and local governments	
Education	24
Highways	11
Public welfare	6
Other	24
	65

[a] Excluding intergovernmental expenditures.
SOURCE: *Economic Report of the President*, 1965.

and the private sector is the subject of serious debate. There is no market that provides relative prices for automobiles and schools or for swords and plowshares. J. K. Galbraith is the best known and most articulate exponent of the view that we systematically starve the public sector.[19] But the reverse view has its defenders as well. The debate contains a mixture of testable statements about what people want and how best they can get it, and value judgments about the nature of the good life toward which we should all be striving. Most of the empirical controversies that are testable in principle are extraordinarily complex ones that are not easily resolved in practice. We consider the

nature of this debate further in Chapter 58.

Another very large part of the public budget goes for transfer payments such as public-welfare payments, social-security payments, and so on. Because of the nature of these payments, there is little doubt that low-income groups receive proportionally more of them than do those with higher incomes.

Whether or not the total volume of government expenditure is a net force for increasing the equality of the income distribution and is thus progressive (in the sense that the proportion of services received declines as income increases) is not clear. A study of U.S. Government expenditures from this point of view was made with 1946–1947 data, and the author concluded that, over-all, expenditures were sharply progressive for incomes up to $2,000 and mildly progressive thereafter.[20] But these data are now far out of date. A recent study, by Richard M. Titmuss, showed that, in the U.K., public expenditure tends to be regressive at low-income levels.[21] To what extent the difference between these two studies reflects international differences and to what extent it reflects differences over time is not clear. With our present empirical knowledge, we cannot offer a firm conclusion about the over-all progressivity or regressivity of public expenditure.

Finally, in discussing public expenditure, we must note that here, too, as with taxes, government policies may change market incentives. Government price supports in agriculture, which are primarily intended to redistribute income, raise farm prices and increase supplies over what they would be. Government warehouses bulge with commod-

19. His book, *The Affluent Society* (Houghton Mifflin, 1958), is probably the most influential and provocative economics book that has been read by the general public in many years.
20. John H. Adler, in Kenyon E. Poole, ed., *Fiscal Policies and the American Economy* (Prentice-Hall, 1951).
21. Richard M. Titmuss, *Income Distribution and Social Change* (Allen and Unwin, 1962).

ities that have been purchased to maintain prices. Government subsidies to airlines and to the merchant marine are of some importance. Government guarantees of loans through the Federal Housing Authority (FHA) and the Veterans' Administration (VA) have had a significant effect on the volume of residential construction.[22] Of major importance, we suspect, are the expenditures of the federal government on basic and applied research and development.

The National Science Foundation provides fellowships and training grants for the education of scientists; it makes research grants to individuals and institutions; and it provides research facilities, including buildings. The Office of Naval Research, the Office of Education, the National Institutes of Health, and other agencies also spend funds to encourage and facilitate research. Industrial research is aided and in some cases partly financed by contractual arrangements between government agencies and particular firms. And many governmental facilities (such as the Bureau of Standards) engage directly in research.

A Final Word: Microeconomic Policy

We have in this chapter, despite its length, merely touched on some public policies that affect microeconomic behavior. The most difficult problem for the student of the U.S. economic system is to maintain his perspective about the scope of government activity. There are literally tens of thousands of laws, regulations, and policies that affect firms and households as they seek their own welfare in a complex world. But seek it they do, and with an enormous amount of discretion about what they do and how they do it. One pitfall is to become so impressed (or obsessed) with the number of ways in which governmental activity impinges on the individual that one fails to see these as merely relatively small changes in the signals and the constraints under which the decision-maker operates within a system that basically leaves him free within that vast area of the economy called the private sector. In the private sector, the individual chooses his occupation, earns his living, spends his income, and lives his life. In this sector, the firm, too, is formed, chooses its products, and lives, grows, and sometimes dies. The opposite pitfall is to fail to see that the highly significant sums paid by the private sector to the government as taxes also buy services and goods that add to the welfare of the individual and his society. By and large, the public sector is complementary to the private sector, doing things the private sector would leave undone, or would do very differently. The public and private sectors compete, of course, in the sense that both make claims on the real resources of the economy.

The particular collection of policies in operation at any time is not the result of a single master plan that specifies precisely where and how the public shall seek to complement, help along, or interfere with the workings of the market mechanism. Rather, as individual problems arise, the government

22. See the study by George F. Break, *The Economic Impact of Federal Loan Insurance* (Washington: National Planning Association, 1961).

attempts to meet them by passing ameliorative legislation. These laws stay on the books, and some of them become obsolete and unenforceable. This is true of systems of law in general. As a result, it is always possible and often easy to find outrageous examples of inconsistencies and absurdities in any system. A distinguished Professorship at Harvard gives its incumbent the right to graze a cow in Harvard Yard. Laws still exist that permit the burning of witches. Neither is enforceable. Many anomalies exist in our economic policies; for example, laws designed to support the incomes of small farmers have created some agricultural millionaires. Nei-

ther individual policies nor whole programs should be free from criticism.

But it is also true, in our view, that, in the main, the myriad policies and regulations reflect the consensus that the areas where they apply require some form of collective (public) action and that, by and large, they are operating in the intended directions. Fundamentally, we retain a free-market system that we value for its lack of coercion and for its ability to do much of the job of allocating society's resources. But we are not mesmerized by it; we feel free to intervene in pursuit of a better world in which to live.

Summary

1. There are several basic reasons for interfering with the free market: market imperfections, differences between individual and collective values, a desire for collective consumption goods, the fact that the cost of collecting revenue from users may be so high as to make production unprofitable to private enterprise, and compassion.

2. Major policy tools that can affect the nature of what goods are produced and how they are distributed can conveniently be classified under the headings *rule-making*, *taxation,* and *public expenditure*. An objective may often be achieved by different policies that may well have different side effects.

3. Public policy toward monopoly is studied as an example of microeconomic rule-making. The basic tool of antitrust policy is a series of laws that seek to make illegal practices that lead to monopoly. The over-all effect of antitrust policy at any time rests upon three things: the nature of the laws themselves, the attitude and interpretation of the

courts, and the vigor with which prosecutions are brought by the Justice Department. By comparison with the British experience, we conclude that the evidence suggests, but does not prove, that American antitrust laws have been more nearly successful in inhibiting restrictive practices than in altering the basic structure of the economy.

4. Tax policy is studied as another main example of micro policy. Proportional taxes take money from people in direct proportion to their income, progressive taxes take a larger percentage from people, the larger their income, and regressive taxes do the opposite. These are positive terms. Taking state, local, and government taxes together, the American tax structure is roughly proportional: Federal government taxes are progressive, while the others are regressive. If the purpose has been to distribute income from rich to poor, the system has not been a success; but if its aim has been to be neutral with respect to the distribution of income, it has

been successful. Tax policy also affects the allocation of resources, but we do not yet have comprehensive quantitative information about these effects.

5. Public expenditures can likewise be a tool of microeconomic policy through the goods they produce, through the changes they bring about in market signals and incentives, and through their direct effect on the distribution of income.

QUESTIONS FOR DISCUSSION

1. What justifications might there be for government interference in the areas of education, medicine, defense, man-power training, public parks, egg production, logging, electricity generation, foreign investment, child labor, and the location of a privately financed toll highway?

2. Give a few examples of types of aid to the distressed Appalachian region that could serve as examples of the different types of government tools to effect allocation. Try the same thing with the economic status of the American Negro.

3. What does the evidence show about the effect of antitrust policies? How conclusive is the evidence?

4. In the farm program for 1965, President Johnson had originally intended to ask for an additional subsidy on wheat production, to be paid by the buyer. Successful lobbying brought about a large outcry against what was termed a "bread tax," and the President and Secretary of Agriculture Freeman agreed to withdraw the proposal that the buyer pay. They agreed, instead, to have the subsidy paid from government funds. Since almost everyone buys bread, does it really matter whether they pay the cost of the subsidy via higher prices or higher taxes?

5. What *is* the fallacy in the argument about a tax on cigarettes on page 511?

6. If the government wishes to curtail the consumption of cigarettes, and believes the elasticity of demand to be very low, what other tools does it have at its disposal?

7. Why might the government elect to subsidize private housing, rather than build more public housing? Why might it *not* do the same for elementary education? What case could be made for the alternative decision in each situation?

8. In what senses are the public and private sectors competitive? In what senses are they complementary?

9. In most states, liquor is subject to heavy taxes. How would you test the hypothesis that the main incentive for levying these taxes was concern over public health and a consequent desire to severely limit—even if not to stop altogether—the consumption of intoxicating beverages?

Chapter **44** THE SOUTH COL[1]

THE ECONOMY OF THE UNITED STATES IS A fantastically complex mechanism. To use the analogy of a machine, it is a mechanism with over 200 million moving parts. The parts—the individuals, households, firms, unions, etc.—are not all directed by a single hand; each is operating with substantial independence of action. Yet they fit together, and they function reasonably smoothly most of the time.

In the preceding sections of this book, we have been looking at these parts, how they behave, and how they interact. Our central concern has been with the factors that make the economy function. In the remaining sections, we have the identical concern, but we approach it from a different point of view. Let us pause and see where we have been and where we are going and why we are changing direction at this time.

Microeconomics and Macroeconomics Distinguished

Microeconomics is concerned with a detailed study of the working of individual markets and of the relation between these markets. The central problem is that of the allocation of scarce resources between alternative uses, which in turn is related to the problem of the determination of prices and quantities in all the markets of the economy. We now move our attention away from a study of the interrelations between the various bits of the economy, and toward a study of the behavior of a number of broad aggregates and averages, such as the level of total employment and unemployment, the total quantity of output (possibly divided into the

total quantity of consumption goods and the total quantity of capital goods), and the average level of all prices in the economy. These broad averages and aggregates are usually referred to as *macro quantities* or *macro variables;* the theory that deals with their behavior is called *macroeconomic theory*.

There is no really clear-cut line between macro- and microeconomics. The division between the two is a matter of convenience, for the problems of these two branches of economics differ, as do the methods of analyzing them. The basic problem in microeconomics is the determination of the structure of relative prices; the basic theory is that of de-

1. The South Col of Mount Everest is the final assault station for mountaineers climbing the world's highest mountain. Here the Himalayan climber gathers his strength, changes the direction of his climb by 90°, and (with luck and skill) reaches the summit.

mand and supply. The basic problem in macroeconomics is the determination of the flow of income; the basic theoretical structure is the model of the circular flow of income.

MICROECONOMIC AND MACROECONOMIC VARIABLES

In distinguishing between micro- and macroeconomics, it is common to distinguish between micro and macro variables. The expenditure of one household is an example of a micro variable, and the aggregate expenditure of all households is an example of a macro variable. In general, we can observe the economy at any level of aggregation. For example, we could consider separately the expenditure of each household, or we could deal with households classified along any one of a number of dimensions. We could arrange households regionally and compare total household expenditure in different regions; we could arrange them by occupations and compare, say, total expenditure of all white-collar workers with total expenditure of all factory workers; we could arrange households by age and compare expenditure patterns where the head of the household is young with those where the head of the household is old; and so on. In general, we should think of micro and macro variables as representing a continuum of more or less aggregated data ranging from the expenditure of a single individual on a single commodity to the total expenditure of all households in the world on all commodities. Up to this point in our study of economics, we have varied the level of aggregation from single households and firms to all households buying a certain commodity and all firms producing that commodity. In the remaining chapters, we deal at a higher level of aggregation and consider the total expenditure on certain classes of purchases of all households and of all firms in one country.

Before we move on, let us review the process of circular flow in microeconomics.

How the Economic System Functions: The Microeconomic View

In microeconomics, we start with households whose members have needs and desires for goods and services. They want commodities to keep them fed, clothed, housed, entertained, healthy, and secure; they want them also to educate, edify, beautify, and otherwise to improve themselves. They have, in varying amounts, resources—income, assets, time, and energy—with which to attempt to satisfy these wants. But, their resources are insufficient to permit them to satisfy all their needs and desires. They are forced, therefore, to make choices, and this they do through markets where they are offered myriad ways to spend their money, their energy, and their time. The signals to which the members of households respond are market *prices;* for each given set of prices, they will make a given set of choices. In so doing, they also, in the aggregate, affect those prices. These prices serve as signals to firms of what goods they may profitably provide. Given technology and the costs of factors, firms must choose among the products they might produce, among the ways of producing them, and among the various quantities (and qualities) they can supply. In so doing, they affect prices. Firms demand factors of production, the quantities demanded depending on the output decisions, which, in turn, depend upon consumers' demands. These *derived* demands for factors will in turn affect the prices of labor, managerial skill, raw materials, buildings, machinery, use of capital, land, and all other factors. The owners of factors (or the possessors of the skills that can provide the factor services) respond to factor prices and make *their* choices about where to offer their services. These choices determine factor supplies. Payments by firms to factor owners provide the owners of the factors with incomes. The recipients of these incomes are people who have needs and desires for goods and services. . . . We have now come full circle!

This *circular flow*, as it is called, is the mechanism that makes the economy work.

In the chapters to this point we have had many insights into how the mechanism works. But we have also neglected certain key issues. We have said nothing about the size of the flow, or of what forces tend to increase it or decrease it. We have not examined the conditions under which the flow will be constant from year to year or the conditions that will make it fluctuate. We have spoken of increases and decreases in demands, but where do they come from? The circular flow is in some degree a misleading phrase, for the circularity is influenced by *injections* into and *withdrawals* from the flow. The reasons why the flow increases or decreases, remains stable or fluctuates, constitute some of the most compelling issues of economic theory, economic research, and economic policy. These are the central issues of macroeconomics.

The Basis of Macroeconomic Theory

In answering many general questions about economic systems, we are interested perforce in the aggregated behavior of large groups of households and firms. A group is made up of its components. If we had perfect knowledge, we could aggregate or disaggregate at will to find out how *any* subgroup or supergroup would behave. Because we do not have any such perfect knowledge, we attempt to side-step such *aggregation* (and disaggregation) *problems* by hypothesizing stable behavior patterns at the aggregate level.[2] We assume, for example, that individual households will behave in such ways that stable relations will be found to exist between the total expenditure of all households and the total incomes of all households.

The hypothesis that stable relations exist between macro variables is the basis of macroeconomic theory. If such stable relations are found to exist, there will be a large payoff for economic policy. The payoff will take the form of being able to influence the size of certain macro variables in which we are interested by changing the size of other macro variables that can be influenced by policy. We can hope, for example, to influence the over-all level of unemployment in the economy by regulating the over-all size of the government's budget deficit or surplus. Where such stable macro relations are not found to exist, we shall have to fall back on a more detailed study of smaller groups of households, firms, and markets before we can understand enough

2. Thus it is to some extent true to say that the division between micro- and macroeconomics arises from our ignorance and is to be accepted only as a working rule that enables us to make progress in understanding certain problems.

about the economy to be able to know what policy measures will achieve our goals.

A detailed study of all the interrelationships in all the markets in the economy would be, at best, extremely laborious; at worst, it would be impossible in our present state of knowledge. Macroeconomics is a search for a shortcut. Policy-makers find it possible to affect certain aggregates; by cutting income taxes, for example, they can increase the total amount of income left in the hands of households. But the behavior of households in the aggregate depends upon what each one of 53 million households does. It may be that it is necessary to predict the behavior of individual households before we can predict their aggregate behavior accurately.[3] It may be, on the other hand, that we can predict the aggregate effect with sufficient accuracy even though we are unable to make highly detailed predictions about the differences in behavior between individual units.

THE VALUE OF THE MICRO-MACRO DISTINCTION

As is usually the case, the value of any procedure is judged by whether or not it

works. If individuals do behave in such a way that macro variables show stable relations with each other, then a theory based on such an hypothesis is likely to prove workable and useful. If individuals do not so behave, then our theory will soon be refuted when we try to use it to predict the outcome of various changes in the economy. Our test is thus a pragmatic one: "Does the theory work?" In the longer run, however, we are seeking a fuller understanding of the behavior of the economy. This means that we must try to move constantly between levels of aggregation. We want to know what a theory that is successful in predicting at one level of aggregation implies about behavior at other levels. In particular, if a theory contains only macro variables, we want to know what it implies about the behavior of *individual* households and firms. Once we have done this, we shall know whether or not the theory is consistent with the observations we already have about the behavior of individual units. This knowledge may lead us to formulate further tests of the theory in cases in which there are definite implications about behavior at other levels of aggregation but no existing observations.

The Problems of Macroeconomics

Why has the level of unemployment in the United States since 1947 oscillated between a low of 2.9 percent of the labor force and a high of 6.8 percent, while at the same time there has been a general trend toward progressively higher wages? Why, during the early 1960s,

were there approximately 4 million persons unemployed in the United States? What have been the effects on unemployment of the recent tax cuts? Is it really possible that a country can spend itself out of trouble? Why did prices double between 1941 and 1947 and

3. This is the hypothesis of one group of able economists. For a very forceful statement of this view, see G. H. Orcutt, "Microanalytic Models of the United States Economy: Need and Development," *American Economic Review,* May, 1962. Right or wrong, it is at this stage a distinctly minority view.

why have they continued to increase, but at a slower rate, since that time? Why do some South American countries experience a more or less permanent inflation, with prices doubling every few years? To what extent do the actions of bankers affect the lives of ordinary citizens? How and why does the Federal Reserve System seek to control the actions of bankers and of consumers? Is poverty in Appalachia and heavy unemployment in Maine and Michigan the inevitable price of economic progress? Will the economies of Germany and Japan continue to enjoy rates of economic growth well in excess of that ruling in the United States, or were the conditions of the fifteen years 1950–1965 exceptional ones, not to be repeated? If the experience of the postwar period does continue into the future, how long will it be before the United States loses its position as the country with the highest average standard of living in the world? If Germany and Japan do overtake the United States in standard-of-living level, will Russia follow as well?

These questions all come within the field of macroeconomics. Perhaps the best way of indicating the scope of this branch of economics is to list the most important sets of problems with which we shall be concerned in the remainder of this book, and to contrast these where possible with the related problems dealt with in microeconomics.

1. *Problems relating to fluctuations in the level of resource use, particularly fluctuations in the level of employment of labor.* In microeconomics, we take the total volume of employment as given and consider how it is allocated among various sectors of the economy.

2. *Problems relating to fluctuations in the average level of prices—problems, that is, of inflation and deflation.* In microeconomics, we take the absolute price level as given and account for the structure of relative prices.

3. *Problems relating to fluctuations in the general level of money wages.* In microeconomics, we are concerned with the relation between wages in different areas, occupations, and industries.

4. *Problems relating to the allocation of resources between the production of consumers' goods on the one hand, and the production of capital goods on the other.* This is an allocation problem similar to the one encountered in microeconomic theory. The level of aggregation is, however, different; here we are dealing with the allocation of resources between two sections that together account for the whole economy, whereas in microeconomic theory we split up the economy into many small sectors.

5. *Problems relating to the rate of growth of productive capacity.* These problems have already been considered in Chapter 20, but they reoccur in the context of macroeconomics.

6. *Problems concerning the relation between international trade and the levels of employment, prices, and growth in the economy.* In Chapters 38–41, we saw how international trade affected domestic prices of certain goods and thus affected the domestic allocation of resources.

7. *Problems concerning the control by the central authorities of the level of activity in the economy, the tools of control being fiscal and monetary policy.* In Chapter 43, we considered government economic policy in relation to the problems studied in microeconomics. In the remaining chapters, we consider government economic policy in relation to the problems studied in macroeconomics.

QUESTIONS FOR DISCUSSION

1. How do we distinguish between micro- and macroeconomics? Where do we draw the boundary?

2. What do we mean when we say that a division between micro- and macroeconomics arises from our ignorance? Why do we call macroeconomics a short cut?

3. Turn to the questions on pages 3 and 4. Which of them seem to you definitely macroeconomic? Which seem microeconomic?

4. On what main hypothesis is macroeconomics based? Is it possible to hypothesize the opposite? What follows then?

5. Can you classify the questions on pages 519–520 into the problem headings on page 520? Take one or two of the problem headings and see if you can think of additional questions that come under the headings.

6. What does microeconomics take as "given" that macroeconomics considers? What would you say about the reverse question?

THE CIRCULAR FLOW OF INCOME

Chapter 45 THE MODEL OF THE CIRCULAR FLOW OF INCOME

IN OUR ECONOMY, BOTH COMMODITIES AND factors of production are constantly being exchanged for money. If one individual buys a currently produced commodity from another, he hands over money in return. The seller of the commodity has now earned this money; it is his income. He may in turn spend the money, passing it on to someone else in exchange for some other currently produced commodity. The second seller has now earned

the money and he may in turn spend it. And so it goes on, the money passing from individual to individual in exchange for commodities; each time money changes hands in return for currently produced goods and services, it is income for the recipient. The money flows from hand to hand in much the same way as water flows through a pipe or electricity through a circuit.

Goods and Money Flows Between Individuals

Imagine a simple economy that consists of four households, *A, B, C,* and *D,* each of which makes a different commodity. Assume

that there is only one dollar bill in the economy. Household *A* buys goods valued at $1 from *B,* giving the dollar bill in return. This dollar is income for household *B*, and it spends this income by buying a dollar's worth of goods produced by household *C*. Household *C* has now earned a dollar that it uses to buy goods produced by *D*, and *D* in turn buys a dollar's worth of goods produced by *A*. The flows of goods and money in this economy are illustrated in Figure 1. Goods flows are shown with broken lines and money flows with solid lines. A single dollar bill has passed round the circle and has been used for four separate transactions. Each household has earned $1 as its income, and each has spent $1. If these are all the transactions over, say, a week, then the total income earned by all individuals in our economy over the week is $4. Note that the total income exceeds the quantity of money ($1) because the same dollar bill was used for more than one transaction. This illustrates an important fact: Total income does not equal total quantity of money, because a single unit of money can create income each time it changes hands. Thus, if the typical unit of money changes hands more than once during the period under consideration, income earned will be greater than the amount of money in existence. When we refer to the number of times that money changes hands over some time period, we speak of the *velocity of circulation* of money.[1]

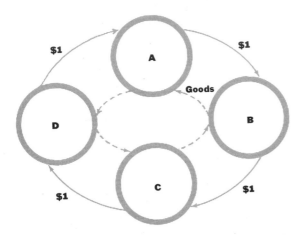

FIGURE 1 **REAL AND MONEY FLOWS AMONG FOUR INDIVIDUALS**

Goods and Money Flows Between Households and Firms

In a real economic system, production is organized by firms; each separate household does not earn its income by making its own goods for sale. Instead, firms make the commodities that households consume. Firms purchase the services of factors of production from the households that own them, paying wages, rent, interest, and profits in return, and then use these factors to make commodities that are sold to households. Households

---

1. The quantity of money is a *stock*, and income is a *flow*. Think of a circular pipe filled with a certain quantity of water that is being forced around the circuit by a pump. The quantity of water in the circuit is a stock; it might, for example, be 100 gallons. But the amount of water passing any one point during some period of time is a flow; it might, for example, be 400 gallons per hour. If the stock of water remains unchanged, but the pump is speeded up so that the water moves faster around the circuit, then the flow will be increased to, say, 600 gallons per hour. In this example, the stock of water is analogous to the quantity of money, and the flow is analogous to its velocity.

Since income is a flow, it must have a time dimension. For simplicity, we shall measure everything in terms of years. Thus, when we speak of the income of a firm or a household, we mean the amount of income that is earned by that firm or that household in one year.

earn income by selling factor services to firms; they spend this income by buying goods and services from firms.[2]

These transactions give rise to a flow of money in one direction, and a flow of goods and services in the other. (See Figure 2.) Money flows from firms to households in return for the factor services purchased from households by firms. Money also flows from households to firms in return for commodities purchased from firms.

Money paid for factor services becomes income for households, and the money paid for commodities becomes the income of firms. Money flows around the circuit, passing from firm to household and back again; thus we speak of the *circular flow of income*. Macroeconomic theory is concerned to explain this flow of income between firms and households.

In this chapter, we shall construct a theoretical model of the circular flow of income in the economy. Like all models, this one will be an abstraction from, and an extreme simplification of, the actual flows in the world. We hope, however, that this model retains the most important elements and abstracts only from the less important ones. The proof of whether or not it is a useful abstraction will depend on how well it is able to predict the outcome of those changes in the economy in which we are interested. If the abstraction is a poor one, the predictions of the model will tend to be refuted when they are confronted with real-world observations. If the abstraction is a successful one, the predictions of the model will tend to conform with what we actually observe.

In constructing the basic model, we identify, and allow for, the most important complications. In subsequent chapters, we examine

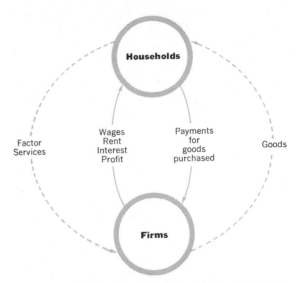

FIGURE 2   **REAL AND MONEY FLOWS BETWEEN HOUSEHOLDS AND FIRMS**

the conditions for equilibrium of the circular-flow model and consider in some detail hypotheses about the behavior of the determinants of circular flow. Once we have built up our theory, we can see how it behaves as various changes, such as an increased desire to spend on the part of households, occur. This will allow us to predict how corresponding real-world magnitudes will vary when the change occurs in the world.

STAGES IN PRODUCTION

We begin by considering a simple economy that consists of three firms and several households. This economy is illustrated in Figure 3. The first firm, *R*, uses factors of production that it purchases from the households to produce raw materials that it sells for $100 to firm *I*. Firm *I* uses factor services to work

---

2. This is usually but not always the case. People in domestic service, for example, earn their income by selling their services directly to other households.

these raw materials into a semimanufactured state and then sells them to firm F for $130. Firm F employs factor services to turn the semimanufactured goods into a finished state, and then sells the goods to the households for $180.

The total value of all sales made by the three firms comes to $410. The total value of final goods produced and sold to households is, however, only $180. How do we arrive at the figure? We might do so in two ways: first, by looking at the sales made by firm F to households, and, second, by summing the *values added* by each of the three firms, R, I, and F. In our example, firm R starts from scratch and produces goods (raw materials) valued at $100; the firm's value added is $100.

Firm I starts with raw materials valued at $100 and produces semimanufactured goods that it sells for $130. Its value added is $30, because the value of the goods is increased by $30 as a result of the firm's activities. Firm F purchases the semimanufactured goods for $130 and works them into a finished state, selling them for $180. Firm F's value added is thus $50. In general, the value added by the productive activities of a firm is defined as the difference between the value of the goods that it produces and the value of the materials that it purchases from other firms.

Our model of the circular flow aggregates transactions between firms that represent stages of production. It displays only the output of goods and services by firms in general.

Factor Incomes

The money that flows from firms to households pays for the factor services sold by households to firms. Payments for the services of factors such as land and labor are made soon after the factors are hired. In the case of labor, for example, payment is customarily made weekly or biweekly in the case of wage earners and once a month in the case of salaried employees. The quantity of factor services hired by firms varies as current production varies.[3] Thus the incomes of the owners of such factors will also vary with production, rising when production rises and falling when production falls. The households that hire factor services out to firms receive

payments from firms in return for providing the factor services that help to produce current output.

Now, take the goods currently produced by some firm, value them at current market prices, and subtract the cost of all materials and hired factors that the firm uses. The amount left over is the firm's remuneration for the use of its own factors, plus any pure profits that it might have earned. The firm regards this whole sum as profits, but the economist regards much of it as the cost to the firm of using its own factors.[4] These "profits" do not, of course, actually accrue to the firm until the goods are sold. Once the profits do accrue,

3. In the case of fixed factors, these statements are true only if there is a very long time lag. A great deal of research has been done recently on the reaction of labor inputs, and hence of labor income, to changes in production. Although it has supported the general statement made in the text, the research suggests that the adjustment of labor inputs to a change in output is spread over a considerable period of time. In the terminology of Chapter 12, we can say that it is true as a general rule that $E = f(Q)$, but that it is also true that E is related to Q by a long distributed time lag (E is employment of factors and Q is quantity produced).

4. This is discussed in detail in Chapter 17.

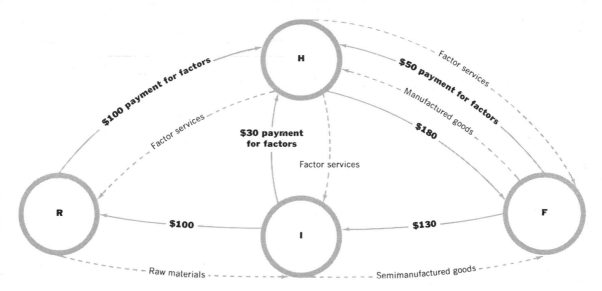

FIGURE 3   **REAL AND MONEY FLOWS BETWEEN HOUSEHOLDS AND FIRMS REPRESENTING DIFFERENT STAGES OF PRODUCTION**

they are income for the households that own the firm (i.e., those households that hold shares in the firm). Business profits thus differ from other factor incomes with respect to the time at which they are earned. Factors that are used in the course of production gain their incomes while they are producing goods; a rise in production will lead to a rise in the incomes of these factors. Profits are obtained when goods are sold; a rise in production will not lead immediately to a rise in profits and thus will not lead at once to an increase in the income of households that own firms.

When a firm hires factor services, it pays income to the households supplying the services. A rise in output produces, after only a short lapse of time, a flow of income actually paid out to households (except in rare cases, such as bankruptcy). In the case of households that have a claim to the firm's profits, the link between changes in output and payments to households is not so precise. Often, firms retain profits that belong to the owners and use them for various purposes. These *undistributed profits* belong to the households that own the firms, but they are never received by households as income.

A Digression on Terminology

In dealing with the circular flow, we are necessarily concerned with certain aggregate concepts of the values of goods and services and of the volume of expenditures made by households. A few definitions are, therefore, in order at this time. (The national-income accountant, as we shall see in the appendix, needs and uses a more detailed set of distinctions.)

VALUE OF TOTAL PRODUCTION

We shall use interchangeably the terms *total income*, *gross national product*, and *national income* to mean the total value of goods and services produced by the economy (including both consumer goods and capital goods) in some period. *Total income* is the sum of the values added at each stage in production ($180 in the example treated in Figure 3); it is the value as well of the final goods produced (also $180 in the example). Notice two important things about this concept: First, it is less than the money value of all transactions ($410 in the example). Second, it does not distinguish between new capital goods and those that are replacements for used goods. We use the total- (or gross-) income concept when we are concerned with, say, the total demand for factors or the level of employment: Building a machine demands labor and raw materials, whether the machine is intended to replace a worn-out one or whether it is a net addition to the capital stock.

Net income (or *net national product*) is simply total income less that portion of the value of goods produced to replace capital that has been used up in production. We use this concept in discussing such matters as the maximum we could have consumed while still leaving the capital stock intact.

DISPOSABLE INCOME OF HOUSEHOLDS

Households demand goods and services, and they also wish to save money. How much income do households actually have available for such purposes? The aggregate equivalent of take-home pay is called *disposable income*. The difference between total income and disposable income is made up of undistributed profits, taxes paid by corporations, and income taxes of households.

In the appendix to this chapter, we provide careful definitions of these rough conceptual distinctions as they are used by the national-income accountants and statisticians. Students who wish may study these now, but it is not necessary to do so in order to follow the discussion in the text.

A Simplified Model of the Circular Flow of Income

We shall build our model in stages. We first consider a simple economy described by the following assumptions: (1) Households spend *all* their incomes on the purchase of goods and services produced by firms; (2) firms keep production exactly equal to sales so that there is no change in inventories; (3) firms pay out to households in wages, interest, and profits all the money they receive from the sale of goods and services. In this econ-omy, the payment to factors is equal to the value of current production. Total income is equal to disposable income. Since households spend all their incomes on goods, firms' incomes will be the same as households' incomes. All the money that is paid out to households comes back to firms when households spend their incomes. Since production is equal to current sales, all the money that comes into firms is paid to households by way of profits, interest, rent, and wages. Clearly, this circular flow of income, once begun, can continue at the same level forever; there is no reason why it should change. To take an example, suppose current production is $1,000 per week, of which $650 is a payment for factor services hired by firms and $350 is business profits, which includes a compensation to the owners of their firm for the use of their capital. Households' incomes will be $1,000 per week. Households' expenditure will also be $1,000 per week. This expenditure becomes the incomes of firms, and this income must therefore be $1,000 per week. Since production is assumed to be at the same rate as sales, $1,000 will continue to accrue to households as their income in return for supplying the necessary factor services.

The circularity of this process should be readily apparent. Furthermore, nothing in the argument depended on the *levels* of the flows. If all the figures in this example are multiplied by 10 (or by 100, or by any other number), the same argument can be reapplied. The new flows will continue indefinitely.

The circular flow of income is the flow from domestic households to domestic firms and back again.[5] As long as households spend all the money that they receive on buying goods and services from domestic firms and as long as firms pay out to domestic households all the money that they receive, the circular flow can go on unchanged forever. All money received by one group is passed on to the other in return for goods received or services rendered. There are neither *withdrawals* from, nor *injections* into, the flow.

A *withdrawal* is any income that is *not* passed on in the circular flow. Thus, if households earn income and do not spend it on goods and services, this income is withdrawn

from the circular flow. Similarly, if firms receive income from the sale of goods, and neither spend this money on purchasing factor services nor distribute it as profits, they have withdrawn it from the flow.

An *injection* is an addition to the income of households that does not arise from the spending of firms or to the income of firms that does not arise from the spending of households. An injection occurs, for example, if firms borrow money from banks to pay households for the use of factor services. Household income is increased not because households are buying more goods from firms, but because firms are borrowing money from outside the circular flow to hire additional factor services.

Figure 4 shows our circular-flow model amended to include injections and withdrawals. Injections are shown as additions to the circular flow of income and are labeled J. Withdrawals are shown as subtractions from the circular flow of income and are labeled W.

Withdrawals represent income received by households and not passed back to firms (upper right-hand arrow) and income received by firms and not passed back to households (lower left-hand arrow). If households elect to put some of their incomes aside rather than spend it all, they withdraw it from the flow. If firms do not pay out profits to their owners but hold the money back for use at some future time, they withdraw this money from the flow.

Injections create incomes for households that do not arise from the spending of firms (upper left-hand arrow) and create incomes for firms that do not arise from the spending of households (lower right-hand arrow). An example of the first sort of injection would occur if some households gained income by

5. *Domestic* is used in distinction to *foreign*.

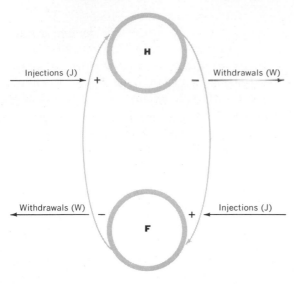

Injections (J)   +   Withdrawals (W)

Withdrawals (W)   −   +   Injections (J)

FIGURE 4

selling their services to foreign firms, for such income clearly does *not* arise from the spending of domestic firms. An example of the second sort of injection arises if some firms borrow money from banks and use the money to purchase goods produced by other firms. In this case, the incomes of firms go up without there having been any increase in the spending of households.

The flow of income increases or decreases according as the volume of injections exceeds or falls short of the volume of withdrawals. It should be obvious that, if we are withdrawing more than we are injecting, the volume of the flow of income around the circuit will be diminishing, whereas, if we are injecting more than we are withdrawing, the volume of the flow around the circuit will be increasing. Only if the two flows of injections and withdrawals are equal will the flow of income around the circuit be unchanged. In formal language, the equilibrium condition for the circular flow of income to be constant over time is that the volume of injections should equal the volume of withdrawals. This will be elaborated upon and illustrated in subsequent chapters.

Saving

If households save some of their income, then they must be spending less on goods and services than they receive as income. Savings are a withdrawal from the circular flow. Of course, some of the savings may eventually find their way back into the circular flow, if, for instance, households lend the money they save to firms and firms use it to build new factories. On the other hand, some of the money saved will not be returned to the circular flow, if, for example, households hoard it in their mattresses.

Firms as well as households can save money. If firms do not distribute all their profits, the undistributed part represents business savings. This money, too, will find its way back into the circular flow, if, for example, the firms use it to build new factories. On the other hand, it need not be returned to the circular flow if, for example, the firm puts it aside for some anticipated "rainy day."

Whatever subsequently happens to the money, the act of saving withdraws funds from the circular flow of income. In our model, we thus treat all savings as a withdrawal.

Investment

Investment is the expenditure on goods not for current consumption.[6] The principal forms of investment are increases in the *inventories* of raw materials, goods in process, and finished goods, and expenditures on *capital goods*, such as plant and equipment. Investment in capital goods is sometimes broken down into *replacement investment* and *new investment*. (The distinction between net and gross national product rests upon this division.) Total investment, or *gross investment*, as it is often called, includes all of these kinds of investment. *Net investment* is gross investment minus replacement investment.

Money for investment expenditure comes from many sources. Virtually all firms accumulate reserves for depreciation as fixed equipment wears out. Some actually set money aside in *sinking funds* to provide funds for replacement investment, but it is more common not to segregate funds. Except for such earmarked sources of funds, investment may be made from borrowed money, from funds currently received but not distributed to households, or from funds accumulated in the past.

In all cases, the expenditure of money on investment adds to the revenues of those firms selling the investment goods and thus in turn adds to the incomes of households selling factor services to these firms. Investment expenditure represents an addition to the circular flow of income. It creates income for households, but, since the goods are sold to other firms and not to households, it does not arise directly out of the expenditure of households. If, for example, firms spend funds accumulated in the past in order to build plant and equipment now, households' in-

comes will rise even though there was no increase in the spending of households.

From the point of view of its effect on the circular flow of income and on employment, it does not matter what the purpose is of the capital goods created by the new investment. A machine might be bought to replace one just worn out, it might be bought to replace one now regarded as obsolete, or it might be bought to increase capacity to produce consumers' goods. In all cases, the flow

In our model of income flows, gross investment is regarded as an injection, since it adds to the circular flow of income without there being any change in the spending of households on goods and services.

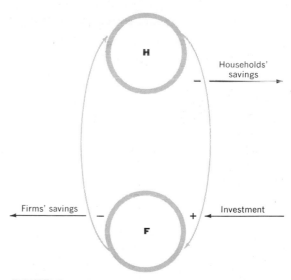

FIGURE 5

6. This can be a slippery concept.

of money is affected by the purchase of the investment goods.

These flows are illustrated in Figure 5. We have two savings withdrawals, since both firms and households save, but we have only one investment injection, since virtually all investment expenditure represents the sale of capital goods from one firm to another.

Foreign Trade

Domestic households may spend part of their income on goods produced by foreign firms, and domestic firms may sell part of their output to households located in foreign countries. The first set of expenditures results in *imports* of goods and services (to which we assign the symbol M) and the second results in *exports* (to which we assign the symbol X).

Imports constitute a withdrawal from the circular flow because, when households spend their incomes on imported goods instead of domestic ones, they create incomes for the foreign firms that make these goods instead of for domestic firms. If, to take an extreme example, households were suddenly to decide to spend all of their incomes on imported goods, no money would be passed back to domestic firms, the income of these firms would fall to zero, and, once they ceased to produce goods for the accumulation of inventories, income paid out to households would fall to zero. To take a less extreme example, assume that American households decide to buy fewer Chevrolets and more Volkswagens. This means that a smaller proportion of the income received by American households will be passed back to the General Motors Corporation and a larger proportion will be withdrawn from the circular flow in the American economy. General Motors will now earn less income and will hire fewer factors so that incomes of U.S. households will fall as well.

Whatever subsequently happens to the money, the act of importing withdraws funds from the circular flow. In our model, we treat all imports as a withdrawal.

One country's imports are another country's exports. Exports constitute an injection into the domestic circular flow of income. In the previous example, there was an increase of imports into the U.S., but there was simultaneously an increase in exports of Volkswagens from Germany. This increase in exports means that the German car company gains an increase in its income and, since

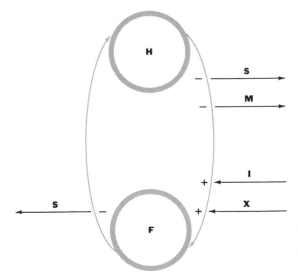

FIGURE 6

more factors will be needed to produce more Volkswagens, there will also be an increase in the income of German households. This increase in the circular flow in Germany did not arise because of any change in the expenditures of German households (it was the expenditure patterns of U.S. households that changed), and so it constitutes an injection into the German circular flow of income.

Whatever subsequently happens to the money, the act of exporting injects funds into the circular flow. In our model, we treat all exports as an injection.

Figure 6 shows imports and exports added to the model of the circular flow of income.

Government Activity

In some aspects of its behavior, the government can be regarded as just another producer buying factor services from households and selling goods to households. This is the case, for example, with the Post Office. In other cases, the government gains its revenue by exercising its right of taxation. Taxes take money from firms and households and so reduce the amount that they can spend on purchasing goods and services. The government uses some of the money it raises through taxation to purchase goods and services. Sometimes the goods and services are consumed directly by government bodies, as is the case with defense goods, and sometimes the goods and services are distributed to households, as is the case with education and the services of most roads and bridges. Some of the money may also be distributed directly to households and firms in the form of grants, pensions, and subsidies. These are *not* paid out in return for currently produced goods and services. Such payments are referred to as *transfer payments*.

Taxes withdraw money from the circular flow of income in just the same way as do savings and imports. If the government taxes firms, part of the money received by firms is not available to be passed on to households.

If the government taxes households, part of the money received by households is not available to be passed back to firms. Of course, some of the tax revenue may find its way back to the circular flow if the government subsequently spends it on commodities purchased from firms or on factor services hired from households. On the other hand, if the government does not spend the money but merely lets it accumulate as a reserve against some future expected expenditure, it will remain outside of the flow.

Whatever subsequently happens to the money, the act of taxing withdraws funds from the circular flow of income. In our model, we thus treat all taxes as a withdrawal. Such taxes are assigned the symbol T.

Government expenditure to buy the services of households or to buy commodities produced by firms represents an injection. It creates income for firms that does not arise out of the expenditure of households. If, for example, the government borrows money from banks and spends this money buying missiles from private firms, the incomes of these firms will rise, as will the incomes of those

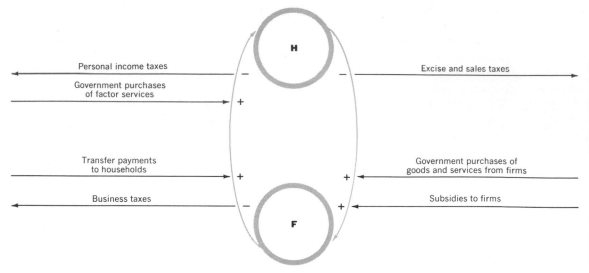

Personal income taxes	−	−	Excise and sales taxes
Government purchases of factor services	+		
Transfer payments to households	+	+	Government purchases of goods and services from firms
Business taxes	−	+	Subsidies to firms

FIGURE 7

households that work on the rocket project. Clearly, this expenditure represents an injection into the circular flow.

_____

In our model, all government expenditure on goods and services is treated as an injection. Such expenditure is assigned the symbol G.

_____

We must now incorporate these various government activities into our simple model of the circular flow. Figure 7 represents various governmental injections into and withdrawals from the circular flow. We shall include government commercial activities, in which factor services are hired and the resulting production is sold to households, in the *firm* sector. Thus when we talk of the activities of firms, we now mean the activities of all bodies, public or private, that buy factor

services from households and earn their incomes by selling their output on the market. All other activities of government are treated as withdrawals or injections.

In order to incorporate the role of the government into our general circular-flow analysis, we shall combine all of these different withdrawals and injections into aggregates, and merely show G entering as one injection in each branch of the circular flow, and T as one withdrawal in each branch.

In Figure 8, we combine the various elements we have discussed in this chapter. Compare this figure with the simple circular flow in Figure 2. There are many different withdrawals from and injections into the circular flow; the level of the flow and whether and why it rises or falls are complex and difficult matters, important aspects of which we shall explore in the next six chapters.

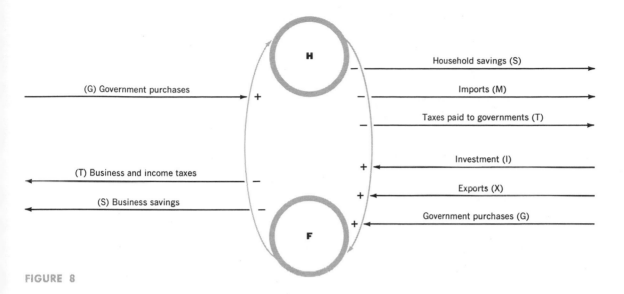

(G) Government purchases

Household savings (S)

Imports (M)

Taxes paid to governments (T)

Investment (I)

Exports (X)

Government purchases (G)

(T) Business and income taxes

(S) Business savings

H

F

FIGURE 8

Summary

1. This chapter is an introduction to the model of the circular flow of income, which we define as the flow of income from domestic households to domestic firms and back again.

2. When all money received by firms and households is passed on again through their spending, we say there are neither injections into nor withdrawals from the circular flow. Injections are defined as either income of domestic households that does not arise from the spending of domestic firms or income of domestic firms that does not arise from the spending of domestic households. Withdrawals are defined as any income received that is not passed on in the domestic circular flow.

3. We shall use the terms total income, gross national product, and national income interchangeably to mean the total value of goods and services produced by the economy in some period. Net income, or net national product, is simply total income less that portion of the value of goods produced to replace capital that has been used up in production. A further useful concept is disposable income, which is the total income actually available to the households for expenditure.

4. Whatever subsequently happens to the money, funds are withdrawn from the circular flow by savings (S), imports (M), and taxes (T).

5. Wherever the money comes from, investment (I), exports (X), and government expenditure (G) inject money into the circular flow.

6. Figure 8 represents all the elements discussed in this chapter.

QUESTIONS FOR DISCUSSION

1. How can the income of an economy ever be greater than the amount of money in the system?

2. How do we measure the value added by the productive activities of a single firm? Of what use is this concept? Do you think this measure could ever be negative?

3. What is the difference between net and gross national product? Which concept is the better one?

4. Where would you show the following in a diagram of the circular flow of American income?
a. the wages paid by General Motors to its employees;
b. the amount spent on automobiles by consumers;
c. the money families put in savings accounts;
d. corporation taxes;
e. the money spent in Vietnam on defense by the U.S. Government;
f. the money spent in the U.S. on materiel for the war in Vietnam;
g. the money spent by the Greek post office on obtaining the services of an American team of efficiency experts;
h. the money spent by the Chrysler Corporation on retooling for next year's production.

5. Review the examples in Question 4 from the point of view of the circular flow of income in countries other than the United States.

6. For each of the eight examples in Question 4, try to find a current newspaper article or similar item that discusses something in the same category.

APPENDIX TO CHAPTER 45 MEASURING NATIONAL INCOME

Why Measure National Income?

THE PRESIDENT, IN HIS ANNUAL economic report, relies heavily on the so-called national-income accounts to describe the state of the U.S. economy. The main reason for attempting to measure the volume of goods and services produced is to provide policy-makers with information as to whether the economy is performing smoothly or whether some sort of crisis is developing. Although the economic history of most Western countries is, in the long run, a series of triumphs, the short-run behavior is much less impressive. The general upward march of these economies has been interrupted by periods of depression and recession that take a heavy toll in human welfare and by periods of inflation that drastically affect the distribution of income. Economic theory is concerned with understanding these things; economic policy is concerned with preventing them. Even if our theories were perfect and our policy tools wholly adequate, we would need measurements, such as the national-income accounts, to tell us when and where trouble spots were developing. The Council of Economic Advisors constantly studies the latest changes reported in these various accounts. As economists, we are interested in them because they provide the data for testing our theories.

Governmental interest in national-income accounts dates from the Great Depression. Today, the collection of national-income data is one of the major activities of the Department of Commerce; the most recent figures are published in the Department's publication, *Survey of Current Business.*

The Concepts of National Production and Income

In Chapter 45, we drew an analogy between the flow of income and of goods and services through the economy and the flow of water through pipes. To measure the volume of water going through a system of pipes over a certain period of time (say, one year), we might attach a meter to one point in the system to record the volume of water passing that point. As long as the flow of water is in equilibrium—as long as it is the same from hour to hour or from day to day—it does not matter at which point the meter is attached.[1] The flow past every point will be the same.

So it is with the economic flows. When the flow of income is constant, the flow past any point in the economy is the same as the flow past every other point. Just as we can measure the flow of water at a number of different points, so are there a number of related ways of measuring national income. For example, in the very simple economy described in Chapter 45, we might measure the following:

1. The flow of goods and services—the oranges, automobiles, television sets, haircuts, and so on—from firms to households. In order to estimate the value of this flow, we have to convert the goods and services into a common unit, such as their money value.

2. The payment for goods and services made by households to firms. *The payment for the goods and services will be exactly the same as the value of the goods and services,* for it represents the opposite side of the same transaction: Every dollar's worth of goods that is sold by a firm to a household leads to a dollar's worth of payment from the household to the firm.

3. The total value of all payments to factors of production, including wages, interest, profits, etc. If we include all payments, including profits, *this too should be the same as the previous totals,* for every dollar received by the firm is either a payment for some factors of production or an addition to profits.

A real economy is more complex: Not all goods that are produced are sold; some sales by firms are to other firms instead of to households; not all goods or factors used are actually paid for; and so on. But, with appropriate adjustments, even a complex economy can be measured. Let us look at some specific measures.

GROSS NATIONAL PRODUCT (GNP)

GNP is defined as the *market value* of all *final goods and services* produced in a given period of time. The choice of *market value* as the measuring rod to add up different commodities is justified, because market values reflect the value that the consumers of the goods place upon them. For goods that are produced and sold, this is clear enough. For goods that are produced and held in inventories (for sale next year, perhaps), the assignment of market value anticipates their sale (and thus goes against the conventions of accountants), but it is justified because the *value* of a Ford in the dealer's showroom is just as great as the identical Ford that is sold to you. The concept of *final goods and services* is difficult and is treated somewhat arbitrarily. All sales to households are treated as final products. Business-investment expenditures are treated as final products. And all government expenditures are treated as final products. Intermediate goods purchased by business for further processing are not treated as final products. Thus when a firm buys a machine or a truck, the purchase is treated as a final good; when it buys a ton of steel, however, the steel is not treated as a final product. The reason for excluding intermediate goods is that we wish to avoid double counting: If the steel is used to make a refrigerator, we will count its value as part of the refrigerator, and do not wish to count it as steel as well.

EXPENDITURE APPROACH TO MEASURING GNP

One way in which the Department of Commerce estimates GNP is by adding up the

---

1. The qualification is important. In disequilibrium, the flows will be different at different points.

Personal consumption expenditures	399	
Durable goods		57
Nondurable goods		177
Services		165
Gross private domestic investment	88	
New construction		49
Producers' durable equipment		35
Change in business inventories		4
Government purchases of goods and services	129	
Net exports	7	
TOTAL GNP	623	

SOURCE: The source for this, the following five tables, and Table A8 is the *Survey of Current Business.*

expenditures on those kinds of purchases that are classified as final goods and services. The basic formula is:

GNP = Consumption + Investment + Government Purchases

or, $GNP = C + I + G.$ (1)

Actually, a somewhat more elaborate series of categories is used, as shown in Table A1.

The major difference between this table and equation (1) is that sales of goods to foreign buyers are not incorporated into the accounts. The reason we include only *net* exports (that is, the value of exports minus the value of imports) in GNP is that gross imports are included in the consumption data.[2]

These same totals can be derived another way (and they *are* so derived as a check on the accuracy of the method). This alternative way is to use the *value added* in all production. (The distinction between value and value added was discussed on pages 527–528. You should review it at this point.)

FACTOR PAYMENTS APPROACH TO MEASURING GNP

We have seen that, in principle, we should be able to estimate total GNP by measuring payments made by firms. Table A2 provides the data in this form.

Table A2 includes all the items that enter the cost side of the production process. "Other compensation of employees" includes fringe benefits (such as contributions to pension funds) and social-security taxes. "Rental income" includes rent payments by those who rent homes or property; it also includes an estimated imputed rental on owner-occupied housing. "Net interest" is the total of interest payments *minus* the government's payment of interest. Government interest payments are considered to be *transfer* payments rather than payments for goods or services.

All business taxes, whether indirect or direct, are included as costs or profits and thus en-

TABLE A2   **FACTOR PAYMENTS APPROACH TO GROSS NATIONAL PRODUCT, 1964, IN BILLIONS OF DOLLARS**

Wages and other compensation of employees		362
Rental income		12
Net interest		27
Income of unincorporated enterprises		52
Depreciation changes		53
Corporate profits before taxes		58
Dividends	20	
Undistributed profits	12	
Corporate income taxes	26	
Indirect business taxes		59
TOTAL GNP		623

2. If the data concerned only domestic consumption, we would need to include gross exports to reflect the total value of goods and services produced in the United States.

ter into GNP. Although this often troubles students, it should not. One way of looking at such taxes is that they are payments for the services governments provide to firms. We regard them as the other side of the coin of the government expenditures, which we included in Table A1, Expenditure Approach to GNP. Another way of looking at them is that every dollar of taxes paid either increases the price of goods or decreases the profits of the firm, the balance between these two effects depending upon the extent to which the tax is shifted onto the consumer. The sum of the two effects for each dollar of tax is, by definition, one dollar.[3]

Note that all profits, whether paid in dividends or plowed back into the business, are included in GNP.

THE INTERPRETATION OF GNP

GNP, a convenient and widely used measure of the productive activity of the economy during a stated period, can, as can almost all useful things, be abused and misinterpreted. Let us note some of the things it does not measure:

1. It does not measure human welfare. There are many reasons why it does not, among which are the following: (a) One aspect of human welfare is the quantity of goods and services available *per person*, but GNP measures only the quantity available for the whole population. (b) GNP does not measure leisure, an-

other indicator of human welfare. A shorter workweek, and the leisure it entails, increases human well-being. However, the shortening of the workweek over the last 50 years from 60 hours to 40 hours would (other things being equal) have decreased by one-third the output of goods and services. Fortunately, other things were not equal, and we have increased both our goods and services *and* our leisure, although the GNP does not indicate this twofold effect. (c) GNP does not allow for the capacity of different goods to provide different results. A million dollars spent on a bomber or a missile makes the same addition to GNP as a million dollars spent on a school or a concert stadium or candy bars. But, from a welfare point of view, the same $1 million produces different effects. A society that could trade swords for plows, narcotics for food, and fallout shelters for houses would be richer, in the welfare sense, but such trades would not make for a larger GNP. (d) GNP is independent of the distribution of income among people. Old-age assistance and other transfer payments are not included in GNP, but most people agree that they increase the over-all welfare of the population.

2. GNP does not measure the value of *all* the goods and services produced. The food a farmer grows for his own consumption and the services a housewife provides her family are not included.[4] GNP is lim-

ited (with a few exceptions) to goods and services that are exchanged in markets. If we use the GNP as a measure of the behavior of the market, the exclusion of nonmarket transactions is desirable.

3. GNP is measured in market prices; thus, it is no better a measure of values than are the market prices involved. One problem is with comparisons of GNP over time whenever there has been inflation or deflation, a problem we will return to later in the appendix.

NET NATIONAL PRODUCT

GNP includes all expenditures in investment goods produced in a given year, whether they are designed to replace existing goods or whether they are net additions to the economy's capital stock. Net National Product is GNP less allowances for "capital consumption" (which is a somewhat generalized term for depreciation).

For many purposes, it is useful to distinguish between investment expenditures that merely replace equipment that

TABLE A3   NET NATIONAL PRODUCT, 1964, IN BILLIONS OF DOLLARS

Gross national product	623
Less capital consumption allowance	53
Net national product	570

3. The value of a final good is, by *definition:*

$$\text{Value of final good} \equiv \text{All costs except profits and taxes} + \text{Profits} + \text{Taxes}.$$

Therefore, we must include taxes to make the two approaches give the some result.

4. One of the best examples is that, when a man marries his housekeeper, GNP declines.

TABLE A4   **PERSONAL INCOME AND DISPOSABLE INCOME, 1964, IN BILLIONS OF DOLLARS**

Wages and other labor income, less contributions for social security	334
Rental income	12
Interest income, including government interest payments	36
Income of unincorporated enterprises	52
Dividends	20
Transfer payments to individuals (social-security payments, etc.)	38
Personal income	492
Less personal taxes	60
Disposable income	432

to GNP and also as a generic term to embrace a whole series of concepts. We will continue to do so, because it seems use-

TABLE A6   **ALLOCATION OF DISPOSABLE INCOME, 1964, IN BILLIONS OF DOLLARS**

Consumption		399
Consumer durables	57	
Consumer non-durables	177	
Services	165	
Savings		33
Disposable income		432

wears out and those that produce a net increase in the capital stock. Rather than try to make such a distinction on every investment expenditure, government statisticians estimate the amount of depreciation (or "capital-consumption allowance") that should be charged in a given period and subtract it from GNP to get Net National Product. See Table A3.

Approximately 9 percent of the total of GNP goes to replacing assets that wear out, such as machines, tractors, and houses. Depreciation in 1964 accounted for about 60 percent of gross investment. In some years it exceeds gross investment. For example, in 1932, gross investment was less than $1 billion, but depreciation was $7 billion. This means that net investment was minus $6 billion; the economy as a whole was drawing down its stock of

capital by failing to replace equipment as it wore out.

NATIONAL INCOME
(Technical Definition)

We have used the term nation income as being equivalent

ful. But national income accountants use the term in a special sense: as Net National Product minus indirect business taxes. Because this is not a concept that has any special relevance to economists, we shall not discuss it further.[5]

TABLE A5   **NATIONAL INCOME ACCOUNTS, 1964, IN BILLIONS OF DOLLARS**

Gross national product		623
Less capital consumption allowances	53	
Net national product		570
Less indirect business taxes	59	
National income		511
Less corporation, income, and social-security taxes	54	
Less undistributed profits	12	
Plus government interest payments	9	
other transfer payments	38	
Personal income		492
Less personal taxes	60	
Disposable income		432

5. There is no clear reason that we know of for excluding indirect taxes and including direct taxes and income taxes.

PERSONAL INCOME AND DISPOSABLE INCOME

Personal income includes all income received by persons. (See Table A4.) It does not include the following GNP items: depreciation, business taxes, undistributed profits, and employers' contributions to social security. But it does include some items that GNP does not measure: interest payments by the government (as on savings bonds) and social-security payments to elderly persons, both of which are income to the recipients.

Disposable income is the income people have for spending. It is personal income minus the taxes that are paid by individuals.

Table A5 shows how the various measures are interrelated, omitting only a few minor items. Table A6 shows the distribution of disposable income into major classes.

National Income Over Time

Table A7 presents, for the years from 1929–1964, several of the measures discussed in this chapter. They reflect the economic history of this period. One difficulty in interpreting these figures is the problem of price changes. For example, GNP in 1934 was $65 billion; in 1964, it was $623 billion. How much of this increase represents a change in the volume of goods and services produced and how much reflects shrinkage in our measuring stick, the dollar?

To answer this question, we have to "deflate" the GNP series, which means to adjust it for the change in the level of prices. This is done for selected years in Table A8. We see that the increase in the flow of goods and services from 1934 to 1964 was between three- and fourfold, not the almost tenfold increase shown in the money figures. GNP in

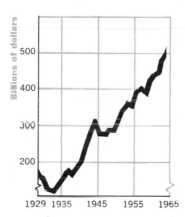

FIGURE A1   GNP IN CONSTANT 1954 DOLLARS

constant dollars is shown in Figure A1. This provides impressive evidence of the growth in the volume of goods and services we produce.

What of the material well-being of the average American? GNP has increased, but so have

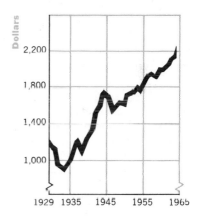

FIGURE A2   DI PER CAPITA IN CONSTANT 1964 DOLLARS

the size of the population and the amount of money the government takes as taxes. Figure A2 shows disposable income per capita in 1964 dollars. This measure is adjusted for price changes, population changes, and income-tax changes.

TABLE A7 **SELECTED STATISTICAL SERIES FOR
THE UNITED STATES, 1929–1964**

Year	GNP	NNP	DI	Population in thousands	GNP per capita in dollars
	Billions of dollars				
1929	104	96	83	121,875	856
1930	91	83	74	123,188	739
1931	76	68	64	124,149	615
1932	59	51	49	124,949	468
1933	56	49	46	125,690	446
1934	65	58	52	126,485	514
1935	73	65	58	127,362	569
1936	83	75	66	128,181	645
1937	91	83	71	128,961	704
1938	85	77	66	129,969	656
1939	91	83	70	131,028	695
1940	101	93	76	132,122	761
1941	126	117	93	133,402	943
1942	159	149	118	134,860	1,180
1943	193	182	134	136,739	1,408
1944	211	199	147	138,397	1,527
1945	214	201	150	139,928	1,526
1946	211	200	161	141,389	1,490
1947	234	221	170	144,126	1,626
1948	259	244	189	146,631	1,769
1949	258	241	190	149,188	1,730
1950	285	266	208	151,689	1,876
1951	329	307	228	154,283	2,132
1952	347	323	239	156,947	2,212
1953	365	339	253	159,559	2,289
1954	363	334	257	162,388	2,236
1955	398	366	274	165,276	2,405
1956	419	385	293	168,225	2,492
1957	443	405	309	171,278	2,585
1958	445	406	318	174,154	2,552
1959	483	442	337	177,080	2,726
1960	503	460	350	180,684	2,781
1961	519	474	365	183,756	2,822
1962	556	508	385	186,656	2,979
1963	584	533	403	189,375	3,083
1964	623	570	432	192,072	3,241

SOURCES: *Historical Statistics of the United States*, p. 139; and *Economic Report of the President, 1965*, pp. 204–205.

TABLE A8   STATISTICAL DEFLATION OF GNP, SELECTED YEARS

Year	GNP in billions of current dollars (1)	Index of prices, 1954 = 100 (2)	GNP in billions of 1954 dollars (1) ÷ (2)
1934	65	46.9	139
1944	211	66.5	317
1954	363	100.0	363
1964	623	120.7	516

QUESTIONS FOR DISCUSSION

1. What does GNP *not* measure?

2. Why do we exclude from GNP the purchase by a baker of grain?

3. Compare the expenditure approach with the factor-payments approach in measuring GNP.

4. Why do we sometimes want to remove the effects of price changes from our measures of the GNP?

5. "They have accumulated many goods and yet their joy in the world has grown less." (From Fëdor Dostocvski, *The Brothers Karamazov.*) What warning about the use of GNP statistics does this passage point to?

Chapter **46** EQUILIBRIUM IN THE CIRCULAR FLOW

IN CHAPTER 45 WE LAID OUT THE BASIC model of the circular flow of goods and income. In the present chapter we study the determination of the equilibrium level of the flow and examine how this level changes in response to changes in the level of each of the components we discussed in Chapter 45.

In subsequent chapters we will consider in detail theories about the behavior of each of the major magnitudes in the flow.

In order to move quickly to the core of the theory of the circular flow of income, we shall make some simplifying assumptions about the behavior of output and prices. Later we will be able to work without these assumptions, but in the meantime they allow us to study the behavior of national income within a simple and yet empirically relevant framework.

Supply and Prices: Some Simplifying Assumptions

We shall assume, first, that the prices of all goods and services are constant and that changes in the demand for goods are met by changes in output. If we think in terms of demand and supply curves, we are supposing that "aggregate supply" is a horizontal line, and thus that the level of output is demand-determined. This is a roughly acceptable assumption if we think of the economy as having a margin of unutilized capacity with less than full employment of all resources. It would not be acceptable in a situation of full employment. We discuss such a situation in Chapter 55.

We shall assume, second, that the size of the labor force is constant. A consequence of this assumption is that (given our first assumption), a rise in the demand for goods, which increases output, increases employment and decreases unemployment. (This assumption is relaxed in Chapter 56.)

We shall assume, third, that inventories remain constant. The consequence of this assumption is that the value of output produced in a given year is the same as the value of output sold in the same year. We discuss situations where this assumption is inapplicable in Chapter 49.

In summary, we assume that we are dealing with situations of unemployment; that prices do not change so that fluctuations in the value of output represent fluctuations in quantities of output; that output is demand-determined, by which we mean that it adjusts passively to fluctuations in total demand in the economy; and that employment of labor fluctuates directly with output, whereas unemployment fluctuates inversely with it. *Under these assumptions, a theory of the fluctuations in aggregate demand provides a theory of fluctuations in the level of national income and of employment.*

Withdrawals, Injections, and Aggregate Demand

In the previous chapter we described three main withdrawals and three main injections in the circular flow. These are summarized in Exhibit 1, first in words and then by assigning a symbol to each.

Aggregate demand is the total of all the demand in the economy. In the simplified model we are considering, aggregate demand determines the volume of income and em-

EXHIBIT 1   **WITHDRAWALS FROM AND INJECTIONS INTO THE CIRCULAR FLOW**

Withdrawals = Savings + imports + taxes.

$$(W = S + M + T)$$

Injections = Investment + exports + government expenditure.

$$(J = I + X + G)$$

EXHIBIT 2   AGGREGATE DEMAND IN THE CIRCULAR FLOW

Aggregate demand = Total demand for goods and services produced by the economy.

Aggregate demand = Expenditure arising from within the flow + injections into the system.

$(AD = C + J)$

Aggregate demand = $\dfrac{\text{Expenditure of households on}}{\text{domestically produced commodities}}$ + investment + exports + $\dfrac{\text{government}}{\text{expenditure.}}$

$(AD = C + I + X + G)$

---

ployment. Demand has two main components: the demand that is injected into the system and the demand that arises from within it because of the spending of households. Total demand in the economy is thus *total injections plus household expenditure on domestically produced goods and services.* See Exhibit 2, where the concept is set out both in symbols and in words.

We study the behavior of the components of the circular flow in subsequent chapters; in the meantime some very simple hypotheses and assumptions allow us to study the determinants of national income. The basic hypothesis is as follows: Everything that originates within the circular flow is assumed to increase as income increases, and everything that is injected from without is assumed to be unaffected by a rise in income. Thus, all withdrawals and consumption expenditure vary directly with income, and all injections are constant with respect to income changes. Consider these one at a time.

1. Consumption is assumed to rise as income rises: The greater the income of a household, the greater the number of dollars it will spend on purchases from domestic firms.

2. Household saving is assumed to rise with income. The greater the household's income, the greater the number of dollars it saves.

3. Imports are assumed to rise with income, because, as incomes rise, households spend more on all kinds of goods, including goods produced abroad.

4. Tax revenue is assumed to rise with income, because, with all tax rates held constant, a rise in household income will increase the yield of income taxes, a rise in household spending on imports will increase the revenue from tariffs, and a rise in spending on domestic consumption will increase the revenue from excise taxes.

Now consider injections. We hypothesize that exports depend on the prices of our goods and on the incomes of foreign households. For the moment, we hold both of these things constant, so exports must be constant. Government expenditure depends on decisions of governments, whereas investment expenditure depends on decisions of firms. Both of these are important determinants of aggregate demand. We shall have a great deal to say about them later, but in the meantime we assume them to be constant, because we do not yet have a theory of how and why they change. These injections, which do not depend on domestic income and which for the moment are assumed to be constant, are often

Components	Behavior as total income rises
Withdrawals	
Savings	Rise by hypothesis
Imports	Rise by hypothesis
Taxes	Rise by hypothesis
Consumption	Rises by hypothesis
Injections	
Investment	Assumed constant (for this chapter)
Exports	Assumed constant (for this chapter)
Government expenditure	Assumed constant (for this chapter)

Locate all those points showing expenditure equal to income. This line, which is labeled $E = Y$, makes an angle of 45° with

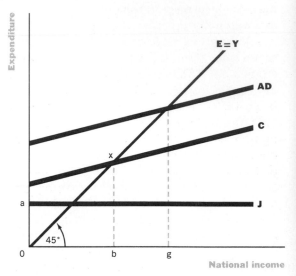

FIGURE 1

referred to as *autonomous expenditures*. They affect the system but are unaffected by it.[1] These assumptions and hypotheses are summarized in Exhibit 3.

GRAPHICAL REPRESENTATION OF WITHDRAWALS, INJECTIONS, AND AGGREGATE DEMAND

Our various assumptions and hypotheses about behavior are plotted on Figure 1. National income is plotted on the horizontal axis and expenditure on the vertical. We measure both of these flows as amounts per year, and we use equal distances to measure a dollar of income and a dollar of expenditure. Any point on this graph shows a combination of income and expenditure. For example, point x shows Ob of income combined with bx of expenditure.

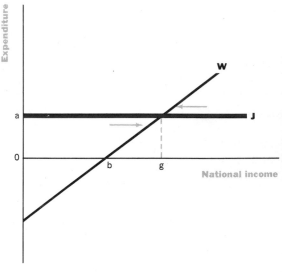

FIGURE 2

1. Autonomous has the same connotations as exogenous. See the appendix to Chapter 3.

the Y-axis and is often referred to as the 45° *line*. Points above or to the left of the 45° line show combinations for which expenditure exceeds income; points below or to the right of the 45° line show combinations for which expenditure is less than income.

Injections are assumed to be independent of income; they are shown as a horizontal straight line, which, in Figure 1, is labeled *aJ*. They are equal to the same amount (*Oa* in Figure 1), whatever the level of income.

Consumption expenditure[2] is shown as an upward-sloping line, indicating that the larger the national income, the larger the consumption expenditure. At the low levels of income below *Ob*, consumption expenditure exceeds income, indicating that households must either be borrowing money or using up their savings. At incomes above *Ob*, consumption expenditure is less than income. Since the 45° line shows points where expenditure equals income, the vertical gap between the consumption line and the 45° line shows the amount by which consumption expenditure falls short of income.[3]

In order to represent aggregate demand, we must add consumption to the injections at each level of income. Since injections are constant, the aggregate-demand line has the same slope as the *C* line (i.e., aggregate demand varies with income only insofar as consumption expenditure varies), but it is shifted upward by the amount of the other injections. That is, the vertical distance between *AD* and *C* is equal to *Oa*.

We have now represented every one of our components on the graph except withdrawals. We have defined a withdrawal as "any income *not* passed on." *Withdrawals are by definition the difference between Y and C.* In Figure 1, withdrawals at each level of income are represented by the vertical distance between the 45° line and *C*. At income *Ob*, withdrawals are zero: All of income is passed on. To the right of this income level, withdrawals are positive and get larger as income rises. To the left of income level *Ob*, consumption exceeds income, and therefore withdrawals are negative. What does this mean? It means that, in order to spend more than they receive, households must either borrow money or use their savings. Either result is regarded as a negative withdrawal. Because Figure 1 is getting crowded, we plot the withdrawal schedule on Figure 2. The scale is exactly the same as in Figure 1, and the points *O*, *a*, *b*, etc., are precisely the same.

The withdrawal line rises with income, as we hypothesized it would.† The withdrawals schedule shows for any level of income the amount of that income not passed on through spending on domestically produced goods. The consumption schedule shows the amount of income that is passed on through spending on domestically produced goods. Clearly, the amount that is not passed on plus the amount that is passed on must equal the whole of income. Therefore, the addition of the *W* line to the *C* line must yield the 45° line, indicating that the total of the amounts spent plus the amounts not spent must account for all of national income.

---

2. Remember that we have defined consumption as "expenditures of domestic households on domestically produced goods."

3. We have drawn the relation of consumption to income as an upward-sloping straight line with a slope of less than 45°. The hypotheses that underlie this particular shape are discussed in Chapter 47.

† We leave as an exercise to the student to show that it does so as a direct result of the fact that we drew the *C* schedule with a slope flatter than the 45° line. We shall discuss the matter in the next chapter.

The Equilibrium Level of Income

We can now determine the level of national income (the volume of the circular flow) at which income is in equilibrium—that is, the level at which there is no tendency for it either to rise or to fall. This equilibrium can be represented in three ways:

1. *Withdrawals equal injections.* If the volume of withdrawals from the circular flow of income equals the volume of injections, then income will remain unchanged. In Figure 2, the level of income for which withdrawals equal injections is *Og*.[4] If more is being withdrawn than is being injected, however, the flow of national income will be declining. If less is being withdrawn in terms of savings, imports, and taxes than is being injected in terms of autonomous expenditure, then income must be rising. Since withdrawals rise as income rises and injections are constant, it follows that at all incomes in excess of *Og* withdrawals will exceed injections and income must be falling. Thus, the arrow to the right of the point of intersection of the *W* and *J* lines in Figure 2 indicates a downward pressure on national income. By the same argument, at incomes below *Og*, withdrawals must fall short of injections and an upward pressure must exist on national income. The equilibrium level of national income is given by the intersection of the withdrawals schedule and the injections schedule; at any other level of income there will be pressure pushing income in the direction of the equilibrium level.

2. *Aggregate demand equals income.* The second way of looking at equilibrium in the circular flow is to find the level of income for which aggregate demand, which determines expenditure in the economy, is equal to the current level of income. If we think again of the circular flow of income, we know that total demand determines the amount of output, the amount of output determines the amount of income earned, and the amount of income earned determines the amount of demand. If the amount being demanded is equal to current incomes, then there is no reason for output, income, or demand to change. If the amount demanded exceeds output and incomes, then output will rise as will incomes earned by households. If, on the other hand, total demand is less than current output and income, then both output and income earned will fall.

The level of income for which aggregate demand equals income is *Og* in Figure 1. At higher levels of income, aggregate demand is less than current incomes so that a downward pressure is exerted on incomes. At lower levels of income, aggregate demand exceeds current incomes and an upward pressure is exerted on national income.

3. *Income last "period" equals income this "period."*[5] The reason why national income can be at a level other than its equilibrium one is because adjustments do not occur instantaneously. A rise in aggregate demand leads, after a lapse of time, to a rise in output. After a further lapse of time, the rise in output places more income in the hands of house-

4. The same result is also apparent in Figure 1. At income *Og*, the distance between *C* and the 45° line is exactly equal to the distance between *C* and *AD*.

5. This section may be omitted.

holds and this after a while leads to a rise in households' spending. If all of these adjustments occurred instantaneously, we would always be at the equilibrium level of national income. Since they do not, we describe this by saying that there are lags in the circular flow of income.

In a full theory of the circular flow, we would allow for these lags, some of which are quite complex. In a simple theory, we can show the essence of the problem by stating very simple lags. We divide time into periods

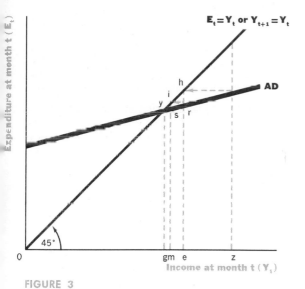

FIGURE 3

called months. The expenditure of households this month is a function of income earned this month, and income earned next month is equal to expenditure this month. In other words, expenditure adjusts to income without a lag, but income adjusts to expenditure with a lag of one month.

This circular-flow system is shown in Figure 3, which has the same scale as Figures 1 and 2. On the horizontal axis, we have income at month t. On the vertical axis, we have expenditure at month t, which will become next month's income (income at time $t + 1$). The aggregate-demand function shows expenditure at time t as depending on income at time t. The 45° line shows all those points for which expenditure at t equals income at t or all those at which income at $t + 1$ equals income at t, which is the same thing. Equilibrium in national income can only occur when income remains constant—that is, at a point where $Y_t = Y_{t+1}$. All such points fall along the 45° line. The equilibrium level of income is now given by the intersection of the two lines on the diagram. To see this, take a level of income above the equilibrium level, say Oz. At that level of income, expenditure is less than current income, so that income generated next period is less than Oz. It will, in fact, be eh. When income is eh (which by the construction of the 45° lines is also Oe), then expenditure is only er. In the following month, income falls to $er = mi$ and, at that level of income, expenditure falls to ms. And so it goes, with income continuing to fall as long as expenditure is less than income, but with the gap between expenditure and income steadily narrowing until, at income Og, expenditure equals income (point y), and equilibrium is attained. The broken arrow shows the sequence of steps we have described.

Repeat the analysis for a case in which income begins at a level below the equilibrium one, and show that income will rise steadily because expenditure exceeds income until, at point y, expenditure and income are equal.†

† This is a case where a little algebra goes a long way. Our assumed lag model says:

$$E_t = f(Y_t) \qquad (1)$$

(footnote continued)

SUMMARY

The nature of the equilibrium of the circular flow can be represented in several alternative ways. They all show the same thing, of course. In subsequent chapters, we shall use two approaches: the one that defines equilibrium where injections equal withdrawals (as pictured in Figure 2), and the one that defines it where aggregate demand crosses the 45° line. You should always draw the diagrams both ways to become completely familiar with both approaches.

The Effects on Income of Changes in Injections and Withdrawals

What happens to national income if there are changes in the expenditure patterns of households, firms, or the government?

We can use the same analysis for any autonomous injection of expenditure, whether it be an increase in investment, exports, or government expenditure. In Figure 4, this is shown by an upward shift in the injection schedule from J_1 to J_2. At the original level of income, Og, injections exceed withdrawals and income will rise. As income rises, withdrawals, which are a function of income, also rise, as shown by the upward slope of the withdrawal function W. The rise in income continues until withdrawals are again equal to the (now higher level of) injections. This is at income Od in the figure.

We can analyze a fall in investment, exports, or government spending by assuming income to start at Od; autonomous expenditure then falls from J_2 to J_1.

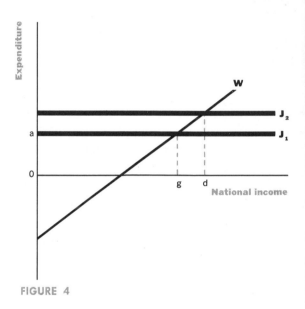

FIGURE 4

We have now derived two predictions from our theory:

(*continued*)
and

$$Y_{t+1} = E_t.$$ (2)

But for equilibrium, we require:

$$Y_{t+1} = Y_t.$$ (3)

By substituting (2) and (3) into (1), we get:

$$E_t = Y_t = f(Y_t).$$ (4)

One of the equations in (4), $E_t = Y_t$, defines the 45° line. Another, $E_t = f(Y_t)$, defines the expenditure function. Equation (4) tells us that to be in equilibrium *both equations must be satisfied*. This is only possible where the expenditure function intersects the 45° line—the result sought.

1. A rise in investment expenditure, exports, or government expenditure, ceteris paribus, will raise the level of national income.

2. A fall in investment expenditure, exports, or government expenditure, ceteris paribus, will lower the level of national income.

A downward shift in the withdrawals schedule because of a fall in the desire to save, import, or levy taxes will raise income. A fall in the withdrawals schedule in Figure 5

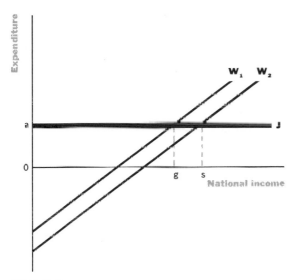

FIGURE 5

from W_1 to W_2 means that at the original level of income, Og, current withdrawals are less than current injections and income will rise. In the figure, income rises to a new equilibrium at Os.

The same analysis can be carried out using aggregate demand. A fall in the withdrawals schedule means a rise in the aggregate demand schedule. If, at any level of income, less is expended on savings, taxes, and imports, more must be being spent on consumption.

The rise in aggregate demand means that, at the old level of income, expenditure exceeds income and income will rise.

A rise in the withdrawals schedule is shown by starting from the schedule W_2 with income Os and letting the withdrawals schedule rise to W_1, so that income falls to Og. A rise in the withdrawals schedule must mean a fall in aggregate demand, because it must mean that less money is available for consumption expenditure at each level of income.

We have now derived two further predictions:

3. A fall in the withdrawals schedule accomplished by a fall in tax rates, or the desire to save, or the desire to import requires a rise in the domestic consumption schedule and a rise in the level of national income.

4. A rise in the withdrawals schedule accomplished by a rise in tax rates, or the desire to save, or the desire to import requires a fall in the domestic consumption schedule and a fall in the level of national income.

COMPENSATING SHIFTS IN INJECTIONS AND WITHDRAWALS

The level of national income is in equilibrium when the total volume of withdrawals equals the total volume of injections. As far as equilibrium in national income is concerned, there is no need for any particular withdrawal to equal any particular injection. The equilibrium condition $S + T + M = I + G + X$ does not imply that $S = I$, or that $T = G$, or that $M = X$. This means that it is possible to have compensating changes in various withdrawals and injections. Indeed, if any injection changes, an equal and opposite change in another injection will leave total injection, and hence total income, unchanged. Also, an equal change in some withdrawal, but in the same direction as the change in injections, will leave income unchanged.

Consider, for example, an equilibrium situation in which full employment rules, and both the budget and international payments are in balance. This means $G = T$, $M = X$, and, since in equilibrium total withdrawals must equal total injections, it follows that $S = I$. Now, assume a decrease in the desire to invest on the part of private firms. Our theory predicts that, *ceteris paribus*, this will lead to a fall in income and employment (see Prediction 2 above). But other things do not have to remain equal. There are two possible offsetting policies. First, the central authorities can increase governmental spending by exactly the same amount as I has decreased. Total injections will be unchanged, and national income will not depart from its full-employment level. In the new position, income will be unchanged, but $G > T$ and $I < S$, so that the fall in investment is exactly compensated for by a government budget deficit. The second possible policy is to cut taxes sufficiently to compensate for the fall in investment expenditure. In this case, there is a fall in withdrawals to compensate for the initial fall in injections. Again, income will not change, but the government will end up with a budget deficit, this time because its tax revenues fall, whereas its expenditures remain unchanged. These compensating changes in injections and withdrawals are extremely important, and they form the basis of governmental full-employment policy. We shall consider them in detail in Chapter 51. In the meantime, the student should not read on until he has used the equilibrium condition.

$$S + M + T = I + X + G$$

to show what the central authorities should do to G or to T in order to offset a rise or a fall in each of the other four withdrawals and injections. In each case, will the government's offsetting action lead to a budget deficit ($G > T$) or to a budget surplus ($G < T$)?

The Multiplier: The Magnitude of Changes in Income

We considered above the effect, specifically, the direction of the effect, on national income of various changes in injections. What can we learn about the magnitude of these changes? If the annual flow of autonomous expenditure changes by some amount, say ΔJ, *by how much* will income change? It is important to know this in order to determine the effects of changes both in private and in government expenditure. For example, in the 1957 recession, gross private investment fell by over $4 billion. How much of a drop in income would have resulted had nothing been done?[6] Or, to take another example, when the government cut taxes in 1964 by $8.4 billion in order to increase aggregate demand and thus to raise income and employment, it had to know, if it was to predict the effect on employment, by how much demand would increase. If the government overshoots the mark, demand can rise too rapidly: Full employment may be achieved with demand still rising. This would have an inflationary effect, since no further increase in output can occur

6. As we shall see in Chapter 58, in situations of this sort public investment is often increased as a matter of policy.

to meet further increases in demand. If the government greatly undershoots its target, much time will have been wasted and there is a danger that its policy will be discredited as ineffective. For these reasons, it is important to form a fairly accurate estimate of *by how much* income and employment will rise for *any given* increase in aggregate demand, whether this increase is accomplished by increasing government expenditure or by increasing private expenditure by cutting taxes. This estimate is provided by the multiplier.

A VERBAL STATEMENT

The following hypothesis sounds plausible: If injection expenditure rises *permanently* by $X million per year (owing, say, to a rise in investment), income will rise by exactly that amount. But it is one easily shown to be mistaken. If an additional amount is spent each year on investment, then income and employment in the investment goods industries will rise permanently by that amount, since new employment will be created to meet the new demand for capital goods. However, most of this new income will be spent by the households who receive it. They will buy more clothing, food, entertainment, cars, television sets, beer, and a host of other goods. Expenditure on these goods will create income for the households that help to make them. These households will in turn spend some of their new income, thus creating new income for yet other households. And so the process continues; the original rise in incomes in the industries that make investment goods spreads out over the whole economy until national income and employment have risen by some multiple of the initial rise in investment expenditure.

What will be the effect on income if, for example, in a period of heavy unemployment, the government spends an additional $10 million *per year* on road building, without any corresponding increase in tax revenues? First, incomes in the construction industry will undergo an increase of $10 million *per year*. The people newly employed in the construction industries will spend much of their new income on consumers' goods. Say they *spend* $4 million, and the other $6 million is withdrawn through taxes, savings, and imports. This means that there is $4 million of extra sales in the consumption industries. Formerly unemployed resources will be put to work to produce these new goods. These newly employed workers will in turn spend some of *their* newly acquired incomes, thus giving rise to a yet larger increase in total income.

This might lead us to put forward an alternative hypothesis: New government expenditure will, through the further rounds of expenditure that it sets off, lead to an indefinite rise in income, for each time someone gets new income he will be led to make new consumption expenditures that are new income for someone else, and so on, *ad infinitum*. But this hypothesis, like the first one, is also easily shown to be wrong: Not all of the extra income is passed on in extra consumption spending. If an average of 40 percent of the new income is spent—the remaining 60 percent being withdrawn in one form or another—the workers in the construction industry will spend only $4 million out of the additional $10 million that they earn each year; the workers in the consumers'-goods industries will spend only $1.6 million out of the $4 million that *they* earn (40 percent of 4 million), and the recipients of the $1.6 million of new expenditure will spend only $0.64 million (40 percent of 1.6 million). Clearly, this process will converge to a limit.[7] Income

---

7. Not all infinite declining series have limits. For example, the series $1 + \frac{1}{2} + \frac{1}{4} + \frac{1}{8} \ldots$ has a limit of 2. The series $1 + \frac{1}{2} + \frac{1}{3} + \frac{1}{4} \ldots$ has no limit. The multiplier series *does* converge.

will not grow to infinity because each recipient of new income hands on, through his spending, only a fixed fraction of what he receives as a result of other people's spending.

The ratio of the increase in equilibrium income to the increase in the injection that brought it about is known as the *multiplier*, which we will denote by K. In general, the multiplier depends on the fraction of additional income that is spent on domestically produced goods, and that thus remains in the circular flow, and on the amount that is withdrawn from the flow. The multiplier will be higher the greater the proportion passed on, and lower the greater the proportion withdrawn. Let us denote the fraction of additional income that is *not* passed on by w. Thus we have

$$w \equiv \frac{\Delta W}{\Delta Y}.$$

w is called the marginal propensity not to pass on income; ΔY is a change in income; and ΔW is the consequent change in withdrawals. The larger is w the less money is passed on by each recipient of new income and hence the lower the final increase in income. If, to take an extreme example, w were equal to 1 (so that new income gave rise to no new consumption spending), then the final increase in income would equal the initial increase in government expenditure. Under these circumstances, if the government spent $10 million on roads, then the incomes of construction workers would rise by $10 million, but *none* of this amount would be spent on consumption, since all of it would be withdrawn in the form of savings, taxes, and/or imports. If w is one, the value of the multiplier is *one*. The smaller is w, the larger is the value of the multiplier.

At equilibrium, withdrawals must equal injections. If autonomous expenditure rises by

ΔJ, withdrawals must also rise by ΔJ before the new equilibrium is reached. Thus, the rise in income must be sufficient to induce new withdrawals equal to ΔJ. If w is unity, then a rise in income equal to ΔJ will be sufficient. If w is $\frac{1}{2}$, then income must rise by $2\Delta J$ before new withdrawals can equal ΔJ; until income does so rise, total withdrawals will fall short of total injections, which is the condition for a rise in income. If w is $\frac{1}{10}$, then income must rise by $10\Delta J$ before withdrawals can equal injections. We conclude therefore that K varies inversely with the propensity *not* to pass on income and that, as the previous examples show, K is equal to the reciprocal of w, where w is the fraction of a change in total national income that is not passed on through new spending.

A GRAPHICAL STATEMENT

The withdrawal and injection function is depicted in Figure 6. When the equilibrium level of income is Oa, withdrawals are $ae =$

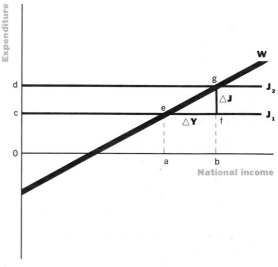

FIGURE 6

Oc. Now assume that injections rise by *cd.* The new equilibrium level of income is given by the intersection of *W* and the new injection schedule J_2. Income is now *Ob.* The rise in income is *ef* (= *ab*) and the rise in injection is *fg.* In the figure, the change in injection is indicated by ΔJ and the change in income by ΔY. The multiplier is the ratio of the change in income to the change in injection, or $\dfrac{\Delta Y}{\Delta J}$. The slope of the line *W* is the ratio $\dfrac{\Delta J}{\Delta Y}$; thus the multiplier is the reciprocal of the slope of the *W* function. The slope of the *W* line is the ratio of the change in withdrawals (ΔW) to the change in income (ΔY), which is the fraction of any new income that is withdrawn from the system and to which we have given the symbol *w.* The multiplier is thus the reciprocal of *w.*

To see the influence of the slope of withdrawal on the multiplier graphically, look at Figure 7, where we examine two different functions. The one marked *W'* has a steep

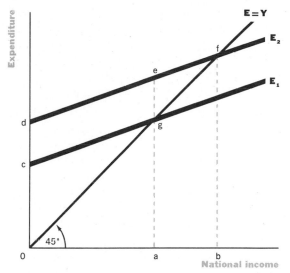

FIGURE 8

FIGURE 7

slope, the one marked *W''* has a very flat slope. In each case, suppose the injection schedule is J_1, and the equilibrium income level is *Oa.* Now, *in each case,* suppose injections increase to J_2. The new income level is *Ob'* in the case of *W'* and *Ob''* in the case of *W''.* The multiplier is much greater for the flatter curve. The common sense of this is that the flatter the curve, the greater the increase in income necessary to bring forth an addition to withdrawals equal to ΔJ.

The concept of the multiplier is an important one, but students often find it difficult to understand. Let us examine it in another way, using Figure 8. Suppose expenditures shift upward from $\bar{E}_1$ to $\bar{E}_2$. Equilibrium income rises from *Oa* to *Ob,* an increase of *ab.* The ratio $\dfrac{ab}{cd}$ is the multiplier. The *steeper* the expenditure curve, the greater the value of the multiplier. The reason is that the steeper the slope of the expenditure function, the farther to the right will be the new intersection with the 45° line. Students sometimes find it helpful to view the increase in income as having two stages: The shift from E_1 to E_2 raises expenditure from point g to point e. In order to restore equilibrium, income must grow to Ob, and we move to the right along E_2 until we reach point f. The multiplier essentially describes the movement along the E_2 curve.

AN ALGEBRAIC STATEMENT

The same analysis can be done somewhat more formally by using a bit of elementary algebra. Although we have avoided using algebra in the text of this book, the present use is so simple and so satisfactory in proving the multiplier that it is worth your time to study it.

In equilibrium we have

$$W = J, \qquad (1)$$

which says that the volume of withdrawals must equal the volume of injections. Now, if J increases by ΔJ, then W must increase by the same amount in order to re-establish equality (1). The symbol Δ means "a change in," so ΔJ refers to a change in injections. Thus we have

$$\Delta W = \Delta J. \qquad (2)$$

This says nothing more than that, if withdrawals equal injections originally, and if injections rise by ΔJ (say by $10 million per year), then withdrawals must rise by the same amount in order to preserve the equality of W and J.

According to our theory, withdrawals depend on income; thus the *change* in withdrawals depends on the change in income. Thus we may write

$$\Delta W = w\Delta Y \qquad (3)$$

If, for example, 20 percent of extra income is not passed on through new spending, then $w = 0.2$, and the change in withdrawals will be 20 percent of the change in income. Expression (3) merely says that, of any new amount of income, some fraction will not be passed on in new spending but will instead be withdrawn.

If we substitute (3) into (2), we obtain

$$w\Delta Y = \Delta J,$$

or, by dividing both sides by w,

$$\Delta Y = \frac{1}{w}\Delta J. \qquad (4)$$

Thus, if we write

$$\Delta Y = K\Delta J, \qquad (5)$$

we have

$$K = \frac{1}{w}, \qquad (6)$$

where K is the multiplier. This demonstrates that the value of the multiplier is equal to the reciprocal of the fraction of income withdrawn from the circular flow. If w is, for example, $\frac{1}{5}$, then the multiplier is 5; if it is $\frac{1}{3}$, then the multiplier is 3, and so on.

CONCLUSIONS OF THE MULTIPLIER ANALYSIS

We now have derived two further important predictions:

5. *The larger the marginal propensity to pass on income (the smaller is* w*), the greater the fluctuations in income for any given shift in aggregate demand.*

6. *The value of the multiplier is equal to the reciprocal of the fraction of income not passed on (*w*).*

If we know, or can estimate, the marginal propensity to pass on income, we can estimate the magnitude of the effect on income of a change in any injection or of a shift in consumption.

Summary

1. In order to develop our theory, we assume that there is some unemployment of all resources and that prices do not change. Under these circumstances, the value of output can change only if the quantity of output changes. We also assume that employment fluctuates directly with, and unemployment inversely with, the quantity of output.

2. Under the conditions outlined in Point 1, the levels of output, employment, and unemployment are all determined by the level of aggregate demand. A theory of aggregate demand becomes a theory of employment, unemployment, and output.

3. We define aggregate demand as the total of all demand in the economy: total injections, plus household expenditure on domestically produced goods and services.

4. Consumption expenditure and all withdrawals are hypothesized to vary directly with income. All injections are assumed to be independent of income changes (i.e., they do not vary with income). Expenditures that do not vary with income are often referred to as autonomous expenditures.

5 The circular flow is said to be in equilibrium when there is no tendency for income to rise or fall. The condition for equilibrium in the circular flow can be stated in three ways: injections equal withdrawals, aggregate demand equals income, and income "last period" equals income "this period' (i.e., income is unchanged from period to period).

6. The theory predicts that a rise in injections (investment expenditure, exports, or government expenditure) will, *ceteris paribus*, raise the level of national income, and that a fall in injections will lower the level of national income.

7. The theory also predicts that a fall in the level of withdrawals associated with each level of income (i.e., a downward shift in the withdrawals schedule) will raise the level of national income, while a rise in the level of withdrawals associated with each level of income will lower the level of national income.

8. A change in one withdrawal (or injection) can be offset by an equal and opposite change in another withdrawal (or injection). A fall in private investment expenditure can, for example, be offset by a rise in government expenditure, leaving income and employment unaffected.

9. The ratio of the increase in equilibrium income to the increase in the injection that brought it about is known as the multiplier. The multiplier theory predicts that the larger is the marginal propensity to pass on income, the greater will be the fluctuations in income for any given shift in aggregate demand, and that the value of the multiplier is equal to the reciprocal of the fraction of income not passed on (i.e., withdrawn from the circular flow).

QUESTIONS FOR DISCUSSION

1. What assumptions do we begin with?

2. Which variables are assumed to be endogenous, which exogenous?

3. Why do we draw a 45° line? If we drew our axes so that a dollar of expenditure was represented by one inch, but a dollar of income was represented by $\frac{1}{2}$ inch, what would replace the 45° line?

4. Why, on the basis of the theory developed in Chapter 46, is our aggregate demand line parallel to the consumption line?

5. What does our theory predict to be the effect on national income of each of the following? (a) a rise in exports; (b) a fall in imports; (c) a fall in investment expenditure; (d) a rise in domestic consumption expenditure. Depict each graphically. What change in taxes would be necessary to offset the effects on national income and employment of each of these changes?

6. If a single individual is thrifty, we normally expect him to be better off than if he is a spendthrift. The theory developed in Chapter 46 predicts that the thriftier people are in the aggregate (the more they try to save at each level), the lower total income will be, while the more spendthrift they are (the less they try to save at each level of income), the higher their total income will be! The theory also predicts that the actual amount of savings that they make will be the same in equilibrium, whether they are thrifty or spendthrift. Derive these predictions, which are often referred to as the paradox of thrift, graphically.

7. What is the value of the multiplier when the marginal propensity to consume is 1, and when there are no imports and no taxes? Explain your result.

8. What would be the equilibrium effect of government expenditure of $10 million on roads in one year only? What would happen at first? Why does the result differ from a case in which $10 million is spent on roads each year?

Chapter **47** HOUSEHOLD CONSUMPTION

ABOUT 65 PERCENT OF TOTAL EXPENDITURE in the U.S. is made up of purchases by U.S. households of goods and services produced in the U.S. Even very small percentage fluctuations in such an important volume of expenditure can have important effects on the level of U.S. national income and employment. If households were to reduce their consumption expenditure by 2 percent, total expenditure would be reduced by 1.3 percent. Combined with a multiplier of, say, 2.5, the U.S. national income would decline by 3.25 percent. Perhaps this doesn't sound like very much. But if employment were to change in proportion to income, this could change a situation of 3 percent unemployment, which is near the low achieved in postwar U.S. experience, to one of over 6 percent, which is near the high achieved over this same period.[1] Clearly, even very small percentage fluctuations can have

an important effect on the economy; if we are to understand the behavior of national income in our economy, we need to know what determines consumption expenditure.

The Consumption Function

To say that X depends on Y is to say that X is a function of Y. A consumption function is nothing more than a statement of the relation between consumption expenditure and those factors that influence it; it is a statement of the way in which consumption depends on other things.

Many factors influence aggregate consumption expenditure: the level of household income, the household's stock of wealth, advertising, the ease or difficulty in obtaining credit, the outlook for the future, the weather, and so on.

Following the procedure we have used so often before, we start by focusing on the relation of consumption to one variable in which we are particularly interested. The one we choose is disposable income. Although disposable income is not the only determinant of consumption, it is shown by empirical studies to be an important one. Changes in other variables can also have an important

influence on consumption. But we have seen before that changes in other variables can be regarded as shifting the simplified function about: Recall in Chapter 7 how, after examining a functional relationship between demand and price, we allowed changes in income to shift the demand curve.

CONSUMPTION AS A FUNCTION OF DISPOSABLE INCOME[2]

That consumption (C) is a function of disposable income (Y_d) is an hypothesis that every study has confirmed. Let us start by stating three more specific hypotheses about the nature of the relationship.[3]

Hypotheses:

1. *The greater disposable income, the greater aggregate consumption.*

2. *For some low enough levels of income, consumption will exceed disposable income*

1. The figures are for illustrative purposes only. The value of the multiplier tends to vary over the time one allows to elapse, but 2.5 is close to estimates of the multiplier effects of some changes in spending, allowing a year or two for the effects to be felt. The relation between changes in income and changes in employment is more conjectural. (Considerable work is being done in this field.) If we are to intervene in the economy in an attempt to control unemployment, we must know how much change in employment will result from a given change in income and output. Our estimates above assumed that the labor force (unemployed plus employed) was constant. In fact, however, it is rising year by year. This accentuates the effect of a downward shift in the level of consumption on employment. One of the reasons why solving the U.S. unemployment problem is so difficult is that the first million new jobs created each year are needed for the new entrants into the labor force.

2. Both consumption and disposable income were defined in Chapter 45, pp. 529–530. If you do not recall the distinction between total income and disposable income, or if you do not recall that consumption excluded purchases of imported goods, you should reread that section.

3. The basic function we are dealing with is $C = C(Y_d)$.

(i.e., households in aggregate will be going into debt or using up past savings), but beyond some level of income not all of the income received by households will be spent on consumption.

3. *Any given rise in income will cause a less than proportionate rise in consumption. To state this another way, any rise in income of X dollars will cause consumption expenditure to rise by an amount greater than zero but less than X dollars.*

GRAPHICAL REPRESENTATION OF THE CONSUMPTION FUNCTION

Figure 1 (i) and (ii) presents two curves (labeled *C*), each of which conforms to the hypotheses just stated. We shall describe the straight line in (ii), but everything we say about it applies as well to the curve shown in (i). At low levels of income, consumption expenditure exceeds income. The income level, *Oa* in our diagram, at which consumption equals income, is sometimes called the break-even level of income. As income rises above this break-even level, the consumption function lies below the 45° line, indicating that total consumption is less than total income.

THE AVERAGE PROPENSITY
TO CONSUME (APC)

APC is the proportion of total income spent on consumption. To calculate this value, we take total consumption expenditure and divide it by total income.† If, for example, out of an income of $100 million, expenditure is $95 million, the average propensity to con-

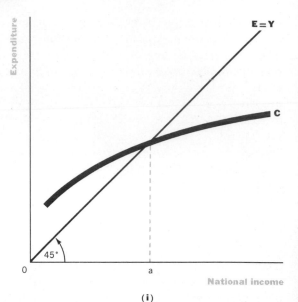

(i)

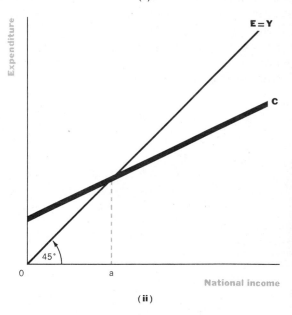

(ii)

FIGURE 1

---

† In symbols, $APC = \dfrac{C}{Y}$.

sume is 0.95; if income rises to $200 million and consumption rises to $180 million, the APC falls to 0.90. We may divide consumption expenditure either by total national income, in which case we have the average propensity to consume out of total income, or by disposable income, in which case we have the average propensity to consume out of disposable income. Which of these concepts is being used is almost always obvious from the context.

THE MARGINAL PROPENSITY TO CONSUME (MPC)

MPC measures the relation between changes in consumption and changes in income. It tells us not how much of total income is consumed, but how much of the last dollar's worth of income is consumed.[†] Say we start from an income of $100 million with consumption expenditure of $05 million, and move to an income of $110 million with consumption expenditure of $103 million. The APC moves from 0.95 to 0.936; the MPC is 0.8 ($\Delta Y = 10$ and $\Delta C = 8$). This tells us that when income is $110 million, just over 93 percent of it is spent on consumption, even though only 80 percent of the last $10 million of income was devoted to consumption. Note that we need only one value for Y and C to calculate the APC but that, since the MPC is concerned with changes, we need two values for Y and C to calculate it. The MPC may be stated as a propensity to consume out of either total income or disposable income. Which of these concepts—total income or disposable income—we are dealing with will usually be obvious from the context.

The hypotheses stated above may now be translated into this new terminology:

1. The MPC exceeds zero at all levels of income.

2. The APC exceeds unity at low levels of income.

3. The MPC is less than unity for all levels of income.

The Consumption Function for the Community and for the Individual[4]

An aggregate consumption function shows how the community's total consumption expenditure varies as its total disposable income varies. Conceptually, the society's function is aggregated from all the functions of the individual households that compose it in just the same way as the market demand curve is aggregated from the demand curves of individual households.

Is this a valid thing to do? Can we really expect to find a stable community relation emerging when changes in income affect individual households in different ways? What are the conditions under which we will get a stable community consumption function? Basically, there are two conditions, either of which is sufficient. The first condition is that all households should have the

[†] In symbols, $MPC = \dfrac{\Delta C}{\Delta Y}$.

4. This section may be omitted.

same marginal propensity to consume. In this case, changes in the distribution of income between households will have no effect on the level of total consumption expenditure. If, for example, all households have an MPC of 0.8, then redistributing a given national income among households will leave the aggregate level of consumption unchanged, for any household that loses a dollar of income cuts its expenditure by 80¢, while any household that gains an extra dollar of income raises expenditure by 80¢. Thus, in this situation, the level of total consumption depends only on the level of total income; it is independent of the distribution of this income among households: To every level of national income there corresponds one and only one level of aggregate consumption.

If households have different marginal propensities to consume, then aggregate consumption depends not only on aggregate income but also on the distribution of this income among households. If, for example, $1 is taken from a household with a marginal propensity to consume of 0.5, and given to one with a propensity of 0.9, then total consumption is increased by 40¢, although total income is unchanged. In this case a change in the *distribution* of income will cause a change in the aggregate level of consumption expenditure associated with any given *level* of national income. When the MPC's differ,

as among households, a sufficient condition for a stable community consumption function is that the distribution of income between households does not change. Thus if national income rises or falls by 10 percent, each household's income will rise or fall by 10 percent, and total consumption expenditure will be uniquely related to total income. But this is a very strong assumption, and a weaker one is sufficient. We do not need to assume that the distribution of income is constant, as long as changes in it are related to changes in national income. If for each level of income there is only one associated distribution of income, then there will be only one associated level of total household consumption.

Thus the use of a stable community consumption function that relates national income to total consumption expenditures, in a world in which MPC's are known to vary among households, requires that most changes that do occur in the distribution of income are themselves associated with changes in the level of incomes. There is considerable empirical evidence that the distribution of income changes only slowly, so that it is fairly stable from one year to the next, and also that such changes as do occur are mainly related to short-run changes in income. For these reasons, we have substantial confidence in our ability to estimate a reasonably stable aggregate consumption function.

Consumption Functions: Empirical Observations

Over the last thirty years a vast amount of attention has been devoted to studying the relation between consumption and income. A detailed survey of this work is beyond the scope of this book. We can, however, mention some of the most important points.

The statistical data available are of two main types: *cross-section* data and *time-series* data. Cross-section data show at any instant of time how different households' expenditures have been related to their incomes. Time-series data show how consumption and income have changed over time; time-series data could be for a single household (i.e., we could observe a household's income and consumption expenditure each year for, say, fifteen years) or for any aggregation of households. Much of the time-series data we work with is aggregate data showing total consumption and total income for the economy as a whole.[5]

Cross-section data are made available by budget studies of samples of households. Many such studies have been made and they all tend to support the following general conclusions:

1. There is a considerable amount of variation between the consumption expenditures of different households that *cannot* be associated with differences in incomes between households. Of three households with an income of $6,000, the first might have total consumption expenditures of $7,000, the second of $5,700, and the third of $4,000. This suggests that, in making their consumption expenditures, households are not solely influenced by the size of their incomes.

2. On the average, household expenditure does tend to vary in a remarkably consistent fashion as income varies. We can remove individual variations by grouping households into income groups (putting all households earning an income of less than $2,000 in the first group, all households earning between $2,000 and $4,000 in the second group, and so on) and averaging the consumption expenditure for all the households in each group.[6] When this is done, we find that average household expenditure on consumption goods rises steadily as income rises, but *not as fast as* income rises. Cross-section data

very strongly confirm the hypotheses stated on pp. 561–562; the shape of the curves in Figure 1 apply directly to cross-sectional studies.

The data from these studies are valuable in suggesting that income does have a significant effect on consumption expenditure. Cross-section data show, however, how consumption expenditure varies as we move up and down the income scale at any moment of time. They do not necessarily show how consumption varies as the incomes of all households change over time. For direct evidence of this we must go to time-series data.

Data for total consumption and expenditure and total income are available for many Western economies starting some time around 1930. Many analyses of these data have been made. Perhaps the most significant conclusion is that the consumption function is different according to the length of time over which data are averaged. The principal findings are summarized below.

LONG-RUN CONSUMPTION FUNCTION: DECADE-TO-DECADE CHANGES

By using five- to ten-year averages for consumption and income, so that each observation consists of average consumption over, say, a five-year period and average disposable income over the same period, we can abstract from many short-run influences on consumption. Such observations reveal a close relation between income and expenditure. We find that the marginal propensity and average propensity to consume are less than unity, but that *the average propensity to consume does not decline as income rises*. We also find

---

5. See the appendix to Chapter 4 for a discussion of cross-section and time-series data. Data about an identical group of households over time are called *panel* data.

6. See Chapter 4, page 49, for an example in which this procedure is followed.

that APC and MPC are very nearly equal.† These data thus confirm the first and the third hypotheses, but tend to refute the second. We call this function a "long-run" consumption function. Look at Figure 2 for a stylized picture of one (curve C).

Let us note in passing that the long-run consumption function might have had the shape pictured in Figure 2 by curve C^1. This curve illustrates a hypothetical case in which both the average and marginal propensities to consume fall as incomes increase. We discuss, in a later chapter, a theory that was based in part on this hypothetical shape.[7] The empirical evidence gives such a shape no support.

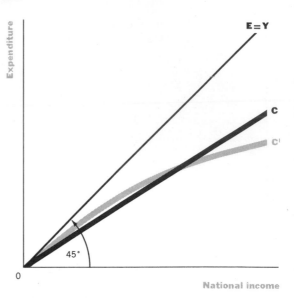

FIGURE 2   **THE LONG-RUN CONSUMPTION FUNCTION**

SHORT-RUN CONSUMPTION FUNCTION: YEAR-TO-YEAR CHANGES

When we use annual data (i.e., when each observation consists of total income over a year and total consumption expenditure for the same year), we find a close relation between consumption expenditure and income. In general, years with the highest levels of income tend to be years with the highest levels of consumption. The observed marginal propensity to consume is less than unity, but larger than that typically found in cross-section studies. The average propensity to consume declines as income rises. The three hypotheses tend to be confirmed. Figure 3 represents this consumption function in a stylized way.

The most significant difference between the long- and the short-run consumption functions is in the relation between the MPC and

the APC. In the long-run function, MPC equals APC, so that households consume a constant fraction of their income, whatever the level of their income, whereas, in the short-run function, MPC is less than APC, so that households consume a lower fraction of their income, the higher their income is.

VERY SHORT-RUN VARIATION OF CONSUMPTION WITH INCOME

When we use quarterly figures (so that each observation consists of data for Y_d and C over a period of three months), we find that the association between C and Y_d is very much weaker than for any of the other observations mentioned above. This suggests that short-run variations in consumption expenditure are

† Prove that in a consumption function of the form $C = aY, (0 < a < 1)$, the MPC and the APC are equal to each other, are less than unity, and do not change as income changes. This function is shown graphically as a straight line through the origin.

7. See the discussion of secular stagnation, pp. 619–620.

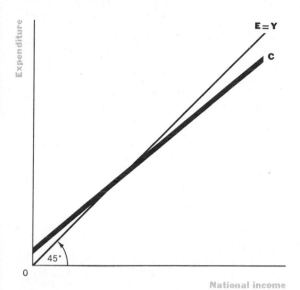

FIGURE 3   **THE SHORT-RUN CONSUMPTION FUNCTION**

number of influences, such as interest rates, size of down payment required, and expected changes in income that do not influence non-durable purchases. (3) The factors just mentioned seem to be more important than income in explaining short-term variations in the purchase of durables.[8]

SUMMARY OF EMPIRICAL FINDINGS

These results suggest that income does exert a significant influence on consumption. At any rate, we are not wasting our time building a theory based on this assumption. They also suggest that factors other than income influence consumption expenditure. For purposes of building a theory of very short-run changes from one quarter to the next, our hypotheses may be too far removed from the facts to be useful. For explaining such short-run changes, more subtle consumption functions may be necessary. The data also suggest (although this is still subject to debate) that, in the long run, income and consumption expenditure may change in proportion to each other (so that $\frac{C}{Y}$ is constant in the long run). They also suggest that although income fluctuates with the business cycle, variations in income are accompanied by less than proportional variations in consumption (so that $\frac{C}{Y}$ varies over the cycle).

Thus it may be necessary to think not of *the* consumption function, but of one function suitable for year-to-year variations in income,

not determined mainly by short-run variations in income. Why are the hypotheses about the consumption-income relationship refuted under very short-run conditions? Over the past decade, many economists have tried to answer this question. One of their findings indicates that it is fruitful to divide consumption expenditure into expenditure on durables (automobiles, refrigerators, television sets, etc.) and expenditure on nondurables (food, entertainment, etc.). Such a division leads to three observations: (1) Much of the short-run variability in consumption expenditure is in the durable category. (This is not surprising since it is very easy to postpone durable purchases for a few months.) (2) Purchases of durable goods seem to respond to a

8. These findings, and others, have lead Professor Milton Friedman to put forward the "permanent-income hypothesis." Part of this hypothesis says that short-run behavior in consumption will be more stable than income, because households, individually and in aggregate, maintain consumption despite either reverses (such as temporary periods of unemployment) or windfalls. The relative stability of consumption can be said to be fairly well established. Whether Friedman's theory is the best one (there are others) is still a matter of debate among economists.

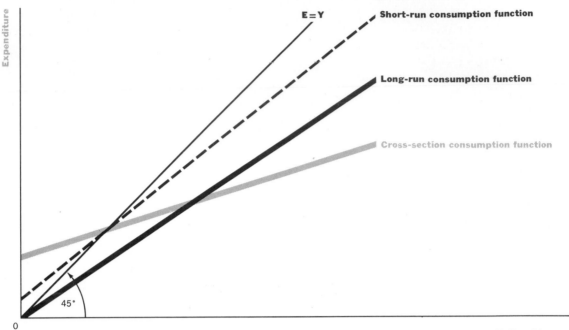

FIGURE 4

of another suitable for decade-to-decade changes, and of yet another suitable for cross-sectional problems, such as the effect on consumption of a redistribution of income. Figure 4 illustrates three consumption functions: the long-run, the short-run, and the cross-sectional.[9]

In the work that follows, we shall use a single consumption function. The function we shall use is most appropriate to describing changes in income from one year to the next. The use of this single function will simplify matters when we are constructing our theory and will also be most appropriate when we use the theory to account for year-to-year changes in national income and employment.

Consumption as a Function of Disposable Income and Total Income

In Chapter 46 we drew a graph relating consumption expenditure to total national income. In the present chapter we have advanced the hypothesis that in fixing their consumption expenditure, households react to their disposable income. Since disposable income is directly related to total income, we can use a relation between C and Y even

9. We have drawn no function for the "very short" period because the relationship, if it exists, is so un-stable as to be misleading.

though the behavior of C is related to Y_d as long as Y_d is itself related to Y.[10] We must remember, however, that anything that changes the relation between total income and disposable income will *shift* the relation between consumption and total income. For example, a cut in income-tax rates will mean that, for any given level of total income, disposable income will be higher than before; this means that, for any given level of total income, consumption expenditure will also be higher than before.[11]

Can Shifts in the Consumption Function Be Controlled?

There are many factors that can cause shifts in the kinds of consumption functions we have shown. Some of these factors can be controlled by government policy and others cannot.

Typical of the uncontrollable, and often unforeseeable factors, would be a sudden shift in the decision to spend on the part of households. In 1962, expenditure on automobiles accounted for 4.0 percent of total household expenditures and 3.8 percent of annual U.S. income. Households may decide that they do not like this year's model car and may save the money they were going to spend on a new car this year until next year. The consumption function will shift downward this year. Incomes earned in Detroit (and many other places) will fall, and unemployment will rise. The unemployed auto workers will cut their spending on other products, and a multiplier process will be set up that will magnify the original cut in spending on new automobiles into a general fall in income and employment.

Typical of the controllable factors would be a change in taxes. If personal-income taxes are lowered, households' disposable income will rise even though total national income is (at first) unchanged. Consumption expend-

---

10. Consider an example in which households always spend 80 percent of their disposable income and in which the withholding from total income (taxes, undistributed profits, etc.) amounts to 10 percent. This gives us

$$C = 0.8Y_d \tag{1}$$
$$\text{and } Y_d = 0.9Y. \tag{2}$$

Substituting (2) into (1) gives C as a function of Y:

$$C = 0.72Y. \tag{3}$$

11. Assume that, in the example of footnote 10, a cut in the tax rate increases disposable income to 95 percent of total income. This gives us the following:
Equation (1) is unchanged:

$$C = 0.8Y_d, \tag{1}$$

but a new equation (2) is needed:

$$Y_d = 0.95Y. \tag{2a}$$

Substituting (2a) into (1) gives a new relation between C and Y:

$$C = .76Y. \tag{3a}$$

Consumption has increased, without any change in households' propensity to consume out of disposable income.

iture will rise and income will rise. On the other hand, a rise in taxes will shift the consumption line downward and income will be reduced. Tax variations have been used as an instrument of policy in both the United States and Great Britain since World War II.

Summary

1. In this chapter, we examined more closely the hypothesis that consumption is a function of disposable income. Three more specific hypotheses about the nature of this relationship were introduced. (a) The marginal propensity to consume (MPC) exceeds zero at all levels of income. (b) The average propensity to consume (APC) exceeds unity at low levels of income. (c) The MPC is less than unity for all levels of income.

2. We can expect to find a stable aggregate consumption function, even when changes in income affect individual households in different ways, *if* either all households have the same MPC, *or* if each level of income is associated with a particular distribution of income.

3. The empirical evidence relating to these hypotheses is discussed, and the results are summarized on pp. 567–568.

4. Anything that changes the relationship between total and disposable income will shift the relationship between consumption and total income. Thus, a lowering of personal income taxes will cause a rise in the average propensity to consume out of total income. Other uncontrollable factors, such as a change in households' decisions to spend and save, will also shift the consumption function.

QUESTIONS FOR DISCUSSION

1. Draw consumption functions to illustrate the following cases:

   a. MPC and APC are constant for all levels of income.

   b. MPC is constant for all levels of income, and APC declines as income rises.

   c. MPC and APC decline as income rises.

   d. MPC and APC rise as income rises.

2. Can we go from an individual consumption function to a community function easily? What do we need? Construct a hypothetical example with just two households to illustrate the situation.

3. With the recent revision of national-income figures, many people were surprised to discover that consumers are spending a greater percentage of their after-tax dollar now than they were in the 1950s. Why might this be surprising? What are some of its implications?

4. What does the empirical evidence suggest about our hypotheses about the relation between income and consumption expenditure? What explanations might be proposed for the differences between time periods?

5. According to our original hypothesis, what would happen to the value of the multiplier if there were a redistribution of income toward greater equality, with all other things staying the same?

6. Illustrate graphically the effect of a successful campaign urging households to save more out of each dollar they earn. Would this be a desirable thing in a time of heavy unemployment, such as that experienced in the U.S. in the early 1960s?

Chapter **48** INVESTMENT AND SAVING

IN 1929, THE TOTAL INVESTMENT EXPENDI-ture of firms and households in the U.S. economy was $16.2 billion. This was almost double the amount of expenditure needed to replace the capital goods that were used up that year in the process of production. The U.S. economy, in 1929, was thus adding rapidly to its stock of new capital equipment. Three years later, in 1932, total investment expenditure was less than $1 billion. This was less than 15 percent of the amount needed to keep the stock of capital intact. The U.S. economy in 1932 was thus rapidly reducing its stock of capital equipment. Such enormous fluctuations in the volume of investment have not been recorded since that time, but the variations have nonetheless been large. Investment expenditure fell by 15 percent between 1957 and 1958; it fell by just over 4 percent between 1960 and 1961; and it then rose by nearly 15 percent between 1961 and 1962. By 1964, total investment expenditure had reached $87.7 billion, which was just less than 15 percent of the gross national income of the U.S.

Why do these variations in investment

expenditure occur and what are their effects?

We saw in Chapter 46 the main short-run effect of these changes. Investment expenditure is an important component of aggregate demand, and changes in it will cause multiplied changes in the level of income and employment. If investment is 15 percent of total expenditure, a 15 percent fall in investment represents a 2¼ percent fall in total expenditure; and given a multiplier of 2.5, this would reduce income by just over 5½ percent and raise unemployment from (say) 4 percent to about 10 percent of the labor force. The long-run effects of changes in investment are felt in terms of economic growth. These problems are discussed in Chapter 56; nothing further will be said about them at this point. In this chapter, we concentrate on the short-term effects of variations in investment expenditure on the level of activity and employment in the economy.

Why do these changes occur? This is a difficult question to answer and it takes us into the theory of the determinants of investment, which is the main subject of this chapter.

The Financing of Investment

Generally, in speaking of the circular flow we speak of withdrawals and injections in pairs: We speak of imports and exports, of

government expenditure and government revenue, and of saving and investment. This pairing is no accident and, in the case of saving and investment, it reflects the fact that the savings of firms and households are the major source of finance for investment. When households and firms save funds, the money must go somewhere; when firms spend on investment, the money must come from somewhere. Generally, the money spent on current investment projects comes from the current savings of firms and households.

Money required for investment expenditure may be raised in several ways. One is for the firm to save the funds itself (by not distributing all its profits to its shareholders). A second way to raise funds is by borrowing the savings of other units in the economy, mainly households. This can be done either directly by selling bonds to households, or indirectly by borrowing from financial institutions money deposited by households in these institutions. If the expenditure on investment is equal to the money saved by households (and by all other units that save out of current income), then the funds spent on investment can be raised completely from funds currently saved with nothing left over.

If the volume of investment expenditure exceeds the volume of funds currently saved, where does the money come from? Basically there are two main sources: The money may come from funds accumulated in the past by firms or households, or it may be money *newly created* by the banking system. In Chapter 53, we shall study in detail how the banking system can create and destroy money within very wide limits. In the meantime, we must note that, if banks can create money, they can lend this money to firms for investment expenditure without there being any corresponding saving of funds on the part of households and firms.

There is one more possibility: Investment may fall short of savings. In this case all of the money saved cannot be passed back into the circular flow by way of investment expenditure. The excess of savings over investment will pile up as idle funds owned either by households or firms and held by them or by financial institutions on their behalf.

What Determines Savings?

Savings represent income earned and not spent. There are many motives for saving: Firms may save in order to have funds for new investment or for replacing their capital stock. Households may save for emergencies or for the education of their children or to provide life insurance and income for retirement. These are important aspects of the behavior of individual units. But, when dealing with *aggregate* income expenditure and saving, if we have a theory that succeeds in explaining the portion of income spent, we shall have an implied theory of savings as well. That is, since income is equal to expenditures plus savings, a theory that explains the proportion of income expended will also explain the proportion of income not expended (i.e., saved). For that reason we do not require a separate theory of aggregate saving.

Should we wish to focus on the relation between saving and income, we may readily do so. For households, for example, we could hypothesize that savings are a function of disposable income; that as income rises, savings rise, but not as rapidly as income; and that the percentage of income saved rises as income rises. These hypotheses are implied by the hypotheses stated at the beginning of Chapter 46, *if* we assume that savings and consumption are the only two elements of disposable income that vary with income.

Once we have a savings function, we can define both an average propensity to save and a marginal propensity to save. We shall have occasion to use these concepts later.

What Determines Investment?

What determines the amount of investment? In Chapter 46, we treated investment as constant and autonomous in order to examine the nature of the equilibrium of the circular flow. We now relax this assumption.

What effect does the rate of interest have on the level of investment? In Chapter 36, we explained the relation between the rate of interest and the demand to borrow money for investment purposes. (Review pages 401–402 before reading on.) We now draw, in Figure 1, a downward-sloping investment schedule plotted against the rate of interest. According to this figure, the amount of investment rises as the rate of interest (which represents the cost of borrowing money for investment) falls. In order to explain some of the variations in the amount of investment, it is necessary to explain variations in the rate of interest.

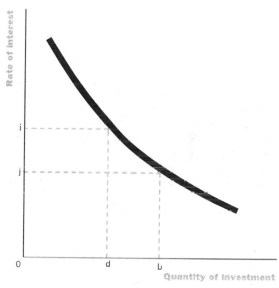

FIGURE 1

Savings and Investment and the Rate of Interest

The rate of interest is to a great extent controlled by the central authorities, particularly the Federal Reserve System and the Treasury.[1] In Figure 1, the rate of interest is Oi. This gives a rate of investment expenditure of Od. If the authorities now force the interest rate down to Oj, the rate of investment expands to Ob. This change in the

rate of investment expenditure in response to a change in the interest rate will be shown as an upward shift in the aggregate demand function in Figure 8, in Chapter 46. Thus interest variation can cause investment variation of the sort we have considered in a previous chapter.

How does the rate of interest respond to the

1. We ask the student to accept that this is so until he reads Chapter 53.

current amount of saving and investment? Assume that when investment exceeds current saving, interest rates rise because there is a shortage of funds to borrow. Would-be lenders will outbid each other to offer favorable terms to attract the existing funds to themselves. Assume also that when investment falls short of current savings, interest rates will fall because some savers will be unable to lend their money at all and so will be prepared to ask lower rates of interest rather than leave their money idle. This hypothesis makes the interest rate a factor helping to restore equilibrium when savings and investment are not equal.

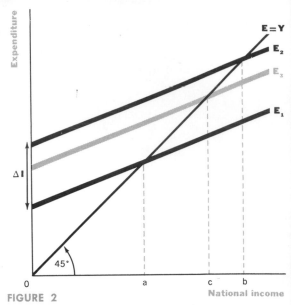

FIGURE 2

INTEREST CHANGES AS A FACTOR IN RESTORING EQUILIBRIUM

In Chapter 46, we saw that an autonomous rise in investment would raise income until new withdrawals sufficient to restore equilibrium had been created. The magnitude of the rise in income depends on the value of the multiplier.

If the rise in investment raises the rate of interest as we have just hypothesized, then this will tend to restore equilibrium by choking off some of the extra investment expenditure.

This is shown in Figure 2. Suppose the aggregate demand function is the one labeled E_1. The equilibrium income is Oa. Now investment increases by ΔI, thus shifting the aggregate demand function to E_2. If all of the adjustment were thrown onto income changes, income would have to rise to Ob. But if interest rates rise, and investment falls, the aggregate demand function will shift downward to E_3, and the new equilibrium will be reached at the lower level of income Oc. If, when investment increases, the rate of interest rises quickly and this rise in costs greatly reduces investment, then income need

not change much to generate the extra withdrawals to match the (small) increase in investment. On the other hand, if the rate changes only a little or very slowly, and if the change in costs does not affect investment much, then most of the burden of adjustment is placed on changes in income.

Let us look at these conclusions in another way. In Figure 3, the current investment schedule is assumed to be I_1, the current rate of interest is Oa percent per year, and the current quantity of investment is Ob dollars per year.

Now assume that the investment schedule shifts to I_2. If the rate of interest remains unchanged at Oa, investment rises by bc. This amount, bc, is the autonomous ΔI of Figure 2. If interest rates remain unchanged (or if the schedule I_2 is completely inelastic), then the whole of the burden of adjustment is thrown onto national income, and income will rise by the multiplier process until new withdrawals equal to bc are generated. If, however, interest rates rise to Od, then investment falls by ec. Investment is now only above its original level

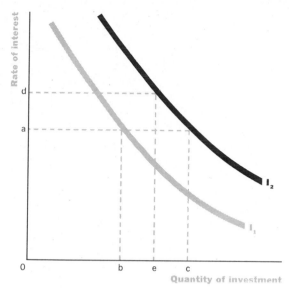

Rate of interest

d

a

0   b   e   c

Quantity of investment

FIGURE 3

by *be,* and the change in income necessary to restore equilibrium is correspondingly reduced. We now have derived the following predictions:

The change in income in response to an autonomous change in investment will be smaller, the greater is the change in interest rates in response to the change in investment and the more sensitive is the quantity of investment expenditure to changes in the rate of interest.

TWO LIMITING CASES OF THE RELATION BETWEEN INVESTMENT AND THE RATE OF INTEREST[2]

The "classical" theory of the workings of the economy prevailed (at least in Anglo-American economics) prior to the publication in 1936 of John Maynard Keynes's *General*

2. This section may be omitted.

Theory of Employment, Interest, and Money. Historians are quick to point out that there were many disagreements among the economists of the time and that to talk of *the* classical theory is to caricature a complex situation. Most economists were, however, more or less in agreement, and the term "classical theory" is now used to describe one version of the views prevalent at that time. The present book is not a treatise on the history of economics, and we would not bother to describe the classical theory of investment and saving were it not for the fact that it is still regarded as not refuted, at least in some of its aspects, by many present-day economists.

THE CLASSICAL THEORY

The basic assumption of the classical theory is that changes in investment and saving cause changes only in the rate of interest.

The classical theory can be summarized as follows: (1) The desired level of investment falls as the rate of interest rises. (2) The desired level of savings rises as the rate of interest rises. (3) The rate of interest changes smoothly and rapidly in such a way as to keep the volume of investment always equal to the volume of saving. As long as the rate of interest always keeps savings and investment equal, there is no reason for changes in either savings or investment to cause changes in income. Consider one case by way of example. Assume that there is an investment boom with a greatly increased desire to invest. With the increase in the desire to invest, firms will be trying to borrow much more money and they will quickly bid up the rate of interest. As the rate of interest rises, the quantity of money firms wish to borrow and spend on investment falls (since the cost of borrowing rises) and the quantity households are prepared to save and loan to firms increases. The rate of interest continues to rise until the diminished investment is exactly equal to the augmented quantity of saving. The whole process happens quickly enough so that there is no significant rise in income generated during the time in which investment exceeded saving. (Work out for yourself the effects of the other three shifts: a fall in the desire to invest, and a rise and a fall in the desire to save.)

The classical theory of saving, investment, and interest is built on two important assumptions about the real world: the assumption that the investment schedule is sufficiently interest-elastic, so that suitable variations in the rate of interest can bring about investment sufficient to match any volume of savings that may be forthcoming, and the assumption that the rate of interest is perfectly free to vary, so that saving and investment are quickly brought into equality.

Considerable doubt can be cast on both of these assumptions. First, most empirical studies that have been made seem to suggest that variations in interest rates *over the range actually experienced* do not cause very large variations in the level of investment. Other factors, such as expectations and the level and rate of change of current demand for consumption goods, seem to exert a major influence on investment decisions, with interest-rate variations having only a small effect. In other words, the investment schedule in Figure 1 is rather interest-inelastic. Second, there is some doubt whether the rate of interest is free to vary so as to equate the flow of current savings with the flow of current investment. The central financial authorities—the Federal Reserve System and the Treasury—exert considerable influence on interest rates, manipulating them in many ways, as we shall see in Chapter 53. Among

the most important of these ways is the sale and purchase of bonds on the open market. It is quite possible that an increase in saving might coincide with an attempt by the central authorities to raise interest rates (lower the price of bonds) by selling bonds on the open market. If the sale of bonds was in an amount equal to the new savings, the entire amount of new savings would pile up as idle balances held by Federal Reserve Banks. In this case, the rate of interest would not move to equate current savings with current investment.

THE KEYNESIAN THEORY

The theory that the interest rate will fluctuate so as to equate saving and investment is directly challenged by Keynes's theory of interest rates. By putting forward a plausible alternative theory of the determination of interest rates in a free market, Keynes showed, at the very least, that the classical theory could not be accepted as obviously true. There were now two contradictory theories to choose between, but there was no way to choose between them in the absence of a careful empirical testing of either theory.

The extreme version of the Keynesian theory was that the interest rate was completely stabilized by the speculative actions of bondholders. Bondholders have an idea of the normal rate of interest, he said, and, whenever fluctuations in current savings and investment cause even small changes in the price of bonds, they would buy or sell from their existing stocks of bonds, thus preventing the actual rate from diverging far from what they believe to be the normal rate.

If bondholders could prevent the rate of interest from changing rapidly, then what would restore equilibrium when there was a large shift in either savings or investment? The equilibrium-restoring mechanism was income fluctuations of the kind analyzed in

Chapter 46. Although the theory that all adjustments take the form of changes in the level of income is generally regarded as too extreme, it focused attention on what has come to be understood as an empirically very important mechanism for adjusting savings and investment (even though there may be others). Fluctuations in the level of income and employment are observed to occur in response to fluctuations in the levels of saving and investment.

The balance of empirical evidence seems to most economists to support a modified version of Keynes's theory. According to this theory, fluctuations in savings or investment cause fluctuations *both* in interest rates and in income. Although most economists agree that, as a general rule, more of the burden of equilibrating the system falls on changes in income rather than on changes in interest rates, the relative importance of these two mechanisms varies between times and places according as the interest rate is free to change in response to changes in savings and investment and as the volume of savings and investment reacts to changes in interest rates.

Investment and the Level of Income

Empirical evidence tends to indicate that investment plans are more responsive to the level of demand for goods than to interest rates. When national income, and hence the demand for consumers' goods, is high, businessmen are likely to spend a great deal on investment; when national income, and hence the demand for goods, is low, businessmen may be unwilling to spend heavily on investment. This makes investment a function of the level of national income.†

The theory that investment will be related to the level of national income has two aspects. First, the higher the level of demand and income, the more *willing* businessmen will be to invest in new risky enterprises because they will have favorable expectations about the future. Second, the higher the level of demand, output, and hence of profits, the more businessmen will *be able to* invest. This aspect of the theory assumes that most businessmen are not able to (or do not wish to) borrow all the funds they require at the current rate of interest; in fact, so goes the hypothesis, they are severely limited in the quantity of funds they can borrow at any moment of time. In technical language, they do not borrow funds in a perfect market. As a result of this, the businessman is forced to look within his own firm for funds to finance many of his desired investment projects. These funds can be obtained by not distributing profits to shareholders. If we now add to this the hypothesis that profits will tend to be high when demand and income are high, we obtain the hypothesis that investment will depend on the level of income.††

The theory that investment is influenced by the level of profits has been subjected to considerable testing and has occasioned much

† In symbols, $I = I(Y)$, where I is the volume of current investment and Y is the *level* of national income.
†† In symbols, $I = f(R)$, where R stands for profits; if we add the hypothesis that profits vary with income, $R = R(Y)$, we obtain $I = I(Y)$, which is the result assumed in the previous footnote.

controversy. The discussion is complex, and much of it concerns the statistical difficulties in determining whether the observations conform to the predictions of the theory. One of the main problems is that the observation that investment is high when profits are high is not necessarily evidence supporting the theory. The causal connection could be in the opposite direction: High investment causes a high level of income (by the multiplier process), which causes high profits. The argument has not yet been settled, and all that we can say at this stage is that there is no really compelling evidence to date that would lead one to reject the theory.

Investment and the Rate of Change of Income: The Accelerator Theory

According to the "accelerator" theory, it is not so much the *level* of national income that affects investment, but, rather, the *rate of change* of national income. The theory is based on the following line of argument: When income is increasing, it will be necessary to invest in order to increase capacity to produce consumption goods; investment may also be high because business *expectations* based on the rising trend of sales may be favorable. On the other hand, when income is falling, it may not be necessary even to replace capital equipment as it wears out; furthermore, expectations based on the falling trend of sales may be unfavorable. For both of these reasons investment expenditure need not be great. Thus according to the accelerator theory, investment is a function of changes in income.†

The basic idea of the accelerator theory is not a difficult one; it can be elaborated as follows: When income is constant, it will not be necessary to expand existing plant and equipment; investment will be limited to replacing existing machinery as it wears out (and installing improved machinery for producing the existing level of output, which we ignore at this stage for simplicity's sake). Investment will be constant and will be equal to that fraction of the existing stock of capital equipment that wears out and that needs replacing each year. If, however, income starts to rise, it will be necessary to invest in new plant and equipment in order to expand the existing capacity to produce (once the expansion of demand is sufficient to employ all of the existing capacity). After this point, every additional rise in income will give rise to additional investment expenditure in order to increase productive capacity. Further, an increase of $1 in income may lead to an increase of more than $1 in investment expenditure; this is because a machine has a long life and may have a value considerably in excess of the value of its output over one year. A machine that has a value of $40,000 may produce an annual output of, say, $10,000. The entrepreneur who wishes to increase his output by using these machines must therefore spend $4 on investment for every $1 that he wishes to add to his annual output. (This is not necessarily a losing proposition, because he only pays once for the machine, which goes on producing goods over all the

---

† In symbols, $I = I(\Delta Y)$.

years of its life.) In our example, once existing capacity is used to its fullest, every $1 increase in income would entail $4 of additional investment expenditure. In more general terms, new investment is said to be some multiple, a, of the change in income. The multiple a is called the accelerator coefficient.† This may be expressed in symbols as follows:

$$I_n = a\Delta Y \qquad (1)$$

when I_n is new investment, ΔY is the change in income, and a is the accelerator coefficient, which depends on the ratio of the value of capital equipment to the annual value of its output.

The accelerator theory has two aspects: (1) that the level of new investment will be a multiple greater than one of the change in income (because the value of a machine is usually well in excess of the value of its *annual* production), and (2) that the level of new investment varies with the change in income (because *new* capital is needed to expand rather than to maintain output).

In Chapter 49, we shall find that even such a simple theory of investment as the accelerator raises the possibility of dynamic fluctuations, and even of unstable behavior, in the circular flow of income.

THE ACCELERATOR: EMPIRICAL EVIDENCE

Many attempts have been made to test the accelerator theory of investment. Tests have been made for single industries and for the economy as a whole. Most of the tests of the simple form given in equation (1) above have shown the theory to be a poor explanation of observed fluctuations in investment. On the basis of these tests, many economists have concluded that the actual evidence was unfavorable to the theory.[3]

There are, however, a number of complications that make it unlikely that so simple a relation as equation (1) could accurately describe real data. The theory does not apply to investment to replace worn-out equipment, nor does it apply to investment in new techniques (investments that reduce costs of production without necessarily increasing capacity). The theory only applies to some part of net investment—that part that increases the capacity to produce goods. The accelerator will not necessarily apply to increases in demand and output thought to be temporary. (The businessman will build new plant to meet new demand only if he expects the new demand to be maintained long enough for the investment to pay for itself.) The theory may not apply at all when there is excess capacity, because a rise in demand will not lead to a rise in investment when there already exists more capacity than is needed to satisfy the original demand *and* the extra demand. Finally, and most important, all the new capacity will not be established immediately after there is a rise in demand. It takes time to plan an increase in capacity, to let contracts, and to have plant

† The basic assumption of the accelerator is that there is an optimal relation between the stock of capital (B) and the level of income, i.e., $B = aY$. Now assume we start from equilibrium so that at period t the actual stock of capital bears the desired relationship to income, i.e., $B_t = aY_t$. Now let income rise between period t and $t + 1$. If the capital stock is adjusted to its new desired level over the same period, $B_{t+1} = aY_{t+1}$. Subtracting these two expressions from each other gives $B_{t+1} - B_t = a(Y_{t+1} - Y_t)$. The change in the capital stock *is* new investment, $I \equiv B_{t+1} - B_t$, and $Y_{t+1} - Y_t$ is the change in income. If we denote $Y_{t+1} - Y_t$ as ΔY, this gives us the relation set out in equation (1).

3. See, for example, A. D. Knox, "The Acceleration Principle and the Theory of Investment: A Survey," *Economica*, August, 1950.

built and machinery installed. Furthermore, the businessman may increase his capacity in a series of stages. He might, for example, need three new factories to meet an increase in demand, and he might not let contracts for the second until the first is well under way, and not let contracts for the third until the second is well under way. Thus, the reaction of investment expenditure to a rise in demand might be spread out over a considerable period of time. When X (in this case, investment) is a function of Y (in this case, changes in income), but when the reaction is spread out over a long period of time, the economist talks of X depending on Y with a *distributed time lag* (see p. 138). The existence of such time lags means that we would not observe a simple relation between investment and income changes of the sort assumed in equation (1). The actual relation would be more complex, and fairly subtle statistical techniques would be needed to observe it if it were present.

More subtle tests have found considerable evidence of an accelerator-type relation, but one complicated by the factors named above. The simple studies that have failed to find evidence of such a relation are, therefore, not conclusive. The existing evidence does point to a fairly strong accelerator-type relation between investment and changes in demand, but one complicated by the fact that the relation is subject to a distributed lag of quite long duration.[4]

Investment and Expectations

Investment takes time. A businessman who decides this year to expand capacity may not see the fruits of his investment for several years. The decision to invest now is thus to a great extent an act of faith concerning the future. If the businessman guesses wrong, the penalties can be great. If he decides not to expand capacity and the market for his product expands, he can fall irrevocably behind his more foresighted competitors. If, on the other hand, he decides to expand capacity and his market does not expand, he can be saddled with unused plant and equipment, the fixed costs of which may bankrupt him. The businessman does his best to predict the extent of his market, but many things can influence it other than the tastes of households. A new Congress may adopt different taxing and spending policies that affect him profoundly; the apparent success—or failure—of a disarmament conference may cause some lines of production to look more profitable and others less profitable. The rise of a new method of transportation, a revolution in South America, or a relapse in the health of President De Gaulle can all influence him in important ways that are hard to predict. By and large, most firms make reasonably accurate decisions about investment most of the time. If they did not, the economic system would exhibit very much more instability than it does now. Occasionally, mob psychology predominates, however, and a feeling of pessimism about the future can snowball into a general cut in investment expenditure, or a feeling of optimism can

4. See, for example, D. Smyth, "Empirical Evidence on the Acceleration Principle," *Review of Economic Studies*, June, 1964.

snowball into an investment boom based on expectations that later turn out to be false.

There is no doubt that the state of business expectations affects investment expenditures and that a general psychological reaction can cause major shifts in investment. We shall see, in Chapter 49, that such changes in expectations are capable of setting off major expansions or contractions in the level of business activity.

Summary

1. Investment expenditure is an important, and quite volatile, component of aggregate demand. In Chapter 46, we studied the effects on income and employment of changes in investment. In Chapter 48, we have examined hypotheses about the causes of such changes and have sought to make investment an endogenous, rather than an exogenous variable.

2. The major source of funds for investment is current savings of households and firms. Investment may also be financed out of funds accumulated in the past and out of money newly created by the banking system and lent to firms. (The process of the creation of money is described in Chapter 53.)

3. There are competing theories of the role of interest rates as a determinant of investment. We derived the prediction that the change in income in response to an autonomous change in the desire to invest will be smaller, the larger the consequent change in interest rates and the more responsive investment expenditure is to such changes. Two extreme theories were studied. In the classical theory, savings and investment are brought into equality solely by changes in (freely and rapidly fluctuating) rates of interest; in the Keynesian theory, the rate of interest is stabilized by the speculative activities of bondholders, and savings and investment are brought into equality by fluctuations in income (which adjust the volume of savings to whatever volume of investment firms have decided upon). The empirical evidence seems to favor a theory that says that changes in the desire to invest exert an influence both on the level of income and on the rate of interest.

4. In considering the determinants of investment, we first dealt with the level of income. One theory that relates investment to the level of income is based on two assumptions: first, that firms are subject to substantial credit rationing and so are forced to finance much of their investment out of undistributed profits; and, second, that the level of profits rises as the level of income rises.

5. A rather different hypothesis relates investment to the rate of change of income. The accelerator theory, which predicts such a relation, is based on the assumption of a desired relation between the size of the capital stock and the level of income, and so predicts a relation between changes in the capital stock (investment) and the changes in income. The empirical evidence does not seem to be inconsistent with some of the more subtle formulations of this theory.

6. Finally, we noted the important effect that the firm's expectations about the future can have on the amount of investment it is prepared to undertake in the present.

QUESTIONS FOR DISCUSSION

1. Why do we speak of savings and investment in the same breath?

2. If $C = .7Y$ and $M = .1Y$, what is the relation between S and Y? (Assume, for simplicity, that there are no taxes and that M equals imports.)

3. What is the importance of interest rates in the theory of investment? What do the theories discussed in this chapter predict about how interest rates behave in response to changes in investment?

4. What conflicting predictions emerge from the "classical" and the "Keynesian" theories of investment?

5. Draw a graph showing investment expenditure varying directly with the level of income. Is investment now an endogenous or an exogenous expenditure? Show that the paradox of thrift becomes even more paradoxical now, in that the thriftier households are (in the sense

defined in question 6, page 560), the less they save when equilibrium has been achieved, whereas the more spendthrift they are, the more they save when equilibrium has been achieved.

6. What is the basic notion of the accelerator theory? Is investment endogenous or exogenous in this theory? Why, when we assume investment to be determined by an accelerator, can we not illustrate the investment function on a simple graph, such as the one you used for question 5? What related magnitude could we plot against the level of income? (Reread the daggered note on page 579).

7. What complications are there in evaluating the evidence about the accelerator theory?

8. If businessmen had believed the statements of some people that the economy was headed for a "stall" in 1966, what effect might this have had?

Chapter 49 FLUCTUATIONS IN THE LEVEL OF BUSINESS ACTIVITY

THE GENERAL TREND OF THE U.S. ECONOMY, as in all industrial societies, is upward: Output, employment, and living standards all tend to rise over time. Compare any year in the 1960s with any year in the first decade of this century, and your overwhelming im-

pression will be one of growth, even if you choose a year of low activity from the 1960s and compare it with a boom year from the 1900s. Living standards are vastly higher now than then.

If, however, you take each year of the 1950s

and 1960s and compare it with the year following, you will find that economic activity proceeds in an irregular path, with forward spurts followed by pauses and even relapses.

The irregular and often violent movements of the economy over short periods of time have long occupied the attention of economists. These movements were once commonly known as business cycles or trade cycles, the word cycle suggesting a regular oscillation of good times and bad. At some times and places, these movements have been remarkably regular. A quick glance at the figure on page 55 will show that unemployment in nineteenth-century Britain showed quite steady

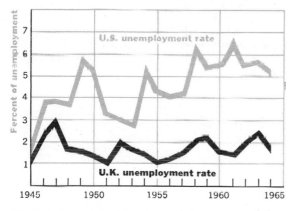

FIGURE 1   PERCENTAGE OF THE U.S. AND U.K. LABOR FORCES UNEMPLOYED, 1945–1964

oscillations, with one period of boom separated from the next by about nine years. At other times, the movements have been more ragged; smooth or ragged, however, they have always been present. Figure 1 shows the percentage of the labor force unemployed in the United States and the United Kingdom for each year since World War II. Fluctuations are present in both economies, but they are

not as regular as the nineteenth-century ones. Indeed, from 1959 to 1964, the U.S. unemployment rate was remarkably steady at the disturbingly high rate of about 5.5 percent. The only exception was in 1961 when the rate rose to 6.7 percent.

The generally irregular movements of the economy are readily apparent in Figures 2 and 3, which show the course of industrial production and of private construction in the present century.

Some students of industrial fluctuations have thought that they were able to discern several types of cycles. One such cycle, which is clearly observable in the British nineteenth-century employment series, had a duration of about nine years from peak to peak. This nine-year cycle was the one usually identified in the past as the *business cycle*. A second type of cycle, for which there is considerable evidence, is one of much shorter duration, lasting anywhere from eighteen to forty months. This cycle is sometimes associated with variations in business inventories: When inventories are being built up, purchases by firms will exceed their sales; when inventories are being reduced, purchases will be less than sales. As we shall see, the building up and running down of inventories can give rise to a regular cyclical oscillation in the economy. Finally, some economists have thought that they perceived a very long cycle of about fifty years' duration. These cycles are thought to be associated with, among other things, major flourishes of investment activity consequent on some fundamental innovation, each burst being followed by a long pause in investment, once all the most obvious new lines have been exploited. Of all the "cycles," this long-wave one is the most conjectural, and we shall say nothing further about it in this book.

FIGURE 2   **INDUSTRIAL PRODUCTION BY MAJOR DIVISION, 1920–1964**

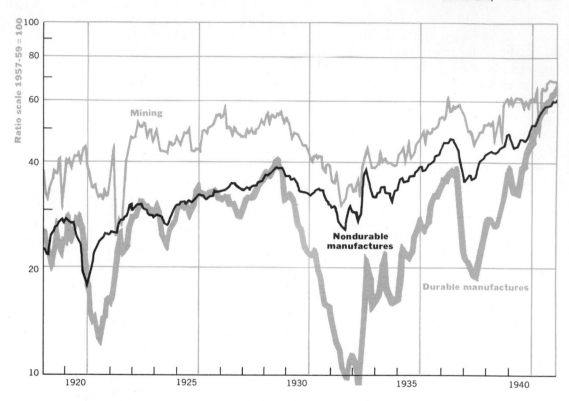

From time to time, many different theories have been put forward to explain these fluctuations in the economy. In the present chapter we can do little more than provide a very general introduction to this interesting and difficult subject.

Phases of the Cycle

Figure 4 shows a stylized cycle and divides it into four periods. We shall first briefly describe the general characteristics of each of the phases of the cycle and then describe one possible theory of the cycle.

DEPRESSION

A depression is characterized by heavy unemployment and a level of consumers' demand that is low in relation to the capacity of industry to produce goods for consumption.

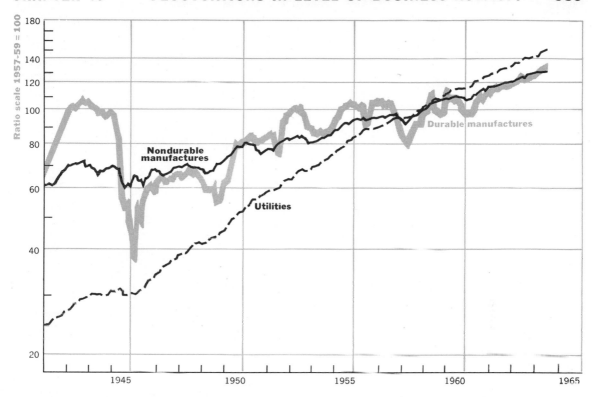

There is, thus, a substantial amount of unused industrial capacity. Some prices may be falling while others will be unchanged, but few if any will be rising. The average level of prices will tend to drift slowly downward. Business profits will be low and, in many individual cases, they will be negative. Confidence in the future will be lacking and, as a result, businessmen will be unwilling to take risks in making new investments. Banks and other financial institutions will have surplus cash that no one whom they consider to be a reasonable credit risk wishes to borrow.

RECOVERY

When something sets off a recovery, we say, as a matter of terminology, that the *lower turning point* has been reached. Once begun, the pace of recovery is likely to quicken. Worn-out machinery will be replaced. Employment, income, and consumers' spending all begin to rise. Expectations will become more favorable as a result of increases in production, sales, and profits. Investments that once seemed risky may now be undertaken as the climate of business opinion begins to change from one of pessimism to one of optimism. As demand expands, production will be expanded with relative ease merely by re-employing the existing unused capacity and unemployed labor. Prices will stop falling and will generally tend to stay constant or else to rise slowly.

BOOM

As the recovery proceeds, bottlenecks begin to occur in various industries: All existing

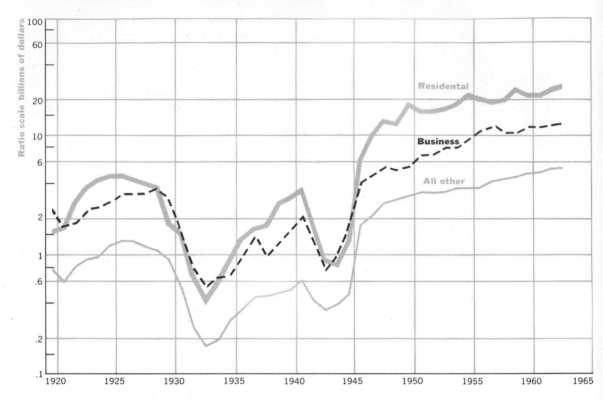

FIGURE 3   VALUE OF NEW PRIVATE CONSTRUCTION, 1920–1963

capacity is fully utilized; labor shortages begin to occur, particularly in certain key skilled categories; and shortages of certain key raw materials develop. It now becomes increasingly difficult to increase output merely by putting unused resources to work, since the supply of unused resources is rapidly disappearing; output can be raised further only by means of investment, which raises the productivity of already-employed labor. Further rises in demand are now met more by increases in prices than by increases in production. As shortages develop in more and more places, a situation of general excess demand for labor develops. Costs rise but prices rise also, and business remains generally very profitable. Losses are infrequent,

since a money profit can be earned merely by holding on to those goods whose prices are rising over time. Investment expenditure will be heavy, investment funds will be in short supply, and interest rates may rise in the face of a heavy excess demand for loanable funds. Expectations of the future are favorable, and much investment may be made that is not justified on the basis of current prices and sales and that requires further rises in prices and demand to render it profitable.

RECESSION

The point at which the boom turns into recession is called the *upper turning point*. Once a recession sets in, it tends to gather its own momentum. Consumption demand

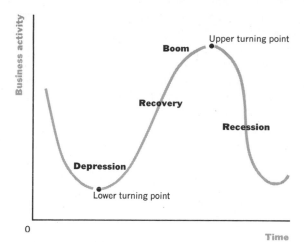

FIGURE 4   **A STYLIZED CYCLE**

Bankruptcies, which were very infrequent in the boom period, now become more common. Production and employment fall as a result and, as employment falls, so do income and expenditure; as demand falls, more and more firms get into difficulties. Prices and profits fall, and new investment is reduced to a very low level. It is very often not even worth replacing capital goods as they wear out, since unused capacity is increasing steadily. When the decline is spent, a period of full depression sets in, and we are back where we began.

This discussion is brief and stylized, but it gives some picture of the typical elements found in the various phases of most cycles, and thus in the theories that seek to explain them. No two cycles are exactly the same. In some, the recession phase is short and the resulting depression is not severe; in others, a full-scale period of stagnation sets in. In some cycles, the boom phase develops into a severe inflation; in others, the pressure of excess demand is hardly felt.

falls off. Investments that looked profitable on the expectation of continuously rising demand and prices suddenly become unprofitable. High interest payments, which seemed easily bearable when sales and prices were rising steadily, now become a heavy burden.

A Theory of the Cycle

Why is it that market economies do not settle down into some position of equilibrium, maintaining more or less full employment at all times? In order to answer this question, we shall develop a theory of the cyclical behavior of the economy—a theory that attempts to account for the fact that such economies tend to progress cyclically rather than smoothly. This elementary theory, which brings together a number of ideas and theories that we developed throughout Part IX, is divided into three parts: first, a theory of cumulative upswings and downswings, explaining why, once started, booms and slumps

tend to carry on of their own momentum; second, a theory of floors and ceilings, explaining why cumulative upward and downward movements are eventually brought to a halt; and, third, a theory of instability, explaining how a process of upward or downward movement, once it is brought to a halt, tends to reverse itself. The theory here presented is but one of the many theories that have been offered. Ultimately, choices among theories must be resolved by appeals to evidence. Because business-cycle theories are highly general and inherently dynamic, they are difficult to test. The theory developed below is a synthesis of several elements of dynamic economic behavior that appear to us to be not refuted by known facts.

CUMULATIVE MOVEMENTS

Why does a period of expansion or contraction, once begun, tend to go on of its own momentum? First, the multiplier process tends to cause cumulative movements. As soon as a revival begins, some unemployed laborers find work again. These people, with their new income, can afford to make much-needed consumption expenditures. This new demand causes an increase in production and creates new jobs for further unemployed workers. As incomes rise, demand rises; as demand rises, incomes rise. Just the reverse happens in a downswing. Unemployment in one sector causes a fall in demand for the products of other sectors, which leads to a further fall in employment and a further fall in demand.

A second major factor is to be found in the accelerator theory of investment demand, discussed in Chapter 48. New investment is needed to expand existing productive capacity and to introduce new methods of production. When consumer demand is low and there is excess capacity, investment is likely to fall to a very low level; once income starts to rise and entrepreneurs come to expect further rises, investment expenditure may rise very rapidly. Further, when full employment of existing capacity is reached, new investment becomes the only way available for entrepreneurs to increase their output. Since a capital good lasts many years, the value of a machine will generally be greatly in excess of the annual value of consumption goods that it produces. If a machine costing $4,000 produces $1,000 worth of goods every year, then it will be necessary to spend $4 on investment for every desired increase of $1 in the annual production of consumers' goods. For these reasons, investment demand may rise by very much more than consumer demand, and even a moderate fall off in consumer demand may reduce desired new investment almost to zero. The volatility of investment expenditure is one of the important causes of fluctuations in market economies.

A third major explanation for cumulative movements may be found in the nature and importance of expectations. All production plans take time to fulfill. Current decisions to produce consumers' goods and investment goods are very strongly influenced by the expectations of businessmen. Such expectations can be volatile. Expectations can, for quite long periods of time, lead to their own realization. If enough people think, for example, that stock-market prices are going to rise, they will all buy stocks in anticipation of a price rise, and these purchases will themselves cause prices to rise; if, on the other hand, enough people think stock-market prices are going to fall, they will sell now at what they regard as a high price and thereby actually cause prices to fall. This is the phenomenon of *self-realizing expectations.* If enough businessmen think the future looks rosy, they may all begin to invest in increasing capacity; this will create new employment and income in the capital-goods industries, and the resulting increase in demand will help to create the rosy conditions the expectations of which started the whole process. One cannot lay down simple rules about so complicated a psychological phenomenon as the formation of expectations. But it is often, if not always, true that they show a sort of band-wagon effect. Once things begin to improve, people expect further improvements, and their actions based on this expectation help to cause yet further improvements. On the other hand, once things begin to worsen, people often expect further worsenings, and their actions based on this expectation help to make things worse.

Variations in the burden of fixed money debts when changes occur in the price level also cause cumulative movements. Debts and other contractual payments are fixed in terms of money. Practically all borrowed money is obtained at the cost of an interest payment fixed in money terms. Prices and costs rise during a boom, but interest payments do not rise in proportion. Thus, if prices and other costs double, profits will more than double, because one element of costs, fixed interest payments, will not rise. On the other hand, if prices and costs fall, profits will fall further, because fixed interest payments will not fall at all. Thus, on the upswing of a cycle, the real burden of fixed money payments diminishes, making it easier to earn profits, whereas, on the downswing, the real burden increases, and profits fall off.

There are other reasons too why recoveries and recessions, once started, tend to build up a momentum of their own, but we shall not go into them here. We note in passing that this tendency complicates government anticyclical policy. It is not sufficient to know *what* measures will stop a boom; it is necessary to apply these measures at just the right time and in just the right strength to curb the boom without setting off a downward spiral that will gather momentum of its own accord.

FLOORS AND CEILINGS

What makes these upward and downward processes come to an end? Once we get started in a boom period, why don't we just go on and on increasing our income and enjoying our affluence? Consider first the revival from a recession.

As long as there is unused capacity, income can continue to rise at a very fast rate. However, once full employment has been achieved, income can rise only as fast as productivity can be increased through new investment. Thus, an automatic check is placed on the rapid expansion of real income once full employment is reached. What about the recession phase? The worst that can happen to gross investment is for it to fall to zero, which *would* happen if no new investment occurred and if no existing machinery were replaced as it wore out. Even in this worst of all possible worlds, however, income would not sink to zero. As income falls, fewer and fewer people save, and such saving as does occur is matched by the dissaving of others. Once the society in the aggregate is no longer saving, consumption will equal income, and income will no longer decrease. This is the lowest conceivable floor to equilibrium income.[1] Although gross investment may sink to zero in some sectors of the economy, it is unlikely to do so in the whole economy. Between 1920 and 1932, investment fell drastically, but at the depth of the depression it was nearly $1 billion. As long as investment exceeds zero in some sectors, it will exceed zero for the whole economy. In some sectors, for example, in the industries providing food, basic clothing, and shelter, demand may remain fairly high in spite of quite large reductions in national income. These industries will certainly be carrying out some gross investment to replace equipment as it wears out, and they may even undertake some net investment. The floor to income occurs at a level of income at which saving is equal to

1. Graphically, it occurs at the point where the consumption function cuts the 45° line.

this minimum level of investment. Thus, although cumulative movements may continue at very rapid rates in either direction for considerable periods of time, floors and ceilings are eventually encountered. The floor stops the contraction while the ceiling slows down the rate of expansion to that made possible by increases in productivity.

TURNING POINTS

Next we introduce a theory that predicts that it is impossible or at least extremely difficult to stabilize the level of national income, and that, once it is prevented either from expanding or contracting at a rapid rate, a turning point will occur. We shall develop such a theory in a moment. When we have it, our theory, which says (1) that things, once started, tend to go off cumulatively in the same direction; (2) that there are limits, floors, and ceilings that slow up or stop upward and downward processes; and (3) that, once such a process is stopped or slowed down, it will reverse its direction, will be complete.

The accelerator theory of investment is probably the best known of the theories accounting for this reversal of direction. This theory was introduced in Chapter 48, and you should now reread pages 578–579.

The accelerator makes the desired level of *new* (not replacement) investment depend upon the rate of change of income. If income

is rising at a constant rate, then investment will be at a constant *level*. If the speed at which income is rising slackens, then the level of investment will decline.[2] This is illustrated in Table 1 for a hypothetical example where $I = 3\Delta Y$. If income merely levels off to a constant level, then *new* investment may be reduced to a very low level. This means that a *leveling off* in income at the top of a cycle

TABLE 1

Period	Y	ΔY	I
1	100		
2	200	100	300
3	275	75	225
4	325	50	150
5	350	25	75
6	360	10	30
7	365	5	15
8	365	0	0

will lead to a *decline* in the level of investment.[3] The accelerator thus provides a theory of the upper turning point, although not one for the lower turning point. The decline in investment at the upper turning point will cause a decline in the level of income that will be intensified through the multiplier process. If the fall in income continues, the floor will eventually be reached. After a while, investment may rise exogenously. If it does not, then, once existing capacity falls to the level

---

2. The concept of a declining rate of increase always causes trouble when it is first encountered. The student familiar with the differential calculus will recognize that it refers to a function with a positive first derivative and a negative second derivative with respect to time. Others will recognize the values of Y in Table 1 as an example of a series that is increasing at a declining rate.

3. Let us consider a further example. Assume that the accelerator relation is $I = 3\Delta Y$. The accelerator coefficient is 3 and the total of new investment occurs in the year in which the rise in income takes place. Now assume that income is *rising* at a constant amount of 100 each year. Investment will be at a *constant level* of 300. If income now continues to rise, but only by 50 each year, the level of investment falls to 150 a year. If income levels off at a constant amount, the level of investment falls, in this very simple example, to zero.

suitable to current output, there will be a revival of replacement demand, and new machines will now be bought as old ones wear out. This rise in the level of activity in the capital-goods industries causes, by way of the multiplier, a further rise in income in response to which new investment will take place, leading to yet further rises in income. So a multiplier and an accelerator combined with "ceilings" and "floors" may be sufficient to set up an endless cyclical process in the economy. To present and develop such a theory formally requires the use of some elementary mathematical tools.[4]

The Inventory Cycle

Business firms all hold inventories of materials and finished goods. These inventories fluctuate widely, as Figure 5 illustrates. Such sharp fluctuations are a major cause of the short-term variations in the level of activity. How does this "inventory cycle" occur? The theory of inventory cycles is very similar to the accelerator mechanism, only we now emphasize investment in *inventories* of goods rather than in plant and equipment.

Start by assuming national income to be in equilibrium with withdrawals equal to injections at the full-employment level. Now assume, in order to get the process started, that there is an autonomous rise in the propensity to save (a fall in the propensity to consume). The first result of the fall in demand will be a piling up of unsold goods on

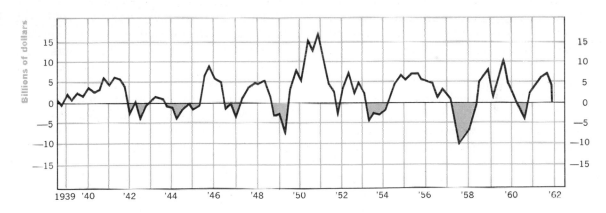

FIGURE 5   FLUCTUATIONS IN INVENTORIES, 1939–1962

4. The student who wishes to see such a theory handled mathematically should consult William J. Baumol, *Economic Dynamics: An Introduction* (2d rev. ed.; Macmillan, 1959).

dealers' shelves. After some time, dealers will reduce their orders so as to prevent inventories from increasing indefinitely: Retailers will reduce purchases from wholesalers and, after wholesalers' stocks have risen, they in turn will reduce their purchases from manufacturers. Manufacturers may maintain production for a while, adding the unsold goods to inventories, in the hope that the fall in demand is only temporary. If this proves not to be the case, manufacturers will cut back on production, laying off some workers and reducing the hours worked by the remainder. Thus income and output will begin to fall and, at this stage, inventories will have risen to an abnormally high level. Once production falls to a level equal to the new (lower) level of consumers' demand, there will be no further rise in the level of stocks. Unfortunately, however, matters will not remain at this point. Stocks will now be too high on two counts: First, because sales will be at a lower level than they were originally, and, second, because stocks will have increased during the transitional process. In order to work off excess inventories, retailers will buy less from wholesalers than they are selling to consumers, wholesalers will buy less from manufacturers than they are selling to retailers, and manufacturers will produce less than they are selling to wholesalers. Thus the current level of output, and hence of income earned by households selling factor services to firms, will fall below the current level of sales. This fall in income will reduce the level of demand still further. As long as production can be held below the level of current sales, then inventories will be falling, even though the level of sales is itself falling. Once inventories are reduced to the desired level, the retailers and wholesalers will increase their orders, so that they are equal to current sales,

thus keeping inventories constant; manufacturers will also increase the level of output until it is equal to the (increased) level of sales, thus keeping their own stocks at a constant level. But this means that production, and hence income earned by households, is increased. As this happens, the demand for goods will rise. The initial impact here will be on inventories, which will be run down as sales rise unexpectedly. Now the whole process is set into reverse. For a while, everyone's inventories will be run down, but then orders will increase, first from retailers, then from wholesalers. Finally, the output of manufacturers will increase. This means that incomes, and with them the level of demand, will rise. Once production is increased to the level of current sales, inventories will no longer be decreasing. But now the level of inventories is too low on two counts: First, because the level of sales is higher than it was when inventories were at the correct level, and, second, because inventories have been run down during the transitional phase. In order now to build up their inventories, retailers will order more from wholesalers than they sell to consumers, wholesalers will buy more from manufacturers than they sell to retailers, and manufacturers will produce more than they sell to wholesalers. This rise in production will raise incomes and thus raise the level of demand still further. As long as production is kept above the level of sales, however, inventories will be rising in spite of the fact that sales are also rising. Once the level of inventories is brought up to the desired level, orders will fall off. Retailers and wholesalers will reduce orders to the level of current sales, and manufacturers will reduce output to that level as well. But this fall in output will reduce incomes and with it demand. For a while, inventories will pile up, but orders and output will be cut back, thus reducing the level of income and demand. If you go back to the beginning of this paragraph and reread it, you will find out what happens next: The whole downward process is set in motion again.

Although this kind of verbal analysis can provide some general ideas of the cyclical process, mathematical tools are essential if we want to carry our analysis much further. In some branches of economics, one can get a long way by means of careful verbal and geometrical analysis. In the field of dynamic fluctuations, one can get practically nowhere. What are the effects of varying the time lags with which firms react to changes in their sales? What if the reaction does not occur suddenly but is *distributed* through time? Un-

der what circumstances will such a cycle die out rapidly so that income *converges* on its equilibrium level? In what circumstances will the self-exciting process continue indefinitely, so that the cycle will itself carry on indefinitely unless stopped by conscious government policy? What will be the effect of government controls built into the system in an attempt to dampen these fluctuations? What difference will it make if the government's control mechanism itself acts with a time lag? To answer such questions, mathematics is indispensable, particularly the sort of mathematics that electrical engineers use to analyze self-exciting (*closed-loop*) control systems. For the student interested in dynamic fluctuations, a knowledge of such techniques has become essential.[5]

Summary

1. The accelerator theory discussed in Chapter 48 leads naturally to the discussion of fluctuations in the level of business activity given in Chapter 49. Economists have often thought that they were able to discern several types of cyclical fluctuations in the economy: a medium-range cycle (lasting about a decade), which has usually been identified in the past as the business cycle; a cycle of shorter duration (eighteen months to three years), usually associated with fluctuations in inventories; and a long-swing cycle of about fifty years' duration, which is much more conjectural than the others.

2. A stylized cycle may be divided into four

phases: depression, recovery, boom, and recession. Each phase has certain characteristic features, although no two real-world cycles will be exactly the same.

3. The rest of Chapter 49 is devoted to describing *one possible theory of the cycle*. This theory has three important aspects: (a) a theory of cumulative upswings and downswings, (b) a theory of floors and ceilings, and (c) a theory of instability. Cumulative upswings and downswings are supposed to be caused by such factors as the multiplier, the accelerator, and the formation of expectations. Floors and ceilings are supposed to provide limits to upward and downward cu-

5. One of the best surveys of the formal economic theory of fluctuations and of the mathematics used therein is to be found in the first half of R. G. D. Allen, *Mathematical Economics* (2d ed.; St. Martin's, 1959).

mulative movements. The accelerator provides one possible theory of instability. It shows how, once an upward expansion is checked, it can easily turn into a downswing.

4. The final section of the chapter provides a description of an inventory cycle, which is similar to an accelerator process, since new investment in inventories depends on changes in the level of income.

QUESTIONS FOR DISCUSSION

1. "The only thing we have to fear is fear itself —nameless, unreasoning, unjustified terror which paralyzes needed efforts to convert retreat into advance. . . ." So said Franklin D. Roosevelt in his Inaugural Address in 1933 at the height of the most serious depression ever recorded in American history. Is this statement consistent with the theory of the business cycle we have developed?

2. If, in the depths of a depression, the government raises expenditure by some fixed amount in an effort to raise employment, which of the following will be most favorable to its efforts? Which least favorable?
   a. Investment is determined mainly by an accelerator relation with an accelerator coefficient of 5.
   b. Investment is determined mainly by an accelerator relation with an accelerator coefficient of 3.
   c. Investment is a function of the level of income.
   d. Investment is autonomous.

3. One of the most controversial statements of the state of the economy in the 1960s was probably the comment made by William McChesney Martin, Chairman of the Board of Governors of the Federal Reserve System, who said, in a speech in mid-1965, that he saw "disquieting similarities" between the boom before 1929 and the boom in the 1960s. Why the concern, and what difference do you think there is between then and now?

4. A great deal of talk in the Great Depression was of "priming the pump." How might a small amount of government expenditure do this? What might happen if business confidence is very, very low?

5. Why do we ever level off, once we get into the downward spiral of a depression?

6. There were, before the escalation of the war in Vietnam, fears of a "high-level stall" of the economy in 1966. Would it be a source of concern if the economy were to level off for a while after a period of rapid increase in output and employment? Why or why not?

7. The Report of the Council of Economic Advisors for 1965 notes that, in the past fifteen quarters (nearly four years), inventories have fluctuated less than previously. What effects is this likely to have had?

8. "No two business cycles are alike. Therefore, it is foolish to talk about them in general." What do you think?

Chapter **50** FOREIGN TRADE AND NATIONAL INCOME

IN CHAPTER 46, WE DEVELOPED PREDICTIONS about the effects of imports and exports on national income. Before continuing, we briefly summarize the analysis of that chapter.

Imports

Imports are regarded as withdrawals from the circular flow of income. When a domestic household purchases a commodity manufactured abroad, it creates income for foreign firms. Imports thus represent money earned by domestic households, but not passed back to domestic firms through consumption expenditure. In that sense, imports withdraw money from the domestic circular flow. If households switch some of their expenditure from domestically produced to foreign-produced goods, the level of national income will fall in just the same way as it will fall if households reduce their expenditure on domestically produced goods. In both cases, the volume of withdrawals from the circular flow of income increases. The effects of the withdrawals are magnified by a multiplier process.

If American households decide to buy more Volkswagens and fewer American cars, American national income will fall. Why? Because fewer American automobiles will be produced, thus fewer workers will be needed in the automobile industry. But this is not the end of the process. Since U.S. auto workers will have less money to spend, they can buy fewer goods: fewer dresses, fewer outboard motors, fewer high-fidelity sets. What happens to the income of firms making these products? It falls too, because the employees of all these firms have to cut *their* spending. The multiplier process continues until the original fall in sales of the auto industry has been magnified into a general fall in sales and incomes throughout the economy.

Exports

Exports are regarded as an injection into the circular flow. When a foreign household purchases a good manufactured in the U.S., it creates income for a U.S. firm. Exports thus represent money earned by U.S. firms that does not arise from the spending of U.S.

households. In this sense, exports inject expenditures into the domestic circular flow of income. When foreign households buy American goods, the level of U.S. national income rises in just the same way as it rises when U.S. firms spend more money on investment. In both cases, the volume of injections into the circular flow of income increases. The effects of the injections are magnified, both directly and indirectly, by a multiplier process. If German households decide to buy fewer Volkswagens and more American cars, American national income will rise. Why? Because more American automobiles will be produced and more workers will be needed in the U.S. automobile industry. This, of course, is not the end of the process. Since U.S. automobile workers will have more money to spend, they will purchase more goods, thus increasing the income of the firms

making these goods. Firms providing such services as night clubs, motel accommodations, and air travel will find their incomes rising, since their sales to auto workers will rise. The employees of these firms will increase *their* spending, and so the multiplier process will continue until the original rise in sales of the auto industry has been magnified into a general rise in sales and incomes throughout the economy.

When we speak of a foreign-trade multiplier, we mean the multiplied effect on national income of a change in either imports or exports. A change in exports has the same effect on national income as has any change in autonomous expenditure. A change in imports has the same effect on national income as has any change in withdrawals from the income stream.†

The Financing of Imports[1]

Imports by Americans must be paid for in foreign currency. The German firm selling Volkswagens to the United States must in the end receive marks in payment so that

it can pay for its factors of production. The foreign money needed to pay for these imports comes from American exports. Exports are sold in the first instance for foreign cur-

† This may be shown formally as follows: Consider a model with only two withdrawals, S and M, and two injections, I and X. (Other withdrawals and injections can be added without affecting any of the following arguments.) In equilibrium, $S + M = I + X$. If there is a change in one of these magnitudes and we then return to equilibrium, then $\Delta S + \Delta M = \Delta I + \Delta X$ (i.e., the change in total withdrawals must equal the change in total injections). We assume that $\Delta S = s\Delta Y$ and $\Delta M = m\Delta Y$, where s is the marginal propensity to save and m is the marginal propensity to import. We also assume that I and X are autonomous. This gives

$$s\Delta Y + m\Delta Y = \Delta I + \Delta X$$
$$\Delta Y(s + m) = \Delta I + \Delta X$$
$$\Delta Y = \frac{1}{s + m}(\Delta I + \Delta X).$$

This expression shows that imports have the same effect on Y as savings, and exports have the same effect on Y as investments.

1. We discussed the problem of financing imports in Chapter 38. If anything in the following summary causes trouble, refer back to pages 430–433 of that chapter.

rency, say, marks. But the American exporter requires payment in dollars in just the same way as the German exporter required payment in marks. American exports thus produce a supply of foreign currency that people are trying to trade for dollars while American imports produce a demand for foreign currency. If, at the current exchange rate, the value of imports equals the value of exports, there will be exactly as much foreign currency earned by exporters as is needed by importers. Thus, imports will be "financed" by exports.

But what if the value of imports does not equal the value of exports? If imports exceed exports, more foreign currency is being spent than is being earned through exports. In this case, one of two things must be happening. Either the difference is coming out of exchange reserves, or it is being provided by foreign lenders. On the other hand, if exports exceed imports, then more foreign currency is being earned than is being spent, and the difference between what is earned and what is being spent must be being used either to add to reserves of foreign exchange or to lend money abroad.

The International Propagation of Depressions and Booms

The foreign-trade multiplier shows that the fates of various economies are intertwined. In Chapter 46, we assumed that imports and exports were independent of each other, but, as we warned at that time, this is a simplification that is not satisfactory.

If the U.S. suffers a fall in national income for some purely domestic reason, U.S. imports will fall. Americans will buy fewer German Volkswagens, fewer British Jaguars, fewer Irish tweed jackets, fewer Swiss watches, fewer French wines, fewer Japanese cameras, fewer Canadian raw materials, and fewer Mexican vacations. As a result, the income of these countries will fall, and they will buy fewer U.S. refrigerators, fewer Dacron shirts, and fewer Florida oranges. Thus, we see that the national incomes of various countries are linked together: A change in income in one country tends to cause the incomes of other countries to change in the same direction. Second, changes in other countries tend to reinforce the initial change; if U.S. income falls, German income falls as well; the Germans then buy fewer U.S. goods and as a result U.S. income falls still further. The extent to which changes in income in one country affect incomes in other countries, and the extent to which these changes reinforce the initial change, depends on the proportion of national income that is devoted to foreign trade. In the United States, this proportion is small and thus the American national income is fairly well insulated from fluctuations in other countries. In many other countries, such as Canada, Japan, and the United Kingdom, the proportion of national income in foreign trade is high, and fluctuations in income in one of these countries are easily translated into fluctuations in the incomes of the others.

Expenditure-Dampening and Expenditure-Switching Policies

In the first half of the 1960s, the United States had a persistent balance-of-payments deficit. Ever since the end of World War II, the United Kingdom has had a recurring tendency for imports to exceed exports. What can any country do when such a persistent tendency exists? Broadly speaking, there are two main sets of policies that can be adopted: First, national income may be reduced by raising taxes or by lowering government expenditure. The fall in income will reduce the expenditure of households on all goods, including imports. This policy is called an *expenditure-dampening policy*; it relies on a general reduction in expenditure to accomplish its goal of a reduction in expenditure on imports. How successful the policy will be depends on the proportion of income that is spent on imports. Where, as in the U.S., this proportion is small, then a large reduction in income will be needed to accomplish a given change in imports. Where, as in Britain, the proportion of income spent on imports is large, then a smaller change in income will be needed to produce any given change in imports.[2]

The second major policy is an *expenditure-switching* one. The expenditures of domestic households on foreign goods can be switched to reduce imports, and the expenditures of foreign households can be switched to increase exports. An expenditure-switching policy is accomplished by changing the prices of foreign goods relative to domestic goods. This can be done by taxing imports and subsidiz-

ing exports, or by devaluing the exchange rate. Expenditure-switching policies were analyzed in detail in Chapter 38.

Expenditure-switching and expenditure-dampening policies can both affect the balance of payments in the desired direction. Both of them, however, have certain side effects.

A policy of expenditure-dampening to reduce imports is somewhat like shooting at a close target with a shotgun. The bull's eye will usually be hit, but so will a lot of other things. Specifically, a general reduction of expenditure will reduce expenditures on all domestically produced commodities. This means that output and standards of living will fall and that unemployment will rise—side effects not usually regarded as desirable, especially by those affected.

An expenditure-switching policy will also have an effect on the level of domestic income, output, and employment. If a devaluation of the American dollar lowers the prices of American goods relative to foreign ones, both foreign and U.S. households will buy more U.S.-produced goods and fewer foreign-produced goods. This will raise incomes in those American industries that produced the newly demanded goods, and, when the extra incomes are spent, a multiplier process will be set up that will raise all incomes in the U.S. On the other hand, if the dollar is appreciated, then foreign and American households will buy fewer American goods. This will lower the income of those sectors of the

2. In general, any change in imports of an amount ΔM can be accomplished by changing income by the amount $\Delta M/m$ where m is the marginal propensity to import. This follows from the relation $\Delta M = m\Delta Y$. Thus if 50 percent of income goes in imports, a change in M of \$1 can be accomplished by changing Y by \$2; if only 5 percent of income goes in imports, then a change in M of \$1 requires a change in Y of \$20.

U.S. economy that produced those goods the demand for which has now fallen. Once the incomes of households in these sectors have fallen, their expenditures will be reduced, and incomes throughout the U.S. will fall. Among the important side effects of such a policy is a redistribution of income among sectors of the U.S. economy.

CONDITIONS FAVORING EACH POLICY

These two policies for removing a balance-of-payments deficit have opposite effects on income. Expenditure-dampening policies lower demand and income and thus tend to recommend themselves to policy-makers in situations of overfull employment, because, in such situations, it may be considered desirable to reduce demand in order to check inflationary tendencies. The use of expenditure-dampening policies in periods when employment is less than or just equal to the level considered to correspond to full employment will have the undesirable effect of reducing employment still further and imposing a sacrifice on the community in terms of foregone domestic output.

Expenditure-switching policies tend to raise demand and national income by increasing the volume of domestic expenditure. Such policies will tend to appeal to policy-makers in situations in which income and employment are below the desired level. A successful expenditure-switching policy in these circumstances will simultaneously improve both the balance of payments and the unemployment situation. If an expenditure-switching policy is to be successful in a period of full employment, however, it must be accompanied by a policy of reducing domestic expenditure. There is no point in switching foreign demand onto your products if you are in a situation in which full employment of resources already persists, because it will not be possible to produce more output to meet the extra demand. The appropriate policy in such a situation is to reduce domestic expenditure by exactly the same amount as the increase in foreign expenditure on domestically produced goods. This keeps national income and employment unchanged, but directs a larger share of total output to exports, thus improving the balance-of-payments situation.

This point was not fully appreciated after the last war, and more than one devaluation was made at times of overfull employment and already existing inflationary pressure. For example, the British pound was devalued in 1949 at a time of full employment when prices were already rising at about 2 percent per year. The devaluation switched expenditure into British goods, but there was little scope to expand output. Devaluation as a method of curing balance-of-payments problems was thus used in a set of circumstances in which theory predicts it had the minimum chance of succeeding. It is difficult, therefore, to accept the evidence of this period as refuting empirically the proposition that devaluations are an effective means of alleviating balance-of-payments deficits.

Imports and Exports: Good or Bad?

It is very commonly argued that exports raise national income and hence are "good," whereas imports lower national income and hence are "bad." The view that exports are beneficial and imports harmful goes back at least as far as the eighteenth century.[3]

When we say exports raise national income we mean that they add to the value of output. But they do not add to the value of domestic consumption. In fact, exports are goods produced at home and consumed abroad, while imports are goods produced abroad and consumed at home.

The issue involved in this section is a most important one, and we shall approach it indirectly by thinking not of exports and imports, but of a farm family that sells produce to the outside world ("exports") and buys goods from the outside world ("imports"). Suppose the farm family sells everything it can grow, but buys nothing. The money will roll in, but the family will get hungrier and hungrier; their car will run out of gas; their clothes will become tattered; and their radio will eventually stop working. Clearly, they cannot be better off than if they used some of their cash to buy needed goods. An extreme case to be sure, but not without some interest.[4]

The standard of living of a person or of all persons in a country depends on the goods and services that they consume, not on what they produce. The *average* material standard of living of the residents of a country may be thought of in terms of the following equation:

$$\text{Average standard of living} = \frac{\text{total of goods and services consumed}}{\text{number of people}}.$$

If exports are really good and imports really bad, then a fully employed economy that obtains an increase in its exports without any corresponding increase in its imports ought to be made better off thereby. This change will, however, result in a reduction in current standards of living, because, when more goods are sent abroad and no more are brought in from abroad, the total goods available for domestic consumption must fall. The view that exports are good and imports are bad implies that the best of all possible worlds would be the situation in which a country exports all its production and imports nothing. No matter how "good" or "bad" this situation is in your eyes, you should not fail to notice that all the inhabitants of the country would soon starve to death, since there would be no goods and services of any kind available for domestic consumption.

What happens if a country achieves a surplus of exports over imports for a considerable period of time? It will be accumulating claims to foreign currency. There are three

---

3. The group of men holding this view were known as the Mercantilists. Adam Smith, often called the Father of Modern Economics, was principally concerned with refuting their propositions.

4. Every so often we read about someone who has been living in utter poverty for decades, but who, when he dies, is discovered to have hundred of thousands of dollars stashed away. We assume he must have been insane.

possible uses for the foreign currency earned by exporting: It may be used to buy foreign goods, to make investments abroad, or to add to foreign-exchange reserves. Foreign-exchange reserves are required for the smooth functioning of a system of fixed exchange rates. Such reserves do not help the functioning of the system if they are accumulated beyond the level necessary to reduce the chance of running out of reserves to a very low level. After that, foreign currencies are useful only if they are spent to purchase useful goods and services. We cannot eat, smoke, drink, or wear British pounds sterling or Indian rupees. But we can spend them. British pounds and Indian rupees can be used to buy British and Indian goods that can be eaten, smoked, drunk, or worn. When such goods are imported and consumed, they add to U.S. living standards. Indeed, as we saw in Chapter 30, the main purpose of foreign trade is to take advantage of the international division of labor; trade allows us to consume more than would be possible if all goods were produced at home. From this point of view, the purpose of exporting is to enable one to import goods that can be produced more cheaply abroad than at home. Exporting more than one is importing makes more sense if the purpose is to obtain funds to invest abroad. (Such foreign investment only makes sense if the return for an equal-risk investment is as high or higher than the return that can be obtained on an investment made at home.) But such foreign investments add to living standards only when the interest earned on them is used to buy imports that do not have to be matched by currently produced exports. From this point of view then, the purpose of exporting more than one is importing in order to make foreign investments is *eventually* to be able to import more than one is exporting!

The living standard of a country depends on the goods and services consumed in that country. The importance of exports is that they permit imports to be made. This two-way international exchange is valuable because more goods can be imported than could be obtained if the same goods were produced at home.

AN ECONOMY WITH UNEMPLOYMENT: AN EXCEPTION?

What about an economy with unemployment, such as the U.S. economy in the early 1960s? Assume there is a rise in that country's exports without any corresponding rise in its imports, perhaps because the government has put a subsidy on exports and increased the rates of tariffs charged on imports. As we saw in the last chapter, this rise in exports will increase income and employment. Surely, in a time of unemployment, this is to be regarded as a "good thing."

Two points need to be made about such a policy. In the first place, the goods being produced by the newly employed workers in the export sector are not available for domestic consumption and so do not raise domestic standards of living. Would it not be better if, instead of subsidizing exports, the government subsidized the production of goods for the home market, so that as well as a rise in employment there would also be a rise in domestic living standards? Or if one objects to the government subsidization of private firms, then the government could create new employment by building more roads, schools, and research laboratories. Again, income and employment would go up, but, again, there would be something more tangible to show for it than the smoke of ships bearing the subsidized exports to foreign markets.

The second point to be made concerns the foreign effects of such a policy of fostering exports and discouraging imports in a situation of general world unemployment. Although the policy raises domestic employment, it will have the reverse effect abroad: It will create unemployment abroad. Such a policy may therefore be referred to as one of "exporting one's unemployment." The foreign countries will suffer a rise in their unemployment, because their exports will fall and their imports rise. This will set up a multiplier process that reduces their levels of income and employment. Even if the governments of these countries are prepared to see their unemployment rise, this policy cannot long continue, because these countries will begin to have a balance-of-payments deficit. They will soon be forced to take steps to remove this deficit. If they do this by restricting imports, the original country will lose the

stimulus that it originally obtained by encouraging exports. If all countries try such a policy of expanding exports and discouraging imports, the net effect is likely to be a large fall in the volume of international trade without much change in the level of employment in any country.[5]

There is, however, one set of circumstances in which the policy could provide a long-run solution. In the early 1960s, the U.S. had heavy unemployment and a balance-of-payments deficit, while Germany had full employment with heavy inflationary pressure plus a balance-of-payments surplus. In these circumstances, an American policy of discouraging imports and encouraging exports to Germany would have raised U.S. employment and alleviated the U.S. balance-of-payments deficit while at the same time reducing inflationary pressures in Germany and reducing her balance-of-payments surplus. This result would have been mutually satisfactory for the U.S. and Germany.

Summary

1. The foreign-trade multiplier refers to the multiplied effect on national income of a change in either imports or exports. Imports are a withdrawal from the circular flow, and exports are an injection into it.

2. If the value of imports exceeds the value of exports, either the exchange reserves are being depleted, or money is being provided by foreign lenders. If exports exceed imports, either reserves are mounting, or money is being lent to foreign borrowers.

3. The international propagation of booms

and depressions occurs by way of the multiplier process. The proportion of a nation's income devoted to exports determines the nation's susceptibility to fluctuations abroad; the amount devoted to imports determines the susceptibility of foreign nations to domestic fluctuations. The United States is not very susceptible to foreign fluctuations, because exports are a small proportion of U.S. national income. Other countries are not so self-sufficient.

4. There are, broadly speaking, two sets of

5. The experience of the 1930s, when many major trading countries did adopt such a policy, was discussed in Chapter 41.

policies a nation may follow when imports persistently exceed exports: expenditure-dampening (which is to reduce the general level of expenditure), and expenditure-switching (which is to switch expenditure from foreign to domestic sources of supply). Both policies have side effects on the level of domestic income, output, and employment. Expenditure-switching tends to raise the level of demand for domestic products, and, at times of full employment, it must be accompanied by some expenditure-dampening to be successful. Otherwise, increasing the demand for domestic goods will do little more than cause inflation.

5. The living standard of the citizens of a country depends on the goods and services consumed in that country. The importance of exports is that they permit imports to be made. This two-way international exchange is valuable, because more goods can be imported than could be obtained if the imported goods were made at home.

6. "Exporting one's unemployment" cannot be successful if all countries try to do it at once. There is one situation in which two nations involved may both find it satisfactory: when one country suffers from both a persistent payments deficit and unemployment, while the other suffers from over-full employment, with heavy inflationary pressures, and a persistent payment surplus. Encouraging exports to, and discouraging imports from, the surplus country might, in this case, be mutually satisfactory to both countries.

QUESTIONS FOR DISCUSSION

1. What would be the effect on U.S. national income of the following?
   a. a change in tastes toward California wines and away from French wines;
   b. a switching of investments from overseas to home;
   c. a decrease in tourist expenditure abroad;
   d. an increase in foreign tourist expenditure in the U.S.;
   e. an increase in the sale of arms abroad;
   f. the sale of U.S. bonds held by the British central authorities in order to meet a balance-of-payments deficit.

2. Considering the above, what is the rationale behind the following *New York Times* headlines?
   a. "Business Men Urged To Curb Overseas Investment Voluntarily"
   b. "Johnson Girls To Help Publicize 'See America First' Campaign"
   c. "Embassies Abroad to Serve California Wines"
   d. "Cut in Tourist Allowance Asked"
   e. "Pentagon Arms Super-Salesmen"
   f. "Offices Abroad To Promote U.S. Travel"

3. What is the purpose, and how would you classify, the following policies of the British Government to end the balance-of-payments crisis it faced in 1965?
   a. a 15 percent import surcharge;*
   b. a subsidy on exports;
   c. an office to advise exporters;
   d. a "credit squeeze," and an exhortation to banks to prefer exporters in granting loans;*
   e. the curtailing of government expenditure on roads, universities, and housing;*
   f. the discouragement of investment abroad, primarily by making it more expensive;*
   g. the strict enforcement of a limit on foreign-exchange facilities for travel abroad;
   h. an increase in the short-term rate of interest in London.

* Measures actually instituted in 1965.

4. Can a country *suffer* from a persistent balance-of-payments surplus?

5. Vietnam was concerned in 1965, over the effects of a sudden influx of dollars. The dollars came from American soldiers, who vastly increased the demand for all kinds of commodities. Surely, since this is akin to exporting, the Vietnamese should be pleased. Why their concern?

6. It used to be said in Europe in the early 1950s: "When America sneezes, Europe gets a cold, but Europe could have pneumonia without America even sniffling." What might be meant by this? (Hint: Consider the proportion of U.S.

income accounted for by sales in Europe and the proportion of European income made up of sales to America in the 1950s.)

7. During the period 1939–1941, the British Government confiscated U.S. securities held by British residents and paid the owners in pounds sterling. The securities were then sold in America, and the dollars obtained were used to buy American-produced war materials needed to defend Britain during the critical period when the United States was not at war with Germany. What was the effect of these crisis measures on the postwar balance of payments between the U.S. and Britain?

Chapter **51** GOVERNMENT AND THE
CIRCULAR FLOW OF INCOME

IN CHAPTER 46, WE STUDIED BRIEFLY THE effects of government taxing and spending policies on the circular flow of income. We learned that government expenditure (G) is an injection into the circular flow of income. It creates income for those firms and households that sell goods and services to the government, but the income does not arise out of the expenditure of households. Government tax revenue (T) is a withdrawal from the circular flow of income. It represents in-

comes of households that cannot be passed on to firms by way of household spending because it is removed from the circular flow by government. A rise in the level of government spending or a fall in the level of taxes will raise national income, for the former represents a rise in the volume of injections and the latter a fall in the volume of withdrawals. A fall in the level of government spending or a rise in the level of taxes will lower national income, for the former represents a fall in

1. If you have any difficulty with these propositions, reread Chapter 46, pages 552–554.

the volume of injections and the latter a rise in the volume of withdrawals. In all cases, the original change in government expenditure or tax revenue will be magnified through a multiplier process so that the final change in national income will be larger than the initial change in G or T.[1]

The Financing of Deficits and Surpluses

The above discussion implies that it is possible to have situations in which government expenditure does not equal government tax revenue. When revenues exceed expenditures, we say that there is a budget surplus; and when revenues fall short of expenditures, we say that there is a budget deficit. If the government spends more than it raises, where does the money come from? If the government raises more than it spends, where does the money go? Basically, the difference between G and T is reflected in changes in the level of the government's debt. If the expenditures exceed revenues, the balance must be borrowed from someone; if revenues exceed expenditures, the balance goes to pay off some of the loans that were made in the past.

A deficit requires an increase in borrowing, for which there are three main sources: the central bank,[2] the commercial banks, and the public. The money raised may represent totally new sources of funds or it may represent money that would have been spent for other purposes. If it represents new sources, there is a net increase in expenditure in the economy; if not, only a rechanneling of expenditure from one stream to another is involved. If the government sells bonds to the central bank, the central bank can pay for these by creating *new* money. The same thing can happen, but within limits, if the government sells its bonds to commercial banks. In both cases, there will be a net addition to expenditure in the economy once the government spends this money. If the government sells bonds to commercial banks or to households and obtains money that would otherwise have been lent to private firms, the expenditure is merely being rechanneled from the private to the public sector of the economy. The new government expenditure still represents an increased injection into the circular flow, but it is matched by an exactly parallel reduction in the injections created by private investment spending.

A surplus allows the government to reduce its outstanding volume of debt. Bonds in the hands of the central bank, the commercial banks, or households may be redeemed. If the money is neither spent by those who receive it nor lent to someone else to spend, there is a net withdrawal from the circular flow. If, on the other hand, the money is spent by those who obtain it, there is a parallel increase in private spending and no net change in total spending.

In what follows, we shall study the common case in which budget deficits cause net increases in the volume of spending, whereas surpluses cause net decreases. Other special cases can easily be analyzed when their particular circumstances are specified.

2. In the U.S., the "central bank" is the Federal Reserve System, which we shall describe and discuss in Chapter 53. The central bank controls the money supply and can increase or decrease it virtually at will.

Revenues, Expenditures, and the National Debt

TABLE 1   **THE U.S. NATIONAL DEBT, 1929–1963, IN BILLIONS OF DOLLARS**

Year	Total gross debt[a] ($)	Debt/GNP %	Year	Total gross debt[a] ($)	Debt/GNP %	Year	Total gross debt[a] ($)	Debt/GNP %
1963	305.9	52.3	1951	255.2	77.6	1939	40.4	44.3
1962	298.2	53.7	1950	257.4	90.4	1938	37.2	43.6
1961	289.0	55.8	1949	252.8	97.9	1937	36.4	40.1
1960	286.3	57.0	1948	252.3	97.3	1936	33.8	40.9
1959	284.7	59.0	1947	258.3	110.2	1935	28.7	39.6
1958	276.3	62.2	1946	269.4	127.9	1934	27.1	41.6
1957	270.5	61.1	1945	258.7	121.1	1933	22.5	40.2
1956	272.8	65.1	1944	201.0	95.1	1932	19.5	33.3
1955	274.4	69.0	1943	136.7	71.0	1931	16.8	22.0
1954	271.3	74.7	1942	72.4	45.5	1930	16.2	17.8
1953	266.1	72.8	1941	49.0	39.0	1929	16.9	16.2
1952	259.1	74.7	1940	43.0	42.7			

a Excludes guaranteed obligations and is based on end of fiscal year, June 30.

SOURCES: 1929–1957—*Historical Statistics of the United States,* p. 720; 1958–1963—*Statistical Abstract,* 1964, p. 403.

We have discussed both budget surpluses and budget deficits. In the United States, periods of deficit are very much more common than periods of surpluses. Table 1 shows two ways of looking at the U.S. national debt. The picture of government indebtedness has varied greatly over time, but the trend in the money value of the debt is strongly upward. Most of the increase was built up during wartime periods, when governments were spending greatly beyond their revenues, and during the Great Depression of the 1930s. In some peacetime periods, the level of indebtedness has fallen for many years at a time.

The size of the national debt, the reasons for it and the consequences of it, is almost surely the aspect of economics about which there is more misunderstanding in the popular press than any other. We must therefore consider it closely.

THE SOURCES AND SIZE OF THE DEBT

In Chapter 43, Table 4, we saw one way of classifying budget expenditures. Let us now consider another.

It is possible conceptually to divide government expenditures into currently consumed items and capital items.[3] The former, such as the costs of running the government, the costs of social-security payments, and the

3. An attempt to classify along these lines is made each year by the Bureau of the Budget. The interested student should examine "Special Analysis D" in the latest issue of the *Budget of the United States.*

costs of operating veterans' hospitals, are used up and add to living standards in the current period. Capital items, such as dams, roads, and schools, last a long time and yield their benefits to firms and households over the whole of their lifetime. Assume for the moment that these capital items are paid for by borrowed money that is to be repaid over the working life of the asset. As a capital item wears out, we will wish to replace it with a new one, especially if it has proved useful. If the value of the capital assets owned and operated by the government remained constant over time, then we would expect the portion of the national debt required to finance capital expenditure to remain constant. Their value does not remain constant, however, and therefore the national debt does not remain constant either. There are several forces that lead to a rising national debt.

First, if prices rise, we would expect that the national debt will have to rise in order to keep the real resources that it represents constant. For example, if the government issues bonds to cover the cost of building a school, and if prices then rise, the cost of *replacing* the school will rise, as will the money value of the debt necessary to cover the cost of replacement.

Second, if the government kept its *relative* importance in the economy constant, we would expect the absolute size of the national debt to grow as the size of the economy and the size of the population grow. Consider an analogy: General Motors makes up 2–3 percent of the total national production of the economy; if General Motors is merely to maintain its relative importance in the economy, then General Motors' production must grow as total production grows. This means that its plant and equipment must be increased, and, to the extent that it finances its activities through borrowed capital, its debt must grow.

Third, if, as we got richer, we wished to spend a larger fraction of our total income on those things produced by governments—education, roads, parks, defense—we would have to increase capital expenditures, and we would thus expect the national debt to grow faster than the national income is growing.

In some countries (Sweden, for example), the size of the debt is tied to government capital expenditures. In the United States, it is not, although many people have urged that some form of *capital budgeting* be used. Are there any reasons why capital budgeting should not be used? One reason, perhaps the most important one, is that it is extremely difficult to agree on what a capital expenditure *is*. Is an investment in the education of children and scientists a current expenditure, or an investment in the future? Is money allocated to research on the causes of disease a current expenditure, or a capital expenditure? Because these things do not correspond to physical assets, many people regard them as not being capital assets. But they represent more of an investment in the future than a nuclear submarine, which, though it is tangible, is providing a current service (defense), not a future one.

The point is that, if we segregate government expenditures into two groups and make it easier to finance one and harder to finance the other, we affect the allocation of resources between the two groups. Almost any set of rules is objected to by some people. To take one example, Senator Wayne Morse of Oregon has several times introduced a bill that would make it easier to finance capital expenditures —defined as projects that provide benefits over more than ten years *and* that repay, by direct revenues, a large fraction of their cost. This may sound eminently sensible to you. But note that probably the only federal government activity that meets the requirement is a public power project. Are dams necessarily more important than public education and public health? Should the government move into producing automobiles and steel (which would fit the definition of favored capital expenditures) and out of conservation and defense? Apparently most senators think not, since Senator Morse's proposal has not been passed.

Fundamentally, there are only three sources of revenue for financing government expenditures: taxing, borrowing, and selling government services. The third is essentially minor.[4] (The postal service and the sale of publicly produced electric power are examples.) The basic question of financing is whether the money that is needed should be raised by taxation or by borrowing.

The question of how to finance expenditures is hotly debated, at least in the United States. Two of the views commonly aired in the press are, first, that the burden of government services should fall on the generation that reaps the benefit, and, second, that there is something morally wrong with a budget that is not balanced. In some cases, these views represent mere value judgments about what ought to be. As such, they are outside the scope of positive economics. More often, they are the product of feared consequences of a rising debt, and it is within the province of positive economics to study whether these consequences are indeed likely to occur. Specifically, it is often feared that a rising debt transfers a burden to future generations and that, if deficits continue year after year so that the debt rises without limit, an impossible burden will eventually

be placed on the country's economy. But what *is* the nature of the burden of the national debt? To what level must it rise before serious economic consequences ensue?

THE BURDEN OF THE DEBT[5]

The national debt represents money owed by the government to those households, firms, and institutions that hold government bonds. In this sense, the national debt is owed by all of us to some of us. The existence of the debt means that households have saved in the past by lending their money to the government and that this money has been spent by the government. These two aspects of the national debt were dramatically illustrated during World War II. The great increase in government debt, financed by the sale of War Bonds, was matched dollar for dollar by the great increase in household savings invested in War Bonds. Many observers at the time praised the rise in savings but condemned the rise in borrowing!

In a very real sense, the cost of government activity cannot be postponed to future generations. We saw in Chapter 1 that the cost of doing something can usually be measured in terms of the things that might have been done instead. If the government uses resources to build dams, schools, rockets, or tanks, the opportunity cost of these is measured by the other things that might have been produced by the resources employed. This real cost in terms of foregone alternatives is incurred, no matter how the money to pay for the project is raised—by taxes, by borrowing from the public, or by creating new money.

4. Some taxes are regarded as "user taxes," in which the incidence of the tax is the payment for the use of a service. This is thought to be the case with gasoline taxes, which pay for the cost of public roads.

5. There is a substantial current controversy about the burden of the debt. For a view different from the one presented here, see William G. Bowen, Richard G. Davis, and David H. Kopf, "The Public Debt: A Burden on Future Generations?," *American Economic Review,* September, 1960.

The method of financing a project dictates how the cost is distributed throughout the community, but it does little or nothing to affect the total current cost.

The problems can best be seen by considering a wartime economy such as that of the United States from 1942 to 1945. During a major war, the government spends vast sums on war materials. A high proportion of the nation's resources are used to produce these materials. The real cost of using these resources to produce war goods is measured in terms of the consumption goods that might have been produced instead. This cost is necessarily borne by the wartime generation, because it as a group has less to consume than it could have consumed if there had been no war. The total cost can be determined only when it is determined how many resources are to be used for war production and therefore not used for the production of consumers' goods or for investments that would yield consumers' goods in the future. During World War II, for example, no passenger automobiles were produced in the United States, because the resources were diverted to war production.

The method of finance cannot significantly affect this total cost, but it does determine who bears the cost and it does allow some group to postpone the burden by persuading other groups to assume the burden in return for some advantage in the future. If the cost of the war is met solely by taxes, then current taxpayers bear the burden by having their consumption of goods and services reduced by taxes. Consumer expenditure will fall by just as much as the output of consumers' goods falls when resources are transferred to the production of war goods. If, on the other hand, the war expenditure is financed by borrowing from households and firms, the reduction in current consumption is suffered by those who lend their money to the government rather than spending it on currently produced goods and services. People who do not buy government bonds do not postpone current consumption and thus do not bear any of the real cost of the war effort.[6]

To the extent that the war is financed by current taxes, the matter is finished once the war is over. Resources can then be transferred back to the production of consumers' goods, and households' disposable income can be allowed to rise by reducing taxes. To the extent that the war is financed by borrowing, the debt remains after the war. It is necessary to pay interest each year to the bondholders and eventually to repay the bonds as they reach maturity. To the extent that interest payments and eventual redemption of the bonds are made from tax revenue, the postwar taxpayers are suffering a reduction in their consumption below what it would otherwise have been, and postwar bondholders are obtaining a rise in their consumption above what it could otherwise have been. The transfer is now reversed: In return for bearing the wartime reduction in consumption, bondholders or their heirs now enjoy a postwar rise in consumption, and taxpayers who are not bondholders suffer a postwar reduction. For a community, the full cost in terms of foregone output is all borne during the war; after the war, total production goes back to normal. The opportunity cost could not be postponed, but some individuals must now

---

6. A third method of financing is by creating new money by selling bonds to the central bank. In this case, government purchases bid up prices, and the costs are borne by the people through the reduced purchasing power of their money incomes.

pay for the war by transferring their claims on current production to other individuals.

Exactly the same analysis applies to the peacetime activities of a government, assuming we are in periods of full employment. If the government builds dams, roads, schools, and rockets, the opportunity cost of these is the cars, television sets, and beer that could have been produced instead. This cost is necessarily incurred by the current generation. But the distribution of the cost can be affected by the method of finance. If all of the expenses are met by tax revenues, then taxpayers are forced to bear the reduction in current consumption. If the costs are met by borrowing, the lenders voluntarily agree to take on the current costs by sacrificing consumption. Taxpayers are then forced to bear the cost slowly over time as funds are raised to pay interest to the bondholders and to provide for the eventual redemption of the bonds. The face value of the bonds represents the consumption originally foregone, and the interest represents the additional payment necessary to persuade bondholders to accept the whole of the burden in the first place.

How do intergenerational issues enter the picture? If you do not choose to buy bonds now, your heirs may be taxed to pay your share of the interest payments to those who did buy them. But this kind of debt is no different from any other kind of debts that your heirs may inherit from you. The interest will be paid to other members of their generation who have inherited the bonds.

Up to now, we have assumed the resources used by the government would otherwise have been used by the private sector to produce goods and services for current consumption. There are two other alternatives. First, the resources might have been used to produce capital equipment to increase output at a future date. This would be the case if the government borrows from households money that would otherwise have been loaned to firms for investment in capital equipment by the firm. In this case, the sacrifice is postponed to future generations. No reduction in current consumption need occur. (The current opportunity cost of the government activity is measured in terms of foregone output of capital goods for the private sector.) If the goods produced by the government add less to future national income than the capital goods the private sector would have produced, there is an added cost that is borne by future generations in terms of a national income lower than it would have been if the government had not borrowed the money, but had left it to be loaned to private firms. If, on the other hand, the capital goods produced by the government add as much or more to national income as would have been added by the capital goods private firms would have installed had they been able to obtain the money that the government raised, then there is no additional opportunity cost of the government activity over and above the consumption goods that could have been produced instead of the capital goods.

The second alternative is that the government borrows money to put unemployed resources to work. If these resources would have been idle in the absence of government spending, then there are no opportunity costs in terms of current production.[7]

---

7. Throughout this discussion we have neglected one real cost to future generations of debt financing. The existence of national debt requires a transfer of income. The government must raise money by taxes and then pay out this money as interest payments to persons holding government bonds. There will be some real cost of collecting taxes and paying out interest. Resources, in terms of tax collectors and inspectors and

SUMMARY

The opportunity cost of any government expenditure is measured in terms of the goods and services that could have been produced by the resources used by the government. If the foregone alternatives were to produce consumers' goods, then the cost is necessarily borne by the community at the time at which the government activity takes place. The total current cost cannot be avoided, but its alloca-tion between groups in the society can be determined. If the expenditure is financed by taxes, then the current cost is borne by tax-payers. If the expenditure is financed by borrowing, then the current cost is financed by lenders, and the cost to taxpayers is post-poned and spread over time. The taxpayers bear the cost when their consumption is re-duced by future taxes levied to pay interest on the debt and to provide for its eventual repayment.

Is There a Limit to the National Debt?

At this time there is a "permanent legal limit" to the United States debt of $285 billion, but there is a "temporary" limit of $325 billion.[8] In fact, such permanent and tem-porary limits are window dressing, and they are raised by Congress as the need to borrow more arises. We are concerned here not with statutory limits, but with economic ones.

To the extent that the money raised by bor-rowing is spent on items that add to money national income, the borrowing creates the extra income out of which extra taxes can be raised to pay the interest. To the extent that the money is spent on items that do not add to our money income, it will be necessary to increase existing taxes in order to provide funds to meet the interest payments. Up to a point, this will not cause any serious prob-lems, since the process of paying interest on the debt involves only a transfer from some citizens (taxpayers) to other citizens (hold-ers of government bonds). That there is a limit beyond which it is not safe to go can be seen by the following example: Suppose the government borrowed a sum equal to 5 per-cent of the national income each year in order to add to the beauty of the countryside, and suppose that national income is growing at less than 5 percent, say, 2.5 percent, per year. If this policy goes on forever, and if no old debt is ever paid off, then eventually the national debt would become so large that cur-rent national interest payments would exceed current national income. In order to raise enough money to meet its interest bill, the government would have to tax all incomes at a rate exceeding 100 percent!

Clearly, then, there is a grain of truth in the worry over the size of the national debt. But this worry applies only to those govern-ment expenditures that do not themselves help to create the extra income out of

accountants and clerks to look after bond issues, will be used for this purpose. These resources could other-wise have been employed to make goods and services for general consumption. Such real costs are but a very small fraction of the interest payments on the national debt.

8. The actual debt at this writing is $319 billion dollars. This is about one-half as large as the national income per year.

which interest payments can be met. And the worry only becomes significant if such nonincome-creating debt is increasing *very much faster* than the national income. Such a situation existed in the country during the crisis periods of World Wars I and II. Both of these periods were, by historical standards, very short. At no other time have we remotely approached a situation in which this class of debt was increasing at a rate anything like the rate at which national income was increasing. In fact, total debt has been declining as a percentage of national income. (See Table 1.)

One measure of whether the size of the debt is approaching dangerous levels is the willingness of borrowers to take government bonds at various rates of interest. Well before a government reached an absolute debt limit (in terms of ability to raise the money to pay the interest on its bonds), the public would lose confidence in the government's ability to pay its debts. One might expect the price of bonds to fall and interest rates to rise as borrowers demanded a premium for risk. (In Chapter 36, we discussed the relation of risk to interest rates. If you have forgotten this, reread pages 406–408.)

The fact that U.S. Government bonds are regarded as the least risky sort of investment available provides compelling evidence that the financial community is not concerned about the size of the debt.[9]

Government Fiscal Policy

Not so many years ago it was generally accepted, and indeed many people still fervently believe, that a prudent government should balance its budget on all occasions. The argument is usually based on an analogy with what seems prudent behavior for the individual. It is a foolish individual whose current expenditure consistently exceeds his current revenue, so that he gets steadily further into debt. It is then argued that what is good for the individual must be good for the nation.[10]

When the government followed a balanced-budget policy, as most governments did until the 1930s, it restricted its expenditure during a slump because its tax revenue would necessarily be falling at that time. On the other hand, during a boom, when its revenue was high and rising, it increased its spending. It rolled with the economy, raising and lowering its expenditures in step with everyone else.

To some people, the government, by going along with the crowd, did not seem to be making the most of its potential to control the economy in a beneficial manner. Why should the government not try to stabilize the economy by doing just the opposite of what everyone else was doing—by buying when everyone was selling, and selling when everyone was buying? This idea seemed particularly sensible in view of the fact that government revenues and expenditures were such an important part of the whole national

9. This is not true of all governments. Municipal government bonds in the U.S. are rated, and the rate of interest that municipalities must pay is variable among cities and over time.

10. Notice that this analogy does not usually hold at the firm level. The debts of most successful and rapidly growing firms will be found to be increasing steadily over time.

income of the country. In the United States, approximately one-quarter of the total national income is accounted for by the government sector; in some other countries, it is even higher. In the United Kingdom, for example, it is 35 percent. The potential to influence the economy of so large a class of expenditures today seems too obvious to ignore.

The government's use of expenditures and taxes in its attempts to stabilize the economy is called *fiscal policy*. It has two aspects: the level of the government's deficit or surplus; and the level of the government's expenditure. To see the difference, imagine a government operating with a *balanced* budget, but at two different levels, say, $90 billion and $110 billion. In each case, the deficit is zero, but the expenditures are different. Let us consider each aspect briefly.

BUDGET DEFICITS AND SURPLUSES

As far as the government budget is concerned, taxes represent a withdrawal from the circular flow of income, and expenditures represent an injection into it. If, in times of depression, the government runs a budget deficit, spending more than it is raising in taxes, then the government will be adding to the circular flow. If the government spends more than it raises, then there will be a net increase in the demand for resources. If, on the other hand, the government raises considerably more than it spends, it will be

causing a net decrease in the demand for resources.

Thus we would expect a government deficit or surplus to have an effect on the level of economic activity. Furthermore, our multiplier analysis allows us to predict that the final effect on the level of income will be greater than the actual amount of the budget deficit or surplus, assuming it to be a continuing one. If the government spends $X million in excess of revenues, this will have an effect similar to that of $X million new investment or any other kind of new injection of $X million; it will start off a multiplier process that will cause national income to rise by some multiple of $X million.[11]

Trying to stabilize the economy by running deficits in periods of slump and surpluses in periods of boom is called a *countercyclical fiscal policy*.

The reaction of some members of the public and of many Congressmen whenever countercyclical budgetary measures are proposed —as they were from 1960 to 1963—is difficult to understand. Evidently, the prospect of governmental budget deficits strikes a deep chord in the American subconscious. Such strong reactions are not aroused in other countries, and it is an interesting sociological problem to explain the strength of the feeling in the United States. In any case, as far as the goals of creating full employment and keeping living standards as high as possible are concerned, there is very little to be said against countercyclical budgeting.[12]

---

11. This assumes that the government goes on with its deficit, for the simple theory of the determination of national income spelled out in Chapter 46 predicts that, as soon as the deficit spending ceases, national income will fall back to where it was before the deficit spending began.

12. Countercyclical budgeting is independent of the question of the long-term change in size of the debt. A countercyclical policy can be imposed on a situation in which the long-term trend of the debt is to rise, fall, or remain the same.

THE LEVEL OF PUBLIC EXPENDITURE AND TAXES

Some people who understand the significance of a budget deficit or surplus believe that, if a government increases both revenues and expenditures in a depression, the level of income and employment will remain unchanged. This view is not necessarily correct.

If the government raises $X million and spends $X million, the circular flow of income will be unaffected only if the whole of the $X million would have been spent by the taxpayers on domestically produced goods. If the government's policy reduces private expenditure by $X million and raises its own expenditure by the same amount, then total expenditure, and hence total activity, will be unchanged. In general, however, we would expect a rise in taxes to cause a fall in consumption, a fall in imports, and a fall in savings. Thus, if we take an extra $10 in taxes away from a consumer, he may reduce his spending on domestically produced goods by less than $10, by, say, only $8, so that he cuts his expenditure on imports and his savings by $2. If the government spends the whole $10 on domestically produced goods, there will be an increase of $2 in total demand. In this case, there is an expansionary effect of the balanced-budget increase in public expenditure.

In general, if the marginal propensity to spend tax dollars is higher for the government than for the taxpayers, there will be an expansionary effect of an increase in the government budget. This effect is sometimes called the *balanced-budget multiplier*. If the government is assumed to spend all its tax revenues on domestic goods, the balanced-budget multiplier is 1: An increase of $X in the government budget will lead to an increase of $X in national income.† But the main point is that government taxing and spending is like a redistribution of income. If we shift command over resources from those with a lower propensity to spend to those with a higher propensity to spend, we increase the circular flow.

CAN A DEFICIT ERASE ITSELF?

The Council of Economic Advisors has in recent years advocated creating a budget deficit (via a tax cut) to reduce the level of unemployment. They have argued that if full employment is once restored there will be a *full-employment surplus* in the budget accounts. Thus an initial deficit may raise income, which will increase tax receipts, which in turn will create a surplus. Let us examine this argument more closely and see what our simple theory of the determination of national income predicts about it.

What the tax cut does is to lower the level of withdrawals associated with each level of income. This is shown graphically by a downward shift in the withdrawal schedule. If autonomous expenditures stay constant, national income will rise until total withdrawals

---

† Suppose the government raises $X by taxes and spends the entire $X on domestically produced goods. Suppose the taxpayers had a marginal propensity to withdraw funds of w (see Chap. 47 if you do not remember this concept). The *initial* effect on the circular flow will be an injection of $X and a withdrawal of $(1 - w)X$. Thus,

$$\text{initial effect} = X - (1 - w)X = wX.$$

But, as with any injection, there is a multiplier effect. The multiplier is $\dfrac{1}{w}$. Thus,

$$\text{the final effect is } wX \cdot \frac{1}{w} = X.$$

The balanced-budget multiplier is 1.

are again equal to the unchanged volume of injections. As income rises, we expect savings, imports, and taxes to rise.

The rise in the tax yield will reduce the budget deficit caused by the initial cut in rates, but, as long as imports and savings rise at all in response to the rise in income, tax yields cannot regain their original pre-tax-cut level (since, in the final position, the total of taxes, imports, and savings must be the same as in the original pre-tax-cut position). Thus, with expenditure unchanged, the final budget deficit must be larger than it was before the tax cut occurred.†

Thus, the theory developed in Chapter 46 leads to the prediction that the deficit cannot erase itself and that the final budget deficit will be greater than zero, although less than the initial deficit.

If there is to be a self correcting deficit, other things must also happen. For example, the tax cut might so stimulate businessmen's or households' expectations that they would increase their expenditures or investments: In other words, they might shift their expenditure plans upward. The accelerator theory of investment provides a possible mechanism

to justify the Council's prediction. It is clear that the prediction depends on there being an induced increase in injection expenditures sufficient to raise national income well above the level predicted by the simple multiplier theory. At the moment, all we can say is that the Council's hypothesis of full-employment surpluses must be regarded as an untested one.

BUILT-IN STABILIZERS

The idea of countercyclical budgeting requires that each year a conscious decision must be made to adjust the budget in a manner designed to stabilize the economy. The political problems involved are too obvious to need enumeration. They were very obvious, for example, in the three years of debate that preceded the tax cut finally enacted by the Johnson Administration in 1964. There are time lags as well. To institute a change in the government deficit takes time, even if there is no political problem. If the President proposes to Congress tomorrow that the government increase its road-building program by $1 billion, it will take a minimum of six

---

† This can be established formally with only the simplest bit of algebra. Let the subscript 1 refer to the initial equilibrium position in which

$$W_1 = J_1. \tag{1}$$

Breaking the withdrawals into three points, we have

$$T_1 + S_1 + M_1 = J_1. \tag{2}$$

Now let tax revenues be reduced by D dollars. This means that, at the original level of income, $W < J$, so that

$$T_1 - D + S_1 + M_1 < J_1. \tag{3}$$

Now let income rise to its new equilibrium level at which withdrawals again equal injections, so that

$$T_1 - D + \Delta T + S_1 + \Delta S + M_1 + \Delta M = J_1. \tag{4}$$

Subtracting equation (2) from equation (4) gives

$$- D + \Delta T + \Delta S + \Delta M = 0.$$

Or,

$$\Delta T + \Delta S + \Delta M = D, \tag{5}$$

which says merely that the induced rise in withdrawals must just cancel the initial reduction (since injections are unchanged).

This gives

$$\Delta T = D - \Delta S - \Delta M,$$

which establishes that, as long as $S + M$ rise at all, the rises in taxes (ΔT) must be less than the initial deficit (D).

months to a year before construction starts, even if Congress passes the legislation the same day it receives the request. It will be longer yet before the construction is completed and the government funds paid out in full. Cuts in taxes may work more quickly, but here too lags between a change in tax policy and the reduced collections may well be substantial. Where taxes are withheld, more rapid adjustment is possible than where taxes are payable at the end of a year or a quarter. Thus the cut in personal income taxes in 1964 came into play more rapidly than did the 1964 cut in the corporate-profits tax.[13]

What about building certain automatic stabilizing devices into the system? For instance, what if the government committed itself in advance to a fairly stable level of expenditure and to a policy of letting revenues fluctuate over the cycle? This would ensure deficits in recessions and surpluses in booms.

Steeply progressive taxes ensure that as incomes rise tax revenues rise more than in proportion, and as incomes fall tax revenues fall more than in proportion. Since expenditures do not adjust instantaneously to revenue, these tax-revenue changes tend to be stabilizing.

The mere fact that a much larger part of total investment is done by governments than in the past has a stabilizing influence, for government investment is not nearly so volatile as private investment. Thus at least part of this potentially very unstable element in national income is made relatively stable.

The stabilizing effect of government activity can be even further increased if some part of government expenditure can be made to vary inversely with income, rising when incomes fall and falling when incomes rise. Important built-in stabilizers that work in this way are unemployment-benefits schemes. When incomes fall, expenditure on unemployment benefits rises; when incomes rise, the expenditure falls. Unemployment benefits ensure that, when workers become unemployed, their consumption expenditure will not fall to zero, since their disposable incomes will not fall to zero. In general, the higher the payment made to the unemployed in relation to the amount they earn when employed, the smaller the fall in their consumption when their employment falls.

Another stabilizer is provided by agricultural policy. When a slump occurs and the demand for agricultural goods falls off, government price-support policies come into action and prevent farm incomes from falling as drastically as they would without such aid. Since agricultural income is more or less stabilized, the expenditure of the agricultural sector is likewise stabilized. Thus, that part of the multiplier process that would have worked through the agricultural sector is frustrated by policies that automatically support agricultural income. These stabilizers are important in countries such as the United States, in which agricultural sectors are large, but are unimportant in countries such as the United Kingdom, in which agricultural sectors are small.[14]

13. Because the government was eager to make a large initial impact with the cut, the reduction in withholding rates was more than the reduction in taxes. This provided a substantial extra increase in expenditure during 1964. In April, 1965, however, most taxpayers (including President Johnson) found themselves owing money to the Treasury.

14. This paragraph assumes that the government agricultural policy does more than merely redistribute a given level of real income from one group to another with the same propensity to spend. While this is theoretically a possible situation, there is abundant empirical evidence that suggests that these policies do reduce the adverse effect that a fall in farm prices would otherwise have had on national income.

Most of these built-in stabilizers are the unforeseen by-products of policies originally adopted for other reasons. The progressive income tax arose out of a concern to make the distribution of income less inequitable. The growth of the government sector has been the result of many factors other than a desire for cyclical stability. Social-insurance and agricultural-support programs were adopted more because of a concern with the welfare of the individuals and groups involved than with preserving the health of the economy. But, unforeseen or not, they work. Even governments can be lucky.

Dynamic Problems of Stabilization Policy

All of the fiscal policies that stabilize the economy, whether they are automatic or the result of conscious policy decisions, work to create *negative feedback*. Negative feedback is a technical term that means that, when any system deviates from its target level, forces are set in motion that push the system back *toward* its target level.[15] Thus, when demand is too high so that inflationary conditions prevail, demand is reduced; when demand is too low so that unemployment prevails, demand is increased. It would be grossly misleading to leave the reader with the impression that providing negative feedback is sufficient to solve all stabilization problems. Negative feedback is a necessary but not a sufficient condition for stability.[16] If any control system operates with delays that are large relative to the period of fluctuations it is seeking to control, it can do the very opposite of stabilizing: The controls can make the system less stable than it would otherwise be; they can actually accentuate rather than check fluctuations.

Controls operate with lags for two main reasons. The first reason is that our knowledge of what is happening is always somewhat out of date. At a minimum, it takes a month or so, and often very much longer, to gather data about current happenings. Our current information thus tells us not what is happening today, but what was happening anywhere from a month to six months ago. The second reason is that it takes time for any policy change to affect the behavior of firms and households. Such lags may vary from a few weeks to a year, depending on the particular measure.

A simple explanation of this problem can be developed along the following lines.[17] Consider a system that is oscillating around a desired level in the way illustrated in Figure 1(i). Time is measured along the horizontal axis, and aggregate excess demand is measured vertically. The fluctuations are such that a boom in which aggregate demand exceeds aggregate supply is followed by a slump in which aggregate demand falls short of ag-

15. The *system* may be anything from an economy to an airplane using an automatic pilot; the *target level* may be anything from a set of natural equilibrium values to a set of values desired and consciously sought after by the central authorities.

16. We illustrated this point in the case of a single competitive market. See page 90, footnote 3, and the discussion of the cobweb theory in Chapter 12.

17. This particular formulation of the problem is taken from A. W. Phillips, "Employment, Inflation, and Growth," *Economica*, February, 1962.

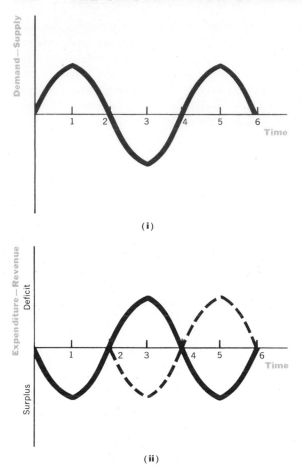

(i)

(ii)

FIGURE 1 (i) **THE RELATION BETWEEN AGGRE-GATE DEMAND AND AGGREGATE SUPPLY, PRIVATE SECTOR;** (ii) **THE GOVERNMENT'S BUDGET DEFICIT OR SURPLUS**

gregate supply. Assume that the government plans to vary its own demand so as to offset these fluctuations exactly. The government wants its plan to have the impact pictured by the solid line in Figure 1(ii). At first, it plans a surplus that will reduce total demand; later, in period 3, it plans a deficit that will raise aggregate demand. If the government's plans are fulfilled instantaneously, then the addition of the solid lines in Figure 1(i) and Figure 1(ii) will produce aggregate excess

demand, for the private plus the public sectors, which is always zero. The government's deficit or surplus exactly counterbalances the difference between aggregate demand and supply in the private sector, so that its stabilization policy is completely successful.

Now, assume that a time lag is involved; further assume, to make the point as clear as possible, that the time lag is equal to half the period of the cycle. Now the planned balanced budget at period zero will not actually occur until period 2; the planned maximum surplus of period 1 will not occur until period 3, when the economy is already in a slump; and the planned maximum deficit of period 3 will not occur until period 5, when the economy is already in a period of boom. Although planned government expenditure still follows the solid line in Figure 1(ii), actual government expenditure now follows the dotted line. Instead of stabilizing the economy as planned, the "stabilizing" policy actually destabilizes it. The combination of public and private demand will give rise to larger fluctuations than would have occurred if the government had done nothing!

This simple example is sufficient to show that the problem of controlling the economy is not so simple as it sometimes seems. In general, policies designed to stabilize individual markets or the whole economy will have quite widely differing effects, depending on the time lags both in the actual working of the economy and in the functioning of the stabilization scheme.

Professor Frank Paish of the London School of Economics has compared controlling the economy to driving a car with blackened front and side windows and only a rear-view mirror from which to see. The car has brakes and an accelerator, but they take effect only a long time after the driver has used them. Thus the driver often has to have the courage to apply the brake when he estimates that he is going uphill and the accelerator when he estimates that he is going downhill, just as the government, in attempting to steer the economy, often has to increase its spending during a boom and decrease it during a slump.

The Hypothesis of Secular Stagnation

So far we have been considering the appropriate governmental policy in the case of cyclical ups and downs in the economy. A much more drastic problem arises if we have a continuous long-term tendency for withdrawals to exceed injections at the full-employment level of national income. Assume that, with international payments in balance and a balanced budget, there is a continuous tendency for saving to exceed investment at the full-employment level of national income. There is nothing logically contradictory in such a situation, all that it requires is that the public should desire to save more than businessmen should wish to invest when the economy is at full employment. It also requires that the gap between full-employment saving and full-employment investment cannot be removed by driving down the interest rate to a very low level. This situation could arise, for example, if as real incomes rise over the years, households wished to save an ever-increasing fraction of their income, whereas businessmen did not wish to make investment expenditure an ever-increasing fraction of national income. If such circumstances were to arise, and if the government insists on following a balanced-budget policy, then there would be a continual tendency for the economy to settle down in an equilibrium (with $S = I$) at less than full employment.

Such a situation is illustrated in Figure 2. At full employment, savings exceed investment by the amount ab. Unless something fills this gap, the economy will move to the

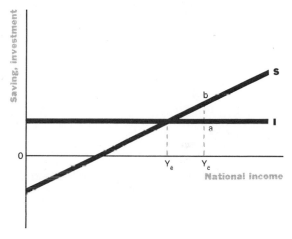

FIGURE 2

equilibrium level of income Y_e, which is less than full-employment income Y_c. Of course, occasional spurts of investment may sometimes raise the economy to full employment, but if the average level of investment is that indicated in the figure, the economy will tend to display chronic unemployment.

If it did display chronic unemployment, what could the government do to remedy this situation? Our national-income theory provides an answer. If the government departs from its balanced-budget policy and adopts a policy of *continuing budget deficits*, national income can be raised to the full-employment level. In this case, resources will not be lying continuously idle; instead, they will be being used to create such public goods as schools, roads, opera houses, universities, defense, rockets, and a host of other goods. Clearly, the policy of continued budget deficits creates a higher level of employment and a higher level of real income than does the balanced-budget policy. Yet the national debt will be increasing year after year. Surely, *this* must matter?

To answer this question, let us consider what the government is doing. It is borrowing that amount of full-employment savings that private businesses will not borrow. The total amount of borrowing is the same as it would have been if full employment had come about because the volume of private investment was higher by the amount ab than the level that it actually achieved ($Y_c a$). All that has happened is that some of the money saved is being channeled into the public sector. The amount that is being so channeled is the amount that the private sector is unwilling to utilize for its own purposes.

Now, there is no reason why such a situation cannot go on forever. There is no reason why the government cannot perpetually borrow and spend those savings that the private sector will not borrow. Indeed, if the private sector will not borrow all the money the public wishes to save, the alternative to budget deficits is that income and employment will shrink and the surplus savings will be removed by the reduction of income and employment to levels sufficiently below the full-employment one that actual savings are reduced to the same volume as that of the investment that the private sector is willing to undertake.

Conditions of a chronic excess of desired private saving over desired private demand have been labeled conditions of secular stagnation. We are not saying here that such a situation is likely to occur in the near future. There has been a long debate in economics about the possibility of such a situation developing. By and large, current opinion is that there is no evidence that such a situation is imminent. The long-run estimates of the consumption function (see pages 565–566) suggest that one of the main postulates of the hypothesis may be factually incorrect. These estimates suggest that, over the long run, the proportion of national income devoted by households to current consumption and the proportion saved tend to remain fairly constant. Furthermore, there is ample evidence that new investment opportunities develop more or less as fast as old ones are utilized. At least, they have so far.

It is important to note, however, that such a situation *could* arise (i.e., there is nothing contradictory in the hypothesis of secular stagnation; it describes a world that could exist). If it did arise, and if the government had a balanced-budget policy, this policy would lead to a higher level of unemployment and a lower level of real income than would a policy of budget deficits.

What If Peace Broke Out?

National defense and defense-related expenditures of the U.S. Government were between $55 billion and $60 billion in 1964. It is a basic tenet of the Marxists that these expenditures alone bolster the American economy and that without them its collapse would be sure and swift. What of this? What does the national-income theory that we have developed predict about the effects of reductions in defense expenditure?

It is perfectly clear that, if the need for defense expenditures fell to, say, $6 billion (the level that they were in 1940 in terms of 1964 prices), there would be problems. Much would depend upon what else happened and how suddenly the change occurred.

If the government maintained its tax rates, reduced its expenditures by $50 billion overnight, and allowed the extra receipts to pile up in idle balances, our theory predicts that the results would be disastrous. With a multiplier of, say, 3, the reduction in national income would be on an order of 25 percent, and unemployment might rise as high as 25 percent of the labor force.

Suppose, instead, that the government reduced both taxes and expenditures equally by $50 billion. Again, our theory predicts an adverse impact on the economy by virtue of the balanced-budget multiplier, but one of lesser (though still serious) magnitude. If the balanced budget multiplier is, say, 1, the reduction in national income would be on an order of 8 percent, and unemployment might rise to 11 or 12 percent of the labor force.

These two situations, of course, do not exhaust the possibilities. In a country that has endless things it would like to do—for itself and for the world—but that it cannot do because of resource limitations, it is perfectly clear that peacetime government expenditures could be substituted for defense expenditures, dollar for dollar if necessary. The level of national income could thus be maintained at the same time as the standard of living rose in response to more civilian goods per capita produced by the government.

In the short run, there would be dangers in returning too much money to the private sector, because the capacity to produce civilian goods would not expand overnight; factories that build rockets do not convert to civilian uses in a hurry. But, could we make, over time, a phased reduction in both taxes and expenditures, with govern-

mental deficits, if needed, to smooth the transition? The long-run evidence about consumption functions and investment opportunities suggests no fundamental problems in doing this. The evidence is that, if consumers' disposable income were raised by 10 percent, the long-run effect would be for expenditure to rise by 10 percent.

The greatest problems would be transitional. First, there would be problems in adjusting the productive capacity and the distribution of resources, geographically and among uses, to a new set of demands upon them. Given what we know about immobility in the economy, we can predict that there would be surpluses in some skills and shortages in others, and that the adjustments would take time and would cause heavy frictional problems. The second problem would be the lack of wisdom of policy makers and economic advisers too. We know much less about the dynamic properties of our economic system than about its equilibrium properties; yet the short-period adjustments are in essence dynamic. Without both wisdom and substantial discretion to act quickly, many problems would persist. We have had little experience of economies faced with sudden changes of such magnitude in peacetime. Such changes in the pattern of demand have, however, occurred during wars, and the evidence seems to suggest that, as long as the level of aggregate demand is held high, substantial reallocations of resources can occur quite rapidly. Although there would be transitional problems, there is no evidence to suggest that they could not be overcome within the space of a few years.

Peace is, of course, unlikely to break out all at once. A gradual relaxation of international tensions and a gradual reduction in required defense expenditure would create less critical transitional problems. We have often had experience with changes of $5 to $10 billion per year, and there seems little doubt that increased public nondefense expenditures combined with tax reductions could accommodate a gradual shrinkage in the size of government spending with gain rather than loss in the standard of living.

Summary

1. When government expenditures exceed government revenues, we say there is a budget deficit; when revenues exceed expenditures, we say there is a budget surplus. A deficit requires an increase in borrowing, which may come from money newly created by the banking system, or from money channeled from existing sources, such as the current savings of households. A surplus allows the government to reduce its outstanding volume of debt.

2. If prices rise, or if real income rises, but if the role of the government in the economy remains constant, we would expect the money value of the national debt to grow.

3. The discussion of methods of financing government debt, and the burden of such debt, is summarized on page 611.

4. The size of the national debt could become a serious problem. This would happen only if the debt incurred to finance expenditures that do not themselves cause an increase in income was increasing much faster than national income. The evidence shows that this is not the case in the U.S. today.

5. A balanced-budget policy would lead the government to restrict its expenditure during a slump and to raise it during a boom. An opposite policy, countercyclical budgeting, is based on the idea that the government could stabilize the economy by having deficits during depressions and surpluses during booms. Deficits and surpluses can be achieved either by varying expenditures or tax receipts, or by both.

6. If expenditures and taxes are raised by equal amounts during depressions and cut during booms, this will tend to stabilize the economy; the amount of this effect is measured by the balanced-budget multiplier. The effect occurs if the marginal propensity to spend tax dollars is higher for the government than it is for taxpayers.

7. The theory developed in Chapter 46 predicts that a government deficit cannot be totally self-erasing, although the final budget deficit will be less than the initial one.

8. It takes time for countercyclical budgeting decisions to take effect, and this obviously creates difficulties. Built-in stabilizers that function automatically may shorten these time lags. All the stabilizers operate on the idea of creating negative feedback, but this is a necessary, not a sufficient condition for stability. If the feedback action is subject to the wrong kinds of lags, the action might conceivably be destabilizing.

9. Secular stagnation is a situation in which the level of savings at full employment consistently exceeds the level of investment. The evidence suggests that such a situation is unlikely to arise today, but, if it did, the doctrine of the balanced budget would lead to a higher level of unemployment and to a lower level of real income than would acceptance of the idea of permanent budget deficits.

10. If defense expenditures fell without compensatory government action, the results could be very severe. But, in a country that

has endless things it would like to do, it is clear that government could substitute expenditure on civilian goods. It would also be possible to diminish the size of the public sector slowly, substituting privately produced goods and services for publicly produced ones. The greatest problems in this case would probably be transitional, but there is no evidence suggesting that they would be overwhelming, particularly if the change were gradual.

QUESTIONS FOR DISCUSSION

1. According to the *U.S. News and World Report*, "Ahead [is] a continuing boom in business fed by guns and by butter. [The] Vietnam build-up, by itself, assures rising business through 1966. The 'Great Society' comes on top of that. If fighting should stop, expect even bigger welfare outlays." If there were no "Great Society" butter plans, would there necessarily be a conflict between having more war goods and more civilian goods? Explain.

2. What is the difference in the "burden" of the following government expenditures? Which do you think are capital expenditures? (a) research into water resources; (b) funds for university buildings; (c) nine new national parks; (d) $4 million for the creation of jobs for unemployed Negro teenagers in New York; (e) Medicare; (f) new fighter planes; (g) Appalachian development in power and electricity; (h) government subsidies for farmers.

3. "It costs more to provide paper towels for the government washrooms today than it did to finance all of George Washington's government." Why?

4. What are the difficulties in countercyclical government policies? What would be the worst possible set of time lags?

5. What is the balanced-budget multiplier? How can national income increase if exactly the same amount is put back into the system through spending as is removed from it through taxes?

6. In his first Inaugural Address, President Roosevelt expounded the doctrine of "sound finance"—that the government's budget should always be balanced. Government spending, however, rose faster than taxes could be increased, and large deficits ensued. Would the effect of the New Deal on employment have increased or diminished if Roosevelt had been successful in keeping the budget balanced throughout his first term by raising sufficient taxes to meet all his new expenditures?

7. "If $1 billion less were spent on road construction each year, we could have $1 billion more in school construction each year." "If $1 billion less were bet on horse races each year, we could have $1 billion more in school construction each year." With which of these statements do you agree? What is the opportunity cost of $1 billion bet on horse races?

8. If Congress passed a law limiting government borrowing in each year to X percent of the national income in that year, would this tend to stabilize or destabilize the economy? Does it matter how large X is?

MONEY, BANKING, & PRICES

Chapter **52** THE NATURE AND HISTORY
OF MONEY

UP TO THIS POINT WE HAVE TAKEN THE SUP-
ply of money for granted. We have assumed
that there was sufficient money to finance
any desired level of consumption and investment expenditure. We now wish to study the
generation of money and credit and the possible effects of these factors on the circular

flow of income. A considerable portion of
both consumption and investment expenditure is made with borrowed money, and one
would expect that the availability and terms
of credit would have an influence on both of
these flows of expenditure. Also, a rise in
output requires an investment of funds in

goods being manufactured but not yet ready for sale. If funds are not available for the purpose, firms may be unable to expand output, even though there is a rise in the demand for their goods.[1]

In this chapter we describe the functions of money and give a brief outline of its history. There is probably more folklore and general nonsense believed about money than about any other aspect of the economy. The purpose of this very stylized bit of history is to remove some of these misconceptions.[2]

What Is Money?

We use the term money to refer to any generally accepted medium of exchange—to anything, that is, that will be accepted by virtually everyone in exchange for goods and services. It is customary to distinguish between money's several different functions. The reason for doing this is that different kinds of money vary in the degree of efficiency with which they fulfill each of these functions; in assessing the efficiency of a particular money system, we have to assess it in relation to each of these functions. The major functions of money are to act as a *medium of exchange*, as a *store of wealth*, and as a *unit of account*.

A MEDIUM OF EXCHANGE

An important function of money is to facilitate exchange. Without money, our complicated economic system, which is based on specialization and the division of labor, would be impossible, and we would have to return to a very primitive form of production and exchange. It is not without justification that

money has been called one of the great inventions contributing to human freedom.

If there were no money, goods would have to be exchanged by *barter*, one good being swapped directly for another. This system is a cumbersome one in which every transaction requires a *double coincidence of wants*. If I have a donkey to trade, for example, I must search not only for a man who wants a donkey, but also for one who has something that I would like to acquire. Furthermore, there is no way to give change on the transaction. If I find someone who wants my donkey, we must agree on a swap rate. If we decide that a donkey is worth nine chickens, then we are in trouble if my trading partner has only six chickens: I can hardly give him two-thirds of my donkey. Thus, goods that are not readily divisible make poor subjects for barter transactions. If we were restricted to barter, we would have to spend a great deal of time searching for satisfactory transactions; we would be unable to specialize in producing some single commodity, for we

---

1. Production does not occur instantaneously; a firm purchases raw materials and factor services at one time and only at a later time does it sell the goods that the factors produce. If there is a rise in demand, the firm must increase its flow of expenditure on factor services and raw materials; and only later, when the finished goods are sold, will the firm's flow of revenues increase.

2. From the point of view of economic theory, this historical analysis represents a digression. Our reason for including it is that a reader who holds one of the major misconceptions about money will find that his understanding of the whole of macroeconomic theory will be distorted. In our own experience, this particular approach provides one of the most effective means of conveying an appreciation of some of the basic facts about money.

could not be certain that we could obtain when we wanted them all the other goods that we required.

The use of money as a medium of exchange removes these problems, as long as money is readily accepted by everyone. If I wish to trade my donkey, then all I need to do is to find someone who wants a donkey. I then hand over my animal and take money in return; it matters not that the individual who takes my donkey has no goods that I require. I now take my money and search for someone who has chickens that he wishes to trade. When I find him, I hand over my money and take his chickens; it does not matter that my provider of chickens has no use for a donkey. The difficulties of barter force people to become more or less self-sufficient; with money as a medium of exchange, everyone is free to specialize and, with specialization in the direction of one's natural talents and abilities, there comes a great increase in the production of all commodities.

If money is to serve as an efficient medium of exchange, it must have a number of characteristics: It must be readily acceptable; it must have a high value for its weight (otherwise it would be a nuisance to carry around); it must be divisible, for money that comes only in large denominations is useless for transactions having only a small value; and it must not be readily counterfeitable, for if money can be easily duplicated by individuals it will lose its value.[3]

A STORE OF WEALTH

Money is a handy way to store wealth; with barter, one must take some other good in exchange. With money, you can sell goods today and store the money until you need it.

This means that you have a claim on someone else's goods that you can exercise at some future date. The two sides of the barter transaction can be separated in time with the obvious increase in freedom that this confers. To be a satisfactory store of wealth, money must have a stable value. If prices are stable, then one knows exactly how much command over real goods and services has been stored up when a certain sum of money has been accumulated. If prices change rapidly, then one has little idea how many goods one will be able to command when previously accumulated money is spent. Clearly, rapid fluctuations in the general level of prices reduce the usefulness of money as a store of wealth.

Money can serve as a perfectly satisfactory store of accumulated wealth for a single individual, but not for the society as a whole. If a single individual stores up money, he will, when he comes to spend it, be able to command the current output of some other individual. The whole society cannot do this. If all individuals saved their money and all simultaneously retired to live on their savings, there would be no current production to purchase and consume. The society's ability to satisfy wants depends on goods and services being available; if some of this want-satisfying capacity is to be stored up for the whole society, then goods that are currently produced must be left unconsumed and carried over to future periods.

A UNIT OF ACCOUNT

Money may also be used purely for accounting purposes without having any real physical existence of its own. For instance, a government store in a truly Communist society might say that everyone had so many

---

3. This last point should be reconsidered after you have studied Chapter 53. In the meantime, you should try to understand why it does not matter if the money can be counterfeited at very high cost.

"dollars" at his disposal each month. Goods could then be given prices and each consumer's purchases recorded, the consumer being allowed to buy all he wanted until his supply of dollars was exhausted.[4] This money would have no existence other than as entries in the store's books, but it would be serving as a perfectly satisfactory unit of account (although it could serve as a medium of exchange between individuals only if the store agreed to transfer credits from one customer to another at the customers' request).[5]

The Origins and Growth of Metallic Money

The origins of money are lost in antiquity; most primitive tribes known today make some use of it. The ability of money to free people from the cumbersome necessity of barter must have led to its early use as soon as some generally accepted commodity appeared. All sorts of commodities have been used as money at one time or another, but precious metals must soon have asserted their ascendancy as the most satisfactory ones. They were in heavy and permanent demand by the rich for ornament and decoration, and they were in continuous supply (since they do not easily wear out). Thus they tended to have a high and stable price. They were easily recognized and generally known to be commodities which, because of their stable price, would be accepted by most people. They were also divisible into extremely small units (gold to a single grain).

Precious metals thus came to circulate as money and to be used in many transactions. Before the invention of coins, it was necessary to carry precious metals about in bulk. When a purchase was to be made, the requisite quantity of the metal would have to be weighed out carefully on a scale. A sack of gold and a highly sensitive set of scales were the common equipment of the merchant and trader.

Such a system, although better than barter, was still rather cumbersome. Coins eliminated the necessity of weighing the metal at each transaction. The prince or ruler weighed the metal and made a coin out of it to which he affixed his own seal, guaranteeing the weight of precious metal in the coin. Thus a certain coin was stated to contain exactly $\frac{1}{16}$ of an ounce of gold. If a commodity was priced at $\frac{1}{8}$ of an ounce of gold, two coins could be given over without any need of weighing the gold. This is clearly a great convenience, as long as traders know that they can accept the coin at its "face value."

The prince's subjects, however, could not let a good thing pass, and someone had the idea of clipping a thin slice off the edge of the coin. If he collected a coin stamped as containing $\frac{1}{2}$ of an ounce of gold, he could clip a slice off the edge and pass the coin off as still weighing $\frac{1}{2}$ of an ounce. ("Doesn't the stamp prove it?," he would argue.) If

4. The use of dollars in this context suggests a further sense in which money is a unit of account. People think about values in terms of the monetary unit with which they are familiar.

5. A fourth function is sometimes distinguished: that of a standard of deferred payments. Payments that are to be made in the future, on account of debts, etc., are reckoned in money. Money is being used as a unit of account with an added dimension in time, for the account is not settled until the future.

he were successful, he would have made a profit equal to the market value of the clipped metal. If this practice became common, even the most myopic of traders would notice that things were not quite what they used to be in the coinage world. Mistrust would grow, and it would be necessary to weigh each coin before accepting it at its "face value"; back would come the scales and most of the usefulness of the coins would be lost. To get around this problem, the prince decided to mint his coins with a rough edge. The absence of the rough edge would immediately be apparent and would indicate that the coin had been clipped. This practice still survives today as an interesting anachronism to remind us that there were days when the market value of the metal in the coin (if it were melted down) was equal to the face value of the coin. The coin itself was nothing more than a guarantee that a certain weight of metal, the value of which did not depend on its being stamped into coins, was contained therein. The subjects, when presented with an opportunity of getting something for nothing, were ingenious enough to surmount even the obstacle of the rough edge: They invented the practice of *sweating*. Sweating involved placing a large number of coins in a bag and shaking the bag vigorously. The dust that flaked off the coins was their reward. This practice seems never to have been as disruptive to the money system as that of clipping, possibly because it was difficult to remove very much metal without defacing the coin, but possibly also because the disruptive effects were eclipsed by the upset caused by the prince's periodic debasement of coinage.

Not to be outdone by the cunning of his subjects, the prince was himself quick to seize the chance of getting something for nothing. Since the prince was empowered to mint the coins, he was in a very good position to work a *really* profitable fraud. When he found himself with bills that he could not pay and that it was inexpedient to repudiate, he merely used some suitable occasion—a marriage, an anniversary, an alliance—to remint the coinage. The subjects would bring their coins into the mint, where they would be melted down and coined afresh with a new stamp. The subject could then go away the proud possessor of one new coin for every one old coin that he had brought in. Between the melting down and the recoining, however, the prince had only to toss some inexpensive base metal into the works to earn himself a handsome profit. If the coinage was debased by adding, say, one part base metal to every four parts of the melted-down metal, then five coins would be made for every four turned in. Thus, for every four coins brought in, the prince could return four and have one left over for himself as profit. With these coins, he could pay his bills.

The result would be an inflation. The subjects would have the same number of coins as before and hence could demand the same number of goods. Once the prince paid his bills, however, the recipients of the extra coins could be expected to spend some or all of them, and this would represent a net increase in demand. The extra demand would bid up prices. Debasing of coinage thus led pretty certainly to a rise in prices. After observing this process in action, early economists propounded the *quantity theory of money*. They argued that there was a relation between the average level of prices and the quantity of money in circulation, such that a change in the quantity of money would lead to a change in the price level in the same direction. We shall have more to say about this theory in Chapter 55.

The Evolution of Paper Money

Another important step in the history of money was the evolution of paper currency. Goldsmiths—craftsmen who worked with gold—naturally kept very secure safes in which to store their gold.[6] The practice grew up among the public of storing their gold with the goldsmith for safe-keeping. In return, the goldsmith would give the depositor a receipt promising to hand over the gold on demand. If the depositor wished to make a large purchase, he could go to the goldsmith, reclaim his gold, and hand it over to the seller of the goods. Chances were that the seller would not require the gold, but would carry it back to the goldsmith for safe-keeping. Clearly, if people knew the goldsmith to be reliable, there was no need to go through the cumbersome and risky business of physically transferring the gold. The buyer need only transfer the goldsmith's receipt to the seller, who could accept it secure in the knowledge that the goldsmith would pay over the gold whenever it was needed. If the seller wished to buy a good from a third party who also knew the goldsmith to be reliable, this transaction too could be effected by passing the goldsmith's receipt from the buyer to the seller. The convenience of using these bits of paper instead of gold is obvious. Thus, when it first grew up, paper money represented a promise to pay on demand so much gold, the promise being made first by goldsmiths and later by banks; as long as these institutions were known to be reliable, such pieces of paper would be "as good as gold." Such paper money was *backed* by precious metal and was *convertible* on demand into this metal.

In the nineteenth century, paper money was commonly issued by banks; in Britain, the commercial banks issued their own notes backed by their own reserves. Also, the Bank of England issued notes backed by the country's gold reserves, for, although it was nominally a private institution until 1947, the Bank always had close links with the government. Since these notes were convertible on demand into gold, the country was said to be on a *gold standard*.

FRACTIONALLY BACKED PAPER MONEY

For most transactions, individuals were content to use paper currency; it was soon discovered, therefore, that it was not necessary to keep an ounce of gold in the vaults for every claim to an ounce circulating as paper money. It *was* necessary to keep some gold on hand, because, for some transactions, paper would not do. If an individual wished to make a purchase from a distant place where his local bank was not known, he might have to convert his paper into gold and ship the gold. Further, if he was going to save up money for use in the distant future, he might not have perfect confidence in the bank's ability to honor its pledge to redeem the notes in gold at that time. His alternative was to exchange his notes for gold and store the gold until he needed it. For these and other reasons, some holders of notes

---

6. All the basic ideas about paper money can be displayed by concentrating on the goldsmiths, although there were earlier sources of paper money in various negotiable evidences of debt.

demanded gold in return for their notes. On the other hand, some of the bank's customers received gold in various transactions and stored this gold in the bank for safe-keeping. They accepted promises to pay (i.e., bank notes) in return. At any one time, therefore, some of the bank's customers would be withdrawing gold, others would be depositing it, and the great majority would be trading in the bank's paper notes without any need or desire to convert them into gold. Thus the bank was able to issue more money redeemable in gold than it actually had gold in its vaults. This was also a profitable thing to do, because the money could be used to make profitable investments. It could be used either to purchase securities that yielded a return, or to make interest-earning loans or advances to households and firms.

This discovery was made early on by the goldsmiths; from that time down to the present day, banks have had many more claims to pay cash outstanding against them than they actually had cash available. A rough rule of thumb is that a 10–20 percent backing for these claims is sufficient. If a bank holds $10,000 worth of gold and has issued $100,000 in notes, it would be perfectly safe in normal times. In such a situation, we say that the currency is *fractionally backed* by gold.

The major problem of a fractionally backed currency is that of maintaining its *convertibility* into the precious metal with which it is backed. In the past, the imprudent bank that issued too much paper money found itself unable to redeem its currency in gold when the demand for gold was even slightly higher than usual. This bank would then have to suspend payments, and all holders of its notes would suddenly find them worthless. The prudent bank, which kept a reasonable relation between its note issue and its gold

reserve, found that it could meet the normal everyday demand for gold without any trouble. It was always the case with fractionally backed currency, however, that, if all noteholders demanded gold at once, they could not be satisfied. Thus, if ever the public lost confidence and en masse demanded redemption of their currency, the banks would be unable to honor their pledges, and the holders of their notes would lose everything. The history of nineteenth- and early twentieth-century banking on both sides of the Atlantic is replete with examples of banks ruined by momentary runs on their cash and gold reserves. When this happened, the bank's depositors and the holders of its notes would find themselves holding worthless pieces of paper. Future social historians may wonder how it was possible, in the face of such a system, that economists could have believed that free-market capitalism provided evidence that the hidden hand of perfection was guiding the economic affairs of mankind.

THE DEVELOPMENT OF FIAT CURRENCIES

As time went on, note issue by commercial banks became less common, and central banks took over a steadily increasing share of this responsibility. The paper currency was, as it always had been, freely convertible into gold. It was also only fractionally backed by gold. The commercial banks retained the power to create money, but this was no longer done by printing paper money; instead, deposit money was created.

During the period between World Wars I and II, virtually all the countries of the world abandoned the gold standard. The reasons for this are historical and cannot be gone into here. (They were mentioned briefly in Chapter 41.) The result of abandoning the gold standard was that currency was no longer convertible into gold.

Some countries (including the United States, until 1965) preserve the fiction that their currency is backed by gold, but none allows it to be converted into gold as a right. The past is recalled by the following statement on some of our currency: "The United States of America Will Pay to the Bearer on Demand Twenty Dollars." The notes are signed by both the Secretary of the Treasury and the Treasurer. (A similar statement appears on the currency of most countries.) If anyone takes this seriously today and demands his twenty dollars, he can hand over his twenty-dollar bill and receive in return a new twenty-dollar bill! In the days of the gold standard, paper money was valuable because everyone knew it could be converted into gold on demand.[7] Today, paper money is valuable because it is generally accepted.[8] Because, by habit, everyone accepts it as valuable, it *is* valuable; the fact that it can no longer be converted into anything has no effect on its functioning as a medium of exchange.

This fact, that present-day paper money is not convertible into anything—that it is nothing but bits of paper whose value derives from common acceptance through habit— often disturbs the student. He feels his money should be more substantial than that; after all, what of "dollar diplomacy" and the "prestige of the pound"? Well, his money is only bits of paper. There is no point in pretending otherwise.

Once it is accepted that modern money is only bits of paper, the next question that comes to mind is: Does it matter? Gold derived its value because it was scarce relative to the heavy demand for it (the demand being derived from both its monetary and its nonmonetary uses). Tying a currency to gold meant that the quantity of money in a country was left to such chance occurrences as the discovery of new gold supplies. This was not without advantages, the most important being that it provided a check on the prince's ability to cause inflation. Gold cannot be manufactured at will; paper currency can. There is little doubt that, if the money supply was purely paper, many governments would have succumbed to the temptation to pay their bills by printing new money rather than by raising taxes. Such increases in the money supply would lead to inflation in just the same way as did the debasement of metallic currency. Thus, the gold standard provided some check on inflation by making it difficult for the government to change the money supply. Periods of major gold discoveries, however, brought about inflations of their own. In the sixteenth century, Spanish gold and silver flowed into Europe from the New World, bringing inflation in its wake. On the other hand, it is usually desirable to increase the money supply in a period of rising trade and income. On a gold standard, this can-

---

7. Originally, the gold had a market value independent of its use as money. Later, however, as large stocks of gold accumulated, gold itself came to have value *because* it was a generally acceptable medium of exchange. There is little doubt that, if at any time in the last few centuries gold had ceased to have value as money (because, say, some superior metal was discovered), the market value of the world's stocks of gold would have fallen very greatly, since the demand for gold for use as a commodity would have been very low in relation to the supply of it.

8. This acceptance may have been helped along at one time in the U.S. by the statement on bills that says "This note is legal tender for all debts, public and private." But the absence of such a statement on the British pound note does not impair its acceptance.

not be done—unless, by pure chance, gold is discovered at the same time. The gold standard took discretionary powers about the money supply out of the hands of the central authorities. Whether or not one thought that this was a good thing depended on how one thought the central authorities would use this discretion. In general, a gold standard is probably better than having the currency managed by an ignorant or irresponsible government, but it is worse than having the currency supply adjusted by a well-informed intelligent one. Better and worse in this context are judged by the criterion of having a money supply that varies adequately with the needs of the economy, but that does not vary so as to cause violent inflations or deflations.

Deposit Money

In most countries today, the money supply consists of notes and coins issued by the government and the central bank, and of *deposit money*. Notes and coins (the market value of the metal in the coinage is but a minute fraction of the face value of the coin) are the inconvertible moneys that we have already discussed. Deposit money is *created* by the commercial banking system. We have already explained how bank notes promising to pay gold on demand circulated as money and how, because most people did not require the actual gold, the banks were able to create money by printing and putting into circulation many more notes than they could redeem in gold at any one time. *When the banks lost the right to issue notes of their own, the form of money creation changed but the substance did not.* Today, banks have money in their vaults (or on deposit with the central banks) just as they always did, only the money is no longer gold; it is the legal tender of the times, paper money. Banks' customers sometimes deposit paper money with the banks for safe-keeping just as, in former times, they deposited gold. The bank takes the money and gives the customer a promise to pay it back on demand. Instead of taking the form of a printed bank note, as in the past, this promise to pay is recorded as an entry on the customer's account. If the customer wishes to pay a bill, he may come to the bank and claim his money in dollars; he may then pay the money over to another person, and this person may redeposit the money in a bank. Just as with the gold transfers, this is a cumbersome procedure, particularly for large payments, and it would be much more convenient if the bank's promise to pay cash could merely be transferred from one person to another. This is done by means of a *check*. If individual A deposits $100 in a bank, the entry, a $100 credit in his account, is the bank's promise to pay $100 cash on demand. If A pays B $100 by giving him a check that B then deposits in the same bank, the bank merely reduces A's deposit by $100 and increases B's by the same amount. Thus the bank still promises to pay out on demand the $100 originally deposited, but it now promises to pay it to B rather than to A. If B now pays C $100 by check and C deposits the check, then the promise to pay (i.e., the credit entry in someone's account at the bank) will be transferred from B to C.

The modern deposit is the equivalent of the old bank note: a promise on the bank's behalf to pay out on demand the money of the time. The passing of the bank's note from hand to hand transferred ownership of the claim against the bank; this is now done by means of a check, which is merely an order to the bank telling it to transfer from one individual to another its obligation to pay cash. It is true today, just as it was in the past, that most of the bank's customers are content to pay their bills by passing among themselves the bank's promises to pay cash; only a small proportion of the bank's customers want cash at any one time. Thus, just as in the past, the bank can create money by issuing more promises to pay than it actually has cash to pay out. The bank can grant a loan by giving the customer a credit on his account equal to the amount of the loan. If the borrower uses the loan to pay bills by check, then the deposit is transferred from person to person. In most circumstances, the bank can have liabilities greatly in excess of the amount of cash that it has in reserve. These deposits can be used to buy goods and services through the medium of checks. Since they are a generally accepted means of exchange, they are money. The great proportion of transactions (by value) take place by check and only a small proportion by notes and coin. Thus, in the modern world, the greater proportion of the money supply is the deposit money that is created by commercial banks. The banks can, if they wish, contract the money supply by not creating deposits, or they can expand it by creating deposits up to the limit of prudence or law (so that there is just enough cash to meet the normal demands

of customers who do not wish to pay by check). It is, of course, in the bank's interest to expand the supply up to the safety limit because every dollar created can be used to grant a loan, to purchase a bond, or to acquire some other asset that pays a return to the bank.

DEMAND DEPOSITS AND TIME DEPOSITS

If a customer has a deposit in a bank, he can keep it in one of two forms: a demand deposit or a time deposit. A demand deposit means that the customer can withdraw his money on demand (i.e., without giving any notice of his intention). The holder of a demand deposit may immediately obtain cash for it, and he may pay his bills by writing a check on it. Such a check instructs his bank to pay without delay a stated sum of money to the person to whom the check is made payable. Banks in most countries do not pay any interest to customers who have money deposited on demand.

The holder of a time deposit (savings account) must legally give notice (thirty or sixty days) of his intention to withdraw his money. Although banks do not enforce this law, they could at any time do so if they wished. Furthermore, the holder of a time deposit cannot pay his bills by writing a check ordering his bank to pay someone out of his time deposit. Banks usually pay interest to customers who have money deposited with them "on time."

An Operational Definition of Money

Earlier in this chapter we defined money as any generally accepted means of payment. We must now make this definition operational

by saying what will be included and what excluded when we reckon the money supply of a country. Clearly, notes and coins are part of the money supply. Demand deposits also fit pretty well into our definition. You can pay for most things by check, although checks are not quite so generally acceptable as notes and coins. You may have trouble, for example, buying a package of cigarettes in a small country store if you offer a check in exchange; you will almost certainly have trouble should you try to walk out of a fur store with a $10,000 mink coat if you have offered a check in payment and you are not known by the store manager. You will not have much trouble if you offer dollar bills in either case.[9] Since demand deposits are a means of ex-change and since checks are widely (if not quite universally) acceptable, it seems reasonable to regard demand deposits as part of the money supply. Time deposits are not so regarded since checks cannot be drawn on them and since, should the bank insist on its legal rights, the deposits cannot be turned into cash with which to make payments until after a lapse of time (the length of which depends on the period of notice). The money supply is, therefore, usually said to consist of three parts, metallic currency (coins), paper money (notes), and demand deposits.

Near Money

Although it is not conventional to include time deposits in the money supply, they are clearly very close to being money. In practice, they can be turned into money without notice merely by filling out a withdrawal slip at one's bank. We thus talk of time deposits as being "near money"—something that is "almost but not quite. . . ." Once we have developed the concept of near money, we realize that there are "liquid assets" other than time deposits, which, although themselves not generally acceptable as means of exchange, are easily convertible into money. Such liquid assets include certain short-term government securities, deposits with savings and loan societies, and a host of other assets that are readily convertible into money. The phenomenal rise in the U.S. of credit cards has helped to make "trade credit" an important near money.

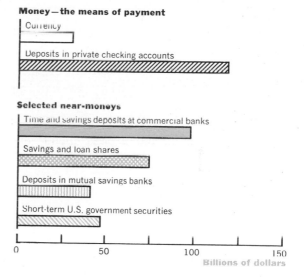

Money—the means of payment

Currency

Deposits in private checking accounts

Selected near-moneys

Time and savings deposits at commercial banks

Savings and loan shares

Deposits in mutual savings banks

Short-term U.S. government securities

0   50   100   150
Billions of dollars

SOURCE: *The Federal Reserve System: Purpose and Functions* (Washington, D.C.: G.P.O., 1963), p. 7.

FIGURE 1

9. On the other hand, you are unlikely to get your cigarettes if you offer a thousand-dollar bill in exchange. If it is Saturday afternoon in a small town in which you know no one, you may have to go without smoking until the bank opens on Monday morning. (It will be able to change your bill, even if no one else can.)

Figure 1 shows for 1962 the quantities of money together with selected near moneys. Perhaps the most striking fact revealed by the figure is the relative insignificance of currency in the total money supply.

There is no need to get into an argument about the definition of money. The way in which we wish to define money and near money depends on the theory we are developing. For many purposes, a narrow definition that includes only currency and demand deposits is useful. On the other hand, near moneys may in many cases be virtually perfect substitutes for money. The matter is an empirical one: Will a theory give generally better predictions using one concept of money rather than another? If so, the theory should be formulated using the relevant concept. There is no right and wrong about definitions, and the relevant questions to ask about them are: "Are they consistent with each other?" and "Do they define classes of things that will be useful in relating our theories to real-world observations?"

Summary

1. The term money refers to any generally accepted medium of exchange. It is customary to distinguish a number of functions of money—the major ones are a medium of exchange, a store of value, and a unit of account.

2. We trace, in a stylized manner, the history of money from the first use of a medium of exchange in a barter society to the use of precious metals as money. We discuss coinage (including some account of the abuses of coinage), the growth of paper money, the important innovation of fractionally backed paper money, fiat currencies, and, finally, deposit money.

3. The following operational definition of money is a commonly used one: The money supply consists of three parts, metallic currency (coins), paper money (notes), and demand deposits.

4. There are many liquid assets, which we call near money; the principal one is time deposits. The dividing line between money and near money is an empirical matter. The important question is: Will a theory give generally better predictions using one concept of money rather than another?

QUESTIONS FOR DISCUSSION

1. "Money is meaningfully defined in terms of how it is used." Do you agree with this statement? If not, how *is* money used?

2. "Demand deposits differ importantly from savings and other time deposits." How? Is this, in your opinion, a fundamental or a minor difference? What developments can you think of that would serve to make the two more nearly similar?

3. There has been, for quite a while, an excess demand for small change in the United States, particularly in the Midwest. One small town started circulating its own wooden nickels, until it was stopped from doing so by federal authorities. Were these wooden nickels money? Considering the economic consequences of stopping the circulation, or of letting it continue, which do you think is the better policy? (Concentrate more on the positive, rather than the normative, as-

pects of the issue.) What must have been the situation for the wooden nickels to be acceptable? How do you think a national shortage can come about? What would you suggest that the town do instead?

4. Congress recently passed a bill allowing the silver content of coins to be reduced. Does this change the status of coins as money?

5. In Greece today, most people pay cash rather than using checks. Greek banks keep more than 50 percent of their deposits in cash. Are these facts related?

6. "I don't see the need for money in my Utopia.

Instead, a very large computer would register the amount and kind of everyone's work, award so many credits, and, when you went into a store, or went to a baseball game, or anywhere else, a register would record your number, and your purchase, and so many points would be charged against your credits." Your idea of Utopia may not coincide with this man's. But what can you say to him about his dream for doing without money? Has his scheme in fact done away with it?

7. "A sound economy requires a sound money system. This can only be provided if the money is adequately backed by the real wealth of the economy, by, say, the value of its natural resources." What do you think?

Chapter 53 THE BANKING SYSTEM AND THE SUPPLY OF MONEY

OUR PRIMARY CONCERN IN THIS CHAPTER IS with the factors that determine the supply of money. In order to study these, we must look at the nature of the banking system, at the way in which banks create deposit money, and at the way in which attempts are made to regulate the money supply through public policy.

The Banking Structure of the United States

Today, there are approximately 14,000 private commercial banks in the United States. These banks accept deposits, make loans, and provide a variety of services to their customers. They are privately owned profit-seeking corporations. They accept sav-ings deposits (often called time deposits) and checking deposits (often called demand deposits). There are also a variety of other kinds of private financial institutions, including roughly 500 mutual savings banks, numerous savings and loan associations, finance companies, and other institutions that accept only time deposits.

The basic unit of the banking system is the ordinary commercial bank. Such banks differ from one another in many ways. Some are very large (the Bank of America has deposits in excess of $12 billion), others are very small; some are located in big cities, some in small towns; some hold charters from the federal government (national banks),

some from state governments (state banks). In an elementary treatment of the subject, we need not be concerned with these differences, and we shall usually speak of *commercial banks* without specifying the type.

The other major element in the banking system is the set of Federal Reserve Banks that constitute the *central bank* of the United States. We shall consider the Federal Reserve System at length later in this chapter.

The Creation and Destruction of Deposit Money by Commercial Banks

One part of the money supply, deposit money, is under the control of privately owned banks. How do these banks *create* deposit money? We have already seen that the ability of banks to create deposit money depends on the fact that bank deposits need to be only fractionally backed by notes and coin. If all deposits had to be backed 100 percent, banks would be nothing more than safety deposit vaults for their customers' money. If a customer deposited $100 in a bank, that bank would give the customer $100 credit on his deposit account, the $100 would go into the bank's vault to "back" the deposit and nothing further would happen. Because the bank does not need to keep 100 percent reserves, it can use some of the $100 that was deposited to purchase income-yielding investments. Just how does the bank do this?

A SINGLE BANK

Consider first a country with only one bank (with as many physical branches as is neces-

sary) and assume that someone makes a new deposit of $100 in cash. Table 1 shows how this transaction will be recorded on the books of the bank. The books show new assets of $100 in the form of cash and new liabilities

TABLE 1   **A NEW DEPOSIT OF $100 IS MADE**

Assets	Liabilities
Cash $100	Deposit $100

of $100 in the form of the customer's deposit. This deposit, and all others like it, is a liability of the bank, since the bank owes this money to the customer and must pay it to him whenever he demands it. Since there is only one bank in the whole country, the bank can immediately create new deposits by some multiple of $100, depending on the legal reserve requirements of the country.[1] Let us say that the law requires a 20 percent reserve. The bank could immediately create further de-

1. If there were no legal reserve requirements, the bank would be able to create deposits up to the ratio proved prudent by experience. In most countries, the banks are required by law to hold reserves to an amount larger than would be dictated by normal prudence. Thus the effective limit on deposit creation is set by law, not by experience.

posits of $400. Assume, by way of example, that the bank loans $200 to a customer and buys $200 worth of bonds in the open market. The bank does this by writing $200 to the credit of the borrower's account (i.e., it loans him the money and deposits it to the credit of his account) and by writing $200 to the credit of the account belonging to the person who sold bonds to the bank. Table 2 shows how these transactions will appear on the bank's books. The bank's assets include the $100 cash of the original deposit, the loan of $200 (it is an asset of the bank, since the borrower owes this money to the bank and must repay it at some stated date), and the bonds to the value of $200 (these are an asset, since they can be sold again for cash). The bank's liabilities are now $500 in deposits, $100 to the account of the original depositor, $200 to the account of the customer who borrowed from the bank, and $200 to the account of the person who sold the bonds

TABLE 2   **$400 IS INVESTED IN LOANS AND BONDS WITH NO CASH DRAIN**

Assets		Liabilities	
Cash	$100	Deposits	$500
Loan	$200		
Bonds	$200		

to the bank. Note that by a few strokes of the pen the bank has created $400 in deposit money. The customers of the bank are now able to spend $400 more than they could yesterday and no one else is forced to spend any less.

The persons who borrowed the money and sold the bonds can be expected to spend their money. In most cases, they will do so by writing checks. The bank honors these checks by reducing the deposit of the person writing the check and increasing the deposit of the person in whose favor the check is written. Thus, if everyone pays by check, the bank can effect these payments merely by changing the accounts of individual customers; no cash ever leaves the bank and the total of the bank's deposit liabilities does not change.[2]

MANY BANKS, A SINGLE NEW DEPOSIT

The whole system is somewhat more complicated when there are many banks. If a depositor in Bank A writes a check to someone in Bank B, then a mere book transfer will not do, because Bank A now owes money to Bank B. By writing the check, the depositor in Bank A is saying, "I claim the money owed me and ask that it be passed over to the man indicated on the check"; when the recipient of the check deposits it in Bank B, he is saying, "I want my money held for me by Bank B";

2. This introductory treatment ignores the fact that people are observed to hold some of their money in cash and some in deposits. If, for example, people hold 10 percent of their money in the form of cash, then the bank can expect a cash drain when it creates new money. This cash drain would mean that deposits could not safely be expanded by $400. If such an expansion were to occur, $40 would be withdrawn by the public, leaving $360 in new deposits. (This would leave the public satisfied, since 10 percent of their new money would be held in cash and 90 percent in deposits, but the bank would have lost $40 in cash and $40 in deposits, leaving it with $60 in cash and $460 in deposits, which gives it a cash-deposit ratio of only 13 percent.) There does exist a smaller deposit expansion that will leave the banks with a 20 percent cash reserve, in spite of the drain of cash to the public. In this case, the bank would only create $285.71 in new deposits. The recipients will then hold 10 percent of their new money in cash (i.e., they will draw cash from the bank) and 90 percent in deposits. For the final position, the bank will have $357.14 in new deposits (the original $100 plus $257.14 that it has itself created) and cash reserves of $71.43, which gives the required reserve ratio. The current holders of the bank's newly created money will have $257.14 in deposit money and $28.57 in cash. Thus cash is 10 percent of their total money holdings of $285.71.

thus Bank *A* must pay the money over to Bank *B*. It is exactly the same as if one individual withdrew cash from Bank *A* and gave it to the second individual who deposited it in Bank *B;* when the transaction is done by check, however, the banks, rather than the individuals, transfer the money.

There are, of course, many such transactions in the course of a day. If the banks are staying the same size in relation to each other, these transfers between banks will tend to cancel each other out. If, for example, Mr. Brown who banks with *A* gives a check for $100 to Mrs. Smith who banks with *B*, and if, at the same time, Mrs. Jones who banks with *B* gives a check for $100 to Mr. Green who banks with *A*, then these two transactions cancel each other out. Bank *A* loses $100 to *B* on account of the first transaction, but gains a like sum from *B* on account of the second. No money need move from bank to bank; all that needs to happen is for *A* to reduce Mr. Brown's account by $100 and increase Mr. Green's by the same amount, and for *B* to reduce Mrs. Smith's account by $100 and raise Mrs. Jones's by the same amount.

Multibank systems make use of a *clearing house* where interbank debts are canceled out. At the end of the day, all of the checks drawn by Bank *A*'s customers and deposited in Bank *B* are totaled and set against the total of all of the checks drawn by Bank *B*'s customers and deposited in Bank *A*. It is only necessary to settle the difference between these two sums. The actual checks are passed through the clearing house back to the bank on which they are drawn. The bank is then able to adjust each individual's account by a set of book entries; a flow of cash between banks is neces-

sary only if there is a net transfer of cash from the customers of one bank to those of another.

What would happen if, in a multibank system, one bank received a new deposit of $100 in cash? In this case, the bank could *not* immediately create another $400 in deposits because, when checks were written on these deposits, the majority would be deposited in other banks. Thus, the bank must expect much of its $100 in cash to be drained away to other banks as soon as it creates new deposits for its own customers.

If the bank that obtains the new deposit has only 10 percent of the total deposits held by the community, then 90 percent of any new deposits it creates will end up in other banks.† If other banks are not simultaneously creating new deposits, then this one will be severely restricted in its ability to expand deposits. The reason for this restriction is that the bank will suffer a major cash drain as checks are written to the favor of individuals who deal with other banks.

If the bank illustrated in Table 1 was only one bank in a system (say with one-tenth of the total deposits in the system) and if the other banks refused to expand deposits, then the final situation would be as illustrated in Table 3.

What has happened between Tables 1 and 3 is that the bank has created $86.96 in new deposits by granting loans. But 90 percent of these have ended up in other banks, so that the original bank ends up with only $8.70 of the new deposits held by its own customers. The remainder is distributed among the other banks. The total increase in deposits is only 86 percent of the original cash deposit, as opposed to 400 percent in

---

† In general, if the bank has X percent of the total value of deposits in the community, then $100 - X$ percent of any newly created deposits can be expected to end up in other banks.

TABLE 3   **BANK A EXPANDS DEPOSITS AS FAR AS POSSIBLE WHILE OTHER BANKS DO NOT**

Bank A		
Assets	Liabilities	
Cash $21.74	Deposits	$108.70
Loans $86.96		
$108.70		$108.70

All other banks in the system	
Assets	Liabilities
New cash $78.26	New deposits $78.26

the monopoly-bank case illustrated in Table 2. This leads us to the following conclusion:

One bank in a multibank system cannot produce a multiple expansion of deposits based on an original accretion of cash, unless other banks also expand deposits.

If all other banks are willing to expand deposits whenever they gain extra cash, the situation shown in Table 3 will not represent an equilibrium position. All other banks in the system will have excess cash: The $78.26 in new cash and new deposits will be spread about equally among them. Thus all banks will have their new deposits backed 100 percent by cash. This should lead all banks to expand deposits simultaneously and produce a different situation from the one shown in Table 3, since there will no longer be a cash drain from one bank to another.

MANY BANKS, MANY NEW DEPOSITS

Assume that, in a system with many banks, each bank obtains new deposits in cash (possibly because of a general increase in the money supply due to a change in government policy).[3] Say, for example, that the community contains ten banks of equal size and that each receives new deposits of $100 in cash. Now each bank is in the position shown in Table 1 and each can begin to expand deposits based on the $100 of reserves (each bank does this by granting loans to customers and by buying bonds and other income-earning assets). Since each bank does one-tenth of the total banking business, an average 90 percent of any newly created deposit will find its way into other banks as the customer pays by check to other people in the community. This will represent a cash drain to these other banks. On the other hand, 10 percent of each new deposit created by each other bank should find its way into this bank. Thus, if all banks receive new cash and all start creating deposits simultaneously, no bank should suffer a significant cash drain to any other bank. Thus all banks can go on expanding deposits without losing cash to each other; they need only worry about keeping enough cash to satisfy those depositors who occasionally require cash. Thus the expansion can go on, with each bank watching its own ratio of cash reserves to deposits, expanding deposits as long as the ratio exceeds 1:5 and ceasing when it reaches that figure. The process will come to a halt when each bank has created $400 in additional deposits, so that, for each initial $100 cash deposit, there is now $500 in deposits backed by $100 in cash. Now *each* of the banks will have entries in its books similar to those shown in Table 2.

We can think of this process taking place in a series of steps. During the first day, each bank gets $100 in new deposits and the

---

3. The ways in which such changes in the money supply can be effected are discussed later in this chapter.

books of each bank show entries similar to those shown in Table 1. During the second day, each bank makes loans, expecting that it will suffer a cash drain on account of these loans. Indeed, 90 percent of the new loans made by Bank *A* do find their way into other banks when the borrower pays money to people who are customers of other banks, but 10 percent of the new loans made by each other bank finds its way into Bank *A* as those borrowing from other banks pay money to people who are customers of Bank *A*. Thus, there is no net movement of cash between banks. Instead of finding itself in a position such as that shown in Table 3, each bank's books at the end of the day contain the entries shown in Table 4.

Cash is now just over 50 percent of deposits instead of being only 20 percent as

TABLE 4   EXPANSION OF CREDIT IN EXPECTATION OF A 90 PERCENT CASH DRAIN TO OTHER BANKS WHEN NO CASH DRAIN ACTUALLY OCCURS

Assets		Liabilities	
Cash	$100.00	Deposits	$186.96
Loans	$ 86.96		
	$186.96		$186.96

is desired. Thus each bank can continue to expand deposits in order to grant loans and to purchase income-earning assets. As long as all banks do this simultaneously, no bank will suffer any significant cash drain to any other bank, and the process can continue until each bank has created $400 worth of new deposits and then finds itself in the position shown in Table 2.[4]

Central Banks

Banks of the kind we have been discussing are private, profit-seeking firms. Most advanced free-market economies also have a *central bank* whose primary purpose is to regulate the flow of money and credit in the economy. The central bank is always an instrument of the central government, whether it is in fact owned publicly or not. The Bank of England, "the Old Lady of Threadneedle Street," is the oldest and most famous of the central banks. It began to operate as the central bank of England in the sixteenth

century.[5] In the United States, the central bank is the Federal Reserve System (or the "Fed" as it is often called). The Federal Reserve System was organized in 1913.

All central banks perform the same functions, but they have different forms of organization. We shall first mention the general functions of central banks, and then we shall look somewhat more closely at the way in which these functions are performed in the United States by the Federal Reserve System.

4. Textbooks often take a case in which one bank creates a deposit on the basis of an accretion of cash, and all of this ends up in a second bank, and the second bank then creates deposits, all of which end up in a third bank, and so on. Two objections can be raised against such a case. First, the situation in which all banks get extra cash is much more common in the real world than the situation in which one bank gets a significant amount of extra cash. Second, even if one bank did get extra cash, the deposits it creates should end up by being distributed evenly throughout all other banks, and thus the cash drain should be evenly spread among the other banks. Thus, after round one, we are immediately in the case of many banks and many new deposits, rather than in a case in which Bank B is the sole holder of a new deposit.

5. It was nationalized only in 1947.

BASIC FUNCTIONS OF A CENTRAL BANK

1. BANKER TO COMMERCIAL BANKS

Banks need a place to deposit *their* funds; they need a mechanism for transferring funds to other banks; and they need a place to borrow money when they are short of liquid funds. The central bank accepts deposits from commercial banks and will, on order, transfer these funds to the account of another bank. In this way, the central bank provides commercial banks with the equivalent of a checking account and with a means of settling debts to other banks.

Commercial banks often need liquid funds, and one way of getting these is to borrow from the central bank. Such borrowing takes one of two forms, either "rediscounting" a note (or IOU), which represents a loan made to some individual or firm, or by giving the central bank the commercial bank's own note, usually backed by the security of government bonds. The rate of interest the commercial bank must pay to the central bank is known as the rediscount rate.[6] The central bank is on occasion a stern banker, and can refuse to lend money to a commercial bank, or it can demand that loans made in the past be paid off now. Such actions are particularly important because the central bank is the "lender of last resort." Central banks to some extent arose in order to provide a lender of last resort—to prevent a bank that had sound assets (such as government securities) but not enough ready cash from being forced into failure by a sudden demand for cash from its depositors. The history of banking in this country, before the establishment of a central bank, is replete with "panics" in which bank after bank failed because depositors demanded cash that the banks could not provide.[7] The other side of the coin is that the central bank can, as we shall see below, use its lending power to regulate the commercial banks.

2. BANKER TO THE GOVERNMENT

Governments, too, need to hold their funds in an account into which they can deposit checks and on which they can write checks. Most government funds are on deposit with the central bank. When the government requires more money, it too needs to borrow, and it does so by printing bonds. Some of these are sold directly to the public, but the more usual way in which the government raises funds is to sell bonds to the central bank, which "buys" them in the sense of giving the government a deposit in the amount required.[8] As of July 1, 1963, the Federal Reserve System held over $32 billion in U.S. Government securities. These securities play an important role in the monetary system, as we shall see.

---

6. The discount rate is merely the rate of interest. If a bill promising to pay $100 in three months' time is sold (at a discount) for $99, then the rate of interest is clearly 1 percent for three months or 1 percent per year. If, at the end of two months, the bill is resold (i.e., rediscounted) for $99.50, then the rate being charged is 50¢ for one month or 6 percent per year. The original borrower, of course, receives only 50¢ for parting with $100 for two months or 3 percent per year, although, had he been able to wait a further month, he would have received his full $100.

7. The severe panic of 1907 led to the formation of the Federal Reserve System.

8. Suppose the government wants $100 million. It prints bonds for that amount and turns them over to the central bank, which increases by $100 million the deposit of the treasury. "As easy as printing money," you may say, and, indeed, it is the same thing, if you remember that deposit accounts *are* money. Congress has the power to limit the amount of borrowing the government may do.

3. CONTROLLER AND REGULATOR OF THE MONEY SUPPLY

The major function of central banks is to control the money supply. They do so in a number of different ways: by controlling the issue of currency, by regulating what banks may do, and by selling or purchasing government bonds *on the open market*. We shall discuss these different techniques at some length later in this chapter.

The Federal Reserve System

In its role as the central bank of the United States, the Federal Reserve System is the arm of the U.S. Government responsible for our monetary policy. If you remember nothing else about the system, remember that. We stress this at the outset because things are not always as they seem, and the organizational structure of the system appears, at first glance, to consist of a number of banks that are privately owned and over which commercial banks rather than the government have basic control.

The basic elements in the system are: (1) the Board of Governors; (2) the twelve Federal Reserve Banks; (3) the Federal Open-Market Committee; and (4) the 6,000-odd member banks.[9]

THE BOARD OF GOVERNORS

The Board consists of seven members appointed by the President and confirmed by the Senate. Appointment is for fourteen years and, in 1965, the salary was $20,000 per year. The length of term is of some importance, since each member of the Board necessarily serves beyond the term of the President who appoints him. The Board members are top-level public servants who usually, but not inevitably, come from the world of business or banking. Indeed, the newest member of the Board, Sherman Maisel, is an economist from the University of California.

The Board is responsible to Congress, but it works in close association with the Department of the Treasury. The Board supervises the entire Federal Reserve System and exercises general policy control over the twelve Reserve Banks.

THE RESERVE BANKS

The twelve Federal Reserve Banks serve the twelve districts into which the country is divided. Federal Reserve Banks are located in Boston, New York, Philadelphia, Cleveland, Richmond, Atlanta, Chicago, St. Louis, Minneapolis, Kansas City, Dallas, and San Francisco. Each of these banks is nominally, owned by the member banks in its district. Each commercial bank that is a member of the system is required to purchase Reserve Bank stock to an amount equal to 3 percent of the member bank's own capital. The commercial banks receive a flat 6 percent dividend on this investment. Each Federal Reserve Bank has nine directors: three bankers elected by the member banks, three representatives of business, agriculture, or industry, and three public members appointed by the Board of Governors. *Although they are technically*

9. We shall ignore the Federal Advisory Council, which has no real powers; its twelve members advise the Board of the views of commercial bankers.

privately owned and operated, the Reserve Banks are actually operated under guidelines set down by the Board of Governors in what is thought to be the public interest. Each of these banks serves as a branch of the central bank in its district.

THE OPEN-MARKET COMMITTEE

The Open-Market Committee consists of twelve members, five of whom are presidents of Reserve Banks, the other seven of whom are members of the Board of Governors. This committee determines the open-market policy of the system, which deals principally with the question of how many bonds the Reserve Banks should buy or sell on the open market.

THE MEMBER BANKS

The 6,000 member banks include all 4,500 national banks (a national bank must be a member) and 1,500 state banks that have chosen to join the system by agreeing to conform to its regulations. Approximately 8,000 banks in the U.S. are not members, but most of them are very small; in aggregate, they account for only 16 percent of the total demand deposits of the banking system.[10]

Tools for Controlling the Supply of Money

CURRENCY CONTROL

In most countries, the volume of currency is wholly determined by the central bank, which has no limits on its power to issue money. This is not quite the case in the United States, but it is substantially so. Look at the next ten pieces of paper money you see and the odds are very great that at least nine of them will have the words "Federal Reserve Note" on them. About 85 percent of the currency in circulation is in the form of Federal Reserve Notes. The great bulk of the rest is *coinage*, issued by the U.S. Treasury, and *silver certificates* (once the principal form of dollar bill, but now fast disappearing). A $5 Federal Reserve note says that the United States will pay the bearer $5 on demand. But, as we have seen, the note *is* $5. By law, the Federal Reserve note is required to have gold backing to the extent of 25¢ on the dollar.[11] This is supposed to put an upper limit on the amount of currency that can be issued, but in practice the limit is not binding. Should it ever become binding—i.e., should there ever be an insufficiency of gold to back the currency needs of the nation— Congress would merely change the law. The law makes some people feel better, but it has no substantive effect. In fact, the quantity of

---

10. Does the fact that so many banks are not members affect our generalization that the Federal Reserve is *the* central bank? The answer is No. The nonmember banks come under indirect control for the following reason: They are almost always small banks, and they maintain accounts as *correspondents* with large member banks. For them, the member bank is their lender of last resort and their clearing agency. In this sense they *are* linked into the over-all system. They are affected by Federal Reserve policy, but at one step removed, since the effect reaches them when it alters the behavior of the member bank to which the nonmember is linked.

11. The gold itself is in government vaults, much of it at Fort Knox. The federal government merely has "gold certificates" that assert that the gold is there.

currency is contracted or expanded to meet the demands for currency of American households and businesses; it is not used to control the over-all money supply.[12]

RESERVE REQUIREMENTS

Deposits that member banks hold at a Reserve Bank constitute the member bank's cash reserves. The federal government can set reserve requirements within specified limits. At present, reserve requirements range between 12 percent and 16 percent and average about 15 percent. The way in which the legal reserve requirements limit the commercial banks' freedom to create deposits was discussed earlier in this chapter. One means of central-bank control lies in varying the legal ratio of reserves to deposits. If this ratio is raised, the banks will have to reduce their volume of loans and other asset holdings in order to reach the new ratio (assuming that they have no excess supplies of cash). Thus, with a given amount of cash, there will be fewer bank loans than before; hence, people's ability to spend will be reduced, as will their actual demands for goods.

OPEN-MARKET OPERATIONS

The most important tool that the central bank has for influencing the supply of money is the purchase or sale of government bonds on the open market. We noted that the federal government held $32 billion in government securities in July, 1963. In 1960, it held only $25 billion. During 1962, it bought and sold $17 billion worth of government securities. What is the effect of such purchases and sales?

If the central bank wishes to increase the cash reserves of the private banks, it buys bonds in the open market. If the bank buys a bond from a private citizen, it pays for it with a check drawn on the central bank and payable to the seller. The seller will deposit this check in his own bank. The commercial bank will present the check to the central bank for payment, and the central bank will make a book entry increasing the deposit of the commercial bank at the central bank. At the end of these transactions, the central bank will have acquired a new asset in the form of a bond and a new liability in the form of a deposit by the private bank. The individual will have reduced his bond holdings and will have raised his cash holdings. The commercial bank will have a new deposit equal to the amount paid for the bond by the central bank. The commercial bank will find its cash assets and its deposit liabilities increased by the same amount. The bank will now be in exactly the same position as the bank illustrated in Table 1, and thus will be able to expand deposits.

If the central bank buys a large volume of bonds in the open market, then the whole banking system will find itself in possession of new deposits; cash assets and deposit liabilities will be increased by the same amount and hence the ratio of cash to deposits will be increased.[13]

If the central bank wishes to reduce the

---

12. Until 1965, all deposits of the Federal Reserve Banks were backed to the extent of 25 percent by gold certificates. This "gold backing" of deposit money was eliminated in 1965 to free gold for other purposes. The motive for the change was the gold drain caused by the balance-of-payments deficit. It illustrates nicely the way in which the fiction of gold backing gives way when it proves inconvenient.

13. Assume, for example, that a bank formerly had $200,000 in cash reserves and $1,000,000 in deposits and that new cash deposits of $100,000 are made. Thus, cash rises to $300,000 and deposits rise to $1,100,000. The cash ratio rises from 20 percent to 27.27 percent.

cash reserves of the private banks, it sells bonds in the open market. If the central bank sells a bond to a private citizen, it gives the bond to the individual and receives in return his check drawn against his own deposit in his bank and payable to the central bank. The central bank presents the check to the private bank for payment. The payment is made merely by a book entry reducing the private bank's cash held on deposit at the central bank.

Now the central bank has reduced its assets by the value of the bond it sold and reduced its liabilities in the form of cash owed to private banks. The individual has increased his holding of bonds and reduced his cash on deposit with his private bank. The commercial bank has reduced its deposit liability to the individual and reduced its cash assets (on deposit with the central bank) by the same amount. Each of the asset changes is balanced by a liability change. Indeed, everything balances! But the private bank finds that by suffering an equal change in its cash assets and its deposit liabilities, its ratio of cash to deposits falls.[14] If this ratio was previously at the legal minimum, it will now have fallen below the minimum and the private bank will have to take immediate steps to restore its cash ratio. The necessary reduction in deposits can be effected by not making new investments when old ones are redeemed (e.g., by not granting a new loan when old ones are repaid) or by selling (liquidating) existing investments (e.g., by selling bonds to the public and receiving payment in checks, which reduces the deposits held by the public).

OTHER TOOLS

The Federal Reserve Banks can affect the supply of money and credit through a variety of other devices that operate through interest rates and through so-called selective credit controls. Although these devices are much less important than open-market operations or reserve requirements, they are used from time to time.

One such tool is control over the rediscount rate. Generally, the central bank can exercise an immediate influence on all rates of interest charged on *short-term* loans (i.e., loans for periods up to, say, a year or so) by changing the rediscount rate. The reason why this can be done is partly custom and partly the fact that, if those making short-term loans should have to borrow from the central bank, they do not wish to be in a position of charging their customers too much less than the bank will charge them (for to lend money for any length of time at a lower rate than one is paying for borrowing the same money is a sure way to financial ruin). Furthermore, the central bank can force the commercial banking system to borrow from it by engaging in sufficiently vigorous open-market operations. These changes in the short-term rate of interest will have certain effects on the economy; in particular, they will influence the flow of foreign funds. A rise in the short-term rate in New York will induce people throughout the world who have money to lend for short periods to transfer the money to New York and lend it out there. This means that these lenders must turn their currencies into dollars and, hence, there will be an increased supply of

14. If, in the previous example, the bank with $200,000 in cash and $1,000,000 in deposits suffered a cash drain (because its depositors were buying bonds from the central bank) of $100,000, then its cash would fall to $100,000 and its deposits to $900,000. Thus its cash ratio falls from 20 percent to 11.11 percent. If we suppose the bank wished to maintain a 20 percent reserve ratio, deposits would have to be reduced by a further $400,000 in order to restore the desired ratio.

foreign funds available in the New York market. A fall in the short-term interest rate has the reverse effect.[15]

Whether or not rediscount-rate policy can have an effect on industrial development, which is usually financed by long-term loans, depends on the relation between short- and long-term rates of interest. Here the evidence is not conclusive, but, on balance, it tends to suggest that the long-term rate does not respond very much to changes in the short rate as long as these changes do not persist for very long periods of time.

Open-market operations designed to affect the quantity of money also have an effect on interest rates. Buying large quantities of bonds tends to force up their price. This, as we have already seen, is equivalent to forcing down the rate of interest.[16] Selling large quantities of bonds, on the other hand, tends to force down the price of bonds and force up the rate of interest. Thus, an open-market policy designed to expand the money supply also tends to lower interest rates, and a policy designed to contract the money supply tends to raise interest rates.

There are a variety of selective credit controls that are designed not to regulate the over-all volume of money or credit, but rather to limit (or encourage) particular forms of it. Stock-market fluctuations can be controlled to some extent through margin requirements; consumer credit, which can be highly volatile, can be controlled in several ways. From World War II to 1952, the Federal Reserve had authority to specify minimum down payments and maximum terms of loans. It does not have this authority at the moment, but a bill is before Congress urging the reinstitution of it.[17]

The final tool that we need to mention here is direct order or suggestion. If the commercial-banking system is prepared to cooperate, the Federal Reserve Banks can operate a tight money policy merely by asking banks to be conservative in granting loans; when the restrictive policy is removed, the commercial bankers can then be told that it is all right to go ahead granting loans and extending deposits up to the legal maximum. The use of "moral suasion" is not necessarily mere exhortation. Member banks do depend upon the Federal Reserve Banks for loans, and noncooperation with FRB "suggestions" can prove costly to a bank in the long run.

In all of these ways, the Federal Reserve *seeks* to control the money supply in a country.

A Theory of the Determination of the Money Supply

We can now develop a theory of what determines the size of the money supply. We do this by making a series of assumptions about the behavior of the various units we have already studied. Our theory is based upon four behavioral assumptions:

1. *The Federal Reserve Board can control the supply of cash reserves in the hands of*

---

15. See the appendix to Chapter 38 for an analysis of the effects of these international movements of short-term capital.

16. See page 375.

17. Both of these tools of control are actually used by the British central authorities in their stabilization policies.

the private banks. We have seen a number of ways in which the Fed can control reserves. In the following discussion, we shall assume that they use open-market operations for this purpose.

2. *Commercial banks are profit-maximizers.*[18] Profits are maximized by expanding deposits up to the legal limit as long as there are reasonable-risk investments available, since newly created deposits can be used to purchase income-earning assets. For instance, the bank could grant a loan to a customer ("purchasing" the customer's promise to pay) and in return receive an interest payment from the customer. This assumption of profit-maximization gives private banks an incentive to expand their deposits up to the legal limit.

3. *The public's demand for loans fluctuates widely and is influenced by a number of factors, one of which is the state of activity in the economy.* When sales and profits are high and rising, the demand to borrow money will be high and rising, but when profits and sales are low, the demand to borrow money will be low. This means that the bank's ability to expand deposits by making loans to the public will be limited by the public's desire to borrow money and that this desire will fluctuate considerably over time.

4. *Banks will refrain from purchasing bonds if they think the price of bonds now is too high relative to what it will be in the future.* If the current price of bonds is very high (the rate of interest is very low), banks may prefer to hold cash rather than to buy bonds. If, for example, the price of bonds is expected to fall by 3 percent within 6 months and the bond pays its holder an interest of 2 percent over a 6-month period, it might be better to hold the cash now and buy bonds in 6 months' time, when their price has

fallen. This means that at times when the interest rate is thought to be unusually low (the price of bonds unusually high), banks may not be willing to expand deposits by purchasing bonds.

The theory can now be stated as follows: The central bank can, through its control of banks' reserves, expand or contract the maximum amount banks may lend. Banks will usually be motivated to expand their loans and deposits to this maximum amount. Whether they in fact do so will depend upon the state of demand. Let us see how this works out.

Assume that the central bank wishes to reduce the level of aggregate demand in the economy because it believes there is too much inflationary pressure at the moment. What is the sequence of events?

1. The central bank enters the open market and sells bonds.

2. The central bank receives checks from the public in payment for the bonds. When it presents these checks for payment, this causes a reduction in the cash reserves of the private banks.

3a. If cash reserves are already at their legal minimum, then commercial banks will have to contract deposits by a multiple of their loss of reserves in order to restore their reserve ratio.

3b. If cash reserves are above their legal minimum, then no contraction of deposits need occur until cash reserves are reduced below their legal requirement. However, any desired contraction of deposits can always be achieved by sufficiently large sales of bonds on the open market.

4. The reduction in the supply of deposit money will affect total spending in the economy. People who would have borrowed money

---

18. This is a rather strong assumption. All that is really needed is the weaker assumption that, *ceteris paribus*, private banks prefer more profits to less profits.

in order to spend it on consumer goods or on investment projects will now be unable to do so. Total spending will be less than it otherwise would have been and this will have a contractionary effect on the economy.

Now assume that the central bank wishes to increase the level of demand in the economy, possibly because there is heavy unemployment. The bank buys bonds, thus increasing the cash reserves of the private banks. The private banks are then able to expand deposits by lending money to members of the public. If, however, no one wishes to borrow

further money, the expansion of deposits will not occur.[19]

Our theory of the control of the money supply has led to two important predictions:

1. *A contractionary monetary policy can always force banks to reduce the supply of deposit money.*

2. *An expansionary monetary policy permits banks to increase the supply of deposit money, but does not force them to do so.*

The Problem of "Near Money"

The validity of the theory outlined above has been questioned in recent years. Critics point to many highly liquid assets held by banks, firms, and households that can easily be converted into money. Thus, say the critics, a contractionary monetary policy will have its effects offset by a liquidation of these near-moneys in order to restore desired cash positions. If this happens, none of the other predicted effects will follow, because the monetary authorities will not succeed in permanently reducing cash ratios of banks, firms, and households. This theory is too complicated to spell out in detail in an elementary textbook and it is still the subject of debate

and testing. At this stage, however, it does serve to warn against accepting as definitely proved the predictions of the orthodox theory of the control of the money supply that we have developed above. Choice among competing theories must rest on evidence, and much work is yet to be done in this field. As yet, it is too early even to guess at the conclusion that will emerge; at any rate, it is not yet possible to dismiss the views of the critics of the orthodox theory who state that near moneys have greatly altered the workings of a tight money policy and reduced its effectiveness, at least in the short run.

19. In these circumstances, the private bank *could* expand deposits by purchasing bonds. The price of bonds will, however, already have been driven very high by the central bank's purchasing policy. The private banks may well decide that they do not wish to buy large quantities of bonds at what may seem to them an abnormally high price. In this case, the extra cash that accrues to them because of the central bank's open-market operations merely swells their cash reserves; it does not result in an expansion of deposit money. This is where assumption 4 becomes important, because banks *can* always expand deposits up to the limit, providing they do not mind what price they have to pay for the bonds they buy.

Summary

1. The basic unit of our banking system today is the commercial bank; the other major element is the set of Federal Reserve Banks that constitute the central bank of the U.S.

2. Fractionally backed reserve systems make it possible for banks to create deposit money. We examined the case, first, in which there is only one bank in the banking system. A new deposit of cash enables an expansion by a multiple of this amount, the exact result depending on the reserve requirements.

3. In a multibank system, one bank cannot produce a large multiple expansion of deposits based on an original accretion of cash unless all other banks also expand deposits whenever they have excess cash reserves.

4. In a multibank system, we end up with a result similar to the one in which the system is composed of but one bank, as long as all banks expand deposits whenever they have excess cash reserves.

5. The central bank is banker to commercial banks, banker to the government, and controller and regulator of the money supply.

6. The Federal Reserve System is composed of the twelve reserve banks, the Board of Governors, the Open-Market Committee, and the 6,000 or so member banks.

7. Among the "Fed's" tools for controlling the quantity of money are its power to control the quantity of currency, reserve requirements, selective credit controls, the rediscount rate, "moral suasion," and, most important, open-market operations.

8. If the central bank wishes to increase the cash reserves of the private banks, it buys bonds in the open market. If it wishes to reduce the cash reserves of the private banks, it sells bonds in the open market.

9. A theory of the determination of the size of the money supply leads to two important predictions: A contractionary monetary policy can always force banks to reduce the supply of deposit money; an expansionary monetary policy permits banks to increase the supply of deposit money, but does not force them to do so.

10. Finally, we noted that there is a great deal of controversy over the validity of the theory, propounded by the critics of orthodox monetary policy, that the existence of "near moneys" greatly alters the workings of a tight money policy. Empirical and theoretical work is proceeding on this controversy, but, as yet, the issue is unresolved.

QUESTIONS FOR DISCUSSION

1. What do we mean when we say that banks can create money? Some people advocate that banks should be required to keep 100 percent cash reserves behind all their deposits. What would be the effects of such a policy?

2. The Board of Governors of the Federal Reserve announces that commercial-bank required-reserve ratios will rise by 3 percent. In one town, a newspaper interviews the bank manager, who says that, as far as he can see, he'll have to call in very few loans. Why might he say this? A few days later, he gets a circular from the bank of which his is a branch. The circular tells him to be prepared to call in far more loans than he had thought necessary. What insight does his head office show that he did not?

3. In Great Britain, in April, 1965, the Bank of England told the commercial banks that they would have to pay in to their accounts "special deposits," which have the effect of increasing their reserves by £90 million. The next day, the headline in the *Guardian* read, "Banks' ability to make loans cut by £90 million." What do you think of this? Suppose the banks raised all the money for their special deposits by restricting loans? Suppose, on the other hand, all they did was to sell government bonds in their possession, the price of which the Treasury was committed to keep fairly steady?

4. What is the object of the following actions of a central bank?
a. selling bonds in the open market;
b. lowering the required reserve ratio;
c. urging Congress to pass a law permitting it to specify that down payments on installment-plan buying may not be less than one-third of the price of the item bought;
d. exhorting commercial banks to give preference in lending to exporters.

How is each supposed to work?

5. An American folk-song about banks has, as one key line, "and the vaults are stuffed with silver." Comment.

6. In what way can you say that there is an asymmetry between the Federal Reserve's ability to induce a contraction and an expansion in the money supply?

7. If all depositors in all U.S. banks tried to withdraw their money tomorrow, what would happen? What would have happened if they had tried to do this in 1900?

8. Recently, while watching firemen battle a blaze in a small-town bank, one of the authors heard a bystander remark worriedly, "I sure hope they get that fire out. My money is deposited in there." Would the man's worries have been eased or aggravated if he had taken a course in the economics of money and banking?

Chapter **54** THE DEMAND FOR MONEY

IF A HOUSEHOLD OR A FIRM HOLDS A MONEY balance either in the form of cash or of a demand deposit, it incurs an opportunity cost, the cost being measured in terms of foregone alternatives. The minimum cost of holding cash is measured by the rate of interest on low-risk securities, which in most countries is something on the order of 5 percent. This means that for every $1,000 held in cash by the household or the firm at least $50 is sacrificed per year in terms of earnings foregone on alternative uses of the money. In the case of a firm subject to credit

rationing,[1] the foregone earnings may be very much higher than the rate of interest on low-risk securities. If the firm is unable to raise all the money it would like to use, the return on additional money invested in the firm may be as high as 15 or 20 percent. In this case, each $1,000 held by the firm as cash or demand deposits costs the firm $150 to $200 per year in foregone profits. Why then do firms and households hold any cash at all? If we are to answer this question, we must develop a theory of the demand for money.

1. See Chapter 36, page 403.

Reasons for Holding Money

Virtually all transactions in our economy are settled with money. Money is passed from firms to households and back again to firms in order to pay for the factor services supplied by households to firms and the goods and services produced by firms and sold to households. This is, of course, the circular flow of income, which we studied in Part IX. These transactions force both firms and households to hold cash balances.

If we let Friday stand for the day on which the wage bill is paid to households, then the cash balances held by firms will build up through the week as money is received and will fall sharply on Friday when wages are paid to households. The balances held by households will run down through the week as purchases are made and will rise sharply on Friday when wages are received. Firms must make payments other than wages, and the timing of these is not as predictable as is the timing of periodic wage payments. The receipts of cash from the sale of goods are not perfectly predictable, because one never quite knows either how much will be sold or when the goods sold will actually be paid for. The receipts and disbursements of firms are, therefore, subject to considerable random fluctuations. It is necessary to hold cash balances in order to be able to carry on business when disbursements are unexpectedly large, or when receipts are unexpectedly small.

It is important to notice that the above discussion implies that cash balances are held for two different reasons. One reason is the nonsynchronization of receipts and disbursements; the holding of balances on this

account is *unavoidable*. The second reason is the uncertainty about the exact timing of receipts and payments; the holding of balances on this account is *avoidable* (provided the firm is willing to be temporarily embarrassed when receipts are unexpectedly delayed or payments unexpectedly advanced). With this general introduction in mind, let us now consider in more detail each of the reasons for holding cash.

UNAVOIDABLE BALANCES

The minimum level of cash balances that must be held depends on the pay period and the size of the wage bill. Assume, for purposes of illustration, that firms pay wages weekly and that households spend all their wages on the purchase of goods and services with the expenditure being spread out evenly over the week. Thus, on Friday morning, firms must hold balances equal to the weekly wage bill, while on Friday afternoon households will hold these balances. Over the week, households' balances will run down as a result of purchasing goods and services. By the same token, the balances held by firms must build up as a result of selling goods and services until, on the following Friday morning, firms will again have amassed balances equal to the wage bill that must be met on that day. On average, over the week, firms will hold balances equal to half the wage bill and so will households; thus total balances held will be equal to the total weekly wage bill.

The size of these unavoidable balances thus depends on the size of the wage bill. If the wage bill doubles, either because twice as many people are employed at the same rate or because the same number is employed at twice the wage rate, then the balances held must double. The size of the wage bill tends to vary directly with the level of national income.

In order to see the importance of the pay period on cash holdings, assume that wages are paid daily, instead of weekly, as we assumed above. On the average, the total balances required will be equal to the total *daily* wage bill, which is, of course, only a fraction of the weekly wage bill.

Balances of the kind we have been discussing must be held, because payments and receipts are not perfectly synchronized both for firms and households. The more often wages are paid, the more nearly synchronized payments and receipts will be and thus the smaller the balances will be that need to be held.

These balances are virtually unavoidable[2] and would exist in a world in which everyone was perfectly certain of the timing of all receipts and payments as long as such inflows and outflows were not perfectly synchronized. We have conducted the argument in terms of the wage bill, but a similar analysis holds for payments for all other factor services.

AVOIDABLE BALANCES

The second reason for holding balances arises because of the uncertainty about the exact timing of receipts and payments. Most goods and services are sold on credit, and the seller can never be quite certain when these goods will be paid for, while the buyer can never be quite certain of the day of delivery and thus of the day on which payment will fall due; nor can he be certain of the degree to which his suppliers will be pressing for prompt payment at the time at which such payment is due. In order to be able to continue in business during times in which receipts are abnormally low and/or disbursements are abnormally high, firms carry cash balances that enable them to weather such periods by making payments out of cash reserves. The larger the cash reserves, the greater is the degree of insurance against being unable to pay bills because of some temporary fluctuation in either receipts or disbursements. Cash balances held for this purpose are avoidable. If the firm is pressed for cash or has other very profitable uses for its funds, it may run down these balances and thus take a higher risk of being caught by some temporary fluctuation in receipts and disbursements. How serious this risk is depends on the penalties of being caught without sufficient reserves by some temporary fluctuation. A firm is unlikely to be pushed into bankruptcy, but it may have to incur considerable costs when it is forced to borrow money for short periods in order to meet such temporary crises. The cost depends on the lines of short-term credit that are open to the firm. The firm might also lose goodwill if it is unable to pay some of its bills until short-term credit has been arranged.

The size of the balances held depends on the degree to which payments and receipts are subject to random fluctuations and on the volume of payments and receipts. If the volume of transactions rises, then a given cash holding will provide less and less protection. To provide the same degree of protection as the volume of business rises, more

---

2. Firms could loan out the money as it accrued through the week by making very short-term loans repayable on Friday, but, given the present institutional setup, and the cost of making loans, such a means of reducing cash balances can be adopted only by a few of the very largest firms.

cash is necessary. Thus we expect the firm's demand for cash to rise as its own business rises. In the aggregate, we expect it to rise as national income rises.

SPECULATIVE BALANCES

One other major reason for holding cash is in order to speculate on the course of future events. The future is never certain, so that any transaction that takes place over time is necessarily somewhat speculative. If we think prices are now very low and will soon rise, the tendency is to buy now or to put off selling until prices rise. If we think prices are high now and will soon fall, the tendency is to sell now and to postpone buying until prices have fallen. This applies to anything that is bought and sold, including stocks and bonds. If the price of bonds is very high (the rate of interest is very low) in relation to what people think is the normal price, the tendency will be to sell bonds now and postpone intended purchases until prices have come down. In such a situation, large quantities of cash will be held in anticipation of a more favorable chance to purchase stocks and bonds in the future. If, on the other hand, the price of bonds is very low in relation to what is thought to be the normal price (the rate of interest is high), the tendency will be to buy bonds now and to postpone sales until a more favorable price can be obtained. In this case, the tendency will be to hold as little cash as possible and hold bonds instead.

Thus we would expect the holding of cash for speculative purposes to vary with the rate of interest; the lower the rate of interest (the higher the price of bonds), the more cash will the public wish to hold.

Determinants of the Demand for Money

We have discussed some of the main reasons for holding money. We now define the demand for money as the total amount of money that all the households and firms in the economy *wish to hold*. We may summarize the previous discussion by listing our hypotheses about the main factors that determine the demand for money:

1. *The demand for money depends on institutional arrangements*. If, for example, households were paid daily instead of weekly, then unavoidable balances would be much less than they now are.

2. *The demand for money depends on the level of income*. The larger the income, the larger the amount of money held in unavoidable balances. The larger the income, the larger the amount needed to provide a given level of security against unforeseen fluctuations in receipts and payments.

3. *The demand for money depends on the rate of interest*. For firms that can borrow all the money they require at the going rate of interest (i.e., for firms that are not subject to credit rationing), the rate of interest measures the opportunity cost of holding cash. The higher the rate of interest, the higher the cost to these firms of holding cash and the less cash they will wish to hold. For all firms and households, the rate of interest influences their decision whether or not to hold cash for speculative purposes. The lower the rate of interest, the less attractive bonds will seem to be and so the higher the demand will be to hold cash instead of bonds.

4. *The demand for cash varies with those factors, other than the rate of interest, that determine the opportunity cost of holding cash.* If a firm is subject to credit rationing (i.e., if it cannot borrow all the cash it wishes to borrow at the going rate of interest), the opportunity cost of holding cash will not be measured by the rate of interest. It will be measured by the return to the firm of an-

other dollar invested in the firm. The opportunity cost will be higher, the higher the internal rate of return and the more severe the credit rationing to the firm. If, for example, a tight monetary policy makes it very hard to borrow money for investments, then firms that feel the effects of this policy will find the opportunity cost of keeping cash holdings increased. They will be tempted to reduce their cash holdings, using the cash thus freed to fulfill at least some of their investment plans, which, before the tight money policy, they were planning to fulfill by spending borrowed money.

A graphical expression of these hypotheses about the demand for cash is given in Figure 1. The demand for holding cash is shown *ceteris paribus* as varying directly with income, inversely with the rate of interest and inversely with the opportunity cost of holding cash.

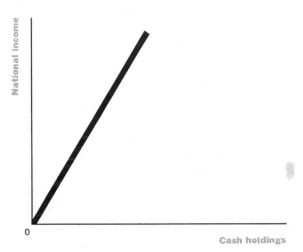

(i)

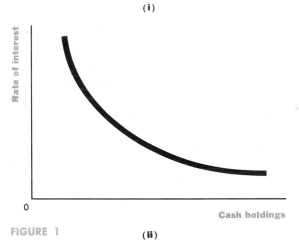

FIGURE 1   (ii)

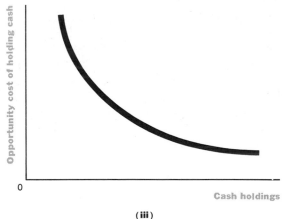

(iii)

Summary

1. We developed a theory of the demand for money in order to answer the following question: Why do households and firms hold *any* money, in view of the opportunity cost involved? Our answer to this question in a nutshell, is that, in some cases, they cannot avoid holding money, whereas, in other cases, the money held confers a benefit to the holder equal to or greater than the opportunity cost.

2. We divide balances into avoidable, unavoidable, and speculative balances. Avoidable balances are held because of uncertainty in the timing of receipts and payments; they provide an insurance against being unable to meet one's obligations when either receipts are unexpectedly small or payments unexpectedly large. Unavoidable balances arise inevitably out of the nonsynchronization of receipts and payments. Speculative balances are held in order to take advantage of opportunities to buy at favorable prices in the future.

QUESTIONS FOR DISCUSSION

1. What things can you think of that determine the opportunity cost of holding cash?

2. If there is a cost to holding cash, why do people hold avoidable balances anyway?

3. Why do we say that some balances are unavoidable? Do they have an opportunity cost too? What significance does this have?

4. What does our theory predict would be the effect on the demand for money of each of the following?
   a. a rise in the real level of output, prices constant;
   b. a rise in the level of prices, output constant;
   c. a rise in the rate of interest;
   d. a credit squeeze that makes it difficult for firms to borrow money for investment purposes;
   e. a trend toward monthly payment of wages;
   f. the wider use of credit cards.

5. Make a list of macroeconomic observations that would refute the theory described in this chapter. Would an economist hope that there are a great many such observations or very few of them?

Chapter **55**   **THE DETERMINATION OF THE PRICE LEVEL**

IN THIS CHAPTER WE DISCUSS NOT RELATIVE prices, but the *price level,* the average level of all prices. If all prices were doubled, relative prices would be unchanged but the absolute price level would be doubled. A rise in the price level is often referred to as an *inflation* and a fall in the price level as a *deflation.* What determines the absolute price level? What causes it to change?[1]

Price levels often change dramatically. Table 1 shows the average rate of change in the price level of twenty-one countries over the eight-year period from 1954 to 1962. It also shows the most and least rapid rise in the price level from one year to the next. Probably the most striking thing about the table is that it indicates the great range and variability of experience among countries. Evidently, there is no mechanism in the modern world to keep price levels even roughly the same across countries.

In Chapter 45, we pointed out that variations in the circular flow of income could result either because of changes in the quantity of goods bought and sold, or because of changes in the prices of these goods. Up to this point, we have assumed that there were

TABLE 1   **RATES OF CHANGE IN PRICE LEVELS OF TWENTY-ONE SELECTED COUNTRIES, IN PERCENTAGES**

Country	Average annual rate, 1954–1962	Maximum rate of increase	Minimum rate of increase
Brazil	26.3	53.2	12.4
Canada	1.3	3.1	0
Chile	29.3	78.9	0.7
China	8.1	13.8	0
Denmark	1.3	3.2	−1
Ecuador	0.5	5.1	−1
France	4.2	11.1	0
Germany	0.9	2	−1
India	3.1	14	−8.8
Iran	0.5	6.2	−2.9
Italy	0.3	3	−3
Japan	0	5	−6.5
Mexico	4.4	14.2	1
Netherlands	0.4	3	2
New Zealand	1.3	3.2	0
Norway	1.5	4.2	−2
Sudan	−1.1	9	−14.5
Syria	0.2	7.2	−7.3
U.K.	2.1	3.9	0.5
U.S.	0.9	3.2	0
Yugoslavia	1.5	4.2	1

1. At this point you might review your understanding of the distinction between absolute and relative prices by rereading pp. 150–152.

unused supplies of all factors of production and that variations in the circular flow of income resulted from changes in quantities produced, not prices. We now wish to take account of the observed fact that fluctuations in aggregate demand often affect the level of prices, as well as the level of output and employment.

Money, Aggregate Demand, and Prices

Very early in the history of economics, changes in the price level were linked to changes in the quantity of money. Thus the theory of the determination of the price level was related to the theories of the demand for and the supply of money. There is, however, an intermediate link in the relation between money and prices. A change in demand for or supply of money is thought to affect aggregate demand, and a change in aggregate demand is thought to affect the price level. Past and contemporary economics contains many controversies about the relation between money and prices. These controversies are more easily studied if we first consider the link between aggregate demand and prices, and then go on to consider the link between money and aggregate demand.

THE RELATION BETWEEN AGGREGATE DEMAND AND THE PRICE LEVEL: A SIMPLE THEORY

A simple theory that makes a strict dichotomy between changes in output and employment on the one hand, and changes in the level of prices on the other, is commonly used in elementary macroeconomics: Below "full employment," prices are assumed to be fixed, and fluctuations in aggregate demand are assumed to cause only fluctuations in output and employment; at "full employment," output and employment are assumed to be fixed, and fluctuations in aggregate demand are assumed to cause only fluctuations in the price level. Let us consider each of these situations.

In periods of less than full employment, excess supply exists in most markets, and the simple competitive theory of price outlined in Part II predicts that each individual price, and hence the average level of all prices, will be falling. We now assume, however, that prices are sticky in a downward direction. When there are unemployed resources, prices either do not fall at all, or else they fall so slowly that, for all practical purposes, they can be regarded as being constant over a period of several years.

The constancy, or at least the extreme stickiness of prices in a downward direction, is assumed to be caused by trade-union resistance to a reduction in wages, by government price-support policies, particularly those in the agricultural sector, and by manufacturers' resistance to a fall in prices. As a result of the downward inflexibility of prices, variations in aggregate demand below the full-employment level will cause variations in the level of output only. Thus the circular-flow theory of the previous chapters provides a theory of the level of output and employment in the economy.

Once the economy reaches full employment, further increases in output become impossible in the short run. A rise in aggregate demand cannot now be met by a rise in output, so prices rise instead. The theory assumes no stickiness of prices in an upward direction.

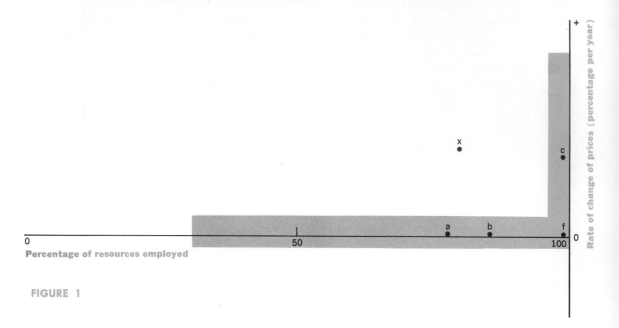

Percentage of resources employed

FIGURE 1

This theory is illustrated in Figure 1. In this figure, the level of resource utilization is plotted on the X axis and the rate of change of the price level is plotted on the Y axis. Each point thus indicates the percentage utilization of resources and the accompanying amount of inflation or deflation observed in the economy. According to the theory, all observations should be clustered in the shaded band drawn around the axes. When there are unemployed resources, the price level should be observed to be constant. A change in aggregate demand will change the percentage utilization of resources, moving the economy, say, between points *a* and *b* without causing any change in the price level. Prices only rise when full employment exists, so that all observations of inflationary price changes should be clustered in the narrow vertical band at or very near 100 percent utilization of resources. What is not allowed by the theory is a situation such as that shown by point *x* in which

a significant degree of inflation is combined with a substantial amount of unutilized resources.

The "L-shaped" relation of Figure 1 has two important policy implications. The first is that inflation can never be reversed. Prices rise when there is excess demand, but they do not fall when there is excess supply. We say in this circumstance that the price level displays a *ratchet effect:* It can move only in one direction. The second and more important implication of the L-shaped relation is that there is no conflict between the two policies of full employment on the one hand and maintaining a stable price level on the other. If there is unemployment in the economy, aggregate demand can be raised until full employment occurs, without any consequent inflationary pressures. Inflation will result only if demand is increased in a situation in which full employment already exists. The economy can be kept in a position such as *f*

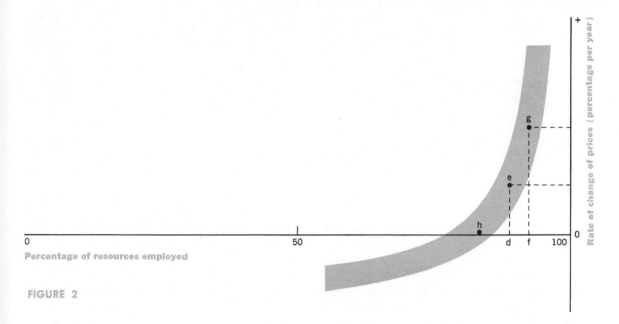

FIGURE 2

in Figure 1 with full employment and stable prices. If the economy is at *a* with unemployment, then aggregate demand needs only to be expanded to move it to *f;* if the economy is at *c* with an inflation under way, then aggregate demand need merely be reduced until the inflation stops and the economy returns to *f.*

AGGREGATE DEMAND AND CHANGES IN PRICES AND OUTPUT: THE EVIDENCE

The theory of the **L**-shaped curve has been subjected to a great deal of testing in the last decade. The testing of any interesting theory almost always raises complicated technical problems. It is fairly clear, however, that the simple dichotomy, changes in output only at less than "full employment" and changes in prices only at "full employment," has not stood up well to testing. As a matter of ob-

servation, it appears that changes in aggregate demand usually cause changes both in output and in prices. The closer the economy is to full employment, the more likely it is that any change in demand will cause a price change and the less likely it is that it will cause an employment change, but, no matter how high the level of resource use is, it is always possible to expand the rate of production a little bit, so that a rise in demand is always accompanied by some rise in output.

The actual observations for any economy seem to lie more in the curved band illustrated in Figure 2 than in the **L**-shaped band of Figure 1. The relation between the level of employment of resources and changes in the price level illustrated in Figure 2 shows prices falling slowly for large amounts of unemployment in the economy; for some smaller volume of unused resources, the price level remains steady, while the price level rises when resource utilization is at a high level.

The higher the level of resource utilization, the more rapid the rise in prices, but it is always possible to obtain a further increase in resource utilization at the cost of a more rapid rise in prices. If, for example, excess demand were causing an inflation of *de* percent per year, and the percentage of resources used was *Od* percent, then a further rise in excess demand would raise the rate of inflation to, say, *fg* percent, but simultaneously raise the level of resource use to *Of* percent.

According to the relation shown in Figure 2, the economy does not suddenly move from a situation of underemployment of resources and constant prices to a situation of full (constant) employment with varying prices; instead, the economy moves by degrees from one to another. Any increase in demand will lower unemployment to some extent, and so raise output, but the lower the level of unemployment already achieved, the less will any rise in aggregate demand affect unemployment and the more will it affect prices.

We conclude that the evidence supports the theory that variations in the level of aggregate demand cause variations in both prices and output; the lower the level of unemployment, the larger the change in prices and the smaller the change in unemployment; the higher the level of unemployment, the more will changes in demand cause output variations and the less will they cause the price level to vary.

Situations such as the one shown by points *e* and *g* in Figure 2 represent disequilibrium positions: If the inflation does eventually eliminate the excess demand, the level of resource utilization will fall back to that compatible with a stable price level. This does not affect the fact that, if the central authorities are prepared to take steps to allow the inflation to continue, they can achieve a level of unemployment lower than that which would obtain if there were no inflation. Also, the more rapid the rate of price inflation the authorities are willing to take steps to maintain, the lower the rate of unemployment they need to accept. Of course, to *maintain* a level of unemployment below *h* percent, the authorities must take steps to ensure a continuing disequilibrium with continuing inflationary pressures in the economy.

Note that the policy implications of this relation differ from those of the L-shaped relation of Figure 1: The control of inflation and the maintenance of the highest possible level of employment are now conflicting policy objectives. If the economy is at point *e*, for example, with $100 - d$ percent unemployment and with *de* percent inflation per year, then the inflation can be slowed down at the cost of increased unemployment; on the other hand, the level of unemployment can be reduced, but only at the cost of more inflation. We shall have more to say about the problems raised by this relation when we discuss macroeconomic policy in Chapter 58.

The Relation Between Money and Aggregate Demand

So far we have discussed the relation between aggregate demand and the price level. In this section we discuss the relation between money and aggregate demand.

In Chapters 53 and 54, we developed theories of the supply of money and the demand for money. If the demand for money is equal to its supply, everyone has the quantity of money he wishes to hold, and a situation of equilibrium exists. Problems arise when we are not in equilibrium: If the demand for money is not equal to its supply, households and firms either have more money than they wish to hold (supply exceeds demand) or less money than they wish to hold (demand exceeds supply); in both cases they can be expected to do something about it. In the former case, we would expect them to use the surplus money for some purpose; in the latter case, we would expect them to try to make up their deficiency by attempting to obtain more money from one source or another.

QUANTITY THEORY AND KEYNESIAN THEORY OF MONEY: A PREVIEW

One important feature that distinguishes among different theories of money is the hypothesis made about what happens in a situation in which the demand for money is not equal to the supply of money. We would expect households and firms to do *something*, but different theories make different behavioral assumptions about what they will do.

We shall study two extreme hypotheses: The first is that all the effects of a difference between the demand for and the supply of money are manifested solely in changes in aggregate demand for goods and services. This behavioral hypothesis is associated with the *quantity theory of money*. It is based on an assumption that, when firms and households have more money than they need to hold, they will spend the excess on currently produced goods and services, while, when they have less money than they wish to hold, they will try to build up their balances by reducing their expenditure on goods and services to

an amount less than their current incomes, adding the difference to their cash holdings. According to this theory, disequilibrium between demand for and supply of money causes changes in aggregate demand for currently produced goods and services.

The other extreme hypothesis, which is associated with the *Keynesian theory of money*, is that a difference between the demand for and the supply of money is manifested solely in the demand for and the supply of securities.[2] According to this theory, when firms and households do not have sufficient cash balances they attempt to build them up by selling bonds, and, when they have more cash than they need to hold, they attempt to invest the surplus in bonds. Thus, a difference between demand for money and its supply will not have any direct effect on aggregate demand for goods and services. There may, however, be an indirect effect. The attempt on the part of households and firms either to buy or to sell bonds in large quantities will affect the price of these bonds. A change in the price of bonds is, as we have already seen, the same thing as a change in the rate of interest. Insofar as investment decisions are affected by the rate of interest, there may be an effect on aggregate demand. The links between money and aggregate demand are less direct in this theory, and the quantitative effect on aggregate demand of a difference between demand for and supply of money is likely to be small, because it depends on the fairly weak link between changes in the rate of interest and changes in investment expenditure.

The significance of these two hypotheses is great. If one believes the quantity hypothesis, one believes that changing the money supply will have a strong and direct effect

2. That is, stocks and bonds. In this text we shall talk about bonds.

on aggregate demand. This makes monetary policy a tool of control of great potential power. If one believes the Keynesian hypothesis, one believes that changing the money supply will have only a weak and indirect effect on aggregate demand and only on that part of it that is composed of investment expenditure. This makes monetary policy a much less potent tool for controlling the economy than it appears to be to supporters of the quantity theory. This is probably the most important difference between the quantity and the Keynesian theories, and it is what the student really needs to understand. It is now necessary, however, to elaborate on these two theories in order to develop the differences and in order to consider the relevance of each theory to actual observations.

THE QUANTITY THEORY

The two basic assumptions of the theory are (1) that the demand for money is proportional to the level of transactions in the economy, and (2) that an excess demand for, or supply of, money is reflected in aggregate demand for currently produced goods and services.

THE DEMAND FOR AND THE
SUPPLY OF MONEY

It is assumed that households and firms wish to hold cash balances equal to some constant fraction of the annual value of their transactions. We indicate this proportion by the symbol k. Thus the demand for money is merely k times the money value of transactions, and the demand curve for money is the one shown in Figure 1(i) in Chapter 54. Assume that k is $\frac{1}{10}$. If transactions are $1

billion, then $100 million will be required as cash balances; if the money value of transactions rises to $2 billion, then $200 million will be demanded for cash balances. The value of k depends, in this theory, on institutional factors such as the pay period. In the examples given in Chapter 54, for example, transactions regarding the earning and spending of wages required that households and firms hold balances equal to $\frac{1}{52}$ of the wage bill when the pay period was once a week, and $\frac{1}{365}$ when it was once a day. If these were the only transactions in the economy, k would be just less than .02 (2 percent) when wages were paid weekly. As it is, there are other transactions, each type requiring the holding of some characteristic proportion of cash balances. For the whole economy, k is the average of all these, and it expresses the over-all need to hold balances as a fraction of the total value of all transactions in the economy.

Next let us take the money value of transactions and split it into two parts: a real part, T, which is the *number* of transactions that occur over some stated time period, say, one year, and a value part, P, which is the average *price* at which these transactions take place. We can now express the demand for money in the following equation:

$$M_d = kPT. \qquad (1)$$

In this equation, M_d is the demand for money, PT is the annual money value of transactions, and k is the fraction of this value required to be held in transaction balances. It should be noted that we have now related the amount of money held in balances, M_d, which is a stock, to the money value of transactions, which is a flow.[3] The job is done

3. One of the trickiest problems in monetary theory is to distinguish between stocks and flows (see pages 37–38) and to discover relations between stocks of money and assets on the one hand and flows of expenditure on the other.

by the humble little k, which seems so insignificant but which actually is so powerful. The hypothesis that the cash balances one needs to hold are some fraction of the annual value of transactions creates a link between the stock of money and the flow of income.

Next we assume that the supply of money is an exogenous constant determined by the central authorities. To show this, we write:

$$M_s = \overline{M}, \qquad (2)$$

where M_s is the supply of money and $\overline{M}$ is some constant amount (measured in dollars). Equation (2) merely says that the supply of money does not depend on any other factors in the economy; it is simply what the central authorities want it to be.

In equilibrium, it is necessary that the supply of money should equal the demand for it. Thus we can write as an equilibrium condition

$$M_d = M_s. \qquad (3)$$

When (3) holds, households and firms will have just the amount of money balances they require. When (3) does not hold, they will have too much or too little money, and we expect them to try to do something about it.

EXCESS DEMAND FOR MONEY
AND AGGREGATE DEMAND
FOR COMMODITIES

The second basic assumption of the quantity theory is the one we have already mentioned: Differences between demand for and supply of money bring about changes in aggregate demand; if the supply of money exceeds the demand, firms and households will try to spend their excess money on goods and services, and this raises aggregate demand; if the demand for money exceeds the existing supply, households and firms will cut down on their purchases of goods and services in order to build up their balances of money. This will reduce aggregate demand.[4]

VELOCITY AND BALANCES

The equilibrium condition in (3) above says demand for money must equal supply of money. If we substitute into equation (3) our theories about what determines the demand for money, equation (1), and the supply of money, equation (2), we obtain

$$kPT = \overline{M}, \qquad (4)$$

which says that, in order that the demand for money should equal its supply in equilibrium, the fixed stock of money ($\overline{M}$) should be a fraction, k, of the annual money value of transactions, PT.

In many treatments, equation (4) is not used. Instead of dealing with (4), k is inverted and called the velocity of circulation. Let us see how this is done. Take (4) and divide both sides by k to give equation (5):

$$PT = \frac{1}{k} \cdot \overline{M}. \qquad (5)$$

Next, as a simple matter of terminology, let us use the symbol V to stand for $\frac{1}{k}$. This gives us equation (6):

$$PT = VM. \qquad (6)$$

---

4. In the terminology of Part IX, an excess demand for money creates a withdrawal from the income stream. Firms and households save some of the money that they receive in order to increase their cash holdings. An excess supply of money creates an injection. Firms and households receive and spend their extra money, which is an addition to their expenditure made from current incomes.

It makes no difference whether we work with (4) or with (6). In (4), we have k on the left-hand side of the equation; in (6), we have $\frac{1}{k}$ ($= V$) on the right-hand side. Although it is as simple as that, we have to be very careful about the way in which we interpret V and k.

In order to see what is involved, consider a simple example. Assume that 6 million transactions occur each year at an average price of $2 per transaction, making an annual value of transactions of $12 million. Assume that k is $\frac{1}{12}$ ($= .0833$) so that desired money holdings are $\frac{1}{12}$ of the annual value of transactions and that the total quantity of money in existence is $1 million. This economy is in monetary equilibrium, since the demand for money is equal to its supply, as is shown by substituting the following values into equation (4):

$$\overline{M} = \$1 \text{ million}$$
$$P = \$2$$
$$T = 6 \text{ million}$$
$$k = .0833.$$

If we now replace k by V, we obtain $V = 12$; substituting into equation (6), we also find, of course, that the economy is in equilibrium. We now see that V must be interpreted as the average number of times that a unit of money changes hands in order to effect the total value of transactions. In our present economy, the typical unit of money must have changed hands 12 times in order that $12 million worth of trade could be done with a money stock of $1 million.[5] Thus we give the

name *velocity of circulation* to V. V tells us the average number of times each unit of money must have changed hands in order that a given annual volume of business could be accomplished.

DISEQUILIBRIUM BEHAVIOR

Now consider what happens to an economy not in equilibrium. Assume that, in the above example, the money supply is increased to $2 million. Firms and households now have more money than they wish to hold and, according to the assumptions of the theory, they try to spend the extra on goods and services. If we make the simplifying assumption that the economy is completely employed so that no more can be produced, then all that can happen is that prices will rise.[6] Transactions will remain constant at 2 million and prices will rise. As long as the price level remains below $4, firms and households will be trying to spend some of their balances, which means that they will be spending in excess of their incomes. This continues the upward pressure on national income. Once the price level has doubled (so that in our numerical example the average price of all transactions is $4), all the money will be required for transactions balances, the demand for money will equal its supply, and the economy will again be in equilibrium. This can be seen by substituting the new set of values into equations (4) and (6):

$$\overline{M} = \$2 \text{ million}$$
$$P = \$4$$
$$T = 6 \text{ million}$$
$$k = .0833 \ (= \tfrac{1}{12})$$
$$V = 12.$$

5. For another example, turn to Chapter 45, pages 525–526. It should help considerably to reread the first few pages of Chapter 45 at this point.

6. We assume, that is, that we are at the full-employment point on the L-shaped curve of Figure 1.

THE PREDICTIONS OF THE QUANTITY THEORY

So far we have made three basic assumptions: first, that the supply of money is exogenously determined; second, that the desired ratio of cash holdings to transactions, k, is a constant; and, third, that disequilibrium situations with respect to demand for and supply of money cause disequilibria in the market for goods and services. If we make one further assumption, we can develop a simple quantity theory. This assumption is that the economy is always fully employed so that T remains constant at the level of transactions appropriate to full employment.[7] Thus changes in aggregate demand affect only prices.

These assumptions now give rise to the most famous prediction of the quantity theory: Changes in the quantity of money will induce exactly proportional changes in prices. To derive this prediction, take equation (4), which expresses the condition for monetary equilibrium,

$$kPT = \overline{M}, \qquad (4)$$

and divide both sides by kT to obtain

$$P = \frac{\overline{M}}{kT}. \qquad (7)$$

Since k and T are constant, we see that, in equilibrium, M and P must vary in proportion to each other.†

Thus any given percentage change in M will, according to this theory, cause an equal percentage change in P. Furthermore, as long as M is clearly determined exogenously by, say, the supply of gold (under the gold standard), the direction of causation is clear: Variations in M cause the variations in P, not vice versa.

The predictions of the quantity theory have been applied to two somewhat different sets of circumstances: long-term changes in the price level, where the problem is to predict changes from one decade to the next over a span of anything from fifty to several hundred years, and short-term changes in the price level, where the problem is to predict changes from year to year (or even from month to month) over a span of, say, five or ten years. Each of these applications raises its own characteristic problems, which we now consider in turn.

THE QUANTITY THEORY APPLIED TO LONG-TERM CHANGES IN THE PRICE LEVEL

The long-term application of the quantity theory is based on a number of behavioral assumptions: (1) T is determined by the economic growth of the economy; changes in T due to growth are large relative to those caused by temporary lapses from full employment, thus T can be taken to be exogenously growing at the long-term growth rate, which will be around 2 or 3 percent per year for the typical Western society; (2) although V can vary from year to year, it is a trend-free variable (i.e., we hypothesize that its average expected value in the 1950s is the same as it was in the 1850s);[8] (3) variations in the money supply were (until very recent times)

---

7. For one justification of this assumption, see Chapter 56, pages 679–680.

† One can write $P = a\overline{M}$, where $a = \dfrac{1}{kT}$.

8. This formulation is more restrictive than is necessary. We do expect V to change in the long-run because of various institutional shifts such as changes in the pay period. These changes, however, will be occasional, discrete, exogenous, and easily identifiable.

exogenously determined because the money supply was linked to the gold supply by the requirement of convertibility. Thus, T can be determined, V can be predicted (with an ascertainable margin of error) to be constant, and P will be observed to vary directly with M. Therefore, our theory states that

$$MV = PT,$$

where V is a constant, M is the exogenously determined stock of money, and variations in T are determined by the economic growth of the economy.

There is considerable favorable evidence linking long-term trend changes in the price level to trend changes in the quantity of money. Four of the most dramatic cases may be mentioned. During the period when the Spanish were importing gold and silver from the New World, a major increase in the quantity of money occurred followed by a major rise in prices. The influx of gold caused a great rise in spending without any corresponding increase in output; therefore, prices rose. The first two-thirds of the nineteenth century was a period of rapid economic growth in Europe and America, but it was a period in which the money supply did not expand rapidly because the world's gold supply was rising only slightly. Thus T was growing faster than M, and the theory predicts that a downward pressure should have been exerted on prices. That such a downward pressure did occur is clearly observable in the price levels of most of the world's major countries. Later in the nineteenth century, gold strikes in America, Canada, and South Africa brought a more rapid increase in the money supply, and the price level responded, as the theory predicted it would. After World Wars I and II, the governments of several countries found themselves unwilling to

raise by taxes the money they were committed to spending. Large budget deficits occurred, which they financed by borrowing from the central bank, which in turn created the requisite amounts of new money. Very rapid increases in the money supply ensued that were immediately followed by the effects predicted by the quantity theory. Many such periods have been documented, and they provide impressive evidence of the close link between major changes in the quantity of money and major changes in the price level.

THE QUANTITY THEORY APPLIED TO SHORT-TERM CHANGES IN THE PRICE LEVEL

The major problem in using the quantity theory to predict the short-term behavior of the price level is that the actual velocity at which money circulates varies. We must be very careful to distinguish here between the actual and the desired velocity of circulation. The V that we have been speaking of so far has been the desired V based on the desired ratio of cash holdings to transactions (desired k). *For any economy whatsoever, there will be a velocity that relates the observed money stock to the observed value of transactions.* If we say that V^* is the observed velocity of circulation and that $k^*(= \dfrac{1}{V^*})$ is the observed ratio of money in the economy to the value of transaction, we can write

$$k^*PT \equiv \overline{M}, \qquad (4^*)$$

and
$$PT \equiv V^*\overline{M}. \qquad (6^*)$$

The identity sign is used here because these relations are necessarily true; they always hold by virtue of the way in which k^* and V^* have been defined. For example, if we observe an economy in which $PT = \$1$ billion and $\overline{M} = \$100$ million, then we say that observed $V^* = 10$ or observed $k^* = .1$. If, for this economy, $\overline{M}$ increases to $200 million and nothing else happens, we merely say that V^* has fallen to 5 or k^* has risen to .2, which is the same thing. Expressions (4^*) and (6^*) do not constitute a theory of money and prices; they are true by definition and do not allow us to predict anything about the economy.

To have a theory of prices we need a theory about desired V (or k). This is what the simple quantity theory provides by hypothesizing that desired k is a constant, and this gives rise to the prediction that in equilibrium a change in the quantity of money will cause a proportional change in the price level. The observed variability of V^* from year to year refutes this simple quantity theory. We cannot predict the relation between changes in M and changes in P because we cannot assume that V^* will remain constant from one year to the next, even though its average value may be constant from one decade to the next.

There is, however, another possibility. We may accept the short-run variability of V^* and develop a theory that predicts how it will vary by linking desired k (and hence desired V) to other observable quantities in the economy. As long as we have a theory that predicts how actual V^* will change, we can predict changes in P on the basis of changes in M, since we know what to expect V^* to do. Seen in this light, the simple theory that V is constant is just a special case of the more general class of quantity theories, all of which attempt to link changes in M to changes in P and all of which require, in order to do this, a theory of the behavior of V.

Some economists have tried recently to restore the quantity theory on these lines by developing a theory of how V changes. They have hypothesized that V changes in a predictable fashion because it is a function of certain observable economic variables.[9] According to these economists, the quantity theory will be useful in predicting the short-run behavior of prices because short-run changes in V will themselves prove to be predictable. Evidence is still being gathered on this sophisticated attempt to restore the quantity theory as *the* general theory of the price level, but it is still too early to say how successful the attempt will prove to be.

We may summarize our discussion of the quantity theory as follows: (1) The theory that states that long-run movements in the price level can be explained by changes in the quantity of money has stood up to testing. (2) The theory that states that short-run movements in the price level can be associated with changes in the quantity of money because V is reasonably stable has not stood up to testing. (3) The theory that states that short-run changes in the price level can be associated with changes in M and *predictable changes* in V is at present the subject of debate and testing.

THE KEYNESIAN THEORY OF MONEY

The Keynesian theory of money diverges in two critical ways from the quantity theory. The Keynesian theory accepts that the demand for money depends partly on the value of transactions, but it adds that it also de

9. Professor Milton Friedman of the University of Chicago is the champion of this attempt.

pends on the rate of interest (see Figure 1(ii) in Chapter 54).

We have already mentioned the second basic assumption of the Keynesian theory concerning how firms and households behave when the demand for money does not equal supply. In the quantity theory, firms and households alter their expenditure on goods and services; in the Keynesian theory, they alter their behavior in the market for monetary assets. If the demand for money exceeds its supply, people try to sell bonds, thus adding to their stocks of cash. If the supply of money exceeds its demand, people try to buy bonds with their excess stocks of cash. It is, of course, quite possible for one individual to adjust his money holdings by dealings in the bond market. But all individuals cannot do this simultaneously unless the total supplies of money and bonds vary. If they do not vary, we get a situation in the bond market analogous to the one that arises under the quantity theory when conditions of full employment in the goods market prevail. If the quantity of bonds is pretty well fixed, then variations in the demand for bonds can only affect their price. In the quantity theory, it is the price level of goods and services that is affected when the demand for money does not equal its supply; in the Keynesian theory, it is the price level of bonds.

Consider this point in more detail. If a single firm is short of cash balances, it can sell some of its monetary assets and immediately replenish its stocks of cash. On the other hand, if the firm has excess stocks of cash, it can invest these forthwith by buying bonds or other assets on the open market. If everyone tries to do this simultaneously, it will not be possible unless the stocks of money or bonds change. If the stocks of money and bonds are fixed, then general attempts to add to or subtract from bond holdings will only succeed in altering their price. Assume, for example, that all firms and households are short of cash. They all try to sell bonds in order to add to their cash holdings. This causes the price of bonds to fall. A fall in the price of bonds is the same thing (as we have already seen) as a rise in the rate of interest. As the rate of interest rises, people will try to economize on cash holdings; they will also tend to reduce speculative balances of cash, since bonds now seem like very good investments. Eventually, the rate will rise high enough so that people will no longer be trying to add to their cash balances. The demand for money will again equal supply. There will no longer be an excess supply of bonds, so the interest rate will stop changing. The net effect of the original excess demand for money will have been an increase in the rate of interest. *Aggregate demand will be affected only insofar as consumption or investment is affected by the change in the interest rate.*

Now consider a case in which people have too much cash. They decide to spend the excess on buying bonds; if everyone tries to do this, however, they will force the price of bonds up (i.e., force the interest rate down). When this happens, people are prepared to hold more cash, both because the opportunity cost of doing so is reduced and because bonds now look like a bad buy, so that people will hold large speculative hoards of cash in expectation of more favorable bond prices in the future.

Thus, according to the Keynesian theory, a monetary policy that expands the money supply does not lead to any direct increase in aggregate demand, as it does in the quantity theory; it leads only to a fall in the interest rate until everyone is prepared to hold the expanded supply of money. Any effect on aggregate demand occurs insofar as investment or consumption expenditure responds to the change in interest rates.

EVALUATION

In the quantity theory, a shortage of money causes firms and households to try to replenish cash stocks by not spending all the money they receive. Thus an excess demand for cash causes aggregate demand for goods and services to fall. In the Keynesian theory, an excess demand for cash causes firms and households to try to replenish their cash balances by selling bonds. This causes the rate of interest to rise (the price of bonds to fall) and affects demand for goods and services only insofar as demand for consumption and investment goods is sensitive to changes in the rate of interest.

The determinants of the demand for money and the effects on the economy of monetary disequilibrium have both been studied intensively. Many of the problems are beyond an elementary treatment of the subject. There does, however, seem to be ample evidence that the demand for money is influenced both by the value of transactions (which is directly related to the level of income) and by the rate of interest. On the effects of monetary disequilibrium, the studies do not seem to support either of the extreme views. To some extent, both the goods and the bond markets seem to be affected when firms and households have either too little or too much cash. If there is an excess supply of cash in the system, there does appear to be an increase both in the demand for bonds and in the demand for goods and services, and if there is an excess demand, there appears to be a reduction in the demands both for goods and services and for bonds. The continuance of the present debate about the effectiveness of monetary policy as a tool of short-run control of the economy reflects the fact that, although neither extreme position can be held, we are not yet sure where the balance lies between them. Is the bulk of the impact of an increase in the quantity of money felt in the market for goods and services or in the market for bonds, and how fast is each effect felt? Here we must wait and see; and here we must recognize that the results of a current debate on practical economic policy turn on future academic work on how the economy behaves in response to changes in the monetary sector.

Summary

1. In examining the relation between the quantity of money and the price level, it is convenient to consider it in two stages: the effect of the quantity of money on aggregate demand, and the effect of aggregate demand on price levels.

2. Two theories of the relation between the level of demand and the rate of inflation are considered. The evidence at present goes against the L-shaped relation and favors the curved one, in which changes in demand affect both the level of activity and the rate of inflation. The higher the level of activity, the more will the effect of a further increase in demand be felt on prices and the less will it be felt on output and employment.

3. The major policy implications of the favored theory is that controlling inflation and maintaining the highest possible level of employment are conflicting objectives. It is always possible, however, to raise output and cut unemployment a bit more at the cost of more inflation.

4. To discuss the relation between money and the level of demand in the economy, we again considered two theories: the quantity theory and the Keynesian theory.

5. In the quantity theory, the demand for money depends on the level of income; the supply of money is an exogenous variable, and excess demand for, or supply of, money causes excess supply or demand in the markets for goods and services. The theory predicts that the price level will change in proportion to changes in the quantity of money.

6. In the Keynesian theory, the demand for money depends on the level of income and the rate of interest. The supply of money is exogenous, and an excess demand for, or supply of, money causes changes in the offers to buy or sell in the bond market.

7. In evaluating the two theories, we note that there does seem to be ample evidence that the demand for money is influenced both by the value of transactions and by the rate of interest. We also note that there is considerable evidence linking long-run changes in the price level with changes in the quantity of money. The studies of the effects of monetary disequilibrium do not seem to support either extreme view. Markets for bonds and markets for goods and services both seem to be affected when there is an excess demand for, or supply of, money. We are not yet sure where between the two positions the balance lies; so, the debate about the short-run effectiveness of monetary policy continues.

QUESTIONS FOR DISCUSSION

1. In 1952, two British economists wrote that "the only practical alternative to recurrent general unemployment is persistent inflationary pressure." On what theory were they relying for this prediction? How could such a theory be tested?

2. "The sole cause of inflation is increases in the supply of money." Does this assertion conform with the predictions of any of the theories we have studied in this chapter? What observations would refute this assertion?

3. What are the different behavioral assumptions of the quantity and the Keynesian theories? What predictions are made by each? Which predictions are in conflict?

4. In what way can the quantity theory be stated so that it is compatible with all states of the universe? Since, in this form, it can never be proved false, why might we wish to change it? What changes will make it into a testable (i.e., falsifiable) theory?

5. The Revolutionary War was financed to a great extent by increases in the money supply, rather than by increases in taxes. What does the quantity theory predict must have happened to the price level at that time? Check this prediction against the facts as stated in any history book.

6. "A change in the value of money, that is to say in the level of prices, is important to Society only in so far as its incidence is unequal," declared John Maynard Keynes in an essay written in 1932. Do you agree? Explain carefully.

7. An editorial in the London *Times* in April,

1960, asserted that even mild inflations must be prevented, because "they will rot everything in the end." What do you think the writer of the editorial might have had in mind? Assuming that you could formulate it in a precise enough fashion as to be interesting, how would you go about testing this view? (Hint: Look again at Table 1, page 660.)

9. Almost all wars in history have been accompanied by major increases in the price levels of the belligerent countries. Given this observation, what does the quantity theory predict about the method of financing wars that has usually been adopted? Check this prediction against the available evidence on a few selected wars.

APPENDIX TO CHAPTER 55 MICROECONOMIC IMPLICATIONS OF VARIOUS AGGREGATE RELATIONS BETWEEN DEMAND AND PRICES

ONE OF THE BASIC POSTULATES of economics is that decisions are made by firms and households and that any observed or hypothesized behavior must be capable of being traced back to decisions made at this microeconomic level. (See page 519.) In this appendix, we shall briefly consider what behavior of individual markets is implied by the relations we have been considering. The theory of the L-shaped relation has implications about behavior at the microeconomic level that we need to notice. To study the first relation, turn back to Figure 1 in Chapter 55. Concentrate on the band along the X axis, which indicates that a zero rate of change of prices is associated with anything less than full employment of resources. This indicates that the price level does not fall even when the percentage of resource utilization falls to a very low level. The micro implication of this is that excess supply does not cause price to fall in

any single market of the economy. To see this, consider a situation in which aggregate demand is so low that there is excess supply in all markets. In this case, no individual price would be rising and if some prices were falling then the whole price level would also be falling. Thus we see that the assumption that the *price level* does not fall implies that price does not fall in any individual market when there is excess supply. The second implication concerns the possibility of the economy existing at a point such as f (where there is a kink in the curve) where full employment is combined with a stable price level. Full employment implies that there is no excess supply in any markets; a constant price level (combined with the previous implication that prices never fall) implies that there is no excess demand in any market. Thus each and every market in the economy must be in equilibrium when the economy is at

the point of full employment without inflation indicated by f in the figure. To see this, imagine the economy starting at a point of heavy unemployment with excess supply in all markets. Now, consider an increase in aggregate demand that causes a rightward shift in the demand curve in each individual market. The theory we are considering implies that expansion of demand occurs in such a way that excess supply decreases equally in each market, for, if it did not, then the price level would begin to rise before full employment had been reached. Indeed, it must rise as soon as excess demand occurs in some market. Clearly, the microeconomic relations for the L-shaped curve are very special ones.

There are two microeconomic implications that follow from the relation shown in Figure 2 in Chapter 55. First, notice that the relation implies that prices do fall in individual markets when there is excess supply.

The macroeconomic relation states that the price level does fall when aggregate demand, and hence the degree of resource utilization, is very low. If the average level of prices is to fall, then at least some individual prices must be falling. Some price rigidities are possible; though it is not necessary that all prices should fall when there is excess supply, it is necessary that some should.

The second implication concerns the relation *among* individual markets when the percentage utilization of resources is high. To see what is involved, consider an economy with such a low level of aggregate demand that there is excess supply in each and every market. Now consider an expansion in aggregate demand that raises the over-all percentage utilization of resources. The rise in aggregate demand will mean a rightward shift in the demand curve in each individual market. These shifts reduce excess supply and raise output and employment in each part of the economy. As aggregate demand goes on increasing, excess demand will develop in some market and price will begin to rise in that market. This will happen while there is still excess supply in other markets. As aggregate demand goes on increasing, more and more markets will begin to develop excess demand. In everyday language, we might say that bottlenecks and shortages be-

gin to develop in some parts of the economy. Eventually, prices will be rising in enough markets to offset the effects of price reductions in other markets, so that the average level of prices will begin to rise. As long as excess supply exists in any market, the level of resource utilization can be increased (i.e., the level of unemployment lowered) by raising aggregate demand. But the more markets there are in which excess demand already exists, the more any further rise in demand will serve merely to increase excess demands in these markets (and so speed up the rate of inflation) and the less it will serve to reduce excess supplies in other markets (and so increase the level of resource use). Thus, the higher the level of aggregate demand, the greater the effect on price and the less the effect on employment of yet further increases in demand. We see, therefore, that the microeconomic implication of the relation of Figure 2 is that markets are not in a state of perfect equilibrium relative to each other. To make the theory work, it is necessary that markets should be in a state such that excess supplies could exist in some markets while excess demands exist in others. Should we be surprised by this? No, not as long as the economy is subject to the kinds of changes that necessarily accompany economic growth.

As productivity grows, some

supplies expand faster than other supplies, and as real incomes grow, some demands expand faster than other demands. Except in the most unlikely of circumstances, we would expect these changes to bring about a reallocation of resources. Since such changes do not happen instantaneously, we would expect some markets to be exhibiting excess supplies while other markets exhibit excess demands.[1] Because demand and supply curves are shifting continuously, due to the reasons mentioned above, and because adjustments take time to accomplish, we would never expect all markets to be in equilibrium simultaneously. If the theory of price is correct, we do expect that prices will work as a mechanism to direct resources to where demand is greatest so that there is a continual movement in the direction of equilibrium, but since the equilibrium values are themselves always changing, we never expect equilibrium to exist simultaneously in all markets. Thus we should not really be surprised that the empirical evidence at the macro level refutes the idea of the L-shaped curve shown in Figure 1 and supports the idea of the smooth curve shown in Figure 2. Indeed, the micro implications of the L-shaped curve are so special that it would upset many of our ideas of micro relations in the economy if the L-shaped curve were observed at the macro level.

---

1. This point is elaborated in Chapter 56. It was also discussed at some length in relation to the long-term problems of agriculture in Chapter 11.

ECONOMIC
GROWTH &
ECONOMIC
DEVELOPMENT

Chapter **56** ECONOMIC GROWTH

TURN BACK TO PAGE 543 AND STUDY FIGURE A2 again. What you cannot help noticing is the dramatic growth that has characterized the American economy since 1929. The growth experience of the United Kingdom, Japan, the Soviet Union, Germany, France, Italy, Holland, and indeed for most Western countries, is strikingly similar. These countries' peoples comprise about 20 percent of the world's population. For the rest of the world, for China, India, and most of Africa and South America, a history of growth is singularly absent over the same period of time. In this chapter and the next, we discuss the nature of economic growth, its causes and its consequences.

Aggregate Demand and Aggregate Supply

The *productive capacity* of an economy is defined as the gross national product that can be produced when all of the economy's resources are fully employed. In Parts IX and X we concentrated on *short-term* changes in national product. We developed a circular-flow theory by taking as given the economy's productive capacity and by concentrating on fluctuations in the *demand* for goods and services. Such demand-induced variations in income lead, we found, to variations in either employment or prices or both. We now wish to consider *long-term* changes in national income and other macro variables. These changes are mainly associated with the changes in the productive capacity of the economy rather than with changes in the demand.

The difference between the subject of Parts IX and X and the subject of Part XI, Growth and Development, can be illustrated by considering investment expenditure. One of the critical variables in the circular-flow theory developed in the earlier parts is the level of investment. Variations in investment expenditure cause variations in employment in the investment industries, variations in the incomes of households employed by these industries, and variations in the expenditures of these households. These variations, through the action of the multiplier, cause further variations in national production and in total employment. In that analysis, we concentrated on the effects of investment expenditure on *aggregate demand*.

It is important to remember, however, that investment expenditure will, after a lapse of time of anywhere between one and five years, also affect *aggregate supply*. Variations in the productive capacity of a country will be affected by changes in both the quantity and the quality of the capital stock available. Such variations are brought about through investment expenditure. Once new capital is built, installed, and put in operation, the effect of investment is to raise the productive capacity of the country—i.e., to raise the level of full-employment aggregate supply. In the theory of growth, we concentrate on the long-term effects that investment expenditure has on aggregate supply just as, in the theory of the circular flow, we concentrated on the short-term effects that investment expenditure has on aggregate demand.

Because the productive capacity of a country changes slowly, it is possible, when considering variations in income over a few years, to ignore such changes. When considering longer-run changes—over ten, twenty, or fifty years, say—we cannot ignore changes in productive capacity. Indeed, the longer the period of our interest, the more important is productive capacity and the less important is the degree of utilization of that capacity.

Growth Rates: Some Sources of Popular Confusion

The distinction we have made between the causes of short-term and long-term variations in income should be clear enough. It is, however, often overlooked in practical discussions about the growth performance of a particular economy. If one looks at the growth in national income of an economy over three or four years, it will be the net effect of two distinct changes: changes in the productive capacity and changes in the percentage utili-

zation of this capacity. If there have been large changes in the latter, we will observe very high rates of increase in national income, but these rates will not be sustainable once capacity is being 100 percent utilized.

A great deal of confusion would be avoided if the term growth rate were used to refer only to the growth rate of productive capacity, and if comparisons of national-income figures for one country over several years were divided into two parts: changes due to the growth rate, and changes due to variations in the employment of productive capacity. Even when we eliminate the problem of variations in the percentage utilization of capacity, there are a number of related concepts among which it is important to distinguish.

Part of any increase in the money value of full-employment output is due to a rise in prices rather than to a rise in output. If we are concerned with variations in a country's capacity to produce goods and services, then we must try to remove the effect of price changes from our calculations. If, for example, the level of a country's income rises from $1,000 million to $2,200 million while at the same time the average level of prices doubles, we would say that *money* national income has increased 120 percent, but that *real* national income has increased by 10 percent, since, if we value the new output at the original set of prices, it would only be worth $1,100. In everything that follows, we are concerned with variations in real national income, which is money national income corrected for changes in the average level of prices.

Even when we are dealing with variations in real national income, we may have to concern ourselves with a number of different but related concepts: the total amount of output, the total output per person in the total population, total output per person employed, and total output per hour worked. As an example of the relations between these concepts, note that a doubling of real national income combined with a doubling of the population would mean no change in per capita income in spite of a large change in total income. Very often

we are more concerned with per capita income than with total income. If we are thinking of living standards, we are certainly concerned with per capita income. The average living standard of a country depends on real income per head of population. The growth in real income per head, however, is likely to understate the growth in productive capacity for at least two reasons. First, as standards of living rise, the proportion of the population actually employed will tend to fall as training periods are extended, as retirement age is reduced, and as every member of the family does not find it necessary to work in order to provide subsistence for the household. Thus, national income per head of population may rise more slowly than income per head of working population because a progressively smaller portion of the population is actually working. Second, as national income rises, those who are working may work fewer hours, taking part of their increase in living standards in terms of an increase in leisure. If this occurs, we should expect the rise in national income per head of employed population to be less than the rise in national income per hour worked by the labor force.

The rise in real national income per hour worked by the labor force shows the rise in the capacity to produce goods and services through human effort and is called a rise in *labor productivity;* the rise in national income per head of population shows the rise in the actual goods and services produced per person. When we are speaking of economic growth in this book, we mean the rise in the productive capacity of a country on a per capita basis.

The Cumulative Nature of Growth

One of the most important aspects of economic growth is that it is cumulative. If one country grows faster than another, the gap in their living standards will widen progressively.[1] By way of contrast, if one country has a less efficient allocation of resources than another, the gap between their national incomes will not widen progressively on this account. Let us assume that, for one reason or another, country A uses its resources 5 percent less efficiently than does country B. On this count, therefore, the real national income of A will always be 5 percent below that of B. If, on the other hand, country A uses its resources so that it grows 5 percent faster than does B, then the gap in incomes will widen progressively. If the two countries start from the same income, and B grows at 5 percent per year and A grows at $5\frac{1}{4}$ percent (i.e., A's growth rate is

TABLE 1   **EFFECT OF DIFFERENT RATES OF GROWTH**[a]

Year	Percentage rate of growth per year				
	1	2	3	5	7
0	100	100	100	100	100
10	110	122	134	163	197
30	135	181	243	432	761
50	164	269	438	1,147	2,946
70	201	400	792	3,043	11,399
100	270	724	1,922	13,150	86,772

[a] National income in year 0 equals 100.

TABLE 2   **AVERAGE GROWTH RATES IN REAL NATIONAL INCOME, 1953–1962**

	Percentage rate of growth of per capita national income	Year in which U.S. will be overtaken, should the growth rates in Column 1 persist
Japan	8.4	1995
Yugoslavia	6.5	2048
Germany	5.5	2005
Italy	5.4	2025
Austria	5.4	2065
France	3.6	2045
Denmark	3.3	2154
Mexico	3.1	2134
Netherlands	3.1	2142
Venezuela	2.7	2235
Belgium	2.4	2236
U.K.	2.1	2139
Philippines	1.8	2590
Turkey	1.1	5735
Canada[a]	1.1	4366
U.S.A.[a]	1.0	—

SOURCE: Calculated from the *U.N. Statistical Yearbook*, 1963.

[a] The growth rate for the U.S. and Canada is understated because 1953 was a year of high activity and a high percentage utilization of resources, whereas 1962 was a year of low activity and a lower percentage utilization of resources. The growth in full-employment productive capacity was probably closer to 2 percent per year over the decade than to 1 percent. Even this rate is very low by international standards; if it grows at this rate, the U.S. will not for long maintain its position as the country with the highest standard of living in the world.

1. If the faster growing country starts from a lower level of income than the slower growing one, the gap will at first narrow; it will widen only after the former has overtaken the latter.

5 percent greater than B's), then in 10 years A's income will be 2.5 percent higher than B's; in 50 years it will be 12.2 percent higher, and in 301 years it will be *double* B's. Such are the long-range effects of tiny differences in percentage rates of growth. If we now pick figures closer to currently observed rates of growth, the comparison becomes even more striking. Consider two countries starting with the same level of income, but having different rates of growth. If A grows at 3 percent while B grows at 2 percent per year, A's income will be twice B's in 72 years. You may not think it matters much whether we grow at 2 percent or 3 percent, but your grandchildren will. Table 1 shows the dramatic effect of different rates of growth on levels of income.

Table 2 shows the average rates of growth of real national income in a number of countries during the period 1953–1962. In many ways, this was an unusual period, dominated as it was by the recovery of so many countries from the devastating effects of World War II. In order to illustrate the powerful long-run effects of observed differences in growth rates, we have given, in Column 2, the year in which each of the countries will pass the per capita national income of the United States *if* the growth rates of the decade should continue indefinitely.

Growth as a Goal of Policy

Great concern is often expressed over rates of growth. For many countries, a high rate of growth is an important policy goal, and the performance of different economies is often compared by comparing their growth rates, the one that is growing fastest being regarded as the most successful. It is probably true that, *ceteris paribus*, the majority of people would regard a fast rate of growth as preferable to a slow one, but policy goals are seldom obtained without cost. If a faster rate of growth is only obtainable at a sacrifice in terms of *present* living standards, it becomes a matter of choice as to how much present sacrifice it is worth making to obtain some specified future gain. In these circumstances, the best policy (in terms of what individuals want most) is unlikely to be the one that secures the fastest rate of growth. In fact, it is unlikely that anyone would want the very fastest rate of growth that could be achieved by sacrificing all other goals and pursuing growth at all costs. The question then is not "How can we grow as fast as possible?" It is, rather, "What are the benefits of growth and what are the costs?"

Economic growth is a means of achieving various objectives. One primary reason for desiring growth is to raise the general living standards of the population. A country whose per capita output is growing at 3 percent per year is doubling its living standards every 24 years.

The extreme importance of economic growth in raising income can be emphasized by comparing the real income of a father with the real income of the son who follows in his father's footsteps. If the son neither rises nor falls in the relative income scale compared with his father, then his share of the country's national income will be the same as his father's. If the son is 30 years younger than his father, then he can expect to have a real income about twice as large as that which his father enjoyed when his father was the same age. These figures assume that the father and son live in a country such as the United States, where the growth rate is in the neighborhood of 2 percent per year. If they live in Japan, where growth has been going on at a rate of more than 8 percent per year, the son's income will be about 10 times as large as his father's: From the point of view of raising the absolute living standards of the poorer sections of the community, growth is clearly more important than the redistribution of income. A redistribution of the sort that seems practicable might cause a maximum, once-and-for-all rise in the incomes of lower income groups of, say, 10 percent. The same rise would be accomplished in about three years with economic growth of 3 percent per year. Of course, not everyone benefits equally from growth, and many of those who are poorest will be out of the labor force and thus least likely to share in the higher wages that are the primary means by which the gains from growth are distributed. Thus, redistributional policies may be required even in a growing economy. But growth makes it much more

feasible politically to do something about poverty. If existing income is to be redistributed, then someone's standard of living will actually have to be lowered. If, however, there is economic growth and if the increment in income is redistributed (through government intervention), then it is possible to reduce income inequalities without actually having to lower anyone's income. It is much easier for a rapidly growing economy to be generous toward its less fortunate citizens—or neighbors—than it is for a static one to do so.

A further reason for wanting growth may arise out of the problems of national defense. If your country is competing with another for power or prestige, then rates of growth are important. If your national income is growing at 2 percent while the "enemy's" is growing at 3 percent, then all he has to do is to wait while your relative strength dwindles. Khrushchev had this in mind when he said, "We will bury you." Also, the expenses of an arms race, or a space race, are easier to bear, the faster the country is growing.

The Causes of Growth

Our knowledge on this subject is far from complete, but there is substantial agreement that certain things have marked effects on the growth of an economy's productive capacity. The cause of growth traditionally emphasized by economists is capital accumulation. If the state of knowledge remains constant and some of the society's resources are devoted to new investment, then more and more capital equipment can be accumulated. This capital will be productive in all sorts of ways, and it will have the effect of raising the productivity of labor and so will cause a rise in real national income. Eventually, if there is no growth of

knowledge, all the most productive investments will be used up, and, as capital accumulation continues, the marginal productivity of capital will decline and eventually will approach zero. In the meantime (which is likely to be a very long time), new capital will contribute to a rise in national income.

New knowledge and inventions also contribute markedly to the growth of national income. In order to see this, assume that the proportion of the society's resources devoted to the production of capital goods is just sufficient to replace capital as it wears out. Thus, if the old capital was merely replaced in the same form, the capital stock would be constant and there would be no increase in national income. Now assume, however, that there is a growth of knowledge so that, as old equipment wears out, it is replaced by different, more productive, equipment. In this case, national income will be growing because of the growth of knowledge rather than because of the accumulation of more and more capital.[2] This sort of increase in national income can come about either by advancing knowledge locally or by importing it. Underdeveloped countries can adapt techniques already used abroad but not in current use at home. Developed countries, which cannot often copy superior techniques from elsewhere, must develop new techniques by research and invention.

The causes of growth mentioned so far have concerned the quantity and quality of physical capital. What about human capital? The productivity of labor can be greatly increased by education and by improved health standards. The scope is greater the lower the existing standards.

Social habits also affect economic growth. Certain religious patterns, for instance, are more conducive to economic growth than are others.[3] It has been argued that the "Protestant ethic" encourages the acquisition of wealth and is thus more likely to encourage growth than is an attitude that directs activity away from the economic sphere. The student must beware of jumping to the conclusion that the social and religious structures should be changed so as to maximize the possibility of growth. Economists are interested in the existence of such relationships. If people derive satisfaction from living in a culture that does not produce growth, we cannot prove that they ought to alter their culture. All that we can say is that *if* they want growth, their culture is likely to inhibit it and that the goals and techniques of another culture are more likely to encourage it.

Legal institutions may likewise affect growth. The pattern of ownership of land and natural resources may greatly affect the way such resources are used, and thus may affect their productivity. To take but one example, if agricultural land is divided into very small parcels, one per family, it may be much more difficult to achieve the advantages of modern agriculture than if they are available for large-scale farming.[4] Many economists are thus concerned with patterns of *land tenure*. Here, too, we meet a conflict of values. If we value a society in which every man owns his own land, we may have to pay a price for it. In America, where land is relatively plentiful, the Jeffersonian ideal of the family farm is much less "expensive" than in, say, India, where land is scarce relative to the population. On the other hand, the concentration of land ownership in the hands of a few absentee landowners who are not concerned to maximize their profits can be detrimental to growth. If the landlord's holdings are so vast that he can obtain all the income he desires without using his land effectively, he may

---

2. We do not need to engage in a futile argument about whether the "quantity" of capital is constant in this case. When a worn-out piece of capital equipment is replaced by a physically different piece of equipment, the concept of the quantity of capital becomes a convention that may or may not be useful for the problem at hand. It is neither interesting nor profitable to argue whether the "real quantity" of capital has gone up or has remained constant when we all agree about what has actually happened in the world.

3. See, for example, R. H. Tawney, *Religion and the Rise of Capitalism: An Historical Study* (Holland Memorial Lectures, 1922 [London: Murray, 1926]). This work is also available in a New American Library paperback.

4. In many countries, collective farms appear to be more productive than the family farms they replaced.

have little motivation to introduce advanced techniques. In many societies where this system of land ownership obtains, land reform, which usually implies the confiscation, nationalization, or communization of land, becomes a necessary condition for growth. Not surprisingly, such reforms are seldom supported by existing governments, which tend to support the interests of the economically powerful. Land reform can often be accomplished only in the wake of a political revolution.

The Costs of Growth

In a world of scarcity, almost nothing is free. Growth usually requires an investment of resources in capital goods, in education, and in health. Such investments do not yield any *immediate* return in terms of goods and services for consumption. Growth, which promises more goods tomorrow, is achieved by consuming fewer goods today. For the economy as a whole, this is the primary cost of growth; we shall consider it in detail in a moment.

For many individuals, there is another and more personal set of costs of growth. If an economy is growing, it is also changing. Innovation leaves obsolete machines in its wake, and it also leaves partially obsolete people. A rapid rate of growth requires rapid adjustments, and these can cause much upset and misery to the individuals affected. The decline in the number of unskilled jobs makes the lot of the untrained worker much more difficult, and when he loses his job, he may well fail to find another, particularly if he is over fifty. No matter how well equipped you are at age twenty-five, in another twenty-five years you are likely to be partially obsolete. Many skills become completely outdated and unneeded. One aspect of this problem is called "structural unemployment," and we shall consider it later in this chapter.[5]

THE OPPORTUNITY COST OF GROWTH

Let us suppose that the central authorities of an economy can establish within limits the growth rate they desire by choosing the allocation of resources between the production of investment goods and consumption goods. Further, assume that the economy is a fully employed one. In this case, every dollar diverted to investment goods means that one dollar less can be spent on consumption goods. Figure 1 shows a production-possibility boundary summarizing the choices open to the economy. Assume the economy is initially producing at the point x, where the rate of annual consumption is Oa, and productive capacity is growing at 2 percent per year. This means that every year the production-possibility boundary will move out by 2 percent; if the economy continues to devote the same fraction of its resources to investment goods, the path of growth will be along the ray labeled "2 percent growth rate." In twenty years the economy will reach point x'.

5. Since this is a book about economics, we shall not discuss the noneconomic costs of growth, although they exist. Unspoiled landscapes become spoiled, the simpler life of family farming gives way to urbanization and slums, the frustrations of a complex and changing world harm some people, and so on.

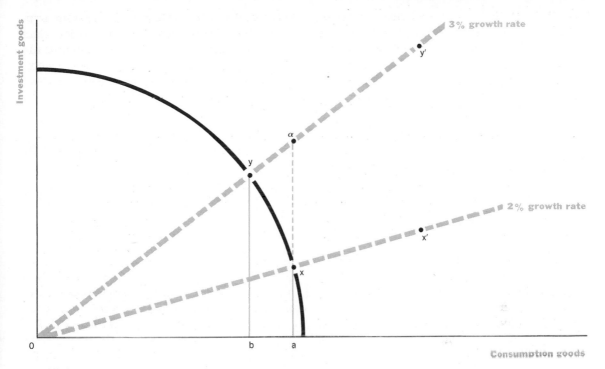

FIGURE 1

Should the central authorities be prepared to reduce the rate of consumption by the amount *ab* and increase the rate of investment, production would be shifted to point *y*. Since more investment goods are being produced, the growth rate will be increased. In this example, the rate of growth rises to 3 percent, and in twenty years the economy will be at point *y'*. The more rapid rate of growth is purchased at the expense of a lower rate of current consumption. Is it worth it?

To see the issues involved in answering this question, assume that, at point *x*, 15 percent of the country's resources were being devoted to investment goods and 85 percent to current consumption. To shift to point *y* would require devoting 23 percent to investment and only 77 percent to current consumption. How long will it take to regain the loss in consumption

if the shift to point *y* is made? This depends upon what one means by "regaining the loss." On the assumed figures, it takes only $3\frac{1}{3}$ years to reach point *a*, where consumption is again *Oa*. Thus the actual reduction in living standards lasts only $3\frac{1}{3}$ years. Of course, had the reallocation of resources not occurred, income would have expanded along the 2 percent growth path and, thus, although the actual cut is restored in less than 4 years, consumption is still well below what it would have been if the reallocation in favor of investment had not occurred. In fact, it takes 10 years for the actual level of consumption to catch up to what it would have been had no reallocation been made. This is seen more clearly in Figure 2, where we chart the two growth paths over time: After ten years the growth paths cross. But the economy has

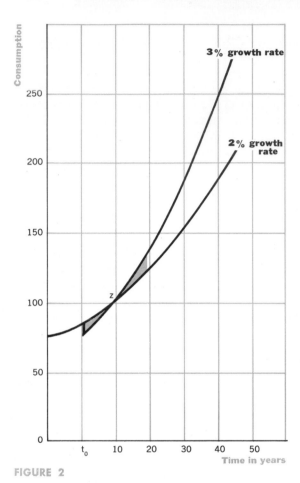

FIGURE 2

total consumption over the whole period is as large as it would have been if the economy had remained on the 2 percent path.[6] From year nineteen on, the initial sacrifice yields bigger and bigger dividends.

Such a policy of sacrificing present living standards for a gain that one does not begin to reap for nineteen years is hardly likely to appeal to any but the very young. Of course, the quantities are only hypothetical (although they are not unreasonable in the light of present knowledge), and it may be that a smaller diversion of resources would achieve the increase in growth rates so that the time taken to break even would be somewhat shorter. This example is only intended to illustrate some of the costs involved in achieving faster growth through a reallocation of resources, to suggest approximate orders of magnitude, and to suggest that the case for pursuing a faster rate of growth *by this means* is possibly not as universally acceptable as it might at first sight seem.

Many governments have followed this route: The Germans under Hitler, the Russians under Stalin, and the Chinese under Mao Tse-tung adopted four- and five-year plans that very consciously shifted resources from consumption to investment. Many countries are using such plans today. They are particularly important when actual growth rates are very small (say less than 1 percent), for without some current sacrifice there is little or no prospect of real growth.

not yet broken even: The darkened area to the left of point z in Figure 2 represents the cumulative loss in consumption over the decade. It takes an additional nine years before

6. This comparison looks only at actual amounts of consumption. If we *discount* the future, preferring to have a quantity of goods now to a somewhat larger quantity in the future, then it will take longer than nine years to *compensate* consumers for the loss of goods during the first ten years.

Ways of Changing the Rate of Growth

Each of the factors that are thought to affect growth can be the object of policy action. Investment can be stimulated by various measures, such as special tax treatment. In the U.S., "investment credits" and accelerated depreciation have been used. An attempt can be made to stimulate innovation and the growth of knowledge by encouraging research. Education and health can be improved in many ways. The effectiveness in influencing growth rates by these means depends on two basic things: first, how important, *quantitatively*, each of these factors is in influencing growth; and, second, how easily each of these factors can be changed by government policy.

A great deal of research is currently being directed to discovering the quantitative importance of the various factors influencing economic growth.[7] There are many technical problems involved in this work, and there is still uncertainty about the validity of the procedures used to produce the estimates. The existing work does suggest, however, that the accumulation of capital is less important and that such factors as innovation and education are more important than had previously been thought. In fact, the best guess based on current knowledge is that substantially less than half of the increase in productive capacity in the United States is due to capital accumulation, while over half is due to other things.

Growth and the Allocation of Resources

We have been discussing growth in the aggregate. Growth also has important microeconomic implications: *Growth will normally result in a reallocation of resources throughout the economy.*

This reallocation of resources is caused by the fact that the rate of growth of the productive capacity of each industry will not exactly match the rate of growth of demand for the product of that industry, except by a very unlikely coincidence. There is thus a supply and a demand side to this reallocation problem.

Consider first the supply side. The rate of growth of an economy is nothing more than an average of the rates of growth of the individual industries composing the economy. The rates of *investment and innovation* will differ among industries and so the rate of growth of productive capacity will also differ among industries. Thus if the allocation of resources among industries did not change, the rate of growth of *production* would vary among industries.

Now consider the demand side. If the central authorities follow a fiscal and monetary policy that keeps the economy at or near full employment, then real income will rise in line with the rise in productive capacity. What happens to the demands for various goods

7. A path-breaking work along these lines is E. F. Denison, *The Sources of Economic Growth in the United States* (New York, 1962).

will depend on the income elasticities of demand for these goods. The larger the income elasticity of demand for a particular commodity, the more rapidly will the demand for that commodity grow as real income grows. In general, demands for commodities with income elasticities of less than unity will be expanding less rapidly than the average rate of growth of productive capacity in the economy, whereas the demands for commodities with income elasticities greater than unity will be expanding faster than the average rate of growth of productive capacity.

One should take care not to confuse total output with total employment in this growth context. As long as an industry's income elasticity of demand exceeds zero (i.e., as long as the commodity is not an inferior good), output will rise as economic growth proceeds. Employment, however, will not increase unless demand expands *faster* than productivity. An industry in which productivity is growing at 3 percent per year and in which demand is growing at 2 percent per year will be an expanding industry in terms of output but a declining industry in terms of employment.

It is an observed fact that income elasticities are different among industries and that they do not remain constant as real income rises. It is also an observed fact that the rate of productivity increase is not the same among industries. Together, these facts lead to rather dramatic shifts in resources over time. The decline of agriculture and the rise of services in the U.S. employment picture are notable examples. Table 3 shows the distribution of the labor force among the major sectors of the U.S. economy each decade over the last 9 decades. The table shows that economic growth has led to a decline in labor employed in agriculture for a long period of time. A

long-term trend has also been observed for the quantity of resources employed in manufacturing to increase. This trend was broken in the 1930s. This means that for a very long time demand was expanding faster than productivity in manufacturing, but that more recently there has been a tendency for demand to expand less rapidly than productivity.

TABLE 3   **DISTRIBUTION OF TOTAL CIVILIAN LABOR FORCE, 1870—1960, IN PERCENTAGES**

Year	Agri-culture	Manufac-turing	Services and all other
1870	50	17	33
1880	50	18	32
1890	42	20	38
1900	37	22	41
1910	31	22	47
1920	27	26	47
1930	22	23	55
1940	17	23	60
1950	12	26	62
1960	8	25	67

SOURCES: 1870–1940—*Historical Statistics of the U.S.,* Series D-57-71; 1940–1960—*Economic Report of the President,* 1965, Tables B21, 26.

GROWTH AND THE PROBLEM OF STRUCTURAL UNEMPLOYMENT

We have seen that growth requires reallocation of resources. Such reallocations are not achieved without cost. The cost to human beings with heavy investments in education and experience in particular occupations can be enormous. A man of forty-five or fifty whose skills are special to a declining industry may, should he lose his job, find the market value of his services cut drastically. Further, if the declining industry is a major part of the economy of a particular geographical area, then the whole area may be a declining one, and all of its residents may suffer because of the decline in demand for all goods and services in this area. For example, if the man wishes to move to an area where jobs are plentiful, he may be quite unable to sell his house and furniture for anything like what their value would be in a growing area. He thus will not be in a position to buy a comparable house and furniture in his new area.

Argument about the effect of economic growth on employment is as old as growth itself. The first thing the displaced worker sees is that technological change is destroying *his* job. This is, understandably, what is of immediate concern to him. What he is likely to conclude is that growth destroys jobs in general and thus raises the average level of unemployment in the economy.

His conclusion is not easy to test. What we can be certain of is (1) that in all growing Western economies over the last century, lapses from full employment have been temporary; (2) that there has been no tendency for average levels of unemployment to rise decade by decade in spite of a prolonged period of sustained growth; and (3) that comparing across countries over the last few years, there has been no clear tendency for higher growth rates to go along with higher unemployment rates. Furthermore, even if it were established that, in a *laissez-faire* economy, higher growth did mean higher levels of unemployment, the macro theory that we have studied in this book provides the central authorities with the fiscal and monetary tools whereby full employment can be pursued as a conscious object of government policy, even if it does not occur spontaneously. In such circumstances, the cost of growth need not be measured in terms of higher levels of unemployed resources, but only in terms of what the resources used to create investment goods might have made had they been used to produce goods for current production and in terms of the human cost involved to those who are left behind in the march of progress.

In the last few years, there has been a revival of the theory that growth raises the average level of unemployment. The revival has occurred in an attempt to explain the disturbingly high average level of unemployment recorded in the United States since 1958.

The first argument is that the rate of growth has been accelerating and that there has been a resulting increase in the number of individuals displaced from those industries in which the volume of employment is declining. Since it takes time for such persons to move, retrain, and enter a new job, it is argued that the average level of unemployment will be higher the higher the rate of growth. A major drawback to this theory is that it is by no means certain, in spite of all the advances of the new "industrial revolution," that the growth rate is significantly higher than the average rate achieved over the last hundred years.

The second argument is that the quality of technological innovation has changed. In the first industrial revolution, so goes the argument, technology destroyed the jobs of skilled artisans by inventing machines to do the work, and created jobs for unskilled workers who could operate the machines. In other words, formerly skilled jobs were broken up into a series of unskilled ones to be done by men and machines. Although the artisan might suffer a reduction in real income, he was not lacking in employment opportunities, since he was always capable of performing one of the unskilled tasks on the machines. The new industrial revolution, so the argument continues, has reversed the technological trend. Now the production process is being reintegrated. The machine in the automated factory now performs all the unskilled tasks, and only a few highly skilled men are necessary to operate the machine and repair it when trouble develops. Thus the unskilled are the immediate sufferers from modern technological advance, and the new jobs are not ones into which they can step without long preparation. Thus, the argument concludes, modern technological advance is destroying the jobs of the unskilled and, even if demand and output are expanding everywhere, the jobs for which demand is expanding are not the jobs that the unskilled can perform. At very best, therefore, we would expect to find a rising level of (mainly unskilled) persons unemployed for long periods of time, and, at worst, there may be a rising number of persons who can never acquire the skills necessary to fit into the new industrial processes.

The first point to make about this argument is that it cannot be ruled out on logical grounds alone. It is not self-contradictory, and it describes a state of affairs that could exist in the world. This makes the discussion of its relevance to today's world a question of fact: Does the argument describe our world, or does it contradict certain observations that we already have? There can be no question that the demands for skilled labor have been rising and that job opportunities for the unskilled have been shrinking. Supplies have also been changing, however, and the labor force today is much better educated and much more highly trained than it was twenty or fifty years ago. There is no solid evidence that the gap between the skills and education levels demanded by employers and supplied by workers is any greater now than it was in earlier times. Second, although the statement about the changing nature of technology *may*

be acceptable as a generalization, it ignores the fact that, in terms of employment, the most rapidly expanding sector of the U.S. economy is not manufacturing but services. Thus, although it may be very depressing to contemplate a fully automated manufacturing plant and wonder how to create jobs for the displaced unskilled workers by inducing further increases in demand for the output of the automated plant, it becomes somewhat less depressing if one realizes that a large fraction of any increment in demand will fall on service industries in which there are still many employment opportunities for the unskilled and semiskilled. Finally, it must be recognized that workers are not completely immobile and that the pattern of demand is not firmly fixed and independent of the structure of relative wages and relative prices. When general demand is high (as it was *not* in the early 1960s in the U.S.), there will be an incentive for employers to assist workers to prepare themselves for jobs for which they may not be equipped by their present training, and to vary the demands of jobs wherever possible. Also, there may be a change in the relative wages between scarce skilled workers and plentiful unskilled workers. These changes in relative factor prices will provide an incentive for employers to economize on skilled workers and to use less skilled ones wherever possible.

The weight of present evidence and the almost universally accepted opinion among economists who have studied the problem is that there is no need for the policy of achieving a low over-all rate of unemployment to conflict with the policy of achieving a high rate of economic growth, nor is there any significant evidence that there has been such a conflict in the United States in the twentieth century.

Summary

1. The productive capacity of an economy is defined as the gross national product that can be produced when all of the economy's resources are fully employed.

2. In Parts IX and X, we considered the effect of investment on aggregate demand. In the theory of growth, we concentrate on the long-term effects of investment on aggregate supply.

3. A frequent source of confusion in the discussion of "growth rates" is the failure to distinguish between changes in productive capacity (which is what we refer to as growth) and changes in the percentage utilization of that capacity caused by fluctuations in aggregate demand.

4. One of the most significant features of growth is that it is cumulative. The enormous effects of small differences in growth rates cumulated over 100 years is illustrated in Table 1, page 682.

5. Securing a fairly rapid rate of growth is one of the goals of economic policy. Growth is a potent means of raising living standards of successive generations; the redistribution of income may also be easier in a growing economy than in a static one.

6. Some of the important causes of growth are capital accumulation, new knowledge and innovation, education, improvement in health standards, and changes in social habits and legal institutions.

7. The opportunity cost of growth in a fully employed economy is a reduction in the level of present consumption. The costs may be high, and it is not clear that more rapid growth is always worthwhile.

8. Growth will normally result in a reallocation of resources; if the necessary reallocation cannot occur, structural unemployment will result. It is the conclusion of most investigators who have studied the problem that there is no necessary conflict between the goals of securing a rapid rate of growth and the lowest possible level of unemployment.

QUESTIONS FOR DISCUSSION

1. In view of what you have learned in this chapter, what do you think was the material standard of living enjoyed by the average citizen in the "good old days," when your great-grandparents were young?

2. If a centrally planned economy decided to hold living standards constant for twenty-five years, what would happen to the percentage of its resources devoted to the production of capital goods, and what would happen to the rate of growth of its gross national product?

3. Investment played a major role in the discussion of the circular flow. In what way has our discussion in this chapter been different?

4. "Growth should take priority over all other goals." What do you take this statement to mean? Discuss this view.

5. A popular concept today is "investment in human capital." What do you think it means? What different sorts of investment can you think of that would fall under this heading? Of what importance is this concept to growth?

6. What problems may come with growth? What can we do about them?

7. "In no other period of history have the problems associated with growth been so severe, and never have they descended on us so rapidly." Do you agree?

8. "A strict *laissez-faire* attitude was the cause of America's rapid growth in the nineteenth century. What we need is a return to this rugged individualism, this pioneer spirit. This way lies prosperity." From your knowledge of nineteenth-century American history, do you think the first sentence is true? Suppose it is true. Do you think the second and third arguments follow logically?

If you think they don't follow, but are valid, construct an intervening argument. How might you go about testing your theory, now that you have constructed it?

9. In the twelve months from Summer, 1963, to Summer, 1964, Britain's gross national product rose by 5 percent. Many commentators expressed satisfaction at this rapid rate of growth. They were also pleased to note that, at the same time, the level of unemployment fell from 2.5 percent to 1.5 percent. What do you think happened and what do you think the prospects were of such a favorable rate of growth being maintained after that date?

Chapter **57** UNDERDEVELOPED ECONOMIES

THE PROBLEMS OF ECONOMIC GROWTH THAT we considered in Chapter 56 are of particular concern to the poorer countries of the world. In our civilized and comfortable urban life, most of us lose sight of the fact that a very short time ago (very short in terms of the life span of the earth, that is) man lived like any other animal, catching an existence as best he could from what nature threw his way. It is only 8,000 years since the agricultural revolution when man turned himself from a food gatherer into a food producer, and it is only within the last centuries that any significant proportion of the population of the world could look forward to anything but unremitting work in wresting an existence from a reluctant nature. The idea of leisure as a right to be enjoyed by everyone is very new in human history. There are 3 billion persons living today in different parts of the world, but the wealthy parts of the world, where

people work no more than forty or fifty hours per week and enjoy substantial amounts of leisure and a level of consumption at or near that attained by the citizens of the U.S., contain only about 20 percent of the world's population. Most of the rest struggle for their very subsistence. About 2 billion people exist at a level at or below that enjoyed by peasants in the more successful civilizations of 5,000 years ago.

If one were studying the effect of variations from year to year in rainfall, one would find that, for a rich country like the United States, such variations would be reflected in farm output and farm income; for each inch rainfall fell below some critical amount, farm output and income would vary in a regular way. In poor countries, such as China and India, variations in rainfall are reflected in the death rate. Indeed, many live so close to the subsistence level that slight fluctuations in the food supply bring death by starvation to large numbers.

The fact that fluctuations that are measured in dollars in rich countries are often measured in lives in poor ones makes the problems of the economy look very different in different countries. It also makes the problems of economic growth very much more urgent in poor countries than in rich ones. Reformers in poor countries often feel a sense of haste not felt by their counterparts in rich countries. To get those citizens now alive off a bare subsistence standard in a very poor country requires an immediate change to a very rapid rate of economic growth.

The Meaning of Underdevelopment

We must now see what light economics can shed on the problem of raising living standards in poor countries. It is often thought that an important step in dealing with the problem of underdeveloped economies is to find the "true" definition of underdevelopment. Books on underdevelopment often start by raising the conceptual problem of how to define *underdevelopment*. The only reason we wish to make clear the meaning we attach to the term *underdeveloped* is that we wish to delimit our area of concern—to say, "We are concerned with these countries and these problems, and not with those countries and those problems." Of course, different investigators could concern themselves with different groups of countries and different problems, and it would be utterly futile to argue which set of problems should be described by the term *underdevelopment*, and which set by other terms. One investigator, for example, defines an underdeveloped country to be one with a per capita national income of less than $500. Another confines his study to countries with substantial quantities of underdeveloped resources. Each of these groups of countries can be studied, and it is completely futile to argue which is the one that is properly defined as underdeveloped.

Underdevelopment has many aspects. We may measure development in dozens of different ways, among them income per head; the percentage of resources unexploited; capital per head; savings per head; conduciveness to growth of social system; conduciveness to growth of local religion; amount of "social capital" (i.e., roads, railroads, schools, etc.); degree of education of the working classes, and so on.

Countries that are "underdeveloped" in one of these ways may not be underdeveloped in another of them. For example, one country may have a lower income per head than others, but have a higher percentage utilization of existing natural resources than others. For this reason it is futile to seek a unique ranking of the various countries in terms of degree of development. We cannot say one country is more underdeveloped than another as long as all of these characteristics affect our view of underdevelopment. Furthermore, the problem of raising the income of a country that has low capital per head, much unemployed labor, but no unexploited natural resources (Pakistan, say) is likely to be very different from that of raising the income of a country like Australia, which is underpopulated and has many unexploited natural resources. In either case, the problems will be more difficult if the country has a religious system that places a low value on economic activity and savings. Instead of trying to define *the* problem of underdevelopment, we should look for some common problems in various groups of countries and be prepared to find major differences in both the problems and the solutions in whatever group of countries we study.

Fostering Growth: Planning or Laissez Faire?

Once the authorities of an underdeveloped country decide to try to raise the growth rate, they will immediately face a fundamental question: How much government control over the economy is necessary and desirable? Practically every shade of opinion from "the only way to grow is to get the government's dead hand out of everything" to "the only way to grow is to get a fully planned, centrally controlled economy" has been seriously advocated. Such extreme views are easily refuted by factual evidence. Many economies have grown with very little government assistance. Perhaps the United Kingdom and Holland are the best examples here. Others, such as modern Russia and Poland, have shown sustained growth with a high degree of centralized control of the economy. Considering other countries, we find almost every conceivable mix of government and private initiative in the growth process. Government fostering of transportation systems is very common, to take but one example of a typical form of government intervention designed to encourage growth.

What sense can we make of these apparently conflicting historical precedents? Probably the only satisfactory answer is that the appropriate action depends on the circumstances presently ruling in the country. In some cases, ineffective governments may have been interfering with the economy to the point of discouraging private initiative, in which case growth may well be enhanced by a reduction in government control over the economy. In other cases, where major quantities of social capital are needed or where existing institutional arrangements such as land tenure are harmful to growth, active intervention by the central authorities may be essential to encourage growth. There are many possible mixes between state and private initiative that have been used successfully at various times and places. On the question of what is the best mix at a particular time and in a particular place, there is likely to be much disagreement.

One of the reasons why governments wish to intervene is to produce a higher level of savings than would ensue if saving decisions were left solely to private individuals. In a fully employed free-market economy, investment is limited by the quantity of savings households and firms will voluntarily engage in. When living standards are low, savings are likely to be low. Central governments can intervene and force the public to save at a much higher rate than they otherwise would. This compulsory saving has been one of the main aims of most of the "Plans" of Communist governments. Those who believe in the individual's freedom of choice may balk at this compulsory sacrifice of the living standards of present generations for the benefit of future ones. The justification offered by the planner is that, with complete freedom of individual choice, growth would be slow or nonexistent, and the present generation would have the power to inflict a low living standard on all future generations. The goal of the five-year plans of Russia, Poland, and now China is to raise savings, and thus to lower current consumption below what it would be, given complete freedom of choice. The ultimate goal is to make future generations better off than they would be if they inherited only the stock of capital that would be voluntarily left to them by present generations.

The Means of Growth

How can an underdeveloped country raise its growth rate?

EDUCATION

The efficiency of labor of all kinds can be raised greatly by education. As modern techniques are introduced, a large rise in the educational standards of the work force is necessary. A man who cannot read or write or do simple calculations will be much less efficient in many jobs than one who can. A manager who knows something of modern methods of bookkeeping, inventory control, and personnel management is likely to be much more effective in getting the most output from a given input than one who is ignorant of these techniques.

HEALTH

A large increase in productivity can be achieved by raising the health standards of the labor force.[1] Less time is lost and more effective effort is put in during the hours that are worked when the labor force is healthy than when it is not.

NATURAL RESOURCES

Natural resources are, of course, important for growth. A country that has a large supply of easily developed resources will find growth easier than one that has fewer and less accessible resources. Developing such resources as are available is a means of fostering growth.

TECHNOLOGY

More modern techniques of production and distribution can be introduced and can make a large contribution to growth. An underdeveloped country does not need to spend vast sums on research and development. It can go a very long way merely by adapting techniques already in use in more developed countries.[2] The most advanced countries, on the other hand, can only institute a new technique when it has been investigated and per-

---

1. But health gains also lower death rates and lead to population growth. In the short run, this makes growth more difficult, as we shall see.

2. We use the word *adapting* rather than *copying*, for an underdeveloped country will often have resource endowments different from those of a developed one and thus should use different techniques. As we pointed out in Chapter 18, in India, where labor is abundant, it does not always make sense to introduce labor-saving techniques.

fected—often at great cost. In this respect, at least, it is easier for a poor country to grow fast than it is for a rich one to do so.

TRANSPORTATION

Specialization of labor and of production and the advantages they bring cannot be realized until the country develops the means of transporting quickly and efficiently men, materials, and finished goods. Roads, bridges, railroads, and harbors play a key role in any industrial economy. Perhaps the most dramatic evidence of this is seen in wartime when belligerents always place highest priority on destroying each other's transportation networks.

The Importance of Capital

All the elements that contribute to growth have in common the need to use large quantities of resources that will not produce an increase in consumption goods for a long period of time. Machines, factories, schools, hospitals, roads, and railroads all require major capital investments. Indeed, because of this, it is common to describe the problem of development as the problem of capital accumulation. This concept can be misleading unless one remembers that it includes human capital (education and health, for example) and social capital (roads, for example) as well as machines and factories. Indeed, what makes the problem of development so difficult is that human and social capital are needed before industrialization can get under way, but they take a long time and a lot of investment to achieve. The impatience of the countries of the world for development now is never more evident than when they face the choice between building a steel industry or educating their children. The second seems like a very slow road to development, yet without it the chance of having a usable steel industry is small.

The need for such painful choices is caused by the scarcity of capital. Perhaps the most visible common feature of practically all underdeveloped countries is the very low amount of capital per head. An increase in the amount of capital would raise productivity and thus raise national income. But, at the present, the accumulated amount of productive capital is small. And the supply of funds for capital investments is much too small to do all the things required. It may take as much as $1,000 of capital to increase national income by $100 per year. If this is so, it will take $100 billion of capital to raise average income per year by $100 in a country of 100 million people. The shortage of investment funds is the bottleneck on the road to development.

The Vicious Circle of Poverty

If capital is to be created at home by the country's own efforts, it is necessary to divert resources from the production of goods for current consumption. This requires a cut in present living standards. If living standards are already virtually at the starvation level, then such a diversion will be difficult and at best only a small proportion of resources can be reallocated to the production of capital goods. Such a situation is often described as the vicious circle of poverty: because a country has little capital per head, it is poor; because it is poor, it can devote only a few resources to creating new capital rather than producing goods for immediate consumption; because little new capital can be produced, capital per head remains low; because capital per head remains low, the country remains poor. Notable examples of countries that have broken this vicious circle by their own efforts are Britain and the Soviet Union—Britain slowly over centuries and Russia rapidly over decades. The fact that it is possible to break the circle does not, of course, mean that it is not a very serious problem.

Growth Through Imported Capital

Another way of accumulating the capital needed for growth is to borrow it from abroad. If a poor country, *A*, borrows from a rich country, *B*, it can use the borrowed funds to purchase capital goods produced in *B*. Country *A* thus accumulates capital and does not need to cut its current output of consumption goods. When the new capital begins to add to current production, it may be possible to pay the interest on the loan and also to begin to repay the principal out of the increase in output. Thus, income can be raised immediately, and the sacrifice postponed until later, when part of the increased income that might have been used to raise domestic consumption is used to pay off the loan. This method has the great advantage of allowing a poor country to have an initial increase in capital goods far greater than it could possibly have created by diverting its own resources from consumption industries. Examples of countries that have grown rapidly, largely at first through the help of foreign capital, are the United States (British capital) and Canada (U.S. and British capital).

Many underdeveloped countries are, however, suspicious of foreign capital, for many of them fear that the foreign investor will

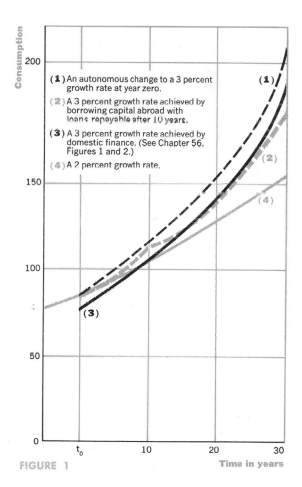

(**1**) An autonomous change to a 3 percent growth rate at year zero.

(**2**) A 3 percent growth rate achieved by borrowing capital abroad with loans repayable after 10 years.

(**3**) A 3 percent growth rate achieved by domestic finance. (See Chapter 56, Figures 1 and 2.)

(**4**) A 2 percent growth rate.

FIGURE 1

gain control over their industries or their government. The extent of foreign control depends on the form that foreign capital takes. If the foreigners buy bonds in domestic companies, they do not own or control anything; if they buy common stocks, then they do own part or all of the company; if they subsidize a government, they may feel justified in exacting political commitments. Whether or not foreign ownership of one's industries carries political disadvantages is a subject of debate.[3] The economic advantages are, however, quite clear. Accumulating a given amount of capital by domestic saving leads to a different time path of domestic living standards from accumulating it by foreign borrowing. The domestic method requires greater current sacrifice, but pays a higher return later; foreign financing requires no present sacrifice,[4] but produces lower gains in living standards later. Figure 1 shows the time paths for consumption when a given amount of investment is financed

by domestic sources and when it is financed by foreign sources. The figure is based on all the assumptions used to construct Figures 1 and 2 in Chapter 56 as well as two alternate assumptions: the capital is produced at home, and the capital is borrowed from abroad.

Getting foreign capital is easier said than done in the early stages of development. America and Canada were underdeveloped in the sense of being underpopulated and having many unused resources, but they were latent giants and held promise of rich returns to foreign investors. It is hard to see similar investment opportunities in Pakistan, say, where overpopulation has been a problem for centuries and where the soil is severely damaged by centuries of irrigation without proper drainage. The ability of such a country to borrow from private sources is small. Foreign capital is playing a role, but it is capital provided by foreign governments and international agencies, not by private investors.

Growth Through Contributed Capital

Investment funds for development are being received today by underdeveloped countries from the governments of the more developed countries acting both unilaterally (as in the U.S. Agency for International Development and in a similar Soviet program) and through international agencies, such as the

International Bank for Reconstruction and Development and the Export-Import Bank. American contributions amount to about $2 billion per year, at the present time.[5] Why do we give? Some say for political gain, some say for economic gain, and some say from compassion. Possibly all are correct in part.

3. In Canada, for example, there has been much debate over the political effects of having much of Canadian industry owned by U.S. nationals who are presumably more open to pressure from U.S. central authorities than from Canadian ones.

4. See the discussion in the appendix to Chapter 38, pp. 442–444, for a description of what happens when capital is borrowed from abroad.

5. Is this a lot or a little? It is less than 1 percent of our GNP. It is, however, about 1 percent of the income of the 2 billion people who live in the underdeveloped nations of the world.

1. POLITICAL

There is little doubt that in the Cold War the struggle for the political allegiance of the uncommitted countries is intense. Since most of the uncommitted countries are underdeveloped and urgently desire to grow, the political system that gives the best promise of growth is likely to have the strongest appeal. The prospects for the vast majority of the world's population of obtaining any living standard above bare subsistence depends critically on the possibility of inducing quite rapid economic growth; there is no doubt that political and social systems will be judged to a great extent by their success in inducing this growth.

2. ECONOMIC

Does a country that gives aid to underdeveloped countries thereby increase its own living standards? Or does it have an economic interest in keeping the poor countries poor so that they can be more effectively exploited? The theory of international trade leads us to predict that there will be a gain if the poorer countries get richer, for as incomes rise in poorer countries the market for our exports will grow. By and large, the volume of international trade tends to grow—in spite of tariffs and other forms of interference—as countries get richer. The larger the productive capacity of the world, the greater the scope for the operation of the international division of labor, and the larger the gains from trade.

On the other hand, growth can *hurt* advanced countries with special positions to protect. A country with a monopoly in the production of some commodity can suffer when competitors arise in other countries. Also, firms from advanced countries that operate in underdeveloped ones often have a lot to lose from growth. The United Fruit Company would undoubtedly lose profits if successful industrial development in Nicaragua so raised the earnings of agricultural labor that the real wage paid to workers on banana plantations doubled. There is, of course, a big difference between having a reason to fear development and actively trying to prevent it. At any rate, this discussion is sufficient to show that there is not a clear case that developed nations *always* gain when underdeveloped countries grow.

3. COMPASSIONATE

There is no doubt that part of the interest of people in developed countries in the fate of people in underdeveloped countries stems from genuine altruism. We believe that a minimum standard of living is necessary to preserve human dignity and to allow development of the human personality. We are disturbed when we see the citizens of whole nations falling below this standard. We do not sit idly by; we try to do something about it.

Perhaps the best evidence that this motive exists is the success of voluntary appeals for food, funds, and clothing for persons in stricken areas of the world. Although this is not a new concern, as we have grown richer, the size of our contributions has grown. It is a policy of our government, and one more or less accepted by both political parties and by the majority of the American people, that we devote some of our resources to alleviating poverty throughout the world.

Population and Economic Development

Capital is a necessary but not a sufficient condition for the economic growth of an underdeveloped country. An underdeveloped country must accumulate enough capital, and of the right kinds, to break the vicious circle of poverty. Once the country does break the circle, it will generate further investment funds from the savings that its population makes from its own growing incomes, and it may also begin to attract private capital from foreign investors.

But first the country must begin to grow. Many of the countries of the world have a standard of living no higher than they had a hundred or even a thousand years ago. They have more national income, but they also have more mouths to feed. The average Vietnamese is as hungry as his great-grandfather was. The growth problem faced by these countries is how to get off the treadmill and onto the escalator. You might think that even modest gains in the size of the capital stock would *eventually* add up to enough to get a sustained growth going. But you would be wrong. For it is the amount of capital *per person* that determines whether living standards will rise, and we must thus be concerned about the growth rate *per capita.* Population growth is a central problem of economic development. If population expands as fast as does the national income, then per capita income will not increase. If population does expand rapidly, a country may make a great effort to raise the quantity of capital only to find that a corresponding rise in population has occurred, so that the net effect of its "growth policy" is that a larger population is now maintained at the original low standard of living. An increase in living standards occurs if capital, and possibly other resources, expand faster than the increase in population. This explains the great importance attached to population policy in many underdeveloped countries.

This population problem has led economists to talk about the "critical minimum effort" that is required not merely to increase capital, but to increase it fast enough so that the increase in output outraces the increase in population.[6] The problem arises because population size is not independent of the level of income. If population control is left to nature, nature solves it in a cruel way: Population increases until many are forced to live at a subsistence level; further population growth is halted by famine, pestilence, and plague. This grim situation was perceived early in the history of economics by Thomas Malthus. In some ways, the population problem is more severe today than it was even a generation ago. Advances in medicine and in public health have brought sharp and sudden decreases in death rates.[7] In Mexico today the birth rate is more than three times as

6. Harvey Leibenstein is the author of the phrase "critical minimum effort." See his provocative book *Economic Backwardness and Economic Growth* (John Wiley, 1957). (Also available in a Science Editions paperback.) W. W. Rostow has used the phrase "take-off" to express a very similar notion.

7. It is ironic that much of our compassion for the poor and underprivileged people of the world has traditionally taken the form of improving their health, thereby doing little to avert their poverty. We laud the medical missionaries who brought modern medicine to the savages, but the elimination of malaria, though surely a boon to the world, has doubled the rate of population growth in Ceylon. No one would argue against controlling disease, but we must recognize that other things must also be done if the child who survives the infectious illnesses of infancy is not to die by starvation in early adulthood.

high as the death rate, and population is growing at more than 3 percent per year. A rise in production of 3 percent per year is required for Mexico to "break even."

There are only two possible ways to solve this problem. One is to make such a massive push that we achieve a growth rate well in excess of the rate of population growth. The second is to control population growth. The problem *can* be solved by restricting population growth. This is not a matter of serious debate, although the means of restricting it are, for there are religious considerations involved. Positive economics does not decide such issues, but it can describe the consequences of any choice that is made. Both

Sweden and Venezuela have death rates of about 10 per 1,000 population per year. The birth rate in Sweden is 14; in Venezuela it is 45. Thus the net increase of population per year is 35 per 1,000 (3.5 percent) in Venezuela, but only 4 per 1,000 (0.4 percent) in Sweden. If each country achieved an over-all rate of growth of production of 3 percent per year, Sweden would be increasing her living standards by 2.6 percent per year, while Venezuela would be lowering hers by 0.5 of 1 percent per year. Today, Sweden's standard of living is more than twice as high as Venezuela's.[8] The gap will widen rapidly, if present population trends continue.

Balanced or Unbalanced Growth?

Should a developing country push expansion in all sectors of its economy (balanced growth), or should it specialize in certain sectors (unbalanced growth)? The decision is an important one, and the government is surely in a position to affect it, either because it is directly the channel of investment or because it uses its tariff and taxing power to influence the allocation of funds.

The principle of comparative advantage (see Chapters 39 and 40) provides the traditional case for the desirability of unbalanced growth. In reaching a decision, however, the central authorities will also take the following considerations into account:

1. The greater the degree of imbalance in growth, the greater will be the country's dependence upon foreign trade. Too much specialization means putting all one's eggs into

one basket and makes the economy vulnerable to fluctuations in world demand and supply for the product in which it is specialized and also vulnerable to technological changes that may render the product obsolete.

2. Specialization is necessary if one is going to reap the gains from trade that accrue when countries specialize in the range of products in which they have a comparative advantage. Balanced growth pursued to the extreme of self-sufficiency is then likely to result in a lower living standard than will result from some degree of specialization.

3. Countries often push certain lines of production either for prestige purposes or because of a confusion between cause and effect. Because most wealthy nations have a steel industry, it does not follow that having a steel industry will make a nation wealthy.

8. And Venezuela is the wealthiest country in South or Central America at the present time. It has an average income per person of about $700. (This compares with the U.S. figure of about $3,000, and with the figure for India of about $100.)

Indeed, if one has a serious comparative disadvantage in steel, then having a steel industry will make one poor. Whether or not one really gains international prestige by having an uneconomic steel industry or national airline is difficult to ascertain. It is very probable, however, that in the long run, prestige goes to the country that grows rich rather than to the one that stays poor but that produces at high cost a few prestige commodities that are regarded as signs of wealth.

4. In deciding what sectors of the economy to push, due regard must be paid to potential future comparative advantages, as well as to current ones. Many skills can be acquired, and the fostering of an apparently uneconomic domestic industry may, by changing the characteristics of the labor force, develop a comparative advantage in that line of production. Where there is excessive concentration on current comparative advantages, one consequence may be an excessive defense of the *status quo* in the pattern of international specialization.

Summary

1. Underdevelopment has many aspects. We may look for common problems in various groups of countries, but we must be prepared to find major differences.

2. At the start of an attempt to raise the growth rate of an underdeveloped country, the government faces a fundamental decision: planning or *laissez faire*? Of course, it is possible to opt for almost any conceivable mixture of free market and central control.

3. Some governmental policies that might help an underdeveloped country are intervention to produce a higher level of savings than would be adopted voluntarily, improvements in education, improvements in health services, development of natural resources, the fostering of technological advances, and improvements in transportation facilities.

4. In order to begin rapid growth, an economy may need to break out of the vicious circle of poverty: Because an economy has little capital per head, it is poor; because it is poor, it cannot increase its capital per head. . . . One way to break out of this circle is to borrow capital from abroad; another way is to make use of contributed capital.

5. Developed countries give economic aid to underdeveloped countries for many reasons: political, economic, and compassionate. Contributed capital is playing a large role today in the process of the economic development of underdeveloped countries.

6. "Critical minimum effort" refers to the effort necessary to increase capital fast enough so that the increase in output outpaces the increase in population. The only other way to secure a permanent increase in living standards is to control the growth of population.

7. The issue of whether a country should push expansion in all its sectors (balanced growth) or concentrate on certain sectors (unbalanced growth) is an important one. The theory of comparative advantage provides the traditional case for unbalanced growth. There are, however, goals other than the one of making current income as large as possible that might lead a government to pursue a policy of balanced growth.

QUESTIONS FOR DISCUSSION

1. What do you think is the significance of the slogan, "Trade not aid"?

2. News media have recently been reporting that Nigeria is ready for a "take off." What do you think they mean?

3. What makes a country underdeveloped?

4. An American economist, Professor Milton Friedman, commented in a speech that the recently built Egyptian steel mills, were like "modern pyramids." What do you think he meant? In order to prove that the investment was economically unwise, would it be sufficient to show that it would be cheaper for Egypt to import steel now, rather than to build the plants? If it was economically unwise, was it necessarily irrational? Are pyramids irrational? What advice can an economist give to the Egyptian Government about the establishment of such industries?

5. Construct a short argument between an advocate of balanced growth and an advocate of unbalanced growth.

6. Of what relevance to growth are the following news items?
a. China to give money to Tanzania for a railroad;
b. India to begin manufacture of contraceptive devices;
c. AFL-CIO aids programs to unite small landholders in Dominican Republic.

7. What is the "population explosion"? Why do you think that it has occurred now, rather than 200 years ago? Why do we worry about it? What can be done about it?

8. "There is no need to worry about the population problem, because, with every new mouth that comes into the world, there also comes a pair of hands to do the necessary work." What do you think?

CONTEMPORARY PROBLEMS OF MACROECONOMIC POLICY

Chapter **58** MACROECONOMIC POLICY

ECONOMISTS STILL DEBATE THE CAUSES OF the Great Depression, just as historians still debate the causes of World War I. But the overwhelming majority of economists agree that another episode like the crash of 1929 and the painful decade that followed it need not happen again. If the economists are right, it is an impressive bit of evidence in favor of economic analysis, because it means that we do believe we understand the workings of the economy well enough that it can be effectively controlled so as to avoid such extremes of economic performance.

In this chapter we are concerned with macroeconomic policy. Experience with past

policies not only constitutes our economic history, but also provides the material for testing our economic theories. Macro theories lead us to predict how various policies will affect certain aggregate variables. If we are now confident that we can make the correct diagnoses, it is because the evidence appears to conform, at least in broad outline, with the major predictions of the theories.

In examining and evaluating this evidence, we have a great scarcity of data. For this reason, attention not only to the U.S. experience but to the experience of other Western countries that have acted on the basis of similar theories is worthwhile, for it extends greatly the number of cases in which we may study the relation between a policy action and the reaction of the economy to it.[1] Just as the distinction between macro- and microeconomic theory is to some extent arbitrary, so the distinction between macro- and microeconomic policy is to some extent arbitrary. Of course, government policy ranges from things affecting single households and firms to things affecting the society as a whole. Our concern in this chapter will be with four major aggregate variables that economic policy seeks to influence: the level of unemployment, the price level, the balance of payments, and the rate of growth of the economy.

Unemployment

There is virtually unanimous agreement that unemployment is undesirable.[2] It causes a loss of output, it is degrading to the persons suffering the unemployment, and it increases the costs of various welfare programs. We have talked many times in this book about full employment, but every time we have talked about the level of employment we have spoken of such and such a proportion of the labor force as being unemployed. Surely full employment means what it says: No unemployment? The answer to this question is an emphatic No! Various causes of unemployment can be distinguished. Some of them are regarded as unavoidable aspects of the functioning of a market system. Such unemployment is often characterized as *frictional:* A first source of frictional unemployment is labor turnover. People leave jobs for many different reasons. Some quit, and some are fired, but almost all of them find new jobs, though it may take time. Since, at every moment of time, there will be a group of individuals moving from one job to another, there will always be some proportion of the labor force out of work. Of course, if the volume of frictional unemployment stays stable over time, it does not mean that the same individuals are out of work. It has been established that, in the U.S., "between a fourth and a third of all workers change jobs either by choice or by force of circumstances in the course of a year. . . ."[3] If the workers take an average of two weeks to change jobs, this will mean that an average of 1 percent of the labor force is frictionally unemployed at any moment of time. This routine turnover is accentuated by economic growth. As growth proceeds, cost conditions and thus input requirements change; the pattern of demand and thus output requirements change as well. Such changes make it necessary for people to move among occupations, industries, and areas; since this movement often requires retraining, which takes time, the expected amount of unemployment is probably increased on this

---

1. To put this more formally, measurement and testing of macroeconomic theory is made easier because of deliberate policies designed to affect aggregate variables. To give ourselves a large enough sample of "tests," we consider not merely the U.S. experience but also that of the other countries operating under similar kinds of market systems.

2. One occasionally hears a defense of unemployment as necessary to "keep them [the employees] on the ball."

3. Herbert S. Parnes, *Research on Labor Mobility* (New York: Social Science Research Council, 1954), p. 62.

count.[4] A third source of frictional unemployment is the seasonality of some occupations in which year-round employment is not available for all who wish it. Many seasonal workers are out of a job for anything from a few weeks to six or seven months and, although some of them seek fill-in work, they frequently fail to find it. Finally, about 2.5 percent of the labor force every year are new entrants, and it is rare for anyone to walk out of school and into a job without some delay.

For these reasons—because people move from job to job and because the structures of demand and of costs are constantly changing—some minimum level of unemployment must always occur in an economy. Full employment is usually said to occur when this minimum level is achieved. How large is it?

In the United States, it is thought to be around 3 percent of the labor force. Since there has not been a prolonged period of unemployment of 3 percent, this view has not really been tested. In Britain, "full employment" was defined in the White Paper on Employment Policy published by the Government in 1944 as existing when recorded unemployment fell to 3 percent of the labor force. Since the war, monetary and fiscal policies have been used in an effort to control the level of unemployment and, in spite of fluctuations, the rate has never risen above 2.6 percent, and it has several times been below 1.5 percent. The British, therefore, have revised downward their notion of the amount of unemployment that is normal and necessary. Most people now feel that full employment requires no more than 1.2 percent to 1.5 percent of the labor force frictionally unemployed. In Sweden, the postwar unemployment rate has frequently been as low as 1.1 percent; in Australia, it has averaged around 1 percent, never rising above 2 percent.

PAST EXPERIENCE

As far back as we have any records, periods of heavy unemployment have been observed. Until very recently, casual observers and experts alike tended to believe that there was not very much a government could do to affect the level of unemployment, except possibly by interfering even less than usual in the economy when unemployment was particularly high, so that the natural market forces could restore full employment. From 1929 to 1932, President Hoover kept assuring the unemployed that prosperity was just around the corner. Until the 1930s, it was at least possible to maintain the view that the market, left to itself, would restore full employment, because recessions, although often sharp, tended to last only a very few years. (Look again at Figure A5, page 55, and Figure 1, page 583.) The Great Depression of the 1930s dispelled forever the belief that the unaided free market would always restore full employment within a tolerable period of time. Those who believed that the unaided market did guarantee full employment were left to argue that this result would come about "in the long run." To those who waited eight years, from 1929 to 1937, for this problematical "long run" to appear, Keynes provided the practical epitaph for their belief: "Maybe you are right, but in the long run, we shall all be dead."[5] In the postwar years, the governments of all Western countries have accepted full employment as a goal of policy: as something that governments can achieve through their

---

4. This problem was considered in Chapter 56, pages 689–690.
5. This is a slight paraphrase of Keynes's famous quote.

actions and as something that they have a responsibility to attempt to achieve. In 1944, the British Government in the forementioned White Paper accepted a responsibility to maintain full employment by appropriate changes in its fiscal and monetary policies. The American Government accepted the same responsibility in the Employment Act of 1946, which set up the Council of Economic Advisors, which was charged with the responsibility of reporting each year on the state of the economy and advising the government on how the full-employment goal could best be achieved.

CAUSES AND CONTROL OF UNEMPLOYMENT

The sources of unemployment at which policy is directed are, first, deficiencies in aggregate demand, and, second, so-called structural unemployment, both of which were discussed at length in Chapters 51 and 56. Structural unemployment is associated with the forces of growth and change in the economy, and deficient-demand unemployment is associated with a reduction in any of the autonomous components of aggregate demand, such as investment or government expenditure.

Deficient-demand unemployment can be removed merely by raising aggregate demand sufficiently. A rise in aggregate demand raises national income and raises output. This leads to an increase in the level of employment and, provided this is not can-

celed out by increases in the labor force, a fall in the level of unemployment. The quantitative relation of employment to demand is not known exactly. Much labor is overhead labor, and its employment does not fluctuate with output. Generally, we expect employment to change in the same direction as output, but not in proportion to the change in output; and, generally, we expect that the longer the time allowed to elapse after the change in output, the greater the reaction in employment. Although the magnitudes are somewhat uncertain, there is no doubt about the direction. It is generally agreed that an available policy to combat unemployment is to raise aggregate demand.

Structural unemployment is harder to remove. Indeed, it has been present throughout the whole postwar period in the United States.[6] Schemes such as retraining programs, moving allowances, and information centers all have the effect of increasing labor mobility and, probably, of reducing structural unemployment. Such schemes have been tried most extensively in Sweden, which has had one of the lowest levels of postwar unemployment in the Western world.

_____

Were unemployment the only major goal of the policy-makers, it would not be difficult to maintain full employment by a policy aimed at maintaining aggregate demand and by selected policies designed to deal with structural unemployment where it exists.

_____

6. See R. A. Gordon, "Has Structural Unemployment Worsened?," *Industrial Relations*, III (May, 1964), 53-77.

The Price Level

Changes in price levels tend always to have a redistributive effect: Those with fixed incomes suffer in periods of inflation and gain in periods of deflation. The full effects of changes in price levels have been discussed at many points in this book; for a review of the effects of inflations and deflations, the student should now reread pages 150–152.

Most people agree that, *ceteris paribus*, a stable price level is desirable. Most agree that rapid inflations and deflations are undesirable. Although there is some consensus that slow changes in the price level are also undesirable, there is considerable disagreement as to how undesirable they are. Some people believe that mild inflations on the order of, say, 2 or 3 percent per year do not cause serious harm, while others believe that any degree of inflation is serious and that the maintenance of an absolutely stable price level is an important goal of policy.

PAST EXPERIENCE

Practically every form of price-level behavior has been observed somewhere at some time. Probably the most dramatic occurrences are hyperinflations, in which prices rise by factors of a thousand-fold in a matter of weeks. One famous example is the hyperinflation that occurred in Germany in the early 1920s. Most savings were totally destroyed in value by the skyrocketing prices, and the consequent destruction of the middle classes as a social unit did a great deal to upset the social fabric of Germany and pave the way for World War II.

In some countries, an inflexibility of prices in a downward direction appears to exist.

This asymmetry in price behavior, by which prices tend to rise but not fall in response to fluctuations in demand, is a relatively recent phenomenon, dating in America from around 1940. Before that time, price levels rose and fell in response to changes in aggregate demand, as Figure 1 clearly shows. Since the war, despite several recessions, average prices have tended to rise or to be stable rather than to fall. There are many theories as to why this has happened. One is that many key prices and wages are "administered" (rather than market-determined) by powerful firms and powerful unions that choose to maintain prices, even if this means reducing output and employment.

CAUSES AND CONTROL OF CHANGES IN PRICE LEVELS

The price level is closely related to both the level of aggregate demand and the money supply, as we have seen. At or near full employment, increases in aggregate demand tend to be inflationary. Reductions in aggregate demand tend to be reflected more in unemployment than in falling prices. In periods of full employment, a restrictive monetary policy can always restrain aggregate demand, but whether in today's world it will bring prices down is another matter.

We saw in Chapter 52 that the government has controlled the money supply almost since the invention of money. The actions of governments in varying the money supply, and thereby inducing changes in the price level, have long been understood, and the responsibility of governments for what happens to prices has been accepted.

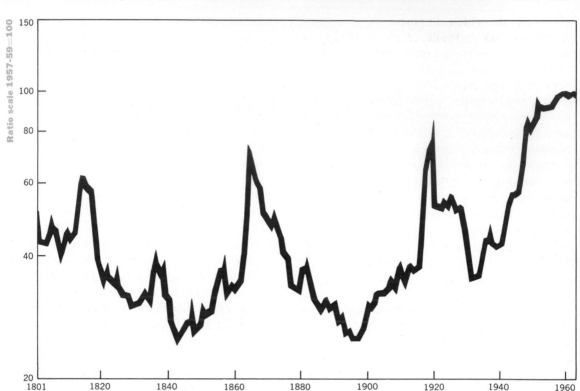

FIGURE 1   **CHANGES IN THE U.S. PRICE LEVEL, 1801–1960**

The tools of public policy potentially available to the central authorities for affecting the price level are numerous. Governments can affect the level of aggregate demand by their expenditures, taxes, or monetary policies. Further, they can use (as they have on occasion) direct price and wage controls. We shall return to the question of which policy tools governments may choose to use later in this chapter.

Were a stable price level the only major goal of public policy, it would not be difficult to achieve it by regulating the level of aggregate demand.

Balance of Payments

Generally, the purpose of international trade is to take advantage of the international division of labor: We export goods in order that we can import those goods that are cheaper to obtain abroad than to produce at home. Flows of long-term capital aside, a large import surplus is regarded as undesirable, as is a large export surplus; a situation in which imports equal exports is regarded as desirable. If a country's present reserves of foreign exchange are thought to be inadequate—a position in which many countries find themselves today—it will regard a mild export surplus as its balance-of-payments target, but, once reserves are at an adequate level, it will aim at an equality between imports and exports.

Even the most enlightened government will not regard an export surplus as anywhere near as undesirable as an import surplus. An export surplus means that foreign exchange is accumulating, an accumulation that can go on more or less indefinitely, as far as this country is concerned. (Of course, some other country must be suffering an import surplus, and that country may be forced to take steps to remove it.) An import surplus can go on only as long as foreign-exchange reserves last. A monthly import surplus equal to, say, 5 percent of the total exchange reserves can last only for 20 months, and, long before that, it will cause a speculative flight of capital in expectation of a devaluation of the currency. An import surplus is generally the occasion for fairly rapid preventative actions, unless there are reasons to believe that it is the result of genuinely temporary factors and will disappear on its own before very long.

PAST EXPERIENCE

We studied past balance-of-payments experience in some detail in Chapter 41. In the past, under the gold standard, governments usually refrained from interfering with the balance of payments. Since the general advent of fixed exchange rates, however, governments have had no choice but to take a major measure of responsibility for the balance of payments.

CAUSES AND CONTROL OF BALANCE-OF-PAYMENTS PROBLEMS

The causes of balance-of-payments problems were discussed in detail in Chapters 38 and 41. For some countries operating under fixed exchange rates, the need to exercise control over the balance of payments is slight: If the country tends to have an export surplus, as Germany has had in the postwar period, it is possible for it to allow reserves to accumulate indefinitely. This was also the case in the United States until the late 1950s. When deficits occur, however, as they began to in the U.S. in 1958, they can be ignored only as long as reserves are adequate. U.S. reserves fell from about $24 billion in 1949 to $16 billion by 1963, and the problem began to appear serious.

Altering the level of aggregate demand and changing the direction of expenditure are the two main policy measures available for dealing with persistent imbalances in the foreign trade of a country. (Review Chapter 38 on expenditure-dampening and expenditure-switching policies, if necessary.)

Were equality in the balance of payments the sole object of governmental policy, it would not be difficult to maintain it either by varying exchange rates or by controlling the level or pattern of aggregate demand.

Growth

By and large, economic growth is accepted as desirable. It is the major cause of changes in living standards. With growth, each generation can expect, on the average, to be substantially better off than all preceding generations. Growth, as we have seen, is not without its costs, and there is a limit beyond which further increases in the rate of growth would not be regarded as desirable. But that limit is probably quite high; at the moment an increase in the rate of growth would probably be generally accepted as desirable in almost all Western countries.

CAUSES AND CONTROL OF GROWTH

Economic growth is the policy variable about which we know least. In spite of a great deal of study and the accumulation of isolated bits of knowledge, we do not really understand the complex causes of growth sufficiently well to be able to alter the growth rate as easily as we can the unemployment rate. No case in which a government has intervened in a free-market society with the purpose of achieving a marked increase in its rate of growth is generally agreed to have been a success. Postwar France, which has had a high growth rate combined with an active planning division, has probably come closest. Many French economists are convinced that their rather loose style of planning has had a significant effect on their growth rate. This is not an easy theory to test, and we can only say at this time that the case is "not proved," one way or the other. Growth, therefore, remains the enigma of macro policy; we agree that it is one of the

most important of all the variables, and we also agree that it is the one we least know how to control.

Certain theories have been put forward. One is that periods of very high demand and mild inflationary pressures are beneficial to growth. It is argued that such periods provide the businessman with both the incentive to invest and the funds (which can be withheld out of profits) with which to finance the investment. Another theory says that periods of moderate excess capacity with an absence of inflationary pressures are most conducive to growth. The argument here is that, when there is some unemployment in the economy, resources for new investment will be readily available, and that innovations in terms of new products or cost reductions in old ones provide the only possible promise of large profits. Research is progressing on these theories, but as yet we really do not know enough to choose between them.

On the negative side, it is clear that a substantial cut in demand, and a recession of any serious degree, has at least a short-run depressing effect on the growth rate. This follows at once from the accelerator theory. (See Chapter 48, page 578.) A cut in aggregate demand can be expected to cut drastically into new investment. It is argued that even if, after a couple of years, a recovery in investment occurs, two years of investment activity will have been lost forever and the growth of the economy will always be two years behind what it otherwise would have been. The evidence with respect to net investment appears to provide support to this proposition.

Since we are not very sure about the causes

of growth, we are not very sure about which policy measures will stimulate it. Almost everyone agrees that anything that increases the rate of new investment will be favorable to growth. In addition to preventing reductions in the level of aggregate demand, investment can be encouraged by providing ample funds at low interest rates, by providing tax advantages to investors, and by encouraging research and development. How successful we think we will be depends on which of the theories of the advancement of knowledge laid out on pages 236–238 we accept.

To encourage growth, we can also seek to change the educational system, the health of the nation, and the attitudes toward invention and innovation, as well as to improve business practices by inventing and publicizing new techniques of business management. We will not know whether or not any already advanced Western nation can succeed in significantly altering its growth rate by adopting a serious program to do so along these or other lines until some country really tries to do so.

If increasing the rate of economic growth were the major objective of economic policy, it is clear that avoiding sharp reductions in aggregate demand would be important and that stimulating invention, innovation, and investment would likewise be desirable. We do not know enough about these processes to be confident of which policies would best achieve the latter objectives.

Conflicts of Policy

Macroeconomic policy is not concerned with reducing unemployment *or* maintaining stable prices *or* reaching an equilibrium in the balance-of-payments position *or* increasing the rate of growth, but, instead, with achieving all of these things simultaneously. Consider the following statement made in the 1965 *Economic Report of the President.*[7]

As 1965 begins, most Americans are enjoying a degree of prosperity unmatched in their experience, or indeed in the history of their Nation. In 1964, some 70 million of them were at work, producing $622 billion worth of goods and services.

The gains of four years of uninterrupted economic expansion had brought fuller pay envelopes, greater sales, larger dividend checks, a higher standard of living, more savings, and a stronger sense of security than ever before. Over that period industrial production grew at an average annual rate of 7 percent, and the total output of all goods and services (valued in constant prices) increased at an average rate of 5 percent. . . . These gains brought jobs to 4 million more persons and raised total consumer income after taxes by 6 percent a year. And all this was accomplished with essentially stable prices.

. . .

The expansion of economic activity during the past four years has carried virtually every economic indicator to a new record level. But this in itself is no cause for complacency. In a growing economy, it should be a matter of course to set new records month by month and quarter by quarter; to be meaningful, economic achieve-

---

7. The annual Report of the Council of Economic Advisors, along with the *Economic Report of the President*, is published every January. It is always worth reading for a statement of the Administration's views as to the central contemporary issues in macroeconomic policy. This excerpt from the 1965 Report is on pages 35 and 38–39.

ments must be gauged against capabilities and objectives.

Unfortunately, the balanced growth of the U.S. economy in recent years, unlike the sustained progress of other industrial economies, has occurred at too low a level. The excessive unemployment and idle capacity with which the current U.S. expansion began have not yet been fully erased. Unemployment at 5.0 percent of the civilian labor force is far better than the 7 percent rate of spring, 1961. But 5.0 percent represents 3.7 million persons seeking work. If unemployment today were at the interim target of 4 percent, the number without jobs would have fallen below 3 million, and the labor force would be considerably larger than it is today, as emerging job opportunities encouraged more people to seek work. Consumer incomes and corporate profits would both be considerably higher. The "gap" of $25–$30 billion that still remains between the nation's actual output and its potential output would be closed. The size of this gap—4 percent of our current potential —is a measure of the primary challenge for economic policy: achieving maximum employment, production, and purchasing power.

A second challenge—not new, but more fully recognized than ever before—lies in the contrast between our great over-all prosperity and the poverty and misery which still afflict too many families, and in the contrast between our great material achievements and the quality of our private and public lives.

A third challenge of pressing importance lies in the fact that, despite considerable progress, we have not yet regained equilibrium in our balance of payments.

To see in general terms why conflicts in policy arise, consider the effects of a sharp increase in aggregate demand in the situation described above. Unemployment should (according to our theories) be reduced by an increase in aggregate demand, and that is clearly desirable. But increasing aggregate demand will lead to upward pressure on prices in the many sectors of the economy where capacity is being fully utilized and where employment is nearly full. Stable prices existed in America at the time that the report was written, but there is no reason why this situation might not give way to one of inflation. Indeed, the rise in aggregate demand makes this more likely. Furthermore, our balance-of-payments position, already unfavorable, would be worsened. As aggregate demand increases, imports will increase, and, if domestic prices rise, exports will be discouraged, and the payments situation will thus deteriorate from both the import and the export sides. If we try to achieve all our policy goals by varying the level of aggregate demand, we will inevitably run into conflict. We will only be able to come closer to some goals at the cost of moving further away from others.

This does not mean that the control of aggregate demand is not a powerful policy tool—indeed, it is perhaps the most powerful one—but rather that a policy that has several goals may have to use several instruments of policy.

MAJOR POLICY INSTRUMENTS

Regulating Aggregate Demand: Fiscal Policy

A rise in government expenditure or a cut in tax revenue increases aggregate demand. Although any increase in expenditure or cut in revenue always tends to increase aggregate demand, the result does not always come about in the same way or in the same amount of time. Public spending can be very narrowly directed so as to increase the demand where it is most needed. If public spending is concentrated in areas where unemployment is very high, where there are no bottlenecks that will lead to price rises, the adverse effect on prices can be lessened. Of course, the multiplier effects cannot be contained to high unemployment sectors; they will tend to spread over the whole economy. A significant proportion of the total effect, however, *can* be contained. If, for example, in the face of heavy unemployment in Appalachia, an extra $1 billion per year is spent in Appalachia, and if the multiplier is 2, then the total change in income and employment will be $2 billion. At least 50 percent of this final figure represents extra demand in Appalachia, although most of the rest may represent extra demand for products, such as television sets, washing machines, and cars, the industries producing which are already fully employed. In principle, an expenditure-oriented policy can be a very fine instrument, injecting excess demand where required.

There are, however, some drawbacks to such a policy. It is difficult to have expenditure of this kind take effect quickly. Quite apart from the political lags in authorizing a project, there are substantial delays in designing and executing large public-expenditure programs. It is not hard to spend $100 million in Appalachia in a summer, but it would be very hard to spend $2 billion there without arousing great public criticism about wastefulness. During the New Deal, the contrast between the Works Progress Administration (WPA) and the Public Works Administration (PWA) was very striking. WPA tried to put income quickly and directly into the hands of the unemployed by creating jobs that they could do at once; PWA attempted to increase aggregate demand by building dams, schools, hospitals, and roads—things of "lasting value." WPA was regarded by many Americans as nearly scandalous ("boondoggle" was the word used to describe some of the projects), whereas PWA was regarded as sound. Yet WPA spent money and thus created income with a much shorter time lag (three months compared to two years, on the average). Although the American people and Congress have accepted the main point that government expenditure policy can be used as a stabilizing device, they are highly suspicious of expenditure that does not produce any direct tangible output. Thus, in America, the limitations of a policy of increasing government expenditure are time lags, when long-term investment projects are used, and public outcry, when the main purpose is merely to get purchasing power into the hands of households, irrespective of what their immediate production might be.

Tax policy, on the other hand, can be made to operate very quickly, once it has been authorized by Congress. The tax cut of 1964 reduced personal tax liabilities by $6.7 billion and corporate liabilities by $1.7 billion. Much of this was made effective at once, by decreases in the rate of withholding. The Council of Economic Advisors anticipated (in its 1964 Report) that a tax cut of $8 billion would have a multiplier effect of about 2 within one year. The expectation was confirmed.

Income tax cuts can be large and quick, but they cannot easily be selective. In the first round, they affect those with income. Their contribution to the poor and the unemployed comes only as the economy expands under the impact of the extra demand. A tax cut that puts an extra $1 billion into the hands of households will, if the multiplier is 2, raise income and employment by $2 billion. But very little of this $2 billion may be spent on products produced in Appalachia or in other depressed areas. It is quite possible that most of the extra demand will have its effect on areas and industries in which the employment situation is already satisfactory. Tax cuts are most effective if unemployment is fairly general throughout the economy and least effective, since their impact cannot be localized, when unemployment is concentrated in regional, occupational, or industrial pockets.

If one is most concerned with the *number* of unemployed, the policy looks more successful than if one is concerned with *who* is unemployed. A change that reduces unemployment in half the country from 4 percent to 2.5 percent and in the other half from 10 percent to 9.5 percent has the same over-all effect as one that reduces unemployment from 4 percent to 3.5 percent in the one half

and from 10 percent to 8.5 percent in the other. But we would prefer the latter over the former if we were concerned with the distribution of unemployment as well as with the total.

There are other issues involved in the choice between expenditure increases and tax decreases. One, which we will treat in the last section of this chapter, concerns the desirable size of the government role in the economy: Some people believe that we devote too few resources to public goods and some believe we have become too much of a welfare state. Another issue concerns the effect on economic incentives. In 1964, the then Secretary of the Treasury, Douglas Dillon, represented much of the business and financial community when he supported the tax cut of 1964 on the basis of what it would do to incentives of people to invest, rather than for what it would do to their level of consumption. As we saw in Chapter 33, evidence of the magnitude of the disincentive effect of taxes is unclear.

In summary, tax changes can be large in size without causing an impossible political uproar, and can take effect relatively quickly. If the propensity to spend is low, a great deal of leakage can occur in translating increases in incomes in the hands of people into aggregate demand. If the propensity to spend is high, a substantial multiplier effect is possible.[8] Direct public expenditure has the potential advantage of being directed to where it is most needed and of being spent with a relatively small amount of withdrawals. It is, however, often regarded as politically difficult, and the lags can prove substantial. Much of actual fiscal policy rests upon a combination of tax and expenditure policies.

8. The reader should satisfy himself that he can demonstrate the following: If the propensity to consume is zero, the final effect of a tax cut of $1 billion on income and employment is zero, whereas the final effect of a rise in government expenditure of $1 billion is $1 billion.

Regulating Aggregate Demand: Monetary Policy

The second major policy tool for controlling aggregate demand is monetary policy. A policy of reducing the money supply, making some loans harder to get, and of raising interest rates is designed to lower the level of demand. A policy of increasing the money supply, making loans easier to obtain, and lowering interest rates is designed to raise the level of aggregate demand. Monetary policy has several advantages over fiscal policy. First, the authority to use it is in the hands of the Federal Reserve Board; thus Congressional delays can be avoided. Second, it is easily adjustable

and thus flexible, because the Open-Market Committee can apply or release brakes gradually if it chooses, and it can reverse its policies on no notice at all. The major drawback is that, although monetary policy can always restrain an expansion by tightening the reins held on the money supply by the central authorities, it cannot force people to spend or invest if they do not wish to. Slacking the reins can create excess funds for the banking system, but it will not necessarily create spending and jobs unless someone wants to borrow and to spend extra money.

Monetary Versus Fiscal Policy

Both monetary and fiscal policy provide tools for influencing aggregate demand and for selectively controlling the pattern of demand. (As examples of the latter, consider control of stock-market borrowing by regulation of margin requirements, and incentives for investment via special tax concessions.) Different tools work differently in different situations and, just as the carpenter carries a variety of tools, so also the policy-maker has a variety at his disposal. This being so, it may seem odd to hear that some of the most bitter debates about economic policy have concerned monetary *versus* fiscal policy. To some extent, this debate has concerned a positive question: In a particular situation, which tool promises the most satisfactory means of reaching agreed goals? That we debate such matters is both proper and necessary. As experience with different policy measures accumulates, this portion of the debate will subside. Much

of the debate, however, has concerned normative issues: The protagonists say, or imply, that monetary policy is in some sense morally better (or worse) than fiscal policy. This is not a matter on which positive economics can shed any light, and we cannot hope to settle it here.

But let us note in passing some of the reasons for the debate. First, the use of fiscal policy implies that governments, through their expenditures, can exert a major influence on the level and distribution of national income. This in turn implies that the government plays a role, and a potentially big one, in economic activity. Some regard this role as highly objectionable; others regard it as desirable, if not essential. Second, monetary policy in the U.S. is carried out by the quasi-independent Federal Reserve System, rather than by the publicly elected Administration. Depending upon one's politics, this may represent an advantage or a disadvantage. Republican hackles still rise at the statement of a prominent Democratic politician that "we will spend and spend and elect and elect." Finally, among economists, the advocacy of fiscal policy reflects the acceptance of the very strong criticisms that Keynesian theory leveled at the existing theories of the time. Keynes was not a tactful man, and bruises still remain.

In every modern society of the West, monetary and fiscal policies are not mutually exclusive, but, rather, complementary. Not all our goals can be obtained by varying aggregate demand alone, no matter how many of the tools of fiscal and monetary policy are used to do the job. We have also seen that particular measures of monetary and fiscal policy usually affect things in the economy other than aggregate demand. For these reasons, the satisfactory attainment of all our goals probably requires that a whole range of tools be used and that the differences between them be exploited fully. For example, if one aspect of fiscal policy has a particularly adverse effect on the balance of payments, it may well pay to substitute a policy that has a better effect on the balance of payments, even though it does not do its primary job of controlling aggregate demand quite so well as the first policy.

We now discuss what can be done to control certain specific policy variables by means other than the regulation of aggregate demand.

Controlling Inflation

We saw in Chapter 55 that, if we attempt to control inflation by controlling aggregate demand, we set up a conflict with the policy of keeping unemployment at a very low level. The major alternative means of controlling inflation is by government intervention. During World War II, all belligerent governments adopted policies fixing prices by decree. These policies were not wholly successful. Price levels did rise during the war, but wartime excess demand was enormous, and there is no doubt that governments succeeded in keeping prices well below what they otherwise would have been. That wartime control of prices through government policy is possible is demonstrated. But is it possible in peacetime? If so, will it require the whole wartime expansion of controls, or can it be accomplished with much less extreme forms of intervention? In order to answer these questions, we need to diagnose the causes of inflation, and we shall digress here to consider this important problem.

THE CAUSES OF INFLATION: DEMAND-PULL, COST-PUSH, OR PRICE-PUSH?

The causes of inflation have been much debated in the last twenty years. The bulk of expert opinion is that the very rapid inflations in many countries, particularly those of South America,[9] have been caused by an expansion of the money supply due to large and persistent governmental budget deficits often incurred to finance a growth plan that

9. See Chapter 55, Table 1.

governments could not or would not finance out of current revenues.

The causes of the mild inflation in the countries of North America and Western Europe have been the subject of great controversy. These inflations have had two characteristics in common. First, money wages have tended to rise at a somewhat more rapid pace than increases in productivity. Second, there has sometimes been an upward movement in prices in spite of the presence of significant amounts of unemployment. The process has been called a "wage-price spiral." Two diagnoses have been put forward: one called *demand-pull,* and one called *cost-* or *price-push.* In essence, the demand-pull theory says that changes in price levels are to be accounted for by disequilibria in markets, such disequilibria usually being caused by changes in aggregate demand. A rise in aggregate demand in a situation of nearly full employment will create excess demand in many individual markets, and prices will be bid upward. The rise in demand for goods and services will cause a rise in demand for factors, and their prices will be bid upward as well. Thus, says the demand-pull school, inflation in the prices both of consumer goods and of factors of production is caused by a *rise in demand.*

To put the matter crudely at first, the cost-push theorists assert that unions have the power to obtain significantly large increases in wages, irrespective of the strength of aggregate demand. This union power is exercised in varying degrees from year to year in response to such economic signals as the popularity of the unions or the relation between unions and the government.[10] When this arbitrary power is exercised, wages rise and, since wages are a large part of the total costs of the firm, prices of commodities rise as well.

What we shall call the price-push theory (it is also called the administered-price theory of inflation) says that sellers have monopoly power and would like to raise prices but are restrained from doing so by fear of antitrust action or adverse public opinion. During labor negotiations, sellers grant wage increases and use them as an excuse to raise prices.

THE EXPERIENCE WITH WAGE-PRICE STABILIZATION

Peacetime controls on inflation are usually referred to as wage-price policies, and they have been tried in most Western countries since the war with varying degrees of seriousness. Believers in each of the theories agree that it is possible, given sufficient controls, to slow down or to stop an inflation. But the kinds of controls and their severity varies with the theory accepted.

One kind of policy may be called "exhortation"; it relies on appeals by the central authorities for moderation in setting prices and wages. In America, the President's price-and-wage guidelines represented such an attempt. The idea that prices can be controlled merely by publishing what the central authorities would like to see happen represents an extreme view of the economic process. It makes most sense if one is either a cost-push or a price-push theorist, because, since the inflation is then assumed to be caused by the exercise of arbitrary power on the part of a few industry or union leaders, it may be possible to persuade them not to exercise their powers. The power of the Presidency can go beyond this, as was seen in 1962 when President Kennedy forced the major steel companies to retract an announced price rise. In Britain in 1949, a wage-restraint policy was

10. The argument has been that if unions exercise too much arbitrary power too often, they will lose public support, and government intervention and regulation will become inevitable.

initiated by the government with the full co-operation of the unions. The rise in wages was very much less than any rise that occurred before or since in the face of the same sort of market conditions. There is little doubt that the policy succeeded temporarily. When co-operation with the unions broke down, very much higher than normal wage increases occurred, so that, by 1951 or 1952, the level of wages was just where one would have expected it to be, given the market conditions that existed, but in the absence of a wage-restraint policy. If one accepts the demand-pull theory, an attempt to hold prices down by talk and propaganda and executive power represents a belief that the whole process of the reaction of prices and quantities to demand and supply, which we have been studying throughout this book, is so flimsy that a few words from the President's office can upset the process and cause the economy to stop functioning in the way that it has functioned for a very long time in the past. When King Canute commanded the tides to halt, he discovered the limits of his own power; this is the fate demand-pull theorists see for a policy of exhortation. Of course, active co-operation on the part of price- and wage-setters can hold back inflation in the face of excess demand for a while. But, according to the demand-pull theorists, this can be only a temporary rear-guard action, and eventually wages and prices will go up by one means or another.

In the United States, controlling the price level has receded somewhat as a major problem. Since the late 1950s, the wholesale price index has been stable, although consumer prices have drifted upward at almost 1 per-

cent per year since 1958. In countries with less unemployment, the pressure on prices has been stronger, and more insistent wage-price policies have been tried.

In the 1950s in Britain, two attempts were made to control inflation by controlling wage increases. These experiments reflected the current acceptance by practically everyone, except professional economists, of the cost-push theory of inflation. In a cost-push situation, control of wages would be sufficient to control inflation, but the problem of how to control wages in a free society has never been solved. The unions did not seriously co-operate in the attempt and the policy broke down; its only significant effects were to get wages in the public sector (whose control was possible) seriously out of line with wages in the private sector (whose control was impossible). The belief that a lot of talk and a minimum of effective action by a few officials could seriously change the operation of the economic system pervaded the whole experiment.[11]

The most serious attempts at wage-price stabilization policies have been made in some countries of Western Europe, particularly the Netherlands and the countries of Scandinavia. Their policies have been pursued with more vigor than have those of the English-speaking countries and generally with more active cooperation from the unions. Even these policies have been far from unqualified successes. There is some disagreement about just what, if any, real success they have had. The main problem that they revealed arises from a phenomenon called *wage drift*. Briefly, this is based on the fact that it is much easier to control negotiated wage rates than it is to control

---

11. At the time of writing (late 1965), a somewhat more determined attempt is being made to control both wages and prices. No serious apparatus of controls and sanctions has been employed, however, and the demand-pull theorist must expect this experiment to have no more significant results than the ones that preceded it.

the earnings of labor. The *wage rate* is the amount a worker gets per hour, and *earnings* are the total amount he gets per week. The officials operating the stabilization policy might decide, for example, that output per man-hour has gone up 5 percent this year, and that they will allow a rise in wage rates of 5 percent in order to keep the increase in purchasing power in line with the increase in output. The average wage is then raised from, say, $2.00 to $2.10 per hour. But if labor is scarce, employers may be bidding against one another to attract new labor and hold onto their existing labor. If they are unable to do this by raising wage rates, they can offer other inducements—such as bonuses and guaranteed overtime pay (whether or not the overtime is worked). If by these devices they can raise average earnings from, say, $80 to $100 per week, then the rise in *earnings* will

greatly exceed the rise in output, and inflation will occur in spite of the successful control over wage *rates*. This tendency for earnings to follow aggregate demand, even though rates do not, is called the wage drift; unless it can be controlled, a wage-stabilization policy becomes nothing more than a legal fiction with household incomes responding just as they always did to market conditions, but with increases occurring because of rises in bonuses, overtime pay, and other extras rather than because of changes in negotiated wage rates.

We have devoted considerable space to the control of inflation, first, because this particular problem illustrates the important aspects of macroeconomic policy, and, second, because, as we shall see below, the policy conflict between inflation and unemployment is one of the most serious problems of macroeconomic policy.

Regulating the Balance of Payments

There are two main tools for regulating the balance of payments: controlling the level of expenditure by controlling aggregate demand, and controlling the direction of expenditure by controlling the relative prices of internationally traded goods (or by interfering with the normal flow of trade with quotas and other quantitative restrictions). We discussed these tools for controlling the level and direction of expenditure in Chapters 38 and 41 and on pp. 715–716 above.

A single country can solve its balance-of-payments problems more easily if it can have recourse to expenditure-dampening and expenditure-switching policies. The ability to apply expenditure-switching policies has, however, been limited to a great extent by

international agreement and even further by certain unplanned postwar events.

International agreement has greatly limited the use of restrictions on imports as a means of switching demand from foreign to domestic sources of supply, and it has also restricted the use of variations in tariffs on imports and of subsidies on exports as a means of switching demand onto domestic sources. It is probably somewhat more acceptable to the international community to use tariff policies than to use physical controls to accomplish this purpose, but there is still great resistance to the use of tariffs. The latest example of such a use was in 1964 when, in the face of a severe balance-of-payments disequilibrium, the British central authorities instituted a 15 percent surcharge on imports. There was a major outcry against this, and the British Government had to give a strong assurance that the surcharge was a temporary measure to meet a temporary imbalance and that it would be removed within eighteen months.

International agreement also restricts the use of exchange-rate variations as a tool of expenditure-switching. By accepting a system of fixed exchange rates, central authorities have completely eschewed the use of this policy to remove *temporary* disequilibria in international payments. Most countries do accept, however, that such changes can be made in order to switch expenditures in the face of long-term persistent imbalances between imports and exports.

The position of the dollar and the pound as reserve currencies puts an added constraint on the central authorities of the United States and Great Britain that restricts their use of devaluation as a means of switching expenditure.[12] A devaluation of the dollar or the pound means a cut in the value of the reserves that other central authorities are holding in the form of claims on dollars or sterling. To be the cause of such losses is not something that would be accepted lightly by either of the two governments. Reluctance is due both to the fact that the central authorities of the two

governments care about public opinion in other countries, and because, to some extent, particularly in the case of Britain, they have encouraged the use of their currency as a reserve currency. To change the exchange rate of a currency with any frequency is to render that currency unsatisfactory as a reserve currency.

There is one further constraint on expenditure-switching that is felt, particularly by the United States. The U.S. military commitments overseas and the program of economic and military assistance to other nations of the world are one of the major sources of U.S. balance-of-payments difficulties. In 1963, between $6 billion and $7 billion was devoted to overseas expenditures of these kinds and more than accounted for the $3 billion deficit in the U.S. balance-of-payments. While it would be easy to "switch" out of these expenditures, we do not choose to do so because of our position as the leading economic power of the Western nations, and because of considerations of national security and defense. But some policies are available, such as reducing the duty-free allowance of American tourists, bringing home servicemen's families stationed overseas, and establishing import quotas. These are, however, minor tools for dealing with a big problem.

CURRENT POLICY ISSUES

Unemployment and Prices: A Persistent Policy Conflict?

The purpose of a wage-price stabilization policy is to allow a high level of employment to be maintained by keeping aggregate demand at a high level, while preventing prices

from rising in spite of the inevitable local shortages. Available evidence seems to suggest that it is not possible at present to operate a really successful wage-price stabilization

12. See Chapter 41, pages 472–473.

policy. This seems to leave us with an irreconcilable policy conflict between full employment and stable prices. What can the economist do in the face of such a conflict?

The first thing he can do is to attempt to discover the quantitative significance of the conflict. The conflict looks very different, for example, if 10 percent unemployment is needed to maintain stable prices than if only 3.5 percent unemployment is needed.[13] The nature of this conflict is shown by the curve in Figure 2 in Chapter 55. Before recent empirical work on this relation was done, it was generally believed that something on the order of 7–10 percent unemployment might be needed to maintain stable price levels. As a result of recent work, our view of the nature of the policy conflict has changed greatly. In Britain, it seems fairly clear that something between 2.5 and 3 percent unemployment would be compatible with stable prices while 1–1.5 percent unemployment might go along with something on the order of a 3 percent annual rate of inflation. For various technical reasons that we cannot go into here, the U.S. results are somewhat less certain, but it appears that rates as low as 4.5 percent unemployment are pretty certainly compatible with stable prices; the minimum rate may be much lower. In this work, we see the economist in one of his most important roles, that of discovering what policy conflicts exist in the present state of the world, and quantifying them by telling us *how much* of this we have to give up to get more of that.

The next thing the economist can do is to study what changes can be made in the economy to reduce the importance of, or to remove altogether, the existing conflict. In terms of Figure 2 on page 663, he is asking how to shift the curve downward. If it could be shifted so that, at a volume of measured unemployment corresponding to "full employment," the rate of increase in wages was no more than the rate of increase in productivity, the conflict would be removed altogether.

One suggested method, that of direct intervention through wage-price policy, has already been considered. Other methods might require less direct intervention. In order to develop such policies, the economist has to understand the actual behavior of individual markets that gives rise to this conflict. A brief outline of this behavior was given in the appendix to Chapter 56, and we briefly recall it here. One reason why inflation sets in before full employment is reached is that in a growing, changing economy, the pattern of consumers' demand is constantly changing, and with it, the pattern of derived demand for factors is also changing. If consumers wish to spend an increasing fraction of their incomes on automobiles and a declining fraction on, say, food, then an increasing proportion of the nation's resources will have to be in auto production and a declining proportion in food. (See pages 131 and 689.) Such reallocations of resources take time and often entail retraining of labor and its movement from one geographical area to another. At any one time, there will be a

13. To measure the extent of the conflict, we need a full theory of the relevant relations in the economy. Here we specify a simplified theory that is enough to illustrate what is involved. More careful work has used more adequate (and necessarily quite advanced) theories. (1) The rate of change of productivity is exogenous. (2) Wages are a major proportion of factor incomes, and other incomes will change in approximately the same proportion as wage incomes. (3) The problem of maintaining a stable price level thus boils down to one of having total wage income (which is the major determinant of aggregate demand) rise at the same speed as productivity (which is the major determinant of aggregate supply). The conflict can then be studied by observing the relation between the level of unemployment and the rate of increase in wages.

supply of unemployed resources that have been released from industries in which they are not required and that have not yet moved to industries in which they are required. Thus, if aggregate demand expands, shortages and bottlenecks and consequent inflationary pressure will develop, even though there are unemployed resources. If movement of these resources can be speeded up, then bottlenecks and shortages would be less likely to occur in expanding areas until over-all unemployment is at a lower level than previously.

The policies to subsidize relocation and retraining in the U.S. have been directed mainly at long-run structural unemployment.[14] They may, however, have the incidental effect of reducing the conflict between a high level of employment and a stable price level. To the extent that these schemes benefit people who would have moved and retrained anyway and allow them to do it faster and more efficiently than they could have done on their own, these policies will have the effect

of lessening the conflict between full employment and stable prices.

Until successful policies for reducing or eliminating the conflict have been designed, it is necessary for society to choose between the two competing policy objectives. How much inflation is it worth having in order to gain a further reduction in unemployment? Here is an area where value judgments tend to predominate. Reasonable men can differ in their evaluation of how bad a bit of inflation is and of how bad a bit more unemployment is. They can also disagree on how to weigh effects on different people—on how, for example, to weigh the harm that inflation does to them against the harm that unemployment does to someone else. These are the kinds of issues on which political parties take stands; once the nature of the conflict has been made clear and ways of removing it studied, the final choice of how we value these two goals relative to each other becomes a political one.[15]

Unemployment and the Balance of Payments

With fixed exchange rates, a major policy conflict can occur between unemployment and the balance of payments. If the country's currency is overvalued so that at full employment there is a balance-of-payments deficit,

then an expenditure-dampening policy will reduce imports and thus alleviate the balance-of-payments problem, but at the cost of raising the level of domestic unemployment. The conflict can be removed by raising aggregate

14. To a great extent, they were motivated by the desire to reduce unemployment in such long-run depressed areas as Appalachia. There, people have often been without work for years and would stand little chance of finding work in their previous occupations and in their present areas even if aggregate demand grew to a level at which inflationary pressures became serious elsewhere in the country. Their only hope of gainful employment is relocation and retraining. To the extent that these people are affected, such schemes are hitting at a permanent hard core of "structural unemployment," which would probably not yield to any of the more general measures of fiscal and monetary policy.

15. This does not mean that rational inquiry ceases at this stage. If you think inflation is more important than unemployment and I think the reverse, we can ask each other our reasons for thinking so. We are then likely to come up with some positive testable statements such as, "I think the effects of each will be thus and so." Such statements are the factual bases on which our judgments rest, and they will usually be testable, at least in principle. It is important in this context that you now reread footnote 1 on page 13.

demand, while at the same time adopting expenditure-switching policies so that international payments are in balance when full employment is achieved. If the central authorities cannot, or will not, adopt expenditure-switching policies, however, there will be no simple way out of their dilemma, and they will have to choose between internal and external balance.

Throughout the 1950s, countries such as the United States and Germany did not face such a conflict, since their currencies were not overvalued at the current exchange rate. Indeed, when full employment ruled at home, both countries tended to have balance-of-payments surpluses. Other countries, including Britain, were in positions in which full employment tended to be associated with payments deficits. As long as expenditure-switching policies could not be adopted, there was pressure to reduce aggregate demand in order to restore balance-of-payments equilibrium. Once this had been restored, there was a tendency to worry about unemployment and to raise aggregate demand. But as soon as the unemployment problem appeared to be solved, the rise in demand, with its consequent rise in imports, brought with it a new payments disequilibrium, and demand would have to be depressed again. The history of macroeconomic policy in Britain during the 1950s and 1960s, and, indeed, in other countries similarly situated, has been a perpetual oscillation between periods of expanding aggregate demand to eliminate unemployment and periods of contracting demand to eliminate balance-of-payments deficits. Fortunately, the level of unemployment at which payments tended to be in balance was not high, so the oscillations were not large. They were frustrating, however, and many econo-

mists believe that the associated uncertainty hurt long-run investment, thus retarding the rate of growth.[16] The whole problem arose because the central authorities (1) would not accept expenditure-switching policies to cure the payments problem, (2) would not admit that this refusal created a conflict between internal and external balance, and (3) would not make a clear decision about how much unemployment they were prepared to accept in order to secure external balance. In such a situation the task of the economist is to point out the policies necessary to achieve both goals, show the conflicts made inevitable by the decision to use only some tools of policy, and press for a clear decision in giving relative values to the two conflicting goals.

In recent times the United States has moved, as we have already seen, to a position in which her international payments tend to be in deficit when income is still below the full-employment level. We expect that reducing the level of unemployment will exaggerate the payments problem. The same conflict that other countries faced in the 1950s has now appeared in the U.S. The problem is greatly eased for the U.S. by the fact that her marginal propensity to import is very small. Since only a small proportion of any change in income is reflected in a change in imports, the American balance of payments is only slightly affected by changes in domestic income. Thus a rise in income and employment in the U.S. will worsen the U.S. payments position only slightly, and such effects can be offset by very mild changes to encourage expenditure-shifting. Nonetheless, the conflict is there, although its magnitude is not great. Other countries with large marginal propensities to import are not in so favorable a position. When their incomes change, a

16. This theory has not yet been satisfactorily tested.

significant proportion of the effect is felt on imports. These countries can have major conflicts between internal and external balance

as long as they are forced to rely solely on policies affecting the level of aggregate expenditure as a means of achieving both goals.

The Composition of Macro Variables

Macroeconomic policy is concerned with the behavior of certain key averages and aggregates such as the average level of all prices and the over-all level of unemployment. In fact, we do not care only about these averages and aggregates. We also care about their composition. Is the over-all level of unemployment made up of very unequal rates of unemployment such as those among industries, occupations, or areas, or is it made up of rates that are very similar across all of these classifications? We would assess a 5 percent over-all unemployment rate in the U.S. very differently if it resulted from 5 percent unemployment in all industries, occupations, and geographical areas than if it resulted from 20 percent unemployment in some classifications and only 2 or 3 percent in others.

Levels of unemployment of 10 or 20 percent are very serious matters, indeed. They are likely to mean that many people will be out of work for very long periods of time and that there is a level of social and personal upheaval that just does not accompany rates on the order of 5 percent. The degree of regional and occupational inequality in unemployment rates in the U.S. has remained quite large throughout the whole postwar period.[17] Clearly, although we should be satisfied that the over-all rate is now falling below 5 percent, we should be very disturbed at the very high rates that persist in some places.

Why does this occur? Why does the market not adjust to bring about approximate equality in unemployment rates? Shouldn't regions and occupations with excess supplies of labor find their relative wages declining so that there is an incentive to employers to hire more of the relatively cheap labor? Does this market mechanism work at all? How fast does it work? Does the shifting pattern of economic growth continue to disturb markets so that the adjustment mechanism can never catch up? Would things be any worse if we interfered in the market mechanism? What government policies would reduce these relative labor-market disequilibria?

A similar set of "disaggregated observations" could be produced for any macro variable, and they would provoke a similar set of questions. But to state just one set is enough to realize that we have now gone full circle and are back at the microeconomics with which we began our study. To tackle these problems, we need to return to market theory, the study of which we began in Part II of the book.

As we stated in Chapter 44, there is no sharp distinction between micro- and macroeconomics. There are merely higher and lower levels of aggregation and a series of questions appropriate to each level of aggregation, with each series shading one into the other.

17. But, contrary to popular belief, it has not increased steadily over the period. See the forementioned article by R. A. Gordon, "Has Structural Unemployment Worsened?"

The Size of Government

In Chapters 11 and 43, we discussed micro-economic policy measures from many points of view, and we examined some of the issues involved in the choice between *laissez-faire* and public intervention. In Parts IX to XII, we have discussed the effects of macroeconomic policy, but have not said much about the government's providing this service. Part of the reason is that the only alternative to government action in the macro sphere is no action at all. We can argue about the relative advantages and disadvantages of having education provided by the private or the public sector, but we cannot argue about the relative advantages and disadvantages of having a full-employment policy administered by a government as opposed to a private firm. The alternative to having a full-employment policy determined by the government is to let unemployment settle at whatever level the private market determines. The evidence of history is that this will mean accepting quite high rates quite often.

In discussing fiscal policy, we have examined government revenues and expenditures as they affect our macro policy goals. We have not discussed the valuation to be put on the ratio of governmental expenditures to national income (which we shall abbreviate as G/Y). It is undoubtedly true that many people place valuations on the size of this ratio. Some think it should be kept down, others think it should be high, and yet others think its over-all size is unimportant as long as each particular public project is acceptable.

What can the economist say about this problem?

First, he can point out that the decision on G/Y cannot be made over-all but can be made only in terms of individual decisions on individual projects. It does not help practical policy to say simply, "The size of the government sector must be reduced by 20 percent"; it is necessary to decide which 20 percent must go. It might be possible, for example, to obtain a sizable majority in favor of cutting government expenditure by 20 percent and yet be unable to find a majority in favor of cutting any particular bit of expenditure.[18] In fact, the aggregate budget of the public sector is built up by approving particular projects. We make piecemeal decisions on Medicare, federal aid to housing, national defense, the space program, national parks, and the budget of a state university.

Many are the senators who want to economize on public expenditures—until they come to a project that will be built in their own state. "Log-rolling" is the name given to trading votes in order to assure a majority in support of *your* project. Perhaps a good illustration is the 1964 Water Resources Research Bill, which provides for federal support in establishing 50 Water Resources Research Centers, one in each state, regardless of the size of the state or the urgency of its water-resource problems.

Those who fear the size of the government sector will be unwilling to accept any particular new measure unless persuaded that its

18. Governors of the several states have discovered this the hard way: Taxpayers want the social services that governments provide, but do not want to pay the taxes required to pay for them. Any governor either arouses the people's wrath by failing to provide wanted programs, or by raising taxes. Winning re-election has become a major problem in many states, for governors of both parties.

particular advantages overweigh their general fears. Those who favor government activity will need less persuasion, but, unless they are dogmatic extremists, they will not accept any measure, no matter how dubious its advantages or how high its costs, just because it is to be provided by the public sector. Those who think the size of the public sector per se is irrelevant will tend to be for or against any particular measure solely on its assumed merits and demerits.

The second thing that the economist can point out is that people's reactions to specific government measures vary over time. When the income tax was first introduced in nineteenth-century Britain, it was at a rate of 6d. on the pound (2.5 cents on the dollar), and the British Parliament expressed profound concern that it would destroy incentives because people would not retain the full fruits of their efforts. When public education was first introduced, many persons felt it was "socialistic" and that such free gifts would destroy the energies and initiatives of the American family. Possibly some people feel the same today, but both the income tax and public education now receive overwhelming support.

What can be of concern when people express opinion on the size of the government sector per se? Partly it is a political matter; people have fears and hopes about government, and they view the importance of government in the economy in terms of their political philosophy. This is without doubt a very important aspect, but it is beyond the scope of the present economic inquiry.

People do debate the size of the government sphere on economic grounds. When they do, it is rarely that they feel a G/Y of 20 percent is better or worse "economically" than a G/Y of 30 percent. It is rather that there usually is a large concealed theoretical structure leading to the prediction that to raise (or lower) G/Y would raise (or lower) living standards, welfare, or whatever is of concern to us. Consider two examples.

Economist A might believe that we have been reasonably successful in getting an ordering of the relative efficiencies with which the public sector can handle certain jobs, but that we have been wildly wrong in judging the absolute efficiency with which it can do any job. This economist would argue that we have long since allocated to the public sector all those things it could do better than the private sector and that, in doing so, we allocated to it lots of things it does worse. He would thus believe that cutting G/Y substantially would raise the over-all efficiency of the economy and add to human freedom by reducing the coercive element in our society.

Economist Z might believe that the goods the public sector provides tend to have high income elasticities of demand so that, if people consumed the bundle of goods they most wanted, the size of G/Y would rise as incomes rose because of economic growth. But, so Z believes, the public fears that a higher G/Y will increase the chances of a Fascist, Socialist, or Communist government being established. If the people's assessment of the political consequences were correct, the decision to go without the goods they want would be a rational one. Z believes, however, that the people are wrong in this assessment of the political effects of raising G/Y. If only G/Y could be increased, the people would see for themselves that their view of the political effects was wrong, and they would then be happy to find themselves able to consume the goods they really want to consume. Z will wish to raise G/Y whenever possible. Faced with a need for a budget deficit to reduce unemployment, he will want to raise G/Y while others may want to cut taxes. The effects on unemployment in the long run will be more or less the same, but the effects on the long-run willingness of the public to accept a different level of G/Y may be very difficult.

Which economist, A or Z, is correct? Indeed, which one of a dozen other views about the short- and long-run economic and political effects of varying G/Y is correct? Only time —and the subsequent research of a host of economists and political scientists of generations to follow ours—will tell.

The Progress of Economics

The general acceptance of the view that the validity of economic theories should be tested by confronting their predictions with the mass of all available evidence is fairly new in economics. At this point, reread the quotation from Lord William Beveridge given at the beginning of this book (see pp. v and vi). The controversy that Beveridge was describing was the one that followed the publication in 1936 of Keynes's *The General Theory of Employment, Interest, and Money*. Keynes's work gave rise to the macroeconomics that we developed in Part IX and on which we have so often relied in subsequent parts. At many points in the present book, we have raised the question of how various parts of macroeconomic theory could be tested; we have also discussed some of the tests that have already been conducted. The student should reflect on how very different this approach to the problem of accepting or rejecting theories is from the approach described by Beveridge.

In the years since 1937, there is no doubt that some—albeit irregular and halting— progress has been made in economics in relating theory with evidence in the world of economic events. This progress has been reflected in the superior ability of governments to achieve their policy objectives. The financial aspects of World War II were incomparably better handled than those of World War I. When President Roosevelt tried to reduce unemployment in the 1930s, his efforts were greatly hampered by the failure of most economists to realize the critical importance of budget deficits in increasing the level of the circular flow of income. When President Kennedy wished to do something about the high levels of unemployment in the 1960s, his main problem was to persuade Congress to adopt what most economists agreed was an appropriate cure —a tax cut; and in 1964, when President Johnson finally persuaded Congress to accept the tax cut, the ensuing rise in output and employment was very close to what the economists on the President's Council of Economic Advisors had predicted it would be. Such important policy areas as the running of wars and the curing of major depressions are places where the general tone of our theories is tested, even if all the specific predictions of them are not. In some general sense, then, economic theories have always been subjected to empirical tests. When they were wildly at variance with the facts, the ensuing disaster could not but be noticed, and the theories were discarded or amended in the light of what was learned.

The advances of economics in the last fifteen years reflect economists' changed attitude toward empirical observations. Today, we are much less likely to dismiss theories just because we do not like them and to refuse to abandon theories just because we do like them. Today, we are more likely to try to base our theories as much as possible on empirical observation and to accept empirical relevance as the ultimate arbiter of the value of our theories. As human beings, the upsetting of a pet theory may cause us much anguish; as scientists, we should try to train ourselves to take pleasure in it because of the new knowledge we gain thereby. It has been said that one of the great tragedies of science is the continual slaying of beautiful theories by ugly facts. As economists, we are all too often swayed by aesthetic considerations. In the past, we have too often hung on to our theories because they were beautiful or because we liked their political implications; as scientists, we must always remember that, when theory and fact come into conflict, it is theory, not fact, that must give way.

Summary

1. Were full employment the only major goal of the policy-makers, it would not be difficult to maintain it by a policy aimed at maintaining aggregate demand and by selected policies designed to deal with structural unemployment where it exists.

2. Were a stable price level the only major goal of public policy, it would not be difficult to achieve it by regulating the level of aggregate demand.

3. Were equality in the balance of payments the sole object of governmental policy, it would not be difficult to maintain it by varying exchange rates or by controlling the level or pattern of aggregate demand.

4. If increasing the rate of economic growth were the major objective of economic policy, it is clear that avoiding sharp reductions in aggregate demand would be important and that stimulating invention, innovation, and investment would likewise be desirable. We do not know enough about these processes, however, to be confident of which policies would best achieve our objectives.

5. If we try to achieve all our policy goals by varying the level of aggregate demand, we will inevitably run into conflict. A policy that has several goals may have to use several instruments of policy, besides the powerful tool of controlling aggregate demand.

6. Both monetary and fiscal policy provide tools for influencing aggregate demand and for selectively controlling the pattern of demand. Much of the debate regarding monetary versus fiscal policy has not really been over positive issues.

7. In order to consider policies for controlling inflation, we must first consider the different theories of the causes of inflation. The three major ones, over which there is much controversy, are the demand-pull, cost-push, and price-push hypotheses.

8. Attempts at wage-price stabilization by policies from exhortation on up have been tried by many Western countries in the postwar period. Demand-pull theorists hold out little hope for such policies. There is also some doubt about what results the policies of countries that have tried moderately vigorous approaches have produced. The main problem is that the actual earnings of labor may often exceed the negotiated wage rates influenced by the policies; this is known as wage drift.

9. Other than controlling the level of ex-

penditure by controlling aggregate demand, the balance of payments may be regulated by expenditure-switching policies. There are, however, many restrictions on such policies, because of international agreements and constraints.

10. We consider two current and persistent policy conflicts: full employment versus stable prices, and full employment versus balance-of-payments equilibrium. The economist's main functions in this are to measure the incompatibility as it stands, and to suggest ways to render conflicting goals more compatible.

11. Lastly, we consider the conflict over the optimal size of the government's activities in the economy. Although debate on this topic is partly political, it also concerns such matters as over-all efficiency and people's desire for public-sector commodities as income rises. Only time and research will tell who is right.

QUESTIONS FOR DISCUSSION

1. "Because flexible and competitive market forces are not alone in affecting prices and wages, a modern economy needs new policies to reconcile the objectives of full employment and stable prices." Discuss this statement from the 1965 Report of the Council of Economic Advisors in terms of the analysis of this chapter.

2. The Council specifically proposed the following wage and price guideposts. *The general guide for wages is that the percentage increase in total employed compensation per man-hour be equal to the national rate of increase in output per man-hour; the general guide for prices calls for stable prices in industries enjoying the same productivity growth as the average for the economy: rising prices in industries with smaller than average productivity gains, and declining prices in industries with greater than average productivity gains.* Discuss what you think the effects of these guideposts on other economic activities are likely to be.

3. "These guideposts," says the Council, "are simple and straightforward, and contain an inescapable economic logic." What is this "inescapable logic"?

4. What do you think is the reasoning behind the following view? "Below 4.5 percent unemployment, wage-restraint policies won't work; above 4.5 percent, you don't need them."

5. In what way is "wage drift" a problem? Do you think it would help to try to eliminate it? How could this be done, even if you don't think it should be done (or would be of any use)?

6. The British National Institute of Economic and Social Research predicted in 1965 that the cost of withstanding a run on sterling would be high that year—virtually no economic growth. In the coming years, it said, the choice was between "quasi-stagnation" of the economy combined with rising unemployment, or an inability to repay its international debts by 1970. Why the dilemma? What policies other than "austerity" are available to the government in the longer run to try to reconcile its two objectives?

7. Why do we say that the question should not be monetary *versus* fiscal policy?

8. We live, say many economists (notably John Kenneth Galbraith), in a country of "private affluence and public squalor." Others claim that the people have the power to choose how they wish the national product to be allocated, and so this represents the free choice of the nation and ought not to be interfered with. Can you write a "pro and con" discussion?

A NOTE ABOUT SUPPLEMENTARY AND MORE ADVANCED READINGS

AN INTRODUCTION TO ECONOMICS ATTEMPTS to convey the scope of the entire subject. In doing so, it barely scratches the surface of each of the specialized branches of economics in which past and current research is going on. In footnotes throughout this book, we have called the student's attention to particular articles or books that take him beyond the point at which we have been forced to leave him.

By and large, we believe that supplementary readings should be suggested by the instructor, for he is in a better position to know the needs and background of his students. One thing on which we feel strongly, however, is that every student of economics ought to buy and read the latest copy of the *Economic Report of the President*. This annual publication discusses the most compelling of current policy issues as they appear to the Council of Economic Advisors and contains a wealth of basic statistical information about the American economy.

The literature of economics is too vast to make even a selected bibliography a sensible thing for an elementary book. But there is more to economics than the principles that we have stressed in this book. How may the interested student explore them? We offer a few suggestions.

I. BY READING COLLECTIONS OF SELECTED ESSAYS

Each of the following general selections enables the beginning student to browse in the economic literature without getting over his depth. Each is available in paperback.

EPSTEIN, R. C., and BUTLER, A. D. *Selections in Economics*. 2 vols. Buffalo, N.Y.: Economica Books, 1958.

HARRISS, C. LOWELL. *Selected Readings in Economics*. 2d ed. Englewood Cliffs, N.J.: Prentice-Hall, 1962.

HARLAN, H. C. *Readings in Economics and Politics*. New York: Oxford University Press, 1961.

SAMUELSON, PAUL A., *et al. Readings in Economics*. 4th ed. New York: McGraw-Hill, 1964.

2. BY INVESTIGATING SELECTED ISSUES OF PUBLIC POLICY

A series of paperbacks published by W. W. Norton introduces the student to a variety of positions on particular issues of public policy in economics. The selections are all chosen with the beginning student in mind. The series is called "Problems of the Modern Economy." The titles are:

BALASSA, BELA (ed.). *Changing Patterns in Foreign Trade and Payments.* 1964.

BOWEN, WILLIAM G. (ed.). *Labor and the National Economy.* 1965.

BUDD, EDWARD (ed.). *Inequality and Poverty.* 1965.

MANSFIELD, EDWIN (ed.). *Monopoly Power and Economic Performance.* 1964.

OKUN, ARTHUR M. (ed.). *The Battle Against Unemployment.* 1965.

PHELPS, EDMUND S. (ed.). *The Goal of Economic Growth.* Rev. ed., 1965.

———. *Private Wants and Public Needs.* Rev. ed., 1965.

RANIS, GUSTAV. *The United States and the Developing Economies.* 1964.

3. BY TAKING A COURSE IN ONE OF THE SPECIALIZED AND APPLIED FIELDS OF ECONOMICS

Among the specialized fields of economics in addition to economic theory are History of Economic Thought, Economic History, Economic Statistics and Econometrics, Economic Development, Comparative Economic Systems, Business Fluctuations, Money and Banking, Public Finance, International Economics, Industrial Organization, Government and Business, Public Utilities and Transportation, Agricultural Economics, Labor Economics, and Economic Demography.

For the student who wishes to go on in one of these fields, there is no substitute for taking a course in it. Most colleges and universities offer courses in many of these fields. The student who wants to know what a particular field covers should ask his instructor to recommend a text in the field and then spend an hour or two with it in the library.

4. BY BECOMING FAMILIAR WITH THE PUBLICATIONS OF THE AMERICAN ECONOMIC ASSOCIATION

The American Economic Association (AEA) has sponsored a two-volume work called *A Survey of Contemporary Economics.* Volume 1 was edited by Howard D. Ellis (New York: Richard D. Irwin, 1948); Volume 2 was edited by Bernard F. Haley (Richard D. Irwin, 1952). These volumes consist of essays by experts summarizing the current research and policy issues in particular fields. The essays may occasionally be difficult for the student who has taken only an introductory course in economics, but for the most part they are manageable. The titles and authors of the essays in Volume 1 are as follows:

HALEY, BERNARD F. "Value and Distribution."

FELLNER, WILLIAM. "Employment Theory and Business Cycles."

GALBRAITH, J. K. "Monopoly and the Concentration of Economic Power."

BAIN, JOE S. "Price and Production Policies."

SMITHIES, ARTHUR. "Federal Budgeting and Fiscal Policy."

METZLER, LLOYD A. "The Theory of International Trade."

REYNOLDS, LLOYD G. "Economics of Labor."

SHOUP, CARL S. "Development and Use of National Income Data."

VILLARD, HENRY H. "Monetary Theory."

SAMUELSON, PAUL A. "Dynamic Process Analysis."

LEONTIEF, WASSILY. "Econometrics."

BERGSON, ABRAM. "Socialist Economics."

WRIGHT, DAVID McC. "The Prospects for Capitalism."

The titles and authors of the essays in Volume 2 are:

BOULDING, KENNETH. "Welfare Economics."

MACK, RUTH P. "Economics of Consumption."

SPENGLER, JOSEPH J. "Population Theory."
ABRAMOWITZ, MOSES. "Economics of Growth."
PAPANDREOU, ANDREAS. "Some Basic Problems in the Theory of the Firm."
JOHNSON, D. GALE. "Economics of Agriculture."
HARRISS, C. LOWELL. "Public Finance."
BUCHANAN, NORMAN S. "International Finance."
BARAN, PAUL A. "National Economic Planning."
RUGGLES, RICHARD. "Methodological Developments."

To supplement these volumes, the AEA has commissioned a series of survey articles published in the *American Economic Review*. The general title of this series is "Surveys of Contemporory Economics." The seven articles that have been published to date are:

SIMON, HERBERT A. "Theories of Decision Making in Economics," June, 1959.
DORFMAN, ROBERT. "Operations Research," September, 1960.
CHENERY, HOLLIS B. "Comparative Advantage and Development Policy," March, 1961.
FERBER, ROBERT. "Research on Household Behavior," March, 1962.
JOHNSON, HARRY G. "Monetary Theory and Policy," June, 1962.
MEYER, JOHN. "Regional Economics," March, 1963.
BRONFENBRENNER, M., and HOLZMAN, F. D. "Survey of Inflation Theory," September, 1963.

More advanced introductions to the journal literature are found in the AEA-sponsored series of volumes of selected readings in particular fields. The titles in this series, all of which are published by Richard D. Irwin, are:

HOOVER, EDGAR M., JR., and DEAN, JOEL (eds.). *Readings in the Social Control of Industry.* 1942.
HABERLER, GOTTFRIED (ed.). *Readings in Business Cycle Theory.* 1944.
FELLNER, WILLIAM J., and HALEY, BERNARD F. (eds). *Readings in the Theory of Income Distribution.* 1946.
ELLIS, HOWARD S., and METZLER, LLOYD A. (eds.). *Readings in the Theory of International Trade.* 1949.
LUTZ, FRIEDRICH A., and MINTS, LLOYD W. (eds.). *Readings in Monetary Theory.* 1951.
STIGLER, GEORGE J., and BOULDING, KENNETH E. (eds.). *Readings in Price Theory.* 1952.
LANE, FREDERIC C., and RIEMERSMA, JELLE C. (eds.). *Enterprise and Secular Change: Readings in Economic History.* 1953.
SMITHIES, ARTHUR, and BUTTERS, J. KEITH (eds.). *Readings in Fiscal Policy.* 1955.
HEFLEBOWER, RICHARD B., and STOCKING, GEORGE W. (eds.). *Readings in Industrial Organization and Public Policy.* 1958.
MUSGRAVE, RICHARD A., and SHOUP, CARL S. (eds.). *Readings in the Economics of Taxation.* 1958.

Unlike the selected essays given in Point 1 above, the articles in these volumes are reprinted in their entirety. They are often advanced, but they are important contributions. A major feature of each volume is an extensive bibliography of works in the field.

Format by Susan Bishop
Set in Linotype Primer with Franklin Gothic
Composed by The Haddon Craftsmen, Inc.
Printed by The Murray Printing Company
Bound by The Haddon Craftsmen, Inc.
HARPER & ROW, PUBLISHERS, INCORPORATED